SPARTANBURGH COUNTY, SOUTH CAROLINA MINUTES OF THE COUNTY COURT 1785 - 1799

by
Brent H. Holcomb, C. A. L. S.

Copyright 1980
By: The Rev. Silas Emmett Lucas, Jr.

All rights reserved. No part of this publication may be reproduced, stored in a retrieval system, transmitted in any form, posted on to the web in any form or by any means without the prior written permission of the publisher.

Please direct all correspondence and orders to:

www.southernhistoricalpress.com
or
**SOUTHERN HISTORICAL PRESS, Inc.
PO BOX 1267
375 West Broad Street
Greenville, SC   29601
southernhistoricalpress@gmail.com**

ISBN #0-89308-175-2

Printed in the United States of America

INTRODUCTION

    Spartanburgh (or Spartan) County was created by the County Court Act of 1785. The court was scheduled to sit beginning on the third Mondays of March, June, September, and December of each year. At this time the court had jurisdiction to record deeds, issue tavern licenses, try small court cases, appoint road gangs or juries, and other duties important to the residents of the county. In 1787, the duties were increased to include probate court. Formerly, residents of this county had had to journey to Ninety Six Court House for probate court. In 1788, it became no longer necessary to prove deeds in open court, but it still could be done. The many dedimi in this particular series of court minutes are excellent clues to persons having immigrated from various counties in North Carolina and emigrated to various counties in Georgia. The sitting of this court was altered in 1791 to be on the second Mondays in April and September for what was them called intermediate court, and the county court to sit beginning the 12th days of January and June.
    These minutes themselves are found in four original volumes, now in the South Carolina Archives. The first volume was 260 pages in length. Only the first 106 pages of the original are now extant (through March term 1787), the remainder exists now only in the W. P. A. copy. The probates were recorded in a separate volumes 1790-1799, an unusual situation for such minutes. The volumes are as follows:

Volume 1784-1799   pp. 1-99
Volume 1789-1794   pp. 100-190
Volume 1794-1799   pp. 191-270
Volume 1790-1799 (probate) pp. 271-307

                              Brent H. Holcomb, C. A. L. S.
                              Box 21766
                              Columbia, South Carolina
                              December 19, 1979

Court Commission. Spartanburgh County.

State of South Carolina   To Baylis Earle, John Thomas Junr.,
    (Seal)   Henry White, John Ford, James Jordan,
William Moultrie.   William Wood, & Henry Machan Wood, Es-
                          quires...in pursuance of an act passed
24 March 1785, to establish County Courts...commissioned, 24
March 1785.   John Vanderhorss, Secretary.

Court Certificate

I do hereby certify that Baylis Earle, John Thomas Junr., Henry
White, John Ford, William Wood, and Henry Machan Wood appointed
Justices to sit in the County Court of Spartanburgh....
April 29, 1785.   Henry Pendleton, Judge.

James Jordan's Certificate.

I do hereby certify that James Jordan, Esquire, one of the
Justices for the County of Spartanburgh, hath taken the oath's
of office and allegiance, agreeable to Law, before Me:
Decemr. 10th, 1785.   Aedamus Burk, Judge.

June Court 1785.

At a Court began to be held at Nichols's Mill, on the third Monday in June 1785, for the County of Spartanburgh, in the State of South Carolina,

Present Baylis Earle, John Thomas Junr., Henry White, John Ford, William Wood, and Henry Machan Wood, Gentlemen Justices.

Court being opened, John Thomas Junr., being previously appointed Clerk, the Court proceeded to the choice of Sheriff for said County, then upon casting of the oaths, Mr. William Young was duly appointed to that office, and Mr. Joseph Buffington duly appointed Coroner for said County.
Court then adjourned until Court in Course. The minutes were signed by Baylis Earle, J.

September Court, 1785.

At a court began and holden for the County of Spartanburgh, at the plantation of Thomas Williamson, on the third Monday in September A. D. 1785.
Present Baylis Earle, Henry White, and John Ford, Gentlemen Justices.

Court being met according to adjournment they proceeded to business, and qualified their clerk. William Young, appointed Sheriff, produced his commission under the hand and seal of his Excellency the Governor, which being read, he was immediately sworn, and gave bond with parties according to Law: which Bond are in the following words (to-wit) - Sheriff's Bond:

...William Young, John Young Senr., and William Wood, are bound to the Treasurers of the State of South Carolina, for ₤ 1500 sterling money in Gold or silver specie, at the rate of four shillings & Eight pence to the Dollar; and one pound one shilling & nine pence to the Guinea...19th day of September 1785.
                           Wm Young (Seal)
  Wit: J. Thomas Junr,   John Young Senr. (Seal)
     Clk of the Court.

James Yancey, Esquire is admited as an attorney to plead in this Court, took the oath prescribed by Law.

Court adjourned until tomorrow morning nine o'clock. The minutes were signed by Baylis Earle, Henry White, John Ford.

Tuesday Morning 20th September 1785, the Court met according to adjournment. Present Baylis Earle, Henry White and John Ford Gentlemen Justices.

On application of Thomas Wadsworth of Belville, praying License to retail spiritous Liquors, ordered that license issue accordingly, authorizing said Wadsworth to Retail according to the rates prescribed by the Court, and that the clerk issue said License on application

Ordered that the following persons do serve as Constables for said County for one year (to wit) Richard Nally, Hancock Smith, Thomas Gordan, Henry Wolf, and Robert Harper. Richard Nally, Henry Wolf and Robert Harper were qualified accordingly.

William Neel came into Court and acknowledged a bill of sale to Daniel Jackson, bearing date the 20th day of Sept. 1785 ordered that the same be recorded which bill of sale are in the following words (to wit)
[abstract]: State of S. C, William Neel of Spartanburgh County for ℔ 200 sterling to Daniel Jackson of Union County, three negroes a negro woman Sue; one girl Riner; one boy Limas, one Feather Bed & furniture, one waggon and Gears, also one white horse branded on the mountain Shoulder 3S, and on the near buttock 113M...20 Sept 1785. Wm. Neel (Seal), Wit: John Motlow, William Prince.

Robert Harper against James Bridges Upon attachment. John Motlow and Samuel Hand being summoned and sworn as Garnashees on said attachment declares they have none of said Bridges property in their hands, or knowledge, etc.

On Motion of James Yancey Esquire praying leave for Michael Miller to Retail spiritous Liquors and keep a private House of Entertainment, Ordered that the clerk issue license accordingly, when applied for.

Court adjourned until tomorrow Morning 9 O'Clock. The Minutes were signed by Baylis Earle, Henry White, John Ford, Wm. Wood.

Wednesday 21st September 1785. the Court met according to adjournment.
Present Baylis Earle, Henry White and John Ford, Gentlemen Justices.

On Application of Capt. William Smith & John Blasingame Esquire, praying to be appointed Guardians of the persons and Estates of the Minors of Joseph Red, decd. Ordered that they be appointed on application.

Ordered the minors of Joseph Polson deceased have Guardians appointed to those under age to choose for themselves that all of the age of 14 & 12 years be bound out respectively to suitable persons applying for the same.

Ordered that George Gordon have License to keep a private House of Entertainment, he conforming to the Rules & Rates of Court.

Ordered that the Ear mark of William Prince be recorded: A smooth or Single Crop in the Right Ear & an under keel in the left.

Ordered that the bond given by the clerk for the performance of his office be recorded. [Abstract:] South Carolina, John Thomas Junior of the County of Spartanburg, Esquire, and Richard Harrison, William Prince & William Smith are bound to the Commisions of the Treasury of the State, for ₤ 1000, 19 September 1785... on condition that the above John Thomas Junior shall faithfully Execute the office of the Clerk of County Court of Spartanburg. John Thoms Junr. (Seal), Richd. Harrison (Seal), William Prince (Seal), William Smith (Seal), Wit: Baylis Earle.

Ordered that the following Rates be observed by all persons who shall or have obtained License to keep Taverns retail Liquors or keep private Houses of Entertainment.

to wit. Comn. cold dinner or supper /8 Hot d' or do. nearly Cookd. 1/ Common breakfast /8 do of Green Tea & loaf sugar 1/ do Bohea do /9 ditto coffee or chocolate /9 Lodging in a clean bed /4 do for 2 in do /3 Each: Jamaica pr Galln. 12/ pr. qt. 3/6 pr. pt. 1/9 half do /9 Gin /5 West India Rum pr gallon 8/ qt 2/ pt. 1/ 1/2 do /6 Gin /4. Northward Rum pr Gal. 5/ qt. 1/3 pt. /8 half do /4. Taffia pr. qt 1/ & so in larger or smaller quantities. Punch made of Jamaica Rum & Loaf sugar pr. qt. 1/4 & so in proportion. Northward Rum & Taffia in punch pr. quart 1/ & so in proportion. Nantz Brandy pr. Gallon 10/ pr. qt. 2/6 etc. Good Country Brandy pr. Galln. 5/ qt. 1/3 pt. /8 etc. Genava pr. Gallon 8/ qt. 2/ pt. 1/ half do. /6 etc. Whiskey pr. Gallon 4/ qt. pt. /6 etc.

Best Medara wine pr. Bottle 4/8 Draught 4/ etc. Common wine pr. qt. 3/ pt. 1/6 Part pr Bottle 3/6 Cherry & Lisbon pr. qt. 3/ Burgandy & Champaign pr. Bottle 4/ Other sweet wines pr. qt. 2/ Porter pr Bottle 3/ Draught do pr. qt. 2/ English Bottles Cyder pr. Bottle 2/ Home made do pr. qt. /6. Stableing an Horse 24 Hours with good & sufficient fodder or Hay 1/6 Corn /2 pr. qt. oats the same.

Ordered that the following persons be summoned to attent the next Court to serve as Grand Jurors. (to wit) Wm. Bensong, George Bruton, William Thomson, David Lewis, Charles James, John Head, William Lipscomb, James Oliphant, Capt. Wm. Smith, Charles Moore, Zadock Ford, Andrew Barry, Wm. Poole (taylor), John Carrick, Thomas Jackson, Edward Mitchison, Obediah Tremia, Israel Morris, Robert Goodlett Senr., John Barry, David Goodlett, Daniel McClarin, Vachel Dilingham, and William Prince.

And the following as Pettit Jurors for March Court--Isaac Bogan, William Lynch, George Roebuck, John Stone, John Tremia, James Hughs, James White, John Shands, John Leech, Thomas Williamson, Samuel Lancaster, David Golightly, Robert McDowall, Thomas Wyatt, Fleming Smith, George Connell, John Nesbit, Isham Foster, Baley Anderson, John Butler, Thomas Davis, Henry Machan, Samuel Culbertson, John Vice, John Banny, John Mapp, John Golightly, Wm. Crocker, John Redman & John Davis.

State against William Turner Thomason. On Recognizance
The defendant appeared in open court according as he was bound in the Recognizance, whereupon no witness or prosecutor appearing against him, he is dismissed without day.

Jeremiah Webb & Mary Crow bound over to this Court to give Evidence in behalf of the State, against William Turner Thomason, their nonattendance, ordered that the clerk issue scire facias, upon their Recognizance both principle & bail.

Issue to Bruton. Road order, from John Head's Ford on Enoree to Isaac Crows, John Head, overseer, Matthew Couch, warnor; from thence to John Pattons on So. Tyger, overseer George Bruton, Alex. Alexander, Warner; from thence to the narrow passage above Nicolas Mill, overseer John Barry, Moses Ward, warden; from thence to Lawsons Fork, at widow Bishops, overseer Robert Jemison, warner, John Goodlett; from thence to So. Pacolate at Kilpatricks old place, overseer James McDowall, warner, William Branham; from thence to the State line by Hoopers Ford, overseer James Hooper, warner, John Earle, Junr.
From Blackstocks ford on Tyger to opposite widow Smiths at Davis' old path, overseer John Bearden, Warner David Pruitt; from thence to Millers old Road, overseer Albertis Bright, warner Nathaniel Davis; from thence to a branch on said Road widow Mrs. Princes, overseer Henry Wells, warner William Underwood; from thence to the Junction with Heads Road, overseer Isham Foster, warner William Tinsley.
From Tates Ferry to opposite William Hickmans plantation, overseer Danl. McClary, warner John Fonderin; from thence to Byares Miller, overseer William Thomson, warner Reubin Smith; from thence to Hammits ford on Pacolate, overseer Malichi Jones, warner William Wooten; from thence to the lower Iron Works, overseer William Poole, J. M., warner Geo. Poole; from thence to the shoal on Fairforest above Mr. Joseph Buffington's, overseer James Smith, warner Fleming Smith, from thence to Duchmans Creek at widow Smith's, overseer Capt. William Smith, warner Thomas Thornton, thence to Blackstocks Road the same & same. (Issued).

Ordered that Major Ford & Samuel FArrow view the Ground & conduct the Road from Blackstocks ford on Tyger to Musgrove on Enoree, overseer Sampson Bobo, warner Edward Hooker.

Ordered that the Clerk issue the orders to the several overseers (Issued.)

Court adjourned until Court in Course. The minutes were signed by Baylis Earle; Henry White, John Ford, Esqrs.

At a County Court began and held for the County of Spartanburgh at the plantation of Thomas Williamson on the third Monday in December, 1785. Court met according to adjournment at three o'clock and at four o'clock adjourned until tomorrow morning at Nine O'clock. Signed Baylis Earle, J.

Tuesday the 20th day of December 1785. The Court met according to adjournment. Present, Baylis Earle, John Ford, and Henry Machan Wood, Gentlemen Justices.

William Shaw, Esquire, produced his Commission to authorize him to be admitted to practice as an Atty. in this State. Ordered that he be Entered on Record and admitted to practice in this Court.

Jacob Brown, Esquire, produced his hand to plead & practice in the several Courts in this State as an Atty. Ordered that the said Jacob Brown be admitted to practice in this Court.

Ordered that James Yancey be admitted to practice as an Atto. in this Court, he producing his license within six months from this date.

Ordered that no Atto. be admitted to practice in this Court in future, unless licensed by the Judges of the Supreme Court according to Law.

Daniel Brown Esquire, produced his Commission to plead and practice as an attorney in this State. Ordered that he be Entered on the Records and be permitted to practice in this Court accordingly.

Mr. Joseph Buffington produced a Commission from his Excellency the Governor, authorizing to act as coroner for the County of Spartanburgh, he was qualified accordingly.

On motion ordered that Mr. Thomas Williamson have license to retail spiritous Liquors and keep a private House of Entertainment on his applying to the Clerk for the same, and conforming to the Rates prescribed by Court.

Grand Jurors drawn to serve this Court. Andrew Braay, John Barry, Charles Moore, Daniel McClary, William Poole, Israel Morris, Edward Mitchison, David Golightly, William Benson, William Lipscomb, Charles James, Robert Goodlett Senr., George Bruton.

The Grand Jury being drawn, impaneled & sworn, the County attorney in behalf of the Court delivered a charge unto them, and forthwith they withdrew.

Robert Harper against Henry Baits. In Case.
Came the plaintiff by James Yancey Gentleman his attor. and the deft. by Daniel Brown Gentleman his attor. who saith he cannot gainsay the plaintiffs action but that it is just, and that he ows the debt mentioned in the declaration, amounting to ₤ 7 s 15 d 7 besides his Costs by him about his suit in this behalf Expended, and the said defendant in mercy.

Thomas Brandon came into Court and proved a lease & Release from John Patton to Zadock Ford. Ordered that the same be recorded.

Thomas Farrow came into Court and proved a lease and Release from Henry Hammilton, to John Farrow Senr., deceased; Ordered that the same be recorded.

William Wood Senr. came into Court and acknowledged a lease and Release unto Thomas Williamson, Ordered that the same be recorded.

Thomas Farrow came into Court and acknowledged a Deed of Gift to William and Samuel Farrow's. Ordered that the same be recorded.

Charles Waters against John Couch. On Petition, Etc.
Came the Plaintiff by Daniel Brown Gentleman his atto., and the defendant failing to appear, it is considered by the Court that the plaintiff recover against the defendant the sum of s 3 besides his Costs about his suit in this behalf Expended, and the said defendant in mercy.

James Betterton against John Bagwell. Petition & Sum.
Came the plaintiff by James Yancey Gentleman his attorney and

the defendant in his own proper person, says that he will not dispute with the Plaintiff or his attorney, whereupon it is considered by the Court that the plaintiff recover against the defendant the sum of Ł 1 s 19 d 10 besides his Costs by him about his suit in this behalf Expended and the said defendant in mercy.

John Elder came into Court and acknowledged a lease & Release to Samuel Farrow, Ordered that they be recorded.

Charles Waters against Vardry Mcbee Petition & Summons. By Consent of the parties and assent of the Court, this action is continued until March Term.

Isaac Cruse & David Brown against Joseph Buffington. On Petition. Came the defendant by James Yancey Gentleman his attorney and the Plaintiff failing to appear, Either in his person or by his attorney, to put in his plea, it is Considered by the Court that the defendant recover of the Plaintiff five shillings damage.

William Gaston against Abrem & Jno Andrews. Summons & Petition. Agreed on the defendants paying all Costs accruing.

Proved by two Evidences a lease and Release from David Cook to Michael Sprinkle, Ordered that the same be Recorded.

Pettit Jurors to serve this Court to wit John Golightly, James Hughs, Samuel Culbertson, John Nesbit, George Connell, John Redman, Henry Machan, Saml. Lancaster, Thomas Williams, John Davis, Fleming Smith, William Crocker.

The petit jurors being sworn to try an Issue of Traverse the State against John Elder, assault & battery, the defendant acquited on paying Costs.

Court adjourned until tomorrow at nine o'clock. The minutes were signed by Baylis Earle, John Ford, Henry M. Wood.

Wednesday the 21st of December 1785. The Court met according to adjournment, present Baylis Earle, John Ford, Henry Machan Wood, Gentlemen Justices.

Charles Moore came into Court and acknowledged a lease and Release to Thomas Moore, ordered that the same be recorded.

Ordered that John Golightly have license to retail spiritous liquors and keep a private house of Entertainment.

Present James Jordan, Esquire, who produced a certificate of his qualification as a justice of the peace for the County of Spartanburgh, Ordered that the same be recorded.

Ordered that a Road be laid out & opened from Thomas Wood, on the middle fork of Saluda to the County line, the said Thomas Wood & George Salmon be appointed Commissioners to lay off said Road, from the above mentioned Woods to McElhanys Shoal, Overseer John Foster Senr., warner Thomas Brammit, from thence to Wm. Young's plantation, overseer Daniel Kelley, warner William Right, from thence to the County line between Reedy River & Brush Creek, overseer James Richey, warner James McElheny.

Mary Crow being cited by scire facias to appear before the Court to Render Reasons why she did not attend at last Court, as an Evidence in behalf of the State on her oath does say she could not attend by reason of sickness, she is acquited accordingly.

Ebenezar Moss rendered such reasons as the Court thought fit to order him acquited also.

Ordered that a Road be straightened and opened from James Alexanders to James McElheny's, from Jas. Alexrs. the usual distance, Overseer John Alexander, warner William Caldwell, from thence the usual distance overseer Saml. Nesbit, warner Robert Nesbit; from thence to the South River overseer William Ursary, warner Robert Ursary, from thence midway, Jno nichols fence, overseer JEREMIAH Dalton (Dutton?), warner Daniel Dalton (Dutton?), from thence to James McElheny, overseer Randolf Casey, warner Levi Casey.

John Nicols is appointed to view & straighten said Road.

Ordered that Thomas Warren be appointed overseer for both Forks of the upper Road, from the North Carolina line to Pacolate River, from thence to the ford on Lawsons Fork at Woffords Iron Works, overseer James Turner, from the line Crossing Pacolate at Hammett's Ford to the said Works, overseer James Blackwell.

Ordered that the several presentments made by the Grand Jury, be put into Execution, by the Clerk issuing the necessary process against them immediately.

Ordered that James Lee be brought into Court to answer to a presentment of the grand jury for calling on God to Damn the said Grand Jurors.

County against James Lee. on a presentment for cursing the G. Jury.
Came the County Atto. Wm. Shaw in behalf of the County & the plaintiff in his own proper person, he being heard, the Court adjudged that the defendant be find in the sum of s 14 and costs.

Ordered that John Childress remain in the Custody of the Sheriff until he finds security for his good behavior & his apperance at next court.

Ordered that the Court House and other Public buildings be Established & Erected on the Lands of Mr. John Wood on the waters of Fairforest, on a small Hill near the said John Wood's dwelling House according to the first appointment.

Ordered that the Jurors for next Court both Grand & Petit be summoned, & that the Clerk issue the necessary venire facias thereupon.

Ordered that a didimus be issued to authorize a justice of peace in North Carolina to take the Evidence of Moses Holcomb Respecting a suit now depending George Parkison against Hugh Price

Court adjourned until the third Monday in March next at Mr. John Wood's, the place appointed. The minutes were signed by Baylis Earle, John Ford, Henry Machan Wood.

At a County Court began to be holden at the plantation of John Wood on the third Monday in March 1786. Present John Ford, James Jordan and Henry Machan Wood, Gentlemen Justices.

The Court proceeded to draw a Grand Jury, they are as follows:

(to wit) Thomas Wadsworth, Joseph Wofford, William Tate, John Gowin, John McElheny, John Timmons, John Nicols, William Smith Capt., George Salmon, William McDowall, Robert Nelson, William Poole J. M., John Russell, William Foster, Henry Wells.

A Deed of Conveyance from James Fanning and his wife to William Lipscomb, proved by the Evidence of Wm. Thomson, & Phillip Martin, Ordered that the same be recorded.

William Thomson came into Court and replevied the Goods of Josiah Tanner, at the suit of the Excors. of Safold.

Charles Goodwin Esquire admitted as an attorney to practice in this Court on his producing admission in the Court of Common Pleas at our next June Court.

Pettit Jurors for March Court, Richard Harrison, Robert Goodgion, William Simpson, Jesse Connell, Christopher Casey, Alexander Vernon, John Smith, Roland Cornelius, James Wofford, John Ward, James White, Isaac Morgan, James Richey, Shands Golightly, James Keen, Joseph Veneble.

Thomas Benson appointed deputy sheriff was duly sworn in Open Court.

A lease & release from Jesse Connell and Ann his wife to George Connell, proved in Open Court by the Evidence of David Golightly and William Ford. And on the Examination of the said Ann Connell she freely pronouncenth her dower before John Ford, Esq., Ordered that the same be recorded.

A lease & release from John Walker to Jesse Connell proved in Open Court by the Evidence of John Smith & Francis Connell. Ordered that they be recorded.

Ordered that a Road be opened from McDowall's Mill on No. Pacolate to Spartanburgh Court House, Overseer Thomas Bennett, warner John Conner.

Two sets of leases & Releases from James Burton to Thomas Williamson, proved in Open Court by the Evidence of William Ford & William Williamson. Ordered that they be recorded.

State against Sarah Bird. In Bastardy.
Ordered by the Court that the defendant Sarah Bird declare on oath the father of her child. On her oath the said Sarah Bird declared William Prince to be the father thereof.
Ordered that the necessary process be issued against the said Wm. Prince Immediately.

James McElhaney against John James. On Attachment.
Ordered that the Goods of the defendant non attached be replevied on the suretys of Robert and Isham Foster. The defendant being Ruled to special bail, the above mentioned sureties Robert & Isham Foster Came into Court and undertakes for the defendant that if he is Cast in this suit they will pay the Cost & Condemnation thereof, or render his body to prison in discharge of the same.

Court adjourned until tomorrow morning nine o'clock. The minutes were signed by John Ford, James Jordan, Henry Machan Wood.

Court met according to adjournment, present John Ford, James

Jordan & Henry M. Wood.

Thomas Tod came into Court & acknowledged a lease & Release from himself and wife to John Thomas Senr. Ordered that the same be recorded.

The said Thomas Tod acknowledged a lease and release to Tilman Bobo. Ordered that they be recorded.

Lease & Release from Samuel Langston & Sarah his wife to Thomas Tod, proved by the Evidences of William Clayton & Edward Hooker. Ordered that they be recorded.

Lease and Release from Samuel Bell to Samson Bobo, proved in Open Court by the Evidence of James Howel & Thomas Tod. Ordered that they be recorded.

Present Henry White, Esquire.

Charles Saxon against Brazal Brashers. Debt.
Came the plaintiff by James Yancey Gentleman his attorney and the defendant by Daniel Brown Gentleman his atto. thereupon he the sd. defendant saith he cannot gainsay the plaintiffs action but that ti is just & true and that he owes the debt mentioned in the declaration, Amountaing to ₤ 8 s 3 d 2 sterling money with interest from the 21st of May 1784 whereupon it is considered by the Court that the plaintiff recover against the defendant the said sum of ₤ 8 s 3 d 2 with interest besides his Costs by him about his suit in this behalf Expended and the said defendant in mercy.

Present Baylis Earle Esquire.

William Graham against Joseph Buffington. In debt.
Came the plaintiff by William Shaw Gentleman his attorney and the defendant by James Yancey Gentleman his attorney Whereupon came a jury (to wit) Richard Harrison, Robert Goodgion, William Simpson, Jesse Connell, James Tichey, Alexr. Vernon, Shands Golightly, John Smith, Roland Cornelius, James Wofford, Joseph Venible, John Ward, who being Elected tried and sworn the truth to speak upon the issue joined upon their oath does say that the deft. does owe the debt mentioned in the declaration amounting to ₤ 50 sterling money, Whereupon it is Considered by the Court that the plaintiff recover against the said deft., the said sum of ₤ 50 sterling, besides his costs by him in this behalf Expended, and the said defendant in mercy.

William Graham against Administratrix of Thomson. In debt.
Came the plaintiff by James Yancey Gentleman his atto. and the defendant by William Shaw Gentleman his atto. saith she cannot gainsay the plaintiff's action but that it is just, and that she owes the debt mentioned...₤ 6 s 14, whereupon it is Considered by the Court that the plaintiff recover.... besides his Costs....

Wm. Lynch noted for non-attendance to serve as a Juror, Came into Court & rendered his Excuses praying to be relieved from the fines and penalties to which he is lyable by Law. His Excuses being Considered by the Court he is relieved accordingly.

Ordered by Court that a Road be laid out and opened from the main Road at or near Major Farrars by Belville to Capt. David McDowalls, thence the nearest & best way across the Forks of Pacolate to the State line into the Road that leads by David

Millers from Major Farrars aforesaid to Lawsons Fork, overseer John Williams, warner Christopher Long, from thence to Pacolate, overseer David McDowall, warner John Conner, from thence to North Pacolate, overseer Hugh Freeman, warner John Carrell, from thence to the State line aforesaid, Overseer John McKnight, warner Robert McMillian.

Ordered that a Road be opened from William Jemisons to widow Bishops on Lawsons Fork, overseer William Jemison, warner Robert Henderson. Court adjourned until tomorrow morning at nine o' clock. The minutes were signed by John Ford, James Jordan, Henry M. Wood.

Present Baylis Earle, James Jordan & Henry M. Wood.
Court met according to adjournment on Wednesday the Twenty-second of March 1786.

Ordered that William Wofford Senr. be Ruled to special Bail in the suit, James McElwayne against Wm. Wofford, and also in the suit, John Elder against said Wm. Wofford, whereupon Joseph Wofford came into Court and undertakes for the defendant that if he is cast in the said action, or Either of them, he will pay the Costs and condemnation thereof or render his body to prison in discharge of the same.

John Timmons came into Court and acknowledged a Deed of conveyance from hismelf to Abner Timmons. Ordered that the same be recorded.

Samuel Porter acknowledged a lease and Release from himself to Uriah Conner. Ordered that the same be recorded.

Piles & McNees against Charles Waters. In Case.
the plaintiff then solemnly called to prosecute this suit, did not appear, neither in his own persons, or by his attorney, Whereupon the Court order the suit to be discontinued at the plaintiff's Costs.

James McElwane against William Wofford. In Debt.
Came the plaintiff by James Yancey his attorney, and the deft. failing to put in his plea, tho. present in his proper person, Whereupon came a Jury (to wit) Richard Harrison, Robert Goodgion, William Simpson, Jesse Connell, James Ritchey, Alexander Vernon, Shands Golightly, John Smith, Roland Cornelius, James Wofford, Joseph Venible, John Ward, who being Elected tried & sworn the truth to speak on their oath does say that the defendant does owe the debt in the Plaintiff's declaration mentioned, amounting to Ł 10 s 11 d 9, Whereupon the Court are of opinion that the said Plaintiff recovere...the sum besides his costs....

Joseph Buffington against Arthur Crocker. In Debt.
By consent of the parties and assent of the Court the trial of said suit is laid over until next Court in Course.

Charles Waters against Vardry McBee.
Came the Plaintiff by his attorney aforesaid, and the defendant by his attorney, and upon the parties being heard it is considered by the Court that the plaintiff recovered against the defendant Ł 3 sterling, besides his costs....

Roger Brown against Charles Hunt. In Petition, Etc.
Came the Plaintiff by James Yancey Gentleman his attorney and the

defendant by Charles Goodwin Gentleman his atto. and upon the
Parties being heard it is considered by the Court that the Plaintiff recover against the defeant ₤ 3 s 11 d 4 besides his Costs

John Farrow against Admors. of Smith. On Petition.
by consent of the Parties & assent of the Court this suit is discontinued at the defendants Costs.

State against Beaks Musgrove & Westwood Waters. Breach of the peace.
Came the defendants Beaks Musgrove & Westwood Waters with Charles Waters their surety, Enters into & acknowledged themselves severally indebted to the State, to be levied on their Goods & Chattles, Lands & Tenements Respectively, ₤ 20 each, also to be forfoeited & recovered of them, unless the said Beaks Musgrove & Westwood Waters does make their personal appearance at the House of John Wood on the third Monday in June next, and from thence not depart until Lawfully discharged by the Court.

Westwood Waters against William Smith. On Petition.
Came the Plaintiff by his attorney Jacob Brown, Gentleman, and the defendant by James Yancey, Gentleman his attorney and upon the parties being heard it is considered by the Court that the Plaintiff take nothing by his bill, but for his false Clamor be in mercy, and that the defendant go hence without day, and recover s 5 damage besides his costs....

Thomas Crow against Andrew Brown. On Petition.
Came the Plaintiff by Jacob Brown Gentleman his attorney and the defendant failing to appear, it is Considered by the Court that the Plaintiff Recover against the defendant ₤ 2 s 16 besides his Costs....

Joseph Buffington against William Wofford Senr. In Case.
By consent of the Parties & assent of the Court, all matters of Controversy is Refered to Richard Harrison, Jesse Connell & John Smith, and their award returnable to next Court, shall be the judgement of the Court.

John Johnson against Amos Space. In Case.
Came the Plaintiff by James Yancey Gentleman his attorney and the defendant by Daniel Brown Gentleman his Atto. Whereupon came a jury to-wit: Richard Harrison, Robert Goodgion, William Simpson, Jesse Connell, James Richey, Alexander Vernon, Shands Golightly, John Smith, Roland Cornelius, James Wofford, Joseph Venible, John Ward, who being Elected, tried and sworn the truth to speak...the Plaintiff recover against the defendant one shillings damage, besides his Costs....

Ordered that Samuel Saratt, John Martin, Obediah Trimia, Thomas Warren, John Ross, Joseph Venible & Capt. Vinson be appointed to lay out a Road from Spartanburgh Court House to the North Carolina line.

Joseph Wofford Came into Court and acknowledged a lease & release from himself to William Lynch, Ordered to be recorded.

Court adjourned until tomorrow morning at nine o'clock. The minutes were signed by Baylis Earle, John Ford, James Jordan.

Thursday the 23rd day of March 1786, the court met according to adjournment. Present Baylies Earle, James Jordan, Henry Machan

Wood.

Ordered that a Road be laid out from Jeremiah Russells to James Tarry's, the nearest & best way, that Joseph Vaughn and said Tarry be appointed to lay out the same, Overseer Joseph Tarry, warner William Cornelius.

State against William Wofford Junr. Adultery.
Came the County Atto. in behalf of the State & the Defendant by his Atto. and upon the Parties being heard it is Considered by the Court that the said defendant be discharged without day, on paying all Costs, Atto. fee paid in Court.

Ordered that Dennis Duff be qualified a Constable for this County, by John Ford Esquire.

Adam Potter Assignee of Thomson against Isham Safold. In Debt on Nonsuit.
Came the Plaintiff by Jacob Brown Gentlemen his atto. and the defendant by James Yancey Gentleman his atto. upon the Parties being heard it was Considered by the Court that the Plaintiff be nonsuited & that the defendant go hence without day, & recover five shillings damage besides his Costs....

John Robinson against John Boyd On Petition, etc.
Came the Plaintiff by Jacob Brown Gentleman his atto. and the defendant failing to appear, either in his person or by his atto., Whereupon it is considered by the Court that the Plaintiff Recovered against the defendant Ł 3 s 14 d 8 besides his Costs....

John Martin against Moses Procter. On Petition Continued until next Court.

William West against James Philips. On Petition Continued until next Court

Thomas Scurry against Benjamin Wofford. On Petition. Continued.

Christaphor Casey against Benjamin Wofford. Tra. Conn.
By consent of the Parties this suit is discontinued at the Plaintiff's Costs. (Septr. 7 Discontind. by Saml Farrow.)

Robert Goodgion against Thomas Davis. On Petition by Acct.
By consent of the Parties & assent of the Court, this suit is Discontinued at Plaintiff's Costs.

Henry Hammilton against Jeremiah Neel. Assault etc. Continued until next Court.

Wadsworth & Company against Frederick Hawkins. On Petition. Continued untill next Court.

Same against Robert Connell. On Petition by Accounty.
Came the Plaintiff by James Yancey Gentleman his attorney and the defendant failing to appear it is considered by the Court that the Plaintiff recover against the said defendant the sum of Ł 1 s 5 d 10 sterling besides his costs....

Wadsworth & Company against Benjamin Stone. On Petition by account.
Came the Plaintiff by James Yancey Gentleman his attorney and the defendant failing to appear Either in own persons or by his attorney, Whereupon it is Considered by the Court that the Plain-

tiff recover against the defendant, the sum of ₺ 2 s 11 d 5 sterling besides his costs....

Wadsworth & Company against John Moore. On Attachment. Court order for the sale of Two Cows and one yearling.

Daniel Symms came into Court & acknowledged a lease and release from himself to Wadsworth and Turpin. Ordered that the same be Recorded.

Ordered that Edmond Craddock have license to keep a Public House of Entertainment by his applying to the clerks office for the same.

On motion of Mr. Shaw Ordered that a new Tryal be admited John Johnson vs Amos Space.

William McDowall against Bartan Coats. In Debt.
Came the Plaintiff by James Yancey Gentleman his attorney & the defendant by Jacob Brown Gentleman his attorney, Whereupon came a jury (to wit) Jesse Connell, Robert Goodgion, William Simpson, James Richey, Alexander Vernon, Shand Golightly, John Smith, Roland Cornelius, James Wofford, John Ward, Obediah Hooper, Martin Armstrong, who being Elected tried & sworn & truly to Enquire of damages upon the issue...the Plaintiff recoer against the defendt. the said sum of ₺ 23 s 6 d 8 with one shilling damage besides his Costs...

Peter Trammel against John King. On Attachment.
On Motion of Mr. Goodwin, as the Plaintiff has not appeared, the attachment is Desolved, & the defendt. have damage on the attachment Bond.

John Elder against William Wofford Junr. Case Default.

Baylis Earle against Thomas Debnard. On Attachment.
The said Writ of attachment is returned by Henry Wolf, constable; Goods levied in the hands of Hugh Peace, Ordered that the said Wolf retain the said goods in his own hand until further orders.

Deed of conveyance from William Dixon to Thomas Farra, proved by the Evidence of James Poole, who on his oath says, he saw Mary Stovaul & Curtis Jury sign the same with himself. Ordered to be recorded.

Joseph Buffington against Thomas Dennard. On Petition.
Came the Plaintiff by James Yancey Gentleman his attorney, and the defendant failing to appear Either in his own person or by his attorney, it is Considered by the Court, that the Plaintiff recover against the defendant, the sum of ₺ 2 s 1 d 7 besides his costs by him in this behalf Expended & the said defendant in mercy.

Francis Nevil Wayland against Thomas Hooper. On Petition.
Came the Plaintiff by Jacob Brown Gentleman his atto. & the defendant failing to appear Either in his own person or by his atto., whereupon it is considered by the Court that the plaintiff recover against the defendant the sum of ₺ 1 s 12 d 6 besides his Costs....

Ebenezar Morse agaisnt John Cooper. Case
Came the Plaintiff by Daniel Brown Gentleman his atto. & the defendant failing to appear, Either in his own person or by his

attorney, thereupon came a Jury to wit, Richard Harrison, Jesse Counnell, Robert Goodgion, Wm. Simpson, James Richey, Alexr. Vernon, Shands Golightly, John Smith, Roland Cornelius, James Wofford, John Ward, Obediah Hooper, who being sworn well & truly to Enquire of damages...the defendant does owe the debt £ 18 s 8 whereupon it is considered by the Court that the Plaintiff recover the debt besides his Costs....

Nathaniel Miller Came into Court and acknowledged a lease and Release to Robert Miller. Ordered to be recorded.

Said Nathaniel Miller acknowledged a lease & release to John Miller. Ordered to be Recorded.

Ordered that George Bruton & David Bruton lay off a Road from John Patton to John Cavins crossing at a shoal on Fergusons Creek above Enoch Floyds. George Bruton appointed overseer of said Road.

Ordered that John Gowin have license to Retail spiritous Liquors and keep a private House of Entertainment, on his applying to the Clerk for the same & conforming to the Rates prescribed by the Court.

Daniel Kelley against Henry Moffatt. In Case.
Came the Plaintiff by Jacob Brown Gentleman his attorney & the defendant by Daniel Brown Gentleman his attorney, who saith he cannot gainsay the Plaintiff's action, but that it is just & that he owe the debt £ 6 s 13 d 11 sterling....

State against Deskin Grant. Breach of the Peace.
The defendant came into Court & acknowledged his fault, fined by the Court, one shillings & all Costs.

Court adjourned until tomorrow Morning at nine o'clock. the Minutes were signed by Baylies Earle, Henry M. Wood, James Jordan.

Friday the 24th day of March 1786, Court met according to adjournment; Present John Ford, James Hordan & Henry Machan Wood.

Israel Morris against Rowland Cornelius. Case Continued 'til next court.

Stephen Williford against John Cooper. Assault & By. Continued until next court.

Richard & Wade Hampton against Thomas Wood. In Debt Default.

John Childress against James Poole Assault & By.
Came the Plaintiff by Daniel Brown Gentleman his atto. and the defendant by James Yancey Gentleman his attorneys and defends the force & Injury & says he is not Guilty of the assault & Battery...thereupon the Parites join issue for the trial of the case at the next court.

James Harrison assignee of Burk against Administrator of John Spurgion. In Debt. Continued until next Court.

Reuben Dixon against Vardry McBee & others. In Debt. Continued until next Court.

Major Parsons against Robert McDowell In Debt. Continued 'till next court.

George Parkison against Hugh Perce. Trover & Conversion.
Came the Plaintiff by Jacob Brown Gentleman his atto. & the
defendant by Daniel Brown, Gentleman his atto. whereupon came a
Jury (to wit) Richard Harrison, Jesse Connel, James Richey,
Shands Golightly, Rowland Cornelius, Robert Goodgion, Alexr.
Vernon, John Ward, James Wofford, David Goodlett, Daniel Symms,
who being Exelcted...say that the defendant is not guilty...
defendant recover against sd. plaintiff five shillings damage....

Ordered that the Clk of the Court furnish the County attorney
with such orders, as the Court have made, Respecting the County
Buildings, a copy of which is given.

Lease and release from William Benson to Richard Harrison, proved
in open Court, by two witnesses, Ordered to be recorded.

Ordered that the Clerk make out Jury lists for June Court and
Issue the venire facias's to the Sheriff of the County.

Ordered that a Didimus Issue to Edward Smith, Joseph Ford & Cornelius Bowman or either of them to qualify Moses Holcom, in the
cause of George Parkison against Hugh Perce- at Blunt Court House
on the second Monday in August next.

Court adjourned until Court in Course. the minutes were signed
by John Ford, James Jordan & Henry Machan Wood.

At a County Court began to be holden for the County of Spartanburgh at the House of John Wood, on the third Monday in June
1786. Present Baylis Earle, Henry White, James Jordan, John
Ford, & Thomas Wadsworth, Gentlemen Justices.

There not being a Grand Jury met, the Court proceeded to Call a
Pettit Jury, which are as follows: Richard James, John White,
Landon Farrow, Moses Timmons, Joseph Barnett, Rowland Johnson,
Francis Nevil Wayland, Isaac Hendrix, Bayley Taylor, Jeremiah
Tilman, Peter Smith, William Smith, Abner Simmons.

Charles Goodwin Esquire produced his admission as an atto.

County against Thomas Williamson. Misdemeaner in Tavern Keeping.
Ordered that Thomas Williamson be summoned to appear at next
Court to answer to such matters as are alleged against him in
Tavern keeping.

James Yancey Esquire produced his license to Please & Practice
as an attorney in the several Courts of Law & Equity in this
State ordered that he be Enrolled, accordingly on the records of
this Court.

Joseph Buffington against William Wofford Senr. In Case
Richard Harrison, Jesse Connell, John Smith to whom was Refered
the settlement of all matters of controversy between the said
Plff. & the sd. defendant & their verdict to be a Rule of Court,
have Returned due to the Pltff. three shillings & four pence
half penney Sterling. Ordered by the Court that the Plaintiff
have judgment for the same, besides his costs....

Thomas Flinn against Paul Garrison Trover Convn. non suit.

William Kerley against History Hilsmore. On Petition.
Came the Plaintiff by Jacob Brown Gentleman his attorney and the
defendant failing to appear, it is Considered by the Court that

the Plaintiff recover against the said defendant one penney damage besides his Costs....

John Head against Peter Brooks. On Petition.
Came the Plaintiff by Daniel Brown Gentleman his attorney & the defendant failing to appear, Whereupon it is Considered by the Court that the Plaintiff recover the sum of ₤ 2 s 9 besides his costs....

Ordered that a Road be opened from Tates Ferry on Broad River to the meadows on the head of peoples Creek on the Cherokee Road, Overseer Nathaniel Robison, warner John Cooper.

Ordered that William Fields be appointed a Constable for this County and he was sworn Immediately in Open Court.

John Wilson against Thomas Lowry. On Petition.
Came the defendant on this action by Charles Goodwin his atto. and the Plaintiff failing to appear Either by his atto. or in his person, Whereupon it is considered by the Court that the Pltf. be nonsuited & pay five shillings damage & all the Costs.
    Millinton Counch is allowed on oath 7/6 for three days attendance on the above mentioned suit.

Elizabeth Casey against Randolf Casey. On Petition by act.
Came the Plaintiff by James Yancey Gentleman her atto. and the defendant failing to appear Either in his person or by his atto. Whereupon it is Considered by the Court that the Pltf. recover against the said defendant the sum of ₤ 1 s 19 besides her Costs.

Baylis Earle against Thomas Dennard. On Attachment
absent Baylis Earle present Henry White. Hugh Perce being summoned & sworn as Garnishee in the said attachment declares he hath in his hands the sum of ₤ 25 old former Currency, the property of the said Thomas Dennard, said attachment was levied in the hands of said Perce; Whereupon came a Jury (to wit) Francis Wayland, Richard James, Landon Farrow, Moses Timmons, Peter Smith, Rowland Johnson, Joseph Barnett, Isaac Hendrix, Wm. Smith, Abner Timmons & William Floyd, who being sworn well & truly... the defendant doth owe the debt ₤ 8 s 11 d 5....

Jesse Davis against Dudley Red. In Debt.
Came the Plaintiff by Jacob Brown Gentleman his attorney & the defendant by Charles Goodwin Gentleman his atto. who saith he Cannot gainsay the Plaintiff's action, but that it is just, & that he owes the debt mentioned in the declaration amounting to ₤ 4 s 13 d 4....

Ordered that Edward Lynch be overseer of the Road from Isaac Crows to Heads Ford on Enoree.
    Absent Thomas Wadsworth.   Present Baylis Earle, Esq.

Wadsworth & Co against Thomas Wood. On Petition by account.
Came the Plaintiff by James Yancey Gentleman his atto. & the defendant failing to appear Either in his person or by his atto., therefore it is Considered by the Court that the Plaintiff recover against the said defendant the sum of ₤ 1 s 11 d 3 besides his costs....

Wadsworth & Co. against Henry Turner Senr. On Petition by account. Came the Plaintiff by James Yancey Gentleman his attorney & the defendat failing to appear, either in his person or by his attorney, therefore it is Considered by the Court that the

Plaintiff recover against the defendant the sum of ₺ 1 s 8 d 9 sterling, besides his Costs...

Wadsworth & Company against Thomas Collins. On Petition. Came the Plaintiff by James Yancey Gentleman his attorney & the defendant failing to appear, therefore it is considered by the Court that the Plaintiff recover against the defendant the sum of ₺ 1 s 12 & d 3 sterling....

Wadsworth & Co. against William Collins. On Petition by account. Came the Plaintiff by James Yancey Gentleman his atto. & the deft. failing to appear Either in own person or by his atto., therefore it is considered by the court, that the Plaintiff recover against the Defendant the sum of ₺ 1 s 13 d 8 sterling besides his Costs....

Absalom Wofford against Zophar Smith. Trover & Convn. The Plaintiff in this action being solemnly called to prosecute his suit, did not appear neither in his person or by his atto., Whereupon it is Considered by the Court that the Plaintiff be nonsuited & that the defendant have five shillings damage....

Thomas Gordon against William Gilbert. On attachment. The defendant being Ruled to special Bail, Robert Prince & John Golightly came into Court & undertakes for the defendant and Replevies the Goods attached, and undertakes that if the defendant is Case in this action, they will pay the Costs & Condemnation thereof, or Render his body to prison in discharge of the same.

Ordered that Rowland Johnson be appointed overseer in the Room of John Williams, David Lewis, warner.

Absent Henry White, Esq. Present Thomas Wadsworth.

Ordered that   Pennington be appointed Constable for this County for one year.

Court adjourned until tomorrow Morning at 9 o'clock. The minutes were signed by Baylis Earle, James Jordan & Thomas Wadsworth.

Tuesday morning 20th June 1786. Court met according to adjournment. Present Baylis Earle, Henry White, Richard Harrison, Thomas Wadsworth & Zadock Ford. Gentlemen Justices.

The Court proceeded to draw Grand Jurors for next Court. Martin Armstrong, Thomas James, Josiah Culbertson, William Foster, William Poole taylor, William Lipscomb, John Gowin, George Bruton, Alexander Ray, Moses Casey, Thomas McKnight, David Lewis, Anthony Coulter, Thomas Williamson, John Redman, Samuel Lancaster, William Tate, Alexander Vernon, Daniel McClain, William Ford (apped.), Thomas Farrow.

Pettit Jurors for September Court 1786. Robert McDowall, James McDowall, William Bird, David Lewis Junr., Samson Bobo, George Connell, Henry Moffatt, William Crocker, William Millinghan, Thomas Millinghan , Samuel Jackson, Peter Elder, Jason Moore, Thomas Hannah, John Moore, Andrew Millinghan, John Golightly, Isham Yearby, John Alexander, James Jackson, Charles Smith, James Smith, Absalom Thomson, James Gilmore. Ordered that the Clerk issue the venire facias against said Jurors to Sept. Court.

17

Ordered that William Turner Thomason do serve this County as a Constable for one year. He was sworn accordingly.

The Court then adjourned until Court in Course. The minutes were signed by Baylis Earle, Henry White, Richard Harrison, Zadock Ford.

At a County Court began to be holden for the County of Spartanburgh, at the Plantation of John Wood, on the third Monday in September Anno. Dommini 1786.
Present James Jordan, Thomas Wadsworth and Richard Harrison, Esquires.

Thomas Peter Carns, Esquire produced his certificate of admission as an attorney and solicitor in the Courts of Law and equity in this State. Ordered that he be Enroled on the Records of this Court.

Sept. 19th. A lease and Release from William McCowin & wife to William Tate senr., proved in Open Court, by the Evidence of Michael Hogin & William Tate Junr. Ordered that the same be Recorded.

Uriah Connor came into Court and acknowledged a Lease and Release from himself and wife to Jeremiah Dalton. Ordered that they be Recorded.

Joseph Morris came into Court and acknowledged a Lease and Release from himself and wife to William Morris. Ordered that they be Recorded.

A Deed of Conveyance from Edward Dickson North Carolina to Bazel Lee proved by the Evidence of Deskin Grant. Ordered to be recorded.

A lease and release from John Kirconnell to Joseph Morris proved by the Evidence of John Morris. Ordered to be recorded.

A lease and Release from Thomas Garvin to Thomas Wadsworth & William Turpin, proved by the Evidence of Thomas Farrar and Daniel Symms. Ordered to be recorded.

A lease & Release from Peggy Lewis to Thomas Wadsworth and William Turpin, proved by the Evidence of Thomas Farrar. Ordered to be recorded.

A Lease & Releas from John Clemins to Thomas Wadsworth and William Turpin. Proved by the Evidence of Daniel Symms & Thomas Benson. Ordered to be Recorded.

A Lease & Release from Polly Lewis to Daniel Symms. Proved by the Evidence of Thomas Farrar. Ordered to be recorded.

William Wofford Senr. came int Court and acknowledged a Lease & Release from himself to Wells Griffith. Ordered to be recorded.

The Court proceeded to draw the Grand Jurors for Septr. Term 1786. whose names are as follows. John Gowin, Foreman. Martin Armstrong, Josiah Culbertson, William Foster, George Burton, Moses Casey, Thomas McKnight, David Lewis, Anthony Coulter, Thomas Williamson, John Redman, William Ford, Thos. Farrow.

Peter Carns Esquire is admitted to practice as an attorney in this Court. On his producing his admission from the judges of the Circuit Court at our next December Term.

James Jordan Esq. acknowledged a Deed of conveyance from himself to Robert Bishop. Ordered to be Recorded.

Present Zadock Ford Esquire. James Jordan, Esquire acknowledged a deed of conveyance from himself to George Devors. Ordered to be recorded.

John Mapp came into Open Court and acknowledged a Lease & Release from himself to John Dickson. Ordered that the same be recorded.

Israel Morris acknowledged a bill of sale of a Negro Man slave to James Jordan Esq. Ordered to be Recorded.

The Court then proceeded to draw the Pettit Jurors, whose names are James Smith, foreman, William Bird, Robert McDowall, Henry Moffatt, Thomas Milligan, Isham Yerly, Charles Smith, Andrew Milligan, David Lewis Junr., Jason Moore, George Connell, James Gilmore.

Nicholas Jasper came into Court and acknowledged a Lease & Release from himself to Peter Howard. Ordered to be recorded.

A Deed of Conveyance from Jesse Tate to John Arnold, proved by the evidence of Henry Robison, Senr. Ordered to be Recorded.

John Brown against William Elder. Case By consent of the Plaintiff & assent of the Court dismissed at Plaintiff's Costs.

William Smith against John Campbell. On Petition.
Came the Plaintiff by James Yancey Gentleman his attorney, and the Defendant saith he Cannot gainsay the Plaintiff's action, but that it is just, and that he owes the debt ₺ 3 s 5 d 10½....

On Motion, ordered that William Poole, Iron Master, have License to Retail Spiritous Liquors and keep a Public House of Entertainment on his applying to the Clerk & giving Bond with approved sureties for his behaviour in the same & conformting to the Rates prescribed by the Court.

The minutes were signed by James Jordan, Thomas Wadsworth, Richard Harrison, Zadock Ford. Court adjourned until tomorrow Morning Nine O'Clock.

Tuesday the 19th September 1786, the Court met according to adjournment. Present James Jordan, Thomas Wadsworth, and Zadock Ford, Esquire.

A lease & Release from John McCullock to Spencer Bobo, proved by the Evidence of Samson Bobo. Ordered to be Recorded.

A Lease & Release from Thomas Davis to Matthias Sulser proved by the evidence of Alexander Ray & Francis Nevil Wayland. Ordered to be recorded.
Present Richard Harrison, Esquire.

Joseph Buffington against Arthur Crocker. In Debt.
Came the Plaintiff by James Yancey, Gentleman his atto. & the defendant by Daniel Brown Gentleman his attorney, whereupon came

a jury (to wit) James Smith, Robert McDowall, Henry Moffatt, Thomas Milligan, David Lewis Junr., Jason Moore, George Connell & James Gilmore, who...upon their oath do say that the defendant doth owe the debt ₺ 6 s 2 d 7....with Lawfull interest from 15 Dec 1783.

Ebenezer Moss against Westwood Waters. On Petition by acct.
Came the Plaintiff by Jacob Brown Gentleman his atto., and the partiés being heard, it is Considered by the Court that the Plaintiff recover against the said defendant the sum of ₺ 2 s 12 d 10 besides his Costs....

Richard and Wade Hamptons against Thomas Wood. In debt.
Came the Plaintiff by James Yancey Gentleman his atto. and the defendant failing to appear, Whereupon came a jury (the same as above), who say that the defendant does owe the debt ₺ 9 sterling money with Lawful Interests from 1 January 1785, until paid with one shilling damage....

John Birdsong on his oath, 15/ is allowed him for Mileage and attendance as an Evidence in the above suit.

A Lease and Release from James Jordan Esq. to Thomas Davis was acknowledged in open Court. Ordered to be Recorded.

A Bill of sale from James Holland of Rutherford County, North Carolina to Thomas Davis proved in open Court by the Evidence of Henry Moffatt & Sarah Bird. Ordered to be recorded.

James Yancey   James Harrison, assignee of Burk   In Debt.
W. Shaw   against Elizabeth Spurgin, admx. of Jno Spurgin
By order of the court this suit is Discontinued at the Plaintiff's Costs.

George Gordon Assignee of Crow against Ebenezer Morse. In Debt.
By order of the Court this suit is Discontinued at the Plaintiff's costs.

Present Baylis Earle, Esquire.

A Deed of Conveyance from Benjamin Brown to Henry Hamilton proved by the Evidences of John Lindsey and Abraham Gray. Ordered to be recorded.

Westwood Waters against Jesse Rakestraw. In Slander.
By the request of the Parties this suit is Discontinued at the Plaintiff's costs.

John Barclay against William Moore. In Trover.
By consent of the Parties and assent of the Court, this action is continued until next Court.

John Campbell against John Huatt. Petition by acct.
The Plaintiff in this case being solemnly called, but failing to appear, Either in his person or by his atto., Whereupon it is Considered by the Court that the Pltff. Be nonsuited and pay unto the said defendant five shillings damage, besides the Costs....

William Bennett against Landan Farrow. In Trover. Continued until next court.

Charles Moore against Benjamin Silman. In Case. By consent of the parties and assent of the Court, this action is continued until December Term next.

William Brazel against Westwood Waters. Case.
By consent of the Parties, and assent of the Court, the trial of this action is referred until December Court next.

Thomas Gordon against Vardry McBee. Debt.
By consent of the Parties and assent of the Court the Trial of this action is Refered until December Term next.

William Couch against Westwood Waters. In Trover.

By consent of the Parties and assent of the Court, the Trial of this action is continued until December Term next.

John Ford against James Ford. On attachment. continued until next Court.

John Farrow against Wm. Tarry & Waldrope. On Petition, etc. Continued until next Court.

John Elder against Benjamin Wofford. Petition by acct.
The Plaintiff on his oath Declares that his accompt. against the defendant of ₺ 1 s 13 is just and true. The defendant being also sworn saith he does not owe the debt nor any part thereof. The Court on due Deliberation ordered the suit to be Dismissed at the Plaintiff's Costs.

James Rakestraw for petty Larceny, with James White & William Elder his sureties, Came into Court and acknowledged themselves severally Indebted to the State in the Terms following...Jesse Rakestraw in the sum of ₺ 100 sterling; James White and William Elder ₺ 25 each to be levied on their goods and chattles, lands and tenements respectively. Yet if the said Jesse Rakestraw shall make his personal appearance at the House of John Wood, To Morrow & there remain until Discharged by the Court, then the above Recognizance to be void... James Porter, D. Clk. of the Court.

On Motion of James Yancey Esquire, Alexander Alexander is allowed to keep a tavern or Public House of Entertainment on his giving Bond with approved sureties for his good Behavior and conforming to the Rates prescribed by the Court.

The minutes were signed by Baylis Earle, Henry White, James Jordan & Zadock Ford, Esqrs. Court then adjourned until tomorrow Morning at Nine O'Clock.

Wednesday the 20th of September 1786, the Court met according to adjournment. Present Henry White, James Jordan, and Thomas Wadsworth. Esquires.

John Snoddy comes into Court and agrees to keep in Repair a certain gut, or piece of Road oposite his Field, on the Road leading from Nickols Mill to Mr. Timmon's to the satisfaction of the Overseer.

Bayley Taylor against John Cooper-Slander.
The Plaintiff in this action being solemnly called, but failing to appear, Either in his person or by his atto., whereupon it is considered by the Court that said Plaintiff take nothing by his bill, but for his false clamour be in mercy.

Bayley Taylor against Robert Hobbs. Slander
The Plaintiff in this action being solemnly called, But failing to appear Either in his person or by his atto., Whereupon it is considered by the Court that said Plaintiff take nothing by his Bill, but for his false clamour be in mercy...the defendant received five shillings damage, besides his Costs....

Ordered that a Didimus Issue to Mecklinburgh County in North Carolina, to take the acknowledgment of George Alexander to a certain conveyance from himself to William McMillin.

Ordered that John Pennington & Henry Hammilton, be Brought into Court to answer to a charge of suffering a Prisoner to Escape. Upon their appearnace the Court ordered that they be holden to Bail for their appearance at the next Court.

State against Ezekiel Wells. Petty Larceny.
Ordered that the Prisoner be Brought ot the Bar & araigned upon his araingnmt. pleads not Guilty, and puts himself upon the Country. Whereupon came a Jury (to wit) James Smith, William Bird, Robert McDowall, Henry Moffatt, Thomas Milligan, Isham Yearly, Charles Smith, Andrew Milligan, David Lewis Junr., Jason Moore, George Connell, James Gilmore...the Defendant is Guilty of Petty Larceny, but recommned him to mercy. James Smith, foreman.
The Court upon the Jury finding the above Ezekiel Wells Guilty of Petty Larceny, adjudge that he receive Twenty Lashes on his bare back at five o'clock this Evening at a certain Tree near the Court House.

State against Beeks Musgrove & Westwood Waters. Troversed.
Beeks Musgrove, Edward Musgrove & James Oliphant Came into Court, and acknowledged themselves to owe the State (to wit said Beeks Musgrove ₺ 50; and Edward Musgrove & James Oliphant ₺ 25 each for the appearance of the said Beeks Musgrove at Next Court.
J. Thomas Junr, Ct.

Westwood Waters, Edward Mitchison & John Pennington Came into Court and acknowledged themselves to owe the State , said Westwood Waters, ₺ 50, and Edward Mitchison & John Pennington, ₺ 25 each for the appearance of said Westwood Waters at next Court.
J. Thomas Junr., Ct.

Martin Williams against Alexander McElheny. On Petition, Etc.
Came the Plaintiff by Jacob Brown Gentleman, his atto., and the Defendant by Daniel Brown Gentleman his atto., the court gave judgment that the Plaintiff take nothing by his bill, But for his false clamor be in mercy, that the said Defendant go hence without day, and receive five shillings damage, besides his Costs....

John Farrow against the Exors. of Ralph Smith. On Petition, Etc.
Came the Plaintiff by James Yancey Gentleman his atto., and the Defendants by Wm. Shaw Gentm. his atto., the Court are of opinion that the Plaintiff take nothing by his Bill, But for his false clamor be in mercy, that the said Defendant...receive five shillings damage besides his Costs....

The Exors. of Safold against the Administrators of Skelton. Case
On Motion of Mr. Goodwin, and of Afadavit made by the Defendant Ordered by the Court that the Trial of said case, be Referred until next Court.

John Shannon against William Gaston. On Petition, Etc.
Came the Plaintiff by Wm. Shaw Gentleman his atto., Also came the Defendant in his own person in open Court, and saith that he will not Dispute with the Plaintiff or his atto., and that he justly owes the Plaintiff ₤ 1 s 11 d 10 with the Costs on the suit.

Thomas Scurry against Benjamin Wofford. Petition, Etc.
Came the Plaintiff by Danl Brown Gentleman his atto., and the Defendant by Charles Goodwin Gentm. his attorney. The court on hearing their alligations, ordered the suit to be dismissed at the Plaintiff's Costs.

The Court adjourned until tomorrow Morning 9 O'Clock. Henry White, James Jordan & Thomas Wadsworth.

The Court met according to adjournment on Thursday the 21st of September A. D. 1786. Present Baylis Earle, Thomas Wadsworth & Zadock Ford, Esquires.

Anthony Coulter, for nonattendance upon the Grand Jury by failing to attend, after being impannaled and came into Court and acknowledged his fault. The Court on Considering the case acquited him of any fine on his paying the fees, Etc.

Present Justice Ford. Absent Justice Wadsworth.

Wadsworth & Turpin against John Elder. On Petition & Summons.
Came the Plaintiffs by James Yancey Gentleman their atto., and the Defendant failing to appear in his person or by his atto., Whereupon it is Considered by the Court, the said Plaintiff Recover judgment against the said Defendt. for ₤ 1 s 14 d 6 Besides his Costs....

Wadsworth & Turpin against Frederick Hawkins. On Petition & Summons.
Came the Plaintiff by James Yancey Gentleman their atto., and the Defendant failing to appear...the Plaintiffs have judgment for ₤ 1 s 17 d 11 besides his costs....

Wadsworth & Turpin against Israel Morris. Case.
Came the Plaintiff by James Yanceys Gentleman their atto., and the Defendant failing to appear...this suit be discontinued at the Defendants costs.

Thomas Moody against Dudley Red. Case. Came the Plaintiff by Daniel Brown & William Shaw Gnetlemen his attornies, and the Defendant by Chas. Goodwin Gentleman his atto., after the Court having heard their alligations, they ordered this suit to be Discontinued at the Plaintiff's Costs.

James Harrison against Joseph Langston. Debt.
Came the Plaintiff by James Yancey Gentleman his atto., and the Defendant failing to appear in his own person or by his atto., whereupon came a Jury (to wit) James Smith, Wm. Bird, Robert McDowall, Henry Moffatt, Thomas Milligan, Isham Terly, Charles Smith, Andrew Milligan, David Lewis Junr., Jason Moore, George connell & James Gilmore...the Defendt. doth owe the Plaintiff ₤ 16 s 5 principle and ₤ 2 s 1 d 4¾ interest...

Present Justice Wadsworth. Ordered that Wm. Tate Senr., serve as an overseer of the Road, leading from his own Ferry towards Spartanburg Court House in the Room of Nathaniel Robison....

John Shannon against John Collins On Petition, Etc.
Continued until next Court at Plaintiff's Costs.

Same against Richard Collins On Petition.
Continued until next Court at the Pltffs. Costs.

The Executrix of Safold against Josiah Tanner. Case
Came the Plaintiff by James Yancey Gentm. her atto. and the Defendant by Danl. Brown & Chas. Goodwin Gentlemen his atto., whereupon came a Jury (same Jury as p. 23)...we find a verdict for the defendant, ...the defendant go hence without Day and Receive his Costs....

Thomas Gordon against William Gilbert On attacht.
The Court gave as their opinion that this attacht. be Dismissed at the Plaintiff's Costs.

A Lease & Release from John Pedan to John Tippins proved by the Evidences of Samuel & David Pedan. Ordered to be Recorded.

Henry Machan Wood against Burwell Thomson. Detimus.
Came the Plaintiff by James Yancey Gentleman his atto. and the Defendant by Charles Goodwin & Wm. Shaw Gentlemen his atto., whereupon came a Jury (same as before)...on their Return on the succeeding Day with their Verdict sealed, upon opening the same the Jury find for the Plaintiff £ 6 s 6 d 8....

In the case above where matters of fact were not clearly proved by reason of the Equivical Testimony of a certain witness, who appeared to be Interested, it was given as the opinion of the Court that the Plaintiff's attorney should have the concluding word, as the Defendant called no Evidences.

Elkenah Hutchison with Nevil Wayland & Joseph Thomson his sureties came into Court and acknowledged themselves to owe the State (viz.) Elkenah Hutchison £ 50 & the sd. Wayland & Thomson the sum of £ 25 each if the said Elkenah Hutchison do not make his personal appearance at the Court House of this County at next Court & from there not Depart until legally Discharged by the Court.

The Minutes were signed by Baylis Earle, James Jordan, Zadock Ford, Esqrs. The Court then adjourned until to-morrow morning 9 o'clock.

The Court met according to adjournment on Friday the 22nd Day of September A. D. 1786. Present Baylis Earle, James Jordan & Thos Wadsworth, Esqrs.

Thomas Gordon against Vardry McBee In Debt.
Came the Plaintiff by James Yancey & Thos Peter Carns Gentlemen his attrs. and the Plaintiff (sic) by Wm Shaw & Peter Carns Gentlemen his attrs., whereupon it is considered by the Court that the Plaintiff suffer a nonsuit. By consent of the Parties and assent of the Court, Reinstated & and so Continued until December Court next.

In the above suit Gordon against McBee Ordered that a Dedimus Issue to Wilks County in North Carolina to William Terrell Lewis, John Brown & Joseph Herndon, Esqrs. or any two of them to Examine Benjamin Herndon on Evidence to papers, relative to above case and that the Defendant have due notice thereof, as the Dedimus is in behalf of the Plaintiff.

James Oliphant against Thomas Farrow & others. in trover
Came the Plaintiff by James Yancey Gentleman his attorney and the
Deft. by Wm. Shaw & Danl Brown Gentlemen, their attorneys, whereupon came a Jury (same as before)...the said Defendant does owe
the Plaintiff Ł 20 s 2 d 4....

Ruled to be observed by the Lawyers in this Court was read and
approved of by the Court and ordered to be Recorded.

Rules and orders of the County Court of Spartanburgh, in the State
of South Carolina, Established 21st September 1786.

Rule 1st, That all persons summoned & appearing to answer as
Garnashees on attachments, shall give in their Return upon oath
in writing.

Rule 2nd. That no writ of Inquiry after an Interlocutory Judgment
shall be executed, nor a Judicial attachemtn be Granted, nor an
order for sale, under an attachment revile, nor a Decree on a
summons & Petition, where the Defendant makes Default pronounced,
nor judgment against a Garnashee for nonappearance, given without
the Sheriff's return being first sworn to before a Magistrate &
rendered on the writ or other process.

Rule 3rd. That the sheriff do make all his returns at least three
Days before the Court to which the writ or other process shall be
Returnable.

Rule 4th. That no Execution shall be issued in any judgment obtained in this Court until the adjournment of the Court, Without
a special order for that purpose.

Rule 5th. That a Copy of every Deed, Bond or Bill or other Writing Declared on shall be filed at the Clerk's office at the time
of filing the Declaration & the Defendant or his atto. shall hand
over of the original if he thinks proper to Demand it.

Rule 6th That no attorney be permitted or suffered to be Bail
for any person whatsoever to the sheriff, on pain of such censure
as the Court shall think proper & the sheriff is hereby Directed
not to take any such bail, or the Bail of any officer of the
Court on pain of being severely fined.

Rule 7. That where more than one attorney shall be employed on
one side, the one that is originally employed shall be entitled
to the Taxed Fee.

Rule 8. That the Plaintiff in any suit shall alwasy be at Liberty to reply in Evidence, but shall not be allowed in such reply
to introduce Testimony foreign to that which the Defendant may
have produced in his Defence.

Rule 9th. That the Plaintiff and the first mover of a question
shall always conclude to the last word.

Rule 10th. That no attorney shall be allowed to speak more than
once in a cause, where more than one atto. are employed.

Rule 11th. That the Civil Docket for the future shall be called
twice over, & the parties shall not be called to Trial untill the
second calling, Provided that this Rule shall not Extend to Summons & Petitions, which shall be placed at the first of the Docket,
& heard at the first calling.

Rule 12. That when the Justices on the Bench proceed to Give their judgments or opinions the youngest Magistrate shall Begin.

Ordered that John Gowin, Samuel Fowler & Thomas Morrow view the ground whereon to open a Road from Jemison's Mill to widow Bishops agreeable to an order of Court for that purpose--Whereof William Jemison is appointed overseer.

John Russell against Henry Prince. Case.
On application of the parties Ordered that Parties in the above case have leave to take their suit out of Court and refer it to the arbitration of John Gowin & James Jordan, Esqrs. with leave for a third person being chose if necessary & their judgment being taken in writing. Returned to the Justices at next term & be considered the judgment of the Court.

State against Jesse Rakestraw. Petty Larceny.
Came the County attorney, William Shaw Esqr. in behalf of the State & the Defendant by Danl Brown Esqr. his attorney, Whereupon came a Jury (same as before)...the Defendt. is Guilty of Larceny, as the Plaintiff by the County attorney complains. Whereupon the Court ordered that the Defendant Receive Fifteen Lashes on his Bare Back, at a certain Tree near the Court House by the sheriff, besides paying the attorney, clerk & sheriff's fees, and the said Defendant be in mercy.

Thomas Wadsworth & Co. against Edward Ballinger. Case.
Came the Plaintiff by James Yancey Gentleman his attorney, and the Defendant failing to appear in his own person or by his attoy., Whereupon it is considered by the Court that this suit be discontinued at the Defendant's costs.

Ordered that the Road from Isaac Crows, along the dividing Ridge between Enoree & Tyger Rivers to the County line, be kept in repair, from Crows to Andersons, overseer Joseph Woodruff, the marked Road of David Anderson, from thence to the Big Pond, overseer Thomas Childress, from thence to the County line, overseer John Redman.

George Gordon assignee of Crow against Ebenezar Morse. In Debt.
Came the Plaintiff by James Yancey Gentleman his attorney, & the Plaintiff by Daniel Brown Gentlm. his attorney, Whereupon it is Considered by the Court that this suit be discontinued at the Pltff. Costs.

The Assignee of Adams against the Admrs. of Jones. In Debt.
On motion of the Plaintiff by Daniel Brown, Esq. leave is granted him to take the Deposition of Robert Adams before Charles McDowall, or Chas. Wakefield, Esqrs. in Burk County, North Carolina, between this and Next Court, on giving Ten Days previous notice to one of the Administrators.

The Minutes were signed by Baylis Earle, James Jordan & Thomas Wadsworth. The Court then adjourned until to morrow morning at 9 o'clock.

Saturday the 23d of September 1786. The Court met according to adjournment. Present Baylis Earle, Thomas Wadsworth & Richard Harrison, Esquires.

Ordered that John & Zadock Ford Esqrs. produce at next December Term, All warrants, Judgments, Executions & other process's whatever had before them against Joseph Hall, since the first day of

March last.

Ordered that the Clerk have the sum of Ł 10 for his Extra services for the year past, & that he retain the said Ł 10 out of the money arising from Tavern Licence.

Present James Jordan, Esqr.

John Johnson against Amos Space. Case
CAme the Plaintiff by James Yancey Esqr. his attoy., and the Defendant by Daniel Brown, Esqr. his atto., whereupon came a Jury (same as before)...we find for the Plaintiff Principle Ł 21 s 8 d 6½ also Ł 5 s 5 interest...

The Court proceeded to Draw the Grand Jurors for December Court 1786, Capt. Wm. Smith, Joseph Wofford, John Conner, David McDowall, Jesse Connell, John Leech, Thomas Haney, Robert Jemison, Robt. Foster, Peter Lewis, Enoch Floyd, Thomas Tod, Absalom Lancaster, Isham Foster, Andrew Barry, Wm. Floyd, Robert Nesbitt, John Shippy.

The Pettit Jurors for December Term 1786. John Miller, Jeremiah Thomson, John Watson(Thickety), Tobias Bright, Andrew Caully, Hugh Freeman, Joshua Hawkins, John Alexander, William Brannon, Charles James, Matthew Alexander, Alexr. McElheny, John Collins, James Alexander, Richard Willis, Richard Barry, William Simpson, Joseph Gilmore, John Butler, James Milligan, Frederick Briggs, Wm. Ford, Wm. Elder, Wm. Snoddy, Thomas Airs, John Snoddy, John Cooper, John Watson, Enoree.

Henry Moffatt against Thomas Wood. Case.
Came the Plaintiff by Danl Brown, Esqr. his atto. and the Defendant failing to appear Either in his person or by his attorney, Whereas it is Considered by the Court that the Plaintiff Recover Judgment by Default.

Hugh Perce against Isaac Brown. Case. Default.

Henry Hamilton against Jeremiah Neel. Asst. & Batty. Default.

Daniel Bennett is allowed Seventeen Shillings & six pence on oath, for 7 days attendance as an Evidence in the suit John Johnson against Amos Space.

Michael Johnson is allowed on oath One Pound Ten Shillings for 12 Days attendance as an Evidence in the suit Johnson vs. Space.

The minutes were signed by Baylis Earle, James Jordan & Thomas Wadsworth, Esqrs. The Court then adjourned until Court in Course.

At a County Court began to be Holden at Mr. John Wood's on the third Monday in December 1786. Present Thomas Wadsworth, Richard Harrison & Samuel Lancaster, Esquires.

The Determination of the Governor & Council, Respectg. the Court House being produced & Read, the Court agreed to adjourn to day & meet at Mr. Thomas Williamson's to Morrow, agreeable to said order, said order filed in the Clerk's office. Signed Thomas Wadsworth, Richard Harrison & Samuel Lancaster. Esqrs. Court then adjourned until tomorrow morning 9 o'clock at Mr. Thos. Williamson's.

Tuesday the 19th day of December 1786, the Court met according to adjournment. Present Thomas Wadsworth, Richard Harrison, &

Samuel Lancaster, Esquires.

A Lease & Release from Joseph Wofford to Thos Brown, proved by the Evidence of John Brown & James Wofford. Ordered to be recorded.

A Lease & Release from James Hardin to Vardry McBee proved by the Evidence of Josiah Tanner laid over for further Proof. At June Court, 1787 This Lease & Release was proved--William Weir. See in Book B, páge 125.

A Lease & Release from Edmund Bishop & Ann his wife to William Bishop, proved in open Court by the Evidences of Stephen Miller & John Bishop. Ordered that they be Recorded.

Richard Chesney came into Court and acknowledged a Lease & Release from himself to Paul Castleberry. Ordered to be recorded.

A Deed of Conveyance from Benjamin Brown to Mary Hannah, proved in open Court by the Evidences of Henry & Peter Hammiltons. Ordered to be recorded.

A Lease & Release from Joseph Kirkland to Ann Hollaway, proved by the Evidence of Thomas Kimbell, laid over for further proof.

The Court proceeded to Draw the Grand Jurors for March Term 1787. Their names are as follows (To wit) James Pharis, David Golightly, Jeremiah Lucas, Alexr. Vernon, John Young Senr., William Prince, Joseph King, Tobias Bright, John Ford, Wm. Benson, Robert Goodgion, Thomas Farrar, Wells Griffith, Ephraim Russ, Martin Oats, Richard Lewis, Geo. Pettis, John Nesbitt, John Smith,(-less) George Devors, David Goodlett, John Golightly, Henry Wells, Wm. Smith, Majr. James Hooper, Giles Connell, Jos. Thomson, David Anderson, John Ford, Thomas Tod, James Huggins.

Pettit Jurors for March Court 1787. Thomas Flinn, Alex. Alexander, Jesse Reams, Thomas Haney, Maximilian Conner, Jonathan Stone, John Cooper, James Norris, Jno. Conwell, James Bruton, Isaac Crow, Joseph Barnett, Robert McMillin, John Timmons, John Bearden, Rowland Johnson, William Hooper, William Sterling, Reubin Dickson, Christopher Casey, James White, Moses Timmons, William Poole taylor, John Wofford, Robert Connell, William McDowall (miller), Josiah Culberson, James Crow, John Williams.

Ordered that the Delinquents belonging to the Grand Jury, be summoned to appear at next Court to make Excuses if any they have.

William Shaw Esqr. against Joseph Buffington. On Petition, Etc. by note of hand.
Came the Plaintiff by Daniel Brown Esqr. his atto., and the Defendant failing to appear Either in his Person or by his attorney, Whereupon it is considered by the Court that the said Plaintiff recover against the said Defendant, The sum of Ł 5 s 1 d 5 besides his costs....

Francis Dodds against William Earnest. Case.
By consent of the parties dismissed at Plaintiff's Costs.

Sarah Guess against Vardry McBee & Wm. Tate Senr. Petition.
Came the Plaintiff by William Shaw Gentleman his attorney, and the Defendants failing to appear, Whereupon it is considered by the Court, that the said Plaintiff recover against the said defendants, the sum of Ł 6 s 14 d 10 with interest from the 20th of August 1786 until paid, besides her costs....

Exors of Safold Deceased. against the Admrs. of Shelton, decd. Case. Continued until next Court at Defendants Costs.

Mary Berkly against William Lindsey. On Petition.
Came the Plaintiff by Jacob Brown Esqr. her attorney And the defendant failing to appear, Either in his own Person or by his attorney, Whereupon it is considered by the Court that the said Plaintiff recover Ł 2 s 7 d 10 & one Penney damage besides her costs....

J'S. Y.   Wettinhal Warner
               against
C. Gasdain Benjamin Wofford. Debt. Etc. Dismissed at Deft. cost.

The Assignee of Adams against the Admrs. of Jones. Debt.
Continued until next Court, by consent of the Parties.

John Thomas Senr. against Major Parsons. In Slander.
Continued until next Court by consent of Parties.

John Farrow, Assignee of Farrow against William Tarry & Jas. Waldrope. On Petition by note.
Came the Plaintiff by James Yancey Gentleman, his atto., and the Defendants failing to appear in their own person or by their atto., ...the Plaintiff recover against the Deft. Ł 7 s 5 d 6 principal and s 15 d 5 interest besides his costs....

Ordered that Jesse Rakestraw be brought before this Court as soon as possible by the Sheriff or other Officer.

The minutes were signed by Richard Harrison, Thomas Wadsworth & Zadock Ford. The Court then adjourned untill to morrow Morning 9 O'Clock.

The Court met according to the last adjournment on Wednesday the 20th day of December 1786. Present Thomas Wadsworth, Zadock Ford, Saml. Lancaster & Richard Harrison, Esquires.

The Court proceeded to Draw the Pettit Jurors for this Court. Wells Griffith, Tobias Bright, Joshua Hawkins, John Alexander, William Brannon, John Collins, Richd. Barry, John Butler, John Snoddy, John Cooper, John Watson, William Ford.

Ordered that John Timmons be appointed Overseer of the Road from the narrow passage to his own House & that Robt. Jemison be Overseer from said Timmon's to the widow Bishops on Lawsons Fork.

Wadsworth & Turpin against Henry Moffatt. Case.
Came the Plaintiff by James Yancey Gnetleman his atto., and the Defendant by Danl. Brown Gentleman his atto., Whereupon it is considered by the Court that this suit be Discontinued at the Defendants Costs.

Israel Morris against Rowland Cornelius. Case.
Discontinued at the Plaintiffs Costs.

John Childress against James Poole. Asst. & Battery.
Came the Plaintiff by Daniel Brown Gentleman his attorney, and the Defendant by James Yancey Gentleman his atto., whereupon came a Jury (to wit) Wells Griffith, Tobias Bright, Joshua Hawkins, John Alexander, Wm. Brannon, John Collins, Richd. Barry, John Butler, John Snoddy, John Cooper, John Watson & William Ford... the Defendant is Guilty of the assault ...they assess the said

Defendant Ł 2 s 1 damage....

Present Henry White, Esqr.

Daniel Hail against John Butler, Trover & C.
Continued until next Court on motino of Mr.Carns, Plaintiff's attorney.

Reubin Dickson against Vardry McBee & Others. Debt.
By consent of the Parties & assent of the Court, the Trial of this cause is Referred until next Court.

John Parker against James Smith. Debt.
Continued until next Court, at the Plaintiff's Costs.

Thomas Gordon against Vardry McBee. Debt.
Continued until next Court at Defendant's Costs.

John Elder against William Wofford, Senr. Case.
Came the Plaintiff by Jacob Brown Gentleman his attorney, and the Defendant by Daniel Brown, Gentleman his atto., whereupon came a Jury (same as before)...this suit be discontinued at the Plaintiff's Costs. Wm. Ford, foreman.

A Deed of Gift from John Elder Senr. to Alexander Elder was acknowledged in open Court by said John Elder. Ordered to be recorded.

John Johnston against Thomas Bennett. Petition, Etc. Came the Plaintiff by Wm. Shaw, Esqr. his atto., & the Defendant by Thomas Peters Carns Esqr. his atto., whereupon it is considered by the Court that the suit be dismissed at the Plaintiff's costs, and the said Plaintiff by Amerced.

Lease & Release from Philip & Phebe Gibbs to Henry Airs proved in Open Court by the Evidences of Peter Elder & Robert Head. Ordered to be recorded.

John Dennard against Hugh Perce. In Debt.
Came the Plaintiff by Jacob Brown Esqr. his attorney & the Defendant by Daniel Brown, Esqr. his atto., the Court on hearing the Parties aforesaid, Ordered the suit to be Discontinued at the Plaintiff's Costs.

Israel Morris against John Kimbell. Case.
Came the Plaintiff by James Yancey Gentleman his atto., and the Defendant by Jacob Brown Gentleman his atto., on hearing the Parties aforesaid, the Court ordered the Case to be Discontinued at the Plaintiff's Costs.

John Shannon against John Collins. On Petition by acct.
At the Request of the Plaintiff by Wm. Shaw his attorney & the assent of the Court, this suit is Discontinued at the Plaintiff's Costs.

Jesse Reams is allow Ł 1 for 8 days attendance as an Evidence in the suit Israel Morris against John Kimbell.

Joseph Venible is allowed on oath s 17 d 6 for 7 days attendance as an Evidence in the suit Morris vs Kimbell.

John Farrow against the Exors. of Smith. On Petition.

This suit is continued until next Court, at the Plaintiff's Costs. Josiah Culbertson proved his attendance to be 8 days in the above suit.

James Adair against Charles Waters. On attachment.
The Court on mature Consideration gave Judgment against the Defendant for ₤ 4 s 10 besides the costs. Ordered that the Sheriff take the goods attached & sell them, or so much of them as will satisfy said sum according to Law.

Ordered that the Court meet on the Twentieth day of January next, in order to let the Public Buildings for this County; and that the Clerk write to Each absent Justice Respectively to attend on that day; To agree on the Method of said Buildings, etc. And that said day be Published as universally as Possible for workmen to attend and undertake.

A Lease and Release from James McDowall to Richard Fryar proved by the Evidences of Thomas Gorman & John Couch. Ordered to be Recorded.

John Barclay against William Moore. Trover & Convern.
By order of the Court Continued until next Term.

The minutes were signed by Henry White, Richd. Harrison, Zadock Ford & Saml Lancaster. Court then adjourned until to morrow morning 9 o'clock.

Tuesday the 21st of December A. D. 1786. The Court met according to adjournment. Present Henry White, Richard Harrison & Zadock Ford, Esqr.

A Lease and Release from William Sterling & wife to Thomas Kery, proved by the evidences of Andrew Thomson & John Elder Junr. Ordered to be recorded.

Ordered that all persons who have obtained orders for License be called to appear at next Court, to pay the Duty due to the county, if not already paid, And those who have obtained License do Continue to sell under the same until next March Term.

State against Beeks Musgrove & Westwood Waters, Defs. Asst. & False Imprisonment.
Came the Plaintiff by Wm. Shaw Esqr. County Atto., and the Defendants by Jacob Brown & Daniel Brown, Esqrs. their atto., whereupon came a Jury (to wit) (same as before)...the Defendants are Guilty of Assault & the false Imprisonment as the County atto., in his pleading complains. Whereupon the Court adjudged that the said Beeks Musgrove pay ₤ 5 and half the Costs and the said Westwood Waters ₤ 2 & the other half of the Costs....

A Deed from George Blanton to James Powell proved in Open Court by the Evidences of John Cooper & Nathaniel Robertson, Ordered to be Recorded.

Henry Hamilton against Jeremiah Neel. Asst. & Battery.
Came the Plaintiff by Charles Goodwin his attorney & the Defendant failing to appear, Either in his own person or by his attorney, whereupon came a Jury (same as before)...we find for the plaintiff ₤ 3 damage besides his costs....

Charles Moore against Benjamin Silman. Case.
By consent of the parties, and assent of the Court, the trial of

this action is referred until next court.

William Bennett admr. of Jno Langston against Landon Farrow. Trover. By consent of the parties and assent of the Court the Trial of this cause is referred until next Court.

John Holcom came into Court and made oath that he saw William Benson sign a Lease & Release to Richard Harrison, Esqr.

Ordered that a Road be laid out and opened from this Court House to the Road leading from the lower Iron Works to Blackstocks, near Connells, Giles Connell overseer & Giles Smith, warner.

John Hightower came into Court and acknowledged a Lease & Release from himself & wife to Thomas Jordan. Ordered to be Recorded.

Jeremiah Silman against John Williams. Trover & C. Came the Plaintiff by Wm. Shaw Esqr. his attorney, & the defendant by Charles Goodwin Esqr. his attorney, whereupon came a Jury (same as before)...the Defendant is Guilty of the Trover & Conversion as the Plaintiff in his Declaration complains. We find for the Plaintiff Ł 10 damage besides his costs....

Mariah Anderson is allowed on oath seventeen shillings and six pence for 7 days attendance as an Evidence in the above suit.

William Wakefield is allowed on oath s 17 d 6 for 7 days attendance as a witness in sd. suit.

Mary Wakefield is allowed on her oath s 15 for 6 days attendance as a witness in the above case.

Mary Francis is allowed on oath s 12 d 6 for 5 days attendance, and s 8 d 4 for 25 Miles Travel from Laurens County.

Ordered that the order Respecting the Court House & other Public Buildings be Reversed until the Determination of the Legislature. Protested against because it originated in an Idea of carrying the Court House back; And because it is finally determined and cannot constitutionally be Taken up again. Richard Harrison.

The minutes were signed by Baylis Earle, Zadock Ford, James Jordan & Thomas Wadsworth. Esqrs. Court then adjourned until to morrow morning 9 o'clock.

Friday the 23rd day of December 1786. The Court met according to adjournment. Present Baylis Earle, Henry White & Richard Harrison, Esqrs.

Ordered that the Clerks Office be kept at Mr. Samuel Porters plantation on Lawsons Fork, being the plantation whereon William McDowall lately lived, until otherwise ordered.

The Admrs. of Jno Lawson Decd. against Isaac Brown. Case.
By consent of the Court and assent of the Parties, the Trial of this cause is Referred until next court.

John Conner Junr. against Robert McDowall. Detimus.
Came the Plaintiff by James Yancey Esqr. his attorney & the Defendant by Daniel Brown Esqr. his attorney whereupon it is considered by the Court that the suit be Dismissed at the Defendants Costs. Present Justice Jordan; Absent Justice White.

John Watson against James White. Slander. Came the Plaintiff by Jacob & Daniel Brown his attorney, and the Defendant by James Yancey & Thomas Peters Carns his attornies, Whereupon came a Jury (same as before)...we find for the Plaintiff ₤ 4 s 7....

Michael Hogan against Peter Edwards. In Debt.
The Trial of this cause is Refered until next Court.

William Hill against George Taylor. In Case.
The Trial of this cause is Referred until next Court.

Charles Waters against Thomas Gorman. damage. The trial of this action is Referred until next Court.

David McDowall against Hugh Freeman. Trover & C.
By consent of Council on Both sides and assent of the Court, a Dedimus Potistatum to the State of Georgia is Granted on behalf of thie Plaintiff on giving the Defendant the names of the witnesses, the County where they live & the names of the Justices before whom they are to be Examined, 15 days before the taking of said Deputations; said order not to be issue until March Term next.

Thomas Wilson against Daniel McClarin. In Debt.
Dismissed at the Defendants Costs.

James McElheny against John James. On attachment. Came the plaintiff by D. Brown Esqr. his atto & the Deft. by C. Goodwin his atto. The Court ordered the attat. to be Dismissed at the Deft. Costs.

David Goodlett is allowed on oath ₤ 1 s 10 for 12 days attendance as an Evidence in the suit James McElheny vs John James.

Ordered that a Road be opened from the mountain shoal on Enoree to cross Two Mile Creek at the convenientest place, Between Morrises and the Mouth of said Creek, and to come into the Waggon Road that leads to Ford Mill, Below Henry Kerly's plantation, And that Alex. Alexander be overseer, and the persons lyable to Law compelld. to work on the same; said Alex. Alexander, Wm. & Isaac Crows, to veiw the Ground & lay off said Road, and the Overseer to appoint a person to warn the Hands to work.

John Hull against Thomas Fortner. attachment. Ordered by Court that the Goods so attached be sold by the Constable Immediately.

The State against Elkenah Hutchison. Receiving Stolen Goods. Acquited by the Court on his paying the Costs.

George Parkison against Hugh Perce. In Trover.
The Court ordered this suit to be Discontinued at the Plaintiffs Costs, as he being an Inhabitant of another State & no security given.

James Harrison against William Smith. In Debt.
Came the Plaintiff by James Yancey Esqr. his attorney and the Defendant failing to appear in his person, or by his attorney, whereupon came a Jury. (same as before)...We find for the plaintiff ₤ 10 s 3 d 3½ principle & s 17 & d 9½ interest....

Ordered that John Snoddy have Leave to Retail spiritous Liquors until next Court.

The State against Jesse Rakestraw. Larceny.
Rakestraw having broken custody, from the Constable, who had him in charge, Ordered by the Court that the Clerk issue an Escape warrant, and the sheriff keep him in safe custody, or on Good Bail, until next Court.

Ordered that the Justices meet on the Nineteenth day of January next to agree on the Plan of the Public Buildings and on the 20th of said January, to let said Buildings as Commissioners, and that the Clerk Advertise the same as General as he can, possibly and that all the absent members of the Court be Notified to appear on the above mentioned days at this place.

The minutes were signed by Baylis Earle, James Jordan & Richard Harrison, Esquires. The Court then adjourned until Court in course.

The Justices whose names are under written met on the 19th day of January 1787 agreeable to an Order of Court Entered on Record the 23rd of Dec. A. D. 1786, (To wit) Baylis Earle, Richard Harrison, Samuel Lancaster & Obediah Tremmier, Esqrs.

A Memorandum of the Dimentions of Spartanburgh Court House as agreed on the 19th of January A. D. 1787, Pursuant to the above order of Court (To wit) 30 feet long by 20 feet wide 12 feet Pitch square Roof The Timbers well proportioned by the Rules of Architictues in a Good and sufficient manner. The Shingles of the Hart of Pine Nailed on with 6d. nails, 21 Inches long, to show 7 inches. Weather Boards 8 inches wide, of quartered plank, to show 6 inches, and Beaded, Nailed with 8d. nails, 2 Doors of a common size, one on each side, Good casings and the Doors plain. 8 Twelve light windows, Good casings, and sashes with glass 10 by 8 inches 2 in the End of the Court Room & one in Each side and 2 in Each Jury Room, 8 feet taken of the length for Jury Rooms, by a Pertition of Plank well confined & that subdivided into Rooms 10 feet by 8 by a light Pertition. The Jury Rooms Elevated 4 feet above the floor of the Court Room, and steps Leading up into Each. The Justices Bench ot be Elevated 4 feet above the floor, done up with plain smooth Plank, in a circular manner, and stairway leading up at Each End, a Jury Bench on the floor, within the circle and convenient Boxes for the sheriff. A Clerk's Table & an attrs. Bar, at a convenient distance in the front of the Justices Bench; The Eaves of the House Boxed and corniced, and the whole done in a workman like manner.

A Goal of 16 feet square, of 10 Inches squared oak Logs, with a Pertition of square oak Timber of the same size, crossing the front at 6 feet Distance from the Door. The Largest Room Divided by a Pertition of Logs of the same size, Through Each Pertition, a Door of 3 feet wide, casings to the Doors 10 Inches by 4 Doors of a proportioned thickness such as are common to jails, and strengthened by Iron Bars, of a moderate size. A common sized jail lock to Each Door. The two lower back Rooms, ceiled with Good 2 Inch oak plank, One of the lower Rooms, in the ceiling to be laid of in Checks of 4 Inches distance and a spike of 4 Inches Long Drove into Each Entersection, The other back Room ceiled with the same kind of Plank, and checked at 12 Inches distance, and spiked in like manner; At the Height of 7 feet, a floor of the same kind plank, and sized Timber, and spiked at four Inches distance over the Back Room. That spiked in like manner, the floors of the others to be spiked as the wall; Five feet from the upper floor, to the Plates whereon the Roof is placed. The Roof to be sheeted with Inch plank & shingles with 21 Inch shingles, to show

7 Inches, Steps from the front Room, up to the upper floor; 4 windows to the Goal, of 10 Inches square, cased with Iron Bars of Half an Inch thickness, Two Bar grates crossing Each other, in Each window; The foundation to be Logs of the same size of the walls, Raised one foot from the Ground, and the under part filled up with large stone.

The whole Timbers to be let into each other, the pertition to be Dovetailed into the walls at Each End. The upper floor to be let into the walls by shoulders, and the whole to be compleated in a workman-like manner.

The Pillory, whiping post & stocks, to be done in a uniform manner to the other Buildings, such as is usual, will answer the purpose. The jail, Stocks & Pillory to be finished in the present year; and the Court HOuse to be compleated in the space of Two years, to commence from the first day of this Instant January 1787.

The sum of ₺ 25 to be paid at the Ensuing June Court, and the Balance to be paid in four Equal payments, at the Expiration of Each succeeding six months. And should paper currency become a Tender in law, and a Depreciation should Ensue the undertaker not to be Injured in the payment, Ordered that the sheriff proceed to let the Buildings to the lowers undertaker, and take Bond with sufficient security for the faithful performance thereof. Baylis Earle, Richard Harrison, Samuel Lancaster, Obediah Trimmier, Esqrs.

Agreeable to the above order, the sheriff proceded to let the buildings. But as the Undertakers that attended, has not time to make proper calculation of the costs, the leting said Buildings are defered untill the 1st of Feb. next....

The Justices met agreeable to the above Order on the first day of February 1787. And let said Buildings to Richard Harrison, Esquire, for the sum of ₺ 204 who gave Bond... They then Received as a Donation from Thomas Williamson, Two acres of Land, for the use of the County, which they then proceeded to law off... Signed Henry White, Richard Harrison, Saml. Lancaster. Esqrs.

At a County Court began to be holden for the County of Spartanburgh at the Plantation of Thomas Williamson on the third Monday in March A. D. 1787. Present James Jordan, Richard Harrison, and Obediah Trimmier, Esquires.

The Court proceeded to draw the Grand Jurors for this Court (to wit) John Ford, James Huggins, Henry Wells, Robert Goodgion, George Pettice, Jeremiah Lucas, Ephraim Ruse, John Nesbit, John Young Senr., James Pharis, Martin Oats, Thomas Tod & William Prince who were sworn and their charge delivered unto them by Wm. Shaw, Esqr.

The names of Pettit Jurors for March Court 1787 (to wit) William Poole, John Cooper, Reubin Dickson, Maximilian Conner, Robert Connell, Thomas Flinn, Rowland Johnston, Moses Timmons, Josiah Culbertson,James White, Thomas Haney & Joseph Barnett.

Grand Jurors for June Court 1787 (to wit) Thomas Pedan, John Golightly, David Goodlett, Robert Sterling, David Anderson, Robert Goodgion, Thomas Farrar, Richard Lewis, David Golightly, Thomas Haney,Wells Griffith, Andrew Barry, James Hooper, William Tate Senr., Nathl. Guyton, Charles Hester, William Benson, Joseph

Thomson, Williwm Smith Majr., & William Thomson.

Pettit Jurors for June Court 1787. William Wood (Fairforest), Wm. Sterling, Jonathan Harris, Thos Farrow, Fleming Smith, John Mapp, Capt. John Bearden, Jas Keen, Reubin Smith, Capt. Jesse Reams, John Wofford, Francis Dodd, Peter Smith, William Wise, Robert McMillin, Absalom Lancaster, Nathaniel Stoaks, John Foster, Jno. Williams, Alex. Alexander, James Norris, Joseph Wofford, William Underwood, William Wofford Junr., Jonathan Stone, James Vernon, Jas. Crow, Joseph Venible, Isham Foster & William Bird.

A Lease & Release from Stephen Vaughn to Alexander Walker proved by the Evidence of Isham Foster & William Foster. Ordered that they be recorded.

A Lease & Release from Jesse Casey to Joseph Couch, prov'd by Benjamine Couch, Laid over for further Proof.

John Golightly came into Court and acknowledged a Lease & Release from himself to Shands Golightly. Ordered to be Recorded.

James Bright came into Court and acknowledged a Lease & Release to John Nesbit. Ordered to be Recorded.

Two sets of Leases & Releases from James McCarley to Jno. Bragg. Both proved by the Evidences of Thomas Doeg, & Peter Bragg. Ordered that they be Recorded.

William Smith came into Court & acknowledged a Lease & Release to James Ham. Ordered to be Recorded.

Alexander Alexander came into Court and acknowledged a Lease and Release to John Nickoll. Ordered to be Recorded.

A Lease & Release from William Venible to Daniel Symmes, proved by the Evidence of Thomas Farrar & George Pettus. Ordered to be Recorded.

William Smith came into Court and acknowledged a Lease and Release to Abraham Moore. Ordered to be Recorded.

Robert Symmes came into Court and acknowledged a Lease and Release to Jeremiah Moore. Ordered to be Recorded.

Reubin Lawson Admr. of Jno. Lawson Decd. against Isaac Brown. In Debt. By order of Court, Dismissed at Defendant's Costs.

A Lease and Release from Westwood Waters & wife to Elizabeth Waters, proved by the Evidences of Thomas Gorman & Mary Gorman. Ordered to be Recorded.

Joseph Logan against James Milligan. In Trover. Dismiss at Plaintiffs Costs; no atto. on Either sides.

An Article of Agreement Between Robert Evins of the one part, and William Young Esqr., Vardry McBee and Jabez Evans of the other, proved in Open Court by the Evidence of Rhoda McBee. Ordered to be recorded.

The minutes were signed by James Jordan, Richard Harrison, Obediah Trimmier & Samuel Lancaster, Esqrs. Court then adjourned until to morrow morning 9 o'clock.

Tuesday the 20th of March 1787. The Court met according to adjournment. Present James Jordan, Richard Harrison & Obediah Trimmier, Esquires.

Ordered that a Road be opened & Kept in Repair from James Harrisons old place up by John Wofford's to Widow Prince's, overseer John Wofford, warner James Wofford.

Ordered that Two Powers of attornies; one from Isham Smith and Elizabeth Osheals, his wife to William Swanson; The other from Thomas Tod, to the said William Swanson, also a probet Elizabeth Osheal, Joseph Wofford & Thos. Tod, all being sworn in Open Court and the whole ordered to be Recorded.

A Lease and Release from Thomas Hightower to Josiah Traylor acknowledged in Open Court and ordered to be recorded.

A Lease and Release from James Foster to John Foster, proved by Two witnesses. Ordered to be Recorded.

A Deed of Conveyance from Edward Dickson to Zachariah Robison, proved by the Evidence of Deskin Grant. Ordered to be recorded.

A Deed from George Turner to William Wilkins, proved by John Headen & Amillira Austell. Ordered to be recorded.

A Deed from George & Ann Turner to Milly Austell, proved by the Evidence of John Headen & William Wilkins. Ordered to be Recorded.

Mr. Thomas Gordon was appointed a Deputy Sheriff for this County and approved of by the Court, and took the oath of aligence and office in Open Court.

A Deed from Vardry McBee to William Wilkins acknowledged in Open Court, and Ordered to be recorded.

Wm. Shaw Esqr. against Stephen Williford. on attacht.
Came the plaintiff by Peter Carns Esqr. his attorney and the Defendant by Jacob Brown Esqr. his atto., who counter-pleads and claims Twenty Bushels of Corn & one cow of the goods attached for Denny Anderson, Whereupon came a Jury (to wit) William Poole, John Cooper, Reubin Dickson, Maximilian Conner, Robert Connell, Thos. Flinn, Rowland Cornelius, Moses Timmons, Josiah Culbertson, James Bruton, Thomas Haney and Joseph Barnett...We find a Verdict, for Anderson, for the said Twenty Bushels of Corn and one cow....

The Grand Jurors Returned with the Different Inditements delivered unto them; with the opinion upon Each of them, whether true Bills or not; upon being Read, as follows.

State against Rhoda McBee. On an Inditement. a true Bill.
Jno. Ford, foreman.

State against Holland Sumner. Inditement. A true Bill.

State against William Walker. Inditement. A false Bill.

State against Benjamin Silman. Inditement. A true Bill.

Thomas Commander Russell against Joseph Buffington. On attachment. The sheriff having Returned the attachment, Executed on Two Negroes the property of the Defendant (to wit) Bobb, A Negro

Man & Phillis, a Negro woman. The Defendant appeared in Court and Replevied the property so attached by giving William Poole, Iron Master, as Special Bail to the action of the Plaintiff. The said Wm. Poole came into Open Court, and acknowledged himself Bound in the sum of ₺ 100 and Special Bail. The Plaintiff puts in his plea by James Yancey his atto. and the Defendant by Jacob Brown Esqr. his atty., comes and defends the force and Injury and says he does not owe the Debt mentioned in the Declaration, as the Plaintiff against him complains, and of this he puts himself upon the County, and the Plaintiff does also the same, therefore, the Parties Join issue for the Trial of the cause at next Court.   Samuel Porter, D. Clk.

John Pennington against David Trammill. Slander. The Court have ordered that this suit be Discontinued at the Defendant's costs.

James Yancey against Isham Safold. Petition by note of hand. The Defendant came into Court & saith that he can not Gainsay the Plaintiff's action, but that it is just & true...the Plaintiff recover the sum of ₺ 4 s 7, besides his costs....

State against Benjamin silman. On an Inditement for Hog Stealing. Came William Shaw Esqr. County attorney, in behalf of the State and the Defendant by Peter Carns Esqr. his attoy., whereupon came a Jury (to wit) (same as before)...We find the Defendant guilty, whereupon it is considered by the Court that the said Defendant pay the sum of ₺ 5 fine besides the Costs.

Ordered that the said Benjamin Silman have until next Court for the payment of his fine on giving approved sureties. Upon which Edward Mitchison & John Pennington came into Court and Entered themselves sureties for the payment of the above sum at next court. Test. Saml. Porter, D. C.

The minutes were signed by James Jordan, Richd. Harrison & Obediah Trimmier, Esquires.
Court ten adjourned until to morrow morning at 9 o'clock.

Wednesday the 21st of March 1787. Present James Jordan, Richard Harrison & Obediah Trimmier, Esqrs.

State against John Gowin. Summs. & C. for Duty Due the county for Tavern License. The Court gave Judgment that the Defendant pay the sum of ₺ 3 Duty to the use of the County &c.

Present Baylis Earle, Esqr.

State against John Golightly. On a Summons.
By order of Court to pay the Tavern License Duty; The Court gave Judgment that the Defendant pay ₺ 3.

State against William Poole. On a Summons to pay the Tavern License Duty, the Court gave Judgment, that the Defendant pay ₺3.

State against Edmund Cradock. On a Summons to pay the Tavern License duty, the Court gave Judgment that the Defendant pay ₺ 3.

State against George Gordon. On a Summons to pay the Tavern License duty, The court gave Judgment that the Defendt. pay ₺ 3.

State against Thomas Williamson. On a Summons to pay the Tavern License duty, the Judgment of the Court is that the Defendant pay the sum of ₺ 3.

Daniel Hail against John Butler. Came the Plaintiff by Peter Carns & Charles Goodwin Esqrs., his attornies, and the defendant by Jacob Brown, his attorney. The Court on hearing their alligations ordered that suit to be dismissed at the Deft's Costs.

Ordered that the Clerk procure a standard of Dry & wet measure, and that he have /6 pr. seal, upon Each of them for puting on the stamp.

ordered that John Thomas Junr., Esqr., be appointed Treasurer for the County, and that he give Bond with Five Hundred Pounds penalty for the due performance thereof.

Frederick Isham & Jacob Isham principles and Jeremiah Silman as surety acknowledged themselves Indebted to the State, the sum of ₺ 25 each. To be void in condition that the Frederick and Jacob Ishams, shall at next Court make their personal appearance to answer to a charge of Petty Larceny, otherwise to be in full force in Law.

Ordered that William Poole, Iron Master, of Lawsons Fork, have License to keep a Tavern. Andrew Barry and Joseph Barnett his sureties for his faithful performance, Gave their Gonds in Open Court.

Ordered that Burwell Thomson have License to keep a Public House of Entertainment. Joseph Wofford & Hezekiah Langston, his sureties, gave their Bonds in Open Court....

Ordered that William Wofford Junr., have License to keep a Public House of Entertainment; Obediah Trimmier & Joseph Barnett, his sureties....

Ordered that the agreement entered into by the Commissioners for the Letting the Public Buildings for the County to Richard Harrison Esquire, who has undertaken to Build the same, is approved by the Court, and that the Inhabitants of this County be assessed one sixteenth of the General Tax, to be collected by the Sheriff, and pay the said Undertaker ₺ 25 at next June Court, and that the said Sheriff be furnished with a List from the Different collections.

A Deed of Conveyance from Robert Evins to Baylis Earle Esqr. was proved in open Court by the Evidence of Felix Walker & laid over for further Proof.

Two sets of Leases & Release from James Jones & Elizabeth his wife to Burwell Bobo, proved in Court, the Evidence of Christopher Casey & Sampson Bobo. Ordered to be recorded.

A Lease and Release from Nathaniel Miller to Saml. Nelly, acknowledged in Open Court. Ordered to be recorded.

State against Holland Sumner. Assault & Battery.
The Court adjuged that the defendant pay the fine of one shilling and all the costs.

A Deed of Conveyance from Susanah Hattaway to George Turner proved by the Evidences of Henry Turner and William Headen. Ordered to be Recorded.

A Deed of Conveyance from John Atkison to Henry Turner, proved by the Evidences of John Headen & William Headen. Ordered to be recorded.

A Lease and Release from Ambrose Barnett to Abraham Nally, proved by the Evidences of David Graham and John Butler.

State against Benjamin Silman. The Jury who found the prisoner guilty of the charge laid in the Bill of Inditement, upon conference with the Court this Day, agreed to leave the point of law to the Determination of the Court (tl wit) Whether the prisoner stole the Hog, therein charged, with a fellonius Intent, or only killed the same, on which the Court Determined that he only killed the same Hog as a Trespass and ordered him to pay the fine of ₺ 5.

Ordered that the clerk pay into the hands of William Young Esqr. Sheriff of Spartanburg, the sum of ₺ 15 for his Extra services, out of the money arising from the fines of Tavern License.

A Lease and Release from Ambrose Barnett to Nathaniel Davis, proved in Court. Ordered to be recorded.

Ordered that William Brannon be appointed, Overseer of the Road, in the Room of James McDowall (Orders to issue immediately) and James Jackson Junr. in the Room of Jas. Hooper.

A Deed from Vardry McBee to William Rickman acknowledged in Open Court. Ordered to be Recorded.

State against Rhoda McBee. On Inditement Petty Larceny.
The Jury being sworn find the Defendant not guilty, the Defendant is ordered to be discharged on paying the Costs.

Wadsworth & Turpin against Peter Martin. Petition &c.
The Court Decreed for the Plaintiff ₺ 1 s 2 d 10 with costs of suit.

John Martin against Moses Procter. Petition &C.
The Court ordered the Pltff to be nonsuited and pay the costs.

William West against James Phillips. Petition &C. By order of Court Discontinued at Defendants costs.

Thomas Pedan against Alexr. McElheney. Petition & C. Came the Plaintiff by Charles Goodwin Esqr. his attorney & the Defendant failing to appear, the Court Decreed for the Pltff. ₺ 1 s 17 d 4 besides his Costs....

David Pedan & David Morton proved their attendce. to be one Day with 30 miles Travel, and the same Returning from Greenville County s/21 9 o'clock.

John Farrow against Ex'ors of Smith. Petition & C. by acct. Continued until next Court at Defendant's Costs, and then to come to trial.

John Bee Holmes against George Taylor. In Debt.
Came the Plaintiff by Charles Goodwin Gentleman his attorney, and the Defendant in his own person came into Court and saith that he cannot gainsay the Pltffs. action, but that it is Just and true and that he owes the Debt ₺ 10 s 17 d 6...

A Deed from Laurens Reddy to William Poole proved by the Evidence of Laurence Esterwood laid over for further proof.

Wilson Rogers against Benj. Burnet Senr., Godfrey & Barnett & Benj. Burnett Junr. Trover & C.
Came the Plaintiff by William Shaw Esq. his atto., & that Defendants failing to appear in their persons or by their attrs., whereupon came a Jury (to wit) William Poole, John Cooper, Reubin Dickson, Maximilian Conner, Robert Connell, Thomas Flinn, Rowland Cornelius, Moses Timmons, Josiah Culberson, James Briton, Thomas Heany & Joseph Barnett...we find for the Plaintiff Ł 12 principle and Ł 8 damage....

Lewis Turner is allowed on oath Ł 1 for Mileage and attendance from Union County in the above suit. Rodgers against Burnetts.

Henry Turner Senr. is allowed on oath seven shillings and six pence for three days attendance in the above suit.

Vardry McBee against Thomas Gordon. Trover & Conversion.
Thomas Gordon against Vardry McBee. In Debt.
By consent of the parties ordered that the said suits, and all matters of controversy...be referred to Obediah Trimmier Esquire, Wm. Thomson & Isham Safold....

John Shannon against Richard Collins. On Petition Etc. by note of hand.
Decree for Ł 50 old currency with Interest from 20th Sept 1783 until paid Besides his Costs by the said Plaintiff Expended....

John Camp against John Chism. Trover & C.
On Motion of Daniel Brown Defendant's attorney, that the Plaintiff give surety for costs, being an Inhabitant of North Carolina, Maximilian Conner, Entered himself as surety for the Plaintiff.

William Young Esqr. against Charles McKnight, Admr. of Trammell, Deft. Petition, Etc.
The Court gave Judgment against the Defendant for the sum of Ł 3 besides his costs....

Robert Head came into Court and proved his attendance to be 6 Days in the suit John Head vs Ebenezer Moss.

James McElwayne & wife against John Shannon. On Petition.
The Court gave Judgment to the Plaintiffs for Ł 3 s 3 d 11¼ besides his Costs....

Michael Hogan against Peter Edwards. Dedymus Potestatum is Granted the Plaintiff to give the Defendant timely notice of the witnesses names and the name of the Justices before whom they are to be Examined, etc.

The minutes were signed by Baylis Earle, James Jordan, Zadock Ford & Richard Harrison. Court adjourned until to morrow 9 o'clock.

Thursday the 22nd of March A. D. 1787. The Court met according to adjournment. Present Baylis Earle, Richard Harrison & Zadock ford.

A Lease and Release from James Bruton to Thomas Williamson acknowledged in Open Court. Ordered to be Recorded.

Ordered that Benjamin Roads & Benjamin Beason be Overseers of the Road from John Pattons to Isaac Crows in the Room of George Bruton to keep said Road in Good Repair by summoning the male Inhabitants within four Miles of said Road to work on the same and that Samuel Jackson be Overseer in the Room of James Hooper. Ordered that orders issue immediately.

Ordered that Ebenezer Moss have License to keep a Public House of Entertainment, Joseph Wofford and John Pennington his sureties for his true performance of the same as Directed by Law.

William Shaw against Stephen Williford. On attachment. William Wood enterpleads and claims one cow and yearling; the Court on hearing the Council on both sides, adjudged the said cow and yearling to be the property of the said Wood and the Sheriff is ordered to Deliver to the said Wood, the said Cow and yearling.

Same against Same   Debt. Judgement for the Pltff. for ₤ 10 and Costs. of suit. Ordered that an order for sale issue for the remainder of the Defendant's Goods, not ordered to the claimants and be sold according to Law.

Absent Baylis Earle, Esqr. Present Obediah Trimmier, Esquire.

Ordered that a Venditis Exponis issue to sell the property of Hugh Perce now in the hands of the Sheriff.

Absent Justice Trimmier, Present Justice Earle.

John Crow against Henry Kirby. Dismissed at the Defendant's Costs.

John Parker against James Smith. Dismissed at Defendant's Costs.

Jordan Monjoy against Thomas Farrow. Dismissed at Pltffs. Costs.

Mary Chumley against John Osheals & others. Dismissed at Pltffs. Costs.

Betsy Chumley against Same & Same. Dismissed at Pltffs. Costs.

John Head against Ebenezer Morse. Dismissed at Defendants Costs.

John Langston against Patty Young, admr. of Nathl. Young decd. contd. at Defts. Costs to June Court 1787.

James Lusk against Hancock Smith. Continued by consent.

John Gowin against Thomas Wood. Continued by consent until next Court.

John Thomas Senr. against Major Parsons. Slander. By consent of the Parties and assent of the Court, continued until next June term.

Thomas Trammill Junr. against John King. Trover & C. Continued until next court by consent.

Benjamin Silman against Charles Moore. Case. Continued until June Court next by consent.

James Barclay against William Moore. Trover & Conversn. By consent of the Parties and assent of the Court continued until next court.

Charles Moore against Benjamin Silman. Case. By consent of the parties and assent of the Court, continued until next June Term.

Bennett, admr. of Langston deceasd. against Landan Farrow. Trover & Convn. By consent of the Parties & assent of the Court. This action is continued until June Court next.

John Langston vs. Patty Young, admr. Joseph Wofford proved his attendance to be four days in the suit. Langston vs. Young.

John Smith proved his attendance to be 3 days in the above suit. Jaconias Langston proved his attendance to be 3 days in the above suit.

James Taylor White assignee of Adams against The Admrs. of Joseph Jones Decd. In Debt.
Came the Plaintiff by Daniel Brown, Esqr. his atty. and the Defendants by James Yancey Esqr. thier attorney, whereupon came a Jury to wit, (same as before)...the sd. Defendants doth owe the debt Ł 452 s 10 old South currency, paying regard to the Depreciation scale with Lawful Interest....

Jonathan Stone proved his attendance to be 4 Days as an Evidence in the above suit.

James Huggins against John Blalock Junr. On attachment. John Blalock Senr. comes into court and claims the property attached, therefore the Court order a Jury to try the same at next Term.

John Brown against James Devine. On Attachment. The Court ordered that the goods so attached be Exposed to sale for the use of the Plaintiff.

John Roebuck against Peter Brooks. On attachment. By consent of the parites, and assent of the Court Contd. until June Court next.

John Bagwell against Littleton Bagwell. Case. Settled at the Defendant's Costs.

William Brown against Benjamin Wofford. fees to be paid by Samuel Farrow.

Paul Smith against Henry Coone. Case. Default.

Wadsworth Turpin against Robert Kimbell. Case. Continued until next Court.

Isaac Buckston against Benjamin Wofford. Trover, Nonsuit 5/ damage & the Costs.

Stephen Williford against Ambrose Dollar. Assault & Battery. Settled at Defendant's Costs.

James Swan against Hugh Perce. Debt. Default.

/Shaw/ Charles McKnight Admr. of Trammell against Thomas Morrow. Case. Default.

John Woottin against David Henry. Slander Settled at Plaintiff's Costs.

James Millican against John Thomas & Nathl. Carrells. Case Contd. until June Court next.

Thomas Whitworth against Peter Edwards. On attachment. Settled at Defendts. Costs.

Wadsworth and Turpin against Peter Martin. Settled and the fees paid.

David McDowell against Hugh Freeman, Admr. of Rodin Trover. Contd. until June Court next.

The Exors of Safold against the Admrs. of Skelton. On Motion of Mr. Goodwin, Defendants attorney and affidavit, the Trial of this cause is Referred until Next Court, at the Defts. Costs.

Reubin Dickson against Vardry McB., Wm. Thomson & Wm Wise. In Debt. Came the Plaintiff by James Yancey & Daniel Brown, Gentlemen, his attornies, and the Defendants, by James Brown & Wm. Shaw, Gentlemen, their attoys., whereupon came a Jury (same as before)...we find for the Plaintiff Ł 400...

Ebenezer Moss against John Cooper. On Execution. Ordered that a writ of venditis Exponis Issue to sell the Land Executed of the Defendants to satisfy said Execution.

William Graham came into Court with Thomas Farrow a surety for Costs in a suit wherein said Graham is Plaintiff & Joseph Buffington, Defendant, as the Pltff. is an Inhabitant of North Carolina.

The Court adjourned until Court in course. The minutes were signed by Baylis Earle, James Jordan & Zadock Ford, Esqrs.

At a County Court began to be held for the County of Spartanburgh at the Court House on the third Monday in June A. D. 1787. Present Baylis Earle, James Jordan, Richard Harrison, Henry White, & Thomas Farrow, Esquires.

A Lease and Release from James Hardin to Vardry McBee proved at December Court by one witness & at this by William Wier. Ordered to be Recorded.

Ordered that the Road from Spartanburgh Court House to McDowell's Mill be extended northwardly to the North Carolina line. Wm. McDowell, overserr and to view the ground for said Road.

A Deed from Samuel Sarratt to John Byars, proved by the Evidences of Thomas Wilson & James Byars. Ordered to be Recorded. Present Saml. Lancaster, Esqr.

A Lease and Release from Robert Goodgion to Wm. Anderson, Acknowledged in Open Court & orderd. to be Recorded.

James Lusk produces a probate made by George Story Senr., respecting the Lands of said Lusk. Ordered to be recorded.

John Ford Esqr. came into Open Court and acknowledged a Lease & Release to James White. Ordered to be Recorded.

A Deed from John Raburn to Henry Hays proved in Open Court by the Evidences of Moses Wood & Thomas Hays. Ordered to be recorded.

Present Obediah Trimmier, Esqr.

A Lease & Release from George Connell & Frances his wife to John Ford Esqr. acknowledged in Open Court the wife being previously examined by Thomas Farrow, Esqr. She truly renounceth her Dower. Ordered to be Recorded.

A Lease & Release from Israel Morris & wife to Wadsworth and Turpin, acknowledged in Open Court and ordered to be put upon Record.

Ordered that the Grand Jurors for the County be summoned to appear at September and March Courts in future.

A Deed from Robert Evins to Baylis Earle Esqr. was proved at March Court last by Felix Walker, Eqr. and at the by Samuel Earle. Ordered to be recorded.

A Deed from John Earle to Richard Raburn, acknowledged in Open Court. Ordered to be recorded.

A Deed of Gift from John Kelley to John Turner proved in Open Court by the Evidences of Samuel Porter & William Young. Ordered to be recorded.

A Lease & Release from William Alderage to Matthew Mackaboy, Acknowledged in Open Court & ordered to be Recorded.

Leonard Adcock came into Open Court and acknowledged a Deed to Jonathan Lowe. Ordered to be Recorded.

Danl. Walker came into Open Court and Acknowledged a Deed of Conveyance to Elisha Smith. Ordered to be put upon the Records of the Court.

Grand Jurors for September Court 1787 were drawn and their names commited to the Minutes (to wit) Andrew Barry, Thomas Pedan, Thomas Farrar, William Tate Senr., Thomas Heaney, James Hooper, Joseph Thomson, Charles Hester, Wm. Smith, Majr. Wells Griffith, William Thomson Gentn., Richard Lewis, William Benson, Robert Sterling, David Goodlett, John Golightly, David Anderson, Robert Goodgion & David Golightly.

Pettit Jurors for Septr. Court, 1787. Isham Foster, Wm. Wood, fairforest, Wm. Wofford Junr., Joseph Wofford, William Sterling, Jonathan Stone, Robert McMillin, John Wofford, William Wier, Jesse Reams, Jas. Norris, Fleming Smith, Joseph Venible, Francis Dodd, Jonathan Harris, James Crow, John Foster, James Vernon, John Mapp, Nathaniel Stoake, John Williams, William Underwood, John Bearden, Reubin Smith, Peter Smith, Absalom Lancaster, James Koon & William Bird.

Mary Wood came into Open Court and acknowledged a Lease and Release to William Poole. Ordered to be Recorded.

A Lease & Release from Jacob Earnest to Thomas Doeg, was proved in Open Court by the Evidences of Alexr. Alexander and David McCarley. Ordered to be recorded.

The will of Moses McCarley was produced in Open Court and proved in the presence of said Court by the Evidences of Samuel and Spencer Fords, to be the said McCarley's last Will and Testament. Ordered to be recorded.

Ordered that a Dydemus Issue to Burke County, North Carolina, to Charles or Joseph McDowell, Esquires, to take the Examination of Elizabeth Belew Respecting a certain matter of controversy between David McDowell, Plaintiff and Hugh Freeman, Administrator of Thomas Rodin Defendant on Giving the said Defendant 15 days previous notice thereof.

The Court proceeded to the choice of a Sheriff, upon casting up the votes, Mr. Samuel Farrow was Duly Elected to that office. Ordered that the Clerk give him a certification accordingly, which was done in Court Immediately.

Edward Hooker against Mark Powell. On attachment. The Court ordered this attachment to be Dismissed at the Plaintiff's Costs.

Ann Alexander against Charles Bragg & Others. Assault, Etc. Nonsuit.

The minutes were signed by by Henry White, James Jordan, Thomas Farrow & Obediah Trimmier. The Court then adjourned until Court in course.

At a County Court began to be holden for the County of Spartanburgh on the third Monday on September 1787. Present Henry White, James Jordan & Richard Harrison, Esquires. Ordered that Thomas Hays serve as Constable During this Court in the Room of David Lewis Junr. who could not attend.

Samuel Farrow produced his commission signed by his Excellency the Governor as Sheriff for this County the Ensuing two years, which was read in Open Court. Ordered that he give bond and surety agreeable to law and qualify accordingly.

Henry Wells was Proposed by Mr. Farrow, the Sheriff, as Deputy Sheriff for said County, who was approved of by the Court and ordered to qualify agreeable to same.

Ephraim Reece against Nicholas Holly. Attachment. For a Debt of Ł 40 sterling.
William Lindsey came into open Court and acknowledged himself Special Bail for the Defendants appearance at next Court.

The Court then Proceeded to draw the Pettit Jurors for next Court, the were as follows (to wit) Samuel Jackson, Jesse Connel, Charles McLain, Thomas Miles, John King, Alexander McCarter, Denny Anderson, Robert Conner, Henry Heirs, John Conner, James Alexander, James Amos, Rowland Johnston, William Clayton, Arthur Hutchins, James Head, Ebenezer Moss, Robert Jamerson, Samuel Jackson Junr., John Ford Junr., James Bennett, Landon Farrow, Christopher Long, Samuel Ford, James Faris, Shands Golightly, George Bennett, Tobias Bright, Edmund W. Clements, Thomas Davis. Grand Jurors Drawn to serve this Court (to wit) William Smith Majr., Thomas Paden, Andrew Barry, David Anderson, William Thomson, Joseph Thomson, Well Griffith, William Tate Senr., David Goodlet, Robert Sterling, Charles Hester, James Hooper, William Benson, David Golightly, Richard Lewis, Thomas Farrow, Robert Goodgion, Thomas Haney, John Golightly.

Pettit Jurors, James Norris, James Keen, James Crow, Reubin Smith, Flemming Smith, William Bird, William Wier, Robert McMillin, Absalom Lancaster, Nathaniel Stokes, William Wofford Junr., Joseph Wofford, Jonathan Stone, John Bearden, William Wood, Joseph Venible, Francis Dodd, Jonathan Harris, John Mapp, William Sterling.

John Smith and Thomas Williams Executors of Moses Span, Deceased, came into Court and Renounced their Executors-ship upon the will of the said Deceased. Therefore came Thomas and Jesse Span, sons of the said Deceased and made application for the administration of the Deceased's Goods and chattels with his will annexed which was granted by the Court accordingly and Thomas Williams and John Bearden were approved of as sureties for the said administration.

The Grand Jurors were Empanneled & sworn & William Shaw Esq, County Attorney, Delivered a charge unto them in behalf of the Court.

The Pettit Jury were drawn, Empannelled, no bisiness being ready for them, they were dismissed until Tomorrow morning at nine o'clock.

Upon the application of Andrew Paul, Ordered that he have license to keep a Tavern, he therefore Produced Jeremiah Thomson and James Smith as Sureties for the same, who were approved of by the Court.

William Clayton came into Court and acknowledged a Deed of Conveyance from himself to Joseph Wofford. The Court ordered the same to be Recorded.

Joshua Smith came into Court and acknowledged a Lease & Release to Owen Forrister. Ordered to be Recorded.

Owen Forrest & wife came into Court and acknowledged a Deed of Conveyance from themselves to Joshua Smith. Ordered to be recorded.

The minutes were read and signed by Henry White, James Jordan, Richard Harrison, Esqrs. Court then adjourned until Tomorrow morning Nine o'clock.

Tuesday the 18th of September 1787. Court met according to adjournment. Present James Jordan, Richard Harrison, and Thomas Wadsworth, Esquires.

Deed of Conveyance from James Head and wife to David Vinson proved by Ralph Jackson, laid over for further proof.

A Deed of conveyance from Samuel Knox and wife to Henry Wells, proved by George Pettus and William Wells, Ordered to be recorded.

Lease and release from David Mcree to John Smith, proved by George Pettus and William Wells. Ordered to be recorded.

Alexr. Alexander and Wife vs Charles & Zebulon Braggs
Charles Bragg vs. Alexr. Alexander & Wife. Assault
State vs. Charles Bragg.
The parties in these three cases submitted the whole of their controversies to the order and arbitrament of John Ford and Andrew Thomson, whose award is that the Defendants pay the sum of ℔ 2 d 6 lawful money and all the costs....

Samuel Farrow, Sheriff for this County came into Court and took the oaths of allegiance and office as prescribed by Law.

Henry Wells came into Court and took the oaths Prescribed by law as Deputy Sheriff for this County.

James Lusk vs Handisck (sic, for Handcock?) Smith. Trespass. This action Discontinued Each paying their own Costs.

James Jordan, Esquire vs John Thomson. On attachment.

Absent James Jordan. Present Baylis Earle, Esquire.

Came the Plaintiff by William Shaw Gentleman his attorney, & the Defendant on his being solemnly called and failing to appear, either in his own person or by his attorney, also came a Jury (to wit) William Wofford Junr., James Norris, James Keen, James Crow, Flemming Smith, William Wier, Robert McMillin, Nathaniel Stokes, Joseph Wofford, Jonathan Stone, John Bearden, William Wood, Joseph Venible, who being Elected, tried & sworn the truth to speak, upon the issue, on their oaths do say That the Defendant does owe the Debt ₤ 19 s 17 d 9 lawful money....

William Walker against Henry Wyatt. Slander. Discontinued at Defendant's Costs.

Present James Jordan, Esquire.

Eleanor Walker against Henry Wyatt. Slander. Discontinued at Defendant's Costs.

Wadsworth & Turpin against Robert Kimbel. Case. Discontinued at Defendant's Costs.

Edward Stokes and Wife against Robert White. Pettition & Summons. Came the Plaintiff by Peter Carns, Gentleman, his attorney and the Defendant by Jacob Brown, his attorney, and upon the Parites being heard it is considered by the Court that the Plaintiff Recover against the Defendant the sum of ₤ 10 Virginia money, Interest and costs of suit. The above sum in sterling ₤ 9 6 10½.

Holland Sumner against Thomas Blasingame. Petition & Summons. Nonsuit.

A Power of Attorney from Thomas Bonner to Vardry McBee proved in Court by William Tate Senr. Ordered to be recorded.

Immediately after the above Vardery McBee came into Court and acknowledged a Lease & Release from himself as attorney of Thomas Bonner to William Tate Senr. Ordered to be recorded.

Wadsworth & Turpin against Thomas Trammel. on a Petition by acct. Came the Plaintiffs by T. P. Carns, Gentl., their attorney, and the Defendant failling to appear either in his own Person or by his attorney, Whereupon it is considered by the Court that the Plaintiff recover against the Defendant the sum of s 3 d 9 besides his costs...

Deed of Conveyance from John McBee to James Jordan proved by Nevil Wayland, laid over for further proofs.

Nathaniel Miller came into Open Court and acknowledged a Lease & Release from himself to Zachariah Walker. Ordered to be recorded.

The minutes were Read & signed by Baylis Earle, James Jordan, Richard Harrison, Esquires.
Court then adjourned until Tomorrow morning at Nine o'clock.

Wednesday the 19th of September 1787. The Court met according to adjournment. Present Henry White, Thomas Wadsworth & Obediah Trimmier, Esquires.

Michael Hogan against John Seratt. Case. Discontinued at Plaintiff's Costs.

Michael Hogan against John Seratt. Trover Discontinued at Plaintiff's Costs.

Deed of conveyance from John McCollock to Edward Hooper, proved by Thomas Todd, laid over for further Proof.

Indenture from Joseph Power & Wife to Edward Smith, proved by Thomas Todd, laid over for further proof.

Indenture from Joseph Power & wife to James Crowther, proved by Thomas Todd; laid over for further proof.

Indenture Peter Smith & wife to William Smith, proved by Josiah Culbertson & Flemming Smith. Ordered to be recorded.

Indenture from William Smith and wife, to James Smith, proved by Josiah Culbertson and Flemming Smith. Ordered to be recorded.

Lease & Release from Elisha Ford & wife to John Posey, proved by William Ford & Charles Moore. Ordered to be recorded.

Lease & Release from Elisha Ford & wife to Robert Goodgion; proved by William Ford & Charles Moore. Ordered to be recorded.

Power of Attorney from Fielding Woodruff to Daniel Brown; Proved in Open Court by Jacob Brown in the following words, "I hereby impower Daniel Brown to make a settlement with William Mitcheson, Esquire, for a certain horse proved away from me, & what he does therein shall bind me." Fielding Woodruff
4th Day of December 1787, which is here Recorded.

Michael Hogan against Peter Edward. In Debt. The Parties by agreement Refered this case to William Tate, Laurence House, Nichols Scurry, Yearby Duberry & Mr. Patrick, and their award to be Returned to next Court, and considered a rule thereof.

State by James Keen against Frederick and Jacob Ison. Larceny. The Defendant by their attorney pray that their trial may come on next Court, they not being ready on this, which was Granted, they giving Security for their appearance then.

Capt. James Smith came into Court & entered himself Bail in the sum of £ 30 for the appearance of Frederick Ison at next Court. Signed James Smith.

The Executrix of Safold against The Administrators of Skelton. In Case. Came the Plaintiff by James Yancey Gentl., her attorney, and the Defendant by Jacob Brown Gentl., his attorney, the Plaintiff for trial, puts herself upon the County, & the Defendants do likewise...whereupon came a Jury (same as before)...we find for the Plaintiff £ 10 lawful money & Costs of suit.

Israel Morriss against Rowland Cornelius. Case. Refered to James Jordan & Thomas Farrer with leave to choose am umpire, and Return the award to next Court to be Considered as a Rule thereof.

Present Baylis Earle, Esq.

Richard Sanders against Peter Martin & Wife. Slander. By consent of the Plaintiff & assent of Court. Dismissed at the Plaintiff's Costs.

Jeremiah Hembrick proved 4 days attendance in Open Court at s 2 d 6 per day in the case. Michael Hogan against Peter Edwards.

James Miller acknowledged a Conveyance from Himself to Robert & William Miller Ordered to be recorded.

Ordered that a Citation issue to Samuel Nesbit to administer on the Estate of John Shannon, Deceased.

Also that a Citation issue to Charles McKnight to administer on the Estate of John Dinkins, Deceased.

Order that an Order of Sale issue to the Sheriff to sell the lands attached by James Jordan Esquire against John Thomson to satisfy the debt and costs demanded by attachment.

A Deed of Conveyance from Joseph Burchfield to James Fannen, proved by Vardry McBee and Isham Saffold. Ordered to be Recorded.

Ordered that the action John Russel against Henry Prince be put on the appearance Docket, and brought on in its Legal Course.

Ordered that Henry Wells, William Wood, & Thomas Underwood, view the nearest and best way for a Road from the Court House, Intersection the Road Leading from the Iron Works to Ford's Mill on Tyger River & that they lay out the same to Intersect said Road, near the Cross Roads & that John Hammet be appointed overseer of the same.

Thomas Gordon against Vardery McBee. In Debt.
Vardery McBee against Thomas Gordon. Trover.
Vardery McBee against Thomas Gordon. Debt.
These three cases Refered by consent of the Parties to the arbitrament of Obadiah Trimmier, William Thomson, and Isham Safford, their awd. to be the Rule of Court.
....We the subscribers being appointed by the worshipful Court of Spartanburgh to settle matters ...between Thomas Gordon & Vardery McBee, do adjudge and say that Vardery McBee is justly indebted to said Gordon the sum of £ 15 s 6 to be paid agreeable to the Instalment Law, and each to pay their own cost in every suit....

Present Henry White, Esquire.

John Camp against John Chisham. Trover. Continued until next Court at Defendant's Cost.

A Bill of Sale from Henry Turner to William Poole; proved in Open Court. Ordered to be Recorded.

A Mortgage from Betty Thomson to William Poole; proved in Open Court. Ordered to be recorded.

A Deed of Conveyance from Vardery McBee to William Wier, acknowledged in Open Court. Ordered to be recorded.

A Lease & Release from William Lewis to John Young. Proved by William Wood and Samuel Porter. Ordered to be Recorded.

William Wier came into Open Court and acknowledged a Power of attorney to Vardery McBee. Ordered to be Recorded.

James Milican against John, Thos & Nathl. Carrels. Case. Submitted to Baylis Earle, James Jordan, William Benson & John Gowin and their award to be returned to next Court, and be considered as a Rule thereof.

Hance Harper against William Fields. Slander. By consent of the Parties and assent of the Court this suit is Dismissed at Equal Costs.

In the affidavit of Stephen Crowder, Ordered that all the suits in which Major Parsons is concerned be continued over to next Court, he appearing by said affidavit to be unable to attend this Court.

Ordered that John Biswel alias Hannah be bound to James Vernon, who now has him in keeping untill he comes of Age.

Ordered that William Thomason be bound out unto William Poole untill he is of the age of 21 years.

Robert Lusk against Nevil Wayland. Assault.
By consent of the Defendant and assent of the Court, this suit dismissed at the Defendant's costs.

Charles Waters against Thomas Gormon. Damage. By consent of the Defendant and assent of the Court this suit Dismissed at the Defendant's Costs.

Minutes were signed by Baylis Earle, Henry White & James Jordan, Esquires. Court adjourned unti-1 Tomorrow Nine O'Clock.

Thursday the 20th of September 1787. The Court met according to adjournment. Present Baylis Earle, James Jordan & Obadiah Trimmier, Esquires.

Frederick Ison against Wm. Davis & Jas. Clark. Trover. Referred to John McElhenny & John Ford with power to choose an umpire and their award to be returned to our next Court, as a Rule thereof.

William Couch against Westwood Waters. Trover. By consent of the Parties and assent of the Court Laid over untill next court.

Dudley Red against Holland Sumner. Attachment. By consent of the Parties & Assent of the court Laid over untill next Court.

Thomas Blasingame against Holland Sumner. Attachment. By consent of the Parties & assent of the Court this suit laid over untill next Court.

James Clark against George Pettus. Case. By consent of the Parties and assent of the Court this suit is laid over untill next Court.

George Pettus against James Clark. Trover. By cosent of the Parties and assent of the Court this suit is Dismissed each paying their own costs.

Henry Hayes against Edward Mitchison. Trover. By consent of the Parties and assent of the Court, this suit is Refered to Baylis Earle & James Jordan with Power to choose an umpire and Return the award to the next Court, as a Rule thereof.

John Pennington against Joseph Hall. Special action on the Case. By consent of the Parties and assent of the Court this action is Refered to the Arbitrament of Benjamine Kilgore & Thomas Tod with power to choose an umpire, and their award to be Returned to next Court and be the judgment thereof.

Henry Hamilton against Joseph Hall. Case. By consent of the Parties and assent of the Court this action is Refered to the arbitrament of Benjamine Kilgore & Thomas Tod with Power to choose an umpire, and their award to be Returned to next Court and be the judgment thereof.

Joseph Hall against Pennington & Rennolds. Malicious Prosecution. By consent of the Parties and assent of the Court this action is Refered to the Arbitrament of Benjamin Kilgore and Thos. Tod with power to choose an umpire....

Ordered that the Sheriff Samuel Farrow enter into bond agreeable to Law. He therefore produced William Smith and George Robuck as his sureties, who were approved of by the Court and assigned a Bond for that purpose in Open Court.

A Bill of Sale from Thomas Brown to Thomas & John Brown, proved in Open Court. Ordered to be Recorded.

Admr. of Langston against Landon Farrow. Trover. By consent of the Parties and assent of the Court, this action laid over untill next Court at Defendant's Cost.

A Deed of Conveyance from James & Ellis Ross to John Tollason proved by two Evidences. Ordered to be recorded.

A Lease & Release from Seth Lewis to John Gosset proved by two Evidences. Ordered to be Recorded.

On motion, ordered that William Bennett be dismissed from his Recognizance on paying costs.

Ordered that the Clerk pay William Young the late Sheriff, the sum of £ 6 s 6 out of the Duty's upon Tavern license as soon as he shall receive a sufficiency for that purpose.

Vardery McBee against Balender's & Seaborne. Trespass. Came the Plaintiff by William Shaw & James Yancey Gentl his attorney's and the Defendants by Daniel Brown Gentl. their attorney and the Defendant pleads to the Jurisdiction of the Court. Plea overruled and ordered to plead substantially therefore the plaintiff moves for an appeal, which is granted accordingly.
    In the above case the Defendant pleads his Habuit in tenements. The plaintiff then demurs judgment for the Defendants on Demurrer.

On the return of the Execution of James McElwayne & wife against John Shannon on mtion of Mr. Yancey, attorney for the Plaintiff for judgement against William Young late Sheriff for £ 3 s 17 d 11¼ the Balance in his hands, the Sheriff confessed Legal Notice & Judgment for the same.

Ordered that John Wood be appointed Overseer to open & keep in good repair the Road from Peter Lewis' on Lawsons Fork to the Court House & that the hands near & contiguous to said Road that ought by Law to work on Roads be under his Direction.

Thomas C. Russel against Joseph Buffington. In Debt. Came the Plaintiff by James Yancey Gentl. his attorney, and the Defendant say he cannot gainsay the Plaintiff's action...he owes the Debt Ł 50 lawful money with interest from 12th Feb 1783 until 20 Sept 1787 together with his costs...

Thomas C. Russel against Joseph Buffington. Petition & Summons. Came the Plaintiff by James Yancey Gentl. his attorney and the Defendant says he cannot Gainsay the Plaintiffs action but that it is just, & that he owes the debt Ł 4 s 2 lawful money with Interest from 1 March 1787 untill 20 Sept 1787...

William Graham against Jas. Buffington & John Thomas Junr. In Debt. Came the Plaintiff by James Yancey Gentl. their attorney & the Defendants say they cannot Gainsay the Plaintiff's action but that it is just & they owe the Debt Ł 45 s 5 lawful money with Interest from 24th March 1786 until 20th Sept 1787....

John Langston against Administrators of Young. Trover.
By consent of the Parties and assent of the Court this suit laid over until To-morrow, then come to trial without fail.

John Gowen against Thomas Wood. Trespass.
Came the Plaintiff by Wm. Shaw Gentl. his atto., and the Defendant by Charles Goodwin and James Yancey Gentleman his attorneys order to the plea of the Defendant be quashed and that he plead the General issue and then came a Jury (to wit) Joseph Wofford, James Norris, James Keen, James Crow, Flemming Smith, William Wier, Robert McMillin, Nathaniel Stokes, Jonathan Stone, John Bearden, William Wood, Joseph Venible, who do say...we find for the plaintiff s 16...

Ordered that a Road be laid out from the widow of Ralph Smith to Musgroves on course crossing Tyger River at Toney's Ford to go the nighest and best way to Musgroves on Enoree and the Inhabitants for 4 miles on each side of said Road be ordered to work on the same, and that Samson Bobo & Stephen Wilson be Overseer of said Road. Issued.

An Indenture of apprenticeship from William Thomson to William Poole was proved in open Court by the oaths of William Shaw & Thomas Farrer Esquires, and was ordered to be recorded.

Wells Griffith proved 3 days attendance as an evidence in the case Fields against Harper.

Thomas Brummet proves his attendance for 20 days amounting to Ł 2 s 10 in case Gowin against Wood. also Samuel Hand proves 17 days attendance amounting to Ł 2 s 2 d 6 in case Gowin vs Wood.

Ordered that the Sheriff expose to sale the Property of Andrew Brown Executor at the suit of Thomas Crow, agreeable to Law.

Alexander Candles proves a deed of conveyance from John McCree to James Jordan. Ordered to be recorded.

James Huggins against John Blailock. Attachment. By consent of the Plaintiff and assent of the Court, this suit Dismissed at Plaintiff cost.

Minutes were read and signed by Baylis Earle, James Jordan & Obadiah Trimmier, Esqrs. Court then adjourned until Tomorrow Nine o'clock.

Friday the 21st of September 1787. The court met according to adjournment. Present Baylis Earle, Richard Harrison & Samuel Lancaster, Esquires.

Ordered that James Holcomb be bound out to John Holcomb and that he learn such Handicraft as the said John Holcomb may follow.

Robert Harper against John McClure. Slander. By consent of the Parties and assent of the Court this suit Dismissed at Plaintiff's Cost.

Samuel Farrow against McBee & Saffold. In Debt.
Came the Plaintiff by James Yancey Gentl. his attorney and the Defendants say they cannot Gainsay the Plaintiff's action...they owe the Debt L 14 s 18 d 10...

John Langston against Administratrix of Young. Trover.
Came the plaintiff by Daniel Brown and James Yancey Gentlemen his Attornies and the Defendant by Charles Goodwin, William Shaw & Peter Carnes Gentlemen her attornies also came a Jury (to wit) Andrew Berry, James Norris, James Keen, Flemming Smith, William Wier, Robert McMillin, Nathaniel Stokes, Jonathan Stone, John Bearden, William Wood, Joseph Venible & William Sterling...we find Nathaniel Young Decd. in his lifetime did convert the property of the said John Langston the plaintff of the value of L 20 ...we submit it to the Court whether action lies against the admx. Andrew Berry, foreman.
On a special verdict for the Plaintiff...ordered that Judgment be entered for the Defendat, with Costs of suit and the Plaintiff is amerced.

George Pettus against David McKneely. Slander. By consent of the Parties and assent of the Court, this suit is Refered to the Arbitrament of two persons, investing them with the power of choosing an umpire & their award to be Returned to out next Court and be considered as a Rule thereof.

George Pettus against David McKneely. Case. (same as preceding)

David McNelly against George Pettus. Ditinue. (same as preceding)

A Lease and Release from John McCullock to James Casey, proved in Open Court by Peter & Sarah Brooks. Ordered to be Recorded.

A Lease and Release from John McCullock to Spensor Bobo, proved by Peter & Sarah Brooks; Ordered to be recorded.

Charles Bruce came into Open Court, and acknowledged a Lease and Release unto James Lusk. Ordered to be recorded.

A Lease and Release from Jacob Dennard to Swann Thomson, proved by one Evidence; laid over for further proof.

On the Return of the Citation obtained by Samuel Neasbitt to administer on the Estate of John Shannon, decd., ordered that he have the administration upon said Estate the same Giving sureties for his faithful administration, he therefore produced Andrew Berry and Thomas Paden who were approved of and that he take the Goods of the said Decd. in to his immediate possession. The admr. gave bond & security, etc., and was qualified in open Court.

Present Henry White, Esquire.

George Carpenter against Joseph Buffington. Debt. This suit is discontinued.

William Poole against Thomas Flinn. Attachment. Ordered that Sire facias issue against William Wofford Junr. and William McDowel, to show what they may have in their hands of the defendant.

Thomas Trammell against Thomas King. Trover. Nonsuit.

John Langston against Administratrix of Young. On Motion. Judgment arrested.

Richard Nalley proved 11 days attendance as an evidence in case Langston against Admx. of Young amounting to Ł 1 s 7 d 6.

David Grimes proved 6 days attendance as an evidence Langston against Admx. of Young amounting s 15.

Richard Chesney proved 15 days attendance as an evidence Langston against Young amounting to Ł 1 s 17 d 7.

John Langston against Patty Young Admr. of Young. Trover. On a special verdict for the Plaintiff subject to the opinion of the Court whether this action lay against the admx. on motion; Court ordered that Judgment be entered for the deft. with costs of suit.

Minutes were then Read & signed by Baylis Earle, Henry White, Richard Harrison, Samuel Lancaster, Esqrs. Court then adjourned untill Court in Course.

At a County Court began to be holden for the County of Spartanburg on the third Monday in December 1787. Tuesday the 18th of December the Court met according to adjournment. Present Baylis Earle, Richard Harrison, Samuel Lancaster, and Thomas Farrow, Esquires.

Ordered that the Sheriff apply to the Different Tax Collectors for a Regular list of all the Taxable Inhabitants; and that he return the same to next Court.

Ordered that the Treasurer pay Mr. David Goodlett the sum of s 8 for the Jury Box out of the County money.

On Return of an attachment, Harrison Culbertson against Francis Amos and no Goods found. Ordered that the officer Executing the same have his fees from the Plaintiff.

An Obligation to make titles in nature of a Mortgage from John McCullock to Robert Kilpatrick was proved in open Court by the oath of Hugh Boid and ordered to be recorded, it being for 1000 acres of Land.

A Lease and Release from William Hendrix to Ebenezer Morse acknowledged by said Hendrix, also proved by two witnesses. Ordered to be recorded.

David Goodlet came into open Court and acknowledged a Lease to John Foster. Ordered to be recorded, and his wife also Privately examined by Richard Harrison Esquire & Relinquished her Dower of the same.

A Lease and Release from James Jones & Wife to Jesse Casey, Proved in open Court by the Evidence of Peter Brooks and wife, Ordered to be recorded.

A Lease and Release from Christopher Casey to Moses Casey proved by Peter Brooks, laid over for further proof.

A Lease and Release from Jesse Casey to Moses Casey, proved by Peter Brooks and wife. Ordered to be recorded.

A Deed of Conveyance from Josiah Tanner to Jonathan Harriss, proved by William Thomson and Michael Hogan. Ordered to be recorded.

Thomas Doeg came into open Court and acknowledged a Deed of Conveyance from himself to James Crow. Ordered to be recorded.

Richard Chesney came into open Court and acknowledged a Lease and Release from himself to John Chesney. Ordered to be recorded.

Jeremiah Lucus and wife came into open Court and acknowledged a deed of conveyance to John Lucus. Ordered to be recorded.

A Deed of Conveyance from John Snoddy & wife to John Lands proved by Jeremiah Lucus and John Osling. Ordered to be recorded.

A Lease and Release from John Hillin & Mary Hillin to James Head, proved by Moses Casey. Laid over for further Proof.

A Deed of Conveyance from Daniel Kelley to John Childs. Proved by one evidence, laid over for further Proof.

A Lease and Release from Daniel Kelley & wife to Hezekiah Childs, proved by one evidence--laid over for further Proof.

John Roebuck came into open Court and Proved a Deed of Conveyance to James Crow, then Heretofore Recorded.

Luerisa Head came into open Court and Proved a Lease and Release from James Head to David Vinson. Ordered to be recorded.

A Lease and Release from Jesse Casey to Joseph Couch. Proved by the evidence of John Watson laid over for further proof.

The Court then Proceeded to draw the Grand Jurors for next Court to wit John McElheney, William McMillin, John McKnight, Thomas McKnight, Andrew Milican, Joseph Thomson, Charles McKnight, Edmund W. Clemons, Charles McClain, William Clayton, James Alexander, James Hooper, James Faris, Robert Jameson, George Bennett, Thomas Underwood, Tobias Bright, John Ross, John Scruggs, John Beach, Shands Golightly.

Pettit Jurors for next Court. Brittain Williford, Thomas Warren, Wells Griffith, William Crow, John Foster, George Lowden, Isaac Crow, Thomas Jackson, John Butter, John Hammet, Andrew Hendrix,

William Wilder, Henry Walker, David Neal, William Wyatt, Shadrack Waldrope, William Abbot, Joel Smith, John Watson.

A Deed of Conveyance from Richard Prince to William Wood proved by the Evidence of Alexander Walker and Henry Walden. Ordered to be recorded.

On the Return of a Citation obtained by Mrs. Ann White, widow of Henry White Esquire, decd. to administer upon the Estate of the said Deceased. Ordered that she have administration of Estate. She producing James Smith, James Lusk, John Mapp & William Wofford Junr. as her securities for said administration who were approved of by the Court.

On application of Mrs. Ann White, widow of Henry White Esquire, deceased, to have the Guardianship of Robert Mitchel, Martha Mitchel, Lemuel Mitchel, Samuel Mitchel & Henry White, minors, children of the said Ann White. Ordered that she have the Guardianship accordingly of the said Minors.

William Graham against Administratrix of William Thomson. In Debt. Ordered that the Judgment and Execution in this cause be set aside with costs, it appearing to the Court that the Judgment was obtained by Fraduality and Circumvention, and also for that this order was made at Last December Court and by neglect of the Deputy Clerk was omitted to be entered on the Records of this Court.

Jurors for this Court. Samuel Jackson, Jesse Connel, Denny Anderson, Henry Airs, John Conner, James Head, John Ford Junior, James Bennett, Samuel Ford, Tobias Bright, Thomas Miles, James Alexander.

John Daniel Came against John Kimbel. Attachment.
Came the Plaintiff by Charles Goodwin Gentl. his attorney and the Defendant say he cannot Gainsay the Plaintiff's action but that it is just and true & that he owes the Debt Ł 17 s 4 d 6 sterling...Signed by himself and Tested by T. P. Carnes.

Charles Hunt came into open Court and proved his attendance having 70 miles journey to attend as a witness in the suit George Berge against George Hunt.

Ordered that a Road be opened through a corner of this County, intersecting a Road from Norht Carolina & a Road through Greenville County distant about 5 miles and that the several inhabitants allowed by Law do work thereon be under the Direction of John Earle, who is appointed overseer of the same. Issued.

Mrs. Ann White came into open Court and took the oath of an administratrix upon the Estate of Henry White Esquires Deceased.

William Graham vs Joseph Buffington & John Thomas Junr. Debt. On Motion of Mr. Daniel Brown for the Defendants and producing several affidavits of the security already given for the Debt and which was approved of by the Plaintiff and also that the Defendants never refused giving security awarding to the Installment Act. It is ordered that the Execution be stayed and that the Judgment stand under the Installment Act, and that the Property Executed be Delivered to the Defendant by the Sheriff Thomas Farrow, Esquires, Descented.

A bill of sale from John Steen to James Lusk for a Hose and Gun.

Ordered to be recorded.

Ann Dewberry vs. William Gilbert. Attachment. On motion of the Plaintiff attorney ordered that a Dedymus Potestatum issue directed to Stephen Williss and   Grant, Esquires, to Examine Thomas Morriss on oath, respecting the above suit on the part and behalf of the Plaintiff, and to return the said Deposition, sealed up to next Court.

Minutes were read and signed by Baylis Earle, Samuel Lancaster, & Thomas Farrow, Esquires. Court then adjourned untill tomorrow Nine O'Clock.

Wednesday the 19th day of December 1787. The Court met according to adjournment. Present Baylis Earle, Richard Harrison & Samuel Lancaster, Esquires.

A Deed of Conveyance from Deskin Grant to Littleton Bagwell, proved by James Smith & Bazel Lee. Ordered to be recorded.

John Bagwell Junr. came into open Court with Mary McAbee, and proved that certain scratches or marks in his back was occasioned by the spurrs of James Lee in a fight between them.

Ann Ford, wife of John Ford Esquire, came into open Court and relinquished her Right of Dower in and to a certain Tract of Land by said John Ford made over to James White.

Ordered that John Farrow act as Constable for this County and qualify accordingly.

Henry Hays came into open Court and acknowledged a Deed of Conveyance from himself to Thomas Calhoun. Ordered to be recorded.

Absalom Bobo came into open Court and proved a Conveyance from John McCullock to Edward Hooker, heretofore Proved.

A Conveyance from Samuel Farrow Esquire Sheriff of this County to Ebenezer Morse, proved by Peter Carnes and Daniel Brown. Ordered to be recorded.

Present Thomas Farrow, Esquire.

Elizabeth Spurgeon Administratrix of John Spurgeon against Mary and John Hillin. Case. Referred to John Ford, Esquire and William Smith with leave to choose an umpire and their award returned to next Court, to be the judgment of the Court.

A lease and release from Michael Sprinkle & wife to William Prince, proved by Peter Elder and Thomas Reece also the wife to Baylis Earle, Esquire (appointed by the Court to Examine her privately & Reports that she freely relinquish her Dower). Ordered to be recorded.

Ordered that a tax equal to one tenth part of the general tax paid by the citizens of this County to the State be assessed immediately, levyed and collected from each citizen within this County for the use of the County in defraying the expenses of the public Buildings, and that the Sheriff make return of the monies so collected against the next Court, or pay the same into the hands of Richard Harrison Esquire, and return the said Mr. Richard Harrison's Receipt to the Treasurer of this County. And it is further ordered that the sheriff return to the Treasurer make out a proper statement of the sheriff's collection & the manner the said monies have been appropriated.

Ordered that a Road be laid out and opened from this Court House to where it will intersect a Road laid out by Greenville Court House towards the ancient boundery line. And that James Jordan Esquire & William Benson is appointed to Examine and mark out the same and that they appoint an overseer.

Michael Hogan against Peter Edwards. Debt. By consent of the parties and assent of the Court this suit Defered untill next Court, a Reference being made last Court.

Ordered that a Bench warrant issue against Andrew Thomson at the Instance of the State Returnable before Richard Harrison, Esquire, for his Further Determination.

A Deed of Conveyance from John Nichols and Jeremiah Neasbitt to Henry Morgan, acknowledged and proved by James Jordan, Esquire. Ordered to be recorded.

William Ford came into open Court and proved 5 days attendance at 2/6 pr day in the suit Lusk against Francis N. Wayland amounting to s 12 d 6 sterling.

Present   James Jordan, Esquire.

James Keen by the State against Frederick & Jacob Isham (sic, for Eison, Ison). Larceny. Came the Plaintiff by William Shaw, County Atto., & the defendant by Charles Goodwin Gentl., his atto., and whereupon came a Jury (to wit) Jesse Connel, Denny Anderson, Henry Airs, John Ford Junr., James Bennett, Samuel Ford, Tobias Bright, Thomas Miles, James Alexander, Ebenezer Morse, John Conner, John Gowen...the Defendant is not Guilty, as by the said Plaintiff Charged...the said defendant be acquited & pay all costs accruing from said Prosecution.

Westwood Waters against John Couch. Trover.
William Couch against Westwood Waters. Ordered that these two cases be refered to the Arbitrament to Robert Hannah and William Montgomery with power of umpirage to be returned to next Court and be considered as a rule thereof.

George Pettus against David McNeely. Case. Same against same Slander. David McNeely against George Pettus. Ditinue.
All these suits of the above parties being refered at June Court to arbitration, the arbitrators award that each party pay their own Costs.

Minutes were read and signed by Baylis Earle, Thomas Farrow, Richard Harrison, Samuel Lancaster, Esquires. Court adjourned untill tomorrow 9 o'clock.

Thursday the 20th day of December 1787. The Court met according to adjournment. Present   Baylis Earle, Samuel Lancaster & Thomas Farrow, Esquires.

William Lancaster as Deputy Clerk of this County was approved by the Court and took the oaths of Office according to Law.

William Shaw against Stephen Williford. On attachment. In this case judgment for costs not being heretofore done the Court adjudged that William Wood who claimed Property attached have his fees.

A Lease and Release from Mason Cox Smithson to Joel Taylor proved by David Goodlett and Isham Foster. Ordered to be recorded.

William Crow against John Cowen. Attachment. By consent of the Parties and assent of the Court this suit Dismissed at Plaintiff's Costs.

George Berry against George Hunt. Attachment. On Motion of Mr. Daniel Brown for Defendant the above suit is Dismissed at Plaintiff's Costs.

William Wilder against Stephen Williford. Case. Discontinued.

David McDowell against Hugh Freeman Admr. of Rodden. Trover. Continued by Consent.

Henry Hays against Edward Mitchison. Trover. Refered as Heretofore.

James Barron against John Moore. Debt. By consent of the Parties and assent of the Court this suit is continued untill next Court.

Paul Smith against Henry Koon. Case. Dismissed at Defendant's Costs.

Charles McKnight admr. of Tramell against Thomas Morrow. Case. The trial of this suit is refered untill next Court by consent of the parties and assent of the Court.

James Milican against Jno Thos & Nathanl. Carrells. Case. By consent of the parties and assent of the Court, the trial of this suit is defered untill next Court.

Leonard Smith against George and John Robuck, Exors. of Benj. robuck, Decd. Case. By consent of the Parties and assent of the Court the trial of this suit is Defered untill next Court.

William Blackstock against William Smith. Trover. Issued. Ordered that a commission issue to Samuel Lancaster and Thomas Farrow Esquires to examine Ralph Smith in the above case on Saturday two weeks, which will be on the 5th day of January next at the house of Ann Smith's and that the plaintiff have notice thereof.

A Lease & Release from Jesse Connell and Ann his wife to Giles Smith Acknowledged in open Court the wife being privately examined, freely Relinquished her dower. Ordered to be recorded.

Major Parsons against Robert McDowell. Debt. By consent of the Parties and assent of the Court the trial of this action Defered untill next Court.

Charles Moore against Benjamine Silman. Case. Ordered that the defendant have a copy of the agreement between the parties.

Present Richard Harrison and James Jordan, Esquires.

Frederick Isam against James Clark. Trover. Refered as heretofore to the Arbitrament of John McElheny and Travill Bull with power of umpirage & their award to be returned to next court and be considered as a rule thereof.

John Barkley against William Moore. Trover. Ordered that this case come to trial the fourth day of next Court without fail.

John Roebuck against Peter Brooks. Attachment. Ordered that Didymus potestatum issue to James Montgomery and   Esquires, to examine Elizabeth Berry as an evidence in the above case, ten days notice to be given to the Defendant of time and place for said examination the above witness to be examined whether she be interested in the event of the suit or not, the same to be returned to next Court.

Issued. Ordered that the following Persons be Recommended Justices for this County, to wit, Andrew Barry, William Smith, William Benson and William McDowel, and the Clerk make out a recommendation to the next Assembly of the said Persons.

Ordered that James Smith have the sum of s 28 of the Public money for running the line between this County and Union and that the draught thereof returned by said Smith be considered the Boundery between said Counties, and the said draught to be filed in the Clerk's Office.

The minutes were read and signed by Baylis Earle, Rich. Harrison, Samuel Lancaster, Esquires. Court then adjourned untill Court in Course.

At a County Court holden for the County of Spartanburgh on the third Monday in March A. D. 1788. Present James Jordan, Samuel Lancaster and Thomas Farrow, Esquires.

The Court proceeded to draw the Grand Jurors, towit Thomas Golightly, Thomas McKnight, John Ross, William MacMullen, Charles MacKnight, Andrew Milican, James Hooper, Thomas Underwood, William clayton, James Faris, John Leech, Charles MacClain, Edward W. Clemons, George Bennett, Joseph Thomson, John McKnight, John Bragg, James Alexander, Tobias Bright & Robert Goodgion.

A Deed of Conveyance from John MacCullock to Samson Bobo, proved in open Court by Burrell Bobo and James Casey, ordered to be recorded.

David Goodlet & William McDowell being appointed Justices for this County, by our Last assembly. Ordered that they be quallified agreeable to Law, which was accordingly done in open Court. William Benson being also appointed at the same time, Declines serving as a Justice for the County aforesaid.

William Tate Esquires admitted as an atto. in the Courts of Law & Equity in this State, produced his credentials as such. Ordered that he be enrolled in this Court accordingly.

Grand Jurors drawn for this Court. Shands Golightly, Thomas MacKnight, William McMullan, Charles MacKnight, Andrew Milican, James Hooper, Thomas Underwood, William Clayton, James Faris, John Leech, Charles MacClain, Edward W. Clemons, Joseph Thomson, Tobias Bright, Robert Jameson.

Ordered that Edward William Clemons be exempted from serving as a Grand Juror for this Court.

Ordered that the affidavit of William MacDowell sworn this day in open Court also a receipt signed by Ricahrd Hodges and witnessed by said William MacDowell and annexed to the said affidavit and also the copy of a certain Bond annexed, also to the said affidavit Be admitted to the Records of this Cout on the oath of the said William McDowell Esquire, one of the Justices of the Court.

Ordered that John Hammett be Dismissed from serving as a Pettit Juror for this Court.

Pettit Jurors drawn to serve for this court, to wit, Brittain Williford, Thomas Warren, Wells Griffith, William Crow, John Foster, George Lowden, John Butler, William Wilder, Henry Walker, David Neel, Shadrack Waldrope & Tod Smith.

A Deed of Conveyance from John Young to Robert Foster, proved by James Jordan Esquire & John Hammett. Ordered to be Recorded.

Ordered that Moses Timmons have License to keep a Tavern and retail Spiritous liquors he giving John Timmons and Joseph Thomson Justices for his Lawful Performance.

A Deed of Conveyance from Arthur Crocker Senr. to William Crocker acknowledged by the said Arthur Crocker. Ordered to be recorded.

A Lease & Release from John MacCarter to James Amos proved by John Leech & Joseph Thomson. Ordered to be recorded.

A Lease & Release from David Prewit to William Brown proved by Aaron Floyd & Benjamine Roads. Ordered to be recorded.

A Lease & Release from David Prewit to Benjamin Roads proved by Enoch and Aaron Floyd. Ordered to be recorded.

A Lease & Release from John Crow to Isaac Crow acknowledged by the said John Crow. Ordered to be recorded.

A Lease and Release from William Bratcher to Nathaniel Wooten, proved by James Smith & Samuel Ward. Ordered to be recorded.

A Deed of Conveyance from William MacDowell and wife to David Lewis acknowledged in open Court. Ordered to be recorded.

Ordered that a Deed of Conveyance from George Alexander to William MacMillin, be recorded, it being heretofore proved in North Carolina.

A Lease and Release from Charles Hunt to John Couch proved in open Court by the Evidence of Henry Meridith, laid over for further proof.

The last will and testament of David Lewis deceased, proved by David Lewis Junr. & Joel Lewis. Ordered to be recorded.

Ordered that Ebenezer Morse have leave to keep a Public House of Entertainment, and to retail Spiritouse liquors, he giving William Wofford Junr. and Alexander Alexander his sureties for his lawful performance.

The minutes were read and signed by James Jordan, Samuel Lancaster, & David Goodlet. Esquires. Court then adjourned untill tomorrow Nine O'Clock.

Tuesday the 18th of March 1788. The Court met according to Adjournment. Present James Jordan, Samuel Lancaster & Thomas Farrow, Esquires.

Ordered that the Clerk Provide a seal for this County and be paid for the same out of the County fund.

A Lease & Release from Christopher Casey to Moses Casey, heretofore proved by one evidence, now proved by the oath of Aaron Casey.

Grand Jurors drawn to serve this Court, to wit, were yesterday impanneled and sworn, Thomas Underwood, Thomas MacKnight, William McMillan, Andrew Milican, James Hooper, William Clayton, John Leech, Charles McClain, John McKnight, Joseph Thomson, John Bragg, Shands Golightly & Tobias Bright.

A Lease and Release from John Livingston and wife to Richard Chesney, proved by the Evidence of Andrew Brown & John Chesney. Ordered to be Recorded.

A Conveyance from Cabel Stone & wife to Mark Powell, proved by the oath of Moses & James Casey. Ordered to be recorded.

Conveyance from John Blalock to William Thomson, proved by the oaths of Joseph Buffington & Richard Thomson. Ordered to be recorded.

Present Obadiah Trimmier, Esquire.

Ordered that the following rates be observed for the Future, to wit, Jamacia Rum per Gallon s 9 d 4, per quart s 2 d 6 per point, s 1 d 3, half pint d 7, Gill d 4.

A Lease and Release from Robert Prince and wife to Wade Hampton acknowledged in open Court by Robert Prince. Ordered to be recorded.

Renunciation of Dower from Mary Prince to Wade Hampton, Esquire, proved in open Court by Thomas Benson. Ordered to be recorded.

William Shaw against Edward Beeks Musgrove. On Petition by Debt. Came the Plaintiff Gentleman Attorney (sic) and the Defendant by James Yancey Gentleman his attorney...the Plaintiff recover against the Deft. ₺ 2 s 3 d 6 with interest and costs of suit....

John Head against Jechonias Langston. Petition and Summons in Debt. On the parties being heard, it is considered by the Court that the Plaintiff recover against the Defendant ₺ 5 with interest besides his Costs...

Thomas Tod against Ebenezer Morse. Petition by Debt. By consent of the Parties and assent of the Court, the trial of this suit is defered untill next Court.

Mary Williams Extx. of James Williams decd. against Nicholas Holley and Benjamin Wofford. Petition and Summons in Debt. Came the Plaintiff by James Yancey Gentleman her attorney and the Defendants by Daniel Brown Gentleman their attorney and upon the parties being heard...the plaintiff recover against the Deft. ₺ 4 s 8 d 9½ with interest according to rate besides the costs....

Bartin Coats against William MacDowell. On a Petition by Account. By consent of the Parties and assent of the Court this suit is continued untill next Court.

Drewry Scruggs against John Wade. On a Petition By Debt. By consent of the Parties and assent of the Court this suit is dismissed at the Defendants costs.

Turner Harris against Drewry Scruggs. On a Petition By Debt. By consent of the Parties and assent of the Court, this suit is dismissed at John Wade's Costs.

Daniel Shaw against John Gowen. Trover. Discontinued at the Defendants Cost, atto. fee excepted.

Daniel Shaw against John Gowen. Trover. Settled at the Defendants Costs.

Alexander Alexander by State against Richard Collins. Assault & Battery. Came the Plaintiff by William Shaw County Attorney, and the Defendant comes and Defends his suit, and whereupon came a Jury (to wit) Brittain Williford, Thomas Warren, Wells Griffith, William Crow, John Foster, George Lowden, John Butler, William Wilder, Henry Walker, David Neel, Shadrack Waldrop & Josel Smith ...the Defendant is Guilty...the defendant pay s 5 besides all costs....

John Roebuck against Peter Brooks. On Attachment. By consent of the Parties and assent of the Court, this suit is continued untill next Court.

Ordered that William Wofford Junr. have license to keep a public House of Entertainment, and retail Spiritous Liquors he giving bond with Jeremiah Thomson and James Fannen for his Lawful performance thereof.

A Deed of Conveyance from William Hamwell Right to James Fannen proved by the oath of Littleton Mapp, laid over for further proof.

A Deed of Feopment from Charles Moore to Thomas Bullian acknowledged in open Court. Ordered to be recorded.

William Burton by State against John McGuire. Petty larceny. Came the Plaintiff by William Shaw County attorney and the Defendant comes and defends his suit, and whereupon came a Jury (to wit) Thomas Underwood, Thomas MacKnight, William MacMillan, Andrew Milican, James Hooper, William Clayton, John Leech, Charles McClain, John McKnight, Joseph Thomson, John Bragg, Shands Golightly, & Tobias Bright...the Defendant is not Guilty...

Ordered that Larkin Lancaster serve as Constable for this County, he being qualified according to Law for that purpose.

Ordered that William Lancaster Deputy Clerk of said Court have the privilege of being three weeks absent from the Clerk's Office in the Month of April.

The minutes were read and signed by James Jordan, Thomas Farrow, & Samuel Lancaster, Esquires. Court then adjourned untill tomorrow 9 o'clock.

Wednesday the 19th of March 1788. The Court met according to adjournment. Present James Jordan, Samuel Lancaster, Thomas

Farrow, Obadiah Trimmier & David Goodlet, Esquires.

James Fannen against Silas MacBee. On Appeal.
Ordered that this action be over untill next Court, and a Dedimus Potistatum issue unto Georgia, Wilks County to three Justices, to examine George Underwood in this case.

On a Memorial exhibited by William Graham against Joseph Buffington and John Thomas Junr., also against the administratrix of Thomson. Ordered that this lie over untill the arrival of the Justices who made the said order, the memorial respecting an order to stay execution last Court. The present Justices does not see cause to make any Decision in said case.

A Lease & Release from William Ford to Daniel Monro, acknowledged in open Court. Ordered to be recorded.

Major Passons against Robert McDowall. On Petition in Debt.
On the Defendants pleading two pleas Non-assumsit and Infamy, the Court ruled to plead only one plea in this case. Whereupon came the Plaintiff by James Yancey Gentleman his attorney and the Defendant by Daniel Brown, Gentleman, his attorney...whereupon came a Jury (same as Alexander bs. Collins)..."agreed by us that the Defendant pay the sum of 1800 Dollars agreeable to Depreciation with Lawful Interest and costs of suit."....

On motion of Joseph Venible as a witness in behalf of Major Passons against Robert MacDowell on oath he is allowed s 12 d 6 for 5 days attendance.

A Lease and Release from Daniel Monroe to James Abanatha, acknowledged in open Court by said Monro. Ordered to be recorded.

Ordered that Wells Griffith serve as Coroner for this County.

A Lease and Release from Vardry McBee & wife to David Allen, acknowledged in open Court, and ordered to be recorded.

Titles from Samuel Farrow Esquire, Sheriff of this County, to James Jordan, Esquire, proved in open Court, by William Shaw & John Thomas Junr. Ordered to be recorded.

Thomas Blasingame Junr. against Holland Sumner. On Attachment.
By consent of the Parties and assent of the Court this mater of controversy is Refered to Colonel Fair, John Montgomery, Nehemiah Howard, Thomas Grier & Stephen Layton, Gentlemen, whose award returnable to next Court shall be the judgment of the Court.

John Farrow against Exors. of Smith. On a Petition.
Came the Plaintiff by James Yancey Gentleman, his attorney, and the Defendant by William Shaw Gentleman his attorney, the parties join issue for trial...refered untill next Court....

On motion of Josiah Culbertson as a witness in behalf of the Plaintiff on oath he is allowed Ł 3 for 24 days attendance in the above suit.

John Thomas Senr. against Major Passons. On Slander. By consent of the Parties and assent of the Court, this suit dismissed at the Defendants Cost, the Plaintiff's attorney fee excepted & the Clerk's fee forgiven.

65

Charles Miles against Vardry McBee. Trover. By consent of the
Parties and assent of the Court, a commission is to be issued to
Examine Evidences Residing without the County in behalf of the
Plaintiff, on his giving the plaintiff 10 days notice of time
and place of examination; the evidences to be examined by any
one Justice in the County where they shall reside.

On application for William Poole for Tavern License, Ordered that
he be furnished with the same by his Giving surities for his
faithful performance according to Law.

Minutes were read and signed by James Jordan, Obadiah Trimmier,
& Samuel Lancaster, Esquires. Court then adjourned untill tomorrow 9 o'clock.

Thursday the 20th of March 1788. Court met according to adjournment. Present Samuel Lancaster, Thomas Farrow, and Obadiah
Trimmier, Esquires, etc.

Ordered that George Ryner have license to keep a Tavern and retail Spiritous liquors he giving Obadiah Trimmier Esquire surety
for his Lawful Performance.

John Pennington against Joseph Hall & Henry Hamilton against
Joseph Hall. Special Actions on the Case.
Joseph Hall against John Pennington & William Reynolds. Malicious
Prosecution. By consent of the Parties and assent of the Court
all matters of controversy is refered to Benjamine Kilgore,
Thomas Farrow and James Jordan Esquires Gentlemen Arbitrators,
whose award returnable to our next Court shall be the Judgment
of the Court.

The Inventory & Sale of Henry White Esquire Deceased returned
into the Court.

A Power of Attorney from Ann White to Major James Lusk & Captain
James Smith, Proved in open Court by the evidence of Spencer
Smith. Ordered to be recorded.

A Deed of Conveyance from Handcock & William Smith to William
Suddoth proved by James & Jane Smith. Ordered to be recorded.
the wives of the above persons which are Jane Smith, wife of
Handcock & Catharine wife of William, being privately examined
by a Justice of the Court, who report that they severally renounce their dower in the above Tracts of Land.

In the two sets of titles heretofore recorded from Peter Smith
to William Smith & William Smith to James Smith (The privay examination of Agnes Smith, wife of said Peter & Catharine wife
of said William Smith) by the Court, who report they freely renounced their dower.

A Deed of Conveyance from Richard Prince to the Executors of
John White proved in open Court by the Evidence of William Wood
& Henry Walden. Ordered to be recorded.

Present   James Jordan, Esquire.

State by John Farrow against Thomas Waldrope, Jesse Hilline,
James Couch & Elizabeth Waldrope. Assaulting the Constable in
his office. Came the Plaintiff by William Shaw, Gentleman, County
Attorney, & the defendants by Thos. P. Carnes, Gentlemen, their
attorney, & came a Jury (same as before)...the Defendants are

Guilty of the assault...the Defendants pay the sum of s5 and costs of suit....

Ordered that Henry Meredith & Edward Lynch view the conveniences & inconveniences that may attend on Turning the road leading from Heads Ford across the Enoree River the upper side of Heads Plantation to the Wier's Creek Road & Return their report to our next Court.

Ordered, that Andrew Paul have Tavern License to keep a Public House of entertainment, he giving Obadiah Trimmier, Esquire, and William Wood, his Justices for his faithful Performance according to Law.

Vardry MacBee against George Taylor & George Taylor against Vardry MacBee. Slander.
By consent of the Parties and assent of the Court these two cases are refered to Zachariah Bullock, William Lipscomb, Obadiah Trimmier Esquire & Adam Potter, Gentlemen or their Umpire whose award returned to next Court shall be the judgment of the Court.

Joseph Burton assignee of Lidson against Maximial Conner & Samuel Porter. On a Petition By Debt. Came the plaintiff by William Shaw Gentleman his attorney & the Defendants by Daniel Brown Gentleman their attorney and upon the parties being heard it is considered by the Court that the Plaintiff recover against the Defendant Samuel Porter Ł 5 with interest from the 5th March 1787, besides his Costs....

Daniel Brown against William Graham. Attachment By Note.
The Plaintiff acknowledged full satisfaction for Debt & Costs the note being for Ł 3 s 5 d 3.

Lease & Release from Thomas Haze to John Foster, acknowledged in Open Court. Ordered to be recorded.

William Lipscomb against JosephBuffington. In Debt. Came the Plaintiff by Daniel Brown Gentleman his attorney and the Defendant says he cannot Gainsay the Plaintiff's action, and that he owes Ł 14 sterling, the Debt contracted in 1787...interest from 20 Nov 1787 until paid...stay execution untill 20 Oct 1788.

Court then adjourned for 15 minutes. Court met according to adjournment.

David Henry against Thomas Brown. On appeal from Esqr. Trimmier. Ordered that the judgment stand as a judgment of the Court.

Minutes were read and signed by James Jordan, Samuel Lancaster, Thomas Farrow & Zadock Ford, Esquires. Court then adjourned untill tomorrow 9 o'clock.

Friday the 21st day of March 1788. The Court met according to adjournment. Present Samuel Lancaster, Thomas Farrow & Zadock Ford, Esquires.

Ordered that Vardry McBee have license to keep a Public House of Entertainment he giving Thomas Warren & James Morriss his sureties for his Lawful Performance thereof.

Ordered that Thomas Williamson have License to keep a Public House of Entertainment he conforming to the Rules Prescribed by Law & giving Charles Moore as surety for the same.

Benjamin Silman against Charles Moore. Case. Came the Plaintiff by William Shaw Gentleman his attorney and the Defendant by Daniel Brown, James Yancey & T. P. Carnes, Gentlemen his attornies, whereupon came a Jury (same as before)...we find for the Plaintiff Ł 13 s 1 d 8....

James Amos maketh oath in open Court that he has not any of the Goods or property of Francis Amos in his Possession, neither is he indebted unto him anything at all by way of contract. Ordered to be recorded.

William Shaw against Stephen Williford. On attachment. On motion of the Plaintiff it is ordered that William Wood pay the fees and expences he was put unto on account of his claim on the property attached.

On motion of Thomas Scurry as a witness in the suit John Couch against Charles Waters, on oath he is allowed s 12 d 6 for 5 days attendance.

Ordered that Thomas Scurry be allowed s 12 d 6 for 5 days attendance as a witness in the suit Beverly Cox against Landon Farrow.

On motion of John Couch as a witness in the suit Beverly Cox against Landon Farrow on oath he is allowed s 21 d 6 for 5 days attendance.

Ordered that Thomas Silman be allowed Ł 2 s 10 for 20 days attendance as a witness in the suit Benjamin Silman against Charles Moore.

On motion of John Brown as a witness in the suit Benjamin Silman against Charles Moore, on oath he is allowed Ł 2 s 10 for 20 days attendance.

Ordered that William Ford be allowed Ł 2 s 10 for 20 days attendance on oath, in the suit Benjamin Silman against Charles Moore.

John Callihan maketh oath that he hat attended 17 days as a witness in the suit Benjamin Silman against Charles Moore, amounting for s 42 d 6. Ordered by the Court that he be allowed the same.

John Camp against John Chism. On a Summons. Came the Plaintiff by James Yancey Gentleman his attorney and the Defendant by Daniel Brown Gentleman his attorney and upon the Parties being heard it is considered by the Court that the Plaintiff recover Ł 2 s 3 d 3¼ besides his costs...

John Camp, Sarah Camp & Reubin Hull is allowed s 12 d 6 each for 5 days attendance in the suit John Camp against John Chism.

William Wilder came into Court and made oath that he hath attended as an evidence in the suit Thomas Tod against Ebenezer Morse 5 days amounting to s 12 d 6. Ordered that he be allowed the same.

Joseph Buffington comes into Court and make the oath that in the case of an attachment Elizabeth Thomson against William Graham he has Ł 2 s 2 d 2 of the property of the said Defendant whereof the said attachment hat been levied and that he is ready to pay it whenver judgment shall be obtained by the Plaintiff for the same.

Minutes were read and signed by Zadock Ford, Thomas Farrow, & Samuel Lancaster, Esquires. Court then adjourned until Court in Course.

At A County Court began and held for the County of Spartanburgh on the third Monday in June 1788. Present Thomas Farrow, William Smith, David Goodlet, and William MacDowell, Esquires.

The Court then Proceeded to Draw the Grand Jurors for next Sept. Court, to wit, George Bruton, Brittain Williford, David MacDowell, John Johnston, Alburtus Bright, John Ford Senior, Samson Bobo, William Poole, Moses Casey, Thomas Jackson, Joseph Woodruff, Thomas Haney, Isaac Young, William Thomson, Isham Foster, Major James Lusk, Thomas Tod, Jeremiah Lucas, Joseph Thomson, John Mapp, Samuel Jackson Junior, Enoch Floyd, William Ford son of John, William Lipscomb & James Alexander of Packolet.

Pettit Jurors drawn to serve next Court, to wit, Zachariah Robertson, Thomas Holcomb, John Cavin, Samuel Fowler, Joel Callihan, Stephen Wilson, Robert MacDowell, Thomas Young, Flemming Smith, John MacClure, William Prince, Henry Turner, James Norriss, William Foster, David Prewit, James Faris, William Jameson, Henry Airs, Charles Bruce, Bazel Lee, James Hughs, Martin Armstrong & John Hammet.

Pettit Jurors drawn to serve this Court, to wit, Ebenezer Morse, Edward Stone Senr., Matthew Couch, Henry Meredith, Thomas Williams, John Williams, Landon Farrow, William Poole, Burrell Bobo, William Mercy, William Simpson, David Andrewson & James Bruton.

George Walker, Esquire, produced his admission as an attorney at Law and Equity in this State which was read and ordered by the Court that he be Enrolled amongst the Gentlemen Attornies of this Court accordingly.

A Conveyance from Timothy Toney to Daniel Grant for two tracts of Land, proved before William Smith, Esquire. Ordered to be recorded

A Lease & Release from Daniel Kelley & wife to Hezekiah Childs; heretofore proved by one evidence now proved by Col. Henry M. Wood.

A Deed of Conveyance from Daniel Kelley & wife to John Childs; heretofore proved by one Evidence now proved by Col. Henry M. Wood.

A Probate proving a certain cornertree of Land now the Property of Major James Lusk proved before Samuel Lancaster, Esquire. Ordered to be recorded.

A Deed of conveyance from Josiah Tanner to William Thomson proved before Obadiah Trimmier, Esquire, by the Evidence of William Turner Thomason. Ordered to be recorded.

The Defaults in appearing as Pettit Jurors to serve this Court, to wit, John Redmund, Tobias Bright, John Shands, John Rainwater, James Hendrix, John Vice, William Lindsey & William Wofford Junr.

Present James Jordan, Samuel Lancaster, Baylis Earle, and Obadiah Trimmier, Esquires.

Thomas Blasingame Junior against Holland Sumner. On attachment. This suit being heretofore refered to the Arbitrament of Col. Fair, John Montgomery, Nehemiah Howard, Thomas Green & Stephen Layton, which was not arbitrated in due time, by consent of the parties, it is ordered that the same persons arbitrate the same ....

Ordered that Col. John Thomas Junr., Clerk of Spartanburgh, make a full settlement of the Estate of John Carley deceased whereof George Bruton was administrator.

Thomas Hamilton & wife against Benjamine Wofford. In a case of Trover. Ordered, that a Dedimus issue, Directed to William Morse and Gentlemen Justices of Wilks County in Georgia, to examine Benjamine Arnold, as a witness for and in behalf of the Plaintiff giving Ten days notice to the Defendant of time and place of examination.

A Lease and Release from Reubin Lawson to Joseph Mitchel, proved in open Court by the evidence of William Poole & Zachariah Sparks. Ordered to be recorded.

A Lease and Release from Reubin Lawson to Zachariah Sparks, proved in open Court by the evidence of William Poole and Joseph Mitchel. Ordered to be recorded.

Samuel Nesbitt Admr. of John Shannon Decd. against Thomas Still. On attachment.

John Earle Esquire of North Carolina being summoned as Guarnishee came into Court & Made oath that he hath Property of the Defendant in his Possession sufficient to satisfy said attachment.

A certificate from under hand of Thos. C. Russel being Produced & read in open Court which specifies that he hath received full satisfaction for all suits that he hath commenced against Joseph Buffington the said Buffington to pay all Costs that have occurred in the Prosecution of the said suits....

Ordered that Joseph Venible and John Wood serve as Constables for this County they being qualifyed in open Court according to Law.

John Patton's Last Will and Testament being Proved in open Court by the evidence of John Cavin & Alexander Evins. Ordered to be recorded.

Samuel Stewart against Avery Connell. On attachment. Thomas Farrar Esq. being summoned as Guarnishee in this case came into Court & made oath that he hath in his posession property of the Defendant sufficient to satisfy said attachment.

Minutes were read and signed by James Jordan, David Goodlett, & Wm. MacDowell. Esquires. Court then adjourned untill Tomorrow Nine O'Clock.

June the 17th 1788. Tuesday Nine O'clock the Court met according to adjournment. Present Samuel Lancaster, Obadiah Trimmier & Thomas Farrow, Esquires.

John Farrow against the Executors of Smith. By Petition & Summons. The Court agreeable to the rule of last Court proceeded to give

Judgment in this case, & after due consideration they do accordingly give Judgment in favor of the Defendant.

Present Baylis Earle, Esquire.

William Shaw heretofore County Attorney hath now resigned; the Court assented to the same, and ordered to be recorded.

Present Richard Harrison, James Jordan & David Goodlet Esquires.

Charles McKnight against William Prince. Ordered that a Dedimus Potestatum issue to two Justices in North Carolina, Rutherford County, to Examine Jeremiah Fields as a witness for & in behalf of the Plaintiff giving the Defendant ten days notice of the time & Place of Examination.

Frederick Ison against William Davis & James Clerke. Trover. Ordered that a Dedimus issue to two Justices of Rutherford County in North Carolina to examine Matthew Harper as a witness for and in behalf of the Plaintiff Giving Ten days notice to the Defendants of time & Place of Examination.

Bennett Langston of Union County came into Court and proved his attendance as a witness in the suit William Bennett administrator of John Langston against Landon Farrow amounting to ₤ 3 s 3 d 6 (according to Law). Ordered that he be allowed the same.

A Deed of Conveyance from Zachariah Bullock to Josiah Tanner acknowledged in open Court by said Bullock. Ordered to be recorded.

John Earle Esquire being summoned as Guarnishee and hath made oath that he hath property in his Possession sufficient to satisfy an attachment leveyed on said Property at the suit of Samuel Neasbitt administrator of John Shannon against Thomas Still, ordered that he keep the Property in his possession untill next Court.

Ordered that the Clerk of this Court receive all Papers from John Earle, Esquire, relative to the settlement of the Estate of John Wood, deceased; and report a statement of the same to next Court.

Thomas Tod against Ebenezer Morse. On Petition. Ordered that John McCravies affidavit be taken in behalf of the Plaintiff & that Testimony to be admitted on Trial.

John Dewberry came into Court and proved his attendance in the suit Michael Hogan against Potter Edwards for 3 days, amounting to s 7 d 6. Ordered that he be allowed the same.

Thomas Farrow Esquire proved 17 days attendance in the suit, the administrators of Langston against Landon Farrow at 2 shillings d 6 per day, amounting to ₤ 2 s 2 d 6.

Ordered that Samuel Farrow Sheriff repay to Mrs. Elizabeth Thomson the money which arose from the sale of her Property, sold by an execution obtained by William Graham against the said Elizabeth Thomson, Widow.

Vardry McBee against John Wooton. Attachment. By consent of the Parties, and assent of the Court this suit is dismissed at the Defendants Costs.

Silas McBee against James Faning. On an appeal. Ordered that this suit Discontinue at the Plaintiff's costs.

William Poole against William Henderson. Case. The Defendant came into court and confessed judgment for ₺ 11 s 12 d 9 sterling and costs of suit.   Wm. Henderson.

A Lease & Release from John Roson to William Poole, proved in open Court by the evidence of James Jordan, Esquire, & Nevil Wayland. Ordered to be recorded.

Peter Brooks came into Court and proved his attendance as a witness in the suit Leonard Smith against the Executors of Roebuck, amounting to ₺ 4 d 4 also proved his attendance in the suit Alexander Alexander against Richard Collins for ₺ 1. Ordered that he be allowed the same.

Israel Morriss against Rowland Cornelius. Case. This case being heretofore refered to the Arbitrament of James Jordan Esquire and Thomas Farrar they making no Decision, Ordered that James Jordan Esquire & Col. Henry Wood arbitrate the same & Return their award to our next Court, to be considered as a rule thereof.

Ordered that the Estrays be sold at six months credit, only the fees to be paid at the time of sale.

Ordered that the sheriff collect the seventh part of the general Tax & deliver the same to Richard Harrison Esquire by the first day of January next, in order to defrat the Expense of the County Buildings.

Ordered that William Bratcher be appointed & ordered in place of John Beardan; the road leading from Blackstocks ford on Tyger River to the Cross Roads opposite the Widow Smith's.

Ordered, that Josiah Culbertson be appointed overseer of the Road leading from the shoal of Fairforest to Wilies Fork.

Ordered that Thomas Williams be the Overseer of the Road leading from Wilies fork to where it intersects the Road leading to Blackstocks ford on Tyger River, in the Room and stead of William Smith, Esquire

John Camp against Thomas David. Trespass. This case refered to the arbitrament of John MacKinney & John McElheny with power of Umpirage, Their award tobe returned to our next court to be considered as a rule thereof.

William Shaw Esquire having resigned as County Attorney the Court Proceeded to appoint a Person to succeed him in the said office When Thomas Peter Carnes was unanimously appointed.

Minutes were read and signed by Richard Harrison, Samuel Lancaster, William McDowell, Esquires. Court then adjourned until Court in Course.

At a County Court began and held for the County of Spartanburgh on the third Monday in September 1788. Present Baylis Earle, William Smith, David Goodlet & Richard Harrison, Esquires.

The Court then Proceeded to draw the Pettit Jury for next Court George Haden Jr., Walter Burrell, Bayley Taylor, Jordan Gibson, James Casey, JosephBlackwood, Thomas Cook, Robert Sterling,

Rowland Cornelius Junr., William Duncan, Reubin Dollar, Benjamine Beson, John Collins, William Brashers, William Hendrix, William Brandon, Isaac Crow, Robert Morrow, John Leech, Joshua Prestrage, Alexander Floyd, Henry Pettit, Robert Neasbitt, Benjamine Stone, Joseph Neasbitt, Nevil Wayland, James Fannen, Malichi Jones, Getis Smith, Jeremiah Lucas, Edwd. W. Clemons, Benjamin Carley, Wm. McWilliams, Brederick Brigs, Thomas Brown & Thomas House.

The following persons being summoned as Grand Jurors for the County Court aforesaid hath now appeared, to wit, Thomas Tod, foreman, Brittain Williford, David McDowell, John Johnston, Samson Bobo, William Poole, Isaac Young, Isham Foster, Joseph Thomson, William Ford, William Lipscomb, James Alexander, John Mapp, Major James Lusk, & Jeremiah Lucus.

Ordered, that John Childs Oversee & keep in Good repair the road leading from Lawsons Fork to South Packolate in the room & stead of Thomas Bennett.

The appearance Docket called over the first time.
Present Thomas Farrow, Esq.

Ordered that Thomas Farrar & John Davis qualify that they saw the Delivery of a certain tract of Land conveyed by Indenture from Samuel Farrow sheriff of this County, to James Jordan, esquire, which was accordingly done in open Court.
This tract of land was sold by Farrow as Sheriff & Bought by Mr. Jordan.

Ordered that Ann Dewberry have Letters of Administration upon the Estate of Giles Dewberry deceased upon Giving Necessary Securities which she did & came into Court & took the oath of office accordingly.

The Last Will & Testament of John Cannon Deceased was Proved in open Court by Leonard Adcock and George Lamkin, Senior.

The Persons who being summoned as Pettit Jurors ahve Been called & have now appeared to wit, Zachariah Robertson, Thomas Holcomb, John Cavin, Stephen Wilson, Robert McDowell, Thomas Young, Flemming Smith, John McClure, Henry Turner, Jas. Norriss, William Foster, David Prewitt, Henry Aires, Charles Bruce, Bazel Lee, James Hughes, Martin Armstrong, John Hammett.

The Last Will and Testament of Jechonias Langston being proved in open Court by the Evidence of Benjamine Beson. The Executors in this case took the oath of administration in open Court.

Philemon Martin against Obadiah Oliphant. Case. Ordered that this suit be refered to the Arbitrament of William Thomson & William Lipscomb, Senior, with leave of choosing an Umpire, Their award to be returned to our next Court to be considered as a judgment thereof.

James Harrison Esquire assignee of Thomas Brandon against Joseph Wofford. In Debt. The Defendant came into Court and confessed judgment for the sum of ₺ 17 s 17 with Interest according to Specialty from 1 July 1788 until paid & Costs of suit, with stay of Execution untill March Court.

Ordered that Peter Bookes's attendance amounting to s 20 which he proved in case of Alexander Alexander against Richard Collins.

Minutes were read and signed by Baylis Earle, Wm. Smith, Thomas Farrow, Esquires. Court then adjourned untill tomorrow 9 o'-clock.

Tuesday the 16th of September 1788. The Court met according to adjournment. Present Baylis Earle, Richard Harrison, Samuel Lancaster, Thomas Farrow, David Goodlett & William Smith, Esquires.

Baylis Earle Esq. against Peter Lewis. Case. Ordered that a commission issue to Rutherford County the second day of Court to qualify Abel Lewis & George Lewis on the Behalf of the Defendant by mutual agreement, Both parties to meet there for that Purpose.

Kate, Plaintiff against James Henderson. On a Breach of the Peace. The Defendant being brought into Court to give Bail & refusing to do so, was ordered to Goal by the Court.

Thomas Flynn against Barton Coats. On Petition. Nonsuit.

Barton Coats against William McDowell. On Petition. Nonsuit.

State against Dennis Lindsey. On Fornication. The court fined the Defendant ℔ 5 sterling money, & ordered that he give Bond & security for ℔ 40 to keep the child off the County.

John Conner Assignee of Barton Coats against William McDowell. Petition by Note. Ordered that this suit be Dismissed at the Plaintiffs Costs.

Ordered that a Cpias issue against Rachel Childers to appear at next Court on account of Bastardy.

Leonard Smith against the Executors of Young. Petition. Ordered that this suit be Dismissed at the Defendants Costs.

Landon Farrow against Benjamine Wofford. Petition. Came the Plaintiff by Thomas P. Carnes, Gentl. his attorney, & the Defendant by Daniel Brown and Peter Carnes his attornies & upon the parties being heard, it is considered by the court that this suit be Dismissed at the Defendants Costs.

Thomas Farrar assignee of Morse agaisnt George West. Petition. By consent of the Parties and assent of the Court, this suit is dismissed at the Plaintiffs Costs.

Joel Callihan against Francis N. Wayland. Petition. By consent of the Parties & assent of the Court, the trial of this cause is Defered untill next Court.

Ordered that Thomas Grant be allowed the sum of s 23 d 4 for the County seal.

Ann Arnett Admr. of Edwd. Arnett against William Clayton & the Executors of Roebuck. Petition. On motion of Thomas P. Carnes Gentleman an attorney for the Plaintiff ordered that this suit be continued untill next Court.

Dennis Lindsey & Henry Earnest came into Court and acknowledged themselves indebted to the County of Spartanburgh in the sum of ℔ 40 sterling each to be void on condition that he the said Dennis save the County Harmless in keeping & maintaining a Bastard Child begotten on the Body of Rachel Childers for 10 years from this date.

Mary Williams Exors. James Williams against William Bracher.
Petition. Nonsuit.

Mary Williams Excx. of James Williams decd. against Henry Kerley.
Petition. Nonsuit.

Andrew Paul assignee of John Paul against William Poole. Petition by Note.
Came the Plaintiff by Thomas P. Carnes Gentl. his attorney & the Defendant by William Shaw Esquire his attorney and upon the Parties being heard it is considered by the Court that the Plaintiff recover against the Defendant the sum of Ł 8 sterling with Interest & Costs of suit....

Thomas Tod against Ebenezer Morse. On Petition. By consent of the parties and assent of the Court the trial of this Cause is Defered untill next court.

On Motion of George Walker Gentl. Attorney for the Administrator of William Dorgan, ordered that the Inquest summoned by the Sheriff to try the right of Property in a certain Negro Girl called Venus be recorded. "We the Jury being sworn to try the right of Property of a Certain Negro Girl called Venus, between Samuel Farrow Sheriff & Kemp Strawder, Administrator of the Estate of William Dorgan, Deceased, after mature consideration of the matter, do determine that she is the Property of the said administration. Richard Harrison, John Gowen, Obadiah Trimmier, Andrew Barry, Ephraim Rees, James Lusk, John Golightly, William Lipscomb, William Thomson, Thomas Tod, Brittain Williford, William Poole.

John Camp against John Chism. Petition. Ordered that this suit be discontinued.

John Gowen and John Ford of Greenville came into Court & entered themselves as securities for the appearance of James Henderson next Court, the said Henderson in the sum of Ł 50 and the securities in the sum of Ł 25 each.

Robert Cooper against Abram Nalley & Walter Burrell. On Petition. By consent of the Parties and assent of the Court the trial of this suit is laid over untill next Court.

John Thomas Junior against Joseph Buffington. On Petition. Joseph Buffington came into Court and confessed Judgment for the sum of Ł 4 s 16 d 5 with Interest and Costs of suit.

Isaac Cruce against Solomon Crocker. On Petition.
By consent of the Parties & assent of the Court this suit is Dismissed at the Defendants Costs.

Philip Tipping against Nicholas Holley. On Petition.
By consent of the Parties and assent of the Court this suit stands over untill next Court.

Joseph Buffington assignee of Thomas Flynn against Maximilian Conner. On Petition. Dismissed by Nonest Inventus.

James Harrison Esq. against William Wofford Sernior. On Renewal of Judgment. The Defendant came into Court and acknowledged that a Judgment heretofore obtained by the Plaintiff against him is still in force & is unpaid and also Joseph Wofford came into Court and entered himself Bail for the Payment of the Judgment Interest & Costs of the above....

State against James Poole On a Breach of the Peace.
James Poole, William Crocker and Leonard Adock came into Court and Entered themselves to owe to the State, to wit, James Poole Ł 40, and Leonard Adcock & William Crocker Ł 20 each for the said James Poole's keeping the Peace and Good behaviour to all People, particularly toward Comfort Holeman acknowledged before J. Thomas Junr.

Holland Sumner & Ann his wife against Buckner Smith. On a Special action on the case.
By consent of the Parties & assent of the Court this suit is refered to the Arbitrament of Thomas Williams, Stephen Wilson & Samson Bobo, Gentlemen Arbitrators, their award to be returned to our next Court & be considered as a rule thereof.

Present Baylis Earle, Esquire.

An amount & calculation of the Estate of John Wood deceased returned to Court & ordered to be recorded.

Israel Morriss against John Kimbell. Case. Ordered that this matter of controversy be refered to the Arbitrament of Rowland Johnston, Isham Foster & Thomas Wyatt, Gentlemen Arbitrators, their award to be returned to our next Court & be considered as a rule thereof.

John Chism appellant against Silas McBee appellee. On an appeal from the Judgment of Esq. Trimmier. Ordered that this suit be Dismissed at the appellants Costs.

State against Jordan Gibson. On an Indictment. The Grand Jury presenting him for Basterdy, It is therefore ordered that a Capias issue for his appearance in Court to answer to the said Indictment.

State against Michael Miller. On an Indictment. The Grand Jury finding a Bill against him for unlawfully marking Hogs; It is therefore ordered that a Capias issue to Bring him to trial on said Indictment.

William Graham against Jordan Gibson. On Attachment. James Terrill Special Bail for Replevying the Property attached. P. Carns, Atty for Defendant.

Present Thomas Farrow Esquire.

John McElheny against John Gowen. Case. By consent of the Parties and assent of the Court the trial of this cause is laid over untill March Court.

The Grand Jurors for this Term made the following Presentments. to wit, The overseer of the road from the Cherokee Ford on Broad River to this Court House for not keeping the same in repair. Ann King for having two Bastard children. Agnes Taylor for having one Bastard child. Polley Williams for having one Bastard child. Lucy McBee for having two Bastard children. Polley McBee one Bastard child, Polley Burk for having one Bastard child. Betty Laxton one Bastard child, Emmy Evans two Bastards, Betsey Morris one Bastard child. We recommend to the Court to appoint Proper Persons to value the necessary Bridge lately Built across South Packolate River, so that the Court may pay the workman for the same. We present Jane Walker for having one Bastard child. Elizabeth Graham one Bastard child, Lydia Hubburt for having two

Bastard children. Thomas Tod, foreman, William Poole, Brittain Williford, James Lusk, John Mapp, William Lipscomb, Samson Bobo, James Alexander, David McDowell, John Johnston, Isham Foster, Isaac Young, Joseph Thomson, Jeremiah Lucus.

Landon Farrow Appellant against Beverly Cox, appelle. On appeal from Esq. Lancaster. The Papers Being mis laid it is therefore ordered that they be produced by request of the attornies of the said appellant, who are ready to prosecute the appeal.

Ordered that the Property attached in the hands of John Earle, Esquire, be Exposed to sale & the money arising therefrom, remain in the Hands of the Sheriff untill next Court.

Ordered that Matthew Guttery & Thomas Wilson view the most convenient & Best way for a road Leading from this Court House by William Poole's now Iron Works to William Camps Plantation on Broad River & Make a return thereof to next Court.

William Graham against Jordan Gibson. On Attachment. Ordered that a Dedimus Potestatum issue to Rutherford County in North Carolina, to Robert Ervin or George Moore, Esquires, to examine Sundry witnesses on oath upon a certain action depending before this Court, between William Graham Plaintiff and Jordan Gibson Defendant on the part of said Plaintiff.

Ordered that a Dedimus Potestatum issue to Rutherford County in North Carolina in Behalf of Jordan Gibson in the above case.

Ordered that the Clerk deliver to William Graham Esquire a certain Note of hand given him by William Thomson and upon which the said Graham brought action in this Court against the administtatrix of the said Thomson.

On motion of James Blackstock as a witness in behalf of William Blackstock against William Smith Esq. on oath he is allowed Ł 3.

Richard Sanders came into Court and acknowledged a Deed of Conveyance from himself to Luke Browning. Ordered to be recorded.

Ordered that David McDowell, Joshua Young & Thomas Bennet value the Bridge across South Packolate River, Built by Baylis Earle Esquire & make a return thereof to next Court.

Ordered that Samuel Lancaster, Esquire be allowed the sum of s 9 d 4 for making out a List to the Sheriff of all the Taxable inhabitants which came to his knowledge as collector in this County, & be paid the same out of the County fund.

David Evin being summoned as Guarnishee by virtue of a writ of attachment William Simmons against William Flannagan On oath saith in open Court that he hath not any of the Property of the Defendant in his Possession.

Minutes were read and signed by Baylis Earle, Thomas Farrow, David Goodlett, Esqrs. Court then adjourned untill 9 o'clock tomorrow.

Wednesday the 17th day of September 1788. The Court met according to adjournment. Present Baylis Earle, William Smith & David Goodlett, Esquires.

Edward Smith against Peter Brooks On Slander. Ordered that this suit be refered to the Arbitrament of Edward Beeks Musgrove,

Abram Gray, James Crowther, Brittain Williford, William Clayton & William Bracher, Gentlemen Arbitrators, their award returned to our next Court, shall be a judgment thereof.

Thomas Tod against Ebenezer Morse. In Debt. Came the Plaintiff by William Shaw Esquire his attorney & the Defendant say he cannot Gainsay the Plaintiff's action, but that it is just & that he owes the Debt specifyed according to Note, whereupon it is considered by the Court that the Plaintiff recover against the Defendant 4 Dollars & a half pr. Hundred for the Tobacco specifyed in the note, amounting to Ŀ16 d 3 sterling with interest from the 15th Nov 1786 untill paid, subject to the Installment Law with stay of Execution three months besides his costs....

Wells Griffith being heretofore appointed Coroner for this County, refuseth to serve, it is therefore ordered that Isham Foster serve in place of said Griffith & take the necessary oath of office according to Law.

John Roebuck against Peter Brookes. On attachment. By consent of the Parties & assent of the Court, this matter of controversy is laid over untill next Court.

Joseph Wofford against John Roebuck. In Debt. By consent of the Parties and assent of the Court the Trial of this Cause is defered untill next Court.

Frederick Eison against William Davis & James Clerke. In Trover. By consent of the Parties and assent of the Court this matter of controversy is laid over untill next Court.

Charles Miles against Vardry McBee. Trover. Continued untill next Court by mutual agreement.

John McGuire against William Burton. False imprisonment. By the consent of the Parties and assent of the Court the Trial of this cause stands over untill next Court.

John Barkley against William Moore. Trover. Came the Plaintiff by Peter Carnes Gentl. his attorney & the Defendant by William Shaw, Gentlemen his attorney, whereupon came a Jury, to wit, Thomas Holcomb, John Cavin, Robert McDowell, Thomas Young, Flemming Smith, John McClure, Henry Turner, James Morriss, William Foster, David Prewit, Henry Aires & Bazel...We find a Verdict for the Plaintiff Ŀ 15 with costs of suit....

State against Michael Hogan. For Petty Larceny. The Grand Jury having examined the Parties, & finding the Defendant Guilty, Present him to the Court for said Petty Larceny.

State against Thomas Dougherty. Assault & Battery. The Grand Jury finding a true Bill against the Defendant Present him to the Court for further trial on the said assault & Battery.

We the Grand Jury for the County of Spartanburgh September Term 1788 Do present as follows, viz: A Grievance that this County is obliged to pay the County Tax immediately in Gold and Silver, a money which at this time can hardly be said to be in circulation, and do request that the time for collecting the said Tax may be prolonged so that those liable to pay the said Tax may have time to carry their produce to market to enable them to pay the said Tax. Frances Holmes for having one Bastard Child. Thomas Tod, foreman.

Landon Farrow appellant against Beverly Cox Respondant. An appeal from Squire Lancaster.
Came the Plaintiff by Thomas P. Carnes Gentleman his attorney & the Defendant by William Shaw his attorney...it is considered by the Court that the respondant recover against the appellant ₤ 2 s 2 d 2 with each party paying equal costs.

Ordered that the time of collecting the third assessment of the County tax be Prolonged untill December next.

Charles Waters against John Couch. Trover. By consent of the parties and assent of the Court this trial is refered to the arbitrament of John Ford & William Ford with power of umpirage their award returned to our next court shall the the judgment thereof.

William Couch against Westwood Waters. Defendant. On motion of Peter Carnes attorney for Plaintiff & By consent of the Parties & assent of the Court, this suit is dismissed at the Plaintiffs costs.

State against Michael Hogan. On Indictment. Michael Hogan principle & Reubin Dickson Security came into Court & acknowledged themselves indebted to the County of Spartanburgh in the sum of ₤ 25 sterling to be void on condition that Michael Hogan personally appear at next Court to answer a Bill of Indictment for Petty Larceny.

Charles Moore against Benjamine Silman. Case. Came the Plaintiff by Daniel Brown Gentleman his attorney & the Defendant by William Shaw Esquire his attorney, the parties join issue for trial, whereupon came a Jury, to wit...(same as before)...for Verdict, refer to page 213.

William Bennett administrator of John Langston vs. Landon Farrow. Case. The Parties enter into agreement to wit: William Bennett chooses William Wilder & Landon Farrow chooses Moses Casey to Value a certain Brown Bay mare that said William Bennett sued Landon Farrow for, & if they cannot agree in Value of said mare, they may accept of the Deposition of two mens oaths in with their Judgment, & also the same too men is to value another Horse and if the Horse is valued over sd. made William Bennett is to pay up in Trade by the value of the same men, also if Landon Farrow's Horse is under the value of said mare, said Landon Farrow is to pay up in trade to the value of said mare by the same men in value of the horse to said Bennett the two men may choose an Umpire- also if the men allows Interest for the sd. mare sd. William Bennett is to deduct out of the Interest from the same. Also Landon Farrow is to pay Samuel Farrow s 12 for said Bennett. The above Business is to be done at Moses Caseys on the Last Saturday in October next. Also I give in my attendance, Thomas Farrow.
              Landon Farrow

                 his
            William X Bennett
               mark

On motion of Alexander Alexander as a witness in the case Isaac Hendrix against George Roebuck on oath he is allowed s7 d 6 for 3 days attendance.

On motion of William Wilder as a witness in behalf of Thomas Tod against Ebenezer Morse on oath he is allowed s 5 for 2 days attendance.

Robert Thomson & William Barkley came into Court & Proved 30 days attendance each as witnesses in behalf of John Barkley against William Moore, taking into account each coming to Court & returning 80 miles.

On motion of Thomas Farrow Esquire as a witness in Behalf of Landon Farrow against Beverly Cox, on oath he is allowed s 10 for 4 days attendance.

William Williamson came into Court & acknowledged a Power of Attorney from himself to John Alexander. Ordered to be recorded.

Articles of Agreement between Thomas Williamson & John Tipping, proved in open Court by the evidence of Wm Williamson. Ordered to be recorded.

Minutes were read & signed by Baylis Earle, Wm. Smith, & David Goodlett, Esquires. Court then adjourned untill Tomorrow 9 o'clock.

Thursday the 18th of September 1788. Court met according to adjournment. Present Richard Harrison, William Smith, & David Goodlett, Esquires.

Ordered that John Gibbs serve as Constable for this County & qualify accordingly, which was done in open Court.

State against Thomas Dougherty. On Assault. The Defendant came into Court in proper person & confessed the assault laid against him in his indicement, whereupon it is considered by the Court that the Defendant pay the sum of one Penny & costs of the said Indictment: William Young, Esquire, and Peter Carnes, Esq., entered themselves security for costs of said suit.

Charles Waters against John Couch. Trover. This case being refered to the Arbitrament of John Ford and William Ford, Gentlemen Arbitrators, with power of umpirage, they choosing John Golightly as umpire and awarded that this suit be Dismissed at the Plaintiffs Costs.

Westwood Waters assignee of Morrison against Major Passons. Debt. By consent of the Parties & assent of the Court, this suit is Dismissed at the Plaintiffs Costs.

Michael Hogan against Peter Edwards. Debt. By consent of the parties & assent of the Court the trial of this cause is defered until next Court.

William Hill against George Taylor. Debt. Ordered that this suit Discontinue at the Plaintiff's costs.

Jeremiah Brashers against Holland Sumner. Trover. Ordered that the suit be discontinued at the Plaintiff's Costs.

Thomas Calhoun against Benjamine Wofford. Trover. Ordered, that this suit be refered to the Arbitrament of Jonathan Downs, Joshua Saxon, Robert Hannah & John Lindsey, Gentlemen, Arbitrators, with leave of umpirage, their award returned to our next Court shall be considered as a rule thereof.

David McDowell against Hugh Freeman, Administrator of Rodden. Trover. Ordered that this suit continue untill next Court.

Jacob Pennington against Joseph Hall. Case. Ordered that this suit be Dismissed at the Plaintiff's Costs.

John Waldrop against Robert & Sarah Sterling Admr. & Adm.x of James Elder. Case. Came the Plaintiff by Peter Carnes, Gentleman, his attorney & the Defendant by George Walker, their attorney, whereupon came a Jury, to wit, James Hughes, Martin Armstrong, John Hammett, William Milican, Josiah Culbertson, Thomas Silman, James Miller, Thomas Haney, Samuel Ward, Samuel Culbertson, John Foster & Joseph Barnett, ...We agree that Each Party shall pay their own costs, the suit shall be Discontinued...Peter Carnes the Plaintiffs Attorney motioned for a new Trial.

Present Baylis Earle.

Rowland Johnston against Wells Griffith. Special action on the case. By consent of the Parties & assent of the Court this suit is Dismissed at equal costs.

Thomas Hamilton & Temperance his wife against Benjamin Wofford. Trover. By consent of the Parties and assent of the Court this matter of controversy is refered to Talley Joice, Benjamin Rainey, Ebenezer Morse & William Michison Gentlemen with leave of umpirage their award to be returned to next Court & became a judgment thereof.

Henry Hays against Edward Michison. Trover. Ordered that this suit Discontinue at the Plaintiffs Costs.

Charles Moore against Benjamine Silman. Case. The Jury having been absent all night and having agreed in their Verdict returned the same in to Court in the following words, viz: "We agree that Charles Moore Plaintiff & Benjamine Silman Defendant each party pay their own cost and quash the action: which was ordered to be recorded, to which each Party agreed in open Court.

On motion of Edward Beeks Musgrove as a witness in Behalf of William Couch against Westwood Waters on oath his (sic) allowed the sum of Ł 5 for his attendance.

He also on oath was allowed the sum of   for 13 days attendance in the case Westwood Waters against John Couch for   miles times for coming without the County to his Court.

Edward Beeks Musgrove against David Golightly. Case. On motion of William Shaw attorney for Defendant, by consent of the Plaintiff by his attorney Peter Carnes Esquire ordered that a Dedimus Potestatum issue to two Justices of Wilks County in George to Examine Paul Garrison in Behalf of the Defendant in the above case.

Edwd. Beeks Musgrove against David Golightly. Case. Ordered that the affidavit of John Wade as a witness in the above case be taken by Richard Harrison Esquire on the Behalf of the Plaintiff, & that the Defendant have notice of the time & place of Examination that he may have the Liberty of Cross Examining said witness.

Isham Foster being heretofore appointed Coroner for this County, came into Court & took the Necessary oath of office according to Law.

George Salmon against Richard Harrison. On Petition, Etc. By consent of the Parties and assent of the Court this suit is continued untill next Court at the Plaintiffs Costs.

Leonard Smith against George & John Roebuck Executors of Benja. Roebuck, Defendant, Deceased. Case.

Came the Plaintiff by Peter Carnes and Daniel Brown Gentlemen his attorny & the defendants by George Walker Gentleman their attorney, whereupon came a Jury, to wit, Thomas Holcomb, John Cavin, Robert McDowell, Thomas Young, Flemming Smith, John McClure, Henry Turner, James Norris, William Foster, David Prewit, Henry Aires, & Bazel Lee...We agree that the Defendant shall pay ₤ 12 s 16 d 4 sterling with Lawful Interest from the year '84 with costs of suit....

Edwd. Beeks Musgrove against David Golightly. Case. By consent of the Parties and assent of the Court this matter of controversy wherein Edward Beeks Musgrove is Plaintiff and David Golightly Defendant is refered to the Arbitrament of John Lindsey & William Smith Esquire with Powers of Umpirage, their award Returned to our next Court shall stand as a judgment thereof.

Ordered that a certificate from under the hand of John Blasingame, Esquire, be entered on record, viz: Spartanburgh County. I hereby certify that Persuant to a report of a Committee appointed by the General assembly March 1787, Colonel Thomas Beardon (sic for Brandon) & myself were authorized to appointed Commissioners & a surveyor to run a line between said County & County of Union that Mr. James Smith were Imployed to run sd. line who completed the said Business was 6 days in running the straight line. Certifyed the 18th day of September 1788, which is hereby recorded.
John Blasingame (Seal)

William Simmons against William Flannagan. On attachment. Judgment by Default. Ordered that the Property attached be exposed to sale, and the money arising therefrom remain in the Constables hands untill next Court.

On motion of Peter Brookes as a witness in the case Leonard Smith against the Executors of Benjamine Roebuck, on oath he is allowed s 12 d 6 for 5 days attendance.

John Wood against Thomas Hanna. Trover. By consent of the Parties and assent of the Court, this cause stands over untill next Court.

On motion of John Butler as a witness in the case Leonard Smith against the Executors of Robuck, on oath he is allowed ₤ 1 s 17 d 6 for 15 days attendance.

James Miller on oath is allowed ₤ 1 for his attendance as a witness in the case Leonard Smith against the Executors of Roebuck.

Joseph Howell on oath is allowed ₤ 5 s 3 d 6 for 28 days attendance in the case Leonard Smith against Exrs. of Roebuck, & for 100 miles in coming to Court.

William Crocker on oath is allowed s 12 and d 6 for 5 days attendance in the suit Andrew Paul against William Poole.

Joshua Pettit on oath is allowed s 12 for 5 days attendance in the suit Andrew Paul against William Poole.

Minutes were read and signed by Saml Lancaster, William Smith, David Goodlett. Court then adjourned untill Tomorrow 9 o'clock.

At A County Court began and Held for the County of Spartanburgh on the third Monday in December 1788. Present Baylis Earle, William McDowell, David Goodlett, & Richard Harrison, Esquire.

James Dougherty Esquire produced his Credentials as an attorney at law and equity in this State was thereupon admitted and enrolled to practice in this Court.

The Court then proceeded to draw the Grand Jurors for March term to wit, Charles McKnight, John James, William Thomson Gentl., James Hooper, Andrew Barry, Alexander Walker, Vardry McBee, John roebuck, George Bruton, Tobias Bright, John Snoddy, Giles Connell, Samson Bobo, Moses Foster, John McElheny, George Roebuck, Francis Dodd, Josiah Culbertson, Charles Moore, Robert Cooglett, William Suddeth, Thomas Paden, John Beard, John Posey, James Alexander, Tyger.

Pettit Jurors. John Williams, Thomas Cole, Thomas Robertson, Robert Miller, Jesse Spencer, Daniel Gilbert, John Haden, Thomas Haze Junr., James Beard, Micajah Taylor, John Smith, Christopher Long, John Brooks, Benjamine Jones, Leonard Adcock, John Atkison, Alexander Evin, Thomas Jones, Ezekiel Young, Drewry Prewit, Thomas Moore, Peter Elder, James Wyatt Junr., Charles Smith, John Wofford, William Bryant, James Burton, Abraham Fowler, Reubin Smith, Moses Casey.

The Persons that were summoned to appear at this Present Court, to serve as Pettit Jurors are as follows to wit, George Haden Junr., Walter Burrell, Bayley Taylor, Joseph Blackwood, William Dundan, Reubin Dollar, Benjamine Beson, Isaac Crow, John Leech, Joshua Prestrage, Alexander Floyd, Henry Pettit, Benjamine Stone, Joseph Neasbitt, Nevil Wayland, James Fannen, Malachi Jones, Edmund W. Clemons, Benjamine Carley & William M. Williams.

William Webb against George Hughey. Petition. Dismissed at the Plaintiff's Costs.

Peter Carnes Esquire vs Joseph Buffington. Petition. The Defendant came into Court in his proper Preson, and confessed judgment for the sum of Ł 2 s 14 d 4 with costs of suit (attorneys fees excepted).

The appearance Docket called over the first time.

Pettit Jurors drawn to serve this Court, to wit, Bayley Taylor, James Fannen, John Leech, George Haden Junr., William Duncan, Isaac Crow, Walter Burrell, Benjamine Carley, Joseph Neasbitt, Reubin Dollar, Malachi Jones, Benjamine Stone, Joshua Prestrage, William McWilliams, Alexander Floyd, Benjamin Beson, Francis Nevil Wayland.

A part of the Inventory, amount & sale of the Estate of William Wofford Junr., deceased, returned into open court by William Wofford Senr., Administrator & the said administrator was allowed untill next Court to make a return in full.

A Deed of Conveyance from John Pack to Thomas David acknowledged in open Court by said Pack. Ordered to be recorded.

Minutes were read and signed by Baylis Earle, Richard Harrison,

& William McDowell, Esqrs. Court then adjourned untill Tomorrow 9 o'clock.

Tuesday the 16th of December 1788. The Court met according to adjournment. present Richard Harrison, David Goodlett, William McDowell, Samuel Lancaster, & Baylis Earle, Esquires.

The last will and testament of James White Deceased was proved in open Court by the Evidence of James Smith. Ordered to be recorded.

The State against John Dotey. On an Indictment. John Dotey pinciple, Reubin Barrett & Joseph Dotey, sureties, came into Court & acknowledged themselves to owe to the State to wit the said Dotey Ł 50, and the said Sureties Ł 25 each for the appearance of the said John Dotey to next Court, to answer to an Indictment against said Dotey.

The State against John Dotey. On an Indictment. Thomas Davis being recognized last court for the appearance of the Defendant to this Court, the Defendant appearing, the said Davis was thereupon dismissed from his recognizance.

The State against Richard Harrison, Esq. On an Indictment. The whole of the recognizance in this case continued untill next court.

The State against William & Samuel Redman. Petty Larceny. The whole of the recognizance in this case continued untill next court.

John McElheny against the administrators of Joseph Jones. Debt. The defendant came into open Court and confessed judgment for 6000 Dollars old South currency, with Interest thereon from the 1st day of May 1780, which time the debt became due; whereupon it is considered by the Court, that the Plaintiff recover against the said Defendant the said sum of 6000 dollars old South currency (paying regard to the scale of depreciation) which is equal to Ł 42 s 13 d 11 sterling, besides his costs...

Edward Smith against Peter Brooks. Slander. This suit being heretofore refered to the arbitrament of Edward Beeks Musgrove, Abram Gray, James Crowther, Brittain Williford, William Clayton & William Bratcher, Gentlemen, arbitrators; hath now awarded that this suit Discontinue at each party's paying their own costs.

Philemon Martin against Obediah Oliphant. Case. This case being refered to the Arbitrament of William Thomson and William Lipscomb Senior awarded that the Plaintiff pay one shilling damage, and costs of suit.

Ann Arnett Admx. of Edward Arnett against William Clayton & the Exrs. of Roebuck. Debt. The defendants came into open court in their Proper persons and confessed judgment for Ł 6 s 9 and costs of suit.

William Bennett admr. of John Langston against Landon Farrow. Trover. Ordered that this suit Discontinued.

Ordered, that a road be laid out agreeable to the course marked and laid off by Matthew Guttery & Thomas Wilson who were appointed to do the same.

Michael Hogan against Peter Edwards. Debt. Nonsuit.

Frederick Eisen against William Davis & James Clerke. Trover. On motion of William Shaw Gentleman Attorney for the Plaintiff and upon hearing the alligations of both parties. Ordered that this suit be dismissed at each party paying their own costs.

Ordered, that Robert McMillan oversee the road leading from William McDowell's Mill to the North Carolina line; in the Room of the said William McDowell Esquire, & that Lepord French warn all people which are liable by law to work on Roads to work thereon under his jurisdiction.

Ordered That Robert Harper oversee the Road from the widow Bishops on Lawsons fork to the Bridge on South Packolet in the room of William Brandon also that Thomas Jackson oversee the said Road from said Bridge to the No. Carolina line in the room of Samuel Jackson. Likewise that the hands directed in the original order to work on said Road do work thereon under them And the said overseers be furnished with a copy of the original order without loss of time.

David McDowell against Hugh Freeman Admr. of Rodden. Trover. Came the Plaintiff by William Shaw Gentlemen Attorney and the Defendant by Thomas Peter Carns, Esquire his attorney, whereupon came a Jury, to wit, Benjamine Stone, Joseph Neasbitt, Isaac Crow, Walter Burrell, William Duncan, Joshua Prestrage, James Fannen, Bayley Taylor, Malachi Jones, George Haden Junior, Reubin Dollar, & John Leech...the plaintiff shall have ₤ 7 with costs of suit...

John Camp against John Chism. Case. Ordered that a Dedimus Potestatum issue to Rutherford County in North Carolina, to Examine John Camp, Thomas Camp, Susannah Camp, Reubin Hill & Sarah Camp on the part and Behalf of the said Plaintiff, He being also required to give the Defendant Ten days notice of the time and place of Examination.

On motion of William Borland, as a witness in the suit Ann Arnett Admx. of Edward Arnett against William Clayton and Exrs. of Benjamine Roebuck, on oath was allowed s 5 for 2 days attendance & s11 d8 for mileage.

The State against Daniel Stephenson. Petty Larceny. The Defendant came into Court with Thomas Moore & John Smith as his sureties, and acknowledged themselves to owe to the State to wit the said Stephenson in the sum of ₤ 50 and the sureties in the sum of ₤ 25 each, for the personal apperance of the said Stephenson to next Court to an indictment against him.

Robert Goodgion against Israel Morris. Debt.
Israel Morris against Robert Goodgion. Debt.
Ordered that all matters of controversy between the said parties both in Law and otherwise, be referred to the arbitrament of William Benson, Isham Foster, & Thomas Farra, Gentlemen Arbitrators, & if either of them should fail to appear, the two meeting are to choose an umpire and arbitrate the said cases on the first or second days of January next, and if either the Plaintiff or Defendant should fail in appearing, the said arbitrators are to proceed to decide the same; & their award returned to our next Court, shall be a judgment thereof.

The State against William and Samuel Redman. Larceny. The defendants came into open Court & acknowledged themselves to owe to the State ₤ 50 lawful money each, also John Conner their surety in the sum of ₤ 25 like money, for the personal appearance of the said defendants at our next County Court to answer to said Indictment.

Joel Callihan against Nevil Wayland. Petition. Nonsuit.

Ordered that a road be laid out and opened from this Court House to the County line, to intersect a road from Union Court House between Mr. Burtons & John Nails, and that Absalom Lancaster, James Smith & William Simpson view and mark out the same, and instruct the overseers accordingly, and that David Brown & Charles James be the overseers of said road, & divide the Ground between themselves.

On motion of Benjamine Barton of Greenville, as a witness in the suit Joel Callihan against Frances Nevil Wayland, on oath was allowed five shillings for 2 days attendance & s 5 for milage.

Ordered that Wells Griffith oversee the Road leading from this Court House, by his mill to the Iron ore ford on Packolate River, warner William Turner Thomason, and that Malachi Jones oversee from thence to a place marked out by the Commissioners, warner Hiram Jones & that William Wier to oversee from thence to the flat sholes on Cherokee Creek warner Frederick Gurrery and Alexander Davidson to oversee from thence to William Camps plantation on Broad River, warner Absalom Hines also that all persons within four miles of said, to work thereon under the Jurisdiction of said overseers.

Israel Morriss against Rowland Cornelius. Case. Ordered that the trial of this suit be refered to the arbitrament of Rowland Johnson & Isham Foster with power of umpirage their award returned to next Court, shall be a rule thereof.

On motion of William Grant as a witness in the case Bazel Lee against Richard Harrison Esquire on oath was allowed s 5 for 2 days attendance & s 11 d 8 for milage.

John Camp against Thomas Davis. Trespass. Ordered that this suit be dismissed at each Party paying their own cash.

Minutes were read & signed by Baylis Earle, Obadiah Trimmier, & David Goodlett, Esquires. Court then adjourned until tomorrow 9 o'clock.

Wednesday the 17th of December 1788. The Court met according to last evening's adjournment. Present Baylis Earle, Thomas Farrow, & William Smith, Esquires.

William Nunn against Landon Farrow. Trover. By consent of the parties and assent of the Court, the trial of this cause is defered untill next Court.

On motion of Isham Saffold as a witness in the case Thomas Gordon against William Gilbert, on oath he is allowed ₤ 1 s 5 for 10 days attendance.

Present Richard Harrison, David Goodlett, Obadiah Trimmier & Zadock Ford, Esquires.

Ordered that the County treasurer pay the constable s 6 for summoning a Guard to guard the prisoner in jail, to wit, McMeekin Hunt & that the guard be allowed s 3 each for guarding the said prisoner) who were Samuel Ward, James Laxton, Samuel Ward Junior, & George Thomason.

Ordered that Yearby Dewberry oversee the Road leading from Buises Mill to Hammett's Ford on Packolate River on the Room of Malachi Jones.

David McDowell against the Admrs. of Rodden. Trover. On motion of Thomas Peter Carnes Esquire attorney for the Defendant for an arrest of Judgment obtained by the Plaintiff yesterday. Ordered, that the said judgment be arrested.

James Rice against Thomas Davis. Assault. Came the plaintiff by his attorney & the defendant by his attorney likewise, whereupon came a Jury to wit, Benjamine Stone, Joseph Neasbitt, Isaac Crow, Walter Burrell, William Duncan, Joshua Prestrage, James Fannen, Bayley Taylor, Malachi Jones, George Hadon Junior, Reubin Dollar & John Leech...we find for the plaintiff with costs of suit....

James Huggins against John Blalock. Attachment. By consent of the parties and assent of the Courts, this suit is dismissed, at each party paying their own costs.

Henry Wolf against William Neal, John Motlow & Daniel Jackson. Debt. Ordered, that this suit be dismissed at each parties paying their own costs.

James Barron against John Moore. Debt. By consent of the Parties & assent of the Court, the trial of this cause is defered untill next Court.

Wadsworth & Co. against Moses Wood. Case. Ordered, that this suit discontinue at the cost of the Plaintiff.

John Roebuck against Peter Brooks. Attachment. Ordered that this suit discontinue at the Plaintiff's Costs.

Israel Morriss against John Kimbell. Case. By consent of the parties and assent of the Court, the trial of this cause refered to the arbitrament of Rowland Johnson & Isham Foster with Power of umpirage, their award returned to our next Court shall be a Judgment.

Ephraim Reece against Nicholas Holley. Attachment. Peter Carnes attorney for the defendant, acknowledged the Declaration to be filed in time & puts in his plea in the following words "Comes and defends the force and injury, etc., & moved to the Court for a nonsuit, for want of a Declaration, also for want of sufficient Bond to ground the attachment & further moves that the attachment be dismissed because it was levyed on land, which is not subject to an attachment by the County Court Law, which plea the Court & looked upon it to be a frivolous plea, & ordered him to plead substantially."

On motion of Rowland Johnson & William Wood as witnesses in the case Wadsworth & Co. against Moses Wood, on oath they were allowed Ł 1 s 5 each for 10 days attendance

Aquilla White against James Wofford & Wife. Executors of Mahany. Case. Ordered that this suit be dismissed at the plaintiff's costs.

Ephraim Reece against Nicholas Holley. Attachment. Came the plaintiff by George Walker, Gentleman, his attorney & the Defendant by Peter Carnes Esquire his attorney, whereupon came a jury to wit (same as before)...we find for the Plaintiff Ł 20 with costs of suit...Nevil Wayland, foreman.

Edward Michison came into Court and proved 10 days attendance as a witness in the above case, amounting to Ł 5 s 5.

On motion of Joshua Morgan as a witness in the said case, on oath, was allowed Ł 1 for milage & Ł 2 s 5 for 18 days attendance.

Holland Sumner & wife against Buckner Smith. Special action on the case. This suit being heretofore refered to the arbitrament of Thomas Williams, Stephen Wilson & Samson Bobo, who hath awarded that the said defendant pay the said Plaintiff s 9 d 4 & the said Plaintiff pay all costs of suit.

John Camp against John Chism. Petition. The suit being determined at last September Court, whereupon an execution issued & was levyed on property of the defendant, on motion of him by his attorney. Ordered that the suit be reinstated & the property under Execution be delivered up to the said Defendant.

Robert Bolston against Thomas Price. attachment. Benjamin Wofford and Samuel Thomson being summoned as Guarnishees came into Court & made oath that they oweth not, nor hath any of the Property of the defendant in their possession.

Minutes were read & signed by Zadock Ford, Thomas Farrar & William Smith, Esquires. Court then adjourned untill Tomorrow 9 o'clock.

Thursday the 18th of December 1788. The Court met according to last nights adjournment. Present Baylis Earle, William Smith & Thomas Farrow & also Richard Harrison Esquires.

Thomas Tod against Ebenezer Morse. Petition. Came the Plaintiff by William Shaw Esquire attorney for the Plaintiff and the Defendant by Peter Carnes Esquire his attorney and upon the parites being heard, it is considered by the Court that the defendant recover against the Plaintiff s 7 and one penny besides his Costs ....

Whereas a petition from a small number of inhabitants of that part of this County formerly considered part of the County of Union is exhibited to the Court stating that before the line between this and Union County was ascertained they were called on to pay their County tax to an officer of Union, and that they have absolutely paid the same. Ordered That when any person shall be called on by the sheriff of this County for the County tax, if they or any of them produce a receipt from the aforesaid officer of Union to the sheriff of this County it shall be a sufficient voucher for him.

William Graham against Jordan Gibson. Attachment. Came the Plaintiff by William Shaw Gentl., his attorney and the defendant by Thos. P. Carnes Esquire his attorney and upon the parties being heard, it is considered by the Court, that this suit be dismissed at the defendant's Costs.

John Thoms Junr. being summoned as a guarnishee upon an attachment Joshua Petty against Hugh Flanagan comes into Court and confessed that he is justly indebted to the said Flanagan; therefore the said Thomas is ordered to pay the debt to no other person but to the said Petty. (whenever he lawfully obtains judgment against the sd. Flanagan) & if the said Thomas cannot take in his note given for the debt upon discharging the same, This shall be a sufficient voucher for his discharging the said debt.

Charles McKnight admr. of Trammell against Thomas Morrow. Case. Came the Plaintiff by William Shaw Gentl. his attorney and the defendant by Thomas Peter Carnes, Esquire, his attorney, whereupon came a Jury, to wit, Benjamin Stone, Joseph Neasbitt, Isaac Crow, Walter Burrell, William Duncan, Joshua Prestrage, Benjamine Beeson, Bayley Taylor, Malachi Jones, George Haden Junr., Reubin dollar & Francis Nevil Wayland...

Samson Bobo against Benjamine Wofford & Henry Earnest. Trover. Ordered that this case be refered to the arbitrament of Thomas Tod, Robert Hannah, John Lindsey & Moses Casey with power of umpirage, their award returned to our next Court shall be a rule thereof.

William Shaw Esquire attorney for Earnest one of the defendants, objects against the above reference as to his part.

Ordered, that Travice Morse act as Constable for this County & take the oath of office accordingly.

David Golightly Exr. of William Golightly against William Wofford Senr. Debt. The defendant came into Court & confessed judgment for ₺ 200 old South currency, the Debt contracted 24 Feb 1778, and due 1st day of the ensuing May. Whereupon it is considered by the Court that the Plaintiff recover against the defendant the said sum of ₺ 200 old South currency, paying regard to the scale of depreciation, which is equal to ₺ 8 s 14 d 8 3/4 with interest thereon untill paid....
Execution not to issue untill June Court.

Ordered, that on appeal from a justice below, no new matter shall be produced on the trial thereof.

Ordered, that a road be opened from Hammett's ford on Packolate River to William Thomson's on Thickety to go the nearest & best way by John Weston's & that Irby Dewberry lay out & oversee the same.

State against Jordan Gibson. On a Breach of the Peace.
The defendant appeared in his own person pleads Guilty and the Court having received exculpatory affidavits, find the defendant one shilling & costs of suit. John Lefever came into Court & entered himself Bail for the fees in the above case, acknowledged before. Wm. Lancaster, D. C.

Robert Cooper against Abraham Nalley & Walter Burrell. Petition. Ordered that this suit discontinue at the Defendants costs.

Philip Tipping against Nicholas Holley. Petition. By consent of the parties & assent of the Court, the trial of this suit, is defered untill next Court.

Thomas Tod against Ebenezer Morse. Petition. Richard Burgess came into Court and proved 3 days attendance in the above case amounting to s 7 d 6 & s 16 d 8 for milage.

On motion of Buckner Smith as a witness in the above case on oath is allowed s 2 d 6 for 1 days attendance.

On motion of Joshua Smith as a witness in the above case, on oath is allowed s 7 d 6 for 3 days attendance.

On motion of Nathaniel Henderson as a witness in the above case, on oath was allowed s 7 d 6 for 3 days attendance.

Wadsworth, & Co. against Joseph Buffington. Petition. On motion of Thomas Peter Carnes Esquire attorney for the Plaintiff ordered that the Plaintiff recover against the deft. Ł 3 besides his costs...

Minutes were read and signed by Baylis Earle, Zadock Ford, Thomas Farrow, Esquires. Court then adjourned untill Tomorrow 9 o'clock.

Friday the 19th December 1788. The worshipful Court met according to adjournment. Present Baylis Earle, William Smith, Thomas Farrar & David Goodlett, Esquires.

Ordered that all recognizances which are now returnable to this Court be continued untill next Court & that where recognizances are taken for the appearance of the Principle that the Magistrates take care to recognize all the witnesses in behalf of the State to appear also.

Ordered, that the following be an established rule of the Justices of this County to establish a line of conduct to be observed by the subscribers as Justices of the County or any others who may hereafter adopt it with respect to strays.

We agree upon the following particulars. That if the strays appears to be abused, the appraisers ought to view them ascertain the damage, & the person so abusing to make it good The appraisers are to be nominated & do their business without expense.

Cows Hogs & sheep may be sold at Home by the Justice before whom they were Toll'd, giving the taker up a preference of keeping them at the appraisment price. The terms of private sales to be the same as those adopted by the Court & the Justices make his return to each succeeding Court.

The intention of the above is not to prevent the owner getting their property at all times, if proved within the lawful time.

Signed by Baylis Earle, Richard Harrison, Obadiah Trimmier, Wm. Smith, Thomas Farrow, David Goodlet, & Zadock Ford, Esquires.

Thomas Gordon against Ralph Cobb. Assault.
Ralph Cobb against Thomas Gordon. Slander.
By consent of the Parties these two cases Refered to the arbitrament of William Wier, William Poole, Matthew Guttery, Reubin Matthews, William Poole Taylor & John Huitt, their award to be returned to next Court & become a Judgment thereof.

Ephraim Reece against Nichols Holley. On an arrest of Judgment. Peter Carnes, Esquire attorney for the defendant moved for an arrest of Judgment, in the above case, decided on Wednesday & after mature consideration by the court of the matter, & reasons assigned Declare & ordered that the Judgment shall not be arrested, but stand according to the verdict of the Jury & the judgment become subject to the installment Law.

Ordered that s 16 be paid Mr. Thomas Williamson for to defray the expence of guarding the Goal by the Sheriff.

Richard Harrison against Bazel Lee. On an appeal from a Justice Below. Ordered that the Trial of this Cause lie over untill next Court.

Robert Harper against Charles McKnight. Case. Ordered, that a Dedimus Potestatum issue to Wilks County in Georgia to any two Justices there to examine Jason Wilson in the above case & one to Burk County in North Carolina to any two Justices there to examine Thomas Parker; Both on the part & Behalf of the Plaintiff he being required to give 10 days previous notice to the defendant of the times & places of Examinations.

Ordered that the sheriff summon a sufficient Guard to take the prisoner now in jail (who is McMeekin Hunt) to the jail at Cambridge & that the jailer of said jail take him into custody.

Minutes were read & signed by William Smith, Thomas Farrow, David Goodlett, Esquires. Court then adjourned untill Court in Course.

At a County Court began and held for the County of Spartanburgh on the third Monday in March 1789. Present Richard Harrison, William Smith & David Goodlett, Esquires.

Whereas experience hath proved the inconvenience of holding Court in this County at the June Term, the Inhabitants of the County being generally engaged at that period with their Harvest; To remedy which it is ordered, that the Jurors be drawn this Court to serve at the next September Term and that all Process issued by the clerk returnable to next Court, be brought forward on the September appearance docket and that all causes undetermined at this Court be continued over, in the same manner to September Term as if a Court should not be held in June & that the clerk put up a copy of this order at the door of the Court House tomorrow morning, Ordered that they be drawn Accordingly.

Grand Jurors. John Brown Gentl., Jonathan Harris, David McDowell, John Young, Majr. John Gowen, Nathaniel Robertson, Samuel Neasbitt, William Hamby, Jonathan Neasbitt, Alburtus Bright, Thomas Williamson, Joseph Barnett, Thomas Wyatt, Martin Armstrong, Charles Hester, Jesse Connell, Thomas Milican, William Tate, Stephen Wilson, & William Lipscomb.

Pettit Jurors. Nathaniel Gentry, Isaac Hamby, Ebenezer Morse, Richard Barry, Samuel Smith, David Henry, Thomas Kimbell, Littleton Mapp Junr., JosephPowers, Charles Carter, Landon Farrow, Solomon Crocker, James Henderson, Thomas Sherley, Matthew Alexander, Hugh Flannagan, Anthony Colter, William Earnest, William Ford no. Tyger, Benjamine Couch, Rowland Johnson,John Callihan, Mason Cannon, Henry Earnest, Joseph Morriss, Jesse Tate, Thomas Warren, Drewry Hutchison, Benjamine Northward & William Gaston.

James Terrill against Vardry McBee & William Beekum. Debt. On motion of Thomas P. Carnes, Esquire, in behalf of the Plaintiff. Ordered that this writ renew & issue against McBee & William Rickman instead of Beckum.

Bavester & Elizabeth Barton against Mary & John Hillen. Special action on the case. Ordered that this suit be dismissed at the Plaintiff's costs.

On having the Petition of Mr. Charles Moore of Tyger River, setting forth he is 64 years of age & much deprived of his hearing Ordered that the said Charles Moore be struck off the Jury list & hereafter exempted from serving as a Grand or Pettit Juror for the County.

Edward B. Musgrove against David Golightly. Case. Non-suit.

On motion of William Turner Thomason as a witness in the above case, on oath he was allowed s 15 for 6 days attendance.

Rowland Jenians on oath was allowed s 30 for 12 days attendance in the above case.

Ordered that Moses Timmons have license to keep a Public House of entertainment & retail spiritous liquors he giving Bond & security to conform with the rates prescribed by Law.

John McElheny came into open Court and acknowledged a lease & Release from himself to John & William Armstrong. Ordered to be recorded.

Ordered that William Pool, taylor, have license to keep a public House of entertainment, he giving Bond & security for his Lawful performance.

County duty paid Colonel Thomas.

Ordered that William Pool, Iron Monger, have Tavern license, he giving approved security for his lawful performance.

Minutes were read & signed by Wm. Smith, David Goodlett, & Saml. Lancaster, Esquires.

Tuesday the 17th of March 1789. The worshipful Court met according to last evenings adjournment. Present William Smith, Thomas Farrow & Samuel Lancaster, Esquires.

Grand Jurors to serve this Term, to wit, Andrew Barry, John James, James Hooper, Alexander Walker, George Burton, John Snoddy, Giles Connell, Samson Bobo, John McElheny, Francis Dodd, Thomas Paden, John Beard, John Posey, William Suddoth & Josiah Culbertson.

Thomas Calhoun against Benjamine Wofford. Trespass. By consent of the parties and assent of the Court, the trial of this case is continued untill next Court.

Israel Morriss against John Kimbell. Case. Came the Plaintiff by George Walker Esquire, his attorney & the defendant by Thos. P. Carnes, his attorney; and after the Jury being empanneled & sworn & there being no witnesses in behalf of the Plaintiff he thereupon drew a Juror and suffered a Nonsuit.

Israel Morriss against Rowland Cornelius. Case. By consent of the parties and assent of the Court, the trial of this cause is continued untill next Court.

Robert Goodgion against Israel Morriss. Debt. This case being left to the arbitrament of Isham Foster, William Benson & James Jordan, Esquire Gentl., arbitrators; who award that the Plaintiff recover against the Defendant ₺ 56 s 13 d 5 sterling with lawful Interest, that is to say, ₺ 30 from 2 Feb 1789, also ₤ 16 s 13 d 4 from 1 Dec 1788....

Ordered that George Haning have license to keep a Public House of entertainment & retail spiritous liquors, he giving approved securities for his Lawful performance. Paid.

James Swann against Hugh Pierce. Debt. Ordered that this suit be Dismissed at the Plaintiff's Costs, after allegations being heard by parties.

Rhoda McBee against George Taylor Slander. Nonsuit.

On motion of William Shaw Esquire for letters of administration for Rispy Foster, to collect and take care of the property of James Foster, who is a Lunatic & gone out of the State, the Court denying they being of opinion they had no power to do the same.

Jesse Davis against James Ward. detinue. Came the Plaintiff by Thos. P. Carnes, Esquire, his attorney, & the Defendant by William Shaw, Esquire, his attorney; Whereupon came a Jury to wit, Robert Miller, John Haden, Thomas Hayes Junr., James Beard, John Smith, Benjamine Jones, Leonard Adcock, Peter Elder, James Wyatt Junr., Charles Smith, John Wofford, and Reubin Smith... we find for the Plaintiff as follows, that the defendant give up the said Horse or pay the Plaintiff ₤ 7 with costs, etc....

Edward Balenger on oath was allowed ₤ 2 s 15 for 22 days attendance in the above case.

David McDowell against Hugh Freeman administrator of Rodden. Special action on the case. Ordered that a Dedimus Potestatum issue to Georgia Burk County to Two Justice for said County, to examine John Golding, Ann Golding & Elizabeth Balue on the behalf of the Plaintiff he giving 10 days notice to the Defendant of the Time & Place of Examination.

Zachariah Taliaferro proved his credentials as an attorney at Law & Equity in this State. Ordered, that he be enrolled amongst the attornies of the Court.

Philip Tipping against Nicholas Holley. Petition. By consent of the Parties and assent of the Court, the trial of this cause is continued untill next Court.

The State against William Patterson. Petty Larceny. John White & Charles Bruce as his surety, came into Court & acknowledged themselves to owe to the State the sum of ₤ 25 each for the personal appearance of said White, to give Testimony in behalf of the State against the said Defendant upon a bill of Indictment prefered against him by the Grand Jury.

Joseph Buffington against Maximilian Conner. Petition. Ordered that this case be continued at the Defendant's Costs.

George Salmon against Richard Harrison. Petition. The defendant pray a verdict of the jury in this case, which was accordingly granted by the Court.

Ordered by the Court that Reubin Smith be fined the sum of s 5 for his failure as a Juror, which he paid in open Court.

Bills Given to the Grand Jury.

The State against John Doughty. Petty Larceny. True Bill.

The State against James McElheny. Petty Larceny. True Bill.

The State against Thomas Price. Petty Larceny. True Bill.

The State against Michael Miller. Petty Larceny. No Bill.
                                    Andrew Barry, foreman.

George Salmon against Richard Harrison, Esquire. Petition. Came the Plaintiff by Thos. P. Carnes his attorney and the Defendant by William Shaw Esquire his attorney, Whereupon came a Jury to wit (same as before)...& Jesse Hammett (instead of Reubin Smith)...we find for the plaintiff the within sum of ₺ 6 s 11 & costs of suit....

William Shaw Esquire attorney for the Defendant moved for an Arrest of Judgment.

Martin Armstrong, as an evidence in the above case on oath is allowed s 30 for 12 days attendance.

The State against William Reynolds. Petty Larceny.
Thomas Penny came into Court & entered himself surety in the sum of ₺ 10 for the defendant's Personal appearance to abide by the Judgment of this Court upon the charge of said Larceny.

Joseph Howell as an evidence in the case John McElheny against John Gowen on oath is allowed s 37 d 6 for 15 days attendance and s 41 d 8 for milage from Greenville County.

Joseph Venible and Jesse Reams as evidences the case Israel Morriss against John Kimbel on their oaths was allowed s 7 d 6 each for 3 days attendance.

William Moore & George Bruton Junr. as evidences in the case Philip Tipping against Nicholas Holley on their oaths was allowed s 5 each for 2 days attendance.

Ordered that a note of hand from Thomas Price to Robert Rolston as delivered up to said Rolston as there was a suit commenced by said Rolston against said Prisoner in Goal, and dismissed at the Plaintiff's Costs.

Marsoncock Smithson as an evidence in behalf of the State against Michael Miller on oath was allowed s 19 d 2 for 3 days attendance & s 11 d 8 for milage.

The State against Thomas Price. Petty Larceny. Ordered, that the bill of Indictment be traversed & that the tryal be postponed untill next Court.

Jane Dill came into Court and acknowledged a power of attorney from herself to David Leech, Esquire. Ordered to be recorded.

Minutes were read & signed by Saml. Lancaster, Wm. Smith, Thomas Farra, David Goodlett, Esquires. Court then adjourned untill To-morrow 9 o'clock.

Wednesday the 18th of March 1789. The worshipful Court met according to last evening adjournment. Present Samuel Lancaster, William Smith & David Goodlett, Esquires.

John McElheny came into Court and proved six days attendance as a witness in the case Frederick Eison against William Davis & James Clerk.

John McElheny against John Gowen. Case. John Timmons being summoned as a witness in this case, & not being capable of coming to Court. Ordered, that his Testimony be taken in writing & be admitted of on trial.

John Couch against Charles Waters. Trover. Execution, being issued & the Sheriff levyed the same on a tract of land & advertised for sale, Ordered, that 300 acres so executed be exposed to sale.

William Blackstock against William Smith, Esquire. Trover. By consent of the Parties and assent of the Court, the trial, of this cause is refered to the arbitrament of Nehemiah Howard, & John Blasingame, Esquire, Gentlemen Arbitrators, with power of umpirage, to be arbitrated the first Saturday in April next at the Widow Roebuck's; their award returned to next Court shall be the judgment thereof.

Samuel Stewart against Avery Connell & Thomas Farrar, Guarnishee. Attachment. Came the Plaintiff by William Shaw his attorney & the Defendant failing to appear, judgment entered according to Specialty for Ł 7 s 13 d 4 with interest & costs of suit....

Joshua Petty against Hugh Flanagan. Attachment. Judgment by Default in behalf of the Plaintiff for Ł 11 s 4 d 7 with interest & cost of suit.

The State against James McElheny. Indictment. Came Thos P. Carnes, Esquire in behalf of the State and the Defendant by Peter Carnes his attorney, Whereupon came a Jury (same as before) ...do say not guilty. John Smith, foreman. The Defendant payed all costs....

The State against John Doutey. Indictment. Came Thos. P. Carnes in behalf of the State and the Defendant by Peter Carnes his attorney, whereupon came a Jury, (same as before)...do say Not Guilty....

William Burton against Richard Lee. Slander. The Parties by agreement left their case to the arbitrament of Benjamine Wofford and Thomas Farrow who say that the suit shall be dismissed at the Plaintiff's Costs.

James Clerk against George Pettus. Case. By consent of the Plaintiff, this suit is Dismissed at his Costs.

Ann Arnett Admx. of Edward Arnett against Benjamine & Joseph Wofford. Debt. The Defendant came into open Court & confessed Judgment for Ł 14 s 10 & costs of suit...the plaintiff agreeing to stay execution until December Court next.

Richard Harrison Esquire against Bazel Lee. appeal from a Justice. Came the Plaintiff by William Shaw, Esquire, his attorney & the Defendant by Peter Carnes his attorney and upon the Court hearing the allegations of each party & after mature consideration, consideration confirmed the judgment which was for ₤ 4 s 1 d 10 & costs of suit.

The Jurors for the Grand inquest of the Body of Spartanburgh, make the following Presents.

The State against Elizabeth Trammell. Indictment. A true Bill.

The State against William Patterson. Petty Larceny. A true Bill.

The State against John Whittemore. Petty Larceny. A true Bill.

The State against John White. Indictment on assault & Battery. A true Bill.

The State against William Reynolds. Petty Larceny. No Bill.
       Andrew Barry, Foreman.

Ordered that the Defendants be taken into custody by the Sheriff.

Henry Hoof as a witness in behalf of the State against John Doutey on oath was allowed s 12 d 6 for 5 days attendance & s 33 d 4 for milage.

Charles Bruce as an evidence in the Case Richard Harrison Esquire against Bazel Lee on oath was allowed s 20 for 8 days attendance.

Josiah Robertson as a witness in the case Richard Harrison Esq. against Bazel Lee on oath was allowed s 20 for 8 days attendance.

A Presentment of the Grand Jury.
The State against Richard Harrison. Indictment. A True Bill.

Minutes were read & signed by Thomas Farrow, Wm. Smith, David Goodlett, Esqrs. Court then adjourned untill Tomorrow 9 oclock.

Thursday the 19th of March 1789. The Court met according to adjournment. Present William Smith, David Goodlett, & Thomas Farrow, Esquires.

Samuel Jentry against John Chesney. Case.
Ordered, that this suit be dismissed at the Plaintiff's Costs.

Jesse Davis presents a mare raised by Stephen Miller, Ordered that he be allowed s 20 pr. year for 2 years out of the sale of said mare.

Reubin Dickson being bound for the appearance of Michael Hogan to answer to a Bill of Indictment prefered against him by the Grand Jury & the said Hogan failing to appear, It was thereupon ordered by the Court, that the Recognizance be forfeited & that the legal steps of the law be taken against the said Dickson.

Benjamine Wofford against John Farrow. Debt. Ordered, that this case be continued by consent of the parties & that the evidence of Landon Farrow be taken debeniesse in writing.

Ordered that the Treasurer pay the High sheriff of this County, the sum of ₤ 5 s 12 d 8 for removing McMeekin Hunt & John Wade from the Goal of this County to the District Goal at Cambridge & for his extingent expenses thereon.

On motion of Joseph Howell as a witness in the case the State against James McElheny on oath was allowed s 10 for 4 days attendance & s 3 d 4 for milage from Greenville County.

The State against Elizabeth Trammell. Indictment. Came Thos. P. Carnes, Esquires, attorney in behalf of the State and the defendant by Zachariah Toliaferro her attorney, and also came a Jury (the same as before)...We do not find the Defendant Guilty.
John Smith, foreman.

Ordered, that Charles Bruce serve as a Constable for this County, and that he qualify accordingly, which he did in open Court.

Ebenezer Morse having obtained judgment against Thomas Tod, Ordered that execution be stayed untill next Court. Present Justices Richard Harrison, William Smith & William McDowell, Esquires.

Jonathan Harriss against Ralph Cobb. Petition. Settled at the Plaintiff's Costs.

William Grant as a witness in the case Richard Harrison Esquire against Bazel Lee on oath was allowed Ł 1 s 6 d 8 for 6 days attendance & milage.

James Wofford against John Collins. Trover. By consent of the parties & assent of the Court the trial of this cause is continued untill next Court.

The State against William Trammell. Indictment. Thos P. Carnes Esquire County attorney came in behalf of the State and the defendant by Peter Carnes his attorney, whereupon came a Jury (same as before)..."Not Guilty."

Henry Conner as a witness in behalf of the State against William Trimmall on oath was allowed s 13 d 4 in the case the State against Elizabeth Trammall, likewise s 13 d 4 in the case the State against James McElheny.

Thomas Brooks against Moses Wood. Trover. On motion of Thomas P. Carnes attorney for the Defendant, Ordered that a Dedimus potestatum issue to three Justices in the State of Georgia, Wilks County (there to examine General Elijah Clerk) directed to John King, Henry Monger & Sidner Cosby, Esquires or any two of them; said witness to be examined in behalf of the Defendant he giving 10 days notice of time & place of Examination to the Plaintiff.

William Venible against Isham Saffold. Case. By consent of the parties and assent of the Court, the trial of this cause is continued untill next Court.

The State against Richard Harrison Esquire. Indictment. Came Thomas P. Carnes in behalf of the State & the Defendant by William Shaw, Esquire his attorney, who confessed the assault & submitted himself...the Defendant pay the fine of Ł 1 s 1 d 9 & be acquitted.

Andrew Paul against William Poole. Case.
Same against Same. Special action on the case.
By agreement of the parties. Ordered that the above two cases be refered to the arbitrament of William Smith, Esquire, Joseph Barnett & Henry McCray, Gentlemen arbitrators and their award

returned to next Court shall be a rule thereof.

Bazel Lee came into Court and proved 7 days attendance as a witness in the case State against Richard Harrison, Esquire amounting to s 17 d 6.

On motion of William Grant as a witness in a case the State against Richard Harrison Esquire on oath was allowed s 22 d 6 for 9 days attendance also s 5 d 8 for milage.

The State against John Whittemore. Trespass. Thos P. Carnes Esquire came in behalf of the State and the defendant came by Peter Carnes his attorney, whereupon came also a Jury, to wit, (same as before)..."We find the Defendant not Guilty"....

The State against William Patterson. Indictment. The Defendant, & Jonathan Harriss his surety came into Court & acknowledged themselves indebted to the State the sum of ₤ 25 each for the personal appearance of the Defendant at our next Court to answer to said Indictment.   Wm. Lancaster, D. C.

The State against John White. Indictment on assault & Battery. The Defendant by Peter Carnes his attorney came into Court & confessed the assault & Battery, & submitted himself to the mercy of the Court, whereupon it is ordered that the said Defendant pay the fine of s 5 & costs of said Indictment....

Ordered that the mark of Thomas Collins be entered on record, to wit, a crop in the right ear & a upper half crop in the left.

Ordered that Thomas Hayes be allowed s 4 d 8 for wintering an estray yearling & cost be paid out of the sale of the same.

Ordered that John Collin's mark be recorded, which is a upper half crop in the right ear & a crop in the left.

Ordered that the sheriff put in the hands of the County attorney all notes due, on account of estrays, and that he commence suit thereon.

Ordered that Henry McCray have license to sell spiritous liquors upon his giving James Wofford & Benjamine Wofford his sureties for his lawful Performance.

Ordered that a scire facias issue to summon the defaulters in appearing as Grand and Pettit Jurors to show cause if any they have, why they did not appear.

Minutes were read & signed by William Smith, Thomas Farrow, & David Goodlett, Esquires. Court then adjourned untill Court in Course.

END OF VOLUME.

VOLUME 1789-1794

At a County Court began and Held for the County of Spartanburgh on the third Monday in June 1789. Present Justices Baylis Earle, Richard Harrison, William Smith, David Goodlett, William McDowell, Obadiah Trimmier, Zadock Ford, James Jordan & Thomas Farrow Esquires.

John McElheny against John Gowen. Case. The Parties came into Court and prayed dismission of this action, therefore its Ordered that the said action discontinue, each paying their own costs, and the Execution be not issued untill next Court.

Andrew Barry being nomination by the Legislature as a Justice for this County, according to Law, came into Court & took the oath of office accordingly.

A Bill of Sale from Joseph Buffington to Caroline Matilda Buffington, was presented to the Court to be recorded, Ordered that the said bill of sale be recorded accordingly.

Bazel Lee against Benjamine Few. Petition & Summons. Ordered that a Dedimus Potestatum issue to Two Justices of the County of Richmond in the State of Georgia to Examin any Witnesses that may be brought before them touching the above case.

Ordered that Obadiah Watson serve as Constable for this County upon his taking the necessary oath of office, which he accordingly did in open Court.

William Barton being appointed by the Court to act as Constable for this County came into Court and took the necessary oath of office accordingly.

A Bill of sale from John Saunders to Jordan Gibson being proved in open Court by the evidence of Henry Gibson was thereupon ordered to be recorded.

A Bill of Sale from Joshua Hawkins to Rowland Johson(sic) being Proven in open Court by the evidence of John Walker was thereupon ordered to be recorded.

Jeremiah Fowler and wife against Samuel Farrow Esquire. Trover By request of the Parties, its Ordered that this case be refered to the arbitrament of Col. John Thomas Junr, William Benson Esqr., & Mr. Charles Bruce; Their award made & returned the second or Third day of next, shall be a Judgment thereof.

Jordan Gibson against John Sanders. Attachment. James Terrill came into Court and Entered himself special Bail for the delivery of the Property attached at next Court.

The sheriff having levyed an Execution on Property supposed to be James Wards, at the Instance of Jesse Davis, But a Daughter of the said Ward laying claim to part of said property Executed, to wit, a Cow & it appearing to the Court that she had a right to the same, Ordered that the Cow be given up by the Sheriff to the Daughter of the said Ward.

The Court proceeded to Elect a Sheriff to succeed the Preceeding one, to wit, Samuel Farrow Esquire, and upon casting up the votes it appeared that William Benson Esquire was duly Elected; Ordered the the Clerk give him a Certificate of the same.

The minutes were read and signed by Baylis Earle, Wm. McDowell & James Jordan, Esquires. Court then adjourned untill tomorrow 9 O'Clock.

Tuesday the 16th of June 1789. The worshipful court met according to last evenings adjournment. Present Justices Baylis Earle, Richard Harrison, James Jordan, David Goodlett, William McDowell, Obadiah Trimmier, William Smith and Samuel Lancaster.

William Blackstock against William Smith Esquire. Trover. This case being heretofore refered to the arbitrament of John Blasingame & John Martindale, who award that the suit discontinue at the Plaintiff's Costs.

William Lipscomb against Joseph Buffington. Debt. Ordered that Judgment be entered up against the Sheriff in this case as heretofore against the defendant, with stay of Execution for 3 months.

Ordered that a road be opened from the Boiling Spring, the nearest and best way to this Court house, & William Wood Junr mark and lay out said Road, and that John Childs oversee & keep in good repair the same.

Ordered that all the money arising from the sale of Estrays, be paid to Richard Harrison Esquire untill the balance due him for Public Buildings be discharged.

Robert Goodgion against Israel Morriss. Debt.
Israel Morriss against Robert Goodgion. Debt.
Agreeable to an order of the Court of Spartanburgh, we the arbitrators Isham Foster, William Benson and James Jordan hath arbitrated all disputes between Robert Goodgion Plaintiff and Israel Morriss Defendant, and Israel Morriss Plaintff & Robert Goodgion Defendant now depending in the said Court, and all other disputes Do adjudge that the said Morriss pay the said Goodgion ℔ 46 s 13 & /4 with Lawful interest to wit, ℔ 30 from Feb. 2 1788 and ℔ 16 s 14 & /4 from Dec. 1788 and all costs.
We the arbitrators having some time past returned our award, in which we omitted, altho' we intended to make it appear all the disputes between the parties were comprehended, we do now certify they were.

Ordered, that John Gibbs cease in his office as Constable, and act no more only to sell the Property now Executed by him, and make due return of his proceedings.

Ordered that John Young and William McMillan oversee a road from Charles McKnights to Wadsworth old store, in the room of Hugh Freeman.

Ordered that Baylis Earle Esquire be allowed the sum of s 40 for keeping a stray Horse.

The State by James Terrill against William Hewitt. Indictment for assault. The defendant came into court with John Hewitt as his Surity, and acknowledged themselves to owe this County ℔ 50 on condition that the said William Hewitt do not personally appear at the next Court, to answer an assault and battery on Capt. James Terrill. John Thomas Junr. C. C.

The State against John Hewitt. Indictment Insulting Justices. The defendant came into Court and acknowledged his fault and prayed mercy. The Court therefore dismissed him on paying fees.

Ordered that two of the Prisoners now in Goal, to wit, William McElheny and David Trammall, be given into the Custody of the Sheriff, to be conveyed to North Carolina, and that he summon a sufficient guard to convey them to Lincoln Goal in order to be imprisoned in the Goal of the County or District where they committed the Felony and that Mr. James Conner the Gentleman whose store was robbed (as it is said) by the said prisoners give a Bond of ₤ 500 to prosecute the said prisoners: to take the legal methods to cause his Brother Henry to appear against them as an evidence, & also others from this State & further that the officer be directed to take a Receipt of the Delivery of said prisoners.

Ordered that Judgment be entered up against the absent Debtor, and that 200 A of land be bound in the hands of Thomas Farrar Esquire & that the said Farrar is to shew the land, Identify it, and make Titles agreeable to Law. Further that the property now under Execution belonging to said Farrar be released from the embarrassment.

A receipt from William Floyd to Thomas Farrar Esquire acknowledged in open Court. Ordered to be recorded.
Viz. Received of Thomas Farrar ₤ 70 sterling agreeable to the award of John Golightly, Charles Bruce, John Thomas Junr., David Goodlett & Isham Foster umpire, also ₤ 5 towards the cost of suit (except the cost of suit) it being the full consideration of all Debts dues and Demands from the Beginning of the world to this day dec'd. this 16 June 1789. William Floyd. Test Isham Foster.

Court of Ordinary the 16th of June 1789.

Ordered that William Prince admr. upon the Estate of Philip Ford decd., do immediately give into the Clerks office of this Court Bond of ₤ 1000 with two good & sufficient surities for his Just and Lawful admn, as the said Prince is about to leave the State And on refusal of so doing that an attachment issue from any Justice of this Court to detain the said Estate untill such surity is Given.

Ordered that a Horse & all that went with him at the time of the imprisonment of William McElheny which was his property, now in the hands of John Collins be given to the Sheriff to remove the said McElheny to North Carolina, and to discharge the expences of the imprisonment of said McElheny. And Further that the said John Collins be allowed s 25 out of the price of the Horse when sold for keeping said Horse.

The Commissioners appointed to examine the Records of this County, to wit, Samuel Lancaster and David Goodlett Esquires, have reported to the Court accordingly, & given in the paper, which is ordered to be filed the Clerks office.

Ordered that Thomas Williamson make Lawful titles to the two acres of Land laid out for the Public use, and that he acknowledged the same at next Court.

The minutes were read and Signed by Baylis Earle, Richard Harrison, David Goodlett, Esquires. Court then adjourned untill Court in Course.

At a County Court began and held at the Court House for Spartanburgh County on the third Monday in September A. D. 1789. Present Justices Baylis Earle, Richard Harrison, William Smith, James Jordan, William McDowell, Thomas Farrow, Andrew Barry & David

Goodlett Esquires.

Pettit Jurors drawn to serve next December Court, to wit, John Ford Junr., Reuben Newman, John Colwall, Thomas Miles, Stephen Philips, Handcock Smith, Robert Milikan Junr., Jason Moore, Stephen Cruce, James Head, Hugh McKein, William Colwall, Ephraim Elder, Samuel Thomson, John Brown, Benjamin Busey, Charles Bragg, William Waldrope, James Patterson, Andrew Colley, Jacob Pennington, William Harriss, Benjamine Spencer, William Lockart, Ellis Johnson, Samuel Snoddy, John Pipes, Randolph Johnson, Christopher Clerke, John Beardan, Junr.

William Benson Esquire produced his commission as Sheriff for this County, came into Court and took the necessary oath of office accordingly.

Ordered that Thomas Bennett, John Young & Joseph Venible view the two roads laid out from the mill of William McDowell Esquire to this Court House, and make a return thereof at our next Court which is the most suitable to be kept in repair.

William Tate being noted to attend as a grand Juror, came into Court and rendered an excuse, upon which the Court thought fit to exempt him from serving this term.

The State against Robert Roberts, William Roberts & Thomas Roberts. Assault and Battery.
On motion of the County Attorney stating that William Roberts & Thomas Roberts were taken and recognized to appear this Court to answer the above charge & that Robert Roberts is returned not to be found.

Ordered that a Bench warrant issue to apprehend the said Robert Roberts and have him before this or the next Court with full power and authority to summon so many Persons as the officer may think proper for apprehending him.

Ordered that John Foster oversee the Road that John Timmons formerly did.

Ordered that the appearance docket be called over the first time which was accordingly done.

Thomas Colhoun against Benjamine Wofford. Trespass. Ordered that the case be dismissed at the Palintiffs costs, the Defendants attorney fee excepted.

William Patterson against John White & Jeremiah Dickson. Assault. Ordered that this case discontinue at mutual costs.

Ephraim Ramsey Esquire admitted as an Attorney at Law and equity in this Court.

The last will and Testament of Henry Hargrove deceased proved in open Court by the evidence of William Hammett & William Thomson Ordered to be recorded.

A Deed from Elias Legate to John Cobb acknowledged in open court by said Legate. Ordered to be recorded.

Another deed of conveyeance from Elias Legate to John Cobb, acknowledged in open Court by said Legate. Ordered to be recorded.

James Allison as a witness in the case Thomas Calhoun against Benjamine Wofford on oath was allowed s 27 d 6 for 11 days attendance and s 26 d 8 for mileage from Laurens County.

David Lewis against Charles Bruce. Appeal from the Judgement of Squire Goodlett. The Plaintiffs property being advertised for sale by virtue of an Execution. Ordered that the sale of the same be Postponed untill To morrow two O'Clock, for a proper investigation of the matter.

A Deed of Conveyance from Thomas Farrow Esquire by virtue of his office of Sheriffatty for the District of Ninety Six, to himself as an individual, Ordered to be recorded.

The minutes were read and signed by R. Harrison, Thomas Farrow, & David Goodlett, Esquires. Court then adjourned untill To morrow Eight O'Clock.

Tuesday the 22nd day of September 1789. Court met according to last evenings adjournment. Present Baylis Earle, Samuel Lancaster & Thomas Farrow esquires.

John Lindsey against Vardry McBee & William Tate. Debt. The Defendants came into Court and confessed Judgment according to Specialty, The debt being for 6000 wieght of Tobacco delivered at the Congaree Ware-House, at s 18 d 8 P. Centum; Due the 21 Dec 1787, whereupon it is considered by the court, that the Plaintiff recover against the said Defendants ₺ 56 sterling with Interest thereon untill paid, besides his costs...

The State against Rebekah Sullivan. Bastardy. The Defendant came into open court and made oath that the child unlawfully Begotten of her body was got by John Hembry and to the best of her knowledge and belief on the 4th of Dec. 1788. Ordered that she be fined ₺ 5 proclamation money, defering execution nine months on her giving surety for the payment thereof.

Present James Jordan, William Smith & David Goodlett Esquires.

Rebecca Sullivan as principle, and Abraham Fowler & Ezekiel Sullivan her surities came into Court and acknowledged to owe to the State ₺ 5 proc. money as aforesaid, for a fine imposed upon said Rebekah for Bastardy.

David Lewis against Charles Bruce. Appeal from the Judgment of Squire Goodlett came the plaintiff by Ephraim Ramsey Esquire his Attorney and the Defendant by Charles Goodwin Gentleman his attorney and upon proper investigation of the matter. Ordered that the Judgment be revised and that the defendant pay all costs thereby accrued.

William Smith against Joseph Warren. Case. The Parties prayed this case to be refered to the arbitrament of Jonathan Law, Leonard Adcock & Ralph Cobb. Ordered, that the award of said arbitrators returned to next Court, be the judgment thereof.

Present Zadock Ford, Esquire.

A Deed of conveyance from Nowel Johnson and wife to John Nelson acknowledged in open Court by said Johnson. Ordered to be recorded.

Philip Tipping against Nicholas Holley. Petition. Ordered that the Deposition of George Burton Junior be taken Debeniesse in writing by some Justice; and that George Bruton Senior cross examine him in behalf of the Defendant.

A Deed of conveyance from Samuel Miller to James Jordan Esquire acknowledged in open Court by said Miller. Ordered to be recorded.

Joseph Erwin against John Naile. Petition. The Sheriff having returned the writ nonest, the Plaintiff by his attorney prayed a dismission, and that an alias issue, which was accordingly done.

James McGowen attorney for Erwin against John Naile. Petition. The Sheriff returning the writ nonest, the plaintiff by his attorney motioned for a Dismission, & that an alias issue, which accordingly granted by the Court.

Henry Hayes against Mary Wood. Case. By consent of the parties ordered that the deposition of Mary Buffington, George Salmon, Martin Armstrong, Moses Wood, & John McElheny be taken Debeniesse in writing to be read as evidence on trial.

The grand Inquest to wit, William Lipscomb, John Harriss, David McDowell, John Young, Samuel Neasbitt, William Hamby, Thomas Wyatt, Thomas Williamson, Joseph Barnett, Martin Armstrong, Charles Hester, Jesse Connell, Thomas Milikin & Stephen Wilson make the following persentments.

The State against Michael McGaughey & John McGaughey. Petty Larceny. A true Bill.

The State against John Roebuck & John Chumler. Petty Larceny. A True Bill.

The State against William Hewitt. Assault. A true Bill.

The State against Thomas Gordon. Assault. a true Bill.

The State against William Roberts & Thomas Roberts. Assault. a True Bill.

The State against John Whittemore. Trespass. A true Bill.
       William Lipscomb, Foreman.

The minutes were read and signed by William Smith, Thomas Farrow & William McDowell, Esquires. Court then adjourned untill tomorrow nine O'Clock.

Wednesday the 23d of September 1789. Court met according to last evening adjournment. Present Richard Harrison, Thomas Farrow, Samuel Lancaster, William McDowell & David Goodlettt Esquires.

Ordered that the Sheriff make proclamation that the Court is now setting as a Court of Ordinary, which was accordingly done.

On motion of Sarah Boid for administration on the estate of John Boid Deceased, Ordered that she have letters accordingly, upon her giving John Camp and James Wofford surities for her lawful administration, which was accordingly done.

Court set as a Court of Common pleas.

Ordered, that Thomas Williamson have licence to keep a Public House of Entertainment, upon his giving approved surities for his lawful performances.

The State against John Roebuck & John Chumler. Indictment for Petty Larceny. The defendants came into court and acknowledged themselves to owe to the State ₺ 20 each and William Bracher and Joseph Power as their Surities, acknowledged to owe to the State ₺ 10 each provided the said defendants shall not personally appear at next Court, and abide by the Judgment thereof on said Indictment.

Ordered that James Miller serve as a Constable for this County upon his taking the necessary oath of office, which he accordingly did in open Court.

Thomas Gordon against Ralph Cobb. Assault. By consent of the parties, and assent of the Court, this suit is discontinued at the Plaintiffs Costs.

Ralph Cobb against Thomas Gordon. Slander. Dismissed at the Plaintiffs Costs.

Pettit Jurors to serve this Term to wit, Isaac Hamby, Richard Barry, Samuel Smith, Littleton Mapp Junr., Joseph Powers, Charles Carter, Solomon Crocker, Anthony Coulter, William Earnest, Thomas Shurley, William Ford & Rowland Johnson.

The State against John Whittemore. Trespass. Came Thomas P. Carnes in behalf of the State and the defend. by his Councellers also a Jury to wit (jury listed above)...Guilty. William Ford, foreman.

The State against Polley Burk. Bastardy. On motion of the Defen= dant by Ephraim Ramsey Esquire her Attorney stating that she never had a Bastard Child and there being no informed mentioned by the Grand Jury in their presentment, Ordered that she be discharged.

The State against Polley McBee. Bastardy. On motion of Ephraim Ramsey Esquire, Attorney for the Defendant, stating that she never had a bastard Child, and there being no informed mentioned by the Grand Jury in their presentment, Ordered that she be acquitted.

A Deed of Conveyance from William McDowell to William Pool J. M. acknowledged in open Court by said McDowell Ordered to be recorded.

Sarah Boid came into Court and acknowledged a power of attorney from herself to Benjamine Wofford, Ordered to be recorded.

Ordered that William Wofford be taken into Custody by the Sheriff untill he gives good and sufficient common bail for his appearance to answer to an action brought by David Golightly against him.

The State against William Roberts & Thomas Roberts. Indictment. William Allen bail for the appearance of Thomas Roberts surrendered him up to the Court, whereupon said Allen is discharged from his surityship. and Robert Robert had came into Court and acknowledged to owe to the State the sum of ₺ 10 provided the said Thomas Roberts does not appear to this Court when called upon to answer and abide by the Judgment of the Court, on said Indictment.

The State against Michael McGaughey & John McGaughey. Petty Larceny. Came Thos. P. Carnes Esquire in behalf of the State and the defendants by their counciling Gentlemen, whereupon came a jury (same as before)..."The Defendants are Guilty."
William Ford, foreman.
The Court therefore ordered that Michael McGaughey receive twenty five lashes on the bare back, and that John McGaughey receive ten lashes on his bare back, by the sheriff at the Common whipping post, between this time and sunset.

The State against John Whittemore. Trespass. John Williams came into court and acknowledged to owe to the State Ł10 if the Defendant does not appear at this Court tomorrow morning in his proper person to abide by the Judgment thereof.

The Grand Inquest for this County make the following Presentment, to wit,

The State against Daniel Stephens. Petty Larceny. No bill.

The State against Matthew Landers. Indictment for Assault and Battery. A true Bill.

We David McDowell and Thomas Bennett appointed to value and appraise a bridge built over SouthPackolate River, do appraise the same at Ł 5 s 10 sterling done 26th Oct 1788 by me
David McDowell
Thomas Bennett

Ordered that the said sum be paid to Baylis Earle Esquire for that purpose.

Ordered, that John Moore and Henry Young warn the men to work on the Road from the Bridge of South Packolate to the North Carolina line under the directed of Thomas Jackson who is the overseer of the same; and that the orders issue immediately to said Jackson and that Matthew Alexander, Ephraim Lewis and Robert Harper have orders also, as they appear not to have issued.

Daniel Joslin against John Hewitt. Case. Ordered that this suit discontinue at the Defendants costs.

On motion of Nathan Neasbitt as a witness in the case Jonathan Neasbitt against Thomas Daugherty and Arias Brown on oath was allowed s 12 d 6 for 5 days attendance.

Ordered that the clerk issue the orders to Benjamine Beason as an overseer of a road, as they appear not to have issued.

Edward Arnold as a witness in the case Thomas Hamilton and Temperance Hamilton against Benjamine Wofford on oath in open Court, was allowed s 27 d 6 for 11 days attendance.

Martin Armstrong against Benjamine Davis. Attachment. Dismissed at the Plaintiffs costs.

Spartanburgh County against Thomas Crowther & John Kimbell. Petition. Ordered, that this case continue untill next Court.

Jane Lowry, came into Court on a charge of Bastardy. She says she is a married woman, and no informer appearing, Ordered that she be acquitted.

Samuel Neasbitt against John Earle. attachemtn. The constable returned "I have sold a Horse of the property of the Defendant for seven pounds ten shillings." William Fields Consta.

Ordered that the road go round the plantation of Charles Bruce, instead of going through.

John Garner as a evidence in the case Andrew Paul against William Pool, on oath in open Court was allowed s 22 d 6 for 9 days attendance.

Hugh Pierce against Thomas Gordon. Attachment. John White came into court and acknolwedged to owe to Hugh Pierce L 23 s 10 if the defendant does not produce the property attached or other property attached or other property sufficient to be exposed to sale to satisfy said attachment' if so ordered by the Court.

Ordered, that the minutes be read, which was accordingly done, and signed by Baylis Earle, James Jordan, Richd. Harrison, William Smith & Thomas Farrow, Esquires.

Court then adjourned untill tomorrow Nine O'Clock.

Thursday the 24th of September 1789 Court met according to last evening adjournment. Present, Justices William Smith, Samuel Lancaster, Thomas Farrow Esquires.

Ordered, that the sheriff make proclamation, that the Court is now setting as a Court of Ordinary, which was accordingly done.

Ordered that William Roberts and Martha his wife late widow of Michael Sprinkle deceased, have the power of administration on the estate of the said Deceased, upon their giving bond and approved surities for the same.

The Court resolved themselves into a court of common pleas. Ordered that Charles Bruce be allowed L 1 s 3 d 4 for making two Goal doors and that he be paid the same out of the County fund.

Ordered that the sheriff be allowed the sum of L 6 s 8 d 6 for the contingent expences accrued by sundry Prisoners in Goal.

Present Baylis Earle Esquire.

John Henderson Esquire against Nathaniel Burton and Charles Burton Attachment. Ordered that this suit discontinued at the Plaintiffs cost and that the attachment bond be given up, which was agreeable to the parties and was accordingly done.

The State against William Roberts & Thomas Roberts. Indictment for assault. Came Thos. P. Carnes Esquire in behalf of the State and the Defendants by their Councellers, whereupon came a Jury (same as before)..."the Defendants are not Guilty." William Ford, foreman.

Joseph Adair against John Serrart. Petition. Ordered, that a Dedimus potestatum issue to Thomas Bush Esquire and two others Justices of the peace in the State of Georgia Green County to Examine Thomas Bonner on the behalf of the Defendant upon his giving ten days notice to the adverse party of the time and place of examination.

On motion of George Walker Esquire attorney for Whittemore, urging for a new trial in the case of yesterday, the State against said Whittemore in trespass. Ordered that a new trial be granted next Court on said Whittemores giving surity for his personal appearance at said term and also that the evidences be summoned to attend at the same time.

John Camp against John Chism. Petition. Continued by consent of the parties.

John Camp against John Chism. Trespass. Continued by consent of the parties untill next Court.

John Camp against John Chism. Case. Continued untill next Court by consent of the Parties.

The State against Thomas Gordon. Indictment for assault. Came the plaintiff by Thos. P. Carnes County attorney & the defendant by his Counsellors whereupon came a Jury (same as before)... "Guilty." William Ford, foreman. The Defendant by his attorney, prayed a new trial which was granted.

James Barron against John Moore. Debt. Nonsuit.

Ordered that s 13 d 4 be paid to Zilpah Trammall wife of William Trammall which was heretofore ordered to Henry Conner for his attendance as a witness in an Indictment prefered against said William Trammall.

Ordered that Baylis Earle Esquire be allowed s 10 for 4 days attenacen as a witness in the case James Barron against John Moore.

Israel Morriss against Rowland Cornelius. Case. Nonsuit.

John Milikin against John, Thomas & Nathaniel Carrells. Nonsuit.

Dudly Red against Holland Sumner. Attachment. By consent of the parties and assent of the Court the trial of this cause is defered untill next Court.

Thomas Blasingame against Holland Turner. Attachment. By consent of the parties and assent of the Court, the trial of this cause is defered untill next Court.

Stephen Williford against William Wood. Mallicious Prosecution. Nonsuit.

James Clerke against George Pettus. Case. Ordered, that this case discontinue at the Plaintiffs costs.

The State against John Whittemore. Recognizance. The Defendant came into Court and acknowledged to owe to the State ₤ 20 and John Williams and Michael B. Roberts as his surities, ₤ 10 each for the personal appearance of the said Whittemore at next Court to abide by the Judgment thereof on said Indictment.

On motion of Isham Foster and Rowland Cornelius Junior as witnesses in the case Israel Morriss against Rowland Cornelius Senior on their respective oaths were allowed to wit, said Johnson ₤ 1 s 10 for 12 days attendance and said Cornelius ₤1 s 5 for 10 days attendance.

John Ward against Thomas Hamilton. Trover. Ordered that a Dedimus Potestatum issue to take the affidavit of John Timmons debeniessee in wirting as he is not able to attend Court at this time and he being a material witness in said case to be read and admitted on trial Provided he should not be able to attend at that time.

The State against William Hewitt. Indictment for assault & Battery. The defendant came into Court and confessed the charge laid against him in the indictment, Whereupon it is considered by the Court that he be fined s 5 and is acquitted upon paying all costs accrued thereon.

Matthew Landers, you acknowledge to owe the State Ł 20; Charles Bruce & William Roberts, each Ł 10 to be leveyed upon your several goods and Chattles Land and tenements by way of recognizance to the States use, upon condition that if you Matthew Landers be and ppear to the next Court....

Philip Tipping against Nicholas Holley. Petition. Came the Plaintiff by THos. P. Carnes Esquire his attorney and the Defendant by William Shaw Gentleman his attorney, and upon a proper in vestigation of the matter, and upon a mature consideration by the Court Ordered that the Plaintiff recover against the Defendant the sum of Ł 10 sterling besides his costs....

The State against William Patterson. Petty Larceny. The Court ordered the County attorney to discontinue this cause, upon the defendant paying all costs accrued thereon, and then be acquitted.

William Moore as a witness in the case Philip Tippings against Nicholas Holley on oath in open Court was allowed s 7 d 6 for 3 days attendance.

Jeremiah Fowler and wife against Samuel Farrow Esquire. Trover. By consent of the parties and assent of the court the trial of this cause is refered to the arbitrament of Thomas Farrow, William Benson, and David Goodlett Esquire, Gentlemen arbitrators. Ordered that their award returned into Court tomorrow morning be a Judgment thereof.

Jacob Bowen and Robert Parker against Carlton Lindsey. Appeal from a Justice below. Came the plaintiffs by William Shaw Esq. his attorney and the Defendant by George Walker Gentl. his attorney, and after a proper investigation of the matter, Ordered that the Judgement be confirmed and that the appelle recover against the appealants Ł 5 besides his costs....

Joshua Lindsey upon oath in open Court was allowed Ł 1 s 10 for his attendance as a witness in the case Robert Parker against Lindsey.

Ordered that a small roan mare tolld before Obadiah Trimmier Esq. be delivered to Mrs. Wilson upon her Proving the property which she accordingly did in open Court.

Ordered that the minutes be read, which was accordingly done and signed by Baylis Earle, Richd. Harrison, Thomas Farrow, Esquires. Court adjourned untill Tomorrow Nine O'Clock.

Friday the 25th of September 1789. The Court met according to appointment. Present Baylis Earle, William Smith, Thomas Farrow & David Goodlett Esquires. The Court resolved itself into a

Court of Ordinary.

Ordered that John Thomas Junior have admn. upon the Estate of Charles Smith deceased, he giving the Security required by law.

Court set as a Court of Common Pleas.

County Treasurer against Matthew Guttery. Petition. The Defendant came into Court in his own proper person, and confessed Judgment for ₤ 2 s 9 d 4 according to Specialty, and prayed the stay of Execution untill next Court which was accordingly granted.

Jeremiah Fowler and wife against Samuel Farrow Esquire. Trover. In persuance of an order of Court to us directed we William Benson, Thomas Farrow & David Goodlett in obedience thereto having examined all matters in Dispute between the said parties do award that all suits and quarrells between them shall cease, and that the said Jeremiah Fowler pay the costs of suit. Given under our hands and seals the 24th Sept 1789. William Benson, Thomas Farrar, David Goodlett, Arbitrators.

On motion of Benjamine Tilman by his attorney, to review the order and record in the case of an Indictment the State against Benjamin Tilman, tryed at March term 1787. The Court came to the following Resolution: That it was their oppinion and the oppinion of the Jury who tried the Indictment, That he only committed a trespass and that the Records meaned nothing more.

Martin Armstrong against John & Rebekah Earle, Admr..& Admx. of Wood. Came the Plaintiff by Charles Goodwin Esquire his Attorney and the defendants by their Gentlemen Attornies: and after hearing the allegations of the parties it is considered by the Court that the Defendants had lawfully administered upon the estate of the deceased, therefore ordered that the suit be discontinued at the Plaintiffs costs.

Vardry McBee against George Taylor. Slander. On motion Charles Goodwin Esquire Attorney for the Defendant, Ordered that this action be dismissed at the Plaintiffs cost.

George Taylor against Vardry McBee and wife. Slander. On motion of William Shaw Esquire, attorney for the Defendants Ordered that this suit discontinue at the Plaintiffs Cost.

George Haning against John Steen. Case. On motion of William Shaw Esquire Attorney for the Defendant Ordered this suit be discontinued at the plaintiffs cost.

Francis Amos against William Fields. Assault. Ordered that this case be dismissed at the Defendants Cost.

David Golightly Executor of William Golightly Decd. against William Wofford. Case. By consent of the Parties, Ordered that this suit be dismissed at mutual costs.

William D. Thomas & Candace Jones Admr. & Admx. of Jos. Jones against William Ford. Case. On motion of Thomas P. Carnes, attorney for the Defendant, this suit is dismissed at the Plaintiffs cost.

On application of Vardry McBee, stating that the saddle sold to defray the expence of the imprisonment of William McElheny and bought by Thomas Williamson on oath of the said McBee that is was his property   Ordered by the Court, that said Williamson give up the said saddle to said McBee, and be allowed the sum of s12 in lue thereof.

George Taylor against Rhoda McBee. Slander. On motion of William Shaw Esquire, gentleman attorney for the Defendant Ordered that this suit be discontinued at the plaintiffs cost.

Rowland Johnson as a witness in the case William D. Thomas against William Ford, on oath was allowed s 12 d 6 for 5 days attendance.

Charles Miles against Vardry McBee.   Trover   Nonsuit

On motion of Benjamine Jones as a witness in the case Charles Miles against Vardry McBee, on oath of said Jones he is allowed Ł 1 s 5 for 10 days attendance, and s 33 d 6 for mileage.

John Russell against Henry Prince. Case. Came the Plaintiff by William Shaw Esquire his attorney, and the defendant by Ephraim Ramsey Gentleman his attorney, Whereupon came a Jury, to wit, Isaac Hamby, Richard Barry, Samuel Smith, Littleton Mapp Junior, James Powers, Charles Carter, Solomon Crocker, Anthony Coulter, William Earnest, Thomas Shurley, William Ford & Rowland Johnson and after being sworn well and truly to try this issue, joined on their respective oaths do say "We find for the Defendant"
                                        William Ford, foreman

Ann Dewberry against William Giber. Attachment. By consent of the parties and assent of the Court, the trial of this cause, is continued untill next Court.

Court adjourned for 20 minutes. Friday afternoon the 25 of September 1789. The court met according to adjournment.

James Chastain, on oath in open court, is allowed Ł 3 s 7 d 6 for 27 days attendance and Ł 1 s 3 d 4 for mileage as a witness in the case John Russel against Henry Prince.

Also Thomas Benson is allowed on oath, s 10 for 4 days attendance and Ł 1 for mileage as a witness Russel against Prince.

The State against Thomas Gordon. Indictment. The Jury finding the defendant guilty Ordered by the Court that he be fined s 5 pay all costs thereon, and be acquitted.

The presentments of the Grand Inquest for the body of Spartanburgh County to wit,

We the grand Jury for the County of Spartanburgh Present to the Court the following grievances, which we consider proper for the Courts attention.

First, we present Elizabeth Graham for Bastardy, living near the Paccolate Springs from the information of William Pool H. S.

Secondly, We present Hugh Pierce for living a Disorderly life with the said Widow Graham and that by their means the Estate of the orphans is wasted And that he the said Pierce lived an Idle dilatory life

Thirdly, We present Ann Carter for Bastardy at the Information of Michael B. Roberts.

Fourthly, we consider it as a grievance that the Road leading from Spartanburgh Court House towards the Cherokee ford on Broad River as far as the County line is much neglected and Desires it may be opened or kept in good repair so that waggons may conveniently & safely pass the same.

Fifthly & lastly, we consider it a grievance that the high way from South Tyger to Heads Ford on Enoree is much neglected

Martin Armstrong	William Lipscomb
Jesse Connell	Jonathan Harriss
Thomas Miliken	David McDowall
Stephen Wilson	John Young
Charles Hester	Samuel Neasbitt
Joseph Barnett	Thomas Williamson
Thomas Wyatt	William Hamby

Joseph Buffington Assinee of Thomas Flynn against Maximilian Conner. Petition Nonsuit

Benjamine Wofford against John Farrow. Debt. Came the Plaintiff by Charles Goodwin Esquire his attorney and upon hearing the matter properly investigated whether the Plaintiff had the liberties of the Laws as a Citizen of this State, which was adjudged by the Court, that he had not; Therefore ordered that the Plaintiff take nothing by his bill, but for his false clamour be in mercy, and that the Defendant go hence without delay....

Henry Meredith as a witness in the above case, on oath is allowed £ 1 s 2 d 6 for 13 days attendance

Benjamine Wofford and Burrell Thomson against Henry Meredith. Debt. Came the Plaintiff by George Walker Esquire his attorney and the Defendant by William Shaw Gentl. his attorney
The Court Divided

Thomas Brooks against Moses Wood. Trover. Ordered that a Dedimus issue to Wilks County in Georgia to Henry Morgan & Sydney Cosby Esquires to examine General Clerk also a Dedimus issue to Burk County in George To any two Justices there, to examine Benjamin Brown in the said case, on the behalf of the Defendant Upon his giving regular & Lawful notice of time and place of Examination

Landon Farrow as an evidence in the case Benjamine Wofford against John Farrow on oath in open Court was allowed s 10 for 4 days attendance.

John Couch came into Court and entered himself special bail in the attachment Henry Domini against John Burt Ordered that the property be Delivered up.

Ordered, that the minutes be read which was accordingly done and signed by Richard Harrison, William Smith, David Goodlett, Esqrs. Court then adjourned untill Tomorrow 8 O'Clock.

Saturday the 26th of September 1789. Court met according to adjournment of last evening. Present William Smith, Thomas Farrow, & David Goodlett, Esq.

Samuel Bell against Administrators of Jones. Appeal from a Justice Below. Ordered that this suit be continued untill next Court.

Ordered that John Roebuck be discharged from serving as a constable for this County be reason of several legal allegations brought against him.

Ordered, that a scieri Facias issue against Travice Morse to appear, to our next Court to answer to the alegations laid against him with respect to his office as a constable, and that he be suspended from said Office untill said Term.

Samuel Farrow against John Gowen. Petition. Ordered that this case be dismissed at the Defendants costs.

James Yancey Esquire against Vardry McBee. Petition Nonsuit

Mary Wood Admr. of James Wood against Obadiah Roberts. Petition Dismissed at the Defendants costs

Henry Domini against John Burk. Attachment. Ordered, that this suit be continued untill next Court

Daniel Brown Esquire against Israel Morriss & Moses Wood. Petition. Came the Plaintiff by James Dohertie Esquire his attorney and the Defendant Israel Morriss appearing in his own Proper Person and after hearing the matter controverted...the Plaintiff recover against the Defendant Ł 8 s 11 and costs of suit. Notwithstanding if the said Defendant bring a Horse to next Court sufficient to satisfy the Debt and costs and Deliver the same to Thomas Farrow & William Smith Esquires (in case the Plaintiff should not attend) The same shall discharge the said Debt

A conveyance from Israel Morriss to Samuel Blakely, Proved in open Court by the Evidence of William Lancaster, Ordered to be recorded.

A note of hand from Stephen Miller to Israel Morriss proved in open court by William Shaw Esquires. Ordered to be recorded which is here inserted.
I promise to pay or cause to be paid unto Israel Morris or his assigns the sum of Ł 20 s 15 sterling, paid in produce for value received 17th Feb 1789 on or before the 25th Decm. 1790.
Test   Henry McCray   Stephen Miller.

This assignment not to prejudice sd. Blakely, Judgment against said Israel Morriss.

I assign this note to Samuel Blakely on his order for value
recd.   Israel Morriss
Wit: William Smith, William Shaw

Bazel Lee against Benjamin Few. Petition. On motion of the Plaintiff in his own proper person, and the defendant failing to appear...the Plaintiff recover against the defendant Ł10 Virginia money, which is equal to Ł 7 s 15 d 6½ sterling, with Interest thereon from 11th August 1785 untill paid, besides his cost by him about his suit in this behalf expended....

Henry Wells against William Colwall. petition

Joseph Erwin against John Naile. Petition Dismist at the Plaintiffs costs

John McGowen attorney for Erwin against John Naile. Petition Dismissed at the Plaintiffs costs.

Andrew Mayes against James Smith & William Alldredge. Petition Ordered, that the trial of this cause be defered untill next Court.

Samuel Farrow Esquire in behalf of the County against William Wofford Admr. of William Wofford. Petition. On motion of the Plaintiff, Judgment is entered against the Defendant for ₺ 2 and costs of suit. Thomas P. Carnes Esquire Attorney in behalf of the County.

Samuel Farrow Esquire in behalf of the County against Jesse Davis, Rowland Johnson, Edmund Fowler & Edmund Clemons. Petition On motion of Thomas P. Carnes Esquire Attorney in behalf of the County Judgment is entered against the Defendants for ₺ 6 s 14 d 6 according to specialty, with interest and costs of suit.

Charles Bruce against Robert Armour. Appeal. Came the plaintiff in his own persons & the Defendant by William Shaw Esquire his attorney and after hearing the parties, Ordered that this cause stand over untill next court

Hugh Pierce against Thomas Gordon. Petition. Nonsuit

William Crocker as an evidence in the case Bazel Lee against Benjamine Few, on oath in open Court, is allowed s 15 for 6 days attendance.

William Wier against John Hembree. Attachment. Ordered that a Scieri facias issue against John Hull to shew cause why Judgment not be entered against him for Debt and Costs.

Jordan Gibson against John Sanders. Attachment. Dismist at Plaintiffs Cost, for want of Prosecution.

George Gibson & Lewis Sanders as evidences in the case Jordan Gibson against John Sanders, on oath in open Court was allowed, to wit, the said George s 15 for 6 days attendance and the said Lewis 17/ & d 6 for 7 days attendance, and s 33 d 4 for mileage

William Benson Esquire Present Sheriff for this County appointed of by the Court; And ordered that he take the necessary oath of office which he accordingly did in open Court.

Charles Bruce against Robert Armour. Appeal. By consent of the parties Ordered that this suit be dismissed at the Plaintiffs cost.

Ordered that the minutes be read, which was accordingly done and signed by William Smith, David Goodlett & Thomas Farrow, Esq. Court then adjourned untill Court in Course.

Court of Spartanburgh, Began and held at the Court House on the 21st day of December A. D. 1789. Present Justices William Smith, James Jordan & David Goodlett Esquires.

The Court proceeded to the choice of the Grand Jurors for next term, to wit, Robert Neasbitt, James Head, George Connell, John Brown, Benjamine McMikin, Josiah Tanner, William Elder, Samuel Miller, John Smith F. F., Shands Golightly, John Neasbitt, William Pool H. S., Samuel Jackson Junior, Samuel Morrow, Joel Traylor, John Tollison, Daniel McClary, John Golightly, Aaron Moore & William Pool Bloomer.

Pettit Jurors for next Court, to wit, Henry Muffatt, Timothy Gowney, James Delling, William Moore, John McCarter, Nathan Ward, Thomas McKnight, John McMahan, John Varnan, Thomas Selman, Snoden Prewit, William Shed, Thomas Williams, Spencer Bobo Senr., Ambrose Dollar, John Cannon, James Wood, David Golightly, Ephraim Lewis, Isaac Wofford, George Grizzle, Disken Grant, William Davison, James Hudgens, Moses Timmons, Littleton Bagwell, Henry Cannon, William Simson, Henry Young & James Terrill.

The State against Ebenezer Morse. Defaulting Juror. The Defendant came into Court & rendered such Excuse as the Court saw cause to Excuse him, upon his paying all costs accured thereon.

Thomas Wyatt & Spencer Casey appointed constables for this County, came into Court and took the necessary oath of office according to law.

The State vs Mason Cannon. Defaulting Juror. The Defendant came into Court & rendered his Excuse: and was thereupon acquitted by the Court, without cost.

The State vs Thomas Kimbell. Defaulting Juror. The Defendant made oath to his excuse & was thereupon Exempted from a fine, and acquitted upon paying Costs.

We the Subscribers being appointed by the worshipful Court of Spartanburgh to Review the different Roads Leading from the court House to North Carolina, and having reviewed the same, are of opinion that the Road leading by the widow Woods old place is the most advantagious Road Witness our Hands this 19th day of December 1789. John Young, Joseph Venible.

The State against Nathaniel Robertson. Defaulting Juror. It appeared to the Court that the Defendant is an Overseer of a Road, He was thereupon Exempted from Serving as a Juror untill the time of his being an Overseer was expired.

William Wier against John Elder. Attachment. John Hull being summoned by a writ of scieri Facias, to Declare upon oath what he was Indebted to the Defendant, upon which Testimony he says he is not Indebted anything...

The State against Jonathan Neasbitt. Defaulting Juror. By affidavit of the Defendant specifying that he was not summoned by the Sheriff Ordered that he be acquitted without costs.

Eli Cook against James Smith. Petition. Ordered that this suit be dismissed at the Defendants costs.

Henry Hayes against Mary Wood Admx. of James Wood Deceased. Case The case is abated by the Death of the Defendant.

Francis Powers against Dennis Sherdon. Attachment. Henry Koon as a guarnishee, came into Court and made oath the he is justly indebted to the Defendant 100 weight of Tobacco payable next Autumn.

Nevil Wayland against McMakin Hunt. Attachment Ordered that the property attached by sold to satisfy the Debt and cost of the Plaintiff

Benjamine Busey against Stephen Williford. Slander. Dismissed at the Plaintiffs Cost by consent.

Ordered that the minutes be read which was accordingly done, and signed by James Jordan, Obadiah Trimier & David Goodlett, Esq. Court then adjourned untill Tomorrow 9 O'Clock.

Tuesday the 22nd Dec 1789. The worshipful Court met according to last evenings adjournment. Present William Smith, Thomas Farrow & David Goodlett, Esq.

William Farrow being appointed Constable for this County, in place of John Farrow Came into Court and took the necessary oath of office according to Law.

The State against William Henderson. Indictment. Ordered that a Capias Issue against the defendant for his Personal appearance at next court.

The State against William Redman & Samuel Redman. Petty Larceny. Ordered that this case continue untill next court

The State against Elizabeth Graham. Bastardy. Ordered that a Plurias Capias issue against the Defendant for her Personal appearance to next Court.

The State against Elisha McAbee. Bail. The Defendant being bail to the Sheriff, in the sum of ₤ 20, for the Personal appearance of Mary McAbee to this Court respecting bastardy as by a Presentment of the Grand Jury, and she failing to appear at the Time appointed, Whereupon a writ of Sciri Facias Issue against the sd. Defendant for him to shew cause why Judgment should not be entered against him for the said ₤ 20. Ordered by the Court that he be acquitted upon his paying all costs accrued thereon.

The State against John Burk. Bail. A Writ of Sciri Facias having Issue against the said Defendant for ₤ 20 as Security for the appearance of Mary Burk, to answer to a Presentment of the Grand Jury respecting Bastardy, Ordered that he be acquitted upon paying all costs thereon.

Petit Jurors to serve this Term. Reubin Newman, John Colwall, Thomas Miles, Stephen Philips, Robert Milikin, Jason Moore, James Head, William Colwall, Ephraim Elder, Samuel Thomson, John Brown & Benjamine Busey.

The State against John Roebuck & John Chumler. Felony. Came Pater Carnes Esquire, appointed by the Court to appear in behalf of the State & The Defendants by their Councellors, whereupon came a jury (same as above)...The Jury find John Roebuck Guilty but recommend him to mercy, and acquit John Chumler.
                                        Jason Moore, Foreman.

The Court resolved into a Court of Ordinary.

Ordered, that Mary Smith, late widow of Edward Smith, Deceased, have Letters of Admn. on his Estate, upon her giving bond with Richard Young & James Crowder as her Surities for her lawful performance.

Court sat as a Court of Common Pleas.

James Henry came into Court and made oath that an Estray he took up and was toll'd before Obadiah Trimmier Esq. is lost, and that he made diligent search for the same and could not find it. Ordered that he sustain no damage thereby; and be acquited of the same.

On consideration of matters of controversy refered to us by Andrew Paul and William Pool, H. S., One for Damages done the other for settlement in account, The first action and both we find to be groundless. Mr. Andrew Paul is to receive s 5 d 7, and pay all costs. Given 5 Nov 1789. William Smith, Joseph Barnett, Henry McCray, Arbitrators.

The State against Matthew Alexander. Defaulting Juror. A writ of Scieri Facias having issued against the said Defendant, for him to shew cause why Judgment should not be entered against him in behalf of the state, but is appearing to the court that he was not summoned as a Juror, Upon which he was dismissed without cost.

Ordered that the Minutes be read, which was accordingly done and signed by William Smith, Thomas Farrow, Andrew Barry, Esq. Court then adjourned untill tomorrow morning 9 o'clock.

Wednesday the 23rd of December 1789. The Worshipful Court met according to Last evenings adjournment. Present Justices William Smith, David Goodlett & Zadock Ford, Esq.

The Court resolved into a Court of Ordinary.

Ordered that Col. Henry Mechan Wood have letters of admn. on the estate of James Wood, deceased, upon his giving John Young Junr. & William Young Esq. as his surities....

John Johnson against John Kimbell. Debt. Ordered that this suit be Discontinued at the Plaintiffs Costs.

John Kimbell against John Johnson. Debt. Ordered that this suit be discontinued at the Defendants Costs.

The renunciation of a Power of attorney from Ann White to James Lusk and James Smith, proved in open court by the Evidence of William Lancaster. Ordered to be recorded

The State against William Waldrope. Recognizance. The Defendant came into Court and ackd. to owe to the State L 20 & Ebenezer Morse as his Surity, L 10...should William Waldrope should fail in personally appearing to next court to answer an Indictment prefered against him by the Grand Jury.

Stephen Miller and George Miller came into Court and proved their attendance as witnesses, to wit, the said Stephen 14 days in two suits John Johnson against John Kimbell and John Kimbell against John Johnson. And the said George three days in only the suit John Johnson against John Kimbell.

The State against Ebenezer Morse. Indictment for Assault. The Defendant came into Court and confessed the assault, Ordered that he be fined s 5 and be acquitted upon paying costs.

The State against John Roebuck. Felony. The Jury having yesterday found him Guilty of said Felony, and recommending him to mercy. Ordered by the Court that he receive five Lashes on his bare back on the second day of next court at the common whipping post between the hours of Twelve and one O'Clock. And be at liberty upon his giving Bond and approved security for his appearance at said Court.

James Lusk against Charles Bruce. Attachment. By consent of the parties, Ordered that this case be refered to the arbitrament of William Smith and Samuel Lancaster, Esq., their award to be a judgment of next Court if returned at that time

William Thomson against Peter Edwards & Daniel Josling. Debt. The Defendant, to wit, Daniel Josling, the Surity came into court and confessed Judgment for L 38 s 2 sterling, the debt contracted 15 Aug 1789, and due 15th Nov. following....

Carlton Lindsey against Robert Parker & Benjamin Wofford. Petition. On motion of Zachariah Toliaferro atty for the Plaintiff Ordered that this cause discontinue at the Plaintiff Costs.

John Roebuck you acknowledged to owe the State L 100, Brittain Williford & John Vice, you and each of you L 50, to be levied upon your several Goods and chattels, lands and tenements by way of Recognizance...if John Roebuck shall fail to be and appear at the next Court to be holden for this County....

Robert Harper against Charles McKnight. Case. Ordered that this case be refered to the arbitrament of Baylis Earle, James Jordan, James Logan & John Bowen Esq. Their award to be a rule of Court.

William Nunn against Landon Farrow. Trover. Nonsuit.

Jonathan Neasbitt against Thomas Daugherty & Arias Brown. Debt. Ordered that the Defendants give special Bail for the Debt & Costs.

The State against John Whittemore. A new trial on an Indictment. Came Peter Carnes Esq. in behalf of the State and James Dohertie Esq. in behalf of the Defendant, whereupon came a jury, Jason Moore, Reubin Newman, John Colwell, Thomas Miles, Stephen Phillips, Robert Milikin, James Head, William Colwall, Ephraim Elder, Samuel Thomson, John Brown & Benjamin Busey...The Jury do acquit the prisoner. Jason Moore, foreman.

Thomas Milikin and William Milikin as witnesses in the case Robert Harper against Charles McKnight on their oaths were allowed to wit, the said Thomas L 2 s15 for 22 days attendance and the said William L 2 s 5 for 19 days attendance in said case.

Thomas Brooks against Moses Wood. Trover. Ordered that a Dedimus Potestatum issue to the State of Georgia Directed to any two or three Majistrates in Burk County, to take the examination of Benjamine Brown, on the part of the Defendant, upon his giving Lawful notice of time and place of Examination.

Zachariah Kirkland against Moses Wood. Debt. Nonsuit.

Thomas Williamson you acknowledged to owe to the State L 100, and Martin Armstrong and Thomas Gordon you and each of you L 50 each to be levied on your several goods and chattels lands and tenements...by way of Recognizance. Condition this that is you Thomas Williamson fail to appear at the next court to be holden at the Town of Cambridge on the 26th day of April next...to answer an indictment for escape of Prisoners out of the Goal of the County of Spartanburgh....

Samuel Stewart against Avery Connell. Attachment. Ordered that a Scieri Facias issue against Thomas Farrar Esq. to shew cause why Judgment should not finally and peremptorily be entered against him in behalf of the Plaintiff.

Landon Farrow as a witness in the case Benjamine Wofford against Henry Meredith, on oath was allowed s 15 for 6 days attendance in said case.

Martin Armstrong against Benjamine Davis. Attachment. Ordered that the property not proven by the interpleader shall be condemned to sale.

James English against James Cullins. Case. Dismissed at Plaintiffs Costs.

Same against Same. Case. Dismissed at Plaintiffs Costs.

Charles Hester against John McGuire. Assault. Dismissed at the Plaintiffs Costs.

John McGuire against Charles Hester. Dismissed at the Defendants Costs.

John McGuire & wife against Charles Hester. Slander. Dismissed at the Defendants Costs.

Ordered that the minutes be read which was accordingly Done and signed by Baylis Earle, Zadock Ford, William Smith, Esq. Court then adjourned untill Court in Course.

Court of Spartanburgh began and held at the Court House of said County, on the 15th March 1790. Present James Jordan, David Goodlett & Thomas Farrow, Esq. The Court proceeded to drawn the Pettit Jurors for next Term, to wit.

Nathaniel Guiton	No.	1	Charles Littlejohn	No. 16
Moses Ward	"	2	John Hamby	" 17
Nathaniel Stokes	"	3	William Monk	" 18
Thomas Langley	"	4	William Hightower	" 19
Henry Foster	"	5	Christopher Rodes Jr.	" 20
William Tacket	"	6	George Newman	" 21
John Couch	"	7	David Brown	" 22
Anthony Crocker	"	8	William Wilder	" 23
Robert Rodgers	"	9	James Betterton	" 24
Edward Stubblefield	"	10	James Ham	" 25
Anthony Piercen	"	11	Robert Hobbs	" 26
James Compton	"	12	Abram Andrews	" 27
Robert Syms	"	13	James Turner	" 28
John Serratt	"	14	Charles Scruggs	" 29
Littleton Mapp Senior	"	15	James Moore	" 30

A Power of Attorney from Benjamine Piper to James Hammett Faugerson acknowledged in open Court by the said Piper, Ordered to be recorded.

Ordered that Thomas Price have Licence to sell spiritous Liquors upon his giving Andrews Thomson & William Shaw Esq. his surities for his lawful performance.

Ordered, that the trial Docket be called over the first time, which was accordingly done.

Samuel Jackson against William Wofford. Debt. Dismissed at the Plaintiffs Cost by his order

Silas McBee against Daniel Joslin. Special action on the case. On motion of Peter Carnes Esq. Attorney for the Defendant and assigning sufficient reasons. Ordered by the Court that the Plaintiff suffer a Nonsuit.

John Thomas Junr. Esq. against Michael Maddox. Attachment. The Defendant being solemnly called, and not appearing himself nor by his attorney, Judgment was thereupon entered by Default and the Guarnishees, to wit, Nathan Veal & Larkin Davis came into Court and made oath that they were indebted certain quantities of Tobacco due some time hence to the said Defendant, which was considered sufficient to satisfy the sum of £ 9 s 1 d 6 the sum due the plaintiff which was accordingly condemned in the hands of the said Guarnishees (when due) for the use of the said Plaintiff.

Francis Powers against Dennis Sherdon. Attachment. There being one brown Horse attached by Thomas Wyatt, the Constable. Ordered that the said Horse be exposed to sale & the money arising therefrom remain in the hands of the Clerk to wait the event of the suit.

Ordered that Thomas Williamson have License to keep a Public House & retail spirituous liquors upon his giving John Golightly & W. Turner Thomason as his surities for his Lawful Performance.

Ordered that Henry McCrary have License to keep Public House of Entertainment and retail spirituous Liquors upon his giving Barzel Lee & George Connell as his surities for his Lawful Performance.

Jonathan Neasbitt against Thomas Daugherty & Arias Brown. Debt. Richard Lewis being special Bail for the appearance of said Brown; and Delivering him up to the Court, Ordered that the said Lewis be acquitted, and John Pace came into Court, and entered himself special Bail for the appearance of said Brown to next Term.

Starling Tucker against Ellis Cheek assinee of Joseph Terry. Appeal. Ordered that the appeal be remanded to the Justice from whence it came.

Ordered that the minutes be read, which was accordingly done and signed by James Jordan, Wm. McDowell & Thomas Farrow, Esq. Court then adjourned untill tomorrow Nine O'Clock.

Tuesday the 16th March 1790. The Worshipful Court met according to last evening's adjournment. Present, William Smith, William McDowell, Andrew Barry & David Goodlett, Esq.

The State against John Roebuck. Indictment. The Defendant being found Guilty of Pettit Larceny, at last Term, and was adjudged to receive five lashes on his bare back on this day between the Hours of twelve & one O'Clock at the common whipping Post: Instead of which he produced a free pardon from his Excellency Charles Pinckney Esq. Governor of this State in the following words, to wit

State of South Carolina By his Excellency Charles Pinckney Esq. Governor and Commander in Chief in and over the State aforesaid. To all and Singular Judges Justices Sheriffs Constables and other officers of Justice in the said State, Whereas, at the last County Court held in and for the County of Spartanburg John Roe-

buck was tried and found guilty of Petit Larceny for which crime has was sentenced to receive five lashes on the bare back on the second day of the meeting of the said Court which is to be held in the said County in March next Now know ye that in consideration of a Petition that has been presented to me in his behalf signed by several of the Magistrates and a number of respectable Inhabitants of the said County I have thought fit to pardon remit and release and by these Presents do pardon remit and release the said John Roebuck as well the crime aforesaid as also the sentence aforesaid, of which all concerned are to take due notice and govern themselves accordingly.
   Given under my hand and the Great seal of the State in the Town of Columbia this 4th Feb 1790.
By his Excellency's Command
Peter Freneau, Secretary   Charles Pinckney.

Whereupon it is considered by the court that he be acquited accordingly, upon paying all Lawful charges accumulated thereon.

The State against John Gowen. Scieri Facias. The Defendant being summoned by a writ of Scieri Facias to shew cause if any he had why Judgment should not be entered against him for his not attending last Court as a Juror. On motion of Peter Carnes Esq. his attorney, Ordered that he be acquitted because it appeared he was not summoned by the Sheriff. The Clerk & Sheriff forgive their fees.

The Court proceeded to the choice of a Grand Jury for this Court, to wit,

John Smith, foreman	No. 1	William Poole, Taylor	No. 10
Robert Neasbitt	2	Samuel Morrow	11
George Connell	3	Joel Traylor	12
John Brown	4	John Tollison	13
Benjamine McMikin	5	Daniel McClary	14
Josiah Tanner	6	John Golightly	15
William Elder	7	Aaron Moore	16
Samuel Miller	8	William Pool J. M.	17
Colo. John Neasbitt	9		

James Smith against Wade Hampton Esq. Case. Ordered, that this suit discontinue at the Plaintiffs cost.

Samuel Stewart against Avery Connell. Attachment. Thomas Farrar, Esq. being examined as Guarnishee acknowledged that he was bound to make titles for 200 acres of land on Bushy Creek in the District of Ninety Six to the said Avery Connell & his Heirs, Whereupon the Court ordered that the said Land be condemned in the hands of the said Farrar for the use of the said Samuel Stewart, and that him the said Farrar do make Titles in fee simple to the Purchaser of said Land, at the sheriff's sale.

A deed of conveyance from Tilley Merrik to John Golightly proven in open Court by the evidence of Thomas Farrar, Esq. Ordered to be recorded

Ordered that a Road be laid out and opened from the No. Carolina line in a straight course from Sloans Ironworks to McDowells Mill on No. Packolate, from thence to David McDowells, from thence the best & Nearest way to this County line in a straight course to Col. John Thomas's Junr., Ralph Cobb overseer from the No. line to Buck Creek, John Jones warner; William Morriss Overseer from Buck Creek to McDowells Mill, Noel Johnson, warner; Isaac

Andrewson overseer from McDowells Mill to David McDowells, James Norriss warner & Matthew Alexander overseer from David McDowells to the County line, leading to John Thomas's Esq, William Alexander warner.

William McKnight Overseer of the Road Leading from McDowells to Poors Ford on Broad River, James McKnight warner, John Johnson overseer of the Road from McDowells Mill to the Boiling Spring meeting House, Thomas Kimbell warner, Edmund Fowler overseer from the Boiling Spring Meeting House to this Court House, Rice Walker warner.

William Coursey against Maximilian Conner & Philip James. Petition by Note of hand. Came the Plaintiff by Thomas P. Carnes Esq. his Attorney, and the Defendant by George Walker Gentl. their Attorney, and after the parties being heard, It was considered by the Court, that the Plaintiff recover against the said Defendants Ł 10 sterling according to specialty which became due 20 March 1786, with lawful interest until paid....

Joseph Adair against John Sarratt. Petition by Note of Hand. Came the Plaintiff by Peter Carnes Gentl. his Attorney and the Defendant by Thomas P. Carnes Esq. his Attorney, and after an investigation of the matter by said Councellors, Ordered that this suit Discontinue at the Plaintiffs costs.

William Birdsong attorney for Isaac Brooks against James Terrill. Trover. By argument between the Councellors of said Parties, Ordered that a Dedimus Potestatum issue to Chatham County in the State of No. Carolina, to three or any two Justices of the Peace for said County to Examine Thomas Brooks & Edward Brya Senr. Also to Orange County in said State to three or any two Justices of the peace for said County, to examine Thomas Dickson. also to Cumberland County in said State to three Justices or any two of them for said County there to examine Micajah Terrill. also a Dedimus Potestatum to Issue to Wilks County in the State of Georgia to any three Justices there or two of them, to Examine Thomas Hill On the behalf of the Plaintiff upon his giving lawful notice to the Defendant of the times and places of Examinations.

John Camp against John Chism. Petition. Came the Plaintiff by James Daugherty Esq. his Attorney and the defendant by Thos. P. Carnes Gentl. his attorney & the Parties agreeing to refer this case to William Moore, John McCarter, Nathan Ward, Thomas McKnight, John McMahan, John Vernon, Thomas Selman, William Shed, Thomas Williams, John Cannon, David Golightly & Moses Timmons Gentl. Jurors, ...We find Ł 9 for the Plaintiff & Cost of Suit....

John Wofford against John Collins. Trover. By consent of the parties and assent of the Court the trial of this case is defered untill next court

James Jordan Esq. proved a mortgage from John Whittemore to Samuel Neasbitt, Ordered to be recorded

Henry Domini against John Burt. Attachment. Nonsuit.

On application of the Deputy Clerk, Ordered that he have leave of absence for five weeks.

A Deed of conveyance from James Jordan Esq. to William Hendrix signed and acknowledged in open Court, Ordered to Record.

John Westmoreland being appointed constable for this County came into Court and took the usual oath of office according to Law.

William Venible against John Conner Junr. On motion of William Shaw Esq. Attorney for the plaintiff, Ordered that the defendant give special bail in the above case.

Matthew Guttery having an Execution issued against him for ₺ 2 s 9 d 4 which was the penalty of a Bond given for an Estray. It is now ordered that he pay only the sum of ₺ 1 s 4 d 8 of the execution now against him, which is the principle of said Bond, & be acquitted upon paying costs.

Ordered that a road be laid out and opened from near James Hams plantation to lead to and intersect a road near Arthur Hutchens Plantation then the nearest and best way to a certain Bridge on Fairforest between William & Handcock Smiths Plantations, thence the best way into the Court House Road between James Smiths & the Baptist meeting house; and that William Smith, James Smith & Arthur Hutchens veiw and lay out the same, Captain William Suddoth overseer of said Road.

Ordered that the minutes be read which accordingly done & signed by William Smith, Zadock Ford & Obadiah Trimmier, Esq. Court then adjourned untill to morrow Nine O'Clock, Wednesday the 17th March 1790. Court met according to last evenings adjournment.

Present William Smith, Thomas Farrow & Obadiah Trimmier, Esq.

Benjamine Wofford & Burrell Thomson against Henry Meredith. Debt. Ordered, that this case continue untill next Court.

Benjamine Wofford & Burrell Thomson against Henry Meredith. Debt. Ordered that a commission issue to any two Justices of this County to take the deposition of Landon Farrow debeneisse in writing to be read in evidence in case of death or sickness, so as to render him incapable of attending Court. On the behalf of the defendant upon his giving lawful notice to the plaintiff of time & place of Examination.

County Treasurer against Thomas Crowder & John Kimbell. Petition. On motion of Thos. P. Carnes County Attorney, Judgment was thereupon entered for the sum of ₺ 1 s 4 d 6 according to specialty, and costs of suit.

Benjamine Wofford against John Farrow. Debt. Ordered, that the note be given up to the Plaintiff.

Hugh Pierce against James Lee. Appeal. Ordered that this continue untill next court.

John Haile Esq. against Ebenezer Morse. Appeal. The Trial of this suit is ordered to stand over untill next Court.

Samuel Bell against the Admrs. of Jones. Appeal. Continued untill next Court.

Joseph Erwin against John Naile. Alias Petition. Ordered, that this suit stand over untill next court.

James McGowen attorney for Erwin against John Naile. Alias Petition. By consent of the parties and assent of the Court, the trial of this cause is defered untill next court.

Bartan Coats against John Conner. Attachment. Came the Plaintiff by James Daugherty Esq. his Attorney, & the Defendant by George Walker Gentl. his Attorney and after hearing the allegations of the parties and a mature consideration of the Court, Ordered that this action Discontinue.

Charles Goodwin Esq. against George Taylor. Petition. The Plaintiff petitioning for the value of 1000 pounds weight of merchantable Tobacco, On motion of George Walker his attorney, Judgment was thereupon entered for Ł 3 s 10 & costs of suit.

The Grand Jury made the return of the following Bills of Indictment.

The State against William Waldrope. Indictment. No Bill.
John Smith, foreman.

The State against Travis Morse. Indictment. A true Bill.

County Treasurer against Jeremiah Walker & Reubin Matthis. Petition. On motion of Thos. P. Carnes Esq. County attorney, Judgment was accordingly entered for Ł 2 s 13 d 6 and costs of suit.

Travis Moss as Principle, and Ebenezer Morse as his Surity, came into Court and acknowledged themselves indebted to the State, to wit the said Travice in the sum of Ł 25 and the said Ebenezer in the sum of Ł 12 s 10 if the said Travice should fail to appear at our next Court, to answer to a Bill of Indictment prefered against him by the Grand Jury.

William Thomson attorney for Adams against Richard Fondrin. Petition. Ordered, that the writ be amended in the name of William Fondrin.

James Lusk against Charles Bruce. Attachment. The defendant came into Court in his proper persons and confessed Judgment for Ł 3 s 10 and also a Heifer & one beef. The value of the beef to be s 40 and cost of suit.

Adam Garner came into Court and acknowledged himself to owe to the State Ł 20 on his failing to appear at next Court to give evidence in the Indictment the State against Travice Moss.

William Thomson Gentl. attorney for Frank Adams. against William Fondrin. Petition. The Plaintiff petitioning for Ł 10 by way of damage, and on motion of Thos. P. Carnes Esq. his attorney (Notwithstanding the allegations of James Dohertie Gentl. attorney for the defendant) Judgment was accordingly entered for the said Ł 10 in behalf of the Petitioner besides his costs....

William Wofford against Handcock Smith. Petition. By consent of the parties and assent of the Court, the trial of this cause is Defered untill next Court.

Benjamine Spencer against William Venible. Petition. The Plaintiff came by Peter Carnes Esq. his attorney, and the Defendant by William Shaw Gentl. his attorney, and after hearing the matter debated...the Plaintiff recover Ł 10 sterling by way of an open account, aggreeable to the supplication of the Plaintiff besides his costs....

The State against George Grizzle. Indictment. No Bill.

The State against Jacob Eisen. Indictment. A True Bill.

The State against Thomas Williamson. On Discharge of recognizance. The Defendant being Recognized at last Court to appear at the Town of Cambridge on the 26th April next at the General Court of Sessions for the District of Ninety Six for the Escape of Prisoners out of the Jail for this County, Now Ordered that he be acquitted from his recognizance upon paying all lawful costs accumulated thereon.

Joshua Smith as an evidence in the case Benjamine Spencer against William Venible on oath was allowed s 7 d 6 for 3 days attendance.

Matthew Mulnex as a witness in the case Benjamine Spencer against William Venible, on oath was allowed s 5 for 2 days attendance.

Buckner Smith on oath was allowed s 7 d 6 for 3 days attendance as a witness in the case Benjamine Spencer against William Venible.

The State against Elizabeth Waldrope. Indictment. Ordered that the defendant and her surities be discharged.

Ordered that the land attached by Samuel Stewart, the property of Avery Connell, be exposed to sale.

Richard Harrison Esq. against Charles Bruce. Case. Ordered that the Bail for the Defendant be acquited, by reason of his being held to bail, without an affidavit.

A covenant and argument between Henry Hayes and James Jordan Esq. proven in open court by the Evidence of Thomas Jackson, Ordered to be recorded.

Vardry McBee against William Rickman. Detinue. Ordered, that this suit be discontinued at the Plaintiffs cost by consent.

Ordered that the minutes be read, which was accordingly done and signed by James Jordan, William Smith & Andrew Barry, Esq. Court adjourned untill tomorrow Nine O'Clock.

Thursday the 18th of March 1790. Court met according to last evenings adjournment. Present Samuel Lancaster, David Goodlett & Thomas Farrow, Esq.

Thomas Blasingame Junr. against Holland Sumner. Attachment. Col. Thomas Brandon as Guarnishee came into Court and made oath that he had not any of the Property of the Defendant in his possession at the time of the attachment being levyed in his hands. Ordered that the Negro woman attached in his hands be released from the attachment, and delivered to said Brandon, and the Bond given by the said Brandon to the Sheriff to try the right of the said Negro be given to said Brandon.

Robert Goodgion against Israel Morriss. Attachment. Stephen Miller as Guarnishee came into Court & made oath that he gave his note to Israel Morriss dated 17 Feb 1789, for ₤ 20 s 15 to be paid in produce, to be paid on or before 25 Dec 1790. The property of the note & debt condemned for the use of the Plaintiff.

A Bill of sale from Mrs. Ann White to William Shaw Esq. for one Negro man called Isaac acknowledged in open Court by said White. Ordered to be recorded.

William Poole J. M. against James Cullins. Case. John Pipes being bail for the appearance of the Defendant, came and surrendered him to the Court upon which he was acquitted.

Robert Harper against Charles McKnight. Case. Ordered, that the arbitration be prolonged, and to be returned to our next Court as a rule thereof.

Dudley Red against Holland Sumner. Attachment. Discontinued at the Defendants costs.

Ordered that the Execution John McElheny against the Admrs. of Jones be renewed.

George Walker Esq. against Michael B. Roberts. Petition. On motion of Peter Carnes Esq. attorney for the Plaintiff (notwithstanding the allegations of James Dohertie & Zachariah Toliaferro Gentl. Councellors of the Defendant) Decreed by the Court that the Plaintiff agreeable to his supplication, recover against the Defendant ₤ 5 s 16 d 8 for Debt, & cost of suit.

Robert Harper against Hugh Freeman. Attachment. Ordered that the property attached be exposed to sale to satisfy said attachment.

Thomas Brooks against Moses Wood. Trover. Ordered that this case continued untill next Court & that a Dedimus Potestatum issue to Burk County in Georgia to any three Justices there, to Examine Benjamine Brown also one to issue to any three Justices in Wilks County in said State to examine Gen. Elijah Clerk on the Behalf of the Defendant, upon his giving lawful notice of times & Places of Examination.

Thomas Gordon against William Gilbert. Slander. Came the Plaintiff by Thos. P. Carnes Esq. his Attorney and the Defendant by his Councellors, Whereupon it is ordered that this suit discontinue at the Plaintiffs Cost for want of witnesses.

Ann Dewberry against William Gilbert. Attachment. Came the Plaintiff by Thos. P. Carnes Gentl. her attorney and the Defendant by his Councellors, whereupon it is decreed by the Court that the Plaintiff recover against the Defendant, ₤ s s 4 with interest thereon from 26 March 1780 untill paid, besides her costs ...the attornies fee paid by the plaintiff

Baylis Earle Esq. against Peter Lewis. Case. Came the Plaintiff by Thos. P. Carnes Esq. his Attorney and the Defendant by Peter Carnes Gentl. his attorney confessed Judgment for s 20 & costs of suit.

Elizabeth Thomson against William Graham. Attachment. Ordered that the trial of this cause be Defered untill next court.

William Venible against John Conner. Debt. Ordered, that a Dedimus potestatum issue to Franklin County in Georgia to any three Justices there to examine William Wood on behalf of the Defendant, upon his giving legal notice of time and place of Examination.

Nicholas Holley against John Bragg. Debt. By request of the party's, Ordered that this suit be refered to the arbitrament of John Lindsey & John Ford Senr. with power of Umpirage their award made at the House of Isaac Crow on the third Monday in May next, and returned to our next Court shall be a rule thereof.

Joseph West against Josiah Culbertson.   Case.
Joseph West against Samuel Culbertson.   Case.
By consent of the parties, Ordered that the above cases be refered to the arbitrament of John Birdsong, William Kenedy, Charles Syms, Samuel Otterson & Drewry Murrell, Their award returned to our next Court, shall be a rule thereof.

John D. Young, Nelly Walker & Harmon Elder came into Court, and acknowledged to owe to the State Ł 25 each if they fail to appear at our next Court, to give evidence in an Indictment prefered by the grand Jury against Jacob Eisen, Acknowledged in open court before W. S. Lancaster, D. C.

Adam Garner as an evidence in the case Samson Bobo against Benjamine Wofford and Henry Earnest, on oath was allowed Ł 1 s 12 d 6 for 13 days attendance.

Carlton Lindsey against Robert Parker & Benjamine Wofford. Petition. Ordered, that all matters of controversy between the Parties be refered to the arbitrament of William Spiler, John Lindsey and Richard Young, Their award to be a rule of Court.

Baylis Earle Esq. against Samuel Porter. Attachment. The defendant being solemnly call'd and not appearing in his own person nor by his Attorney, Judgment was thereupon entered by Default, and on motion of Thos. P. Carnes Esq. Attorney for the Plaintiff, final Judgment was accordingly entered for Ł 12 according to specialty....

Felix Walker assinee of Hane & Burk against Hugh Freeman. Debt. Came the Plaintiff by Thos. P. Carnes Esq. his attorney and the Defendant being solemnly called and not appearing by himself nor his attorney, Judgment was thereupon entered by Default for Ł 12 s 15 d 3 accroding to specialty....

Jacob Eisen as principle and William Smith & Samuel Elder his surities came into court and acknowledged to owe to the State, the said Jacob Ł 100, and the said William Smith & Samuel Elder Ł 50 each if the said Jacob Should fail to appear....

John Lindsey against Vardry McBee & William Tate. Debt. Ordered, that the Property Executed, be sold to satisfy the Execution Levyed.

Thomas Farrow Esq. as an evidence in the case Carlton Lindsey Plaintiff and Robert Parker & Benjamine Wofford defendants on oath was allowed s 10 for 4 days attendance.

Mills Sumner on oath was allowed s 17 d 6 for 7 days attendance as a witness in the case Thomas Blasingame against Holland Sumner.

Paul Castleberry on oath was allowed Ł 2 s 12 d 6 for 21 days attendance as a witness in the case Nicholas Holley against John Bragg.

Joel Hembry as a witness in the case Nicholas Holley against John Bragg on oath was allowed Ł 2 s 7 d 6 for 19 days attendance.

Henry Meredith on oath was allowed Ł 2 for 16 days attendance as a witness in the case Samson Bobo against Benjamine Wofford & Henry Earnest.

Andrew Mayes against James Smith & William Alldredge. Petition. Ordered that the trial of this cause be defered untill next court.

Thos. P. Carnes Esq. heretofore County Attorney, now resigned his office with approbation of the court, who returned Mr. Carnes their thanks for his faithful discharging his office.

Major John Gowen is appointed overseer of the Road from the head of Lawsons fork from Passons's old Road to said Gowens Mill, in the room of William Jameson. James Fowler, warner.

Baylis Earle Esq. is appointed overseer of the Road from the No. Carolina line, to Greenville County line, in place of John Earle.

Thomas Davis appointed overseer of the Road from Passon's old road to where it intersects the Road that leads to the Widow Bishops, the usual hands to work thereon according to the original Division, Isaac Bishop warner.

Ordered, that the Sheriff proceed to the sale of the Estrays.

Ordered, that a Road be laid out and opened from the Court House of this County to meet a Road laid out by an order of Greenville Court Downward to the ancient boundery line near J. Morgans Esquires to be laid out the nearest and best way and that William Benson and James Jordan Esquire be the Commissioners to lay out and mark the same, and appoint the overseers thereof.

Samuel Farrow Esquire in behalf of the County against Thomas Gordon and Littleton Bagwell. Petition. On motion of Thos. P. Carnes Esquire County Attorney, Judgment was accordingly entered for the sum of ℔ 2 s 18 d 6 according to specialty and costs of suit.

Thomas Blasingame against Holland Sumner. Attachment. By consent of the parties, ordered that the trial of this cause be defered untill next court.

George Taylor against Thomas Edwards. Trespass. Nonsuit.

William Pool J. M. against Thomas Flynn. Attachment. Ordered, that the trial of this cause be continued untill next Court.

Joseph Wofford against John Roebuck. Debt. Nonsuit.

Elizabeth Thomson against George Taylor. Case. Nonsuit.

John Spelee against Michael Waldrope. Attachment. Nonsuit.

Vardry McBee against John Steen. Attachment. Ordered, that the trial of this cause stand over untill next Court.

John McElroy against Samuel McClure. Case. Ordered that the trial of this cause be defered untill next Court.

John Cowen against Ebenezer Morse. Special Action on the case. Nonsuit.

Samson Bobo against Benjamin Wofford & Henry Earnest. Trover. By consent of the parties and assent of the Court, the trial of this cause is defered untill next court.

John Wood against Thomas Hannah. Trover. Ordered, that the trial of this case stand over untill next Court.

William Bratcher against Baylis Earle Esq. Exr. of Hampton. Debt. Continued untill next court.

Same against Same. Trover. Continued untill next Court.

Daniel Shaw against John Gowen. Special action on this case. Nonsuit.

John Williams against William Duncan & Moses Biter. Case. By consent of the parties, ordered that this case continued untill next Court.

Thomas Hamilton and Temperance Hamilton against Benjamine Wofford. Trover. By consent of the parties the trial of this cause is defered untill next Court.

John Spelee against Stephen Williford. Attachment. Ordered, that this suit be discontinued.

Vinson Brown against John Ryan. Attachment. Ordered, that this suit be Discontinued.

John Wooton against William Casey. Attachment. Ordered, that this suit be Dismissed.

Edward Hooker against John Collo. Attachment. Dismissed.

Edmund Pugh against John Williams. Special Action on the case. By consent of the parties, the trial of this cause is defered untill next Court.

Thomas Brandon Esq. attorney for Hendrix against Robert Harper and William Byrd. Trover. By consent of the parties, Ordered that the trial of this cause be defered untill next Court.

George Vaughn against William Smith Esq. Detinue. Ordered that this suit be dismissed.

Daniel Jackson against John Chesney. Trover. Nonsuit.

Joshua Hawkins against Holland Sumner. Trover. Ordered that this cause be continued untill next Court.

John McGuire against William Burton. False Imprisonment. Nonsuit.

Spencer Bobo against Samuel Porter. Attachment. Continued untill next Court.

Samuel Neasbitt admr. of John Shannon against Thomas Still. Attachment. Continued untill next Court.

Vardry McBee against John Wooton Senior. Attachment. Continued untill next Court.

Israel Morriss against Major Passons. Attachment. Continued untill next Court.

John D. Carne against Edward Balenger, Uriah Conner & William Young, Esq. Debt. Continued untill next Court.

John Lambert against Henry Moffatt. Trover. Nonsiut.

John Tollason against James Hall and wife. Slander. Continued untill next Court.

Matthew Harper against Stephen Fuller. Attachment. Ordered, that this suit be Dismissed.

William Robbin against John Wade. Attachment. Ordered that this suit be discontinued.

William Venible against Isham Saffold. Case. Ordered, that this case be continued untill next Court.

Joseph Dickson against Joseph Buffington Debt. Continued by consent untill next Court.

Israel Morriss against John McElroy. Debt. Ordered, that this suit be dismissed.

Joseph Means against Benjamine Wofford. Trover. Ordered that this suit be continued untill next Court.

George Lamkin against Joseph Buffington. Debt. Continued untill next Court.

William Walker against Ralph Cobb. Assault. Nonsuit.

John Camp against John Chism. Trespass.
Same against Same. Case.
Ordered, that the above cases be continued untill next Court.

Thomas Jenkins against Maximilian Conner. Debt. Came the plaintiff by Thos. P. Carnes Esq. his Attorney and the defendant being solemnly call'd and not appearing by himself nor his Attorney, Judgment was thereupon entered by default, for the sum of £ 17 s 8 according to specialty in behalf of the said plaintiff, besides his costs in this behalf expended, and the said Defendant be in mercy.

Thomas Brandon Esq. attorney for Hendrix against Robert Harper and William Byrd. Trover. By consent of the parties, Ordered that the trial of this cause continued untill next Court.

Daniel Joslin against Joseph Morriss. Special Action on the case. Nonsuit.

Daniel Brown Esq. against Willis Watkins and Michael Hogan. Case. Came the Plaintiff by Thos. P. Carnes Esq. his Attorney and the defendants being solemnly called and not appearing...Judgment was thereupon entered by Default against the said Defendants....

Jonathan Neasbitt against Thomas Daugherty & Arias Brown. Debt. Continued untill next Court.

John Ward against Thomas Hamilton. Trover. The Plaintiff came by Thos. P. Carnes Esq. his Attorney and the defendant being solemnly called and not appearing...Judgment was thereupon entered by default.

James Terrill against Vardry McBee & William Rickman. Debt. Continued untill next Court.

John Lefever against Peter Edwards. Special Action on the case. Nonsuit.

John Hewit against William Thomson. Special Action on the case. Discontinued the Plaintiffs Attorney fee excepted.

Peter Brooks against George and John Roebuck. Debt. Continued untill next Court.

David McDowell against Hugh Freeman admr. of Rodden. Special action on the case. On motion of Wm. Shaw Esquire attorney for the Plaintiff (after the defendant being call'd and not appearing either himself or by his attorney) Judgment was thereupon entered by default.

Holley Pore against Robert Goodwin. Attachment. Ordered, that this suit be dismissed.

John Holeman against George Lamkin. Debt. Continued untill next Court.

William Smith against Joseph Warren. Case. Continued untill next Court.

John Garner against John Steen. Attachment. Ordered, that this suit be dismissed.

Hugh Pierce against Thomas Gordon. Attachment. Continued untill next Court.

John Gordon, Hugh Quinn & Benjamine Philips against John Pritchett & Jesse Tate. Debt. Came the Plaintiffs by James Dohertie Esquire, their attorney and the defendants being solemnly called and not appearing niether by themselves or their Attorney, Judgment was thereupon entered by default.

Same against Valentine Riznor, Pritchet & Tate. Debt. On motion of James Dohertie Gentl. Attorney for the Plaintiffs, after the defendants being call'd and not appearing by themselves or their attornies, Judgment was thereupon entered by default.

William Wofford against Joseph Buffington. Attachment. Came the Plaintiff by George Walker Gentl. his Attorney and the defendant being solemnly called and not appearing himself neither by his attorney, Judgment was thereupon entered by Default.

William Hill Assinee of Quin against James Terrill. Debt. The Plaintiff came by James Dohertie Gentl. Attorney and the defendant not appearing in his own person nor by his attorney, Judgment was thereupon entered by default.

James Barron against John Moore. Debt. Continued untill next Court.

Joseph Henderson assinee of Kirkendale against Andrew Milikin. Debt. Continued untill next court.

John Henderson assinee of Godfrey Adams against Thomas Brown. Debt. Abated by the death of the Defendant.

Israel Morriss against Rowland Cornelius. Debt.
Same against Same. Case.
Ordered that the plaintiff suffer a Nonsuit in both of the above

cases, by being out of the State and not giving Security for costs.

Michael Miller against John Golightly. Malicious Prosecution Continued untill next Court.

Randolph Casey against Moses Casey. Detinue. Continued untill next Court.

John Thomas Junr. Esq. against Nicholas Holley. Trepass Vi et armis. Continued untill next Court.

Ordered that the minutes be read which was accordingly done & signed by Baylis Earle, David Goodlett & Saml. Lancaster, Esq. Court then adjourned untill Court in Course.

Court of Spartanburgh, began and Held at the Court House of said County on the third Monday in June 1790. Present Baylis Earle, William Smith, Thomas Farrow, David Goodlett, Andrew Barry, William McDowell, James Jordan & Samuel Lancaster, Esq.

Ordered that David Noel overseer the Road from Isaac Crows to Heads Ford on Enoree River in place of Edward Lynch.

Ordered that Ebenezer Morse Overseer the Road from the Mountain Shoals on Enoree River below Henry Carleys Plantation, in place of Alexander Alexander, Obadiah Morse warner.

Ordered that Alexander Nevins overseer the Road from Pattons ford on Tyger River to Alexander Alexanders Plantation, Matthew Patton warner.

Alexander Alexander is appointed overseer of the Road from his plantation to Isaac Crows, Robert Hammon warner.

The Court proceeded to draw the Grand Jurors for next Court, to wit.

Charles James	No. 1	John Gowen	No. 11
John Hightower	2	Jonathan Neasbitt	12
Thomas Tod	3	John Young	13
John Shippy	4	Joel Traylor	14
William Garrett	5	John Golightly	15
William Foster	6	Giles Connell	16
Samson Bobo	7	William Thomson Gentl.	17
Thomas Underwood	8	John Neasbitt Colo.	18
Nathaniel Robertson	9	William Suddoth	19
Samuel Neasbitt	10	John McElheny	20

    Petit Jurors drawn for next Court

Samuel Morros	No. 1	William Carley	No. 11
James Crow	2	James Norris	12
Joseph Venible	3	Abram Byce	13
Edward Stone	4	Edward Clerk	14
Shadrack Waldrope	5	David Smith, Packolate	15
Samuel Elder	6	Jeremiah Moore	16
Henry Jones	7	John Watson	17
Thomas Clayton	8	Robert Foster	18
Frederick Guttery	9	Jonathan Synyard	19
Sherard Holcomb	10	John McKnight	20
Abram Nalley	21	Moses Pervines	26
John Salley	22	John Penny	27

Thomas Brooks	23	Daniel Barnett	28
Micajah Barnett	24	John Castleberry	29
Alexander Copelander	25	Aaron Casey	30

Ordered that Peter Brooks be allowed the sum of ₤ 2 s 16 d 8 for his attendance as a witness in the case Dudley Red agst Holland Sumner: which he made oath to.

A deed of conveyance from Jacob Earnest to Robert Hammon proven before Thomas Farrow Esquire, Ordered to be recorded

Another Deed from Jacob Earnest to Robert Hammon proven before Thomas Farrow Esq., Ordered to be recorded.

A Deed of Conveyance from William Brown to Catharine Grace proven before Thomas Farrow Esq, Ordered to record.

William Roberts is appointed Warner of the Road from the Baptist meeting-House to Arthur Hutchins Plantation, under the direction of William Suddoth, who is overseer of the same.

Ordered that James Turner overseer the Road from Lawsons Fork at Woffords old Iron-Works to Packolate River Warrens Ford, Samuel Turner warner, Joseph Morriss overseer from Packolate River to the N. C. line, Hutchens Forest warner.

Ordered that a Road be laid out and opened from this Court-House the nearest and best way by Pools new Iron-works to the upper Island Ford on Broad River, Thomas Jordan and Isaac Young Commissioners to mark and lay out the same from Packolate to Broad River. William Garrett Senior and James Wyatt to lay out from this Court House to Packolate. Charles Gilley warner, John Jones overseer from Packolate to Broad River, Owen Bowen warner.

Ordered that William McMillin, John Johnson & Thomas McKnight view and report to the next Court which is the most suitable way to open a Road from Slones Iron-works toward Greenville Court House, and where the said Road shall cross the two main forks of Packolate and Broad River, whether at the upper or lower Island fords of said River, which report is to be made on oath.

Ordered, that Richard Barry Overseer the Road from the Narrow Passage on Tyger to Pattons ford on South Tyger in place of Andrew Barry Esq., John Ford & Robert Miller warners.

William Hill assinee of Hugh Quinn against James Terrill. Debt. Execution having issued, ordered that the sale of the property executed be defered untill next Court, by consent.

The Court proceeded to the choice of a County Attorney, when William Shaw Esquire was unanimously appointed.

Robert Harper against Charles McKnight. Case. Persuant to the within order of Spartanburgh Court, we whose names are hereunto subscribed, having met the parties therein named, and heard each of their allegations and the testimoney of their witnesses respecting the case in dispute and due & mature consideration of the affair do award and determine that the within named Charles McKnight pay unto the within named Robert Harper ₤ 4 sterling also the costs of the suit now pending in the court aforesaid, in consequence of which we were appointed referees and that all further disputes and lawsuits subside and be no more between the said parties respecting the matter aforesaid, 29 May 1790.

N. C. the above to be discharged in trade, at the rate of Ł 3 for a cow & calf so far as the sum to be paid Harper.
Baylis Earle, James Jordan, James Logan, John Gowen, arbitrators.

Ordered that William Farrow serve as deputy sheriff for this County, who came into Court & took the necessary oaths of office accordingly.

Joseph West against Josiah Culbertson.
The same against Samuel Culbertson. Case. We the arbitrators ...the said Josiah Culbertson pay unto Joseph West Ł 12 and Samuel Culbertson pay unto said West Ł 14...as appears to us by the oaths of Samuel Jackson & Walter West said sum to be paid on or before the 12th day of December next. 22 April 1790.
John Birdsong, William Kenedy, Charles Syms, Samuel Otterson, Drewry Murrell, Arbitrators.

Nicholas Holley against John Bragg. Debt. Pursuant to the within order of Court...we find it so intricate and difficult, that we may not be proper Judges on which we submit it to a Course in Law. John Lindsey, John Ford, Arbitrators.

Ordered that the Jury be dismissed, on account of Harvest.

Samuel Farrow Esquire who has acted as sheriff for this County near five years, having this day declined acting longer in that office, this Court in consideration of his ill State of health are obliged to accept it, but return to him their hearty thanks for his fidelity and attention in the Execution of his office, and think proper to give him this testimoney of their approbation of his conduct.

Andrew Mayes against James Smith & William Alldredge. Petition The parties came into Court and settled upon the defendants agreeing to pay the interest upon the principle of the note (which was for 1000 weight of Tobacco, equal to Ł 9 s 6 d 8) from the time it became due untill paid, which appears to be 24th day of March last...stay of Execution 3 months.

Henry Foster as a witness in the case Andrew Mayes against James Smith and William Alldridge, on oath in open Court, is allowed s 5 for 2 days attendance.

James Mayes as a witness in the case Andrew Mayes against James Smith and William Alldredge, on oath in open Court was allowed s 5 for 2 days attendance.

John Mayes as a witness in the case Andrew Mayes against James Smith and William Alldredge, on oath in open court is allowed s 5 for 2 days attendance.

Ordered that Major James Lusk have license to keep a Public House & sell spirituous liquors upon his giving John Golightly & Joel Hembry his surities for his Lawful performance.

Ordered that the minutes be read which was accordingly done & signed by Baylis Earle, David Goodlett & William Smith, Esq. Court then adjourned untill Tomorrow Nine O'Clock.

Tuesday the 22nd of June 1790. Court met according to last evenings adjournment. Present William Smith, David Goodlett, Obadiah Trimmier and Baylis Earle, Esq.

Ordered that summons issue against Larkin Lancaster, Turner Thomason, William Fields & Thomas Wyatt Constables, commanding them to attend next Court, in order to serve the same in their official Duties, for that term.

Ordered that Samuel Farrow Esq. be allowed the sum of ₺ 12 s 3 d 8 the Balance of his amount produced by him upon his resignation in office.

Ordered that the Estrays which are liable for sale, be sold at six months credit. Ordered that the minutes be read which was accordingly done & signed by Baylis Earle, Obadiah Trimmier, David Goodlett & William Smith, Esq. Court then adjourned untill Court in Course.

Court of Spartanburgh County, began and held at the Court-House on the third Monday in September A. D. 1790. Present James Jordan, David Goodlett, William Smith, Esq.

The Court proceeded to Draw the Petit Jurors for next Court, to wit.

Henry Aires	1	Newton Bramblett	11
Spencer Bobo Junr.	2	James Buice	12
Thomas Roberts	3	Thomas Prewitt	13
Robert Milikin	4	Richard Prior	14
George Hughey	5	Benjamine Clarke	15
William Floyd	6	Peter Smith	16
John Pennington	7	James McDowell	17
Nathan Langford	8	William Haden Sr.	18
Samson Trammall	9	Joseph Warren	19
Henry Morgan Jr.	10	Thomas White	20
William Wilkins	21	Thomas Bennett	26
William Moore	22	Joseph Cavin	27
William Taylor	23	David Brewton	28
William Bracher	24	Jesse Reams	29
John Brown	25	Oba. Wingo	30

In consequence of an order Issued from last Court to William McMillan, John Johnson and Thomas McKnight, directing them to vew and Report (on oath) to this Court which were the most suitablest way for a Road from Slones Iron Works Towards Greenville Court-House (whether to cross the two main forks of Packolate & Broad River at the upper or Lower Island Fords) In obedience to which they make the Following report.
"We have viewed the Ground for said Road & agree it to come from the upper Island Ford on Broad River to Gores Mill on Buck Creek, from thence to McKnights ford North Packolate, from thence to the Bridge on South Packolate paid by James Norriss.
William McMillan, John Johnson, T homas McKnight, Comssrs.

Ordered, that Samuel Timmons oversee the Road from Mr. Timmons's to the Narrow passage, in place of John Foster.

Ordered that John Collins, Edward Bishop and Thomas Wyatt view a Road from this Court-House to that of Greenville Court-House and report accordingly.

Ordered that Daniel Shippy oversee a Road from his House at the County line up the Green River Road to the Cross Road leading to this place.

Grand Jurors drawn to serve this Court, John Gowen, foreman.

John Gowen	1	Samuel Neasbitt	9
Charles James	2	Jonath Neasbitt	10
John Hightower	3	John Young	11
Thomas Todd	4	Joel Traylor	12
Daniel Shippey	5	John Golightly	13
William Garrett	6	Giles Connell	14
William Foster	7	William Suddoth	15
Thomas Underwood	8		

William Hill against James Terrill. Debt. By a certificate from the plaintiff, Ordered that this suit be dismissed.

Larkin Lancaster against James Smith, Thomas Gordon, William Pool. Petition. Dismissed at the Defendants Costs.

John Camp against John Chism. Trespass. Dismissed at the Plaintiffs Costs.

Ninian Barrett against William Jordan. Detinue. Abated by the Death of the Defendant.

John Camp against Benjamine Wofford. Detinue. Ordered that this suit be discontinued at the Plaintiffs costs by his assent.

The State against William Roberts. Presentment. Order that a capias issue against his Body to be brought to this Court, to answer their charge.

Ordered that Thomas Wyatt, Richard Lewis and James Taylor White appraise the Estate of John Lucas Deceased and make due return of the same.

Edward Stone being summoned as a petit juror to this Court, rendered such Excuse as the Court thought proper to accept and thereupon acquitted him for this Term.

James Norriss is Excused from serving as a Petit Juror for this Term.

Ordered, that the minutes be read which was accordingly done and signed by James Jordan, David Goodlett, Thomas Farrow, Esq. Court then adjourned untill Tomorrow 9 O'Clock.

Tuesday the 21st of September 1790. The Worshipful Court met according to last Evenings adjournment. Present James Jordan, William Smith, Thomas Farrow, Esq.

Thomas Blasingame against Holland Sumner. Attachment. On motion of William Shaw Esq. Attorney for the plaintiff Judgment is entered by Default, The Court ordered a writ of Inquiry to be Executed, whereupon came a Jury to wit, Samuel Morrow, James Crow, Joseph Venible, Shadrack Waldrope, Samuel Elder, Henry Jones, Frederick Guttery, David Smith, Robert Foster, Jonathan Sinyard, John McKnight and Micajah Barnett...we find for the plaintiff L 25 s 18 d 5½ with costs of suit....

Hugh Pierce against James Lee. Appeal. Ordered that this suit be dismissed at the Plaintiffs costs.

Ebenezer Morse against John Haile Esq. Appeal. On an investigation of the matter by the Attornies, to wit, James Dohertie, Esq.

for the Plaintiff, and William Shaw Gentleman attorney for the Defendant, Ordered by the Court that the Judgment be reversed.

John D Carnes & Co. against Edward Balenger, Uriah Conner & William Young. Debt. Dismissed at the plaintiffs costs by consent.

William Pool J. M. against Thomas Flynn. Attachment. On motion of William Shaw Esquire attorney for the Plaintiff Judgment is entered by default, The Court thereupon ordered that a writ of enquity to be Executed whereupon came a jury (same as before)... We find for the plaintiff ℔ 15 & costs of suit....

William Birdsong attorney for Brooks against James Terrill. Trover. Ordered that a Dedimus Potestatum issue to Chatham County in North Carolina, to any two Justice to Examine Simon Terrill, by consent of both parties, upon his the said Plaintiff (on whose behalf the Dedimus issues) giving legal Notice to the adverse party of the time & place of Examination.

Samuel Bell against Elizabeth Jones Admx. of Thomas Jones decd. Appeal. Ordered that the Judgment be reversed.

Thomas Brooks against Moses Wood. Trover. Came the plaintiff by James Dohertie Esq. his Attorney and the Defendant by William Shaw Gentleman his attorney, whereupon came a jury (same as before)...we find for the plaintiff ℔ 12 and costs of suit....

John Tollason against Joseph Hall & Wife. Slander. Dismissed at the plaintiffs costs by his own consent.

William Crocker as a witness in the case Hugh Pierce against James Lee, on oath in open Court is allowed s 17 d 6 for 7 days attendance.

Bazel Lee as an evidence in the case Hugh Pierce against James Lee on oath in open Court is allowed ℔ 1 for 8 days attendance.

A Deed of conveyance from Thomas Williamson to the Worshipful Court for 2 acres of land for the use of the Public Buildings Signed & acknowledged in open Court, Ordered to be recorded.

James Terrill against Vardry McBee & William Rickman. Debt. Ordered that this case be refered to the arbitrament of William Thomson & Adam Potter, Gentlemen Arbitrators, with power of Umpirage, their award to be a rule of Court.

John Bridges against Robert Smith. Attachment. Dismissed at the plaintiffs costs by his request.

Ordered that Burrell McBee a Bastard child, be bound to Vardry McBee, and that the Indentures be taken before Obadiah Trimmier, Esq., and returned to this Court.

Joseph Erwin against John Naile. Petition by Bond. Nonsuit.

James McGowen attorney for Erwin against John Naile. Petition by account. On motion & by the oath of James Dohertie attorney for the Plaintiff, setting forth that the Defendant assumed the payment of the Debt agreeable to the Instalment Law, Judgment was entered accordingly for ℔ 5 s 18 & costs of suit.

Vardry McBee against John Steen. Attachment. On motion of Willaim Shaw Gentleman attorney for the Plaintiff, Judgment is enby Default and the Plaintiff proving his account which was granted by the Court...we find for the Plaintiff ₺ 6 s 13 d 10 with costs of suit....

John McElray against Samuel McClure. Case. Ordered that this cause continue untill next Court at the Plaintiffs Costs.

William Wofford against Handcock Smith. Petition. Ordered that this case be continued.

Carlton Lindsey against Robert Parker & Benjamine Wofford. Petition. Ordered that this case be dismissed.

Hugh Means Esq. against John Hudgens & John Pennington. Petition. Dismissed at the Defendants Costs.

Charles Burton assinee of Potter against Joseph Quinn. Petition. The Defendant came into Court and confessed Judgment for the sum of ₺ 7 s 8 & costs of suit.

William Darby against Charles Burton. Petition. The Defendant came into Court and by James Doherty Esquire confessed Judgment for the sum of ₺ 6 s 15 d 9 & costs of suit. with stay of execution 1 month.

Samuel Miller against Martin Armstrong & John Miller. Petition by Note. John Miller one of the Defendants came into Court and confessed Judgment for the sum of ₺ 7 s 10 and costs of suit subject to the Instalment Law with stay of Execution untill Christmas next.

James Lusk against William Alldredge. Petition. Ordered that the Defendant give special Bail.

Thomas Gordon Assinee of White & McBee against Brittain Williford & John Shands, Exrs. of James White Deceased. Petition.
Ordered that this case be discontinued at the Plaintiffs Costs.

James Lusk against William Aldredge. Petition. Captain William Suddoth came into Court and Entered himself Special Bail for the Debt & Cost of suit, or render the body of the said Defendant in discharge thereof.

William McMullan as an evidence in the case John Bridges against Robert Smith on oath in open Court is allowed s 10 for 4 days attendance.

John Bingham as a witness in the case John Bridges against Robert Smith on oath in open Court is allowed s 7 d 6 for 3 days attendance.

Denny Anderson against William Rountree. Appeal. Ordered that this case continue untill next Court.

(above repeated twice)

John Tollason as an evidence in the case John McGuire against William Burton on oath in open Court, is allowed the sum of ₺ 1 s 5 for 10 days attendance.

William Bryan as a witness in the case John McGuire against William Burton on oath in open Court is allowed ₺ 1 for 8 days attendance.

Mary Brooks as a witness in the case, Thomas Brooks against Moses Wood on oath in open Court is allowed Ł 2 s 5 for 18 days attendance.

Eady Johnson as a witness in the case Thomas Brooks against Moses Wood, on oath in open Court is allowed Ł 2 s 5 for 18 days attendance.

John Kimbell is allowed Ł 1 s 15 for 14 days attendance as a witness in the case Thomas Brooks against Moses Wood.

Greenham Crowder is allowed s 17 d 6 for 7 days attendance as a witness in the case Thomas Brooks against Moses Wood.

An affidavit made in open Court by Major Passons concerning the loss of a Bond, ordered to be recorded.

Ordered that the minutes be read which was accordingly done and signed by James Jordan, Thomas Farrow, David Goodlett, Esq. Court then adjourned untill Tomorrow Nine o'Clock.

Wednesday the 22nd of September 1790. The Worshipful Court met according to last evenings adjournment. Present James Jordan, William Smith, Thomas Farrow, Zadock Ford, Esq.

Charles Bruce as an evidence in the case Ebenezer Morse against John Haile Esquire, on oath in open Court is allowed s 10 for 4 days attendance also the sum of Ł 1 s 6 d 8 from mileage 80 miles in coming to Court, from Greenville County.

Samson Bobo against Benjamine Wofford & Henry Earnest. Trover. The Plaintiff discharged Henry Earnest one of the Defendants in this suit and came by William Shaw Gentleman his Attorney & Benjamine Wofford the other defendant by James Doherty Esquire his attorney and thereupon came a Jury to wit (same as before)... we find for the plaintiff Ł 16 and costs of suit...

Present Baylis Earle Esquire.

Ordered, that John Gibbs serve as a constable for this County, granted by the Court, in consequence of a petition of a number of inhabitants of this County, upon his quallifying accordingly.

Ordered, that William McMullen be overseer of the Road from Charles McKnights to the South Fork of Packolate in the Room of Hugh Freeman, Hugh McMillen warner.

Ordered, that John Young Senior, Overseer the Road from the South fork of Packolate to the Widow Lewis's Mill on a branch of Lawsons Fork, in place of David McDowell, Joel Lewis warner.

Ordered, that William Byrd overseer the Road from the North Carolina line, to near Jameson Mill, where it joins Gowens Road, James Byrd warner.

Peter Brooks against George and John Roebuck. Debt. By consent of the parties and assent of the Court, the trial of this cause is defered untill next Court.

Ordered, that a Road be laid out and opened from the Sandy Ford on Enoree River to Blackstocks Ford on Tyger River and that Samuel Farrow Esquire lay out the same and also that Long John Couch oversee and the same in good repair, Adam Garner warner.

Ordered that a Road be opened from Blackstocks Road, near the South side of Joel Smith's Plantation, to go a direct course to Darby's Store, crossing this County line near Prewit Town, and that Dudly Red open & oversee the same, Moses Prewit, warner.

Adam Garner as a witness in the case Samson Bobo against Benjamine Wofford, on oath in open Court is allowed s 10 for 4 days attendance.

Burrel Bobo is allowed s 27 d 6 for 11 days attendance as a witness in the case Samson Bobo against Benjamine Wofford.

John Casey as an evidence in the case Benjamine Wofford at the suit of Samson Bobo on oath in open Court is allowed Ł 20 for 16 days attendance.

Henry Meredith as an evidence in the case Samson Bobo against Benjamine Wofford, on oath in open Court is allowed s 10 for 4 days attendance.

Edmund Pugh against John Williams. Special Action on the Case. Dismissed at the Defendants Costs by consent.

John Wood against Thomas Hanna. Trover. Zopher Smith as witness subpoened for the Plaintiff having appeared before the Court and the Jury being sworn to try the cause refused to give his Testimoney, in contempt to the Court, norwithstanding an order of Court, refused to give the same untill his attendance were paid. Ordered that he be committed to jail by the oppinion of Baylis Earle, James Jordan, David Goodlett & William McDowell, Esq. Thomas Farrow Esq. descented thereto.

John Wood against Thomas Hanna. Trover. Zopher Smith, as a material witness in this case, refused to give his Testimony, for which the Plaintiff was obliged to suffer a Nonsuit.

Josiah Culbertson as a witness in the case John Wood against Thomas Hanna, on oath in open Court, is allowed Ł 3 s 10 for 28 days attendance.

John Elder is allowed Ł 2 s 17 d 6 for 23 days attendance as a witness in the case John Wood against Thomas Hanna.

James Wofford against John Collins. Trover. Ordered, that the trial of this cause be Defered untill next Court.

William Bratcher against Baylis Earle Esq. Exr. of Edward Hampton. Debt. Nonsuit.

William Bratcher against Baylis Earle Esq. Executor of Edward Hampton. Trover. Nonsuit.

John Williams against William Duncan & Moses Biter. Special Action on the Case. On motion of William Shaw Esquire Attorney for the Plaintiff, Ordered that he suffer a Nonsuit by his request.

Jonathan Neasbitt against Thomas Daugherty & Arias Brown. By consent of the parties, Ordered that this case be refered to the arbitrament of Samuel Clowney, Nevil Wayland, John McElheny, Robert Foster, Thomas Wyatt & James Taylor White, Gentlemen, Arbitrators, with power of Umpirage. Their award returned into Court to morrow, shall be a rule thereof.

Thomas and Temperance Hamilton against Benjamine Wofford. Trover. Ordered that this case stand over untill the day after tomorrow and then come to trial.

John Duncan as a witness in the case John Williams against Willaim Duncan & Moses Biter, on oath in open Court is allowed ₺ 1 s 12 d 6 for 13 days attendance.

Thomas Blasingame as a witness in the case William Brachter against Baylis Earle Esq. Exr. of Edward Hampton Deceased, on oath in open Court is allowed ₺ 1 s 12 d 6 for 13 days attendance.

George Haden as a witness in behalf of Owen Bowen against William Haden on oath in open Court is allowed s 6 d 6 for 3 days attendance.

Daniel Brown against Willis Watkins & Michael Hogan. Case. Ordered, that this cause be discontinued.

John Wood against Thomas Hanna. Trover. In this case Zopher Smith being a material witness refused to qualify to the Jury after they were sworn, was thereupon committed to the custody of the sheriff upon which a nonsuit took place. The Jury being discharged, the said Smith came into Court and made his confession for his contempt. The Court thought fit to discharge him from his imprisonment on that account.

Ordered that the minutes be read which were accordingly done and signed by Baylis Earle, Thomas Farrow, David Goodlett, James Jordan, Esq. Court then adjourned untill Tomorrow Eight O'Clock.

Thursday the 23rd of September 1790. Court met according to adjournment. Present James Jordan, William Smith, Thomas Farrow, Esq.

The State against Travice Morse. Indictment. Ordered that all the Recognizances in this case continue untill next Court.

Jonathan Neasbitt against Thomas Daugherty & Arais Brown. Debt. This case being refered yesterday to the Arbitrators...we ... could not agree; so chose an Umpire William Fields who aver'd as his oppinion that the Bond must be paid by the said Arias Brown together with the Lawful Interest thereon agreeable to the Tenor of the same, and the whole cost of suit, except Jonathan Neasbitts Lawyers fees...22nd Sept 1790 Samuel Clowney, Nevil Wayland, John McElheny, Robert Foster, Thomas Wyatt, James T. White, Arbitrators, William Fields, Umpire.

Benjamine Wofford & Burrell Thomson against Henry Merridith. Debt. The original writ being misplaced so that it could not be found Decreed by the Court that a new writ Issue agreeable to the Declaration & proceed to Trial, and on motion of William Shaw attorney for the plaintiff Ordered that a Nonsuit be entered.

The State against Jacob Eisen. Indictment. By order of Court, no Evidence appearing to support the Indictment, Ordered that a Nolli Prosique be entered by W. Shaw Co. Atty.

The State against William Redman & Samuel Redman. Petit Larceny. Ordered, that capias's issue against the Defendants Returnable to next March Court, & that Scieri Facias's issue against the Bail, and the Capias's issue against Hugh Stephenson, Alexander Stephenson, Jane McCle, David McDowell & Robert McDowell, Returnable before some Justice of the County to appear to March Court next to give evidence in behalf of the State.

The State against Reubin Dickson. Recognizance. Ordered, that his Recognizance be forfeited by reason of his not producing the person indicted for which he was bound.

Elizabeth Thomson against William Graham. Attachment. Nonsuit.

Thomas Brandon Esq. attorney for Hendrix against Robert Harper and William Byrd. Trover. Ordered that this suit be dismissed at the Defendants costs by a letter from the Plaintiff.

Same against Same. Trover. Dismissed at the Defendants costs by a letter from the Plaintiff.

William Venible against John Conner. Debt. On motion of William Shaw attorney for the plaintiff Judgment was entered by default Ordered that a writ of Enquiry be executed in this case, whereupon came a Jury ... N. B. a Repetition is entered in this case.

William Venible against John Conner. Debt. On motion of William Shaw Gentleman attorney for the Plaintiff, Judgment was entered by Default, Ordered that a writ of enquiry be executed in this case, Whereupon came a jury (same as before)...we find for the plaintiff ₤ 18 with lawful interest & costs of suit....

Joshua Hawkins against Holland Sumner. Trover. The Defendant being solemnly called, and not appearing himself nor by his attorney, On motion of Zachariah Toliaferro Gentl. Attorney for the Plaintiff, Judgment was thereupon entered by Default.

William Pool J. M. against William Henderson. Case. Discontinued at the Defendants Costs.

Samuel Nesbitt against Thomas Still. Attachment. Dismissed at the plaintiffs costs, since the Judgment was confessed.

William Ford as an evidence in the case Jonathan Nesbitt against Thomas Daugherty & Arias Brown, on oath in open Court is allowed s 7 d 6 for 3 days attendance.

A covenant and agreement between Seth Lewis, Elizabeth Lewis & Agness Nesbitt and James Nesbitt, proved in open court by the evidence of Jonathan Nesbitt, Ordered to be recorded.

Nicholas Holley against John Bragg. Debt. Came the plaintiff by William Shaw his attorney and the Defendant by Zachariah Toliaferro his attorney the Court on hearing the alligations of each party, Ordered that the plaintiff by Nonprossed.

Thomas Farrow Esq. as an evidence in the case Nicholas Holley against John Bragg on oath in open Court was allowed ₤ 3 s 2 d 6 for 25 days attendance.

Vardry McBee against John Wooton. Attachment. The defendant being solemnly called and not appearing by himself or his attorney, on motion of James Dohertie, attorney for plaintiff, Judgment was thereupon entered by default.

Israel Morriss against Major Passons. Attachment. Ordered that the Plaintiff be Nonprossed.

Jeremiah Shields against Israel Morriss. Debt. The Defendant being solemnly called and not appearing by himself nor his attorney, on motion of William Shaw Gentleman attorney for the plaintiff, Ordered that Judgment be entered by default.

William Venible against Isham Saffold. Case. On motion of Zachariah Tolliaferro attorney for the Defendant, Ordered that the Plaintiff be nonprossed.

Joseph Dickson against Joseph Buffington. Debt. The Defendant being called and not appearing by himself nor his Attorney, on miotion of James Dohertie attorney for the plaintiff, Ordered that Judgment be entered by Default.

Joseph Means against Benjamine Wofford. Trover. Came the plaintiff by William Shaw Gentleman his attorney and the defendant by James Dohertie Esq. his attorney, whereupon came a Jury (same as before)...we find for the plaintiff ₺ 12 with costs of suit.

Robert Head against The Admr. & Admx. of Michael Sprinkle Decd. On a charge of wasting the Estate of said Decd. After the Testimony of Thomas Reece and Henry Aires being Heard by the Court Ordered that the Admrs. appear in this Court Tomorrow and give back security otherwise the admn. will be revoked and Re-administration granted, and the Lawful steps taken with the present administrations.

Charles Burton against Mark Powell. Attachment. By consent of the parties this case is refered to the arbitrament of Adam Potter, Christopher Casey and George Bruton as an Umpire, Gentlemen Arbitrators who are to meet next Friday week at Mr. Prices Store to arbitrate the same, their award returned to next Court shall be a rule thereof.

John Couch as an evidence in the case Benjamine Wofford and Burrell Thomson against Henry Meredith on oath in open Court was allowed ₺ 2 for 16 days attendance.

David Neal on oath in open Court is allowed ₺ 1 s 17 d 6 for 15 days attendance as a witness in the case Benjamine Wofford & Burrell Thomson against Henry Meredith.

Matthew Couch as an evidence in the case Benjamine Wofford and Burrell Thomson against Henry Meredith on oath in open Court is allowed ₺ 1 s 5 for 10 days attendance.

Levi Casey against Benjamine Wofford. Case. By the consent of the parties, Ordered that this case be refered to the arbitrament of Nathaniel Davis, Thomas Tod, and John Lindsey; Their award made at the House of Moses Case on the third Monday in October next, the Arbitrators & parties present to proceed in the business as tho' all were present, and returned to next Court, shall be the Judgment thereof.

George Lamkin against Joseph Buffington. Debt. Ordered that this case be defered untill next Court.

Thomas Jenkins against Maximilian Conner. Debt. Ordered that the defendant be nonprossed.

David McDowell against The Admr. of Rodden, to wit, Hugh Freeman. Special Action on the Case. Ordered that this case be dismissed.

John Holeman against George Lamkin. Debt. Ordered that the Plaintiff be nonprossed.

Samuel Jackson as an evidence in the case Joseph Means against Benjamine Wofford on oath in open Court is allowed Ł 1 s 15 for 14 days attendance, also Ł 1 s 17 d 6 for mileage from Union County.

William Smith against Joseph Warren. Case. The defendant being solemnly called and not appearing by himself nor his attorney, on Motion of James Dohertie Esq. attorney for the plaintiff, Judgment was entered by default.

Hugh Pierce against Thomas Gordon. Attachment. Ordered that the plaintiff be nonprossed.

John Gordon, Hugh Quinn and Benjamine Philips against John Pritchet and Jesse Tate. Debt. Discontinued at the defendants costs, the plaintiff attorney's fee except.

John Gordon, Hugh Quinn, and Benjamine Philips against Valentine Rizner, John Pritchet and Jesse Tate. Debt. Discontinued at the defendants costs, the plaintiffs attorney's fee excepted.

William Wofford against Joseph Buffington. Attachment. Ordered that the plaintiff be nonprossed.

Joseph Henderson assinee of Kirkindale against Andrew Milikin. Debt. This suit is abated by Death of the Plaintiff.

Ordered that the minutes be read which were accordingly done and signed by Baylis Earle, William Smith, James Jordan, David Goodlett, Esq. Court then adjourned untill tomorrow eight O'Clock.

Friday the 24th of September 1790. The Worshipful Court met according to last evenings adjournment. Present James Jordan, William Smith & David Goodlett, Esq.

Ordered that Alexander Copeland act in place of John McKnight as overseer of the Road from North Packolate where Hugh Freeman leaves off working, to the line of the State.

James Barron against John Moore. Debt. On motion of William Shaw Gentleman attorney for the Defendant, Ordered that the Plaintiff be Nonprossed.

Michael Miller against John Golightly. Malicious Prosecution. On motion of William Shaw Esq. attorney for the Defendant, Ordered that the plaintiff be nonprossed.

Randolph Casey against Moses Casey. Detinue. Dismissed at the plaintiffs costs.

John Thomas Junr. Esq. against Nicholas Holley. Vi. et armis. By consent of the parties and assent of the Court, the trial of this case is defered untill next Court.

Robert Goodgion against Israel Morriss. Attachment. Judgment were entered some time agone.

Alexander Ray against Moses Wood. Breaking Close. On motion of William Shaw Gentleman attorney for the Defendant, Ordered that the Plaintiff be Nonprossed.

William Ford against Daniel Monroe. Attachment. The defendant being solemnly called, and not appearing by himself or his attorney, on motion of Zachariah Toliaferro gentleman attorney for the plaintiff, Judgment was thereupon entered by default.

William Poole J. M. against James Cullins. Case. The defendant being solemnly called and not appearing by himself or his attorney on motion of William Shaw gentleman attorney for the plaintiff, Judgment was entered by default & the cause continued untill next Court.

Richard Harrison Esq. against Bazel Lee. Case. By consent of James Dohertie Esq. attorney for the plaintiff, this cause is discontinued at the plaintiffs costs.

Richard Harrison Esq. against Charles Bruce. Case. By consent of the plaintiff by James Dohertie Esq. his attorney this case is discontinued at his own costs.

William Pool J. M. against Joseph Buffington. Attachment. The defendant being called and not appearing by himself or his attorney, on motion of William Shaw Gentleman attorney for the plaintiff, Judgment was entered by default.

Francis Powers against Dennis Sherdon. Attachment. Judgment was entered in part heretofore, Ordered that the property in the hands of the Guarnishee, to wit, Henry Koon, be exposed to sale for the use of the plaintiff.

Robert Goodgion against Israel Morriss. Attachment. Ordered that a scieri Facias issue against Col. Henry M. Wood who was summoned in this case as Guarnishee, to declare what property he hath of the defendants in posession.

Owen Bowen attorney for Stewart against William Haden. Detinue. The parties join issue in this case and continue the same untill next Court.

William Austin against Edward Arnold. Case. Ordered that this cause continue untill next Court.

Samuel Elder against Elisha Smith. Debt. By consent of the parties and assent of the Court, the trial of this cause is defered untill next Court.

Francis Powers against Dennis Sherdon. Attachment. Judgment heretofore in part, the Constable had orders to sell a Horse condemd. to sale for the plaintiff Returns "Sold for £ 2, bought by Francis Powers. "
                              Thomas Wyatt, Const.

Vardry McBee against John Wooton. Attachment. On motion of James Dohertie Esq. attorney for the plaintiff, Ordered that this case be dismissed at the defendants costs.

Joshua Hawkins against Holland Sumner. Trover. On motion of Zachariah Toliaferro attorney for the plaintiff, Ordered that a writ of enquity be executed, whereupon came a jury (same as before)...we find for the Plaintiff £ 10 with costs of suit.

Michael Miller against John Cambell. Attachment. On motion of William Shaw Gentleman attorney for the plaintiff, Ordered that Judgment be entered by default.

Jeremiah Sheals against Israel Morriss. Debt. On motion of William Shaw gentleman attorney for the plaintiff, Ordered that a writ of enquiry be executed, whereupon came a jury (same as before)...we find for the plaintiff ₺ 29 and lawful interest with costs of suit....

Thomas Crowther as a witness in the case Joshua Hawkins against Holland Sumner on oath in open Court is allowed ₺ 1 s 17 d 6 for 15 days attendance.

Ann Arnold as a witness in the case Thomas Hamilton against Benjamine Wofford, on oath in open court, is allowed ₺ 1 s 15 for 14 days attendance also the sum of ₺ 1 s 6 d 8 for mileage.

Ann Arnold likewise as a witness in the case John Ward against Thomas Hamilton on oath is allowed s 17 d 6 for 7 days attendance, also s 13 d 4 for mileage.

Edward Arnold on oath is allowed s 17 d 6 for 7 days attendance as a witness in the case Thomas Hamilton and wife against Benjamine Wofford.

Michael Miller against John Cambell. Attachment. William Simmons as Guarnishee by the Judgment of the Court stand indebted to the defendant ₺ 40 payable in property at Christmas next, Ordered that on the first Monday in Jan. next the said Simmons produce property to the amount of the said Debt after the attachment obtained by Benjamine McMakin and exected by first satisfyed ...to be appraised by John Nichol by appointment of the court on the part of the defendant, and on the part of the Guarnishee such person as he may appoint.

David Golightly as an evidence in the case Michael Miller against John Golightly on oath in open Court is allowed s 12 d 6 for 5 days attendance.

Jeremiah Selman on oath is allowed s 10 for 4 days attendance as a witness in the case Michael Miller against John Golightly.

John Miller on oath is allowed s 10 for 4 days attendance as a witness in the case Michael Miller against John Golightly.

Henry Wells Esq. as a witness in the case Michael Miller against John Golightly on oath is allowed s 12 d 6 for 4 days attendance.

Ordered that a Road be opened the nearest and best way 30 feet wide from this Court House to Portroyal the new buildings belonging to William Shaw and William Benson, Esq.

Spencer Bobo against Samuel Porter. Attachment. Ordered that Judgment be entered by default, and that a writ of enquity be executed whereupon came a jury (same as before)...we find for the plaintiff ₺ 13 and lawful interest with costs of suit.

Ordered that William Shaw County Attorney, be allowed 3 guineas for his drawing the conveyance for the 2 acres of Land for the use of the County, from Thomas Williamson to the Justices of the Court.

John Camp against John Chism. Case. On motion of Zach. Toliaferro Esq. attorney for the Defendant, ordered that this case be discontinued at the plaintiffs costs.

William Smith against Joseph Warren. Case. On motion of James Dohertie Esq. Attorney for the plaintiff, Ordered that this cause be dismissed at the Defendants costs.

Ordered that the Estrays be exposed to sale by the Sheriff, according to Law.

Ordered that the Readministration of the Estate of Michael Sprinkle deceased be committed to Robert Head, upon his giving Samuel Elder and some other sufficient freeholder as his surity for his lawful performance.

Ordered that the Road from Nichol's old Mill to where it intersects the Road from Fords Mill to the Ironworks, be opened and kept in good Repair according to Law by Jeremiah Selman, who is to oversee the same. Thomas Tinsley, warner.

Ordered that the minutes be read, which were accordingly done and signed by James Jordan, William Smith, D. Goodlett, Esq. Court then adjourned untill Court in Course.

Pursuant to a late act of the Legislature of the State of South Carolina, the Honorable Court of Spartan County were Held at the Court House on the third Monday in March 1791. Present the Hon. William Smith Esq.

Ordered that a Grand and Petit Jury be drawn to serve at the Court of Sessions and Pleas to be Held on the 12th day of June next.

Grand Jurors

William Lipscomb	1	John Snoddy	11
Charles Hester	2	Jesse Connell	12
Samuel Morrow	3	Tobias Bright	13
John Posey	4	William Hembry	14
Francis Dod	5	John Jones	15
Alexander Walker	6	Moses Foster	16
Joseph Barnett	7	Robert Nesbitt	17
William Pool, Taylor	8	George Burton	18
Jonathan Harriss	9	William Foster	19
John Beard	10	George Connell	20

Petit Jurors

Thomas Penny	1	David Allen	16
Ellis Cannon	2	John Williamson	17
Burrel Thomson	3	William Bruce	18
Hance Harper Junior	4	James Crowther	19
Travice Reece	5	Aaron Floyd	20
Simson Newman	6	Ephraim Reece	21
Richard Morriss	7	James Smith Capt.	22
Daniel Amos	8	William Stephenson	23
Aaron Pinson	9	John McCarrell	24
Jacob Holmes	10	Samuel Timmons	25
Abram Wyatt	11	Henry Morgan	26
William Fondrin	12	Nathaniel Davis	27
John Grizzle	13	John Byars	28
Isaiah Lewis	14	John Elder	29
John Gibbs not Const.	15	Rowland Cornelius	30

Ordered that the minutes be read which was accordingly done & signed by William Smith, Esqr. Court then adjourned untill Tomorrow Nine O'Clock.

Tuesday the 22nd of March 1791. The Honorable Court met according to adjournment. Present The Honorable William Smith and James Jordan,Esq. who being quallifyed according to Law.

William Lipscomb as principle, John Shippy & Isham Foster as Surities, acknowledge to owe to the State of S. C. ₤ 50...if you personally shall personally appear at the next court of please & sessions to be held for this County ln 12th June next to answer an Indictment for beating the wife of James Fannen so as to make her mis-carry and not depart from thence untill discharged by the same, then this recognizance to be void, else in full force in Law. Wit:
W. Lancaster, D. C.

Ordered that all recognizance taken by the Justices of the peace for this County be returned to the Clerk on or before the first day of every succeeding Court for the future.

Charles Burton against Mark Powell. Attachment. October the 11th 1790. We the Arbitrators on the within case do award that Mark Powell pay the costs & pay Mr. Burton ₤ 10 between this & Christmas in Good Trade. If Mr. Powell & Mr. Burton cannot agree, the property to be valued at Trade Rate. Adam Potter, Christopher Casey, George Bruton, Arbitrators.

Thomas Farrow, Samuel Lancaster, David Goodlett, Isham Harrison, Samson Bethel, Zadock Ford & Thomas Moore Esq. being nominated by the Legislature of this State as Justices of the peace for this County, Hath taken the necessary oaths of office before The Hon. William Smith Esq. and this Court.

The Last Will and Testament of Hezekiah Childs deceased, being proven in open Court by the evidence of Henry Turner & William Turner subscribing witnesses to the same, who made oath that they also saw Thomas Williamson subscribe his name as a witness thereto, Ordered to be recorded.

Jeston Childs & John Childs Exrs. of the Estate of Hezekiah Childs Deceased, came into court and took the usual oath prescribed by Law.

The Court proceeded to the nomination of a Sheriff, when Major John Gowen was unanimously appointed, Ordered that a certificate issue to his Excellency the Governor in order for him to be commissioned accordingly.

Ordered that John Young Senior, William McMillan & David McDowell lay out a Road from Charles McKnights ford on North Packolate River to Cross South Packolate about a mile below James Gilmores ford on said River, and direct the same the nearest and best way to this Court-House.

Ordered that the Estrays be sold by the Sheriff according to Law.

Ordered that an Alias Fieri Facias issue to Union County or elsewhere in the case Thomas Blasengame Junior against Holland Sumner in consequence of an affidavit being provided by said Blasingame that the original was lost.

Absalom Lancaster, Larkin Lancaster, John Westmoreland, John Gibbs & Nathaniel Stokes being appointed Constables for this County, hath taken the oaths of office accordingly.

George Bruton as an evidence in the case John Ward against Thomas Hamilton on oath before a Single Justice, is allowed s 12 d 6 for his attendance.

Ordered that the minutes be read which were accordingly done & signed by William Smith, James Jordan, Esq. Court then adjourned untill the 12th day of June next.

An an Intermediate Court began and Held for the County of Spartanburgh, at the Cour-House, on the second Monday in April 1791.

Present Their Honors William Smith and James Jordan Esq.; John Thomas Junr. Esquire who having heretofore acted as Clerk for this county, came into Court and resigned the said office. The Court therefore thanked him for his faithful attendance & performance in said office, and appointed William Lancaster Clerk of the same, who gaive his hand & took the necessary oaths accordingly.

John Gowen Esquire being heretofore appointed Sheriff of this County produced his Commission, gave his Bond and took the oaths of office prescribed by Law.

Vincent Anderson being Recommended by the Sheriff to the Court, to act as Deputy Sheriff, was apporved of, and quallifyed accordingly.

Ordered that Thomas Mabrey have License to keep a Tavern and Retail spirituous liquors, upon his giving approved surities, which he did accordingly in open Court.

A Deed of Conveyance from Philemon Martin attorney for William Rush to John Gowen, acknowledged in open Court by the said Martin, Ordered to be recorded.

ordered that Thomas Price have Licence to keep a public House of Entertainment & Retail Spirituous Liquors upon his giving approved Surities, which he did accordingly.

Ordered that John Tollison have licence to keep public House & Retail Spirituous liquors upon his giving sufficient Surities & Conforming to the Rates prescribed by Law.

Ordered that Henry McCray have licence to Retail Spirituous liquors & keep public House of Entertainment upon his giving lawful surities, which he did in open Court.

A Lease & Release from William Colwall to Martha McCray proved in open Court by the evidence of Andrew Thomson who made oath he saw the same Legally Executed, Ordered to be recorded.

Ordered that William Haden, Thomas Jordan & Moses Proctor view the Road leading from John Shippy's towards Green River & Report to next Court, what Inconveniences hath arisen by Matthew Guttery turning the same & Direct which way said Road shall Lead.

Ordered that Samuel Fowler Oversee the Road leading from Jamesons old Mill to the Head of Lawsons Fork as far as Passon's Road, in place of John Gowen Esq., John Fowler, warner.

Ordered that William Fields oversee the Road leading from Passon's Road to where it intersects the Road near the Widow Bishop's, in place of Thomas Davis, Thomas Brooks, warner.

Ordered that the minutes be read which was accordingly done and signed by James Jordan, William Smith, Judges. Court then adjourned untill tomorrow Nine O'Clock.

Tuesday the 12th of April 1791. The Honorable Court met according to last Evenings adjournment. Present Their Honors William Smith and James Jordan, Esq.

Ordered that Thomas Williamson have licence to keep public House of Entertainment and retail spirituous Liquors, upon his giving approved Surities, to conform to the Rates and Orders Required by Law.

Ordered that a Deed of Gift from Susannah Spencer to Jesse Spencer which was proven in open Court by the evidence of Griffin Hogan, who made oath that he also saw John McInvail subscribe his name as a witness thereto, Be Recorded.

A Deed of Conveyance from Alexander Kilpatrick and wife to Benjamine Clerk, lawfully proven in open Court by the evidence of John Young Junior, Ordered to be Recorded.

A Receipt on the Back of a Mortgage from John Bullion to Thomas Shurley proven in open Court by the Evidence of Charles Burton, Ordered to Record.

A Deed of Conveyance from Luke Thornton and wife to Nicholas Keating proven in open Court by the Evidence of Andrew Thomson according to Law, Ordered to Record.

William Moore came into Court & acknowledged a Deed of Conveyance to John Curham, Ordered to Record.

Turner Thomason being appointed by the Court to act as a Constable for this County, came into Court & took the oaths of office prescribed by Law.

Ordered that Majr. James Lusk have Licence to keep a public House of Entertainment, and retail spirituous Liquors, upon his giving approved surities, which he did in open Court.

Ordered that the Estrays be sold by the Sheriff according to Law.

Ordered that Alexander Walker serve as Coroner for this County, the next two years ensuing, & that a Certificate issue to his Excellency, for him to be Commissioned accordingly.

Ordered that the minutes be Read which were done and signed by James Jordan, Wm. Smith, Judges. Court then adjourned untill the second Monday in September next.

At a Court of Sessions and pleas, Began and Held at the Court-House of Spartanburgh county, on the 13th of June (the 12th happening on Sunday) 1791. Present their Honors William Smith & James Jordan, Esqr. The Court proceeded to Draw the Grand Jurors for Next January Session, to wit.

Benjamine McMekin	1	John Tollison	11
John Brown	2	William Elder	12
Thomas Milikin	3	Charles McKnight	13
Thomas Paden	4	George Roebuck	14
Aaron Moore	5	Josiah Tanner	15
Shands Golightly	6	Stephen Wilson	16

Thomas Williamson	7	David McDowell	17
Josiah Culbertson	8	James Hooper	18
Thomas Wyatt	9	John Smith F. F.	19
Daniel McClaren	10	Tobias Bright	20

Petit Jurors drawn for next January Session, to wit,

Thomas Jordan	1	James Kean	16
Noel Johnson	2	Arthur Simson	17
Samuel Culbertson	3	Jonathan Gibbs	18
John Shands	4	Francis Clayton	19
George Taylor	5	Samuel Kithcart	20
Spencer Bobo, big	6	Jacob Chamberly	21
Thomas McCrory	7	Jordan Reaves	22
William Crow	8	Alexander McCarter	23
William Casey	9	David Prewet	24
Andrew Ray	10	John Gibson	25
Joseph Buring	11	James Stephenson	26
George Turner	12	Edward Clayton	27
David Humphries	13	Thomas Rodgers	28
Ezekial Wells	14	Job Sossbery	29
John McElwrath	15	John Wood	30

William Shaw Esq. County Attorney, took the oath prescribed by the fourth Article of the late constitution of this State, by order of Court.

The Grand Jury to serve the Present Court, to wit,

William Lipscomb, foreman	1	Jonathan Harriss	9
Charles Hester	2	George Bruton	10
Samuel Morrow	3	John Beard	11
John Posey	4	John Snoddy	12
Frances Dod	5	Tobias Bright	13
Alexander Walker	6	John James	14
Joseph Barnett	7	Moses Foster	15
William Pool, Taylor	8	William Foster	16
		George Connell	17

were sworn, received their charge by the County Attorney, and returned to their chambers.

Thomas Walker Esq. producing his Commission as an Attorney at Law, was thereupon admitted to practice in this Court.

Michael B. Roberts against Charles Bruce. Special Action on the Case. By request of the parties this case is refered to the arbitrament of David Goodlett Esq., James Gibbs & Brittain Williford, their award return to this Court to be the Judgment thereof.

Charles Bruce against Richard Harrison Esq. Mal Pro. Dismissed at the Defendants Costs by Consent.

Levi Casey against Benjamine Wofford. Case. Judgment by award for the sum of £ 10 and costs of suit.

The State against William Lipscomb. Indictment. The parties having compromised the matter, Ordered by the Court that the County Attorney Enter Noli prosequi on the Indictment.

The State against John Conner. On Scire Facias. Ordered that his Recognizance be forfeited in the sum of £ 25 wherein he was bound for the personal appearance of William Redman and Samuel Redman, in which they failed to do.

The State against Samuel Hayes. Escape. Ordered that a Bench warrant issue against the Defendant for Breaking & Escaping from Jail & Imprisonment of this County.

Ordered that the Defendant pay into the Treasury of the County the sum of ₤ 5 proclamation money at the Expiration of 12 months and that she give bond & security in the sum of ₤ 100 to keep the burthen of the maintenance of Her Bastard Child from falling on the County.

Michael B. Roberts against Charles Bruce. Special Action. This suit being Refered to the Arbitrament of David Goodlett Esq., Brittain Williford & James Gibbs who Return their award & say We the Arbitrators are of oppinion that Roberts pay the Cost of the suit & it be dismissed.

Richard Roberts against Thornton McDaniel. Assault & Battery. Dismissed at the Plaintiffs cost by consent.

Joel Hembree against Benjamine Wofford. Case. Discontinued by consent.

Charles Burton assinee of Mangham against Josiah Tanner. Debt. Discontinued at the Defendants costs.

William Birdsong attorney for Brooks against James Terrill. Trover. Dismissed at the Plaintiffs cost by Request.

John Bagwell against Andrew Paul. Attachment. Dismist at the Defendants costs by request of Mr. Henry McCray, who assumes the payment of the same.

Samuel Farrow Esq. against Nicholas Holley & Joseph Wofford. petition on a note. on motion of William Shaw attorney for the plaintiff Judgment was entered according to Specialty for ₤ 6 and costs of suit.

Peter Brooks against George & John Roebuck. Debt. Dismissed at the Defendants Cost by agreement, the Sheriffs fee excepted.

William Pool J. M. against James Cullin. Case.
Same against Same. Case.
Both the above suits dismissed at the Defendants Cost.

Henry McCray against Robert Hobbs. Attachment. William Thomson as Guarnishee in this Case came into Court & made oath that he Justly owed the Defendant by note of Hand two cows & calves which was condemned by the Court for the use of the plaintiff.

The State against James Dohertie. Petit Larcey. The Grand Jury find a True Bill.   William Lipscomb, foreman.

The last will and testament of William Jordan Deceased proven in open Court by the Evidence of John Jordan. Ordered to Record.

A Deed of Conveyance from John Ward to Daniel Barnett, acknowledged in open Court by the said Ward, Ordered to Record.

John Cantrell being appointed to act as constable for this County, came into Court and took the Necessary Oaths of office prescribed by Law.

The State against James Dohertie. Petit Larceny. Col. Thomas Brandon, Richard Powell & William Farrow came into Court and acknowledged to owe to the State Ł 50 each if they fail to appear to give their testimoney...

Ordered that the minutes be read which was accordingly done and signed by William Smith, James Jordan, Judges. Court then adjourned untill Tomorrow 9 O'Clock.

Tuesday the 14th of June 1791. Court met according to adjournment. Present their Honors, William Smith & James Jordan, Esq.

The State against William Redman & Samuel Redman. Petit Larceny. Ordered by the Court that the County Attorney Enter Noli prosequi on this Indictment.

William Sutin against Edward Arnold. Case. By consent of the parties and assent of the Court the trial of this cause is defered untill next Court.

The State against William McClure. Petit Larceny. The Defendant acknowledged to owe to the State Ł 25 and Hugh Stephenson & John McClure his securities Ł 25...by way of recognizance if the sd. William McClure shall fail to appear....

Baylis Earle Esquire being appointed by the Legislature of this State to act as one of the Judges of this County Took the Necessary oathes of his office, prescribed by Law, received his commission & took his seat with his associates.

Petit Jurors Summoned to Serve this Court

Ellis Cannon	1	Abram Wyatt	10
Thomas Penny	2	David Allen	11
Hance Harper	3	James Crowder	12
Travice Reece	4	Ephraim Reece	13
Samuel Timmons	5	John McCarrell	14
Richard Morriss	6	Simson Newman	15
Daniel Amos	7	Henry Morgan	16
Aaron Pinson	8	Nathaniel Davis	17
Jacob Holmes	9	John Byars	18

Hance Harper & Thomas Penny are Excused from serving as Petit Jurors for this Court.

John McElroy against Samuel McClure. Case. Came the Plaintiff by Thomas Walker Esq. his Attorney and the Defendant by William Shaw Gentl. his Attorney, whereupon came a Jury, to wit, Ephraim Reece, foreman; Ellis Cannon, Travice Reece, Samuel Timmons, Richard Morriss, Daniel Amos, Aaron Pinson, Jacob Holmes, Abram Wyatt, David Allen, John McCarrell, & Simson Newman...we find for the defendant, that the Defendant recover of the Plaintiff his Costs and damages in this suit....

The last will and testament of George Lowder proven in open court by the evidence of William Crow, agreeable to an act of assembly in that case made & provided Ordered to Record.

Ordered, that James Saunders have Licence to Retail Spirituous Liquors on his conforming to the Law, and the rates & rules of this Court

William Wofford against Handcock Smith. Petition by Account. On motion of Zachariah Toliaferro Gentl. Attorney, for the Plaintiff, It is Decreed by the Court that the Plaintiff recover of the Defendant, the sum of ₶ 9 s 6 d 3 with legal Interest from 25th May 1789, being the time the Debt became due, besides his costs....

The Last Will and Testament of William Spiller proven in open Court by the Evidence of Warrington Spiller agreeable to Law, Ordered to Record.

Nathan Childs, being appointed by the Court to act as a constable for this County, came into Court & Took the Necessary oaths of his office prescribed by Law.

The State against William Roberts. Incest or Fornication. Ordered that the Recognizance in this case Continue untill next Court.

James Wofford against John Collins. Trover. Came the plaintiff by William Shaw Esq. his Attorney & the Defendant by Zachariah Toliaferro his Attorney, whereupon came a Jury, to wit (same as before)...we find for the plaintiff ₶ 6 & costs of suit....

Baylis Earle Esq. against John Conner. Attachment. On motion of Zachariah Toliaferro & William Shaw Gentlemen attorneys for the Plaintiff, Judgment was entered by Default.

James Lusk against William Alldredge   Petition by Account. The parties came into Court, and settled on each paying their own Costs.

Thomas Gordon against James Lusk. Appeal. Dismissed at the plaintiff Costs by Consent.

Baylis Earle against John Conner. Attachment. Henry Woody came into Court and made oath that he was Justly Indebted to the Defendant the quantity of 8000 wieght of Tobacco, Ordered that the said quantity of Tobacco be condemned in the Hands of the said Guarnishee, for the use of the said Plaintiff.

The State against James McClure. Petit Larceny. Ordered that a Bench Warrant issue against the Defendant returnable before any Judge or Justice of the peace in this County, for him to be bound to appear at next Court....

The State against John McClure & Co. Indictment. Mary Saunders as principle, & John Gowen Esq. as her surity, came into court & acknowledgd to owe to the State ₶ 50 & suritiy in ₶ 25...if the said Mary Saunders shall fail to appear at next Court to give Testimoney in behlaf of the State....

The State against John McClure & Co. Indictment. Lucy Passons as principle, and Samuel McClure as her surity...to give testimony in behalf of the State against the said Defendants.

Miriam Anderson as a witness in the case James Wofford against John Collins on oath in Open Court is allowed ₶ 1 s 17 d 6 for 15 days attendance.

Court adjourned for Half an Hour. Court met according to adjournment.

Thomas & Temperance Hamilton against Benjamin Wofford. Trover. Came the Plaintiff by William Shaw Gent. his attorney, and the defendant by Zachariah Toliaferro his Attorney, whereupon came a Jury (same as before)...we find for the Plaintiff ₤ 10 and costs of suit....

Robert Harper against Joseph Venable. Special Action. By consent of the parties, this case is Refered to the Arbitrament of Baylis Earle Esq., John Gowen & James Hooper, their award to be a rule of Court.

Charity Martin as a witness in the case John Ward against Thomas Hamilton, on oath in open Court is allowed s 7 d 6 for 3 days attendance also s 13 d 4 for mileage.

Peggy Hamilton as a witness in the case John Ward against Thomas Hamilton on oath in open Court is allowed s 7 d 6 for 3 days attendance, and s 13 d 4 for mileage.

Benjamine Arnold a witness in the case Thomas & Temperance Hamilton against Benjamine Wofford on oath in open Court is allowed s 7 d 6 for 3 days attendance, and s 13 d 4 for mileage.

Edward Arnold a witness in the case Thomas & Temperance Hamilton against Benjamine Wofford on oath in open Court, is allowed s 7 d 6 for 3 days attendance

Denny Anderson against William Rountree. Appeal. Continued untill next Court.

John Ward against Thomas Hamilton. Trover. By agreement of the parties this Case is Refered to the arbitrament of Jesse Connell, John Ford, Isham Harrison and Henry Wells Esq. Gentlemen Arbitrators, their award made next Tuesday at the house of William Lindsey, and returned by next Court shall be a Rule thereof.

Ordered that the minutes be read which were accordingly done & signed by James Jordan, Baylis Earle, Judges. Court then adjourned untill Tomorrow 9 O'Clock.

Wednesday the 15th of June 1791. Court met according to adjournment. Their Honors James Jordan & Baylis Earle, Esq.

The State against James Dohertie. Petit Larceny. Ordered, that the Sheriff take the Body of James Dohertie & Bring him personally into Court in order to Stand his trial.

Present his Honor William Smith, Esq.

The State against William Morriss. Indictment. William Morriss as principle and Charles Bruce & Bazel Lee as his Surities came into Court, and acknowledged to owe ₤ 100 and the surities ₤ 50 each....to answer a chrage prefered against him for Horse stealing....

The State against James Dohertie. Indictment. The Defendant being arraigned, and on his Indictment pleaded not Guilty. Ordered that his trial be postponed untill peremptorily the Hour of two O'Clock, at his Request.

Joseph Dickson against Joseph Buffington. Debt. On motion of the plaintiffs councellors for a writ of Enquity...whereupon came as Jury (same as before)...the Plaintiff recover ₤ 33 s 7 d 4 according to specialty with legal interest thereon....

Felix Walker against Hugh Freeman. Debt. Dismissed at the Request of Thomas Walker attorney for the Plaintiff.

James Terrill against Vardry McBee & William Rickman. Debt. Nonsuit.

William Pool J. M. against Joseph Buffington. Attachment. On motion of William Shaw Esq. gentleman attorney for the plaintiff, that a writ of Enquiry should be Executed in this case...jury (same as before)...we find for the Plaintiff according to Specialty with interest & costs of suit...Ł 19 d 1 which became due 2 Dec 1790 with legal interest thereon.

Owen Bowen attorney for Elizabeth Stewart against William Haden. Detinue. Jonathan Bowen came into Court and Entered himself Security for the Costs that might accrue by the Plaintiff in this suit.

Same as above. Nonsuit.

The State against James Dohertie. Petit Larceny.
By the request of the Defendant to be brought out of Jail & to come to trial, Ordered by the Court that the Sheriff bring him into Court immediately & proceed accordingly.

Ordered that a summon Issue against Margaret Johnson for her to shew cause why Judgment should not be entered against her, for the value of a Horse & Mare Taken up by Her as Estrays, and not acting agreeable to Law.

The State against James Dohertie. Pettit Larceny. Came William Shaw Gentl. attorney in Behalf of the State and the Defendant by his Councelors, whereupon came a Jury (same as before)...Guilty, on which the prisoner implor'd mercy from the Court.

Henry McCray against Robert Hobbs. Attachment. On motion of Zachariah Toliaferro attorney for the plaintiff, Decreed by the Court, that he recover Ł 7 d 3 and costs of suit.

Henry McCray against Abram Williams. Appeal. Continued by Order of Court.

Henry McCray against Walter Burrell. Appeal. Continued by Order of Court.

Henry McCray against John Elder. Appeal. Continued by Order of Court.

On motion of William Shaw Esquire, Ordered that Samuel Farrow Esq. & George Riner be Released from their Recognizance in which they were bound for the personal appearance of James Dohertie to this Court to stand his Indictment.

The State against James Dohertie. Petit Lerceny. The Court proceeded to pass sentence which was that the prisoner at the Bar should be taken from thence to the Common Jail of this County where he is to remain untill Friday the 15th day of July next (unless he gives satisfactory security to the Court personally to appear & suffer the sentence of this Court) and to be removed from the said Jail to the public whipping post of this County, and between the hours of Twelve and two O'Clock to recieve on his Bare back five lashes well laid on by the Sheriff.

156

Ordered that for the above & other accusation against the said James Dohertie, that he be forever hereafter silenced from practicing as an Attorney at Law in this Court.

Baylis Earle Esq. against John Conner. Attachment. On motion of Zachariah Toliaferro Attorney for the Plaintiff, that a writ of Inquiry should be executed in this Case...came a Jury (same as before)....we find for the Plaintiff ₤ 15 & costs of suit....

On oath of William Darby stating that James Dohertie called him to the Jail and threating (sic) that he would take the life of one man the moment he was at liberty and stating that he believed the threat was apointed at the said William Darby or William Shaw Esq. having mentioned his name & saying that God had forsaken him & he did not Care what he did, and that the said William Darby swearing that he was in fear of Himself, Ordered that before the said James Dohertie be admitted to his liberty that he enter into Bond of ₤ 1000 with good and sufficient security that he peaceably behave himself to the said William Darby & William Shaw Esq. and all other Citizens of this State & that a Copy of this Order be immediately Transmitted to the Sheriff.

The State against William Morriss. Indictment. James Robertson & Elizabeth Robertson as principles and Joseph Robertson & Zachariah Robertson as surities, James & Elizabeth ₤ 50 each and Zachariah & Joseph ₤ 25 each if the said James & Elizabeth shall fail to appear at next Court of Sessions & pleas for this County to give Testimony in behalf of the State against the said Morriss.

Baylis Earle Esq. against John Conner. Attachment. Ordered that the property in the Hands of the Guarnishee be exposed to sale to satisfy the said Plaintiff, or so much thereof that will satisfy the Debt & on his failing to Deliver the same shall pay to the Plaintiff ₤ 15 & costs of suit said sale of property is subject to be upon the same Terms as the Debt was Originally to be Discharged by Woody to Conner.

William Ford against Daniel Monroe. Attachment. On a motion of Zachariah Toliaferro attorney for the Plaintiff, a writ of Inquiry was executed...we find for the plaintiff ₤ 43 s 12 d8 with costs of suit....

Henry McCray against Abram Williams. Appeal. Ordered, that this suit be Dismissed.

Ordered that the Estrays be exposed to sale by the Sheriff according to Law.

Wells Griffith against William Wood. Attachment. Continued by Order of Court.

John Alexander Esq. against Martin Armstrong. Attachment. Continued by Order of Court.

Samuel Farrow Esq. against John Elder, William Elder, & Alexander Elder. Debt. Continued by Order of Court.

John Williams against William Duncan & Moses Biter. Trover. Discontinued by request of the plaintiff.

Joel Hembree against Nicholas Holley. Debt. Continued by Order of Court.

Winthrop & Co. assinee of Tod. against John Moore. Debt. Continued by Order of Court.

Richard Hampton & Co. against Richard Harrison Esq. Debt. Continued by Order of Court.

Thomas Gordon against William Young. Attachment. William Pool as Guarnishee in this case, came into Court & made oath, that he is indebted to the Defendant some certain sum but cannot Estimate at this time what, But sayes on his oath that whatever he shall fall indebted to the Defendant when he makes a true estimation he will pay to the said Plaintiff in the same manner as he was to pay the same to the said Defendant, which were the Order of Court.

Ordered that John James be paid by the County Treasurer s 10 d 7 for sawing plank & halling the same for repairing the jail, and that Alexander Walker be paid s 35 out of the County fund, for repairing the same.

John Barry being appointed to act as a constable for this County, by the Court, took the Oathes of office accordingly.

Ordered that three Constables be summoned to attend next September Court.

Ordered that the minutes be read, which were accordingly done & signed by Baylis Earle, James Jordan, William Smith, Judges. Court then adjourned untill Court in Course.

At a Court of Sessions and pleas began and Held at the Court-House of Spartanburgh County on the 12th January 1792. Present their Honors James Jordan & William Smith, Esq.

The Court proceeded to draw the Grand Jurors for June Court next, to wit,

John Golightly	1	Daniel McClaren	11
Giles Connell	2	Aaron Moore	12
Samuel Neasbitt	3	David McDowell	13
Josiah Culbertson	4	Samuel Morrow	14
James Hooper	5	Jesse Connell	15
William Elder	6	Frances Dod	16
John Young	7	William Thomson Gentl.	17
Alexander Walker	8	John Posey	18
Jonathan Harriss	9	John Neasbitt Colo.	19
William Hembree	10	George Connell	20

Petit Jurors for next Court

John Smith B. S.	1	William Rampley	16
Ignacious Griffin	2	Paul Castleberry	17
Thomas Jenkans	3	John Hayes	18
William Smith Tyger	4	Joseph Rice	19
John Berk	5	John Center	20
John Pack	6	Robert Connell	21
John Stone	7	Zachariah Carwile	22
William Reaves	8	Samuel Ford	23
Augustine Clayton	9	Peter Edwards	24
David McCarley	10	Jacob Earnest	25
John Earle	11	William McClure	26
William Anderson B. S.	12	William Powers	27
Thomas Cary	13	John Burnett	28
Benjamine Couch	14	Hugh Fourley	29
Joseph Chastain	15	Tobias Bright Junr.	30

Charles McKnight being summoned to this Court, to serve as a Juror, the Court hath acquitted him from ever attending the same in this County for that purpose.

The Grand Jurors that appeared were dismissed untill Tomorrow 10 O'clock.

Abram Nott Esq. produced his commission as an Attorney as Law and equity in this State, Ordered that he be enrolled on the records of this Court to practice the same.

The Last will and testament of Robert McMillin proved in open Court by the evidence of William McMillen agreeable to Law, Ordered to Record.

Ordered that the minutes be read which was accordingly done and signed by James Jordan, William Smith, Judges. Court then adjourned untill To morrow 10 O'Clcok.

Friday the 13th of January 1792. The Honorable Court met according to adjournment. Present Their Honors William Smith & James Jordan, Esq.

Ordered that the County Treasurer pay Charles Bruce s 8 for carrying a Hue and Cry.

The State against Jeremiah Thomson. Indictment for Assault. The parties compromising the matter & the defendant submitting himself to the Judgment of the Court, Ordered that the case be discontinued by his paying Costs.

Grand Jurors to serve **this** Court

John Smith, foreman	1	Josiah Tanner	8
Thomas Milikin	2	George Roebuck	9
Thomas Paden	3	Stephen Wilson	10
Thomas Williamson	4	David McDowell	11
Josiah Culbertson	5	James Hooper	12
Daniel McClaren	6	Tobias Bright	13
John Tollason	7	William Elder	14

Ordered that John Brown a defaulter in attending the Grand Jury, be summoned to next Court to shew cause why he did not attend.

Edward Cross & wife against John Williams. Special Action on the Case. By consent of the parties this case is refered to the Arbitrament of Thomas Moore, Esq., Andrew Barry, William Ford, And John Ford Junr., Gentl., arbitrators, with power of umpirage ....

The County Treasurer against Nathaniel Wooton & William Bratcher. Petition. Debt. On motion of William Shaw, Esq., the Defendant came into Court and confessed Judgment for ₺ 10 proc. money & costs of suit.

Charles Hardy against Landon Farrow. Petition by account. Discontinued at the plaintiff's costs by agreement.

Joseph Wofford against John Clayton. Petition. Debt. On motion of William Shaw, Judgment is entered according to specialty for ₺ 8 s 1 d 11 with interest and costs of suit.

William Bratcher against Burrel Thomson. Petition by Account.

On motion of William Shaw attorney for Plaintiff, decreed by the Court for Ł 5 s16 d 4 & costs of suit.

Henry Bishop against William West. Slander. Dismist at Plaintiff's Costs by Consent.

William West against William Bishop. Breaking Close. Discontinued at Plaintiff's Costs by Consent.

Spencer Bobo against Landon Farrow & Samuel Farrow. Case. Continued, also the Plaintiff by William Shaw Esq. motion for a nonsuit.

Jesse Casey against Joseph Couch. Breaking Close. Discontinued by Consent of the parties.

Petit Jurors to serve this Court

Thomas Jordan, foreman	1	Joseph Boring	7
Noel Johnson	2	David Humphries	8
Samuel Culbertson	3	John McElwrath	9
George Taylor	4	Francis Clayton	10
William Casey	5	Alexander McCarter	11
Andrew Ray	6	Edward Clayton	12

The State against Travice Morse. Scieri Facias. The defendant being summoned to answer a charge of taking unlawful fees, came into Court and Confessed the same & submitted himself to the mercy of the Court, who dismissed him upon paying Costs.

The State against William Roberts. Incest. Ordered that Noli prosiqui be entered in this Case, and the defendant be acquitted on paying Costs.

The State against John McClure the Elder, James McClure, William McClure & Caty McClure. Indictment for Petty Lerceny. The prisoners being arraigned and the jury (same as above listed) ...The Jury find James McClure guilty and the rest discharged. Ordered that he be committed to jail until Tomorrow Eleven O' Clock when the Court will pass sentence. Zachariah Toliaferro his attorney motioned for a new trial at the meeting of the Court tomorrow.

Joseph Kenely came into Court and made oath that a certain dark bay Horse which he found in the possession of Joseph Moore Branded I S on the near shoulder, about 14½ hands high, about 14 or 15 years old was his right and property & that he never sold nor Barter'd said Horse to any person.

William Ford proved two days attendance as a witness in the Case William West against William Bishop, amounting to five shillings.

Ordered that the minutes be read, which was accordingly done and signed by William Smith, James Jordan, Judges. Court then adjourned untill Tomorrow 9 O'Clock.

Saturday the 14th January 1792. The Honorable Court met according to adjournment. Present their Honors, William Smith & James Jordan, Esq.

William Easly being appointed by the High Sheriff to serve as a deputy for this County who was approved by the Court, and was admitted to take the necessary oaths of office accordingly.

The State against James McClure. Petty Lerceny. The Court proceeded to pass the sentence against the defendant for the Frime in which he was yesterday found Guilty...the Hour of one O'Clock then to receive at the whipping post of this County, five lashes on the Bare back by the Sheriff after which punishment you are to return to Jail untill you discharge the Costs of the Indictment.. The Sheriff made his return that he had put the above sentence into Execution.

The State against William Morriss. Theft. Ordered that a scieri Facias issue against the Bail for their appearance to next Court, to shew cause why their recognizance should not be forfeited.

Ordered that the Clerk be at liberty of Issuing Citations in the Intrim of Courts, to those that may make application for the future, for administration.

The State against Samuel Hayes. Breaking Jail. Ordered that a Bench Warrant as heretofore Issued, be renewed and be of force against the said defendant.

The State against Robert Young. Perjury. Ordered that the Sheriff take the necessary steps to have the Body of the said Robert Young before the Judges of the Superior Court of Pinckney District on the first day of April next, at Union Court-House in order to answer said Charge.

Ordered that Alexander Walker be allowed the sum of ₺ 1 s 17 d 4 for the necessary Expenditures in repairing the Jail of this County.

Henry McCray against Walter Burrell. Appeal. The Judgment of the Justice Confirmed by the Court, for ₺ 1 s 18 d 6½ in behalf fo the defendant.

Henry McCray against John Elder. Appeal. The Judgment of the Justice Confirmed by the Judgment of the Court for ₺ 2 s 2 in behalf of the defendant.

The State against William Luallen. Bastardy. Ordered that he pay ₺ 5 proc. money 12 months hence. Matthew Guttery and Frederick Guttery came into Court and Entered surities for the payment of the above sum and Costs.

William Luallen as principle and Matthew Guttery & Frederick Guttery as surities came into court and acknowledged to owe to the State the surities ₺ 25 each if the said Luallen shall fail to indemnify & keep Harmless & clear this County from maintaining a Bastard Child Begotten by Elizabeth Saunders.

The State against Richard & Jane Roberts. Lerceny. Ordered that all recognizance in this case continued untill next court, and a capias issue against Nancy Carter, returnable before some justice of this County for her to enter into recognizance to give testimoney in said Case.

Ordered that all recognizance return'd to this Court, stand over and be of force untill next Court, except those where other orders Interfere repugnant to this order.

Wells Griffith against William Wood. Attachment. Dismissed at defendants Costs by affidavit of the plaintiff.

Thomas Gordon against William Young. Attachment. Dismissed by order of Court.

John Bearden against Thomas Blasingame. Appeal. Judgment confirmed.

Thomas Gordon against Larkin Lancaster. Appeal. On motion of William Shaw Gentleman Attorney for the defendant, Judgment was Confirmed by the Court, for the sum of ₤ 1 s 18 d 6 on behalf of the defendant.

David Golightly against Tobias Bright. Attachment. Ordered that a Scieri Facias issue against Samuel Burns to shew cause why Judgment may not be entered against him in behalf of the plaintiff.

John Bragg against Nicholas Holley. Appeal. The Judgment of the Justice confirmed by the Judgment of the Court, for one Guinea, in behalf of the plaintiff.

John Farrow proved three days attendance as a witness in the case John Bragg against Nicholas Holley, amounting to s 7 d 6.

William Farrow proved three days attendance in the above case John Bragg against Nicholas Holley amounting to s 7 d 6.

George Deavours proved 2 days attendance in the suit Henry Bishop against William West, amounting to s 5.

Peter Green against John Cantwell. Attachment. On motion of Zachariah Tolliaferro attorney for the plaintiff Judgment was entered by the Court for ₤ 5 s 8 d 9 and costs of suit in behalf of the plaintiff, Ordered that the property attached be exposed to sale for the use of the said plaintiff.

John Ward against Thomas Hamilton. Trover. In conformity to an order of Court, we the Arbitrators hereof, to wit, Jesse Connell, John Ford, Isham Harrison & Henry Wells, appointed to settle all matters of Controversy between John Ward and Thomas Hamilton, doth Judge and award that the said Thomas Hamilton do pay the said Ward ₤ 30 for his mare with costs of suit. Given under our hands 21 June 1791, ratified by the Court.

George Bruton proved 12 days attendance in the case John Ward against Thomas Hamilton amounting to ₤ 1 s 5.

William Austin against Edward Arnold. Case. Ordered that this case continue at the defendants Costs.

William King came into Court and made oath that a Certain Bay Horse with a lump under his belly, branded on shoulder & Buttock T Ŧ about 17 hands high 10 years old, was and is the property of Richard Childers of Georgia, and that said Childers never sold nor barter'd said Horse to any person to his knowledge.

Edward Goode, being nominated by the assembly to act as a Justice of the peace for this County, came into Court and took the necessary oaths of office accordingly.

James Hooper being nominated to act in the office of a Justice of the peace for the County, came into Court, and took the necessary oaths of office prescribed by Law.

Ordered that the minutes be read which was done and signed by William Smith, James Jordan, Judges. Court then adjourned untill Monday 10 O'Clock.

Monday the 16th of January 1792. The Honorable Court met according to adjournment. Present the Honorable William Smith and James Jordan, Esq.

Ordered that Alexander Alexander be admitted to retail spirituous liquors and keep a public House of Entertainment upon his giving Ebenezer Morse and John Erwin his surities for his Conforming to the rules prescribed by Law.

George Lamkin against Joseph Buffington. Debt. The defendant not appearing in his own person nor by his attorney on motion of Zachariah Toliaferro, Atty. for Plaintiff, Judgment is entered by default.

John Thomas Junior against Nicholas Holley. Vi et Armis. Dismissed at the defendants Costs by request.

Samuel Elder against Elisha Smith. Debt. Nonsuit.

Robert Harper against Joseph Venable. Special Action. Nonsuit.

Samuel Farrow Esq. against John Elder, William Elder & Alexander Elder. Debt. On motion of William Shaw Gentl. Attorney for the Plaintiff Judgment is entered according to Note, which is ₤ 28 s 14 d 8 due 26 Dec 1788 with giving credit as by a receipt under the hand of the said plaintiff for ₤ 8 25 Dec 1791, also on the Note ₤ 8 12 Oct 1790, which leaves due the sum of ₤ 12 s 14 d 8 besides his costs....

Joel Hembree against Nicholas Holley. Debt. Came the plaintiff by William Shaw his attorney, and the defendant by Zachariah Toliaferro his attorney whereupon came a Jury (same as before)... we find for the Plaintiff ₤ 20 sterling and interest allowing the defendant the Credit on the note.

his
Thomas T Jordan, foreman
mark

Winthrop Tod & Withrop Assinee of Thomas Tod against John Moore. Debt. On motion of William Shaw Gentl. Attorney for the Plaintiff, the defendant by Thomas Walker his Attorney, confessed Judgment according to specialty for ₤ 60 s 8 after deducting the sum of ₤ 2 credit on the note, the debt contracted 21 Jan 1785, with interest & Costs of suit.

Richard Hampton & Co. against Richard Harrison. Debt. Abated by the death of the defendant.

Essix Capshaw against William Wofford. Attachment. On motion of William Shaw attorney for the Plaintiff, and the defendant not appearing in his own persons nor by his Attorney, Judgment was thereupon entered by default.

Ordered that the County Attorney, Clerk & Sheriff be paid whatever sum may be due them in Consequence of trials in behalf of the State against Sundries, as heretofore have been tried under the late act.

Ordered that a Bench Warrant issue against Richard Collins for him to appear at next Court to answer a charge of Beating and assaulting the sheriff in the Execution of his office.

Ordered that letters Testimentary be granted to Thomas Farrow Esq., he having taken the oath of an Executor to the last will and Testament of George Lowther deceased.

Ordered, that all the Estrays which have been provided to the Sheriff be sold by him according to Law.

James Oates being appointed to serve as a Constable for this County, came into Court and took the oathes of office prescribed by Law.

Benjamine Petitt as a witness in the case Joel Hembree against Nicholas Holley, on oath in open Court, is allowed s 7 d 6 for 3 days attendance.

Joel Hembree as a witness in the case Joseph Wofford against John Clayton on oath in open Court is allowed s 5 for 2 days attendance.

Owen Bowen attorney for Elizabeth Stewart against William Haden. Trover. On motion of William Shaw Esq. attorney for the plaintiff & on agreement of the parties, Ordered that the Bail be discharged in this case, and Malachi Jones & Jonathan Bowen came into Court & acknowledged themselves securities for Costs in the above suit.

Ordered that the minutes be read, which was accordingly done and signed by William Smith, James Jordan, Judges. Court then adjourned untill the 12th day of June next.

At a County Court of Sessions and pleas began and Held at the Court-House of Spartanburgh on the 12th day of June 1792. Present their Honors William Smith and James Jordan, Esq.

The Court proceeded to draw the grand Jurors for next January Court, to wit,

John Brown	1	John Snoddy	11
John Hightower	2	Joel Traylor	12
Moses Foster	3	Shands Golightly	13
Vardry McBee	4	William Garrett	14
George Bruton	5	George Roebuck	15
Charles Hester	6	Jonathan Neasbitt	16
John James	7	William Foster	17
Thomas Milikin	8	Nathaniel Robertson	18
Robert Neasbitt	9	Charles James	19
William Pool J. M.	10	Thomas Williamson	20

Petit Jurors for next Court

John Bragg	1	James Cooper	16
Zebulon Bragg	2	William Watkins	17
James Clerke	3	Joel Dean	18
Joseph Alexander	4	Allen Henderson	19
William McGowen	5	Zedikiah Walker	20
Arthur Hutcheson	6	William Shurley	21
Abner Center	7	Joseph Couch	22
Elisha Thomson	8	John Farmer	23
Joel Smith	9	John Conner Senr.	24
Richard James	10	John Miller	25
James Wilson	11	Samuel Gilbert	26

Richard Chesney	12	David Cooper	27		
Thomas Philips	13	David Davis	28		
Josiah Thornton	14	Joseph Buffington	29		
Samuel Serrart	15	William Robison	30		

William Nibbs Esq. producing his credentials as a practicing attorney at Law in this State was thereupon Ordered to be enrolled on the records of this Court to practice the same.

Patrick Michie Esq. producing his Commission as a practicing attorney at Law & equity in this State, Ordered that he be enrolled on the records of this Court to practice the same.

Isham Pulliam against William Watts. Slander. Dismissed at the plaintiffs Costs by request.

The Last Will and Testament of John Brown deceased proven in open Court by the evidence of Nevil Wayland, ordered to record.

The minutes were read and signed by James Jordan, William Smith, Judges.

Wednesday the 13th June 1792. The Honorable Court met according to adjournment. Present their Honors William Smith & James Jordan, Esq.

The persons whose names are immediately following were impannelled and sworn as Grand Jurors, to wit,

James Hooper, foreman	1	Daniel McClaren	9
John Golightly	2	David McDowell	10
Giles Connell	3	Jesse Connell	11
Josiah Culbertson	4	Francis Dodd	12
William Elder	5	William Thomson	13
John Young	6	John Posey	14
Alexander Walker	7	John Neasbitt	15
Jonathan Harriss	8	George Connell	16

The following bills were handed to the Grand Jury who received the same and retired to their Chambers, to wit,

The State against Richard Collins. Indictment for Assaulting & Beating the Sheriff. The Jury aforesaid find a true Bill. The defendant Confessed the Charge & put himself upon the mercy of the Court.

The State against William Morris. Horse Stealing. No Bill.

The State against Peter Davis. Horse Stealing. A true Bill.
James Hooper, Foreman.

The State against Margaret Johnson. Unlawful using Estrays. A Capias having Issued & returned nonest, Ordered that the proceedings discontinue, the defendant having moved out of the State.

The County by William Byrd against Baylis Earle Esq., Richard Saunders, Thomas Divine, James Hooper, William Redman, John Moore & Joseph Moore. Capias for not working on a Road. Ordered that the above Case be dismissed as the Original Order for the Overseer of the Road was Illegal.

The State against Robert Young. Perjury. The proceedings of this case are transfered to Pinckney District Court.

The State against Samuel Hayes. Breaking Jail & C. A bench warrant having issued, and returned not to be found, Ordered that the same be renewed.

The State against Samuel Clerke. Bastardy. (Bond Given) Ordered that the defendant pay into the Treasury of this County, ₺ 5 by Christmas next, & Costs of suit. Matthew Guttery & James Clerke came into Court and entered themselves surities for the debt and costs. Also ordered that the principle & surities enter into a bond of an Hundred pounds to Indemnify the County from being at any Expence with the said Bastard Child.

The State against Susannah Proctor. Bastardy. Ordered that the Clerk inform Samson Bethel Esq. to cause the said defendant to appear before him & enter into recognizance to appear at next January Court, to answer said charge.

The State against Peter Davis. Indictment for Horse Stealing. Ordered that Nathaniel Stokes proceed immediately to summon William Davis & Francis Powers to personally appear in open Court, to give evidence in said case.

The State against John Brown. Defaulting Jurors. Discontinued by Order of Court.

The State against William Walker. Bastardy. Ordered that the Clerk give Information to Esq. Bethel to Bind the said defendant and Salley Larkey to appear at next Court, to answer said Charge.

The State against William Redman & Samuel Redman. Petit Larceny. Ordered that this case be dismissed.

The State against William Smith. Assault. Discharged for want of a prosecutor.

Bills sent to the Grand Jury & returned as follows.

The State against John Duncan. Lerceny. No Bill.

The State against Richard Roberts. Lerceny. No Bill.

The State against Jane Roberts. Lerceny. A True Bill.

The State against Samuel Staggs. Horse Stealing. No Bill.
          James Hooper, Foreman.

Ordered that John Cantrell be find s 20 for not attending as a Constable to this Court, he being summoned by the Sheriff by Order of Court.

James Henderson against Richard Pace. Assault. The defendant being solemnly called, and not appearing neither in his own person nor by his Attorney, Judgment was thereupon entered by default.

Matthew Guttery against John George Reiner. Petition by A/C The defendant by Mr. Nobbs Attorney came into Court & confessed Judgment by default for ₺ 7 s 1 d 4 3/4 with Interest & Costs of suit, with stay of Execution 4 months.

Samuel Farrow against Benjamin Wofford & Samuel Thomson. Debt. The defendants came into Court in their own proper persons, and confessed Judgment for ₺ 12 s 16 d 1 with stay of Execution untill Christmas next, with Interest & Costs of Suit.

Richard James against James Smith. Slander. The defendant being called and not appearing himself nor by his Attorney, Judgment was thereupon entered by default.

John Cantwell against Benjm. Wofford. Detinue. By consent of the parties, the trial of this cause is refered to the Arbitrament of Capt. William Benson, Capt. Henry Wells & W. Giles Connell Gentlemen arbitrators, their award returned to next court shall be the Judgment thereof.

Present Baylis Earle Esq.

Matthew Harper against James Saterfield. Debt. Dismissed at the defendants costs by Consent.

William Henderson against Thomas McKnight. Case. By consent of the parties and assent of the Court, the trial of this cause is refered to the arbitrament of John Gowen, Esq. James Alexander, Baylis Earle Esq. and William Wood Esq. with power of Umpirage their award made on the 18th Oct. next and returned to next Court shall be the Judgment thereof.

John Alexander Esq. against Martin Armstrong. Attachment. Dismist by consent of the Plaintiff.

Elizabeth Spurgion, as a witness in the case Samuel Farrow against Benjamine Wofford & Samuel Thomson on oath in open Court is allowed s 5 for 2 days attendance.

Duncanson & Murry against Spencer Bobo. Case. Ordered that a capias with an affidavit of James Gibbs, issue against the defendant to cause him to give special Bail in this case, for debt Interest and costs of suit, the sum being ₤ 14 s 5 d 6½. Capt. Henry Wells came into Court and entered himself security for the costs of this suit.

Ordered that a warrant of appraisment issue to Thomas Farrow Esq. admr. of George Lowther deceased, and that Thomas Clerk, John Allen, Ebenezer Morse, and Shadrack Waldrope appraise the same.

The State against Peter Davis. Theft. Ordered that Samuel Staggs who is now in jail, be liberated from the same, upon his giving such surities in the sum of ₤ 50 each to be with himself in the sum of ₤ 25 as the Court shall approve for his personal appearance at next Pinckney Court, to give evidence in behalf of the State against Peter Davis for Horse Stealing.

Court adjourned for one Hour. Court met according to adjournment.

A power of attorney from Joseph Thomson Junior to John Slone, acknowledged in Open Court by said Thomson, Ordered to be recorded.

Richard James against James Smith. Slander. Judgment being entered by default, W. Shaw attorney for the plaintiff evaded the same & the parties postpon'd the Trial thereof untill next Court.

Mrs. Anna Harrison, Isham Harrison Esq. & Thomas Williamson came into Court and took the oath of Admn. on the estate of Richard Harrison Esq. decd. Ordered that they have letters of admn....

William Austin against Edward Arnold. Case. The defendant by Zachariah Toliaferro his Attorney confessed judgment for ₤ 33 to be paid in property by the 1st of Jan. next & Costs of suit.

Ordered that John Young and William Wood Junr. be allowed the sum of ₤ 4 s 4 for Guarding the Jail.

Essix Capshaw against William Wofford. Attachment. On motion of William Shaw Gent. attorney for the Plaintiff, that a writ of Inquiry should be executed in this case, the jury, to wit, Ignacious Griffin, Thomas Jackson, William Smith, John Stone, William Reaves, Austin Clayton, David McCarley, Benjamin Couch, William Rampley, Paul Castleberry, Robert Connell & John Burnett ...we find for the plaintiff ₤ 16 s 9 d 7 with interest from the time it became....

John McElheny against Benjamine McMikin. Slander.
Benjamine McMikin against John Davis. Appeal.
By consent of the parties Mr. McElheny in behalf of Davis comes into Court & refers these cases to John Vaughn, Capt. William Benson, Nevil Wayland, and Maj.r John Gowen, with power of umpirage, their award returned to next Court shall be a rule thereof.

James Montgomery against Henry O'Kean. Attachment. Ordered that the property attachment be exposed to sale in behalf of the Plaintiff.

Ordered that John Walker be allowed the sum of s 11 d 8 for repairing Jail Door, also that John Gowen be allowed s 14 4 Jail Locks.

Denny Anderson against William Rountree. Appeal.
On motion of Zachariah Tolliaferro Attorney for Plaintiff and Thomas Walker Esq. attorney for defendant and after an Investigation of the matter by their Councellors, It is thereupon decreed by the Court, that the Judgments be recorded.

William Michison as a witness in the cases Denny Anderson against William Rountree on oath in open Court is allowed s 22 d 6 for 9 days attendance, also 96 miles @ d 2 pr mile amounting to s 16.

Benjamin Kivel as a witness in the cases Denny Anderson against William Rountree on oath in open Court is allowed s 30 for 12 days attendance also s 20 for 120 miles at d 2 per mile for mileage.

The State against Richard Collins. Indictment for assault. The defendant came into Court and pleads Guilty and throws himself upon the mercy of the Court, and the Court adjudged that he pay as a fine into the County Treasury ₤ 5 within 6 months or give good Security for the same otherwise suffer one month Imprisonment.

The minutes were read and signed by James Jordan, Baylis Earle, Judges. Court then adjourned untill Tomorrow 8 O'Clock.

Thursday the 14th of June 1792. The Honorable Court met according to adjournment. Present Their Honors William Smith & James Jordan, Esq.

Ordered that all recognizance which have not been carried into execution this Court stand over untill next Court.

Ordered that James Saunders have licence to retail spirituous liquors upon giving approved surities for his lawful performance, which he did in open Court.

The State against Jean Roberts. Lerceny. The prisoner being arreigned & the Jury (same as before)...William Shaw Esq. County attorney in behalf of the state & the defendant by her Councellors & after the witnesses in behalf of the defendant ....we find the defendant Guilty. Thomas Jackson, foreman. The Court proceeded to pass sentence as follows. That the said Jane Roberts receive three lashes in the usual manner at the Common whipping post immediately, to be discretionally done by the sheriff with respect to decency. The Sheriff made return that he had inflicted the punishment accordingly.

Ordered that Henry McCray have licence to retail spirituous liquors upon giving Littleton Bagwell & Obadiah Trimmier Esq. his surities for his lawful performance, which he did in open Court.

John & Susannah Salley against Richard Saunders and wife and James McClure & wife. Slander. Settled at mutual Costs by agreement.

Thomas White against Buckner Smith. Debt. Settled at Defendants Costs by request.

Ordered that Capt. Henry Wells, Obadiah Trimmier Esq. & George Parkison appraise the Estate of Richard Harrison Esq. deceased & make return thereof to the next Intermediate Court.

Ordered that all of the Estrays produced to the Sheriff this Court be sold by him agreeable to Law.

Richard Roberts husband of Jane Roberts came into Court and made Oath that he was not able to pay the Costs accrued on an Indictment against him & his wife.

David Golightly against Tobias Bright. Attachment. On motion of Mr. Nott attorney for Plaintiff, Judgment was entered in behalf of the plaintiff, for ₤ 7 s 9 d 4 & Costs of suit.

Court adjourned for two Hours. Court met according to adjournment.

Samuel Farrow against Benjamine Wofford. Petition. Debt. The defendant confessed Judgment for the sum of ₤ 9 s 7 with stay of execution untill November next.

Ordered that the value of an Estray which was ₤ 7 s 4 bought this day by William Shaw Esq. be allowed him in discount of fees due him from the County, and that this order be the Treasurers receipt.

John McElheny against Benjamine McMekin. Slander. Nathaniel Stokes as a witness in this case, on oath in open Court is al=lowed s 20 for 8 days attendance.

Ordered that such part of the personal Estate of the late Richard Harrison as the admrs. may deem necessary to be sold for the benefit of the said Estate be sold at the plantation of the late deceased, on the 3rd Saturday of July next, giving a Credit till

1st of March next, taking sufficient security, on the admrs. filing in the hands of the Clerk of this Court, the Inventory and appraisment of the said Estate & advertising the said sale 20 days before the same takes place.

Samuel Staggs as principle, Charles Bruce and William Staggs as surities came into Court and acknowledged to owe the State, to wit, the Said Samuel Staggs ₤ 50 and the sd. Charles Bruce & William Staggs ₤ 25 each if the said Samuel Staggs shall fail to appear at next Pinckney Court to give Testimony in behalf of the State against Peter Davis.
Test W. Lancaster C. S. C.

Elijah Isaacks against Hugh Greenwood. Attachment. The defendant being Called and not appearing by himself nor his Attorney, Judgment was thereupon entered by default.

Ordered that Job Sosbee be allowed s 7 for wintering Estray Bull to be paid out of the County fund by the Treasurer.

Ordered that the fine of John Cantrell be exonerated as it appeared he did not omit attending the Court as a Constable, out of Contempt.

Ordered that Thomas Williamson be allowed ₤ 2 s 2 for boarding William Wood & John Young guarding the Prisoners in Jail.

The minutes were read and signed by Baylis Earle, William Smith, Judges. Court then adjourned untill Tomorrow seven O'Clock.

Friday the 15th of June 1792. Court met according to adjournment. Present their Honors William Smith & Baylis Earle, Esq.

Ordered that Vardry McBee be allowed s 20 for wintering 3 Estrays the last winter to be paid by the Treasurer of the County.

Ordered that Absalom Lancaster servce as coroner for this County, for the Term required by Law.

Ordered that Thomas Williamson be allowed the sum of ₤ 5 d 6 for receiving & victualing William Morriss & Samuel Staggs in jail & keeping five Estrays.

The minutes were read and signed by William Smith, Baylis Earle, Judges. Court then adjourned untill Court in Course.

January Sessions 1793

At a Court of Sessions and pleas began and Held for the County of Spartanburgh at the Court-House the 12th day of January 1793. Present his Honor William Smith, Esq.

The Court proceeded to draw the Jurors for next Term.

Grand Jurors

John Shippy	1	Samson Bobo	8	Joseph Barnett	15
Thomas Wyatt	2	William Suddoth	9	Wm. Poole Tay.	16
William Lipscomb	3	John McElheny	10	Vardry McBee	17
William Tate	4	John Smith F.	11	Jesse Connell	18
John Beard	5	Thomas Tod	12	William Hembry	19
Thomas Underwood	6	Thomas Paden	13	Thomas William-	20
Charles McKnight	7	Stephen Wilson	14	son	

                        Petit Jurors
Benjamine Rhodes Junr.   1   John Butler   16
Isaac Hembree   2   William Morriss Senr.   17
John Streemathead   3   William Fondrin   18
John Hewatt   4   David Grines S. of Jno.   19
Samuel Turner   5   Zachariah Blackwell   20
John Lackey   6   Robert Page   21
David Cook   7   Samuel Miller C. B.   22
Daniel Cornwall   8   William Crocker   23
William Castleberry   9   William Morriss   24
Francis Powers   10   Buckner Smith   25
Andrew Thomson   11   John White, Tyger   26
Samuel Harper   12   Evans Davis   27
Peter Hamilton   13   Brittain Williford   28
John Morriss S. C.   14   Jonathan Law   29
Nicholas Holley   15   John Campbell   30

Ordered that Abraham Nalley have the admn. of the Estate of Richard Nalley deceased, upon his qualifying & giving Bond of ₤ 200 with Nicholas Holley & David Grimes his surities for his lawful preformance, which he accordingly did in open Court.

Ordered that Joseph Wofford, Richard Young & George Roebuck appraise the Estate of Richard Nalley deceased & make due return thereof.

Absalom Lancaster producing his Commission to the office of Coroner for this County, came into Court and took the necessary oath prescribed by Law.

Ordered that the minutes be read which was done & signed by William Smith, Judge. Court then adjourned untill Monday morning 10 O'Clock.

Monday the 14th of January 1793. The Honorable Court met according to adjournment. Present their Honors James Jordan, Baylis Earle & William Smith, Esq.

   Grand Jurors empaneled to serve this Court, to wit,
George Bruton, foreman   1   John Snody   7 Wm. Foster   13
Moses Foster   2   Joel Traylor   8 Nathl. Robert
John Brown   3   Shands Golightly 9   -son   14
Charles Hester   4   John Roebuck   10 Charles James 15
Robert Nesbitt   5   Wm. Garrett   11 Thos. William-
William Poole J. M.   6   Jonathan Nes-   son   16
                                 bitt   12

who was sworn received their charge by the Court and retired to their chambers with several Indictment Bills.

   Petit Jurors drawn to serve this Court, to wit,
John Bragg   1   Richard Chesney   8
James Clerk   2   Josiah Thornton   9
William McGowen   3   John Farmar   10
Arthur Hutchins   4   John Miller   11
Joel Smith   5   David Davis   12
Richard James   6   William Robertson   13
James Wilson   7

The Executors of the Estate of William Tate deceased returned their Inventory, which is ordered to be filed and that the said Exrs. advertise the said Estate 20 days & then sell the same at 12 months credit, except sums under s 15 which is to be paid at the time of sale.

Edward Cross & wife against John Williams. Special Action on the Case. Ordered this case be discontinued.

John Spencer against Andrew Thomson. Case. Ordered that this case be discontinued at the Plaintiffs costs.

Daniel Barnett against Crook & McDaniel. Debt. Dismissed at the Defendants Costs by agreement.

Matthew Guttry. against John Geo. Reiner. Petition. The defendant by Mr. Nobbs his Attorney came into Court and Confessed Judgment for ₤ 7 s 1 d 4 3/4 with costs of suit.

Thomas Price against Thomas Spann. by Appeal. Dismissed at the plaintiffs Costs by consent.

Gabriel Bumpass & Robert Bumpass Petitioning the Court to grant that Augustine Bumpass should be their Guardian which accordingly consented to by the Court.

The State against Richard James. Horse Stealing. Henry McCray, Littleton Bagwell, Jonathan Bowen and John Cantwell, came into Court and acknowledged to owe to State ₤ 25 each if they fail to attend this Court ot give evidence in the same.

Henry Shaver against John Tollison. Petition. Ordered that a Commission issue to the State of Georgia   County to Justices of the same, to examine a witness in this case, upon the defendant giving 10 days notice to the Plaintiff, of the time and place of Examination.

Benjamine McMekin against John Davis. Appeal. The parties came into Court and Consented to a new Trial before David Goodlett & Thomas Moore Esq., on Monday next & their Judgment to be final.

Thomson & Haning against Diskin Grant. Petition by Debt. Ordered that this case be dismissed at the defendants costs by his consent.

James Kemp against Benjamine Wofford. Detinue. Edward Cornwall & William Camp came into Court and acknowledged themselves responsible for the Costs of this suit provided the plaintiff should be cast in the same.

Sarah McDowell widow of William McDowell deceased, came into Court and prayed administration on her deceased Husbands Estate, which was accordingly granted, upon her signing a Bond & taking the necessary oaths of admn., which she did in open court.

Ordered that George McDowell, John Davis and Alexander Roddy appraise the Estate of William McDowell deceased & make due return thereof.

The State against Ann Carter. Lerceny. The Grand Jury find a True Bill. George Brewton, Foreman.

The defendant being arraigned and the Trial postponed untill Tomorrow, Mr. Toliaferro & Mr. Tenant appointed by the Court to plead for the defendant in Caseof high Indigency.

William Peter Tenant and Charles Jones Calcock Esq. practising attornies in this State, as appears by their credentials which was read in Court, was thereupon admitted to practice in this Court, by being enrolled with the attornies of the same.

The State against Richard James. Horse Stealing. The Grand Jury find "No Bill."

Ordered that the admx. of William McDowell deceased proceed to the sale of his Estate after giving 20 days public Notice, at 12 months credit, except sums under s 10 which is to be paid at the time of sale.

Michael B. Roberds as a witness in the case Edward Cross & wife against John William, proved 6 days attendance in the said case at 2 & 6 pence per day.

William Allen & Rhoda Allen proved 4 days attending as witnesses in the case Edward Cross and wife against John Williams.

John Durham as a witness in the Case Edward Cross and wife against John Williams on oath in open Court was allowed s 10 for 4 days attendance in said case.

Ordered that the minutes be read which was accordingly done & signed by Baylis Earle, James Jordan, William Smith, Judges. Court then adjourned untill Tomorrow 9 O'Clock.

Tuesday the 15th of January 1793. The Honorable Court met according to adjournment. Present their Honors, William Smith & James Jordan, Esq.

Littleton Mapp against James Oliphant. Attachment. Came the plaintiff by Patrick Mechie Esq. & the defendant by Mr. Nott Gentl. their attornies...it is decreed by the Court that the Plaintiff recover Ł 3 s 16 d 4 besides his costs....

The State against Margaret Mehaney. Concealing the death of a Bastard Child. The Grand Jury find "a true Bill."

The State against Ann Carter. Lerceny. The defendant being arreigned yesterday & on her Indictment pled not guilty, being now brought to Trial on the same Indictment pleads Guilty & throws herself upon the mercy of the Court, who say that the said Ann Carter receive five lashes on her Bare back by the Sheriff at the Common whipping post, in the space of two Hours. The Sheriff returned that he had put the Judgment of the Court into Execution.

The defendant made oath that she was not able to pay the cost of the above Indictment upon which she was acquitted.

  Present his Honor Baylis Earle, Esq.

The State against Nathaniel Hammett. Assault. No Bill. Ordered that his recognizance be void.

The State against Jonathan Bowen. Assault. A true Bill. This Indictment is Travers'd untill next Court.

The State against Dudly Red. Assault. A True Bill. The defendant came into Court & Confessed the charge laid against him in his Indictment, and submitted himself to the mercy of the

Court who adjudged that he pay s 5 & costs of the Indictment, & be acquitted.

The State against Carlton Lindsey. Lerceny. Ordered that Noli prosiqui be entered by the County Attorney.

The State against Samuel Hayes. Breaking Jail. Ordered that this case be discontinued.

The State against Tully Davis. Bastardy. Ordered that the Recognizance in this case be continued untill next Court.

The State against Salley Lackey. Bastardy. Ordered that the defendant pay into the County Treasury ₤ 5 prov. money at the rate of s 6 d 6 pence to each dollar.

The State against William Walker. Bastardy. The defendant came into Court and Confessed the charge & submitted himself to the mercy of the Court, who adjudged that he pay into the County Treasury ₤ 5 proc. money at the rate of s 6 d 6 to each Dollar.

The State against William, Benjamine, Nathaniel & Elijah Hammett. Peace Warrant. Ordered that the defendants be acquitted from their recognizance.

The State against Robert Harper. Assault. No Bill.

The State against Agness Morse. Assault. The defendant came into Court and confessed the charge & submitted Herself to the mercy of the Court, who say that the defendant shall pay the fine of s 2 d 6 & the Costs of the Indictment & be release from the same.

John Harriss & Daniel Walker came into Court and Entered themselves securities to the County for the sum of ₤ 10 proc. money, the fine imposed upon William Walker for a Bastard child Begotten by Salley Larkey, to be paid 12 months after date; the said surities also agree that the maintenance to the said Bastard child shall not fall on the County nor no part thereof.

John D. Kern against Martin Armstrong & Joseph Venable. Debt. Joseph Venable a defendant in this case came into Court & confessed judgment for ₤ 17 s 4 d 6 & costs of suit.

The State against Bernard Wm. Sweny. Hog Stealing. The Grand Jury find "No Bill" in this case.

The State against Bernard Wm. Sweny. Marking & Disfiguring a Hog. The Grand Jury find "No Bill."

William Clayton against Reubin Newman. Petition. After the allegations of each party by their Attornies, Ordered that this case discontinue at the Plaintiffs Costs.

The State against Elizabeth Saunders. Bastardy. The defendant came into Court & submitted Herself to the mercy of the Court, who adjudged that she be fined ₤ 5 proc. money to be paid 12 months hence. Isaac Young & James Saunders came into Court entered themselves surities for the said sum & costs. They also agree to Indemnify the County from the maintenance of the Bastard child.

Ordered that the minutes be read which was accordingly done & signed by Baylis Earle, James Jordan, Judges. Court then adjourned untill Tomorrow 10 of the Clock.

Wednesday the 16th of January 1793. The Honorable Court met according to adjournment. Present their Honors William Smith & James Jordan Esquires.

The State against The Spann's. Assault. Ordered that a Bench Warrant issue against the defendant returnable to next Court.

The State against James Taylor. Murder. Ordered that the recognizance of this case continue untill next Court.

Ordered that the clerks of this Court take the oath prescribed by law as a Justice of the peace, which the clerks of the County Court are directed, which he did in open Court.

Margaret Campbell against John Jackson. Trover. By consent of the parties and assent of the Court this case is refered to Samuel Neasbitt & George Crezie with power of Umpirage, their award to be a rule of Court.

George Lamkin against Joseph Buffington. Debt. on a writ of Inquiry. Came the parties by their Councellors, and the plaintiff praying that a writ of Inquiry should be executed in this case, which was granted by the Court, whereupon a Jury, to wit Joel Smith, foreman, John Bragg, James Clerk, William McGowen, Arthur Hutchens, Richard James, James Wilson, Richard Chesney, Josiah Thornton, John Farmer, John Miller & David Davis, who on their oaths do say we find for the Plaintiff ₤ 24 s 11 d 6 with interest and costs of suit....

Owen Bowen attorney for Elizabeth Stewart against William Haden. Trover. Continued by affidavit of the Plaintiff untill next Court, at his costs.

William Henderson against Thomas McKnight. Case. Ordered that this Case be continued untill next Court agreeable to an affidavit of the defendant.

John McElheny against Benjamine McMekin. Slander. Ordered that this Case be Continued.

Lucy Thomson against Benjamine Wofford. Continued untill next Court by oath of the defendant.

Joseph Venable against Alexander Copeland. Detinue. Continued by affidavit of the defendant.

An award between Charles Bruce & Richard Harrison deceased, Ordered to be recorded upon Esqr. Earle acknowledging that he sign the same.

William Jackson against Benjamine Wofford. Case. Came the Plaintiff by Zachariah Toliaferro his Attorney, and the defendant by William Shaw, Esq. his attorney, whereupon came a Jury (same as before)...we find for the Defendant....

Hugh Stephenson against James Gilmore Junior & William Gilmore. Breaking Close. Nonsuit.

Peter Varner against Philemon Martin. Slander. Nonsuit.

John Gray against William Wofford. Attachment. By agreement of the Attornies, Ordered that a Dedimus issue to North Carolina, Burk County, to Examine Robert Baker as a witness in this case before Joseph Young Esq. or some other Justice of the peace for said County upon the defendants giving 10 days notice to the adverse party of the time & place of Examination.

Thomas Blasingame Junior against Burrel Thomson. Petition. By agreement of the parties, Ordered that a Dedimus issue to the State of Georgia   County for any two justices of the peace for said County to Examine William Neal as a witness in this case in behalf of the defendant upon his giving 10 days notice to the adverse party of the time & place of Examination.

Richard James against James Smith. Slander. Ordered that this cause be continued untill next Court.

William Owen against Thomas Staggs. Criminal Conversation with Plaintiffs wife. Nonsuit.

James Henderson against John Maxwell. Detinue. Issue joined & Continued untill next Court.

John Jones against James Alexander. Case. Issue Joined & Continued untill next Court.

David McCarley against William Farrow. Assault. Issue Joined & Continued untill next Court.

James Henderson against Richard Pace. A writ of Inquiry on Assault & Battery. Came the parties by their Councellors, also came a Jury (same as before)...we find for the Plaintiff s 5....

Ordered that the Road first opened through John Golightlys Plantation thence through Tinsleys plantation to Intersect the old Road on the Ridge towards Mr. Bowlens, thence to the Cross Road Toward Fords Mill, be the Established Road instead of any other that hath been opened, to lead to said places, agreeable to a petition presented to this Court for that purpose, and that Joel Hurt oversee & keep the same in good Repair.

John McMullen against Benjamine Wofford. Detinue. Nonsuit.

Duncanson & Murry against Spencer Bobo. Case. Came the Plaintiff by William Shaw & Zachariah Toliaferro Gentl. their Attornies, and the defendant by Mr. Nott & Patric Michie his attornies, who mov'd for a Nonsuit & was over ruled by the Court, whereupon came a Jury...we find for the Plaintiff ₤ 11 s 7 with interest from the year 1786 brought under the Instalment Law....

David Hicks against Charles McCarter. Attachment. The parties came into Court & refered this Case to Peter Smith & Nevil Wayland, their award to be a rule of Court.

Drewry McDaniel being appointed a Constable for this County came into Court & took the Necessary oaths of office Prescribed by Law.

Elijah Isaacks against Hugh Greenwood. Attachment. On motion of Zachariah Toliaferro attorney for the plaintiff, Its decreed by the Court that the Plaintiff recover the sum of ₤ 10 sterling & Costs of suit. William Miller being summoned as a Guarnishee in this case, and failing to appear upon which a Scieri Facias against him & he failing to appear after being serv'd with the same, Ordered that Judgment be entered as fully against him for the aforesaid sum as against the original Debtor with Costs of suit.

The minutes were read & signed by Wm. Smith, Baylis Earle, Judges. Court then adjourned until Tomorrow morning Nine O'Clock.

Thursday the 17th January 1793. The Court met according to adjournment. Present their Honors William Smith & Baylis Earle, Esq.

William Jackson against Benjamine Wofford. Case. This case being tried yesterday & a verdict found by the Jury in behalf of the defendant, on motion of Mr. Nott Gentl. attorney, that a new Trial ought to be had on this Case, which was accordingly granted by the Court, Ordered that this cause stand on the trial Docket in rotation as if it had not been tried, and come in rotation to next Court for a new trial.

Benjamine Jones as a witness in the case James Henderson against Richard Pace, on oath in open Court was allowed s 15 for 6 days attendance.

Ordered that Job Sosebee Oversee that part of the Road from here to James Smiths, to where the road from the Iron works to Georgia crosses the same.

Ordered that a capias issue against Samuel Lancaster Esq. for the Sheriff to take him before some one Judge of this County, in order for him to be bound in Recognizance to appear at next Pinckney Court, to answer to a charge of Gambling & Keeping bad house, agreeable to a Presentment of the Grand Jury of this County.

Ordered that the different Overseers of the Roads Presented by the Grand Jury of this Court, be summoned to appear at next Court, to answer the charge of the same.

Ordered that the Estrays be sold by the Sheriff if any liable and given him for sale, at six months Credit.

Ordered that the minutes be read, which was accordingly done and signed by Baylis Earle, Wm. Smith, Judges. Court then adjourned untill Court in Course.

At a Court of Sessions and pleas began and held at the Court-House of Spartanburgh on the 12th day of June 1793. Present their Honors William Smith & James Jordan, Esq.

The Court proceeded to draw the Grand Jurors for next January term, to wit.

Benjamine Busey	1	Alexander McCarter	11
David Allen	2	William Millikin	12
George Kizie	3	Benjamine McMekin	13
John Posey	4	Daniel McClaren	14
John James	5	Joseph Wofford	15
Daniel Harkney	6	David McDowell	16
Drewry McDaniel	7	John Tollison	17
Thomas Gore	8	Ebenezer Morse	18
Stephen Philips	9	Isaac Young	19
William Ford, C.	10	Richard Young	20

Petit Jurors drawn for next January Term

Isaac Hamby Junior	1	Thomas Prewet	16
George Bishop	2	John Woodruff	17
John Redman	3	Amos Cretchfield	18
Nathan Walden	4	John Walker	19
John Young Junior	5	William Bryan	20
Robert White	6	Joseph Boring	21
Joseph Wade	7	Joseph Alexander Junior	22
Robert Wood	8	Ezekiel Standley	23
Henry Young	9	Jeremiah Selman	24
Henry Wood	10	Nathaniel Woodruff	25
William Smith J. C.	11	John Walker Fh.	26
Isaiah Waldrope	12	James Southerland	27
John Wells	13	Edward Stubblefield	28
Jesse Traylor	14	John Tarket	29
Jacob Eison	15	William Sterling	30

Pursuant to the within order, we have reviewed the two Roads in dispute and do say that the Road by John Golightlys House is the best and most suitable to be Established as a public Road, 25th April 1793. John Ford, Jason Moore, Henry McCray.

Ordered that John Walker serve as a Constable for this County in place of Nathaniel Stokes, upon his taking the necessary oaths prescribed by Law, which he accordingly did.

A deed of conveyance from David McCarley to Alexander Alexander acknowledged in open Court by said McCarley, ordered to record.

The last will and Testament of William Reid deceased approved of and proven in open Court by the evidence of John Stovaul according to law, Ordered to record.

A Deed of Conveyance from Andrew Thomson to William Miller acknowledged in Open Court by the said Thomson, Ordered to be recorded.

The State against Moses & Thomas Spann. Assault. The defendants came into open court and plead guilty and throwed themselves upon the mercy of the Court, who fined them s 5 each and costs of suit.

David Hicks against Charles McCarter. Attachment. Refered.

Our oppinion is from the Evidence and circumstances that the doctor return Mr. Hicks his Horse or Ь10 sterling, and pay all charges as it is evident he did not attend him duty as he ought to do, and his hearing of Mr. Hick's being well was no apology for not goint to see, as thereby he might be the better satisfied as to particulars as it really appears also from the last clause of the deposition that he did not care whether he did any more for Hicks or not.

The above is the award of us the underscribeds, being duly appointed by the Honorable Court of Spartanburgh to Arbitrate a certain matter in dispute between David Hicks and Charles McCarter. 19th of January 1793. Nevil Wayland, Peter Smith.

William Lancaster against Isham Babbitt. Petition. The defendant came into Court in his own proper person and confessed judgment according to note for the sum of Ь 6 s 5 with interest & costs of suit.

James Kemp against Benjamine Wofford. Detinue. By consent of the parties and assent of the Court, this case is refered to the arbitrament of Jonathan Downs Hollaway Power & Jesse Dodd, their award returned to next Court to be a Judgment thereof.

Gideon Gibson against Nathan Gibson. Case. Dismissed at equal costs.

John Motlow against John Moore. Attachment. James Hooper Esq. being sworn as a guarnishee in the above case saith on his oath that he hath nothing but 7 pounds of iron and two Deer skins the property of the defendant absent debtor in his hands.

Ordered that the minutes be read, which was accordingly done and signed by William Smith, James Jordan, Judges. Court adjourned untill Tomorrow Nine O'Clock.

Thursday the 13th of June 1793. The Court met according to adjournment. Present their Honors James Jordan, William Smith, & Baylis Earle, Esq.

A Deed of Conveyance from William Benson Esq. to William Shaw, Esq. proven in open Court by the Evidence of Christopher Golightly, Ordered to be recorded.

Ordered that William Wells have licence to retail spirituous liquors and keep public House of Entertainment upon giving Capt. Henry Wells and Bazel Lee his surities for his lawful performance.

Robert Sterling & Wife Admr. & Admx. of James Elder decd. against Philip Hart. Appeal from a Justice. The papers being detained by the Justice thro' a mistake in his duty to return them, but comes into Court and Consents to return them either to this or the next Court, Ordered that this case stand over untill them.

The State against James Taylor. Peace Warrant. Ordered that the defendant continue to be bound to keep the peace as heretofore.

The State against Tullie Davis. Bastardy. On motion of the County Attorney, Ordered that the defendant be find Ł 10 proc. money, to be paid as quick as possible to be collected, and costs of the Indictment.

Ordered that the Road laid out by James Jordan and William Benson Esq., from this to Greenville County line be opened agreeable to their return, to wit, Agreeable to the within, the Road leading from Spartanburgh Court-House to Intersect the Road leading from Greenville Court-House, where it intersects the Road that leads by Isaac Morgans Esq. to the County line at the Ancient Indian Boundery Beginning at Spartanburgh Court-House, thence a direct course acorss Fairforest where it is marked above the Plantation of Benson, Thence a direct course to Mr. Timmon's Mill; thence a direct course by James T. Whites; thence to Mr. Sloans Iron-works, thence to the old ford on South Tyger River, thence to the County line of Greenville; where the Road shall intersect near the maple swamp Branches, James Ward overseer 'till it shall intersect Millers Road, Samuel Jamerson overseer from where it shall intersects Millers Road to James Creek, Michael Miller overseer from Jamies Creek to South Tyger, James Bright overseer from South Tyger 'till it shall Intersect Greenville Road.

The state against Absalom Stokes. Bastardy. The offence being committed in Greenville, Ordered that he be acquitted from his recognizance to appear here, and be bound for his appearance at next Greenville Court, to answer said charge.

The State against George Pool. Bastardy. The defendant came into Court and plead guilty, who was fined ₤ 5 proc. money, to be paid 12 months hence, and costs of the Indictment.

The State against Elizabeth Sinckley. Bastardy. The defendant came into Court and put herself upon the mercy of the Court, who fined her ₤ 5 proc. money and costs of the Indictment, George Pool the father of her Bastard child, came into Court and agreed to pay the same.

James Barron against John Moore. Debt. Came the plaintiff by Zachariah Tolliaferro Gentl. his attorney, and the defendant by William Shaw Esq. his attorney, whereupon came a Jury to wit, William Ford, Benjamin Rhodes, Samuel Turner, John Larkey, David Cook, William Castleberry, Francis Powers, Nicholas Holley, Buckner Smith, John White Tyger, Brittain Williford, & William Crocker...we find for the plaintiff ₤ 21 s 8 d 4 with lawful interest thereon from August 1784 and costs of suit.
                                        Wm. Ford, foreman.

The State against George Pool. Recognizance for Bastardy. The defendant came into Court with Jacob Hames his surity, and they both acknowledged to owe to the County Treasurer ₤ 25 each, if the said Poole shall fail to pay ₤ 10 proc. money which hath this day been imposed upon him and Elizabeth Sinkley (whose fine he assumes to pay) 12 months after, also the costs of the Indictments, and to Indemnify the County from the maintenance of the said Bastard child.

A Deed of conveyance from John Naile and wife to Henry Naile, proven in open Court by the evidence of John McDowell, Ordered to be recorded.

Ordered that all recognizance returnable to this Court that are not carried into prosecution, be continued.

Benjamine McMekin against John Davis. Appeal from a Justice. In pursuance to an order of the Honorable Court of Spartanburgh to us directed we proceeded to consider the matter as a new Trial, and after hearing the defence on both sides, consider that a nonsuit take place. 21 June 1793. David Goodlett, J. P., Thomas Moore, J. P. N. B. Our oppinion is that John Davis pay all costs of suit appeal.

Henry Shaver against John Tollison. Petition. Debt. Came the plaintiff by Zachariah Toliaferro Esq. and the defendant and after a full Investigation of the matter by the Attornies of each, decreed by the Court, that as the debt and interest exceeded a summary Jurisdiction that a nonsuit take place.

Charles Burton against Thomas Price. Case. By consent of the parties and assent of the Court, the cause is refered to John Ford, Tobias Bright, Joseph Woodruff & George Burton, Gentlemen argitrators, with powerof umpirage, to be arbitrated peremptorily at the House of John, the first Friday in August next, their award to be a Judgment of the Court.

Court then adjourned for half an Hour. Court met according to adjournment.

Ordered that John Wofford Junior oversee the Road, in place of his father, from Union line to Gibbs Mountain, and that all hands within three miles work thereon under his jurisdiction.

Rebekah Moody against Dudley Red. Trover. Dismissed by request of the Plaintiffs attorney.

William Henderson against Thomas McKnight. Case. Came the plaintiff by Mr. Shaw Gentleman and defendant by Zachariah Toliaferro his attorney, whereupon came a Jury, to wit, William Ford, Benjamine Rhodes, Samuel Turner, John Larkey, David Cook, William Castleberry, Francis Powers, Nicholas Holley, Buckner Smith, John White, Tyger; Brittain Williford, & William Crocker ...we find for the Defendant... Wm. Ford, foreman.

James Hughes, William Milikin and James Milikin proved their attendancy as witnesses in the case William Henderson against Thomas McKnight, to wit, the said Huggins 7 days, William Milikin 11 days and James Milikin 8 days, at s 2 d 6 per day.

Adam Beard as a witness in the case Henry Shaver against John Tollison, came into Court and proved 8 days attendance in said case, besides 160 miles as he lived out of the County at d 2 per mile.

The State against Peter Bragg & Margaret Floyd. Bastardy. The defendants came into Court (to wit Bragg) and Consented to pay the fine of ₺ 10 rpco. to Thomas Moore Esq. which the Court accepted and acquitted them upon their entering into recognizance before said Esquire Moore for Indemnifying the County for the maintenance of said Bastard.

Ordered that the Estrays returned to the Sheriff this Court, be sold Tomorrow at 4 O'clock agreeable to Law.

Ordered that the mintues be read, which was done & signed by William Smith, James Jordan, Baylis Earle, Judges. Court then adjourned untill Tomorrow 9 O'Clock.

Friday the 14th of June 1793. The Honorable Court met according to adjournment. Present their Honors William Smith, James Jordan, & Baylis Earle, Esq.

William Gowen being presented to the Court by the Sheriff of this County for him to act as under Sheriff, who was approved of, and ordered that he be quallifyed accordingly, which was done in open Court.

William Henderson against Thomas McKnight. Case. A trial being had yesterday and the Jury finding for the Defendant, Mr. Shaw attorney for the plaintiff, motioned for a new trial which was granted, and the costs to wait the event of the suit.

The last will and Testament of Richard Saunders deceased proven in open Court by the evidence of Michael Miles, according to Law, Ordered to record.

The State against Jonathan Bowen. Assault. Came William Shaw Esq. in behalf of the State and came a Jury (same as before)... Guilty, whereupon it is considered by the Court that he pay the fine of ₺ 5 & costs of the Indictment.

The last Will and Testament of Elisha Thomson, proven in open Court by the evidence of Mary McCarter according to law, Ordered to be recorded.

The State against Jonathan Bowen. Assault. Ordered that a Scieri Facias Issue against the surities of the defendant, to shew cause if any they have, why their recognizance in which they were bound for the appearance of the said defendant on an Indictment for assault, should not be forfeited, as he did not appear on trial.

John McElheny against Benjamine McMekin. Slander. Award returned. We the Arbitrators appointed by the Honorable Court of Spartanburgh, met at the House of John Thomas Junior, Esq., to Arbitrate a certain matter of scandal, not agreeing in our oppinion, calld in Capt. Wm. Thomas as Umpire, who decided the matter by agreeing that the Defendant should pay all costs of the said suit that may be lawful, or that may accrue thereon. 30th June 1792. John Vaughn, Wm. Benson, Nevil Wayland, John Gowen, Wm. D. Thomas.

Lucy Thomson against Benjamine Wofford. Case. This case is continued untill next Court by affidavit with a peremtory rule to be tried next Court.

Joseph Venable against Alexander Copeland. Debt. Ordered that this case be refered to the arbitrament of Capt. William Benson, & Turner Thomason Gentl. Arbitrators with power of Umpirage, their award to be a rule of Court.

Richard James against James Smith. Slander. Continued by affidavit of the Defendant, that his witnesses were absent.

John Cantwell against Benjamine Wofford. Detinue. By consent of the parties and assent of the Court, the trial of cause is refered to the Arbitrament of Mr. William Ford and Isham Foster, with power of Umpirage, their Judgment to be a rule of Court.

Richard James against James Smith. Slander. By consent of the parties and assent of the Court the trial of this cause is refered to the Arbitrament of Joseph Barnett and Jesse Connell Gentl. Arbitrators, with power of Umpirage, Their award to be a rule of Court.

John Mason against William Pool. Detinue. Came the plaintiff by Patrick Mechie Esq. his attorney and the defendant by William Shaw, Esq. his attorney, whereupon came a Jury (same as before) ...we find for the Defendant....

John Smith proved 3 days attendance in each case John McElheny against Benjamine McMekin, and Benjamine McMekin against John Davis as a witness in the same.

William Ford as a witness in the case Joseph Venable against Alexander Copeland proved 13 days attendance at s 2 d 6 per day.

Court then adjourned for half an Hour. Court met according to adjournment.

George Devours as a witness in the case Joseph Venable against Alexander Copeland on oath in open Court, is allowed s 30 for 12 days attendance.

Elizabeth Bennett as a witness in the case Joseph Venable against Alexander Copeland on oath in open Court is allowed s 22 d 6 for 9 days attendance.

William Moody against Dudly Red. Assault. Ordered that the plaintiff give security for costs or be non prossed.

Bazel Lee proved 6 days, William Hargrove 4 days, Hugh Hargrove 4 days, William McAbee 3 days and John Henry 4 days attendances as witnesses in the case John Mason against William Pool, at s 2 d 6 per day.

Joseph Howell proved 10 days attendance and riding 52 miles in coming to Court at d 2 per mile, in the case John Cantwell against Benjamine Wofford.

Francis N. Wayland proved 16 days attendance as a witness in the case John McElheny against William Ford.

Francis Dodd proved 10 days attendance as a witness in the case John McElhany against William Ford.

Nevil Wayland proved 3 days attendance as a witness in the case Benjamine McMekin against John Davis.

Nicholas Holley proved 12 days attendance as a witness in the case John Cantwell against Benjamine Wofford.

Rachel Arnold proved 3 days attendance as a witness in the case John Cantwell against Benjamine Wofford.

George Martin proved 3 days attendance as a witness in the case John McElheny agaiinst William Ford.

Ordered that scieri Facias issue against those that have Estrays in their possession, which are liable to be sold as appear by the Estray Book, for them to shew cause if any they have why they do not produce them to be sold according to law, or return the necessary proceedings thereon.

Ordered that the minutes be read which was accordingly done and signed by William Smith, Baylis Earle, James Jordan, Judges. Court then adjourned untill Court in Course.

At a Court of Session and pleas began and Holden at the Court House of Spartanburgh on the 13th (the 12th happening on Sunday) of January 1794. Present their Honors William Smith and James Jordan, Esq.

The Court proceeded to draw the Grand Jurors for June Term 1794, to wit,

Thomas Miles	1	John Pace	11
Michael Wood	2	John Pennington	12
William Lipscomb	3	John Young Senior	13
James Wood	4	William McWilliams	14
Samuel Timmons	5	William Simpson	15
Samuel Miller	6	John McCarter	16
Ransom Tinsley	7	Richard Morriss	17
John West	8	Hugh Stephenson	18
Benjamin Wofford	9	Thomas Tod	19
John Wofford	10	Thomas Williams	20

Petit Jurors drawn to serve next Court, to wit

William Smith by Connells	1	William Stone	16
William Murry	2	John Smith on Tyger	17
Joseph Lively	3	David Neal	18
Thomas Spann	4	John Osheals	19
Benjamine Stone	5	Nathaniel Stokes	20
Young Griffin	6	William McClure	21
Caleb Langston	7	William Massy	22
James Satterfield	8	Daniel Finch	23
Samuel Shurbet	9	Robert Page	24
Charles McClain	10	George Lowther	25
Martin Oates	11	Jonathan Low	26
John Wooton	12	James Nesbitt	27
Bazel Lee	13	Robert Miller	28
Frances Mason	14	Abraham Moore	29
Thomas Price	15	Page Puckett	30

Grand Jurors to serve this Court, Impanneled and sworn, to wit,

John James foreman	1	Alexander McCarter	8
George Kezie	2	William Milikin	9
John Posey	3	Joseph Wofford	10
Daniel Hackney	4	David McDowell	11
Drewry McDaniel	5	Ebenezer Morse	12
Thomas Gore	6	Isaac Young	13
William Ford	7	Richard Young	14
		John Tolleson	15

Petit Jurors to Serve this Court, to wit,

Robert White	1	Jesse Traylor	7
Isaac Hamby	2	Jacob Eisen	8
John Redman	3	John Woodruff	9
Nathan Walden	4	Amos Critchfield	10
Robert Wood	5	Jeremiah Selman	11
John Wells	6	William Sterling	12

Ann Saunders against Noel Johnson. Detinue. Dismis'd at the Defendants Costs.

The last Will and Testament of Martha McCroy deceased proven in open Court by the evidence of Richard Young, Richard Chesney, & Samuel Bell, Ordered to be recorded.

The Executor of the Estate of Martha McCrory deceased, came into Court and took the oaths of office prescribed by Law.

A Deed of Conveyance from Wm. D. Thomas, James Clerk, Mary Clerk, Elijah Clerk, Elijah Stevens & Anne Stephens to Michael Miller proven in Court by Nevil Wayland, Ordered to Record.

Ordered that the minutes be read which was done and signed by William Smith, James Jordan, Judges. Court then adjourned untill Tomorrow 9 O'Clock.

Tuesday the 14th of January 1794. The Honorable Court met according to adjournment. Present their Honors William Smith and James Jordan, Esq.

Ordered that Thomas Miles be allowed the sum of s 20 for keeping an unbroke Estray.

The State against James Taylor Assault.
Same against the Same. Murder. By order of Court, Noli prosequi is entered by the County Attorney.

The State against Benjamine Wofford. Forgery Ordered that this case be transfered to next Pinckney Court and that the defendant give good security for his personal appearance there to answer said charge.

Ordered that Thomas Kemp have the Administration on the Estate of John Waggoner deceased, upon signing a Bond for the complyance with the requisites of the Law, and qualifying which he accordingly did.

The State against Benjamine Wofford. Forgery. The Defendant came into Court with Ebenezer Morse and Andrew Hendrix, as his aurities, and they acknowledged to owe to the State, to wit, the sd. Wofford Ł 100 and the surities Ł 50 each...by way of recognizance, if the said Benjamine Wofford shall fail to appear at next Court to be held at Pinckneyville on 1st April next....

The State against Malachi Jones. Scieri Facias on forfeiture of Recognizance. The defendant with John Humphries came into Court, and confessed Judgment for Ł 10 in discharge of his recognizance for Jonathan Bowen, which was assented to by the Court, and which is in full satisfaction for the fine and costs against Jonathan Bowen.

The State against John Hudgens. Bastardy. The defendant plead Guilty and submitted himself to the mercy of the Court who fined him Ł 5 proc. money & costs of suit.

John Westmoreland being recommended by Zadock Ford Esq. to act as his Constable was approved of by the Court, and took the oaths of office accordingly.

The State against Jeremiah Spann. Bastardy. Ordered that the recognizance continue untill next Court.

The State against Francis Clerk. Bastardy. Ordered that a Bench warrant issue against the defendant to appear at next Court to answer said charge.

The State against William Merchant. Lerceny. Continued by order of Court, also ordered that a Capias issue against Benjamine Hooker, to take him before some Justice to be bound to next Court, to prosecute the said offender.

The State against Saphira Whittemore. Bastardy. Continued untill next Court, and ordered that a Bench warrant issue against her, to be brought to next Court, to answer said charge.

The State against Thomas Buckeby. Bastardy. Mary Powers came into Court and made oath that the Defendant was the father of her Bastard child, and the said defendant appears by Mr. Nott his attorney and defends his cause, and after an Investigation of the matter by him and the County Attorney, Ordered that the said defendant be fined Ł 5 and costs of suit.

The State against John Hudgens. Bastardy. John Hudgens and John Pennington came into Court & confessed Judgment for Ł 5 payable 12 months hence for the said defendant begetting a bastard child on the body of Sapphira Whittemore.

The State against John Hudgens. Bastardy. The defendant with John Pennington came into Court and acknowledged to owe to the State Ł 25 each if the said John Hudgens shall fail to keep harmless this County in maintaining a Bastard child begotten of the Body of Sapphira Whittemore.

The State against Thomas Milikin & Mary Milikin. Bastardy. Ordered that James Hooper send a summons against the Defendants to cause them to be brought before him to be bound to next court to answer said charge.

The County against Demps Bonner. Qui Tam. The defendant having taken up 3 estrays and not returning them according to law to be sold, whereupon a precept issued against him for the same, But as he made it appear that the Estrays, to wit, a Black mare, a Bay Horse Branded DD, and a Bay mare with a wart in her ear, were proven away before Edward Goode, Esq., Ordered that he be acquitted upon paying costs of the same.

The County against Edward Goode, Esq. Qui Tam. The Defendant having taken up a Bay mare, Branded I M and not returning the same, to be sold according to law, whereupon a precept issued against him for the same, for certain reasons given by him to the Court, Ordered that he be acquitted upon paying costs.

The County against James Crook. Qui Tam. For not returning a Bay mare (branded on the near shoulder & jaw A, taken up by him as an Estray) to be sold according to Law, Excused by the Court on the reasons given, upon paying costs.

Same against Same. Qui Tam. For a bay Filley taken up by him as an Estray & not return'd to be sold according to law, Excused by reasons given to the Court, upon paying costs.

The County against Jacob Casey. Qui Tam. For not returning a Bay Horse, taken up by him as an Estray and toll'd Thomas Farrow Esq., excused by reasons given to the Court, upon paying the costs.

The County against Edward Goode, Esq. Qui Tam. For a Roan Hipshotten mare, taken up by him as an Estray & not returning the same to be sold according to law, as it was proven away, but omitted making the necessary return For which reason the Court acquitted him without costs.

The County against David Bruton. Qui Tam. For a Black Horse Toll'd before Thomas Farrow, Esq., which was proven away, and as the return was not made, Ordered that he be acquitted upon paying Costs.

The County against Zachariah Robertson. Quit Tam. For a White Horse, also the cow & two stears posted before Richard Harrison, Esq., It appearing they were sold, Ordered that this case be dismissed at the Counties Cost.

The County against Ellis Cannon. Qui Tam. For a gray Horse tolld before Richard Harrison, Esq., It appearing the same was legally proven away, for that and other reasons, this case is dismissed without costs.

The County against James Alexander Qui Tam. For a Black Horse Toll'd before William McDowell, Esq., the same being lost as appear by the Testimony of Joseph Venable, Ordered that this case be dismissed without Costs.

The Courtn against Henry Bishop, Qui Tam. For a Gray Mare tolld before David Goodlett Esq. the same being proven away, Ordered that this case be dismissed at the defendants Costs.

The County against James Head. Qui Tam. For a Bay Horse, Toll'd before Thomas Farrow, Esq., It also appearing that the same was proven away fore said Farrow, but no return being made, Ordered that this case be dismissed at the defendants costs.

The State against Mary Powers. Bastardy. The defendant plead guilty, and submitted herself to the mercy of the Court, who was thereupon fined Ł 5 proc. money payable 12 months hence and costs of suit.

The County against Landon Farrow. Qui Tam. For a Bay Horse, & Bell Toll'd before Thomas Farrow Esq. who proved that the same was kill'd by accident, Ordered that he be acquitted upon paying costs.

The County against Littleton Bagwell. Qui Tam. For a Dun-coloured Horse tolld' before Richard Harrison Esq. whereas the Clerk saw the Estray given up by his directions, altho' It was not proven away & a return made, Ordered that the defendant be acquitted & the Clerk pay the Costs, Attorney's fee forgiven.

The County against Elisha Smith. Qui Tam. For a Brown mare Toll'd before Obadiah Trimmier, Esq., the defendant made oath that the same was proven away & that he handed the probate to the Clerk, therefore Ordered that the same be dismissed at the Clerks costs, attorney's fee forgiven.

The County against John Trimmier. Qui Tam. For a dark Chestnut mare toll'd before Samson Bethel, Esq. the same being proved away, and the defendant having the probate and not returning it, Ordered that he be acquitted upon paying the Costs.

The County against William Moore. Qui Tam. For a Brown mare toll'd before Thomas Moore, Esq. the defendant made oath that the same was proven away, and as there was no return made, Ordered that he be acquitted upon paying the Costs.

The State against Henry William & John Reynolds. The defendants came into Court and acknowledged to owe to the State Ł 50 each and William Taylor, George Taylor and Lewis Standly as their surities Ł 25 each if the said defendant fail to appear Tomorrow when call'd for, to answer said charge.

The State against Thomas Huckeby. Bastardy. The defendant with John Chumlie and William Avet came into Court and confessed Judgment for the following sum, to wit, Ł 10 proc. money, Ł 5 and costs to be paid 6 months hence, and Ł 5 12 months hence for his and Mary Powers fines for said charge, which remits her fine.

Ordered that the minutes be read which was accordingly done & signed by James Jordan, William Smith. Court then adjourned untill Tomorrow 10 of the Clock.

Wednesday the 15th day of January 1794. The Honorable Court met according to adjournment. Present their Honors William Smith and James Jordan, Esquires.

The last will and Testament of John Grist deceased was approved of and proven in open Court by John Chumler & Thomas Tod according to law, Ordered to be recorded.

The Executors of the Estate of John Grist, deceased came into Court and took the necessary oaths of their office prescribed by Law.

The last will and testament of William Wood deceased who being approved and proven in open Court by the evidences of William Young & John Young, Ordered that the same be admitted to record.

George Salmon Esq. Executor of the Estate of William Wood came into Court and took the necessary oaths of his office as Executor, prescribed by law.

Ordered that John Tap, Thomas Bennett and Daniel White appraise the Estate of William Wood deceased.

The County against Robert White. Qui Tam. For a Small Black mare toll'd before Richard Harrison Esq. deceased, be request of the defendant, Ordered that this case be continued untill next Court.

The County against Mason Morse. Qui Tam. For a Black mare toll'd before Thomas Farrow, Esq. the same being proven away, but no return made, Ordered that the defendant be acquitted upon paying the costs.

The County against James Laxon. Qui Tam. For a Bay Horse toll'd before Richard Harrison Esq. the same being proven away & the probate not return'd, therefore dismissed at the defendants costs.

The Same against Robert Connell. Qui Tam. For a sow & two shoats, which appeared to have been proven away, but no return being made, therefore dismissed at the defendants costs.

The same against Samuel Jentry. Qui Tam. For a Brown mare, by request of the defendant this case is continued, untill next court.

The Same against William McDaniel. Qui Tam. For a Bay Horse, which appeared to have been proven away, but no return made, therefore dismissed at the defendants costs.

The Same against William Taylor. Qui Tam. For a Sorrel Horse, which appeared to have been proven away & no return made therefore dismist at the defendants costs.

The Same against Lewis Standly. Qui Tam. For a Yellow Bay gelding, toll'd before Samson Bethel, Esq. the defendant having given up the Estray with being proven, Judgment was therefore entered against for Ł 6 for the same and costs of suit.

The County against William Moore of Jamies Creek. Qui Tam. For a Bay mare, the same being proven away, but no return thereof, Dismissed at the defendants costs.

The Same against Isaac Young. Quo Tam. For a Bay mare toll'd before Samson Bethel, Esq., Continued by Order of Court.

The Same against William T. Thomason. Qui Tam. For a Sorrel mare toll'd before Isham Harrison, Esq. Continued by Order of Court.

The Same against William Biter. Qui Tam. For a Cow and calf and a stear toll'd before Thomas Moore, Esq., which creatures

it appeared are lawfully dealt by, to wit, the steer dead & the
rest sold but no return thereof. Ordered that the defendant be
acquitted without Costs.

The Same against Richard Harriss. Qui Tam. For a Bay gelding
toll'd before Zadock Ford, Esq., It appearing that the same
was proven away, but no return thereof, therefore ordered that
the defendant be acquitted upon paying the Costs.

The Same against John Chumler. Qui Tam. For a Brown Bay mare
toll'd before Samuel Lancaster, Esq., It appearing to the satisfaction of the Court that the creature tumbled into a River and
was drowned by accident. Therefore the defendant is acquitted
upon paying the Costs.

The Same against William Roberts. Qui Tam. A Sorrel mare,
toll'd before Isham Harrison, Esq., The same being proven away,
but no return thereof, Ordered that the defendant be acquitted
upon paying the Costs.

The Same against Berryman Shoemate. Qui Tam. For a Bay Gelding
toll'd before James Jordan, Esq., which appears to have run away
so that it could become it by the Taker up, Therefore ordered
that he be acquitted upon paying the costs.

The Same against James McHughes. Qui Tam. For four Hogs toll'd
before James Jordan, Esq., Judgment entered against the said
Defendant for s 20 & costs for the said Estrays.

The County against William Ford. Qui Tam. For a Stear, agreeable
to the proceedings of the defendant, The Court acquitted him a
balance due of the Stear for wintering the same, and paying Costs.

The Same against Josiah Tanner. Qui Tam. For a Sorrel Horse,
toll'd before Edward Good, Esq., For reasons given to the Court
this case is dismissed at the defendants costs.

The Same against Ignacious Griffin. Qui Tam. For a Brown Horse
toll'd before Obadiah Trimmier, Esq., the same appearing to be
dead tho' not occasioned by the defendant, Therefore ordered
that he be acquitted upon paying the costs.

The County against Obadiah Wingo. Qui Tam. For an old Black
Horse toll'd before Richard Harrison, Esq., The same being sold
as by the oath of the defendant, Therefore he is acquitted without costs.

The Same against John Lemaster. Qui Tam. For a Sorrel Horse
toll'd before Richard Harrison, Esq., proven away, and the defendant dismissed upon paying Costs.

The State against Benjamine Wofford. Forgery. Ordered that the
recognizance & this case continue in this Court Instead of going
to Pinckney.

Lucy Thomson as principle and Burrel Thomson as surity came into
court and acknowledged to owe to the State, to wit, Lucy Ł 50
and Burrel Ł 25 if the said Lucy shall fail to appear at next
court, to give Testimony against the defendant.

Wednesday the 15th of January 1794.
The last will and testament of William Wood deceased being approved and proven in open court by the evidence of William Young

and John Young, Ordered that the same be admitted to record.

George Salmon Esq. Exr. of the Est. of William Wood deceased came into court and took the necessary oath....

Ordered that the minutes be read which was accordingly done and signed by William Smith, James Jordan, Judges. Court then adjourned untill Tomorrow Nine of the Clock.

See the minutes of the County Court of Spartanburg Book B page 182 & Book C page 5 for the continuation of same days proceedings.

END OF VOLUME.

VOLUME 1794-1799

The State against James Burnett. Lerceny. Alexander Roddy and David Lewis as witnesses in this case in behalf of the State, came into Court and acknowledged themselves indebted to the State ₤ 20 each if they failed to attend next Court to give evidence against the defendant.

The State against John Spelce. Burglary. John Blasingame Esq., acknowledged to owe the State ₤ 20 if he failed to appear at next Court to give Testimony in behalf of the State against the said Defendant.

Benjamine McMekin being summoned as a Grand Juror, was for certain reasons given acquitted by the Court for the term.

Graff Edson & Co. against John James. Petition. The defendant confesses judgment for ₤ 6 s 1 d 6 & costs of suit.

Owen Bowen Attorney for Elizabeth Stewart against William Haden. Trover. William Shaw Esq. motion for a nonsuit and being opposed by Zachariah Toliaferro attorney for the Plaintiff, and after an investigation of the matter, Ordered that a nonsuit be entered against the Plaintiff.

Charles Burton against Thomas Price. Case. Award returned thus "In pursuance of the within rule to us directed, we John Ford, George Bruton, Tobias Bright (the within named Joseph Wofford being absent) & David Burton was chosen by the parties to act in his place, in evidence thereto we proceeded to have the allegations of the parties & their evidence, We do therefore give and award to the within named Charles Burton ₤ 8 s 10 d 5 with all legal costs of suit." 2 Aug 1793.

Philip Hart against Alexander Ray. Petition. The defendant came into Court in his own proper person & Confessed Judgment according to Specialty, with stay of Execution two months.

The state against John Reynolds, Wm. Henry and Furny Reynolds. Indictment for Hog Stealing.
A bill of Indictment being prefered by the County Attorney to the Grand Jury, returned the same thus " A true Bill.
John James, foreman.

The State against William Smith & William Smith Junr. son of Handcock. For a charge of Hog Stealing. Whereas a State Warrant having issued by Isham Harrison Esq. on the oath of Absalom Lancaster, and the Constable returning that he could not execute the same, Ordered that a Bench Warrant issue against the said defendants for them to be brought to next Court.

Robert Goodgion against Javis Cornwell. Debt. Ordered that this suit be submitted to the Arbitrament of James Logan, James Hooper, and William Benson, Esq., or any two of them, whose award made upon any day fixed on by the parties to be a rule of Court.

Thomas Blasingame, Esq. as a witness in this case, Philip Hart against Alexander Ray, on oath in open Court is allowed s 5 for 2 days attendance.

The State against John, William, Henry & Furney Reynolds. Hog Stealing. Ordered that this Indictment be travers'd, unill next Court, and that the defendants be committed to jail untill they give good security for their appearance at that time.

Samuel Turner as an evidence in the case Owen Bowen Attorney for Elizabeth Stewart against William Haden, proved 7 days attendance at 2/6 per day.

Elias Jordan proved 7 days attendance as a witness in the case Owen Bowen attorney for Elizabeth Stewart against William Haden at 2/6 per day.

William Henderson against Thomas McKnight. Capias. Ordered that this case be continued untill next Court at the plaintiffs costs.

Ordered that a Bench warrant issue against Furney Reynolds, to be brought to next Court to answer a charge of Hog Stealing.

John Reynolds, William Reynolds, & Henry Reynolds as principles came into Court with George Taylor and William Taylor as their securities and acknowledged to owe to the State, sd. Reynolds Ł 50 each and sd. securities Ł 25 if the sayd Reynolds failed to appear at next Court to answer the charge of Hog Stealing.

Ordered that Thomas Beddington, Daniel Grant and James Crowder appraise the Estate of John Grice, deceased, and make due return thereof.

Ordered that the Executors of John Grice, decd., proceed to the sale of the said deceased's Estate on the first Monday in Feb next at 12 months credit, except sums under s 5 to be paid at the time of sale.

Ordered that the minutes be read which was accordingly done and signed by William Smith, James Jordan, Judges. Court then adjourned untill tomorrow Nine of the Clock.

Thursday the 16th day of January 1794, Court met according to adjournment. Present their Honors William Smith and James Jordan, Esq.

Abraham Pool against John Tucker. Attachment. Samuel Tucker being summoned as guarnishee came into Court & made oath that he had not any property in his hands of the defendant nor had not at the time he was summoned.

Joseph Wofford a guarnishee in the same case maketh oath that he hath not at this time neither at the time that attachment was levyed in his hands any property of the defendant the absent debtor.

Lucy Thomson against Benjamine Wofford. Case. The parties came into Court and consented to refer the trial of this case to the Arbitrament of John Ford and John Blasingame gentlemen arbitrators, with power of Umpirage to be arbitrated at the House of William Smith, Esq., on the last Friday in March next, their award returned to next Court shall be a Judgment thereof.

Joseph Venable against Alexander Copeland. Detinue. Pursuant to an order from the Hon. Court of Spartanburgh, we the Arbitrators nominated to Determine a case wherein Joseph Venable is plaintiff and Alexander Copeland defendant after hearing the parties and such evidence as was produced by the contening parties, we do arbitrate and award that the plaintiff be nonprossed.

20th July 1793.

William Poole against Reubin Matthis. Case. The defendant being called, and not appearing himself neither by his Attorney on motion of William Shaw, Gentl., attorney for the plaintiff, Judgment was entered by default. and ordered that a writ of Inquiry be executed in this case, whereupon came a jury, to wit, Robert White, Isaac Hamby, John Redman, Nathan Walden, Robert Wood, John Wells, Jesse Traylor, Jacob Eison, John Woodruff, Amos Crutchfield, Jeremiah Selman and William Sterling, who being sworn to well and truly Execute all writs of Inquiry that shall be given them in charge this Court...we find for the plaintiff Ł 49 s 8 and costs of suit. Robert White, foreman....

Richard James against James Smith, Slander. This cause is laid over until tomorrow with a preemptory rule to be tried the first cause.

John Cantrell against Benjamine Wofford. Detinue. The defendant by his attorney motioned for a nonsuit for want of proof that a demand was made for the Horse before suit was brought upon which this action is founded, which he says was not done then nor any other time, But as the plaintiff and defendant came to the House of Nicholas Holley in time of the war to prove the Horse to be the defendant's, which they did not do, the Court supposes that was a demand sufficient, and thereupon over ruled the motion, and ordered that a trial be entered into. The plaintiff by **Mr. Nott** his attorney proceeded to the same, and in examining the evidences of Edward Balenger as a person liable for the Horse, the Jury (same as before)...we find for the defendant ....

Whereas, Sciri Facias's hath issued against those that took up Estrays and did not take the legal steps with the same, for which they are run to much costs thereon, William Shaw, Esq., as County Attorney forgave his fees in said cases; and the Court ordered that a minute be made of the same.

Ordered that William Moore of James Creek be paid the sum of s 20 out of the County fund for the County attornies fee for a Sciri facias issuing & being returned against him for an Estray, as he acted according to law, and the fault lay in the justice before whom it was told (sic), for not making his return in a legal manner.

The County against Vardry McBee. Qui Tam. for Estray. The defendant being made liable to pay costs, ordered that he be acquitted from the same, as it appeared by his information to the satisfaction of the Court, that he had heretofore informed them what became of the Estray & that he did not convert it to his own use.

John McElheny against William Ford. Case. The Jury being sworn and the parties appearing with their Counselors, It was thought advisable by the Attornies and the Court that this suit discontinue, which was accordingly done.

George Martin proved four days attendance as a witness in the case John McElheny against William Ford, a 2/6 per day.

James Laurence proved 10 days attendance as a witness in the case John McElheny against William Ford, at 2/6 per day.

George Lewis against Thomas McKnight. Appeal from a Justice Below. Came the appellant by Patrick McKie his attorney and the Investigation by the Counselors of each party, Decreed by the Court that the Judgment of the Justice be set aside.

Ezekial Farmer against Francis Gilley. Attachment. Dismissed at the plaintiff's Costs by order of Court.

Nevil Wayland proved 4 days attendance as a witness in the case John McElheny against William Ford, a 2/6 per day.

John Vaughan proved 7 days attendance as a witness in the case John McElheny against William Ford at 2/6 per day.

Rachel Arnold proved 5 days attendance as a witness in the case John Cantrell against Benjamine Wofford at 2/6 per day, also 50 miles at two pence per mile as she lives without the limits of this County.

Joseph Howell proved 4 days attendance as a witness in the case John Cantrell against Benjamine Wofford at 2/6 per day, also 50 miles at 2 pence per mile as he lives without the limits of this County.

Hollaway Power proved 4 days attendance as a witness in the case John Cantrell against Benjamine Wofford, at 2/6 also two pence per mile as he lives in Laurence (sic) County.

John Bingham proved four days attendance as a witness in the case Joseph Venable against Alexander Copeland at 2/6 per day, also 60 miles at 2 pence per mile as he lives without the limits of this County.

Ordered that a Capias issue against George Parkison for the Sheriff to take him before some justice of the peace for the County, for him to be bound in recognizance to attend next Court to give evidence in behalf of the State against William Smith Senior and William Smith Junior son of Hancock as a Bench Warrant is to issue against them on a charge of Hog Stealing.

Ordered that s 5 be allowed Alexander Roddy for wintering an Estray yearling to be paid out of the County fund.

Ordered that James Jordan Esq. be allowed s 20 for keeping an Estray Horse.

Ordered that the minutes be read which was accordingly done & signed by Wm. Smith, James Jordan, Baylis Earle, Judges. Court then adjourned untill Tomorrow Nine o'clock.

Friday the 17th of January 1794. Court met according to adjournment, present their Honors William Smith & James Jordan, Esq.

Absent William Smith, Esq.

William Smith Esq. against William Clayton. Petition Debt. On motion of William Shaw, Esq. attorney for the plaintiff, decreed by the Court in favour of the plaintiff according to note allowing s 14 pr lb. for the Tobacco, with Interest & Costs of suit.

William Smith Esq. against Thomas Mabery & Charles Mabery. Petition by account. On motion of William Shaw, attorney for the plaintiff, Decreed by the Court in favour of the plaintiff ₺ 5 s 14 d 4½ and costs of suit, after Deducting the dependants account.

Hardy Owens against William Traylor. Capias Case. Nonsuit.

Nathaniel Henderson against Joseph Wofford. Special Action. Nonsuit.

John Stokes against Hugh Freeman Admr. of Thomas Rodden, decd. Attachment. After a contest by the Counsellors of each party whether the guarnishees in this case should be sworn or not, which the court ruled that they should, Hugh Stephenson and William McWilliams being the persons, who after qualifying on their oaths say, to wit, the said Stephenson rented a plantation and was to give corn to the value of ₺ 5 s 5, and the said McWilliams for the same two cows & calves, which was the property of the Defendant. Ordered that the same be paid to the plaintiff and the attorney for the plaintiff directed that this attachment be struck off the docket, as that is all that can be got.

Graff Edson & Co. against John Johnson. Debt. The defendant being called and not appearing in his own person nor by his Attorney Judgment was therefore entered by Default, and the attorney for plaintiff motioned for a writ of Inquiry to be executed in this case, which was accordingly granted by the Court, whereupon came a Jury, to wit, Robert White, Isaac Hamby, John Redman, Nathan Walden, Robert Wood, John Wells, Jesse Traylor, Jacob Eison, John Woodruff, Amos Critchfield, Jeremiah Tilman and William Sterling, who being sworn to well and truly execute all writs of Inquiry...we find for the plaintiff according to note. Robert White, foreman....

Thomas Blasingame against Burrel Thomson. Petition by account. By consent of the parites and assent of the Court, the trial of this case is refered to the arbitrament of Joseph Woodruff, Thomas Tod, Thomas Moore, Esq., John Ford & George Bruton, at the house of William Smith Esq., the last Friday in next month an award made by any three of them and returned to next Court shall be the Judgment thereof.

Richard James against James Smith. Slander. Dismissed at the defendants costs by consent, attornies fee, except by his direction.

James Henderson against John Maxwell. Detinue. Continued by order of Court at the plaintiffs costs.

Margaret Campbell against John Johnson. Trover. Came the parties by their Counselors, also came a Jury (same as before)... we find for the plaintiff ₺ 5 s 12 d 4 & costs of suit....

Charles Bruce proved 10 days attendance as a witness in the case Margaret Campbell against John Jackson, also 80 miles at 4 pence pr. mile as he lives without the limits of this County.

Thomas James proved 11 days attendance as a witness in the case, Richard James against James Smith, at 2/6 per day.

Samuel Knox against William McGowen. Petition Debt. Decreed by the Court in favor of the plaintiff according to note being ₺ 7 s 17 d 6 allow a reduction of s 24 on account of the defendant from the debt, and costs of suit.

Thomas Wells against John James. Attachment. Settled at the defendants costs by Information of the plaintiff's attorney whose fee is accepted by him.

William Darby against John James. Attachment. Dismissed at the defendants Costs by his consent.

Graff Edson & Co. against John Johnson. Petition. Debt. On motion decreed for the plaintiff Ł 4 s 19 d 11 according to note & costs of suit.

William Benson against John Hammett. Petition Debt. Continued by consent of the parties.

James Kemp against Benjamine Wofford. Detinue. Nonsuit.

Moses Clayton against John Clayton. Case. Continued by affidavit of the defendant at his costs.

William Trountree against Dudly Red. Attachment. The defendant being called and not appearing in his own person nor by his attorney, Judgment was thereupon entered by default and on a writ of Inquiry the Jury (same as before)...we find for the plaintiff Ł 10 s 2 d 8 with interest & costs of suit....

Michael McKie against William Ford. Debt. Ordered that a commission dedimus Potestatum issue to the State of Virginia both for plaintiff and defendant, to be effectual upon either giving the other legal notice of the time & place of Examining the witness or witnesses touching the above case.

Jeremiah Walker against William Pool. Debt. By consent of the parties & assent of the Court the trial of this cause is refered to the Arbitrament of Isham Harrison, Isham Foster, Esq., & Henry Wells, their award to be a rule of court.

Zachariah Robertson against William Wofford. Attachment. Benjamine Wofford came into Court and acknowledged himself special Bail for the Debt and costs or render the body of the defendant in discharge thereof.

James Rountree proved 5 days attendance as a witness in the case William Rountree against Dudly Red at 2/6 per day also 46 miles at 2 pence per mile, as he lived without the limits of this County.

William Moody against Dudly Red. Assault. Ordered that the Defendant be non prossed because he did not give security agreeable to an order of Court.

Zachariah Robertson against William Wofford. Attachment. John Harris being summoned as Guarnishee came into Court and made oath that he acknowledged himself indebted to the Defendant Ł 45 at the time that he was summoned and that he still owes the same which is condemned by the Court for the use of the plaintiff, It being granted on motion that a trial be had by a Jury, to wit, (same as before)...we find Ł 16 s 9 d 11½ for the plaintiff with interest and costs of suit.

Absalom Lancaster proved 15 days attendance as a witness in the case Richard James against James Smith at 2/6 per day.

Thomas Price against Dudly Red. Attachment. The defendant being called and not appearing himself nor by his attorney, Judgment was thereupon entered by default. And on motion of the plaintiff's attorney for a final decree the same was accordingly entered for ₺ 4 s 7 d 4 and costs of suit. Ordered that the property attached be sold, or so much thereof as will satisfy the debt & costs. One feather bed & furniture excepted.

Ordered that the estrays which are given or may be given to the sheriff this Court, which are liable for sale, be sold at the adjournment of Court according to Law.

Ordered that the minutes be read, which was done accordingly and signed by William Smith, James Jordan, Judges. Court then adjourned untill Tomorrow Nine O'Clock.

Saturday the 18th day of January 1794. Court met according to adjournment. Present their Honors William Smith & James Jordan, Esq.

Ordered that William Thomson Gentleman, have license to sell spirituous liquors and keep public House of Entertainment, upon giving Malachi Jones & John Golightly his securities for his lawful performance, which he did in open Court.

Dianna & Millie Mayfield against Stephen and Francis Silvey. Slander. Nonsuit.

Robert Smith against William Wood. Case. This suit is abated by the death of the defendant.

William Rountree against Dudly Red. Attachment. Ordered that the personal property attached in this case be sold to satisfy the plaintiff's debt & costs of suit.

Zachariah Robertson against William Wofford. Attachment. The Counselors for the defendant motioned for a new trial who was overruled, the Court being of opinion that no new trial ought to be had, and the defendant by his attorney prayed an appeal which was granted on his giving an appeal Bond according to law before the final adjournment of this Court, and as the defendants suggested that he inteneded to carry this cause to the Superior Court by a writ of Certiorari, Execution was thereupon stayed untill the first day of April next.

William McGowen assignee of William Wilkison against George Taylor. Debt. Ordered that a commission Dedimus Potestatum Issue the State of Georgia to Examine such witnesses as the plaintiff may require upon his giving legal notice to the adverse party.

Thomas Parks assignee of Philip Wells against Edward Arnold. Petition Debt. The defendant confesses Judgment for ₺ 8 s 14 the debt and costs of suit upon the plaintiff agreeing to pay s 14 of the cost on an attachment, Parks against Arnold and stay Execution 6 months.

John Cantwell against Benjamine Wofford. Detinue. The plaintiff by his attorney motioned for a new trial, but was overruled by the Court, for certain reasons alleged by the defendant's attorney that no new trial ought to be had in this case.

Micajah Barnett against James Pool. Special Action. The defendant by his attorney mov'd for a nonsuit by reason of the writ being ₺ 50 instead of 20. The plaintiff by his attorney plead a special assumpsit to be amended in the writ, who was overruled and ordered that a nonsuit take place.

Eli McVey against Rowland Johnson, David Goodlett & Nathaniel Stokes. Detinue. Dismissed at Plaintiffs Costs.

John Motlow against John Moore and James Moore. Attachment. Came the parties by their counselors, also came a Jury, to wit, (same as before)...we find for the plaintiff agreeable to Specialty & costs of suit.... Also ordered that the property attached be sold or so much thereof as may satisfy the demands of the plaintiff.

Edward Stewart against Eli McVey. Attachment. The parties appeared by their Counselors, a Jury was sworn, a mistrial was made, and the suit continued untill next Court.

Robert Sterling and wife admr. & admx. of James Elder decd., against Philip Hart. Appeal. On motion of the plaintiff's attorney for the judgment to be set aside, and after hearing the allegation of the attorney of the defendant, Ordered that the judgment be recorded.

Ordered that the minutes be read which was accordingly done & signed by William Smith, James Jordan, Judges. Court then adjourned untill Court in Course.

At a Court of Sessions and pleas began and held at the Court House of Spartanburgh County on the 12th day of June 1794. Present their Honors William Smith & James Jordan, Esq.

Grand Jurors drawn to serve next Court, to wit,

John McElwrath	1	George Roebuck	11
William Thomson	2	Alexander Walker	12
John Kain	3	Wm Moore by Woodruffs	13
John Vice	4	Thomas Paden	14
Stephen Wilson	5	Moses Foster	15
James Mayes	6	Nathl. Robertson	16
David Jones, Th.	7	Vincent Wyatt	17
Wm. Jordan, T. G.	8	Benj. Bonner	18
Zachariah Robertson	9	Denny Anderson	19
John Rainwater	10	Wm. T. Thomason	20

Petit Jurors drawn to serve next Court

James Simmons	1	Broadrick Mason	16
Nathan Ward	2	Anthony Pearson	17
John Story	3	William Waldrope	18
William Trailor	4	Hugh Moore	19
James Wilson	5	George Story, Junr.	20
Shadrack Waldrope	6	Thomas Rodgers	21
Iley Waldrope	7	Thomas Young	22
John Stone	8	William Lindsey	23
William Shed	9	Nevil Wayland	24
Jesse Spann	10	Jonathan Neasbitt	25
John Arnold	11	Peter Pinion	26
Thomas Wells	12	Joseph Robertson	27
Edward Lynch	13	John Morris	28
John Jackson	14	Robert Symms	29
Christopher Rhodes	15	Samuel McClure	30

Waddy Thomson, Esquire being licensed to practice the laws of this State was thereupon admitted to practice in this Court.

Grand Jurors to leave this Court.

John Young Senior foreman	1	John Wofford	7
Thomas Miles	2	John Pennington	8
William Lipscomb	3	William Simpson	9
Samuel Timmons	4	John McCarter	10
Samuel Miller	5	Thomas Williams	11
Ransom Tinsley	6	Hugh Stephenson	12
		John Pace	13

Petit Jurors to serve this Court

William Murry	1	Thomas Price	9
Joseph Lively	2	John O'Sheals	10
Thomas Spann	3	William McClure	11
Benjamine Stone	4	Daniel Finch	12
James Saterfield	5	Robert Page	13
Martin Oates	6	James Neasbitt	14
Bazel Lee	7	Robert Miller	15
Francis Mason	8	Abraham Moore	16

Thomas Spann, Benjamine Stone, John O'Sheal & Abraham Moore are excused from serving as Jurors on account of the melitia Election untill Saturday Eight O'Clock.

Enoch Hooper against Charles Littleton & James Hooper. Petition Debt. The defendant James Hooper, Esq. came into Court and confessed judgment for Ł 6 s 5 according to specialty allowing s 10 pr. Ct. for the Tobacco with Interest & Costs.

The County Treasurer against Nathaniel Wofford & James Wofford. Petition. Dismissed.

Alexander Alexander against William Earnest. Detinue. Dismissed at the plaintiffs Costs.

Alexander McBeth against Thomas Maybery & James Gibbs. Debt. Judgment confessed for Ł 10 s 11 d 2 with stay of Execution untill 1st Nov. next.

John Spelcer against Ambrose Dollar Assault. Dismissed at the Defendants costs.

William Lewis against Robert Woods and Thomas McKnight. Debt. Dismissed at the defendants costs.

The County against William T. Thomason. Qui Tam for Estray. Dismissed at the defendants costs, by reasons given on oath of Lawyer Johnson.

The County against Isaac Young. Petition Debt. Dismissed at the defendants, costs, by reason given that the estray proven away.

William Benson against John Hammett. Petition Debt. Came the plaintiff by Mr. Nott his attorney & the defendant by Mr. Shaw his attorney, be request of the parties came also a Jury, Thomas Price, William Murry, Joseph Lively, James Saterfield, Martin Oates, Francis Mason, William McClure, Daniel Finch, Robert Page, James Neasbitt, Robert Miller & Abraham Moore, who on their oaths do say, we find for the plaintiff Ł 6 with interest & costs of suit.....

Samuel Farrow Esq. against William Moody and Dudly Red. Attachment. Settled by the parties, Thomas Price, their security has paid the debt, & assumed to pay the costs.

William Smith Senior as principle and James Smith and James Hickey as his surities came into Court and acknowledged themselves justly indebted to the State, William Smith ₺ 50 and James Smith and James Hickey ₺ 25 each...if the sd. William Smith shall fail to appear and aswer to this Court when call'd upon, for a charge of Hog Stealing.

Len Henley and Richard Bullock against Edward Goode Esq. Petition. Debt. Judgment is confessed for ₺ 5 s 11 d 7 and costs of suit.

Nicholas Holly proved 4 days attendance as a witness in the case John Cantwell against Benjamine Wofford, at 2/6 per day.

Agreeable to a presentment of the Grand Jury, they were dismissed from serving any longer this Court, and also ordered that the State papers in possession of the Clerk, where bills of Indictment have not been prefered, be given to the County Attorney, in order for him to prepare Bills of Indictment for next Court.

Jeremiah Selman as a witness in the case William Benson against John Hammett, proved 6 days attendance at 2/6 per day.

The State against Thomas Lockart. Assault. Dismissed at the defendants Cost by consent.

Ordered that the minutes be read which accordingly done and signed by James Jordan, William Smith, Judges. Court then adjourned untill Tomorrow Eight O'Clock.

Friday the 13th of June 1794. Court met according to adjournment. Present his Honor James Jordan, Esq. Ordered that the minutes be read which was accordingly done & signed by James Jordan, Judge. Court then adjourned untill Tomorrow Eight O'Clock.

Saturday the 14th of June 1794. Court met according to adjournment. Present their Honors James Jordan, Baylis Earle, Esq.

William Darby against William Stewart. Petition. On motion of the plaintiffs attorney Judgment was entered for ₺ 5 s 7 d 3 and costs of suit.

John B. Earle against Edward Goode, Esq. Capias. By consent of the parties and assent of the Court, the trial of this cause is refered to the Arbitrament of John Gowen, Esq. & Gentleman William Thomson with power of Umpirage, their award returned to this Court shall be a Judgment thereof.

Benjamine H. Saxon, Esq., is admitted as an Attorney to practice in this Court, upon producing his commission at next Court.

The last will and Testament of John McElheny decd. is proved in Court by the evidence of Neomi Davis according to Law.

James Jordan Esq. being nominated as an Executor in the last will and Testament of John McElheny decd. refuses to act as such, Ordered that a minute be made of the same.

Francis Lay against Mark Powell & Ebenezer Morse. Petition. Nonsuit.

Robert Goodgion against Jarvis Cornwall. Capias Debt. We whose

names are hereafter subscribed being personally indifferently chosen as well in behalf of Robert Goodgion as Jarvis Cornwall to settle and award all matters of debate now subsisting between then and in particular of a suit now depending in the County Court of Spartanburgh for which they produced an order for the same, and whereas the 21st of March insuing is appointed for arbitration or settling their debates, after hearing the grievances of both parties Do award...all suits by drawn out of Court at the costs of expense of him the said Jarvis Cornwall, and say that sd. Cornwall pay unto sd. Goodgion at his the said Goodgions dwelling House 20 bushels corn as soon as it may be done in the fall at his the said Cornwalls expense, and further we do award that the title to said land for which Goodgion brought suit be made according to Law. James Logan,
James Hooper, Arbitrators

John Cooper against Charles Bruce & John Gowen, Esq. Petition. Continued untill next Court.

The state against John Spelce & Joseph Spelce. Burglary. The prosecutor came into Court and desired that the defendants be dismissed from their recognizance, therefore ordered that they be acquitted.

William Henderson against Thomas McKnight. Case. Came the parties by their Counsellors also came a Jury, to wit, William Murry, JosephLively, James Saterfield, Martin Oats, Bazel Lee, Francis Mason, Thomas Price, William McClure, Daniel Finch, James Neasbitt, Robert Miller & Abraham Moore, who say June 14th 1794 we find for the plaintiff Ł 20 dollars at 6/6 with interest from the date. Thomas Price, foreman.
The defendant prayed an appeal to the Superior Court, which was accordingly granted, upon his complying with the requisites of the law.

Lucy Thomson against Benjamine Wofford. Case. The defendant confessed Judgment for Ł 13 & costs of suit with staying the levy of an Execution 3 months.

James Gibbs against Justice Reynolds. Petition. Came the plaintiff by Samuel Farrow Esq. his attorney and the defendant appearing in his own proper person to defend his action, the allegations of each being heard a decree was entered in favor of the plaintiff for 600 pounds of cotton at d 2¼ per pound, with a deduction of two dollars and costs of suit.

John B. Earle against Edward Goode Esq. Case. We the arbitrators being chosen unanimously between Baylis Earle plaintiff and Edward Goode in a suit taken out of Court, have awarded that the said Goode pay Ł 12 s 10 or 25 head of one year old cattle in 6 months from this date as our award with costs of suit. 14th June 1794. William Thomson, John Gowen, Arbtrs.

Abraham Pool against John Tucker. Attachment. On motion decreed for the plaintiff Ł 6 s 2 and costs of suit and ordered that the property attached in the hands of Joel Hembree be condemned for the use of the plaintiff.

Ordered that William Wells have license to retail spiritous liquors and keep a public House of entertainment upon giving Jesse Connell and Bazel Lee his surities for his lawful performance.

William Jackson against Benjamine Wofford. Case. Continued untill next Court with a peremptory rule to be tried the third day of Court.

Wells Griffith against John James. Attachment.
Same against Same Attachment. Both above cases are dismissed at the defendants costs.

William Jackson against Benjamine Wofford. Case. Ordered that a dedimus potestatum issue to the State of Georgia to examine James Tinsley and others in behalf of the defendant by giving legal notice to the adverse party of the time and place of Examination.

Ordered that the County Treasurer pay to William Shaw Esq. County attorney L 10 in part of fees due to him from the County.

Ordered that William Benson Esq. be appointed Treasurer of this County in place of David Goodlett, Esq., as he has remov'd out of the County with full power and authority to examine adjust and settle the account of the late and all former Treasurers of this County, and with all and every person & persons, whatsoever who have at any time heretofore been Invested with the Collection and disbursement in any way or manner whatsoever for the benefit of this County, And on thorough investigation and examination thereof a fair and correct statement and account by way of Debtor and Creditor be made of past collections & disbursements for the future annually, first for the Inspection of the County and afterwards to be pasted up in some conspicious part of the Court House for the perusal and Inspection of any person or persons who may have an Inclination to do the same.

Bazel Lee proved 2 days attendance in the suit James Gibbs against Justice Reynolds at 2/6 per day.

Jesse Connell proved two days attendance as a witness in the case James Gibbs against Justice Reynolds at 2/6 per day.

William McGowen against George Taylor. Debt. Ordered that a commission dedimus Potestatum issue to the State of Georgia to Examine a witness in behalf of the plaintiff upon his giving legal notice to the adverse party, of the time & place of examination.

Ordered that the Clerk be allowed L 5 s 7 for the contingent services done in his office to the State exclusive of what he has presented to the assembly.

Ordered that Thomas Farrow Esq. be allowed L 1 for keeping an Estray also s 3 for his fee made use of in an order to pay Mr. Shaw.

Ordered that Michael Miller be paid L 10 for building a Bridge across South Packolate River ouf of the County fund.

James Milikin proved 6 days attendance as a witness in the case William Henderson against Thomas McKnight at 2/6 per day.

James Huggins proved 6 days attendance as a witness in the case William Henderson against Thomas McKnight at 2/6 per day.

William Millikin proved 6 days attendance as a witness in the case William Henderson against Thomas McKnight a 2/6 per day.

Ordered that David Goodlett Esq. be allowed the sum of five P. Ct. Commissions for the time he has acted as County Treasurer for money recd.

Ordered that the Executors of the Estate of Arthur Crocker deceased proceed to sell the same on the first Friday in July next upon giving 20 days notice at 12 months credit, all articles sold for a sum less than s 5 to be paid at the time of sale.

Ordered that Rowland Johnson be allowed s 20 for keeping an unbroke Estray.

Ordered that William Turner be allowed s 20 for keeping an umbroek Estray.

Ordered that the Estrays given to the sheriff be sold at the adjournment of Court, at six months credit.

Ordered that Richard Collins have Indulgence for his fine untill otherwise ordered.

Ordered that Lewis Stanley be exempted from a judgment against him for Estray, upon paying the costs, as he produced a satisfactory probate for the same, which showed that is was proven away & not converted to his own use.

Ordered that the minutes be read which was done & signed by Baylis Earle, James Jordan, Judges. Court then adjourned untill Court in course.

At a County Court began to be Holden at the Court House of Spartanburgh County the 12th day of January 1795. Present their Honors William Smith and Baylis Earle, Esq.

The Court proceeded to draw the Grand Jurors for next court, to wit:

Charles Hester	1	Matthew Harper	11		
James Amos	2	William Wilkins	12		
Reason Holland	3	John Nesbitt, Colo.	13		
Joseph Neasbitt	4	Thomas McKnight	14		
Reubin Newman	5	James Crow	15		
John Brooks	6	John McKnight	16		
David Bruton	7	Daniel Ledbetter	17		
Samson Bobo	8	Edmund Bishop	18		
Wm. Poole, taylor	9	Basil Trail	19		
Willey S. Brown	10	Daniel Barnett	20		

Petit Jurors drawn for next Court

William Miller	1	Thomas Kimbell	16		
John Barnett	2	Richard Carver	17		
George Divine	3	James Bruton	18		
William Duncan	4	James Anderson	19		
John Bishop	5	James Cantrell	20		
James Wyatt	6	Robert Rodgers	21		
John Elder	7	Francis Powers	22		
Robert Armour	8	Iven Davis	23		
George Gilbert	9	Francis Clerke	24		
Benjamine Hammett	10	Richard Cox	25		
William Davidson	11	Hugh Gourley	26		
Thomas Woodruff	12	Daniel Cornwall	27		
John Humphries	13	John Davis	28		
William Reaves	14	Matthew Couch	29		
Rowland Jenians	15	Thomas Brice	30		

Grand Jurors to serve this Court

William Thomson Gentl.	1	Moses Foster	9
John McElwrath	2	Nathaniel Robertson	10
John Vice	3	Vincent Wyatt	11
Stephen Wilson	4	Benjamine Bonner	12
William Jordan	5	Denny Anderson	13
Zachariah Robertson	6	Wm. Thomason	14
Alexander Walker	7	Wm. Moore (Woodruffs)	15
Thomas Paden	8		

The Grand Jury being sworn, William Thomson appointed foreman, they received their charge and retir'd. to their room.

Petit Jurors that appeared this Court

Nathan Ward	1	Christopher Rhodes	10
John Story	2	Anthony Pearson	11
William Traylor	3	William Waldrope	12
James Wilson	4	Hugh Moore	13
Shadrack Waldrope	5	George Story	14
John Stone	6	Thomas Rodgers	15
John Arnold	7	Thomas Young	16
Thomas Wells	8	Jonathan Neasbitt	17
Edward Lynch	9	Joseph Robertson	18
		Samuel McClure	19

Ezekiel Johnson against Joseph Morriss. Assault.
The Same against William Jordan. Assault.
By consent of the parties and assent of the Court, the Trials of these causes are refered to the Arbitrament of William Garrett, Reubin Warren, John Hightower, Obadiah Trimmier, Isaac Young, Leonard Adcock, George Kezie, Hugh Stephenson, Thomas Gore, William Barton, Joseph Blackwood, William McDowell, gentlemen, arbitrators; an award returned by any nine of them next Court to be a rule thereof.

Christopher Rhodes being very infirm in body, Nathan Ward rendering a sufficient excuse to the Court, & Hugh Moore being under age, were all exempted from serving as Petit Jurors this Court.

Ordered that Mary Lindsey have the full administration on the Estate of the late deceased Dennis Lindsey upon giving Nathaniel Woodruff & William Moore sureties for the Bond of ₤ 200 for her lawful performance.

Ordered that George Bruton, William Moore & Joseph Woodruff appraise the Estate of Dennis Lindsey deceased & make their return of the same.

Ordered that Jesse Rakestraw receive out of the County fund the sum for which an Estray sold for which he proved to be his in the lawful time, the same being bought by Daniel Stephens after being toll'd before Thomas Moore, Esq. taken up by Richard Cox.

Ordered that the minutes be read which was done and signed by Baylis Earle, William Smith, Judges. Court then adjourned untill tomorrow 9 O'Clock.

Tuesday the 13th day of January 1795. Court met according to adjournment. Present their Honors William Smith & Baylis Earle, Esq.

The State against James McKnight. Assault. Dismissed at the

defendants costs by consent.

The last will and Testament of Joseph Allen deceased, proven in open Court by the evidence of William Ford, ordered to record.

Ordered that James Crook, William McDaniel and John Ward appraise the Estate of Joseph Allen deceased, and make due return thereof.

Ordered that Edward Goode, Esq. be exempted from the sum for which an Execution issued against him for an Estray.

Josiah Leek an Attorney at law is admitted or practice the same in this Court.

The State against Hugh McMullen. Peace Warrant. Ordered that this case be dismissed.

James Saunders against Isham Babbitt. Attachment. Dismissed by request of the plaintiff.

Ordered that Mr. Abram Nott act as County Attorney throughout this Session, as the Common practicing attorney cannot attend by reason of sickness.

The State against Francis Clerke. Bastardy. The defendant came into Court, with James Crow and Samuel Farrow Esq. her Surities and they acknowledged to owe to the State the sd. defendant Ł 25 and the sd. surities Ł 12 each, if the said defendant shall fail to appear at next Court, to answer to the above charge.

Ordered that all the States Business returned before this Court, continue untill the next Court.

The State against Robert Elder. Hog Stealing. The defendant by his attorney prayed a Trial at this Court and the same was continued untill next Court.

The State against William Smith & William Smith son of Hancock. Hog Stealing. The defendants by their attorney prayed a trial and the same was continued untill next Court.

The state against Spencer Casey. Assault. A trial prayed by Samuel Farrow his Attorney and the same was continued untill next Court.

The State against Peter Burrel. Sheep Stealing. The Grand Jury returned "not a true Bill" William Thomson, foreman.

John Jones against James Alexander. Case. Dismissed at the plaintiffs costs by consent of his attorn ey.

Jeremiah Walker against William Pool. Debt. award return'd Pursuant to the within order to us directed after hearing and duly Examining the matter in debate between Walker and Pool, we find after giving Walker credit for the 3,000 Lb. of Tobacco that there is a balance due to Pool of Ł 25 s 6 on back account. 25 Jan 1794. Isham Harrison, Isham Foster, Henry Wells, Arbitrators.

James Wofford against Robert Goodgion. Debt. This suit is withdrawn by the plaintiff.

Obadiah Trimmier Esq. against Essix Capshaw. Attachment. The defendant came into Court in his own proper persons and confessed Judgment for ₺ 9 s 7 d 5 and costs of suit.

The State against the Thomsons. Larceny. Ordered that this case be dismissed.

Samuel Morrow against Josiah Culbertson, John Story, and David Golightly. Debt. Dismissed at the defendants costs by consent.

Ordered that Giles Connell be allowed s 4 for keeping Estray yearlings.

Elizabeth Robertson & Fendol Whitworth is allowed on oath, to wit, the said Robertson s 5 for 2 days attendance, and the sd. Whitworth s 5 for 2 days attendance and 8/4 for 25 miles at 4 pence pr. mile as he lived without the limits of this County, as witness in the case William Walton against Thomas Whitworth.

William Walton against Thomas Whitworth. Attachment. Ordered that this case be dismissed.

The State against Elijah Bruce. Horse Stealing. The defendant came into Court and acknowledged to owe to the State ₺ 100 and George Solmon, Esq. and John Motlow as his surities also acknowledged in Court to owe ₺ 25 each if the said Elijah Bruce shall fail to attend at next Court to answer to & abide by the Judgment & orders of said Court.

A Deed of Conveyance from James Jordan, Esq. to Philip Johnson Junior acknowledged in open Court, ordered to be recorded.

On motion of Rispey Foster for admn. on the Estate of an absent James Foster who was formerly her husband, by Samuel Farrow Esq. and other Councellors in her behalf, And the motion being opposed by Mr. Nott and other Counselors in behalf of the Brothers and kindred of the said James Foster, and after a long & warm debate on the matter, the Court replyed "We will give you our opinion To morrow."

Ordered that the minutes be read, which was accordingly done and signed by Baylis Earle, William Smith, Judges. Court then adjourned untill To morrow 9 O'Clock.

Wednesday the 14th day of January 1795, The Court met according to adjournment. Present their Honors William Smith & James Jordan, Esq.

David Smith against Josiah Tanner. Case. Judgment confessed according to specialty (as by an Instrument of writing under the hand of the defendant by Mr. Lispcomb).

Spencer Bobo against Samuel Farrow & Landon Farrow. Case. Settled at each party paying their own costs.

William Henderson against Thomas McKnight. Case. There being an appeal granted in this case and carried to the Superior Court, and the same remanded to this Court by order thereof, and the clerk of that Court omitting to certify the same to this Court, But all parties consenting that a trial should now be had, the Jury, to wit, Thomas Wells, John Story, William Traylor, James Wilson, Shadrack Waldrope, John Stone, John Arnold, Edward Lynch, Anthony Pearson, William Waldrope, George Story, and Thomas Rodgers... We find for the plaintiff Ł 20 Virginia money and costs of Suit. Thomas Wells, foreman... Ł20 Va. money equal to Ł 15 s 11 d 1¼ sterling....

Samuel Farrow Esq. against Alexander Elder. Debt. The defendant confessed judgment for Ł 11 s 19 d 8 according to specialty and costs of suit.

Graff Edson & Co. against Charles Maybery. Debt. The defendant came into Court in his own proper person and confessed judgment for Ł 16 s 7 d 8 and costs of suit, with stay of Execution until 1st day of April next.

Charles Bruce as a witness in the case Samuel Farrow, Esq. against Alexander Elder on oath is allowed s 30 for 12 days attendance and s 25 for 150 miles in coming to Court, as he lived without the limits of this County.

Essix Capshaw against Alexander Peeler. Attachment. Ordered that on motion of Zachariah Toliaferro, attorney for the defendant that this case be dismissed for want of a return by the Execution officer.

The State against Elizabeth Harris alias Hammett. Lerceny. The Grand Jury find "No Bill."

On the motion yesterday by Rispey Foster alias Joel for admn. on the Estate of James Foster, decided by the Court that admn. cannot be granted to those requesting the same.

Ordered that whereas there was a mistake in a Judgment and Execution in a case William Darby against Edward Stewart that the same be amended.

Ordered that the Estrays which are delivered in to the hands of the Sheriff be sold this evening.

Thomas Farrow, Isham Harrison, Henry McCray and Zadock Ford, came into Court and took the necessary oaths prescribed by law, as Justices of the peace for the County.

William Jackson against Benjamin Wofford. Special Action. Continued untill Tomorrow Ten O'Clock.

A mortgage from Samuel Culbertson to Henry O'Nail proved in open Court by Mr. Abram Nott, ordered to be recorded.

Thomas Moore, Esq. took the necessary oaths of office prescribed by law as a justice of the peace for this county.

James Norriss proved three days attendance as a witness in the case William Henderson against Thomas McKnight.

Ordered that the minutes be read which was done and signed by James Jordan, William Smith, Judges. Court then adjourned till Tomorrow Nine O'Clock.

Tuesday the 16th day of January 1795. Court met according to adjournment. Present their Honors William Smith, Baylis Earle & James Jordan, Esq.

John Trimmier took the several oaths requisite to the office of a Constable for this County.

The State against Drewry Couch. Larceny. The defendant by Samuel Farrow his attorney motioned for a trial but the cause was continued untill next Court.

The State against William Smith. Killing a mare. After a motion of his attorney praying a trial, The cause was continued untill next Court.

The State against Jeremiah Spann. Bastardy. A trial prayed and ordered to be continued untill next Court.

James Henderson against John Maxwell. Detinue. Continued untill next Court.

William Jackson against Benjamine Wofford. Case. Came the plaintiff by Zachariah Toliaferro his attorney and the defendant by Mr. Abram Nott his Attorney, whereupon came a Jury, to wit, (same as before)...We find for the defendant with costs of suit.

Thomas Blasingame against Burrel Thomson. Petition. The defendant came into Court with Benjamine Wofford and Samuel Thomson his surities, who acknowledged themselves responsible for the debt and costs in this action, provided he should be case in his suit, upon which the cause was continued untill next Court.

William Henderson against Thomas McKnight. Case. On motion by the Counsellors of the plaintiff for an appeal, It is the opinion of this Court that as two trials have been had in this Court, and an appeal granted to the Superior Court and the case being remanded back to this Court, and a third trial had here, two of which hath been in favor of the plaintiff by Jurors of this County, that under those circumstances an appeal cannot be granted.

The State against Abraham Fowler & Jacob Fowler. Horse Stealing. A trial prayed by the attorney, and the cause continued untill next Court.

Mason Morse as a witness in the case William Jackson against Benjamine Wofford proved 27 days attendance and 200 miles in coming to Court, as he lives without this County.

William Tinsley as a witness in the case William Jackson against Benjamine Wofford, proved 5 days attendance and 90 miles in coming to Court, as he lived without the limits of this County.

Francis Ley against Mark Powell & Ebenezer Morse. Debt. Continued by request of the defendants.

Ordered that the minutes be read which was done and signed by Baylis Earle, James Jordan, William Smith, Judges. Court then adjourned untill To morrow Ten O'Clock.

Friday the 16th day of January 1795. Court met according to adjournment. Present their Honors William Smith, James Jordan, & Baylis Earle, Esqs.

George B. Moore against Joseph Wofford. Debt. Ordered that a Commission issue to any Justice of the peace in this County, to take the examination of Nimrod Childs Debene Isse in writing (as he is a material witness in this case) to be read at next Court.

James Hooper was qualifyed as a justice of the peace for this County.

David McCarley against William Farrow. Assault. Ordered that this case be continued.

Moses Clayton against John Clayton. Case. Came the plaintiff by Mr. Nott his attorney & the defendant by Zachariah Tolliferro also a Jury (same as before)...we find for the plaintiff Ł 16 and costs of suit...

John Cantwell against Henry McCray. Trover. Ordered that this cause be continued.

Edward Steward against Eli McVey. Attachment Ordered that this cause be continued.

William Lewis assignee of David McKnight against Charles McKnight & John Armstrong. Debt. On motion of Zachariah Tolliaferro attorney for the Defendant, ordered that a nonsuit take place.

James Hooper Esq. against John McGrew. Attachment. Dismist each party paying their own costs, by consent.

Isaiah Lewis against William T. Thomason & Arnold Thomason. Assault. Nonsuit.

Brittain Williford against Thomas Williams. Debt. Settled at defendants costs.

Robert Connell against John Robertson. Assault. Ordered that this cause be continued.

William Poole against William Wofford. Attachment. Dismissed.

John Harden against Benjamine Wofford. Petition, Nonsuit.

Ephraim Elder against Brittain Williford. Debt. Dismissed at the defendants cost by consent.

Alexander McBeth against Essix Capshaw. Attachment. Ordered that this case be dismissed.

James Smith against Richard James. Appeal. Came the appellant by Mr. Nott his attorney and the appellee by Mr. Farrow his attorney. Decreed by the Court that as the appellant did not appear before the Justice with the records of this Court that the Judgment be confirmed.

Bazel Lee & Thomas James proved 3 days attendance each as witnesses in the above case.

Reubin White proved 3 days attendance in the above case.

William Ussery assignee of John Ford assignee of James Green against Thomas Massingale. Petition. Nonsuit.

Samson Bethel took the necessary oaths of office as a Justice of the peace for this County.

The Court proceeded to the choice of a sheriff, when Samuel Miller was duly elected, Ordered that a Certificate be sent to the Governor for him to be Commissioned accordingly.

The minutes were ordered to be read which was accordingly done and signed by William Smith, Baylis Earle, James Jordan, Judges. Court then adjourned untill Court in Course.

At a County Court of Sessions and Pleas began to be Holden at the Court House of Spartanburgh on the 12th day of June 1795. Present The Hon. William Smith, Esq.

The Court proceeded to draw the Grand Jury for next Court, to wit-

James Vernon	1	William McGowen	11	
Richard Williss	2	Robert Foster	12	
William Foster, fairforest	3	John Farrow	13	
Samuel Jameson	4	Thomas Bennett	14	
William Foster, Tyger	5	William Ford, Tyger	15	
Edward Arnold	6	Beverly Lewis	16	
Obadiah Wingo	7	William McDowell, Esq.	17	
Samuel Culbertson	8	Malachi Jones	18	
John Snody	9	Aaron Casey	19	
John White	10	Joseph Barnett	20	

Petit Jurors drawn for next Court

Daniel Allen	1	Joshua Edwards	16
Joseph Champion	2	James Hewet	17
George Bishop Senr	3	Elijah Hendrix	18
James Cowen	4	David Jones	19
David Childers	5	Buckner Smith	20
Spencer Bobo Junr.	6	Joseph Couch	21
George Kirk	7	Rowland Johnson	22
David Humphries	8	Elijah Hammett	23
Josiah Thornton	9	William Davis	24
Thomas Thornton	10	John Cooper	25
Thomas Gillingwaters	11	Zebulon Bragg	26
William (sic)	12	William Bramlet	27
Thomas Betterton	13	Richard Harriss	28
Thomas Clerke	14	Robert Conner	29
Israel Credenton	15	William Casey	30

Ordered that the minutes be read which was done & signed by William Smith, Judge. Court then adjourned untill To morrow Ten O'Clock.

Saturday the 13th day of June 1795. Court met according to adjournment. Present their Honors William Smith and James Jordan, Esq.

Ordered that Evan Davis be ever exempted from serving as a Juror for this County, as he presented an affidavit to the Court sufficient for the same.

The following persons are those of the Petit Jurors who have appeared by virtue of a venire.

William Miller	1	Rowland Jenjans	10
John Barnett	2	Richard Carver	11
John Bishop	3	Robert Rodgers	12
James Wyatt	4	Francis Powers	13
John Elder	5	Francis Clerk	14
Robert Armour	6	Hugh Gourley	15
Benjamin Hammett	7	John Davis	16
Thomas Woodruff	8	Matthew Couch	17
William Reaves	9	Thomas Brice	18

The following persons are those who are drawn to serve as Petit Jurors this Court.

Richard Carver	1	John Davis	7
John Bishop	2	James Wyatt	8
Robert Armour	3	Rowland Jenians	9
Robert Rodgers	4	Thomas Brice	10
Francis Clerk	5	Francis Powers	11
Hugh Gourley	6	Benjamine Hammett	12

The last will and Testament of Francis Tillett, deceased, proven in open Court by the oath of Absalom Lancaster, Ordered to record.

John Davis against John Jones. Special Action. Dismissed at Defendants Costs by consent.

Christopher Degraffenreed against William Taylor. Debt. The defendant came into Court and confessed judgment for Ł 17 s 9 and Interest according to note, subject to such credits as he shall in future establish by his receipts to be produced to the Clerk, with stay of Execution untill 12 Jan. next and costs of suit.

The State against John Elder. Hog Stealing. The former suristies came into court and delivered him thereto, in order to be delivered from the sureties; whereupon came Alexander Elder and Ephraim Hill...John Elder Ł 100, sd. sureties Ł 50 each, if the sd. defendant shall fail to appear before the Judges aforesd. Court when call'd for to answer the above charge....

Ordered that the minutes be read which was accordingly done and signed by James Jordan, William Smith, Judges. Court then adjourned untill Monday Ten O'Clock.

Monday the 15th day of June 1795. Court met according to adjournment. Present their Honors William Smith and James Jordan, Esq.

Ordered that three Constables be summoned to attend next Court to serve the same.

James Henderson against John Maxwell. Detinue. Came the plaintiff by Mr. Abram Nott his Attorney and the defendant by Zachariah Tolliaferro his Attorney, also a Jury, to wit Robert Rodgers, Richard Carver, John Bishop, Robert Armour, Francis Clerk, Hugh Gourley, John Davis, James Wyatt, Rowland Janians, Thomas Brice, Francis Powers & Benjamine Hammett, who sayd we find for the defendant. Robert Rodgers, foreman....

John Hammett against Jeremiah Selman. Slander.
Jeremiah Selman against John Hammett. Slander. By consent of the parties and assent of the Court the trial of this cause is refered to the Arbitration of George Connell, Jesse Connell, Benjamine Piper, Isham Harrison, Isham Foster and Nevil Wayland, Gentlemen, Arbitrators, their award being returned to this or next Court, to be a rule thereof.

The following names are the persons who are to serve as Grand Jurors this Court, to wit.

John Neasbitt	1	William Poole, taylor	8
Charles Hester	2	William Wilkins	9
Reason Holland	3	James Crow	10
Joseph Neasbitt	4	Edmund Byshop	11
Reubin Newman	5	Basil Trail	12
David Bruton	6	Daniel Barnett	13

Samson Bobo   7

William Hammett against Daniel Walker. Slander. Dismissed at the defendants Costs by Consent.

Robert Connell against John Robertson Assault. By agreement of the parties and consent of the Court, the trial of this cause is refered to the Arbitrament of Bazel Lee, Turner Thomason, William Benson & Isham Foster, Esq. their award made at the house of sd. Foster and returned to next Court to be a rule thereof.

Ordered that John Lefever be allowed s 15 out of the County fund for keeping an Estray.

David McCarley against William Farrow. Assault and Battery. Came the plaintiff by Mr. Nott his Attorney & the Defendant by Mr. Dunlap his Attorney, also a Jury (same as before)...we find for the plaintiff Ł 5 damage.

John Gowen against John Bishop & William Stewart. Debt. Dismissed at the Defendant's Costs by Consent.

The State against Robert Baker. horse stealing. The Grand Jury returned thus, "No Bill." John Neasbitt, foreman.

Ordered by the Court that he be dismissed from his recognizance.

Samuel McCall against George Gilbraith. Petition. Debt. The defendant came into Court and confessed Judgment for Ł 3 s 6 d 8 with interest and Costs of suit, with stay of Execution three months.

Thomas Blasingame against Burrel Thomson. Petition. Dismissed at the defendants paying his own costs, the plaintiff's attorney, and the Clerk's and Sheriff's fees.

John Cantwell against Henry McCray. Detinue. By consent of the parties and assent of the Court, the trial of this cause is refered to the Arbitrament of Giles Connell, William Benson, and Capt. James Smith, Gentl. Arbitrators, their award returned to next Court to be a rule thereof.

Henry McCray against Jesse Matthews. Petition Nonsuit.

George Roebuck against William Farrow. Special Action. Ordered that this case be continued untill To morrow evening with a preemptory rule then to be reid.

The State against Spencer Casey. Assault. The Grand Jury say thus " A true Bill. "

The State against John Elder Junr. & Robert Elder. Hog Stealing. The Grand Jury returned thus "No Bill."

William McGowen assignee of William Wilkison against George Taylor. Debt. Came the parties by their Councellors, a Jury being sworn a wits. trial was had and a Nonsuit took place.

Ordered that Jean Simson and James McElwayne have the full admn. with the will annexed, of the Estate of Arthur Simson deceased by quallifying, signing a Bond according to law, which they did in open Court.

Ordered that the Estrays be sold to morrow after the adjournment of Court according to Law.

Ordered that the minutes be read which was done and signed by William Smith, James Jordan, Judges. Court then adjourning untill To morrow Nine O'Clock.

Tuesday the 16th day of June 1795. The Court met according to adjournment. Present their Honors William Smith and James Jordan, Esq.

William Fields qualified to act as a constable for this County before James Jordan, Esq.

Edward Stewart against Elis McVey. Attachment. Dismissed by reason of the attachment being levy'd before the Bond became Due.

George B. Moore against Joseph Wofford. Debt. Nonsuit.

Charles Brice against James Lusk. Assault. Came the plaintiff by Samuel Farrow his Attorney and the defendant by Mr. Dunlap his attorney, also a Jury (same as before)...we find for the plaintiff s 5....

James Bell as a witness in the case Isaac Crow against Zadock Ford and Thomas Parks, proved 4 days attendance and 32 miles at 2 pence pr mile for coming & going to Court as he lived out of the limits of this County.

James Bell proved 2 days attendance as a witness in the case George B. Moore against Joseph Wofford, with 32 miles in coming & going to Court.

Charles Burton against William Farrow. Special Action. Came the plaintiff by Mr. Leek his attorney and the defendant by Mr. Dunlap, also a Jury, to wit (same as before)...we find for the plaintiff L 3 s 4....

Enoch Hooper qualified as a Constable by taking the oath prescribed by Law.

The State against Francis Clerke. Bastardy. The defendant came into Court and made oath that Jeremiah Spann was the father of her Bastard child, and she submitted herself to the mercy of the Court, was fined L 5 proc. money, payable 12 months hence.

The State against Jeremiah Spann. Bastardy. Ordered that a Sciri Facias issue against both the defendant and the sureties to shew cause to the Court if any they have why their recognizance should not be forfeited.

The State against William Lee. Bastardy. Ordered that the defendant be dismissed from his recognizance as the mother of the Bastard child came into Court and made oath that she did when she was delivered of the child, and now does live in the County of Union; and this Court considering they have no jurisdiction over the same.

John Cooper against Charles Bruce. Petition. Nonsuit.

The Grand Jury returned the following Bills of Indictment thus

The State against Henry Turner, Richard Turner, Thomas Green, William Garrett, Abram Wyatt, George Martin & Samuel Turner. Killing a Cow. A true Bill.

The State against William Brittain. Stealing Tobacco. A true Bill.

The State against William Smith Senr. & William Smith son of Hancock. Hog Stealing. A true Bill.

The State against Thomas Langley. Hog Stealing. No Bill.

The State against Jacob Fowler. Horse Stealing. The defendant by Samuel Farrow his attorney motioned for a discharged by the Habeas Corpus act.

Abram Nott Esq. against Henry Huff Junr., John Head & Henry Huff, Senr. Debt. The Defendants by Henry Huff Senr. came into Court and confessed judgment for s 12 d 2 with interest and costs of suit.

John Gowen Esq. against Simson Newman. Special Action. Dismissed at mutual costs by consent.

Ordered that Isaac Crow have license to retail spirituous liquors upon signing a Bond with Brittain Williford and George Roebuck his sureties for his lawful performance.

The State against John Reynolds, William Reynolds, Henry Reynolds & Furney Reynolds. Hog Stealing. Ordered that the recognizance of the defendants be forfeited.

Benjamine Wofford against William Hagan. Replevin. This case by agreement of the parties is refered to the arbitrament of Thomas Farrow, Esq., William Lipscomb, William Thomson, Alexander Alexander, and Henry Wells, Gentl. arbitrators, their award returned to next Court to be a rule thereof.

The State against Jacob Fowler. Horse Stealing. The defendant came into Court with Josiah Thornton, Rowland Jenians and William Fowler as his Sureties, and acknowledged to owe the State the sd. Fowler L 50 and the sureties L 25 each...if the said Jacob Fowler shall fail to appear to this Court when call'd....

The State against Henry Turner, Richard Turner, Thomas Green, William Garrett, Abram Wyatt, George Martin & Samuel Turner. Killing a Cow. Mr. Dunlap appearing in behalf of the State and the defendants by their Councellors, also a Jury (same as before) ...Not Guilty.

Ordered that John Pace be allowed out of the County fund L 1 s 17 d 4 for Blocking up the Court-House and other repairings of the same.

Benjamine Wofford against Henry Earnest. Detinue. Refered by consent to the Arbitrament of George Bruton, David Bruton, & William Ford, their award made at the House of Isaac Crows the first day of August next, and returned to next Court shall be the Judgment thereof.

John Cooper against Charles Bruce and John Gowen. Petition. A Nonsuit having taken place to day and a new action being Instituted, the parties came into Court & agreed to drop the action....

Charles Burton against William Farrow. Special Action. On motion of Mr. Nott for a new trial was accordingly granted and the costs to await the event thereof.

William Thomson against Justice Reynolds. Debt. The defendant came into Court and confessed Judgment according to Specialty the note being for Ł 6 sterling and costs of suit with stay of Execution 6 months.

Francis Ley against Ebenezer Morse & Mark Powell. Petition. Judgment confessed according to Specialty and Costs of suit the note being for   with stay of Execution 6 months.

Joshua Downs against Robert Connell. Petition. On motion of Benjamine H. Saxon, Esq., attorney for the Plaintiff decreed that he recover Ł 5 s 4 d 5 with costs of suit.

Saxon and Wilson against Benjamine Wofford. Petition. On motion of Benjamine H. Saxon their attorney for a decree, which the defendant objected to and praying a Jury, Ordered that the cause continue for that purpose.

Ordered that the minutes be read which was accordingly done and signed by William Smith, James Jordan, Judges. Court then adjourned untill Court in course.

At a County Court began to be holden at the Court-House of Spartanburgh on the 12th day of Jan. 1796. James Jordan and William Smith, Esq.

The Court proceeded to draw the Jurors for next Court.

Grand Jurors:
James Smith, Canpr.	1	Shands Golightly	11
Alexander Elder	2	Culbert Burton	12
Jesse Temples	3	Matthew Patton	13
John Ford, Senr.	4	Lee Clerke	14
John Bragg	5	Francis Dodds	15
Drury Hutchison	6	John Hammett	16
Thomas Cole	7	David Anderson	17
Richard Barry	8	John Vaughan	18
John Ross	9	Robert Elder	19
Richard Barry	10	Samuel Morrow Senr.	20

Petit Jurors:
Robert Kimbol	1	John Kirkland	16
Daniel Amos	2	James Gilmore	17
Nathaniel Hamby	3	John Bruton	18
Andrew Ray	4	Obadiah Gravatt	19
William Brandon	5	John Davis	20
Leonard Adcock	6	James Blackwell	21
Peter Bragg	7	Samuel Colley	22
Thomas Evatt	8	Hance Harper	23
John Carrell	9	Andrew Colley	24
John Farmer	10	Thomas Hunter	25
Jarvis Gilbert	11	John Burk	26
William Allen	12	Nathaniel Henderson	27
Samuel Casey	13	Paul Castleberry	28
William Hammett	14	Richard Chesney	29
Thomas Jordan	15	Henry Earnest	30

The following names are the persons who appeared by virtue of a venire facias for Grand Jurors

Robert Foster, foreman	1	Samuel Culbertson	8
Richard Willis	2	John Snody	9
William Foster, FF.	3	John White	10
James Vernon	4	Thomas Bennett	11
Samuel Jameson	5	Beverly Lewis	12
Wm. Foster, Tyger	6	William McDowell	13
Obadiah Wingo	7	Aaron Casey	14
		Joseph Barnett	15

Petit Jurors drawn to serve this Court, to wit

William Casey	1	James Cowen	7
Daniel Allen	2	Buckner Smith	8
David Childers	3	William Bramlett	9
John Cooper	4	Rowland Johnson	10
Israel Credenton	5	William Davis	11
Joseph Champion	6	George Kirk	12

Whereas William Wilkins hath heretofore been Surity for Josiah Tanner on his admn. on the Estate of Mark Skelton deceased, came into Court and desiring to be released therefrom which was granted him, William Lipscomb was received in his place by consent.

John D. Young against John Ford. Petition by Account. This suit is abated by death of the defendant.

The last will and Testament of William Young, deceased, proven in open Court by the Evidence of Millington Smith, Ordered to record.

The minutes were read and signed by William Smith, James Jordan, Judges. Court then adjourned untill To morrow Nine O'Clock.

Wednesday the 13th day of January 1796, Court met according to adjournment. Present their Honors James Jordan & William Smith, Esq.

Ordered that Alexander Roddy be allowed s 5 for keeping an Estray.

Ordered that the Commissioners of the poor be paid out of the County fund, ₤ 50 as soon as it can conveniently be collected in the Treasury for the support of the poor.

John Cantwell against Henry McCray. Detinue. Continued by rule of reference.

Benjamine Wofford against Henry Earnest. Detinue. In pursuance to the within rule of Court, we George Bruton, David Bruton, and William Ford, hath examined into the matter of Difference wherein the within mentioned Benjamine Wofford is plaintiff and Henry Earnest defendant, Do award the sd. Earnest do pay to sd. Wofford ₤ 16 with the costs of this present suit. 1 Aug. 1795

The Plaintiff came into Court and acknowledged reception of the principle debt of the above award, also that he would see the Clerks and Sheriff's fees paid.

Michael McKie against William Ford. Capias. Debt. Nonsuit

Candace Jones Admx. of Wm. D. Thomas Admr. of Joseph Jones Junr. decd. against William Ford. Debt. Came the plaintiffs by their councellors and the defendant by his attornies, also came a Jury, to wit, George Kirk, William Casey, Daniel Allen, David Childers, John Cooper, Israel Credenton, Joseph Champion, James Carver,

Buckner Smith, William Bramlett, William Davis & Rowland Johnson
...we find for the defendant...

The Grand Jurors...do present and say

The State against George Easlinger. Abusing Horse. No Bill.

Elizabeth Thomson against John Erwin. Attachment. Dismissed at the defendants Costs.

Len Henly & Richard Bullock against George Taylor. Petition. The defendant came into Court in his own proper person and confessed judgment for   according to specialty and all costs except the witness attendance.

The minutes were read and signed by William Smith, James Jordan, Judges. Court then adjourned untill To morrow Nine O'Clock.

Thursday the 14th day of January 1796. Court met according to adjournment. Present the Hon. William Smith and James Jordan, Esq.

Samuel Johnson and James Ditty Admrs. of Gordon deceased against George Gilbraith. Petition. On motion of Mr. Leeke attorney for the defendant, Ordered that a Nonsuit take place.

James Hewet and Thomas Thornton were drawn as Talliesmen to serve as petit Jurors this Court in the room of John Cooper & James Carver, who failed to appear.

Sarah Darby admr. of William Darby decd. against Thomas Bearden. Petition. The defendant came into Court and confessed Judgment for Ł 4 s 14 d 6 3/4 and costs of suit.

George Roebuck against William Farrow. Special Action. Refered by consent to the arbitrament of Thomas Moore, Esq., with power of choosing two men to aid him, their award returned to next Court to be a judgment thereof.

The State against John F. Harmony. Assault & Battery. Ordered that Nole prosequi be entered in this case.

Sarah Darby admrx. of William Darby decd. against Jacob Casey. Petition. The defendant confessed judgment for Ł 7 s 9 d 9¼ and costs of suit, with stay of execution untill 1 June next, Aaron Casey came into Court and became surity for the payment of the same.

Robert McNees against Thomas Chumler & Mary Chumler. Debt. Came the plaintiff by his Councellors, and the defendants by their attornies also a jury (same as before...We find for the plaintiff against Mary Chumler Debt and Costs with all lawful interest.   George Kirk, foreman.
to recover against Mary Chumler Ł 13 d 1½ and costs....Samuel Farrow attorney for the defendant motioned for a new trial.

The Grand Jury returned the following Bills as follows.
The State against Daniel Evans. Hog Stealing. A true Bill Robert Foster, foreman.

The State against John Elder Junior & Alexander Elder. Larceny. A true Bill. Robert Foster, foreman.

Saxon and Wilson against Benjamine Wofford. Petition. The defendant confessed judgment for s 7 d 3 with costs of suit with stay of Execution untill 17th Feb. next.

John Hammett against Jeremiah Selman. Slander.
Jeremiah Selman against John Hammett. Slander.
Pursuant to an order of Court to us directed after hearing the evidences on each side, and considering the same, we do think and award that each person pays his own costs. 9 Jan 1796. J. Harrison, Wm. Foster, Jesse Connell, Geo Connell, Nevil Wayland, B. Piper, arbitrators.

Moses White indorsee of Robert White against John King. Petition. Nonsuit.

Thomas Williamson against Benjamine Wofford. Petition. The defendant came into Court and confessed judgment for Ł 9 s 6 d 8 according to Specialty and costs of suit.

John Timmons Admr. of Thomas Timmons against Robert Connell & Moses Timmons. Debt. Ordered that this cause lye over untill next Court.

Joseph Venable against William Fields. Case. Continued untill Tomorrow.

Whereas Robert Montgomery Junior in a fight with Joseph Venable Junior had a large piece bit out of his left ear, petitioning this Court that the same should be entered on the records thereof, which was accordingly granted as a manifestation to the world that it happened not by corporeal punishment by the laws of the land. The Court therefore desires that all due credit be paid to this memorial.

The minutes were read and signed by William Smith, James Jordan, Judges. Court then adjourned untill Tomorrow Nine of the Clock.

Friday the 15th day of Jan. 1796. Court met according to adjournment. Present their Honors. James Jordan & William Smith, Judges.

William Gist assignee of Samuel Farrow against William Smith, Esq. Dismissed at the defendants costs by consent of Parties.

Benjamine Jones against John Jones. Attachment. Dismissed by request of the plaintiff.

The State against William Smith. Killing a mare. The Grand Jury return thus "No Bill." Robert Foster, foreman.

Morriss Veal against James Smith. Case. By consent of the parties the trial of this cause is refered to the arbitrament of Capt. Ransom Tinsley and Mr. Jesse Connell, with power of Umpirage, their award returned to next Court to be a Judgment thereof.

Jesse and Robert Rakestraw against James Smith. Slander. By consent of the parties, the trial of this cause if refered to the arbitrament of James Lusk, Robert White, and Peter Smith, their award returned to next Court to be a judgment thereof.

Joseph Venable against William Fields. Case. Came the parties by their attornies, and a Jury, to wit, George Kirk, William Casey, Daniel Allen, Daniel Childers, John Cooper, Buckner Smith,

William Bramlet, Rowland Johnson, Thomas Thornton, Josiah Thornton, Thomas Beddenton & Joseph Couch, who say...we find for defendant with costs of suit. George Kirk, foreman.

William Gist, assignee of Samuel Farrow against Ebenezer Morse. Capias Debt. Judgment confessed by the defendants attorney for ₤ 9 s 7 d 9 according to Specialty, and costs of suit.

The State against Augustine Bumpass. Bastardy. The defendant came into Court and put himself on their mercy who fined him ₤ 5 proc. money payable nine months hence, Brittain Williford & Aaron Lancaster came into Court and acknowledged themselves sureties for the same.

The State against Margaret Dodds. Bastardy. The defendant came into Court with Francis Dodds her surity for ₤ 5 proc. money a fine which the Court imposes on her for said charge, also for her taking good care of said child untill it arrives to the age of ten years.

The State against Augustine Bumpass. Bastardy. The defendant came into Court with Aaron Lancaster and Brittain Williford his surities and acknowledged themselves indebted to the State, to wit, the sd. Bumpass for ₤ 50 and the sd. surities ₤ 25 each, if the said defendant fails to indemnify the County in the maintenance of a Bastard child begotten by Margaret Dodds.

The State against Spencer Casey. Assault. The defendant submitted himself to the mercy of the Court who fined him s 20 with indulgence untill next Court.

The State against William Farrow. Assault. Discharged from his recotnizance by order of Court.

The State against Benjamine Wofford. Forgery. Discharged from his recognizance by order of Court.

The State against William Merchant. Larceny. Discharged from his recognizance by order of court.

The State against James Burnett. Larceny. Laid over untill next Court.

The State against George Easlinger. Assault. Discharged for want of a prosecutor.

The same against the same. Abusing a Horse. Discharged for want of a prosecutor.

The State against John Terry. Burning Fence. Discharged from his recognizance by order of Court.

Ezekiel Johnson against Joseph Morriss. Assault. Nonsuit.

Ezekiel Johnson against William Jordan. Assault. Nonsuit.

Isaac Crow against Zadock Ford, Esq. & Thomas Parks. Capias. Debt. Judgment confessed for ₤ 10 s 10 according to Specialty & costs of suit.

Micajah Barnett against James Poole and Isaac Reed. Special Action. The parties appeared by their attornies, also came a Jury (same as before)...we find for the Plaintiff against James

Poole Ł 16 with costs of suit....

Nevil Wayland as a witness in the case, Joseph Venable against William Fields proved 6 days attendance at 2/6 per day.

William McDowell Esq. qualified as a Justice of the peace for this County, agreeable to a late act of assembly before James Jordan & William Smith, Esq.

Ordered that the Estrays be sold To-morrow at the adjournment of Court.

The minutes were read and signed by William Smith, James Jordan, Judges. Court then adjourned untill Tomorrow Nine O'Clock.

Saturday the 16th day of Jan. 1796. Court met according to adjournment. Present their Honors William Smith & James Jordan, Esq.

David Anderson and James Wofford reported that agreeable to an order of Court they have viewed and marked out a Road from Nichol's old mill to David Anderson, and from thence to Enoree near the Governor Shoals, and we marked it according to our directions to Arnold's Mill which is about a quarter of a mile from the Governor Shoals, which appears to be a good way and agreeable to the settlement, and where its mark'd to is opposite where its cleared the other side of the River. Therefore ordered that John Durham open and keep in good repair the same from Nichols old Mill to John Waldrope and that Thomas Paden oversee from thence to Enoree River near the Governor Shoals, all hands within three miles of the same to work thereon under their directions.

David McKnight against John Armstrong & Charles McKnight. Capias Debt. Stands over by consent.

Sarah Darby against Fielding Foster. Attachment. Stands over by consent.

Margaret Johnson against Abraham Hester & Sarah Hester. Slander. Nonsuit.

The Same against Randolph Laurence. Slander. Nonsuit.

Bazel Lee proved 15 days attendance in the suit John Hammett against Jeremiah Selman.

Rebekah Anderson against Benjamine Wofford. Capias Case. Ordered that a Dedimus Potestatum be issued to the State of North Carolina, to Examine Margaret Rice; with his giving the adverse party 10 days notice of the day & place of Examination.

Ordered that Mary Alexander have full admn. on the Estate of Thomas Alexander, deceased, upon her signing a Bond, which she did with Richard Venable and John Gowen as her Surities, and also qualified according to Law.

William Thomson against Essix Capshaw and Jonathan Harris. Capias. Nonsuit.

Swanson Lansford against Benjamine Wofford. Capias. Stands over by consent.

Charles McAbee against William Hagan. Slander. The plaintiff came by Mr. Nott his attorney and the defendant by Zachariah Tolliaferro his attorney, also came a Jury, Rowland Johnson, William Casey, Daniel Allen, David Childers, John Cooper, Buckner Smith, William Bramlet, Thomas Thornton, Josiah Thornton, Thomas Beddenton, Josiah Couch & William Davis...we find for the defendant. Rowland Johnson, foreman.

Essix Capshaw against William Cunningham & Obadiah Trimmier. Capias. Nonsuit.

Benjamin Wofford against William Hagan. Distress for Rent. Continued at Plaintiff's Costs.

Charles Burton against William Farrow. Capias. Came the plaintiff by his attorney and the defendant by his, also a Jury (same as before...we find for the plaintiff Ł 1 s 16.

Ordered that Robert Harper, Samuel Fowler, and Henry Young, appraise the Estate of Thomas Alexander, deceased, and make their return thereon.

William Benson proved 3 days attendance as a witness in behalf of John Hammett against Jeremiah Selman.

Ordered that the County Treasurer pay out of the County fund the sum to William Foster, that Benjamine McMekin was allowed for keeping a certain Negro Anthony who has become a County charge.

Rowland Johnson proved 7 days attendance as a witness in the suit William D. Thomas against William Ford.

James Tanner & George Walker against Matthew Gentry. Appeal. Ordered that the Judgment of the Justice below be recorded.

Joel Hembree against Israel Credenton. Attachment.
Catharine Hacker appeared as an interpleader to try the right of property, Whereupon came a Jury, (same as before)...we find for the plaintiff the mare and one cow.... Ordered that the Sheriff give up the other cow to Catharine Hacker, and that the property found to be Israel Credenton's by the Jury, be sold by the Sheriff and the money arising from the sale thereof be in the hands of the Clerk of this Court....

By application of Samuel Farrow, Esq., ordered that the property executed by the Sheriff of Mark Powell at the Instance of Francis Ley be sold at said Powell's dwellings.

Ordered that the County Treasurer pay John Gowen out of the County fund, Ł 5 for his Extra fees for the year 1795 as he then acted Sheriff for this County.

Martha Gaff served 5 days attendance as a witness in the case Joel Hembree against Israel Credenton.

John Hacker proved 5 days attendance as a witness in the case Joel Hembree against Israel Credenton.

Ordered that John Gillispie and John Turner be released from their imprisonment as there appears no vouchers for their detention.

Ordered that the minutes be read which was done & signed by James Jordan, William Smith, Judges. Court then adjourned untill the 16th day of July next.

At a Court of Sessions and Pleas began to be holden at the Court-House of Spartanburgh County the 16th day of July 1796. Present their Honors William Smith and James Jordan, Esq.

The Court proceeded to draw the Grand Jurors for next Court, to wit.

James Miller	1	Leonard Carden	11	
Alexander Jordan	2	Charles James	12	
Isaac Crow	3	Littleton Bagwell	13	
John Anderson	4	Landon Farrow	14	
James Lusk	5	John Golightly	15	
John Head	6	Richard Frier	16	
Samuel Thomson	7	George Connell	17	
John Leech	8	Joseph Thomson	18	
John Cooper	9	Thomas House	19	
Alexander Roddy	10	Thomas Compton	20	

Petit Jurors Drawn for next Court, to wit

Thomas Brown	1	William Rampley	16
Elijah Kelly	2	John Vanderver	17
Henry Coal	3	John Miller	18
John Grizzle	4	Benjamine Howard	19
Andrew Carver	5	Henry Turner, Lawsons fork	20
Ellis Johnson	6	John Vernon	21
John King	7	John Jennings	22
John Cantwell	8	Charles Whitten	23
John Haden	9	James Crook	24
Benjamine Couch	10	William Stephenson	25
Thomas Harris	11	James Turner	26
John Chesney	12	Elias Jordan	27
John Harris	13	William Hadden	28
Benjamine Clerke Sr.	14	William Buice	29
David Davis Junr.	15	Henry Turner	30

Ordered that the Estate of Obadiah Gravatte deceased be sold, after giving 20 days notice, at 12 months credit, for all sums above 10 shillings.

Ordered that William Nibbs Esq. act as County attorney for this present Term.

Alexander McBeth & Co. against Matthew Gentry. Petition. Settled by the defendant in open Court.

Ordered that John Carmichael have license to retail spiritous liquors upon signing a Bond with Isham Harrison and Isham Foster, Esq., his Aurities for his lawful performance.

The minutes were read & signed by James Jordan, Wm. Smith, Judges. Court then adjourned untill Monday nine O'Clock.

Monday the 18th day of July 1796. Court met according to adjournment. Present their Honors James Jordan & William Smith, Esq.

Grand Jurors empaneled & sworn to serve this Court, to wit

James Smith, foreman	1	Lee Clerk	9
John Bragg	2	Francis Dodd	10
Thomas Cole	3	David Anderson	11
Richard Barry	4	John Vaughan	12

Richard Beardan	5	Robert Elder	13
Shands Golightly	6	Samuel Morrow	14
Cutbert Burton	7	John Hammett	15
Matthew Patton	8		

Samuel Colley attended to serve as a petit Juror, but was dismist from the same by the Court.

Petit Jurors drawn to serve this Court, to wit

Leonard Adcock, fore	1	Peter Bragg	7
William Hemmett	2	Richard Chesney	8
Hanie Harper	3	James Gilmore	9
Nathaniel Henderson	4	John Kirkland	10
Thomas Evatt	5	John Burk	11
Andrew Ray	6	Andrew Colley	12

On a mortgage Bond from John Whittimore to Samuel Nesbitt, for Ł 22 s 5 the said Neasbitt came into open Court, and confessed he had received full satisfaction for the same.

William Ford, attorney for Edward Stewart against Thomas Davis. Case. By consent of the parties the trial of this cause is refered to the arbitrament of James Jordan, Esq., & William Benson with power of umpirage, their award returned to next Court to be a rule thereof.

Thomas Price against Benjamine Connell. Petition. The Defendant came into Court & confessed judgment for Ł 7 s 10 according to Specialty, the note bearing date 6 May 1796, and costs of suit with stay of Execution untill 1st Oct. next.

Thomas Price against Alexander Ray. Petition. The Defendant by information of Manly Ford, confessed judgment for Ł 8 s 10 d 9 according to Specialty, the note bearing date 6 May 1796, and costs of suit, with staying Execution untill 1st Oct. next.

William Fields against William Ford. Special Action. By consent of the parties and trial of this cause is refered to the arbitrament of James Jordan, Esq., and William Benson, with power of Umpirage, their award returned to next Court to be a rule thereof.

The State against Margaret Lewis. Larceny. The Grand Jury say "A true Bill." James Smith, foreman.

The State against Richard Lee. Larceny. The Grand Jury find A true Bill.

The State against Samuel Bruton. Stealing Bee Hive. The Defendant failing to appear Ordered that a Sciri Facias be issued against him & John Spelce compelling them to attend next Court to shew cause if any they have why their recognizance should not be forfeited.

James Henderson against Richard Barnett. Assault & Batty. Dismissed by request of the plaintiff.

George Gordon & Co. against William Stone. Petition. The defendant came into Court confessed judgment for Ł 9 s 5 d 9 agreeable to note, the same bearing date 7 June 1795 & costs of suit.

Samuel Miller, Sheriff against John Conner & Daniel Cornwall. Debt. The defendant to wit, Daniel Cornwall came into Court & confessed Judgment for ₺ 7 s 13 d 11 the costs on the Execution for which he was surity for the delivery of property to satisfy the same & costs of suit.

A Deed of Conveyance from Edward Hooker & wife to John David Nebuhr, acknowledged in open Court, ordered to record.

Ordered that Anne Hendrix have the sum which an Estray sold for, taken up by Abraham Whittimore & Toll'd before Thomas Moore, Esq. bought by John Gowen, Esq. to be paid out of the County fund after deducting the cost.

Absent William Smith, Esq.

William Moore qualified as a Constable for the County.

The last will & testament of Samuel Morrow deceased, proven in open Court by the evidence of Lee Clerke & Thomas Thornton, Ordered to record.

William Smith & George Bruton, Esq., qualified as Exrs. to the Estate of Samuel Morrow, Deceased.

Ordered that Brittain Williford, Thomas Williams and David Trail appraise the Estate of Samuel Morrow, deceased, and be qualified before Samuel Lancaster, Esq.

  Present William Smith, Esq.

Ordered that Thomas Jackson and James Jackson have the full admn. of the Estate of Samuel Jackson, Senr., deceased, upon qualifying and signing a Bond of ₺ 300 with John Spelce and Samuel Jackson his surities; which was done accordingly.

Ordered that James Gilmore, Alexander Copeland and James Hooper, Esq., appraise the Estate of Samuel Jackson, decd., & make due return thereof.

Micajah Barnett against Joel Hembree. Debt. The Defendant came into Court & confessed judgment according to Specialty & costs of suit.

Ordered that the Exrs. of the Estate of Samuel Jackson deceased proceed to the sale thereof after giving 20 days notice, at 12 months credit for all sums above s 10.

William Collins against Byas Boican. Attachment. John Collins being summoned as a guarnishee came into Court and made oath that upon a settlement he fell indebted and is still Indebted unto the said defendant for ₺ 40.

Ordered that the minutes be read which was done & signed by William Smith, James Jordan, Judges. Court then adjourned untill Tomorrow nine O'Clock.

Tuesday the 19th day of July 1796. Court met according to adjournment. Present their Honors William Smith and James Jordan, Esq.

Ephraim Ramsey Esq. against William Venable & Larkin Venable. Petition. Debt. Mr. Nott appeared in favour of the plaintiff and Mr. Toliaferro in favour of the defendants, whereupon the Court decreed against William Venable & entered judgment by default against Larkin Venable.

The State against Daniel Evans. Larceny. Came the parties by their attornies whereupon came a Jury to wit, Leonard Adcock, William Hammett, Hanee Harper, Nathaniel Henderson, Thomas Evatt, Andrew Ray, Peter Bragg, Richard Chesney, James Gilmore, John Kirkland, John Burk, and Andrew Colley, who say "Not Guilty"
                                        Leonard Adcock, foreman.
Ordered that he be discharged from his recognizance.

The State against James Clerke & Leather Tickle. Larceny. The Grand Jurors say "A true Bill." James Smith, foreman.

The State against William Brittain. Assault & Biting a Lip. The Grand Jurors say "A true Bill."
This indictment is traversed untill next Court by Samuel Farrow, attorney, for the Defendant.

Alexander McBeth & Co. against Essix Capshaw. Petition. The Court decreed ₤ 5 s 2 d 3 for the plaintiff & costs of suit.

John Harriss against John Hammett. Attachment. Nonsuit.

Sarah Darby Admx. of William Darby decd. against William Stephenson. Petition. Laid over untill next Court by consent.

Sarah Darby Admx. of William Darby decd. against Hugh Stephenson Junior. Petition. Stands over untill tomorrow.

Daniel Barnett against Benjamine Busey. Petition. Thomas Price came into Court and entered himself Surity for the Costs of the above action provided the plaintiff should be cast in his suit. Ordered that the same be continued by affidavit of the defendant.

Denny Anderson against John Pennington. Capias. The defendant came into Court & confessed judgment for ₤ 11 s 13 d 4 and costs of suit, with staying Execution untill the last day of Oct. next.

Sarah Darby admx. of Wm. Darby against John Bearden Senior. Debt. Settled at the defendant's costs by consent.

Elias Reynolds proved 2 days attendance as a witness in the case Denny Anderson against John Pennington.

Justice Reynolds against Samuel White. Appeal. Zachariah Tolliaferro attorney appeared in behalf of the appellant, and Mr. Abraham Nott, Esq. attorney in behalf of the appelle, and after an investigation on the matter, It is Decreed by the Court that the judgment be reversed.

The State against James Hicks. Horse Stealing. The Grand Jury find "A true Bill"
Ordered that the prisoner be removed to Pinckneyville.

The State against Richard Lee. Sheep Stealing. The Grand Jury find "A true Bill."

Justice Reynolds against Daniel Carmichael. Appeal. Came the appellant by Zachariah Tolliaferro his attorney and the appelle by Waddy Thomson, Esq.,his attorney, whereupon it is decreed by the Court that the judgment be confirmed.

Ordered that no witness be allowed for their attendance except those who appeared before the justice.

The State against James Hicks. Horse Stealing. Moses Cantwell and George Lamkin as principles and Wells Griffith and Richard Turner as their Surities came into open Court and acknowledged themselves indebted to the State, sd. Cantwell and Lamkin Ŀ 50 each and the sd. Griffith and Turner surities Ŀ 25 each....if the sd. Cantwell & Lamkin Esq. shall fail to appear at next Pinckney Court to give evidence in behalf of the State against the said James Hicks....
Test W. Lancaster, C. S. C.

Ordered that the minutes be read which was done & signed by William Smith, James Jordan, Judges. Court then adjourned until Tomorrow Nine O'Clock.

Wednesday the 20th day of July 1796. Court met according to adjournment. Present their Honors William Smith & James Jordan, Esq.

The State against James Clerks & Leather Tickle. Larceny. Came Mr. Nibbs in behalf of the State and the prisoners being arraigned and Samuel Farrow Esq. appearing in their behalf; also a Jury (same as before)...James Gilmore and Andrew Colley on their affirmations do say "Guilty."

The State against John Elder Junior & Alexander Elder. Larceny. Continued until Tomorrow by request of the defendant for want of witnesses, Ordered that Larkin Lancaster go immediately & compel the attendance of Charles Burton, William Rodgers & Elizabeth Sullivan for trial.

John Pace against Nicholas Waters. Capias. Settled each party paying his own costs.

Bazel Scott against Henry Turner Junr. Capias. Dismist by request of the plaintiff.

The State against Margaret Lewis. Larceny. Came the defendant by her attorney, and a Jury (same as before)...Not Guilty.
The grand Jury were dismissed by order of Court for this Term.

The State against Richard Lee. Larceny. Came Mr. Nibbs in behalf of the State and the defendant by his attornies, whereupon came a Jury. Isham Harrison, Esq., Hanee Harper, Nathaniel Henderson, Thomas Evatt, Andrew Ray, Peter Bragg, Richard Chesney, James Gilmore, John Kirkland, John Burk, Andrew Colley, and William Brannon, Not Guilty. Isham Harrison, foreman.

The State against Christopher Stone, Caleb Stone & Philip Huff. Samuel Farrow Esq. attorney for the defendant demanded a trial which was not granted.

Ordered that the minutes be read which was done & signed by William Smith, James Jordan, Judges. Court then adjourned until Eight O'Clock Tomorrow.

Thursday the 21st day of July 1796. Court met according to adjournment Present their Honors William Smith and James Jordan, Esq.

226

The State against Leather Tickle and James Clerke. Larceny. The defendants by their Attornies motioned for a new trial: The Court were of the opinion that the grounds on which the motion was founded were not sufficient for a new trial; Samuel Farrow attorney for the defendants, motioned for an arrest of judgment who was also overruled; and the Court gave their opinion to pass sentence against the prisoners, to wit...you are to be taken from this bar by the Sheriff to the most convenient place for execution and there receive, viz, you James Clerke five lashes on your bare back and you Leather Tickle one, at the discretion of the officer to execute the same. The Sheriff reported that he had Executed the above sentence according to the directions of the Court.

The State against James Dempsey. Horse Stealing. Samuel Farrow, attorney for the defendant demanded a trial, Ordered that the cause stand over.

The State against Thomas Langley. Samuel Farrow, attorney for the defendant demanded a trial, Ordered that the cause stand over.

The State against William Smith Senior and William Smith Junior. Hog Stealing. Mr. Nibbs appeared in behalf of the State and Samuel Farrow and Mr. Nott Attornies in behalf of the defendants whereupon cane a Jury (same as before)...Guilty.
It appearing after the evidences were closed, that there was nothing proven against William Smith Junior, therefore ordered that he be struct out of the Indictment.

Robert White against John King. Debt. Settled by report of the plaintiff.

John O'Nail against Crofford Simson. Attachment. Francis Dodds being summoned as a Guarnishee and failing to appear, Ordered that a Decree be entered against him by default.

Mary Alexander Admrx. of Thomas Alexander deceased against James Alexander. Special action on the case. Dismissed by order of Court.

The minutes were read & signed by William Smith, James Jordan, Judges. Court then adjourned untill Tomorrow Eight O'Clock.

Friday the 22nd of July 1796. Court met according to adjournment. Present their Honors William Smith and James Jordan, Esq.

The State against John Elder Junior and Alexander Elder. Larceny. The prisoners being arreigned and challenging the Jurors, untill a Trial could not be had for want of Jurors, Therefore ordered that their recognizance continue untill next Court.

The State against John Elder Junior and Alexander Elder. Larceny. The defendants came into open Court with Captain Samuel Morrow and Robert Elder their Surities and acknowledged themselves justly indebted to the State...the sd. Elders L 50 and the sd. Morrow and Robert Elder L 25 each...if the sd. John and Alexander Elder shall fail to appear at next Court when call'd....
Test W. Lancaster, C. S. C.

The State against William Brittain. Larceny. Ordered that a Sciri Facias issue against the Surities to shew cause why the principle did not appear.

The State against John Spelce. Stealing Bee Hive. Ordered that a Sciri Facias issue against the Surities to shew cause why the principle did not appear.

The State against David Davis. Rescuing Executed Property. No prosecutor nor witness appearing, Ordered that the defendant be dismissed.

The State against Jeremiah Spann. Sciri Facias for Bastardy. Ordered that Samuel Thomson's recognizance be forfeited and that another Sciri Facias issue against Jeremiah Spann and Burrel Thomson, to shew cause why their recognizance should not be forfeited.

Ordered that the States business be continued untill next Court.

John Gray against William Wofford. Attachment. Nonsuit.

John Cantwell against Henry McCray. Detinue. Continued under the former rule of reference.

John Timmons Admr. of the Estate of Thomas Timmons, deceased against Robert Connell and Moses Timmons. Capias Debt. Came the plaintiff by Mr. Waddy Thomson his Attorney and the defendant by Mr. Nibbs his Attorney, also a Jury (same as before)...we find for the plaintiff $197.50 with costs of suit.

Thomas Farrow Esq. Exor. of Thomas Lowther deceased against John Erwin. Special Action. Nonsuit.

David Goodlett, Esq., of Greenville County, a witness in the suit John Timmons admr. of the Estate of Thomas Timmons decd. against Robert Connell and Moses Timmons, proved 14 days attendance at 2/6 per day also for riding 100 miles at 2 pence per mile.

George Roebuck against William Farrow. Special Action. The award being returned and set aside, Ordered that the case be continued and that a commission issue to the State of Kentuckey to take the evidence of Joseph Howell in behalf of the plaintiff upon giving legal notice to the adverse party.

Morriss Veal against James Smith. Case. Came the plaintiff by Mess. Nott & Thomson his attornies and the defendant by Samuel Farrow Esq. his attorney, whereupon came a Jury (same as before) ...we find for the plaintiff $40 with all costs of suit....

Ezekiel Johnson against William Garrett. Capias Assault. The defendant being called and not appearing in his own person nor by his attorney, Judgment was thereupon entered against him by Default.

Alexander McBeth & Co. against Dennis Sullivan and John Thomson. Petition. The defendant came into open Court in his own proper person and confessed Judgment, according to Specialty, and costs of suit with staying execution untill next Court.

The State against William Smith Senior. Hog Stealing. The argument upon the grounds for an arrest of Judgment is continued untill next Court.

Rebekah Anderson against Benjamine Wofford. Capias. Ordered that a Dedimus Potestatum issue to the State of North Carolina to examine Margaret Cane on behalf of the defendant, upon giving the adverse party 10 days notice.

William Poole against Henry Wyatt. Appeal. On motion of the plaintiff's attorney, Ordered that the judgment of the Justice be confirmed.

James Rutherford against Henry McCray. Petition. The defendant came into Court and confessed judgment for Ł 3 s 16 d 1 with Interest from 17th Feb 1790 which appears to be the sum due according to note and account, and costs of suit.

Ordered that the Estrays delivered to the Sheriff be sold at the adjournment of Court.

Ordered that the Road leading across heads Ford on Enoree River be turn'd above said Heads plantation to cross at the flat shoals, and that Isaac Lynch be appointed overseer of the same, and that all hands within three miles of the same work thereon under his direction.

Thomas Richards & wife against James Beards & wife. Slander. Ordered that a commission Dedimus Potestatum issue to the State of North Carolina to take the examination of Sarah Peters and Anne Chapman in behalf of the plaintiff, upon his giving 10 days notice to the Defendant of the time and place of Examination.

John Tucker against Mary Lindsay. Appeal. The plaintiff's attorney came into Court and moved for an order of this Court against George Burton, Esq., ordering him to certify up to this Court the proceedings in said case, or shew cause why he should not, which was accordingly granted and the cause continued.

James Lusk, William Roberds, Daniel White, Peter Smith, and Spencer Smith proved to wit, Lusk 14, Roberds 14, White 4, Spencer Smith 12 and Peter Smith 12 days attendance as witnesses in the Morris Veal against James Smith, and 2/6 per day.

Elizabeth Fallace proved 9 days attendance as a witness in the case Thomas Richards and wife against James Beards and wife, at 2/6 per day, also 120 miles at 2 pence per mile.

John Strow against Solomon Hill and James Burns. Capias. Ordered that a Dedimus Potestatum issue to the State of North Carolina, Lincoln County to examine George Gilbraith in behalf of the defendants upon his giving the adverse party 10 days notice.

William Fields against William Ford. Capias. Ordered that a dedimus potestatum issue to the Town of Granby to take the examination of Hargrove Arthur and   Brooks in behalf of the defendant, upon his giving legal notice to the plaintiff.

Ordered that the minutes be read which was done accordingly and signed by James Jordan, William Smith, Judges. Court then adjourned untill Court in Course.

At a Court of Sessions and pleas began to be holden at the Court House of Spartanburgh County 12th day of Jan. 1797. Present their Honors William Smith & James Jordan, Esq.

The Court proceeded to Draw the Grand Jurors for next Court, to wit

Michael Miller	1	George Bruton	11
Samuel Neasbitt	2	Henry Foster	12
Jesse Spencer	3	Wells Griffith	13
James Southerland	4	Benjamine Clark	14
Absalom Lancaster	5	Robert Miller, Fork	15
Wm. Poole, J. M.	6	Thomas Underwood	16
Jarayal Barnett	7	Henry McCray	17
Berryman D. Shumate	8	Edmond Fowler	18
William McDaniel	9	George Lamkin	19
Alexander Alexander	10	John Trimmier	20

Petit Jurors Drawn for next Court, to wit

David Cook	1	Joseph Dill	16
John Brown	2	George Grace	17
Joseph Kelso	3	David Brown	18
John Cobb	4	Henry Harden	19
Jesse Austin	5	James Kearn	20
James Henry, Junr.	6	William Crocker	21
Aaron Bawcomb	7	John Cross	22
James Hagan	8	Joseph Venable	23
Henry Cannon	9	William Bishop	24
Richard Barry	10	Benjamine Arnold	25
Thomas Jones	11	Isaac Hamby	26
Samuel Busey	12	Abraham Andrews	27
James Evatt	13	Isaac Couch	28
William Evatt	14	Arias Brows	29
Alexander Evans	15	Nathaniel Burton	30

John Grizzle, Charles Whitten and Henry Turner appeared to serve as Petit Jurors, but were exempted from the same by the Court.

Petit Jurors Drawn to serve this Court

John Chesney	1	Thomas Harris	7
Andrew Cowen	2	David Davis	8
Elijah Kelley	3	John Cantwell	9
Henry Turner L. F.	4	Thomas Brown	10
James Turner	5	John Vernon	11
John Hadden	6	Benjamine Couch	12

Isham Harrison, Esq. being appointed to act as a Judge for this County by the Legislature of this State took the several oaths of office prescribed by Law.

The Last will and testament of Thomas Collins deceased proven in open Court by the evidence of William Traylor and James Jordan, Esq., Ordered to Record.

John Collins and Joseph Collins came into Court and qualified as Executors to the last will and testament of Thomas Collins, decd.

The last will and testament of Alexander Collins deceased proven in open Court by the evidence of William Traylor & Mary Traylor. Ordered to record.

Ordered that Joseph Woodruff have license to retail spiritous liquors upon giving Isaac Crow and John Golightly his surities for his lawful performance.

Ordered that Isaac Crow have license to retail spiritous liquors upon giving Joseph Woodruff and John Golightly his surities for his lawful performance.

Ordered that Mary Ramply have full admn. on the Estate of William Ramply decd. upon giving Joel Hembree and John Beard <u>his</u> surities in ₤ 300 & qualified which was done in open Court.

Graff Edson & Co. vs Robert Garrett & Archer Harris. Petition Debt. The Defendants came into Court and confessed Judgment for ₤ 6 s 17 d 5 with interest from 20th August 1796 and costs of suit.

Ordered that the Minutes be read, which was accordingly done, and signed by William Smith, James Jordan, Isham Harrison, Judges. Court then adjourned untill Tomorrow 9 O'Clock.

Friday the 13th of Jan. 1797. The Court met according to adjournment. Present their Honors William Smith and James Jordan, Esqs.

Ordered that the Clerk be allowed out of the fines and forfeitures of this County, ₤13 s 19 for his services done by Virtue of his office for the State, from June Court 1793 to July Court 1796.

Ordered that James Crowther, James Beard and John Hindman appraise the estate of William Ramply deceased, and make due return thereof.

James Martin against William Rickman. Writ. Debt (₤ 30) The Defendant in his own proper person came into Court and confessed judgment for ₤ 30 according to Specialty with Interest and cost of suit.

Sarah Darby Admx. of William Darby decd. against William Stephenson. Abated by death of plaintiff.

Sarah Darby against Hugh Stephenson Junr. Petition. Abated by death of this plaintiff.

Sarah Darby against John Roebuck. Petition. Abated by death of the plaintiff.

Sarah Darby against Elie McVey and William Anderson. Petition. Abated by death of the plaintiff.

Sarah Darby against Glanley Fewell. Petition. Abated by death of the plaintiff.

Alexr. McBeth & Co. against George Taylor. Writ. Case. Dismissed at plaintiff's costs by consent.

Sarah Darby against Fielding Foster. Attachment. Abated by the death of the plaintiff.

William Tipping assignee of Crofford Simpson against John O'Nail. Writ Debt. Dismissed at plaintiff's costs by consent.

Sarah Darby admx. of William Darby decd. against Joseph Kemp. Writ. Case. Abated by death of the plaintiff.

Present his Honor Isham Harrison, Esq.

Grand Jurors to serve this Court, to wit.

Alexander Jordan	1	Charles James	7
Isaac Crow	2	Littleton Bagwell	8
John Anderson	3	John Golightly	9
James Lusk	4	Richard Fryer	10

John Cooper	5	George Connell	11
Leonard Carden	6	John Leath	12
		Thomas Compton	13

who were empanneled & sworn.

Graff Edson & Co. against John Haden. Petition. Dismissed at Defendant's Costs by consent.

The State against Alexander Elder. Larceny. Came the plaintiff by Mr. Dunlap and the defendants by his attornies, whereupon came a Jury James Turner, foreman' John Chesney, Andrew Cowen, Elijah Kelley, Henry Turner, L. F., John Haden, Thomas Harris, David Davis, John Cantrell, Thomas Brown, John Vernon, Benjamin Couch ...We find the prisoner not Guilty.

William Feals against William Ford. Writ. By consent of the parties & assent of this Court the trial of this Court is refered to the arbitrament of James Jordan, Esq., & James Vernon, with power of umpirage their award made & return'd to next Court to be a judgment thereof.

Andrew Colley against John Bingham. Writ. Continued by consent of the parties.

The State against Daniel White. Assault. The Grand Jury returned a true bill. John Golightly, foreman.

The State against James Burnett. Larceny. The defendant came into Court with John Piper and JohnJohnston his Surity & acknowledged themselves to owe to the State (to wit) the sd. Burnett Ł 50 and sd. surities Ł 25 each...provided the sd. James Burnett shall fail to attend this Court when call'd upon to answer to the above charge. Test: William Lancaster.

The State against Ezekiel Johnston. House Braking. Ordered that a nole prosiqui be entered.

The appraisment of the Estate of Saml. Jackson Senr. decd. returned by the admrs.

Ordered that the minutes be read which was done & signed by James Jordan, Isham Harrison, William Smith, Judges. Court then adjourned untill tomorrow nine O'Clock.

Saturday the 14th day of Jan. 1797. The Court met according to adjournment. Present their Honors William Smith, James Jordan, Isham Harrison, Esq.

Ordered that James Hooper, Esq., be allowed s 30 out of the County fund for wintering an Estray mare taken up by Saml. Young & told before him.

George Roebuck against William Farrow. Special Action. By consent of the parties & assent of the Court the trial of this cause is refered to the arbitrament of William Crow, Isham Foster, & John Rainwater, their award made & returned to be a judgment of this Court.

John Wofford against Saml. Lancaster. Writ. Debt. The Defendant confessed judgment for Ł 25 s 8 d 9 3/4 with interest & costs of suit with stay of Execution untill 1st of March next.

The State against Christopher Stone, Caleb Stone and Philip Huff. Larceny. Stealing Bacon, Rye & a Bee-Hive. The Grand Jury returned no Bill.

John Cnatrell against Henry McCray. Writ. Trover. By consent of the parties and assent of the Court, the trial of this cause is refered to the arbitrament of Isham Foster, James Smith & Giles Connell.

Jesse & Robert Rakestraw against James Smith. Writ. Assault. Continued by affidavit of the Plaintiff, the costs of wait the event of the suit.

The State against William Bridgman. Indictment for Burglary. The Grand Jury returned "A True Bill."

Swanson Lansford against Benjamin Wofford. Writ. Debt. Continued by affidavit of Deft.

The State against James Dempsey. Horse Stealing. Discharged.

The State against Thomas Langley. Horse Stealing.
Joshua Downs against James Henderson. Petition.
The Defendant confessed judgment for the sum of Ł 3 s 5 with costs of suit.

Ordered that Capt. John Lipscomb oversee the road from the County line below Mr. Shippys to William Thompsons (in place of Thos. Gillingwaters) all hands within three miles of the same which are liable by Law to work thereon under his directions at such times & places as he may think necessary for keeping the same in good repair according to Law.

David McKnight against John Armstrong & Charles McKnight. Writ. Nonsuit.

George B. Moore against Joseph Wofford. Writ. Ordered that the plaintiff give security for the Costs of said suit within 30 days.

Rebecah Anderson against Benjamine Wofford. Writ. Case. Came the plaintiff by Z. Toliaferro an Attorney, and the Defendant by Mr. Thomson his Attorney, Whereupon came a jury (same as before)...we find for the plaintiff $31.44 with costs of suit.

The State against Simon Pack. Sheep Stealing. Ordered that an attachment Issue against the body of Sarah Pack to compell her attendance at this Court on Monday next to give Evidence in behalf of the State and that the sum be put in the hands of Bazel Lee to Execute.

David Anderson & Mary ann Anderson proved attendance the suit Rebecah Anderson against Benjamine Wofford (to wit) the sd. David 8 days and the sd. Maryann 7 days @ 2/6 pr. day each.

The State against John Elder. Larceny. Ordered that his recognizance be continued untill next Court.

Ordered that the minutes be read which was done and signed by William Smith, J. Harrison, James Jordan, Judges. Court then adjourned 'till Monday nine O'Clock.

Monday the 16th day of Jan. 1797. The Court met according to adjournment. Present their Honors James Jordan & Isham Harrison, Esq.

Thomas House was excused from serving as a Grand Juror by Reason of sickness & John Leach appeared & was sworn to serve in his place.

Thomas Richards & wife against James Beard & wife. Writ. Slander. Continued by consent of parties.

John Strow against James Barns & Solomon Hill. Debt. Continued by consent of the parties.

The State against William Brittain. Assault & Biting a Lip. Came the plaintiff by John Dunlap states attorney and Saml. Farrow Esqr. defendant's attorney, whereupon came the petit Jurors aforesaid, ...We find the prisoner Not Guilty.

The State against Simon Pack. Indictment for sheep stealing. The Grand Jury...returned No Bill.

Daniel Barnett against Benjamine Bussey. Petition. Continued by consent of the parties.

Andrew Tarrance against John Cook, James Betterton & Archer Howard. Petition. Came the Plaintiff by John Dunlap, Esq., his attorney & the defendants by Waddy Thompson, Esq., their attorney, whereupon a cedree was granted by the Court in favour of the plaintiff for £ 7 s 10 according to specialty with Interest & costs of suit.

The State against William Brittain. Indictment for Stealing Tobacco. The attornies for each party appeared & the Jury aforesaid appeared & being sworn...we find prisoner Guilty. The Defendant's attorney moved for an arrest of judgment.

Ordered that Jonathan Harris have Tavern License upon giving James Smith & William Thomson his Surities for his lawful performance, which he did in open Court.

Jesse & Robert Rakestraw against James Smith. Writ. Assault. On motion of the plaintiff's attorney, Ordered that a Dedimus Potestatum Issue to the State of Georgia to take the Examination of William Hagan of Frankling County & Morris Veal of Oglethorpe upon his giving the adverse party 10 days notice of the time and place of Examination.

The admr. of Mucklehany against The admr. of Jones. Sci Fa for renewal of Judgment. A Scire Facias having issued, ordered that the rule (to shew cause why the judgment in this case should not be renewed) be made obsolete and the judgment be revived.

Robert Connell against John Robertson. Writ. Assault. Ordered that this case continue.

James Clarke against James Henderson. Writ. Slander. Continued by consent of the parties.

Ordered that the minutes be read which was done & signed by James Jordan, Isham Harrison, Judges. Court then adjourned untill Tomorrow nine O'Clock.

Tuesday the 17th day of Jan. 1797. The court met according to adjournment. Present their Honours James Jordan & Isham Harrison, Esq.

The State against William Bridgman. Indictment for Burglary. Ordered that the prisoner be delivered into the possession of Col. William Bratton Sheriff of Pinckneyville District in order to be confined in the common Goal of said District untill further delt with according to law, And that the Sheriff of this County assist with a sufficient guard in conveying him to said Goal.

Ordered that James Vernon, Samuel Miller & Arias Brown appraise the Estate of Thomas Collins, deceased and make due return thereof.

William Rightsford proved 2 days attendance as a witness in the suit David McKnight against John Armstrong and Charles McKnight. also that he rode 63 miles at 4' pr. mile

The State against William Britton. Tobacco Stealing. On motion of Saml. Farrow, Esq., for an arrest of judgment the Court defered their opinion for a further consideration.

Ordered that Sciri Facias issue in all the States business where the defendants & witness did not appear at this Court by virtue of thier recognizances.

The State against William Smith Senr. Hog Stealing. The Court ordered that the defendant be find the sum of £ 5 sterling and that he pay all costs of the Indictment, 3 months given for the fine on payment of costs.

The State against Jesse Davis & David Hicks. Stealing Cow. Ordered that a nole prosequi be entered.

The State against Jeremiah Spann. Bastardy. Sciri Facias. Ordered that the recognizance in this case be Forfeited and Execution be issued against the Defendant for £ 5 proc. money & costs.

Present his Honour William Smith, Esq.

William Wells assignee of Wells Griffith against Justice Reynolds. Writ. Debt. Came the plaintiff by John Dunlap and Waddy Thompson Esq. his attorneys and the defendant by Joseph Gist Esq. his attorney a motion being made for the postponement of the trial was overruled, and a trial was had, and the Jury aforesaid ...we find for the plaintiff $107.15 with interest and costs of suit. The defendant came into Court and confessed Judgment ...the plaintiff paying all costs.

Wells Griffith against Justice Reynolds. Writ. Debt. Came the parties by their Attornies whereupon came the Jury aforesaid who being sworn...we find for the plaintiff £ 32.15 with interest and costs of suit....

John Stron against James Burns and Solomon Hill. Writ. Ordered that a Dedimus potestatum issue to the State of Kentuckey to take the examination of Stanly Fewel in behalf of the Defendants also to the State of North Carolina Lincoln County to take the examination of George Galbraith in behalf as aforesaid, upon giving 10 days notice to the adverse party.

Henry McCray against Obadiah Watson. Appeal. Came the plaintiff by Mr. Nott his attorney and the defendant by Mr. Gist his attorney, and the court defered their decision untill Tomorrow morning.

The State against Jacob Fowler. Horse Stealing. Discharged by the Court.

Ordered that the Estrays produced to the Sheriff be sold at the adjournment of this Court.

Ordered that James Hooper, Esq., have five head of sheep, and one Two years old stear (the sheep taken up by Robert Harper, and the stear by James Fowler) sold and return the Notes to the County Treasurer.

The State againstWilliam Brittain. Stealing Tobacco. A Motion being made for an arrest of judgment, it was accordingly granted by the Court and ordered that the Defendant be dismissed.

Ordered that the minutes be read which was done and signed by William Smith, Isham Harrison, James Jordan, Judges. Court then adjourned untill Tomorrow Nine O'Clock.

Wednesday the 18th day of Jan. 1797. The Court met according to adjournment. Present their Honours James Jordan and William Smith, Esqs.

Ordered that Obadiah Watson be allowed s 19 d 10 out of the County fund for keeping Estrays January Court and July Court Also for keeping James Clarke and Leather Tickle in Goal.

Henry McCray vs Obadiah Watson. Appeal. The Court Defering their opinion untill to day, are now divided in their opinions.

Henry McCray vs John Watson. Appeal. Came the plaintiff by Mr. Nott his attorney and the Defendant by Mr. Gist his Attorney and after a long debate between the parties the Court confirmed the Judgment of the Justice.

William Collins against Tobias Boican. Attachment L 80. John Collins as guarnishee came into Court and acknowledged himself indebted to the absent Debtor L 40 sterling.

A Deed of conveyance from John Gowen Esq. to Abner Henry acknowledged in open Court, Ordered to be recorded.

William Collins against Tobias Boican. Attachment. On a writ of Inquiry the Jury aforesaid on their several oaths do say "We find for the Plaintiff $257.14. Ordered that the money in the hands of the Guarnishee be appropriated to discharge the Debt.

Joroyal Barnett against Moses Timmons and Daniel Carmichael. Writ. Debt. Nonsuit.

Absent James Jordan, Esq.

Alexander Alexander assignee of James Jordan, Esq. against Mary Lindsey Admx. of Dennis Lindsey. Writ. Debt. On motion of Samuel Farrow Esq. attorney for Defendant craving oyer of the note, was overruled being answered by the plaintiff that the note was lost, also that the Defendant had no right to crave oyer of the note when he Demured to the Declaration upon the following ground, that the Declaration was defective inasmuch that it did not shew when the note was given to the said James Jordan, Esq., or when it was assigned by him the said James Jordan to the said Alexander Alexander but being overruled, Ordered that he plead substantially, whereupon came the Jury aforesaid, who being duly sworn on their several oaths do say We find for the plaintiff $65 with costs of suit.

Randolph Brown proved 4 days attendance as a witness in the suit, Wells Griffith against Justice Reynolds at 2/6 pr. day.

Ordered that the minutes be read which was done and signed by William Smith, Isham Harrison, James Jordan, Judges. Court then adjourned untill Tomorrow nine O'Clock.

Thursday the 19th day of Jan. 1797. The court met according to adjournment. Present their Honours James Jordan, William Smith, and Isham Harrison, Esqs.

John Cunningham against John James. Writ. Debt. Order for judgment.

Samuel Hampton & James Matthews against Justice Reynolds. Writ. Debt. The Defendant making oath that the plaintiffs live without the limits of this State, ordered that they give security for costs within 30 days or be nonprossed.

George Gordon & Co. against William Farrow. Writ. Debt. The Defendant confessed judgment for ₤ 11 with Interest agreeable to note & costs of suit.

Boley Conner against Larkin Venable. Attachment. Came the plaintiff by Abraham Nott, Esq., his attorney, and the Defendant by Samuel Farrow, Esq., his attorney, whereupon came the Jury aforesaid, who being sworn, on their several oaths do say We find for the Plaintiff ₤ 8 s 16 d 8 with costs of suit.
A new trial was prayed which was accordingly granted, upon payment of costs and giving special Bail to the action.

The State against Augustine Bumpass. Bastardy. The Court having fined the said Defendant the sum of ₤ 5 proc. money, He applied, and obtained a remitment of the same from under the hand and seal of his Excellency Arnoldus Vanderhorst, Esq., Gov. and produced the same to the Court.

John Cunningham against John James. Writ. Debt. Came the parties by their attornies whereupon came the Jury aforesaid who being sworn on their several oaths do say We find for the plaintiff ₤ 12 s 2

Daniel Barnett against Benjamine Busey. Petition. Accomp't. Came the plaintiff by Mr. Nott his attorney and the defendant by Mr. Gist his attorney, and a Jury being prayed by Defendants came as aforesaid, who being sworn, on their several oaths do say We find for the plaintiff $12.07 and two mills.

Ordered that all the notes in the hands of the County Treasurer which has been on Demand 12 months be collected as soon as convenient.

John Johnson against George Gilbert. Petition. Note. Decree by the Court for ₤ 6 with interest and costs of suit.

Samuel Hampton & James Matthews against Justice Reynolds. William Bostick came into Court and entered himself security for the costs in the above suit, provided the plaintiffs should be case in the same.

John Wright and Micajah Barnett proved attendance as witnesses in the suit Daniel Barnett against Benjamine Busey, to wit, the sd. Wright 13 days and the sd. Barnett 13 days at 2/6 pr. day.

John Harris proved 5 days attendance as a witness in the suit John Johnson against George Gilbert at 2/6 d. pr. day.

Ordered that when a certificate shall be produced from the Commissioners appointed to let the Bridge across Tyger River, that the Undertakers be paid Ł 15 out of the County fund.

Andrew Colley against John Bingham. Writ. Case. Ordered that a Dedimus Potestatum issue to the City of Charleston to take the Examination of John Cunningham in behalf of the Plaintiff upon giving the adverse party 10 days notice of the time and place of examination.

William Smith & George Bruton Esq. against Jason Moore. Writ. There appearing a clerical mistake in the clerk, inasmuch as he mentioned "administrators" in the writ, instead of "Executors" Ordered that the same be amended by striking out "Administrators" and inserting "Executors" in lieau thereof.

Ordered that the minutes be Read which was done and signed by William Smith, Isham Harrison, Judges. Court then adjourned untill Tomorrow Nine O'Clock.

Friday the 20th day of Jan. 1797. The Court met according to adjournment. Present their Honours William Smith and Isham Harrison, Esq.

Morris Veal against James Smith. Fieri Facias. Ordered that for certain reasons that the Sheriff proceed no further in Executing the same untill next Court.

James Moore against William Wofford. Appeal. Dismissed.

Ordered that Tobias Bright, Charles Burton & John Meadows, be the Commissioners to view and lay off the most convenient and best way for a Road from Blackstocks Road to Rodgers Bridge on Tyger River, From thence to the Charleston Road, leading by Isaac Crows, and make their Report next Court of the same.

Ordered that William Turner be allowed out of the County fund $4 for wintering an Estray mare sold this Court.

Ordered that Isham Foster, Esq., proceed to sell an Estray Heifer posted before him, Taken up by William Turner.

Ordered that the Sheriff Employ Workmen to repair the Goal of this County in an complete manner for the use of Holding prisoners.

Ordered that Sheriff Miller be paid out of the County fund the sum of s 18 d 8 for 2 locks he found for the Goal of this County.

Ordered that the minutes be read which was done and signed by

William Smith, Isham Harrison, Judges. Court then adjourned untill Court in Course.

At a County Court of Sessions and pleas began to be Holden at the Court-House of Spartanburgh on the 17th (the 16th happening on Sunday) day of July 1797. Presents their Honours James Jordan & Isham Harrison, Esq.

The Court proceeded to drawn Jurors for next Court.

Grand Jurors for next Court.
William Poole, Taylor	1	Robert Sterling	11
Jonas Bruton	2	Alexr. Alexander	12
Burrel Bobo	3	John Anderson	13
Joroyal Barnett	4	James Mayes	14
William Pollard	5	John Cooper, Thickety	15
Thomas Beardan	6	Denny Anderson	16
John Barry	7	John Pennington	17
David Anderson	8	Samuel Snoddy	18
John Ross	9	Samuel Neasbitt	19
David Allen	10	Reuben Warren	20

Petit Jurors drawn for next Court
Benjamine Howard	1	James Moore	10
Thomas Woodruff	2	George McCarter	11
John Wells	3	Darby Turner	12
Thomas Westmoreland	4	Thomas Hughes	13
Obadiah Morse	5	Thomas Hadden	14
Nicholas Holley	6	Hance Harper	15
Thomas Murry	7	David McCarley	16
Joseph Morris	8	James Hickey	17
Joseph Hughes	9	Richard Traylor	18
Arnold Thomason	19	Richard Turner	25
William Traylor	20	Samuel Turner (P)	26
John Hammett	21	Lacey McAbee	27
Broadrick Mayson	22	Nathaniel McElrath	28
David Davis	23	William Towers	29
James McDowell	24	Henry Harden	30

Grand Jurors to serve this Court
Michael Miller	1	George Bruton	10
Samuel Neasbitt	2	Wells Griffith	11
Jesse Spencer	3	Benjamin Clarke	12
James Southerland	4	Robert Miller	13
Absalom Lancaster	5	Thomas Underwood	14
Jeroyal Barnett	6	Edmond Fowler	15
Berryman D. Shumate	7	Henry McCray, Esq.	16
William McDaniel	8	George Lamkin, Esq.	17
Alexander Alexander	9	John Trimmier	18

The Grand Jury being empannel'd & sworn Received their charge & retired to their Room.

Petit Jurors that appeared this Court
David Cook	1	James Peaks	12
John Brown	2	William Crocker	13
Aaron Bawcomb	3	John Cross	14
Henry Cannon	4	Joseph Venable	15
Richard Barry	5	William Bishop	16
Samuel Busey	6	Benjamin Arnold	17
Alexander Evins	7	Isaac Hamby	18
William Evatt	8	Abraham Andrews	19

Joseph Dill		9	Arias Brown		20
David Brown		10	Nathaniel Burton		21
Henry Harden		11			

Abraham Nott Esq. appointed to act as County Attorney this Court.

Petit Jurors drawn to serve this Court.

David Brown, Form.	1	Aaron Bawcomb		7
William Bishop	2	Joseph Dill		8
Abraham Andrews	3	Arias Brown		9
John Cross	4	William Crocker		10
Joseph Venable	5	William Evatt		11
James Keen	6	Nathaniel Burton		12

Mr. Henry Harden appeared to serve as a Petit Juror, but made his excuse to the Court which was heard, and was thereupon Exempted from the same.

The State against Margaret Dodds. Bastardy. The Defendant being fined by this Court produced a remitment of the same.

The State against Daniel White. Assault & Battery. The Defendant plead Guilty and throwed himself on the mercy of the Court, who fined him five shillings.

Stephen Heard, Esq., a practicing Attorney at Law & equity in this State, was admitted to practice the same in this Court.

George Lamkin Esq., vs Briant Bonner. Appeal. Dismissed.

John McClure against John McCarroll. Slander. Award returned and ordered to be dismissed at Defendant's Costs by his consent.

The Executors and Executrix of the last will and testament of Alexander Ray, Decd., sworn in open Court.

Ordered that Alexander Roddy, James Vernon & Alexander McCarter appraise the Estate of Alexander Ray, decd., and make due return thereof.

Ordered that that part of the Estate of Alexander Ray which is to be sold by virtue of his will be sold after giving 20 days notice at 12 months credit.

William Feals against William Ford. Writ. Case. Dismissed at Defendants costs by consent.

Ordered that the Minutes be Read which was done and signed by JamesJordan, Isham Harrison, Judges. Court then adjourned untill tomorrow 9 O'Clock.

Tuesday the 18th day of July 1797. The Court met according to adjournment, present their Honours James Jordan & Isham Harrison, Esq.

Waddy Thompson, Esq., is appointed to act as County attorney in the cases The state vs James Burnett and the State against John Elder, as the present County Attorney was employed in their behalf previous to his appointment.

John Cantwell against Henry McCray. Writ. Trover. Settled each party paying his own costs.

Nathaniel Wofford against William Vincent. Writ. Ordered that a commission issue to take the evidence of Giles Connell Junr. Debene Isse in writing to be read in evidence, provided the sd. evidence should not be in this State

The State against Mark Powell. Horse Stealing. Ordered that the Defendant & Surities be served with a rule to shew cause if any they have why Their recognizances should not be forfeited.

Jesse & Robert Rakestraw against James Smith. Writ. Assault. Came the parties by their Attorneys whereupon came a Jury, to wit, David Brown, foreman; William Bishop, Abraham Andrews, John Cross, Joseph Venable, James Kean, Aaron Bawcomb, Joseph Dill, Arias Brown, William Crocker, William Evatt and Nathaniel Burton, who being sworn on their several oaths do say We find for the plaintiff s 40 with costs of suit....

The State against Alexander Stewart. Assault & Battery. The Grand Jury returned a true Bill. Henry McCray, foreman.

Morris Veal against James Smith. Fieri Facias. Whereas a Fieri Facias issued in this case and the Court inhibited the Sheriff from proceeding thereon untill this present Term in order to obtain the opinion of the Judge of the Superior Court, and whereas Major William Smith who was to obtain the opinion of the Judge is absent. Ordered that the opinion of Mr. Smith be taken respecting the same and that Execution do cease or issue accordingly.

Casper C. Shute against Thomas Gore. Writ. Debt. The Defendants came into Open Court & confessed judgment for Ł 13 s 10 d 5 and costs of suit.

Thomas Richards & wife against James Beard & wife. Writ. Slander. By consent of the parties and assent of the Court, the trial of this cause is refered to George Bruton, Esq., Isaac Crow, Tobias Bright and Robert Rodgers with power of umpirage, their awards made and returned to next Court to be a judgment thereof.

Robert Elder came into open Court and acknowledged a Deed of Conveyance to James Crowther, Ordered to be recorded.

Betsy McBee against George Walker. Attachment. Decree for $23.43 with costs of suit.

Vardry McBee against Isaac Chapman. Writ. Case. By consent refered to the arbitrament of Obadiah Trimmier, Esq., and John Lipscomb with power of umpirage, their award returned to next Court to be a judgment thereof.

Edward Arnold against William Hendrix. Writ. Case. Dismissed at Defendant's costs.

Mr. Arias Brown a Juror empannelled to serve this Court, being taken very ill in health, was thereupon Exempted from serving as a petit Juror this Court, and Samuel Busey was drawn as a Tallied man to serve in his stead.

The State against John Elder. Indictment. Larceny. Came the parties by their attornies, whereupon came the Jury aforesaid, who being duly sworn on their oaths do saw, we find him not Guilty. David Brown, foreman. Ordered that the defendant and witnesses be discharged from their recognizances.

George Gordan & Co. against Benjamine Wofford. Appeal. Ordered that the judgment of the justice be confirmed.

Moses Hide against William Allen. Special Action. By consent refered to Messrs. Robert Foster and John Durham with power of umpirage their award returned to next Court to be a rule thereof.

Burrel Bobo against Moses Casey. Case. By consent of the parties and assent of the Court the trial of this cause is refered to the arbitrament of George Bruton, Esq., Rubin Dollar and Jesse Spann, their award made at the House of Isaac Crow on the last Saturday in August next, and returned to next Court ot be a rule thereof.

Ordered that the minutes be read, which was done and signed by James Jordan, & I. Harrison, Judges.

Wednesday the 19th day of July 1797. The Court met according to adjournment. Present their Honors James Jordan and Isham Harrison, Esq.

A deed of conveyance from Robert Miller to Samuel Miller, Esq., acknowledged in open Court.

Ordered that Captain William Anderson have license to retail spirituous liquors on giving William Wells and John Vaughn his surities for his Lawful performance.

Andrew Colley against John Bingham. Writ. By consent of the parties and assent of the Court, the trial of this cause is refered to the arbitrament of James Miller, George Kusee, James Logan, and John Gowen, with power of umpirage, their award made and returned to next Court, to be a judgment thereof.

Joel Hembree against Israel Credenton. Attachment. On motion of Plaintiff's attorney, ordered that this cause be continued untill next Court with a preemptory rule then to be tried.

William Thomson against Essix Capshaw. The Defendant, Essix Capshaw being call'd not appearing, Judgment was entered by default, whereupon a writ of Inquiry was executed and the Jury ...we find for the plaintiff $42.88 as principle & $3.69 interest.

The State against Richard Lee. Stealing Corn. Ordered that a Sciri Facias be issued against the defendant his surities in the above case to shew cause if any they have, why their recognizances should not be forfeited.

The State against Alexander Stewart. Assault. Abraham Nott, Esq., appearing in behalf of the State & the defendant by his attorney, whereupon came a jury....we find the defendant Guilty.

Ordered that Michael Miller be allowed out of the County fund, Ł 10 for repairing this County jail.

Robert Connell against John Robertson. Assault. Nonsuit.

Swanson Lansford against Benjamine Wofford. Writ. Debt. Ordered that a Dedimus potestatum issue in behalf of the defendant to the State of Georgia to take the examination of William Merchant.

George B. Moore against James Henderson. Case Nonsuit.

James Clerke against James Henderson. Case. Nonsuit.

John Stone against James Burns, Solomon Hill. Debt. Nonsuit.

The State against John Snowden & others. Larceny. The Grand Jury finding No Bill. Ordered that the be discharged from their recognizances.

The State against James Burnett. Larceny. The Grand Jury say a trule Bill. H. McCray, foreman.

The State against James Burnett. Larceny. Came the parites by their attornies, also a Jury...Guilty. We recommend him to the mercy of the Court. A motion was made for a new trial.

Nathaniel Henderson against John Spears. Petition. After an investigation of the matter by the attorney's of each party, the Court defered their judgment untill tomorrow.

George Roebuck against William Farrow. Special Action. Ordered that the last award be as a Judgment of this Court.

Joseph Gist admr. of Sarah Gist. against William Newman. Debt. On motion of plaintiff, Judgment was entered by default.

John Pepes against Henry Turner. Special Action. By consent of the parties & assent of the Court, the trial of this cause is refered to the Arbitrament of William T. Thomason, John Young, George Lamkin & Isham Foster, Esq., with power of Umpirage, their award returned to next Court, to be the judgment thereof.

Gustavus Boswell against William Chumley. Slander. Came the plaintiff by Zachariah Tolliaferro his attorney and the defendant by Samuel Farrow, Esq., his attorney, also came a Jury....We find for the plaintiff $21.45 and costs of suit.

The Last Will & Testament of Thomas McCrory decd. proven in open Court by the evidence of William Rodgers, who made oath that he saw the Testator Execute the same, and that he Robert Alexander & Elizabeth Hendrix were called on to witness the same. Laid over for further proof.

Jane McCrory, Executrix, Robert Rodgers, & Alexander Alexander Exrs. of the Estate of Thomas McCrory, decd., came into Court & took the necessary oaths of office accordingly.

Merrick Herrington as a witness in the case James Wofford against John Roebuck proved 5 days attendance at 2/6 per day & 48 miles at 4 pence per mile.

David Brock against Nicholas Murry. Petition. Decreed by the Court in favor of the plaintiff $21.45 with interest according to specialty & costs of suit.

John Bird against George Taylor. Attachment. Dismissed at the plaintiff's request.

Daniel McClaren against James Martin. Attachment. William Rickman being summoned as guarnishee came into Court and made oath that he was indebted to the defendant L 30 payable next Jan. and upon the merits of the cause a Jury was prayed.

Samuel Farrow Esq. attorney for James Flinn against John Wright. Debt. Settled by Instructions of the plaintiff.

Hannah Beshears against Daniel White. Assault. Dismissed at the defendants costs.

Wilie Williford against Isaac Beardan. Petition. Dismissed at the plaintiff's costs.

Gustavus Boswell against Jeremiah Wofford & Wife. Slander. Continued by affidavit of the plaintiff.

Mary Nealy against The Executors of James Miller decd. Appeal. Came the parties by their Attorneys and after an investigation of the matter, Ordered by the Court that the Judgment of the Justice be confirmed.

Ordered that the Estrays be sold Tomorrow at the adjournment of the Court.

Ordered that the minutes be read which accordingly done & signed by James Jordan, I. Harrison, Judges. Court then adjourned untill Tomorrow Nine O'Clock.

Thursday the 20th day of July 1797. The Honorable Court met according to adjournment. Present their Honors James Jordan & Isham Harrison, Esq.

A deed of conveyance from Justice Reynolds to Alexander Alexander acknowledged in open Court, Ordered to be recorded.

The State against Alexander Stewart. Assault. The defendant made oath that he was not worth s 5, therefore the Court proceeded to fine him, which they did in the sum of s 5.

Nathaniel Henderson against John Spears. Petition. Decree for the plaintiff for $18 with costs of suit.

The State against James Burnett. Larceny. A new trial prayed by the defendant's attorney, but was over-ruled by the Court.

James Mayes against Benjamin Bearden. Case. Came the plaintiff by Joseph Gist his attorney, and the defendant by Abraham Nott, Esq., his attorney, also came a Jury...We find $3 for Hundred for the Tobacco which is $15.03. David Brown, foreman....the plaintiff recover of the defendant the sum aforesaid agreeable to the Verdict of the Jury, but subject to the cost of s Petition and summons only.

Daniel McClaren against James Martin. Attachment. Decreed against the Defendant for $32.76 which is condemned in the hands of William Rickman, payable in Jan. next & costs of suit.

The State against Samuel Bruton. Larceny. Ordered that the rule to shew cause why their recognizance be forfeited be absolute.

The State against Mark Powell. Horse Stealing. Ordered that a Bench warrant issue to bring him to next Court.

John Bruister against William Rickman. Case. Ordered that a Commission issue to be evidence of Vardry McBee Debene Issee in writing to be read in evidence on trial, provided the said McBee shall be out of the limits of this State at the time of trial.

Philemon B. Waters against William Farrow. Case. Nonsuit.

Betsy McBee against George Taylor. Attachment. Captain Daniel McClaren as Guarnishee made oath that he was $6 indebted to the defendant payable in plank, which is condemned by the Court for the use of the plaintiff.

Ordered that Bazel Lee be paid out of the fines and forfeitures of this County by the Treasurer as soon as convenient the sum of L 5 s 1.

Ordered that a Bench Warrant issue against Arnold Thomason to appear next Court to answer to a charge presented by the Grand Jury.

Ordered that a Bench warrant issue against Edmund Fowler, William Bennett & William McWilliams to answer to a charge, presented by the Grand Jury for retailing spiritous liquors without license.

Betsy McBee against George Walker. Attachment. Ordered that Scire Facias issue against the Guarnishee who failed to appear, to shew cause why Judgment should not be entered against them.

The State against James Burnett. Larceny. The Court proceeded to pass sentence on the defendant, viz: that he be carried from that place & there receive at the common whipping post of this County, five lashes on his bare back, and then to be return'd to jail unless payment of costs for the Indictment is made, The sheriff reported to the Court that he had punctually inflicted the sentence of the Court on the defendant James Burns.

Absalom Stokes against James Henderson, David McDowell. Debt. Dismissed at the defendants costs, except the plaintiff's attornies fees.

Edmund Fowler and William McWilliams being presented by the Grand Jury came into Court with their surities to wit, Edmund Clemons, as Surity for Fowler and William Wells as Surity for McWilliams, who acknowledged themselves indebted to the State, to wit, the sd. principles in the sum of L 25 and the sd. surities L 12 s 10 each...if the said Fowler and McWilliams shall fail to appear when called on by the Court to answer the above charge.

Ordered that William Turner be allowed s 5 out of the County fund for wintereing an Estray Heifer taken up by him & toll'd before Isham Foster, Esq.

William Bennett as principle with Edmund Clemons as Surity came into Court and acknowledged themselves indebted to the State the sum of, to wit, the sd. principle L 25 and the sd. surity L 12 s 10...if the said Bennett shall fail to attend on this Court when called for to answer to a presentment of the Grand Jury.

Ordered that the minutes be read which was done & signed by I. Harrison, James Jordan, Judges. Court then adjourned untill Court in course.

January Session 1798

At a County Court of Sessions & pleas Held at Spartanburgh Courthouse the 12th day of Jan. 1798. Present their Honors James Jordan and Isham Harrison, Esq.

Grand Jurors drawn to serve next Court.

James Turner, Esq.	1	William McGowen	11
Jason Moore	2	David McDowell	12
Thomas Farrow, Esq.	3	John McCarter	13
John Woodruff	4	Thomas Price	14
Richard Thomson	5	Laurence Bankstone	15
Michael Wood	6	Henry Jameson	16
John Wood	7	Adam Sloan	17
Nathaniel Burton	8	David Golightly	18
James Smith, Capt.	9	Thomas Todd	19
David Tanner	10	Alexander Thomson	20

Petit Jurors drawn for next Court

John Nelson	1	Thomas Norton	16
James Brown	2	John Billiss	17
William Wofford	3	Job. Loftis	18
Samuel Prewit	4	John Stone	19
Isaac Wofford	5	Clayburn Johnson	20
Isaac Young	6	John Southerland	21
Alexander Autry	7	Samuel McClure	22
John Wilson	8	Jesse Shambling	23
Anthony Shands	9	Hugh Moore	24
Christopher Stone	10	William Gibson	25
Thomas Stroud	11	John Lee	26
Samuel Kithcart	12	William Stewart	27
Charles Cantrell	13	Drury Couch	28
William Lee	14	Matthew Sparks	29
James Sutton	15	Edward Stone	30

The following names are the persons impannelled and sworn to serve as Grand Jurors this Court.

William Poole, Taylor	1	John Anderson	11
Jonas Burton	2	John Cooper, Thickety	12
Burrel Bobo	3	John Pennington	13
Joroyal Barnett	4	Samuel Snody	14
William Pollard	5	Reubin Warren	15
Thomas Beardan	6		
John Barry	7		
David Anderson	8		
Robert Sterling, afirm'd	9		
Alexander Alexander	10		

Petit Jurors that appeared this Court

James Hickey	1	James Moore	10
Broadrick Mayson	2	Thomas Hughes	11
John Hammett Junr.	3	Nicholas Holley	12
Arnold Thomason	4	Thomas Westmoreland	13
Richard Traylor	5	Benjamine Howard	14
David McCarley	6	Thomas Woodruff	15
George McCarter	7	John Wells	16
Henry Harden	8	James McDowell	17
Darby Turner	9	Samuel Turner	18
		Richard Turner	19
		Nathaniel McElrath	20
		William Towers	21
		Lacy McAbee	22

Petit Jurors drawn to serve this Court

James Hickey	1	Arnold Thomason	7
Thomas Westmoreland	2	David McCarley	8
John Hammett Junr.	3	Broadrick Mayson	9

Darby Turner	4	John Wells	10
Thomas Woodruff	5	James Moore	11
Lacy McAbee	6	Henry Harden	12

Justice Reynolds against Solomon Hayes. Appeal. Ordered that the Judgment of the Justice be continued.

Matthias Rush against William Ford Junior. Petition. Settled by information Mr. Miller.

Andrew Colley against John Bingham. Case. Continued by consent of parties.

Hans Carr against John Sloan. on motion of Waddy Thomson, Esq., Ordered that the writ be amended.

William Ford Atty. for Edward Stewart against Thomas Davis. Case. Dismissed at mutual costs by consent.

Lewis Cockrell, being recommended by Isham Foster, Esq., to act as a constable for this County, he was approved of by the Court, and took the necessary oaths prescribed by Law for that office. Dismissed by consent.

Ordered that the minutes be read which was accordingly done & signed by James Jordan, I. Harrison, Judges. Court then adjourned untill To morrow Nine O'Clock.

Saturday the 13th of Jan. 1798. Court met according to adjournment. Present their Honors James Jordan & Isham Harrison, Esq.

William Venable against Robert McDowell. Petition. A Jury prayed, Therefore ordered that the cause stand over.

Thomas Gore against George Taylor. Case. Nonsuit.

Samuel Neasbitt as a grand juror, came into Court and qualified by affirmation.

Swanson Lansford against Benjamine Wofford. Capias. Case. Came the parties by their Attornies, whereupon came a jury, to wit, Broadrick Mayson, Thomas Westmoreland, John Hammett Junior, Darby Turner, Thomas Woodruff, Lacy McAbee, Arnold Thomason, David McCarlye, John Wells, George McCarter, Henry Harden & William Towers... We find for the plaintiff ₤ 12 with interest & costs of suit.   Broadrick Mayson, foreman.

William Hagan against Benjamine Wofford. for Rent. Nonsuit.

Isaac Hendrix against Ebenezer Morse. Ordered that the plaintiff give security for costs on Monday next or be nonprossed.

James Wofford against John Roebuck. Debt. Ordered that the cause be discontinued.

The Admrs. of John McElheny decd. against John Motlow & John Davis. Capias Debt.

Vardery McBee against Isaac Chapman. Capias. Nonsuit.

John Pipes against Hugh Thomson. Petition. By consent the trial of this cause is refered to the arbitrament of Alexander Copeland, Mr. Kizer, John Young Senior, Isham Foster Esq. & Maximilian Conner to be settled at the Boiling Springs next Saturday week, their award returned to next Court to be a rule thereof.

Gustavus Baswell against Jeremiah Wofford. Slander. Continued by affidavit of the defendant.

The State against Jacob Casey. Assault & Battery. The Grand Jury say "A true Bill." David Anderson, foreman.

The State against Jacob Casey. Assault & battery. The defendant by Samuel Farrow Esq. his attorney plead guilty to the indictment & threw himself upon the mercy of the Court, who proceeded to fine him $4.

Charles Bruce against William Crane. Petition. Dismissed at the defendants costs by consent.

Ordered that the minutes be read which was done & signed by James Jordan, I. Harrison, Judges. Court then adjourned until Monday 10 O'Clock.

Monday the 15th of Jan. 1798. Court met according to adjournment Present their Honors James Jordan & Isham Harrison, Esqs.

Ordered that the Court be adjourned untill Tomorrow ten O'Clock.

Tuesday the 16th of Jan. 1798. Court met according to adjournment. Present their Honors James Jordan & Isham Harrison, Esqs.

A Deed of Conveyance from David Quarles to John Harris, acknowledged in open Court ordered to be recorded.

Michael McElrath came into Court and acknowledged that he hath received the Estate in full out of the hands of Samuel Neasbitt, and John McElrath his guardian.

Ordered that Anthony Foster have license to retail spirituous liquors upon giving Samuel Lancaster & Brittain Williford his surities for his lawful performance.

The sale and statement of the Estate of Henry Hargrove decd. returned by the Executors.

John Pipes against Henry Turner. Case. Ordered that a commission Dedimus potestatum issue to North Carolina,   County to Examine Dempson Crane in behalf of the plaintiff, giving legal notice.

John Jackson against The admrs. of Samuel Jackson, decd. Case. Ordered that a commission issue to the State of North Carolina Rutherfordton (sic) County to take the Examination of Charles Richardson & Joseph Moore, also that the evidence of John McGore Debene isse in writing be taken in evidence, provided he is removed without the limits of this State at next Court.

Ordered that Bernard William Sweny have license to retail spiritous liquors upon giving William Wells & Jeremiah Selman his surities for his lawful performance.

Ordered that Jacob Woodruff have license to retail spirituous liquors upon giving John Williams & Absalom Lancaster his surities for his lawful performance.

Samuel Hampton & James Matthews against Justice Reynolds. Debt. Came Abraham Nott, Esq. in behalf of the plaintiff and Zachariah Tolliaferro attorney & for the defendant also came a jury, to wit (same as before)...we find for the plaintiff ₤72 s 11 d 9¾ with interest & costs....

William Venable against Robert McDowell. Petition. Continued by consent of parties.

A deed of conveyance from Benjamine Wofford to William Earnest, acknowledged in open Court, Ordered to record.

A deed of conveyance from Benjamine Wofford to William Earnest, acknowledged in open Court, Ordered to record.

Samuel Lowrie Esq. against Nevil Wayland. Petition. Nonsuit.

Joel Hembree against Israel Credenton. Attachment. Continued by consent.

James Neasbitt against John Cooper. Special Action. Dismissed by order of Court.

John Pipes against Henry Turner. Special Action. Ordered that this cause be continued under a former rule of reference.

Moses Hide against William Allen. Special Action on the case. An award being returned Ordered to be recorded...in persuance of a rule of the Honorable Court of Spartanburgh, directed to Robert Foster, and John Durham to arbitrate...between Moses Hide and William Allen with power of umpirage, Now know ye that I Andrew Barry, Umpire, indifferent chosen by the said Robert Foster and John Durham, have heard....each of the said parties shall pay & bear his own costs & charges...the sd. William Allen shall deliver or cause to be delivered to the sd. Moses Hide a certain note of hand signed by the sd. Hide for a cow which note is now in possession of sd. Allen, and the sd. Allen shall on or before 1 Jan. next pay to Moses Hide s 14...30 July 1797.

Ordered that Richard Lee be taken into Custody by the Sheriff & there be kept untill he give surity for his appearance when called for to the County Court of Spartanburgh to answer to a presentment of the Grand Jury for stealing a Bagg of wheat.

Ordered that that part of the Estate of William Wood Esq. decd. be sold by the Executor, which hath note yet been sold after giving 20 days notice at 12 months credit.

The State against Richard Lee. Stealing Corn. Abraham Nott, Esq., appearing in behalf of the State and Mr. Gist & Earrow as as Attornies in behalf of the defendant, whereupon came a Jury, to wit, (same as before)...Not Guilty.

Samuel Lancaster Esq. against John Wofford. On an appeal. The Court defered givint their opinion untill Tomorrow.

The State against John Huckeby. Corn Stealing. The defendant is discharged by order of Court.

Ordered that the Estrays be sold Tomorrow Evening.

Ordered that the Minutes be read, which was accordingly done & signed by James Jordan, I. Harrison, Judges. Court then adjourned untill tomorrow nine O'Clock.

Wednesday the 17th of Jan. 1798. Court met according to adjournment. Present their Honors James Jordan & Isham Harrison, Esqs.

Hampton & Matthews against Justice Reynolds. Debt. The defendant agreed to stay Execution 8 months.

Burrell Bobo against Moses Casey. Case. Continued by order of Court.

George Lamkin Esq. against Drewry Scruggs. Appeal. Dismissed at the appellant's costs by consent.

Ordered that Jonathan Harris have license to retail spirituous liquors upon giving Joel Hembree & William Rickman Surities for his lawful performance.

William Smith & George Bruton Esq. exrs. of Samuel Morrow decd. against Jason Moore. Case. Mr. Nott appeared in behalf of the plaintiffs & Samuel Farrow Esq. in behalf of the defendant a Jury being sworn the plaintiffs' Attorney suffered a Nonsuit.

A deed of conveyance from Vardery McBee to James Wofford, assignee of William Wofford acknowledged in open Court, Ordered to be recorded.

Joroyal Barnett against Moses Timmons & Daniel Carmichael. Debt. Came the plaintiff by Mr. Farrow his attorney, the deft. by Mr. Thomson, his Attorney, whereupon came a Jury (same as before)... we find for the plaintiff ₤ 17 s 8 d 10 with interest & costs of suit.

David Goodlett Esq. as a witness in the suit Joroyal Barnett against Moses Timmons and Daniel Carmichael on oath in open Court is allowed s 12 d 6 for 5 days attendance also 60 miles at 2 pence per mile coming from Greenville County.

Daniel McClaren against William Rickman. Debt. This action being brought for debt, Ordered that the writ be amended from that of a debt to that of promises & assumptions.

Ordered that a Bench Warrant issue commanding the Sheriff to take Charles Morgan, William Morgan, Bridges Arnold & Reader Arnold & keep them in his custody unless they give him good surities for their appearance to next July Court to answer to a presentment of the Grand Jury for falling timber across a Road from near Jonathan Harris' House to the Cherokee ford on Broad River.

Daniel McClaren against William Rickman. Writ. Debt. Came the parties by their Attornies, whereupon came a Jury (same as before) ...We find for the defendant costs of suit....

John Spear against Israel Credenton. Petition. Ordered that this cause be discontinued.

Alexander McBeth against John Elder. Case. The defendant being called and not appearing by himself nor his Attorney, on motion of Mr. Nott, attorney for the Plaintiff, judgment was thereupon entered by default.

Richard Harris against Benjamine Turner. Assault. The defendant being called, not appearing in his own person, nor by his attorney, on motion of Mr. Nott, attorney for the plaintiff, Judgment was thereupon entered by default.

Richard Harris against Benjamine Turner. Assault. The defendant being called, not appearing in his own person, nor by his attorney, judgment was thereupon entered by default.

William Bennett against Daniel Carmichael. Attachment. The defendant not appearing in his own person, nor by his Attorney, judgment was thereupon entered by default, and ordered by the Court, that the property attached be sold, subject to the plaintiff's demands.

Noel Hammon against Moses Hide. Attachment. Ordered that the property attached be sold by the officer subject to the plaintiff's demands.

Moses Timmons against Daniel Carmichael. Attachment. Ordered that the property attached be sold subject to the plaintiff's demands.

George Gibson proved 4 days attendance as a witness in the case Nathaniel Wofford against William Vincent, at two shillings & six pence per day.

Ordered that Isham Foster Esq. be allowed out of the County fund $2 for making out the Jury list for tickets to regulate the Jurors for this County.

William Hagan against Benjamine Wofford. Destrain for Rent. Ordered that Execution issue for Ł 15 agreeable to destrain & costs.

Ordered that Execution be detained from issuing in the case the State against William Smith for Ł 5 witherein James Smith, James Hickey were surities, untill July Court next.

William Thomson against Hugh Moore. Case. Ordered that the evidence of Vardry McBee be taken Debene isse in writing to be read in evidence on trial, provided the said Mc Bee shall not reside within the limits of this State at the time of trial.

David Childers proved 3 days attendance as a witness in the case Isaac Hendrix against Ebenezer Morse.

Barnet Dempsy also proved 3 days attendance in the same aforesaid case.

Samuel Lancaster Esq. against John Wofford. Appeal. The Court defered giving their judgment untill next Court.

Charles Burton against Brittain Williford. Certiorari. Ordered that a writ of Certiorari issue against Colo. Thomas Moore, George Bruton & zadock Ford, Esq. to certify up to this Court, their proceedings as Justices of the peace in said case.

Ordered that the Clerk & Sheriff have the liberty of furnishing themselves with an office under the two Jury rooms of this Court-House, by raising the Court-House & cutting away therein to affect the same to purpose, also to build a chimney thereto & every other thing necessary, the Court agreeing to be at equal expense with the clerk & sheriff in accomplishing the same.

Ordered that the County Treasurer put the law in force to collect such debts due to him by virtue of his office, which have been two years standing.

Daniel McClaren against William Rickman. Debt. Ordered that the motion for a new trial be continued untill next Court, upon the plaintiff paying the present costs before he leaves Court.

Ordered that the minutes be read which was accordingly done & signed by James Jordan, I. Harrison, Judges. Court then adjourned untill Court in course.

At a County Court of Sessions and Pleas began and held at the Court-House of Spartanburgh on Monday the 16th day of July 1798. Present their Honors James Jordan, and Isham Harrison, Esq.

The Court proceeded to draw the Grand Jurors for next Court, to wit:

David White	1	Obadiah Trimmier, Esq.	11	
John Underwood	2	Joseph Collins	12	
Clayburn Johnson	3	Benjamine McMekin	13	
George Kizie	4	Penuel Wood	14	
Moses Timmons	5	James Finley	15	
George Connell	6	Richard Venable	16	
James Morse	7	Joseph Wofford	17	
Thomas Moore, Esq.	8	Samson Bobo	18	
John Snody	9	Bazel Trail	19	
Samuel Morrow	10	John King	20	

Petit Jurors drawn for next Court

Charles Morgan	1	Mason Cannon	16	
Robert Wood, Tyger	2	Benjamine Waldrope	17	
Buckner Smith	3	Elijah Thomson	18	
Daniel White	4	Dennis Sullivan	19	
John Beard	5	William Casey	20	
Jason Moore	6	*Nathan Ward, Junr.	22	
Jordan Gibson	7	Ambrose Dollar	23	
James Johnson	8	Liffert French	24	
John Morrow	9	James Lee	25	
William Stone	10	Nathaniel Young	26	
James Oats	11	George Devine	27	
Robert Kimbell	12	Thomas Kimbol	28	
Aaron Templeton	13	Randolph Johnson	29	
John Waldrope	14	Warrington Spiller	30	
Thomas Cook	15	*James Dewberry	21	

Ordered that the admrs. of the Estate of Jesse Chamblin decd. proceed to the sale of the same after giving 20 days public Notice, at 12 months credit for all sums above $4, all others to be paid at the time of sale.

Grand Jurors drawn & impanneled to serve this Court

James Turner, Esq.	1	David McDowell	8	
John Wofford, Affd.	2	Thomas Price	9	
Richard Thomson	3	Laurens Bankstone	10	
John Wood	4	Henry Jameson, Affd.	11	
Nathaniel Burton	5	Adam Sloan	12	
David Tanner	6	David Golightly, Forn.	13	
William McGowen	7	Alexander Thomson	14	

Petit Jurors to serve this Court

Samuel Prewit	1	Samuel Kithcart	7	
Christopher Stone	2	Matthew Sparks	8	

William Lee	3	James Brown	9
William Gibson	4	Isaac Wofford	10
Alexander Autry	5	Drewry Couch	11
John Stone	6	William Wofford	12

Graff Edson & Co. against Joel Hembree. Petition. The defendant came into Court & confessed judgment for ₤ 3 s 17 with stay of execution 3 months.

Thomas Richard & wife against James Beard & wife. Slander. Dismissed at plaintiff's costs by award.

Ordered that Isaac Crow have license for keeping tavern on giving Joseph Woodruff & Brittain Williford his surities, for his lawful performance.

John Montgomery against Alexander Roddy. Case. Ordered that this cause be dismissed.

Gustavus Boswell against Jeremiah Wofford & wife. Slander. Dismissed at defendant's costs by consent.

Ordered that the minutes be read which were accordingly done & signed by James Jordan, I. Harrison, Judges. Court then adjourned untill Tomorrow Nine O'Clock.

Thursday the 17th day of July 1798. Court met according to adjournment. Present their Honors. James Jordan & Isham Harrison, Esq.

Ordered that Matthias Rush have license to keep Tavern on giving James Ward & Bernard William Sweny his Surities for his lawful performance.

Ordered that John James have license to keep Tavern upon giving James Ward & B. Wm. Sweny his Surities for his lawful performance.

Joel Hembree against Israel Credenton. Attachment. Continued upon the affidavit of the defendant.

John Pipes against Henry Turner. Special Action. Ordered that this cause be continued.

Burrel Bobo against Moses Casey. Case. Came the plaintiff by Zachariah Tolliaferro, Esq. his attorney, and the defendant by Samuel Farrow his attorney, whereupon came a Jury, to wit, Isaac Wofford, Samuel Prewit, William Lee, William Gibson, Alexander Autry, Samuel Kithcart, Matthew Sparks, James Brown, Drewry Couch, William Wofford, Isaac Young & John Nelson who being sworn... We find for the plaintiff ₤ 3 s 9 d 4 and costs of suit. Isaac Wofford, foreman....

Isaac Hendrix against Ebenezer Morse. Petition. The Court postponed their decision untill a future period.

Andrew Colley against John Bingham. Case. By consent of the parties and assent of the Court, the trial of this cause is refered to the Arbitrament of William Walton & James Logan with power of Umpirage, their award to be a rule of Court.

Maximilian Conner against John Cantrell. Case. The trial of this cause is refered to the arbitrament of Isham Foster, Esq. & James Smith, with power of Umpirage, their award to be a rule of

Court.

James Henderson against Jacob Knight. Assault. Dismissed at mutual costs by consent.

Brittain Williford against Charles Burton. Appeal from Justices Below. The Court postponed their decision untill they meet To morrow.

The State against Richard Lee. Confind. The surities gave up the prisoner, therefore ordered that he be committed to Goal & there to continue untill he be thence delivered by a due course of Law.

Ordered that Benjamine McMekin be allowed out of the County funds 7 for an Estray stear, toll'd before James Jordan, Esq.

Ordered that the minutes be read which was accordingly done & signed by James Jordan, I. Harrison, Judges. Court then adjourned untill tomorrow 9 O'Clock.

Wednesday the 18th day of July 1798, Court met according to adjournment. Present their Honors James Jordan & Isham Harrison, Esqs.

William Milikin a poor boy appearing to the Court with sufficient testimony that he is of the age of 21 years, Therefore ordered that he be examined from his Indentureship also that Robert Goodlett appear at the next Intermediate Court to shew that he hath complyed with his obligations concerning said Boy.

William Webster against Alexander McKie & Richard Thomson. Case. Nonsuit.

Brittain Williford against Charles Burton. Appeal. The Court having postponed their opinion untill today, Now Ordered that the judgment of the Justices below be reversed.

Ordered that Andrew Barry act as Guardian for James Barry minor, and son of John Barry deceased, and that said Andrew Barry give a Bond with two good surities for the safety of the said minors property.

John Bruister against William Rickman. Case. Nonsuit.

Graff Edson & Co. against Henry McCray, Esq. Debt. Came the parties by their attornies, whereupon came a Jury (same as before)...we find for Defendant. Isaac Wofford, foreman.

William Thomson against Hugh Moore. Case. Came the parties by their councellors, also a Jury (same as before)...we find for the plaintiff $140 & costs of suit....

Samuel Lancaster, Esq. against John Wofford. Appeal. Decreed by the Court that the Judgment of the Justice be reversed.

William Thomson against Hugh Moore. Case. Waddy Thomson, Esq., attorney for the deft. objected to the Instrument of writing on which the suit was brought, going to the Jury, after they were sworn.

Ordered that Henry McCray Esq. proceed to sell an Estray steer toll'd before him by Obadiah Trimmier, Esq.

Nathaniel Wofford against William Vincent. Special Action. Came the plaintiff by Samuel Farrow Esq. his attorney and the defendant by Zachariah Tolliaferro, Gentl. his attorney, whereupon came a Jury...The Jury did not make up their Verdict today.

Ordered that the overseers of the Road from this Court-House to Jamies Creek appear at the next Intermediate Court to shew cause why the same is not kep in good repair they being presented by the Grand Jury.

Ordered that Joel Pearson & William Pearson be taken by the Sheriff and carried before some Justice & there give their recognizance for their good behaviour as they were presented by the Grand Jury.

George Gibson proved 7 days attendance as a witness in the case Nathaniel Wofford against William Vincent.

Charles Bruce against Ebenezer Morse. Petition. Settled at mutual costs by consent.

James Beard & wife against James Wofford. Special Action. Nonsuit.

James Beard & wife against James Wofford & wife. Special Action. Nonsuit.

William Venable against Robert McDowell. Petition. Ordered that this cause continue at the plaintiff's costs, and that a commission dedimus potestatum issue to the State of North Carolina, Rutherfordton County, to examine Thomas Liles in behalf of the plaintiff upon his giving 10 days notice to the adverse party of the time & place of examination.

John D. Young against William S. Wilson. Petition. Settled at the defendant's costs.

Ordered that the Estrays lyable for sale be sold by the Sheriff tomorrow at the adjournment of Court.

Ordered that the minutes be read which was accordingly done & signed by James Jordan, I. Harrison, Judges. Court then adjourned untill Tomorrow Nine O'Clock.

Thursday the 19th day of July 1798. The Honorable Court met according to adjournment. Present their Honors James Jordan & Isham Harrison, Esq.

Nathaniel Wofford against William Vincent. Special Action. The Jury not making up their Verdict while the Court say yesterday this morning returned the same...we find for the defendant...

James Synyard against Nathaniel Henderson. Appeal. Ordered that Moses Casey the justice before whom the cause was tried, appear at next Court to shew cause why he did not grant an appeal, and also certify up to this Court his proceedings in said case.

William Venable against Robert McDowell. Petition. Refered by consent to the arbitrament of Berryman D. Shumate, Esq., George Kezie, Isham Foster, Esq., & Hugh Stephenson, their award to be a rule of Court.

Isaac Hendrix against Ebenezer Morse. Petition. The Court proceeded to give their decree today for Ł 8 s 17 d 4 equal to $38 & costs of suit.

John Wn. Calhoun against Benjamine Wofford. Debt. Came the plaintiff by his Attorney and the defendant by Mr. Gist his Attorney, whereupon came a Jury (same as before)...we find for the plaintiff Ł 11 s 9 d 4 and interest for Ł 8 s 5 d 4 from the date of the writ....

Samuel Lowrie Esq. against Hugh Stevenson. Petition. Ordered that the plaintiff give security for costs in time of this Court or be nonprossed, and that the cause be no more on this docket.

Noel Hammon against Moses Hide. Attachment. Ordered that this cause continue at the defendant's costs.

John Jackson against Thomas Jackson and James Jackson Admrs. of Samuel Jackson, decd. Case. Came the plaintiff by Samuel Farrow and Joseph C. Gist, gentlemen, his attornies, and the defendant by Mess. Nott & Thomson Esq. their attornies, also a Jury ...we find for the defendant....

John James against John D. Young. Debt. Ordered that this cause be continuec on an affidavit of the defendant.

John Sloan proved 2 days attendance as a witness in the case, James Henderson against Arias Brown and Isaac Pace.

Noel Hammon against Moses Hide. Attachment. Dismissed at the defendant's costs upon the plaintiff paying his own witness & the justices' fee with staying execution 1 month.

Ordered that the minutes be read which was accordingly done & signed by James Jordan, I. Harrison, Judges. Court then adjourned untill Tomorrow Nine O'Clock.

Friday the 20th of July 1798. Court met according to adjournment.

Isaac Hendrix against Ebenezer Morse. Petition. Mortion for a new trial overruled.

Samuel Farrow Esq. assignee of Zebulon Bragg against Allen Gentry. Debt. The defendant being called and not appearing in his own person nor by his Attorney, on motion of Joseph C. Gist., Esq., attorney for the plaintiff, judgment was thereupon entered by default.

Samuel Lowrie Esq. against Hugh Stepheonson. Petition. Dismissed by request of Mr. Gist., attorney for the plaintiff.

William McGowen against George Gibson. appeal. Ordered that this case be remanded to the Justice from whence it came upon payment of costs.

L. & W. Wilson against Jacob Casey. Petition. Decree for the plaintiff for Ł 8 s 16 d 7 & costs of suit.

Obadiah Watson against John Lancaster & Absalom Lancaster. Case Nonsuit.

Daniel McClaren against William Rickman. Case. Motion for a new trial overruled.

Henry Eyres against Joshua Downs & William Wells. Debt. Judgment confessed by William Wells according to Specialty the note being for ₤ 18 s 9 d 5 bearing date 23 Jan. 1796 on demand the 1st day of March 1796 and costs of suit.

John Woodruff against Daniel Bragg. Special Action. Came the plaintiff by Samuel Farrow Esq. his attorney, and the defendant by Waddy Thomson, Gent., his attorney, whereupon came a Jury, (same as before)...it is considered by the Court that the sd. defendant recover of the plaintiff his costs in this suit....

Hans Carr against John Sloan. Trover. Ordered that one or more commissions issue to the State of North Carolina, County to examine certain evidence in the above case, on behalf of the Defendant.

Richard Harris against Benjamine Turner. Assault & Battery. On executing a writ of Inquiry, the jry...do say We find for the plaintiff ₤ 5 damage and costs of suit....

George Gordan & Co. against William Wilder and George Divine. Debt. Came the parties by their attornies, also came a Jury... we find for the plaintiff ₤ 13 s 9 d 4 agreeable to note with interests and costs of suit.

Richard Barry assignee of Obadiah Watson against Moses Timmons. Debt. The parties appeared by their attornies, also a Jury... we find for the plaintiff $100 with interest and costs of suit.

David Goodlett Esq. of Greenville County, proved 7 days attendance as a witness in the case Richard Barry assignee of Obadiah Watson against Moses Timmons, and s 20 for mileage.

William Robertson against George Thomason. Slander. By consent of the parties and assent of this Court, the trial of this cause is refered to Thomas Moore and Berryman D. Shumate, Esqs., Gentlemen, Arbitrators with power of Umpirage, their award returned to next Court to be a Rule thereof.

Isham Foster, Esq.,as a witness in the case of Richard Barry, assignee of Obadiah Watson, against Moses Timmons, on oath in open Court was allowed s 12 d 6 for 5 days attendance.

Nathaniel Wofford against William Vincent. Special Action. Motion for a new trial overruled.

Robert Abanatha against Robert West. Debt. On motion of Waddy Thomson, Esq., attorney for the plaintiff, Ordered that this cause be dismissed at the defendant's costs.

Ordered that all notes in the hands of the County Treasurer which have been due 12 months, be called by the Treasurer as quick as possible.

Ordered that Captain James Smith have credit for $6 on a fine of ₤ 5 against William Smith for which he the said James Smith is responsible & that he have indulgence untill next Jan. Court for the Balance.

Bazel Lee as a witness in the case of Obadiah Watson against John Lancaster & Absalom Lancaster on oath is allowed s 5 for 2 days attendance.

Ordered that Bazel Lee be paid out of the County fund Instead of the fines & forfeitures agreeable to a former order for Guarding the Goal of this County.

Ordered that the minutes be read which was accordingly done and signed by James Jordan, I. Harrison, Judges. Court then adjourne untill Court in course.

At a County Court of Sessions and Pleas began to be Holden at the Court House of Spartanburgh County on the 12th day of Jan. 1799. Present their Honors James Jordan & Isham Harrison, Esq.

The Court proceeded to draw Grand Jurors for next Court.

David Jones	1	Joseph Barnett	11
James Keen	2	William Gray	12
Shands Golightly	3	John Turner	13
Charles Hester	4	Samuel Jameson	14
John Westmoreland	5	John Posey	15
Adam Kilby	6	John Wright	16
Jacob Utley	7	John Williams	17
John Barnett	8	Thomas Underwood	18
Osburn West	9	Stephen Wilson	19
John James	10	Landon Farrow	20

Petit Jurors drawn for next Court

Flemming Smith	1	Isaac Cooper	16
John Shippy	2	Alexander Keeler	17
Jesse Temple	3	William Rodgers	18
Thomas Stone	4	John Lynch	19
John Beardan	5	Daniel Rodgers	20
Solomon Crocker	6	William Lemaster	21
John Beard, Cr.	7	Benjamine Cantrell	22
(Blank)	8	John King	23
William Bramlet	9	James Hadden	24
David Allen Junr.	10	John Miller	25
Abraham Moore	11	John Law	26
James Timmons	12	Richard Harris	27
Shadrack Waldrope	13	Samuel Miller	28
John Bennett	14	James Wofford	29
Charles Holt	15	Nathaniel Hamby	30

A deed of conveyance from Samuel Miller, Esq. to Alexander McKie acknowledged in open Court Ordered to be recorded.

Ordered that Alexander McKie be allowed out of the County fund the sum of s 18 for keeping Estrays and John Bingham in Goal.

William Smith against Thomas and David Quarles. Debt. Settled at defendant's costs.

George Lamkin Esq. against John Beckham. Ordered that the Judgment of the Justice be confirmed.

Ordered that the residue of the Estate of Alexander Ray, decd. be sold at 12 months credit after giving 20 days legal notice all sums under s 10 to be paid down.

George Lamkin Esq. being reappointed to act as a Justice of the peace in this County came into Court and took the necessary oaths prescribed by Law.

Alexander Thomson took the necessary oaths as a Constable to act in the County before James Jordan, Esq.

William T. Thomason was qualified according to Law to act as a constable for this County.

Ordered that the minutes be read, which was accordingly done & signed by I. Harrison, James Jordan, Judges. Court then adjourned untill Monday nine O'Clock.

Jan. 14th 1799. Court met according to adjournment. Present their Honors James Jordan & Isham Harrison, Esq.

Justice Reynolds against Samuel Farrow, Esq. Appeal Ordered that the Judgment of the Justice be confirmed.

Andrew McMullen came into Court and took the necessary oaths of office as a Constable to act in this County.

Petit Jurors that appeared this Court.
Charles Morgan	1	Thomas Cook	10
Robert Wood	2	Mason Cannon	11
Daniel White	3	Benjamine Waldrope	12
John Beard	4	James Dewberry	13
Buckner Smith	5	Nathan Ward Junr	14
James Johnson	6	James Lee	15
James Ottis	7	Thomas Kimbell	16
Robert Kimbell	8	Randolph Johnson	17
John Waldrope	9	Warrington Spiller	18

Petit Jurors drawn to serve this Court.
John Waldrope	1	Thomas Cook	7
Nathan Ward	2	James Ottis	8
Randolph Johnson	3	Robert Wood, forem.	9
Warrington Spiller	4	Charles Morgan	10
John Beard	5	Robert Kimbell	11
Thomas Kimbell	6	Daniel White	12

Ebenezer Morse against Isaac Hendrix. Attachment. Joseph Woodruff came into Court and acknowledged himself indebted to said plaintiff Ł 30 to be paid the sd. plaintiff on condition the sd. Woodruff shall fail to pay any Judgment that sd. Morse shall recover in the sd. case. Ordered that the Sheriff pay the money in his hands by virtue of the attachment to Mr. Joseph Woodruff.

Alexander Alexander against John Tucker. Writ. Settled at equal costs by consent.

Richard Tolliaferro Esq. against George Taylor. Attachment. Came the parties by their Attornies and the Guranishee Mr. Sion Cooper being sworn, declared that he was indebted to George Taylor the absentee in two notes of hand, one dated 23 Sept. 1796, the other 24 Sept. 1796, one payable 25 Dec. 1797 the other 26 Dec 1797, for 1000 weight of merchantable Tobacco each, which the Court valued at $4 pr. Ct. Ordered that the property attached be condemned in the hands of the Guarnishee subject to the plaintiff's demand, also Moses Guiton being sworn as a Guarnishee, acknowledged himself to be Indebted to the Absent Debtor Ł 20 to be discharged in trade, also the balance which is in his hands made subject to the same demand.

A Bill of Sale from Margaret McCarter to Alexander McCarter acknowledged before James Jordan, Esq. ordered to be recorded.

A Bill of sale from Margaret McCarter and Matilda McCarter to Mary McCater acknowledged before James Jordan, Esq., Ordered to be recorded.

Mr. Abraham Nott came into open Court and resigned the office of County Attorney, whereupon Waddy Thomson Esq. was appointed.

William Crow against Ebenezer Morse & Mason Foley. Assault & Battery. Settled at equal costs by consent.

Ordered that Thomas Miles have the full admn. of the Estate of Zebulon Bragg decd. upon signing a Bond for that purpose.

John Lipscomb and Aaron Casey being reappointed as Justices of the peace for this County came into Court & took the necessary oaths of their office, prescribed by Law.

William Austell being appointed to act as a Constable for this County, came into Court & took the necessary oaths prescribed by Law.

Ordered that the minutes be read, which was done & signed by James Jordan, I. Harrison, Judges. Court then adjourned untill Tomorrow Nine O'Clock.

Friday the 15th Jan. 1799. Court met according to adjournment. Present their Honors James Jordan, and Isham Harrison, Esqs.

Drewry McDaniel, James Hooper and John Anderson, Esqs. being appointed to act as Justices of the peace in this county came into Court and took the necessary oaths prescribed by Law.

Ebenezer Morse against Isaac Hendrix. Attachment. Mr. Brittain Williford being sworn as guarnishee declares that he had at the time of the attachment being leveyed in his hands $£$ 8 s 16 d 4 of the defendants money, Ordered that it be condemned in his hands subject to a Judgment which the plaintiff may recover hereafter.

Thomas Cook being drawn yesterday to serve as a petit Juror & failing to appear to day, James Dewberry was drawn to serve in his stead.

Joel Hembree against Israel Credenton. Attachment. A bond in this case having never been returned to the Clerk, Ordered that a nonsuit take place, also ordered that the money in the hands of the sheriff arising from the sale of the defendant's property which was attached be returned to said Defendant or his Attorney of record.

Andrew Colley against John Bingham. Case. Came the parties by their attornies, whereupon came a Jury (same as on p. 359)... we find for the plaintiff $£$ 20 bearing interest from date 1783 with costs of suit. Robert Wood, foreman....

James Henderson against Isaac Pace and Arias Brown. Special Action. Dismissed each party paying his own costs by consent.

Zadock Ford and Berryman D. Shumate being appointed to act as Justices of the peace in this County, came into Court and took the necessary oaths prescribed by Law.

Arias Brown being appointed to act as a Constable for this County, came into Court and took the necessary oaths of office prescribed by Law.

Alexander McKie and William Thomson came into Court with Major John Gowen and Capt. Daniel McClaren, who acknowledged themselves indebted to the State of S. C. to wit, sd. McKie & Thomson Ł 100 each, and the sd. surities Ł 50 each...that they keep the peace and behaviour to all the good people of the State, and especially to Justice Reynolds for the term of 1 year....
Signed in presence of Jno. Lancaster.

Jno Pipes against Henry Turner. Special Action. Came the parties by their Attornies, also came a Jury, but the plaintiff's attorney chose to suffer a nonsuit rather than leave the trial of the cause to the Jury.

James Southerland against William Parks. Slander. Dismissed at the defendant's costs.

Samuel Lancaster Esq. being reappointed to act as a Justice of the peace for this County, came into Court and took the necessary oaths prescribed by Law.

Thomas Miles came into Court and took the oath of Admr. on the Estate of Zebulon Bragg, decd.

Ordered that William Wilder, Spencer Bobo, Peter Penial appraise the estate of Zebulon Bragg, decd., and make due return thereof.

Nathaniel Henderson against Moses Casey, Esq. Sciri Facias. Mr. Casey, the defendant came into Court and gave satisfaction to the Court, why he did not grant the appeal for which he was cited. Therefore ordered that he be dismissed from the same.

A deed of conveyance from William Wood to Reubin Lissenby proven in open Court by the evidence of William Pearson, Ordered to be recorded.

Ordered that the minutes be read, which was done & signed by I. Harrison, James Jordan, Judges. Court then adjourned untill Tomorrow Nine O'Clock.

Wednesday the 16th day of Jan. 1799. Court met according to adjournment. Present their Honors James Jordan & Isham Harrison, Esqs.

Henry McCray and William McDowell Esqs. being reappointed to act as Justice of the peace in this County came into Court and took the necessary oaths prescribed by Law.

George Bruton Esq. being appointed to act as a Justice of the peace in this County, took the necessary oaths of office prescribed by Law, before James Jordan, Esq.

John Trimmier being appointed to act as a Constable in this County, came into Court and took the necessary oaths prescribed by Law for that office.

Ebenezer Morse against Isaac Hendrix. Attachment. On motion of Samuel Farrow Attorney for the defendant that the attachment be quashed, because the same was issued when the defendant was absent from the State and not removing or about to remove, as is the digest of laws, page 366, The plaintiff praying a Jury, Ordered that they proceed to trial.

John Taylor, Esq. a practicing attorney at Law in this State, being recommended to and approved of by this Court,Ordered that he be enrolled with the other practicing attornies to practice law in this Court.

Bazel Lee as a Constable for this County came into Court and took the necessary oaths of office prescribed by Law.

Maximilian Conner against John Cantwell. Case. Dismissed by consent.

David Wells against Robert Black. Attachment.
David Wells against Robert Black. Writ.
By consent of the parties and assent of the Court, the trial of these two causes is defered to the Arbitrament of David Goodlett, Jesse Carter, William Lancaster, Esq., and Mr. David Golightly, Gentl. arbitrators, with power of umpirage, their award made and returned to next Court to be a judgment & rule thereof.

The State against Richard Lee. Larceny. Ordered that this trial come on half after two o'clock of this day, and then laid over the trial of the same untill tomorrow morning.

John D. Young against the Exrs. of John Ford. decd. Petition-continued by consent.

John James against John D. Young. Capias Debt. The defendant came into Court and confessed Judgment according to Specialty & costs of suit with stay of Execution 6 months.

Hans Carr against John Sloan. Trover. Continued by order of Court.

Thomas Price against George Tho. Sloan. Case. Settled at each party paying their own costs.

Frederick Hovers against John Lefever. Attachment. Continued by order of Court.

William Hammett against William Turner Thomason. Assault. Came the plaintiff by Mr. Nott his Attorney and the defendant by Thomson his attorney, Also came a Jury (same as before)...We find for the plaintiff $2.50 with costs of suit....

Ordered that Colo. Obadiah Trimmier be allowed out of the County fund s 7 for an Estray stear toll'd before Henry McCray, Esq.

William S. Milson against John D. Young. Debt. Continued by consent of the parties.

Daniel Bragg and John Harris being appointed to act as constables in this County came into Court & took the necessary oaths of office prescribed by Law.

Frederick Hovers against John Lefever. Attachment. Ordered that a commission Dedimus potestatum issue to the State of North Carolina, Lincoln County, to take the Examination of John B<u>ee</u>st in behalf of the plaintiff.

Ordered that the Estrays produced to the Sheriff be sold tomorrow at the adjournment of Court.

Arnold Thomason being appointed to act as a Constable in this County, came into Court & took the necessary oaths of office prescribed by Law.

William Bennett against John Daniel. Attachment. Decreed by the Court in favor of the plaintiff against the defendant the sum of Ł 9 d 4 & costs of suit.

John Pipes against Hugh Thomson. Petition. Ordered that an attachment issue against the body of John Turner of Greenville County, to compell his attendance at next Court as a witness in the above case for his contemptuously failing to appear at this Court.

Gabriel Benson Admr. of the Est. of William Benson decd. against Joel Hembree. Case. By consent of the parties, the trial of this cause is refered to the arbitrament of the Judges of this Court with powerof umpirage, their award returned to next Court to be a rule thereof.

Ordered that the minutes be read, which was accordingly done and signed by James Jordan, I. Harrison, Judges. Court then adjourned untill tomorrow Nine O'Clock.

Thursday the 18th Jan. 1799. The Hon. Court met according to adjournment. Present their Honors James Jordan & Isham Harrison, Esqs.

Hans Carr against John Sloan. Trover. Abated by death of the plaintiff.

Gabriel Benson admr. of William Benson decd. against Joel Hembree. Case. By consent of the parties and assent of the Court, the trial of this cause is refered to Joseph Woodruff and Henry McCray, Esq., Gentl. Arbitrators, with power of Umpirage their award returned to next Court to be the judgment thereof.

Mr. Compty against Benjamine Wofford. Petition. Decreed for the plaintiff Ł 5 according to Specialty & costs of suit.

Ordered that James Galt and William Anderson have license to retail spirituous liquors upon giving Alexander Walker and Henry Wells his surities for their lawful performance.

George Taylor against Sion Cooper and Daniel Amos. Case. The parties appeared by their attornies, also came a jury (same as before)...We find for the Plaintiff $80 with interest and costs of suit....

The State against Richard Lee & others. Sciri Facias. Discharged upon payment of costs.

The State against Richard Lee. Stealing Wheat. Ordered that the Recognizance of the defendant be continued.

Michael O'Barr against Justice Reynolds. Case. Ordered that a commission issue to take the evidence of Robert O'Barr Debene Esse to be read in evidence in Court, provided the said Robert O'Barr shall not be in the County upon giving legal Notice to the adverse party-

Lewis Cockrell being appointed to act as Constable for this County, was qualified accordingly in open Court.

George Roebuck against William Farrow. On Fieri Facias.

Samuel Farrow Esq. attorney, for the defendant came into Court and motioned for a Nonsuit because there was no declaration filed in said case, which motion was overruled, but further motion in which was granted. That the officer proceed no farther with the Execution untill the witnesses came before the clerk and proved their attendance at every particular Court, Viz: How many days they attended at each Court and at which Court, and that the defendant be served with a notice when the said witness will attend to make out their legal demands as aforesaid and that the defendant when made have a fair copy of the same, agreeable to the fee bill of Ninety-one.

Ordered that a commission issue to the Justices of the peace in to examine the witnesses to the last will and testament of John Timmons, decd.

The Court proceeded to Elect a sheriff when Brittain Williford was duly Elected for the term of one year.

Obadiah Morse against Mason Foley. Debt. The defendant came into Court and confessed judgment for $2000 and costs of suit.

Gabriel Benson admr.of William Benson decd. against Joel Hembree. Settled by the parties, upon each paying his own attorney, the plaintiff paying the Sheriff and the defendant the clerk's fees.

Ordered that the minutes be read which was accordingly done and signed by James Jordan, I. Harrison, Judges. Court then adjourned untill Court in course.

At a County Court of Sessions and pleas began to be Holden at the Court-House of Spartanburgh on the 16th day of July 1799. Present their Honors William Smith & James Jordan, Esqs.

The Court proceeded to draw the Jurors for next Court.

Grand Jurors

Charles Burton	1	Alexander Evans	11
Peter Peterson	2	Spencer Calvert	12
Andrew Barry	3	Israel Robertson	13
Joel Traylor	4	Andrew McMullen	14
Charles James	5	George Rowland	15
Robert Harper	6	John Cooper	16
Thomas Jackson	7	John McKnight	17
George Williams	8	Edmund Bishop	18
Peter Gray	9	Jonathan Harris	19
William Farrow	10	Dempsey Bonner	20

Petit Jurors

William Brannon	1	Isaac Hamby	16
John Crofford	2	Francis Mayson	17
Rolley Calvert	3	Samuel Busey	18
Simpson Newman	4	William Barrett	19
Zachariah Groce	5	Matthew Abbott	20
James Landford	6	Peter Peterson	21
David White	7	James Byas	22
John Hamby Junr.	8	James Southerland	23
Michael French	9	Jelson Olliver	24
William Wilder	10	John Roebuck	25
William McDowell	11	Fennell Wilson	26
Richard Whitby	12	Jesse Tate	27
Samuel Gentry	13	William Lewis	28
Joseph Davis	14	James Betterton	29
Isham Clayton	15	Joseph Cavin	30

The following persons names were drawn to serve as Petit Jurors this Court, they being impanneled & sowrn.

Samson Bobo Junior	1	John King, foreman	7
Shadrack Waldrope	2	Samuel Snoddy	8
John Beardan	3	Abraham Moore	9
Thomas Stone	4	William Rodgers	10
John Miller	5	David Allen	11
Daniel Rodgers	6	John Barnett	12

Ordered that in consequence of a petition to the Court by James K. Benson, desiring a guardian for the better procuring his part of his Father William Benson's Estate, that Gabriel Benson act in that place agreeable to the said minors petition.

The following persons names are those that appeared to serve this Court as grand Jurors.

Shands Golightly, foreman	1	Joseph Barnett	7
James Keen	2	William Gray	8
David Jones	3	John Turner	9
Adam Kelby	4	Samuel Jameson	10
Jacob Utley	5	John Poesy	11
Osborn West	6	John Wright	12
		Thomas Anderson	13

Ordered that Sarah Leech and John Collins have the full admn. of the Estate of John Leech decd. upon giving Bond and surities accordingly.

Gabriel Benson against Joel Hembree. Petition Debt. The defendant came into Court and confessed Judgment according to Specialty with costs of suit with stay of Execution 1 month.

John F. Harmoning against Joel Hembree. Petition. Debt. The defendant came into Court and confessed Judgment according to Specialty with costs of suit with stay of Executoin untill the 1st of Jan. next.

Alexander McBeth & Co. against Rolley Horton. Petition. Debt. The defendant's attorney appeared and confessed Judgment according to specialty with costs of suit on staying Execution untill next Court.

Alexander McBeth & Co. against John Elder. Case. Ordered that this action be dismissed at the defendant's costs.

George Gordan & Co. against William Stone. Sciri Facias to renew Judgment. Ordered that the judgment which the plaintiff hath heretofore obtained be recorded against the defendant.

Sarah Leech and John Collins, admr. and admx. of the Estate of John Leech decd. came into Court & took the admn. oaths according to law.

Ordered that Benjamine McMekin, John Davis & John Pace appraise the Estate of John Leech decd. and make due return thereof.

The last will and testament of Erasmus Nobles proven in open Court by the evidence of Samuel Barns who made oath that he and Benjamine Farmer and Benjamine D. Shumate were call'd on to witness the same and did it according laid over for further proof.

Ordered that Gabriel Benson act as Guardian for Robert Benson, Thirza Benson & Nimrod Benson, upon signing a bond for that purpose.

Ordered that Ignacius Stokes act as guardina for Patience Benson and Polley Benson minors & heirs of William Benson decd.

Ordered that Willis Benson act as guardian for Elias Benson minor & heir of William Benson decd.

An appraisment of the Estate of Stephen Wilson decd. returned by the Executor.

Elizabeth Benson made application to the Court for Samuel Miller to be her Guardian, which was accordingly granted.

Abner Benson made application for Gabriel Benson to be his Guardian which was accordingly granted.

Nancy Benson petitioned the Court for Joseph Benson to be her Guardian which was accordingly granted.

Ordered that Jean Eley and William Allen have the full admn. of the estate of John Eley decd. upon qualifying & signing a bond for that purpose.

Flemming Smith appearing as a Juror, gave the Court such satisfaction of his inability to serve as exempted him from serving this Court.

Ordered that the minutes be read which was accordingly done & signed by Wm. Smith, James Jordan, Judges. Court then adjourned untill Tomorrow Nine O'Clock.

Wednesday the 17th of July 1799. Court met according to adjournment. Present their Honors William Smith and James Jordan, Esqs.

Ordered that William Brannon have license to retail spirituous liquors upon signing a bond with Robert McDowell & John Keenum his surities for his lawful performance.

John Barnett and Charles Hester appeared as grand Jurors & were qualified accordingly.

William Robertson against George Thomason. Slander. Continued by affidavit of the defendant.

Frederick Hovers against John Lefever. Attachment. Came the plaintiff by Mr. Nott his attorney, and the defendant by Mr. Thomson, also appeared Mr. Charles Morgan who was summoned as Guarnishee and upon being qualified on his oath saith that he owed the defendant nothing when the attachment was levyed in his hands whereupon came a Jury, to wit, John King, Samson Bobo Junr., Shadrack Waldrope, John Beardan, Thomas Stone, John Miller, Daniel Rodgers, Samuel N. Snody, Abraham Moore, William Rodgers, David Allen & John Bennett...we find Charles Morgan the Guarnishee indebted to John Lefever at the time the attachment was levyed $100. John King, foreman....

Alexander McBeth & Co. against Sion Cooper. Petition. Debt. By consent of the defendant's attorney, decreed by the Court for the debt according to specialty & costs of suit.

The State against Susannah Colley. Assault. The Grand Jury find "A truel Bill." Shands Golightly, foreman.

The State against Nathaniel Powers. Assault. The Grand Jury say "A true Bill."

The State against Moses Snow. Assault. The Grand Jury say True Bill.

The State against Susannah Colley. Robberty. The Grand Jury say No Bill.

John D. Young against William McDaniel. Debt. The defendant came into Court and confessed Judgment according to Specialty, with stay of Execution 9 months & costs of suit.

Zachariah McDaniel against John James. Petition Debt. The Court decreed for the plaintiff according to Specialty & costs of suit.

The State against Samuel Moore. Assault. The defendant came into Court in his own proper person & plead guilty to the Indictmetn, & threw himself on the mercy of the Court, who fined him s 5 and acquitted him upon payment of costs.

A deed of conveyance from Baylis Earle, Esq. to Andrew Colley, acknowledged in open Court, Ordered to be recorded.

William Hammett against Blake Massingale. Assault. The parties appeared by their attornies, also a Jury (same as before)... We find for the plaintiff $20 with costs of suit....

The last will & testament of Erasmus Nobles proven by the evidence of Berryman D. Shumat, Esq., which is complete with the proof heretofore, Ordered to record.

Randolph Casey against Christopher Stone. Special Action. By consent of the parties and assent of the Court the trial of this cause is refered to the arbitrament of John Farrow, Henry Harden, Jesse Spann, Richard Young & Henry Meredith, their award to be a rule of Court.

Ordered that the minutes be read which was accordingly done & signed by William Smith, James Jordan, Judges. Court then adjourned untill Tomorrow Nine O'Clock.

Thursday the 18th day of July 1799. Court met according to adjournment. Present their Honors William Smith & James Jordan, Esqs.

Ordered that Alexander Alexander have license to keep Tavern upon giving Aaron Casey and Moses Casey his surities for his lawful performance.

Moses Casey came into Court and quallifyed as an Executor of the last will and testament of Erasmus Nobles, deceased.

Ordered that James Bright, Berryman D. Shumate and Samuel Burns appraise the Estate of Erasmus Nobles, decd., and make due return thereof.

Moses Casey against Burrel Bobo. Special Action. Samson Bobo being Empannelled and sworn to serve as a Petit Juror, but being a brother of the defendants, was desirous of being exempted this cause, which was accordingly granted and John Snow was sworn to serve in his stead.

Moses Casey against Burrel Bobo. Special Action. Came the parties by their Attornies, whereupon came a Jury....We find for the defendant....

John Lancaster resigning acting any longer as a deputy clerk for this County, and William Toney being recommended by the clerk and approved of by the Court, to wit, as a deputy, Ordered that he take the necessary oaths prescribed by Law, which he did in open Court.

John Pipes against Hugh Thomson. Petition. Decreed for the plaintiff Ł 6 and costs of suit.

John Hamby against Benjamine Wofford. Special Action. By consent of the parties and assent of the Court the trial of this cause is refered to the Arbitrament of David Bruton and William Crow, with power of Umpirage, their award returned to next Court to be made a rule thereof.

Michael O'Barr against Justice Reynolds. Case. Continued by order of Court.

William S. Milson against John D. Young. Debt. Mr. Nott, attorney for the deft. motioned for a nonsuit, but being overruled by the Court, Mr. Thomson appearing as an attorney in behalf of the plaintiff, whereupon came a Jury....We find for the plaintiff $4 with costs of suit....

Ordered that the County treasurer pay out of the County fund the sum of s 36, it being the price of an Estray cow, which was sold and bought by Michael Miller to Mr. Robert Black, which is the sum due after the fees deducted.

The State against William Wofford and Benjamine Wofford Junior. Indictment for Rescue. The Grand Jury say "True Bill."

The State against Benjamine Wofford & Sarah Wofford. Assault.

The State against Levi Snow. Assault. The Grand Jury find a True Bill.

The State against Elijah Herring. Larceny. The Grand Jury find a True Bill.

The State against Hayes Bagwell. Burning Woods. The Grand Jury say No Bill.

The State against Charles Morgan & others. Bench Warrant. The Grand Jury find A true Bill.

Ordered that William Brannon and Joshua Edwards be bound in recognizance to answer the charge of the Grand Jury.

Henry Young came into Court and proved 3 days attendance as a witness in the suit John Piper against Hugh Thomson at 2/6 per day.

The State against Richard Lee. Larceny. Ordered that a Sciri Facias issue against Richard Lee, John Edmundson, Benjamine Wofford & Aaron Templeman to shew cause why their recognizance should not be forfeited.

Alexander Morrison against William Wilder. Petition Debt. The defendant came into Court and confessed judgment according to specialty with staying Execution untill 1st Jan. next.

William Venable against Robert McDowell. Petition. Mr. Gist appearing as an attorney for the plaintiff and Mr. Tolliaferro attorney for the defendant and after hearing the allegations of each party, decreed by the Court $36 and costs of suit in favor of the plaintiff.

Ordered that James Crook, Thomas Stone and Daniel David appraise the Estate of John Ealy, decd. and make due return thereof.

George Roebuck against William Farrow. On a writ of Fieri Facias. Ordered that the Sheriff proceed on an Execution agreeable to the former judgment for which he had an Execution.

Jonathan Harris against William Vincent. Debt. Dismissed at the defendant's costs. Jesse Vincent came into Court & acknowledged himself surity for the costs.

Ordered that the minutes be read which was accordingly done & signed by Wm. Smith, James Jordan, Judges. Court then adjourned untill tomorrow Nine O'Clock.

Friday the 19th day of July 1799. The Hon. Court met according to adjournment. Present their Honors William Smith & James Jordan, Esqs.

William Simpson Esq. being reappointed to act as a Justice of the peace in this County, came into Court and quallifyed accordingly.

Nathaniel Henderson against James Synyard. Appeal. Ordered that the judgment of the Justice be confirmed.

An Inventory of the Estate of James Wood decd. returned by the Executor.

The State against Benjamine Wofford, Benjamine Wofford Junior, & William Wofford. Rescue. Waddy Thomson appeared as the States attorney & Mr. Gist & Tolliaferro, attornies for the defendants Ordered by the Court that a Nole prosequi be entered and that the defendants be discharged from their Recognizances.

The State against Susannah Colley. Assault. By request of the County Attorney, Ordered that the Indictment be quashed.

The State against Moses Snow. Assault & Battery. By request of the County attorney, Ordered that the indictment be quashed.

The State against Nathaniel Power. Assault & battery. By request of the County Attorney, Ordered that the indictment be quashed.

The State against Benjamine Wofford & Sarah Wofford. Assault. Ordered that the Indictment be quashed by request of the County attorney.

The State against Levi Snow. Assault. By request of the County attorney Ordered that the Indictment be quashed.

The State against Elijah Herring. Larceny. By request of the County attorney, Ordered that the Indictment be quashed.

Ebenezer Morse against Isaac Hendrix. Attachment. This cause stands over by consent.

Obadiah Watson against John & Absalom Lancaster. Case. Ordered that Isham Foster, Isham Harrison & Gabriel Benson Esqs. search and adjust the accounts, and bring an abstract to the next Court of the same, and the accounts so adjusted be taken in evidence, and that a commission issue to take the evidence of Sarah Lea Debene esse also that a commission issue to take the evidence of Daniel Carmichael.

Nathaniel Power against Benjamine Wofford. Attachment. Ordered that the cause be dismissed by consent.

Ebenezer Morse against Isaac Hendrix. Attachment. Ordered that a commission Dedimus potestatum issue to the State of Georgia to take the examination of Andrew Hendrix in behalf of the defendant upon his giving the plaintiff 10 days notice of time & place of Examination.

Jethro Osheal against Joel Hembree. Slander. The defendant came into Court and acknowledged the words spoken were in the Heat of passion, and that he never knew anything against the character of the said plaintiff, Ordered that the suit be dismissed at equal costs.

John Cunningham against John James. Sciri Facias to renew judgment. Ordered that the Judgment which the plaintiff hath heretofore obtained against the defendant be revived.

Richard Tolliaferro against George Taylor. Attachment The defendant being called and not appearing in his own person neither by his attorney, Judgment was thereupon entered by default.

John Utley against Pleasant Turner. Attachment. Ordered that this cause be dismissed.

Zachariah Arwood against Mark Brown. Attachment. Nonsuit.

Daniel Hammett against James Acry. Petition. Decreed for the plaintiff for five Barrels & three Bushels of Corn at $3 per Barrel, & costs of suit.

Swanson Lansford against Benjamine Wofford. Sciri Facias. The defendant being called on and now shewing cause why the Judgment which the plaintiff hath against him should not be revived. Therefore ordered that the same be of force & liable to be recovered by Execution.

Ordered that the Estrays which are liable for sale now in possession of the Sheriff be sold at the adjoutnment of Court.

Ordered that the minutes be read which was accordingly done & signed by William Smith, James Jordan, Judges. Court then adjourned untill Court in Course.

END OF VOLUME.

"Order Book For the Ordinaries office and Intermediate Courts commencing in March Term 1790 and in September Term 1791 Intermediate."

1 Court of Ordinary at the Court-House of Spartanburgh, on the third Monday in June 1790.
Present Baylis Earle, WIlliam Smith, Thomas Farrow, David Goodlett, Andrew Barry, William McDowell, James Jordan & Samuel Lancaster Esquires.

 Ordered, that a Citation issue to James Jackson & William Kelso, in order for them to administer on the Estate of Samuel Jackson Deceased. Issued.

 Ordered, that a Citation issue to Rachel Lucus, in Order for her to Administer on the Estate of John Lucus Deceased. Issued.

 Ordered that the Sale of the Estate of Edward Smith Deceased be proceeded to by the Administratrix on the twenty Second day of next month, at Nine months Credit, Unless sums under five Shillings, which is to be paid in ready cash.

 Court of Ordinary then adjourned, untill Court in Course, after the minutes being read & Signed by
        Bayles Earle)
        David Goodlett &) Esquires
        William Smith)

Court of Ordinary for Spartanburgh County Commencing on the third monday in September 1790 Agreeable to the Court of Common Pleas, during which Session, made the following orders.
Present James Jordan, William Smith, David Goodlett, Esquires.

Ordered, that Rachel Lucus have Letters of administration on the Estate of John Lucus Deceased, after producing her Citation which had been published according to Law, and taking the administration oath, which she did in open Court.

2 Ordered, that Thomas Wyatt, Richard Lewis & James Taylor White appraise the Estate of John Lucus Deceased, And make due return of the same.

   Tuesday the 21st of September 1790
Present James Jordan, William Smith, Thomas Farrow, Esquires.

Ordered that James Jackson and William Kelso, who returned their Citation obtained for administration on the estate of Samuel Jackson deceased, with a Certification of the same being Published by the oath of Thomas Jackson, have letters of administration accordingly.

 The administrators of the Estate of Samuel Jackson Deceased hath Chosen William McMullan & Alexander Copeland, to appraise the Estate of the said Deceased. Ordered that they act accordingly.

Court then adjourned untill Court, in Course.

Friday the 24th September 1790
Present James Jordan, William Smith & David Goodlett, Esquires.

Ordered that the Readministration of the Estate of Michael Sprinkle Deceased be committed to Robert Head, Upon his giving Samuel Elder and some other Sufficient freeholder as his Surety for his lawful performance.

Court of Ordinary then adjourned untill Court in Course After the minutes being Read and Signed by
       James Jordan)
       William Smith)
       D. Goodlett)Esquires

3 Court of Ordinary for Spartanburgh County commencing on the third Monday the 21st March 1791 (Pursuant to a late Act of the Legislature of the State of South Carolina) By divers sitting and adjournments, agreeable to the Court of Common Pleas, made the following Orders.

Present. The Honorable William Smith Esquires.

The Last Will and Testament of Hezekiah Childs deceased being proved in Open Court by the evidences of Henry Turner & William Turner, Subscribing Witness's to the same; Who made Oath that they also saw Thomas Williamson Subscribe his name as a witness thereto Ordered to be recorded.

Jeston Childs and John Childs Executors of the Estate of Hezekiah Childs Deceased came into Court And took the Usual Oath prescirbed by Law.

Court then adjourned, untill the Second Monday in June.

Court of Ordinary, Couch'd in an Intermediate Court, held for the County of Spartanburgh on the Second Monday in April 1791 During its Continuation made the following Orders.

Present Their Honors William Smith & James Jordan Esqrs.

Ordered, that a citation issue to Capt. James Terrill in Order for him to administer on the Estate of Israel Robertson Deceased. Issued.

Ordered, that Isham Harrison Esquire, Joseph Venible and William Lancaster appraise the Estate of Hezekiah Childs Deceased and make due return thereof.

Whereas the appraisers heretofore appointed to appraise the Estate of John Lucus deceased, did not proceed to appraise the same & two of them having removed out of the County It is therefore Ordered that James T. White, John Brown & Robert Goodlett appraise the same & Make due return thereof.

The Last Will and Testament of John McCrory Deceased being approved by the Court & Proved by the Testimonies of James Clayton & Tilman Bobo was thereupon Ordered to be recorded.

4   Tuesday the 12th April 1791

Capt. James Terrell having Yesterday Obtained a Citation for Administration on the estate of Israel Robertson Deceased & returned the Publication accordingly Ordered that he have Letters of Administration upon his Giving Approoved surities, which he did in Open Court And took the Administration oath accordingly.

Court then adjourned untill the Second Monday in September next, After the Minutes being Read and Signed by James Jordan Wm Smith, Judges.

Court of Ordinary, Couch'd in the Court of Session and pleas, began and Held at the Court House of Spartanburgh County on the 13th of June (the 12th happening on Sunday) 1791 And from thence continued by divers adjournments to the 15th Instant and while Setting Ordered as follows.

Present Their Honors William Smith & James Jordan, esqr.

The Last will and Testament of William Jordan Deceased proven in open Court by the Evidence of John Jordan. Ordered to Record.

The last will and Testament of George Lowder proven in open Court by the evidence of William Crow agreeable to an act of Assembly in that case made & provided. Ordered to record.

The last will and Testament of William Spiller proven in open Court by the evidence of Warrington Spiller agreeable to Law Ordered to Record.

   Court of Ordinary agreeable to the Court of Common pleas, then adjourned untill Court in Course, after the Minutes being Read and Signed by   Baylis Earle)
                                       James Jordan) Judges
                                       William Smith)

5   At an Intermediate Court began and Held at the Court-House of Spartanburgh County on the Second Monday the 12th September 1791.
Present Their Honors, William Smith and James Jordan Esquires.

Nathan Childs being Summoned to attend this Court to Serve as a Constable, Came into Court and give Satisfactory excuse for his exemption this Court.

Ordered that the sale of the Estate of John Lucus Deceased, be proceeded to by the administratrix on the first Monday in October next, at nine months Credit, where any purchaser purchases articles exceeding Ten shillings, and for all purchases under that sum to be paid at the day of Sale.

Ordered that William Wilkins Oversee the Road from the County line near John Shippys plantation, to that of William Thomson's in place of said Shippy.   Issued.

Ordered that Joseph Price Oversee the Road from William Thomsons to where it Crosses Thicketty.   Issued.

Ordered that Edward Williams Oversee the Road from Thicketty near Gutterys Mill up to the State line, which leads towards Green River.   Issued.

Ordered that Ignacious Griffin Oversee the Road from Thicketty near William Thomsons, to Hammetts ford on Packolate River. Issued.

6   Ordered, that Thomas Cole Oversee the Road from the North side of Thicketty, to the County line as it leads to Broad River Cherokee Ford. Issued.

Ordered that Capt. William Benson be allowed the sum of Ten pounds one Shilling and Six pence for his Extri Services & Contingent expences while Acting as Sheriff for this County. Issued.

A Deed of Conveyance from Frederick Eisen to John D. Young proven in open Court by Jonathan Bowen according to Law. Ordered to Record.

Ordered that Summons's Issues against Baylis Earle Esquire Richard Saunders, Thomas Devine, Thomas Jackson, James Hooper, William Redman, John Moore & Joseph Moore, to Shew Cause why they did not Attend to work on the Road, Under the Direction of William Byrd, who was Overseer.

Ordered, that an Estray Bull taken up by Job Sosby, be sold by a Constable, at Six Months Credit, the purchaser giving bond & Security for the same According to Law.

Ordered that the Administration of the Estate of William Wheeler deceased be granted to Maryan Oates & James Gibbs upon their applying to the Clerk & Signing Bond with such Surities as he shall accept.

A Bill of Sale from Major James Lusk to Josiah Culbertson acknowledged in open Court by the said Lusk. Ordered to Record.

A Bill of sale from Majr. James Lusk to Robert Davison, acknowledged in open court, by the said Lusk. Ordered to Record.

A Deed of Conveyance from Ebenezer Morse to Benjamin Busey, acknowledged in open court by said Morse. Ordered to Record.

7   Ordered that, Vardry McBee be allowed the sum of one pound for his keeping & Preserving an Estray. paid

Ordered that Thomas Williamson be allowed the sum of two pounds three shillings out of the County fund, for maintaining John Tanner in Jail. paid

Ordered that, Edmund Wade Oversee the Road from Broad River at the upper Island Ford, to Packolate River near John Hightowers. Issued.

Ordered that William Garrett Oversee the Road from Hightowers ford on Packolate to this Court-House. Issued.

William Wood by permission of the Court Joined Henry Mechan Wood in his administration Bond, in place of William Young Esquire.

Ordered that the Estrays be exposed to Sale by the Sheriff, according to Law.

Ordered that three Constables be Summoned to attend next Court. Issued.

Ordered that the minutes be read which were done according-

& Signed by   William Smith, James Jordan, Judges.

Court then adjourned untill Court in Course.

8   At an Intermediate Court begun and Held for the County of Spartanburgh at the Court-House on the Second monday in April 1792.
   The Judges not appearing, Court was adjourned untill Tomorrow Nine O'Clock.

   Tuesday the 10th of the same Instant, the Honorable Court met according to adjournment.   Present   Their Honors William Smith & Baylis Earle   Esquires.

   William Lancaster who has acted as County Treasurer while in office of Clerk, produced his account to the Court, falling in debt thereby to the Treasury the sum of Six pounds Nine shillings & three pence   Which the Court Accepted and thereupon acquitted him from serving any longer as Treasurer; And thereupon appointed David Goodlett Esquire to the office of Treasurer for the County, during pleasure.
Ordered that said Lancaster deliver up to said Goodlett such papers as relate to the Treasury & Income of the County.

   Ordered that the County Treasurer pay Majr. John Gowen the Sheriff for this County, the sum of five pounds for his Extri Services for one year.

   The Last will and Testament of William Gowen deceased, proven in open Court by the evidence of Millington Easly, According to Law.   Ordered to Record.

   David Goodlett Esquire having purchased an Estray at last Court for the sum of one pound   five shillings & Six pence for which he gave his note to the County Treasurer, and the Creature being proven within the Lawful limits & given up Ordered that he have his note & be acquitted from the debt of the same.

   Henry Young being appointed to act as a Constable for this County, came into Court & took the Necessary Oaths prescribed by Law.

9   Ordered that Nathaniel Stokes, Turner Thomason & John Cantrell be Summoned by the Sheriff to attend on next June Court as Constables.   Issued.

   Ordered that John Burnett Oversee the Road from this Court-House to the Boiling Spring Meeting-House in place of Edmund Fowler & that all hands within two miles of said Road work under his direction.   Robert Kimbell Warner. Issued.

   Ordered that James Alexander Senior Oversee the Road from the Bridge on Lawson Fork near the widow Bishops to the Bridge on South Packolate in place of Robert Harper, and the Inhabitants within five miles to work thereon under his direction. Thomas Alexander Warner. Issued.

   William Young is appointed Warner under the direction of Thomas Jackson who is an Overseer of a Road from the Bridge on South Packolate to North Packolate Hooper Ford, in place of Henry Young.   Issued.

Ordered that John Poesy Senior Oversee the Road from Buck Branch to where Blackstocks Road leaves Millers Road & those within three miles of said Road to work under his direction Instead of Capt. Henry Wells. Robert Piper warner.

Ordered that Charles Burton Oversee the Road from Ephraim Hills up to where it Intersects Millers old Road, and all persons on the west side of the North fork & main branch of Dutchmans Creek opposite thereto & within three miles on the west side of the Road and Crossing Tyger River, work thereon under his direction   Thomas Moore son of Jason Moore warner.

George Bruton presenting to the Court a poor decriped Negro as a County Charge Considered by the Court, for which they allowed said Bruton at the rate of Eight pounds Pr yer Six months past for maintaining said Negro who is named Anthony To be paid out of the County fund.

10 Ordered that the County Treasurer pay George Bruton the sum of four pounds out of the first Collection for his supporting said Negro.

Ordered that Thomas Williamson be paid by the County Treasurer the sum of forty five shillings for his Contingent expences for Supporting John Tanner in Jail.

Ordered that Capt. Henry Wells have licence to retail spirituous Liquors & Keep Public House of Entertainment upon his giving Isham Harrison & David Goodlett Esquires his Surities for his Lawful performance.

Ordered that Thomas Williamson have licence to retail spirituous Liquors and Keep Public House upon giving Capt. Henry Wells & Isham Harrison Esquire as his Surities for his Lawful performance.

Ordered that all persons within five miles of a Road whereof William Bird is overseer, that are in Spartanburgh County be liable to work thereon under his direction.

The Minutes were read & Signed by William Smith, Baylis Earle, Judges.

    Wednesday the 11th of April 1792
The Honorable Court met according to adjournment. Present His Honor Baylis Earle Esquire.

An account Calculation & Sale of the Estate of Andrew Foster deceased returned to Court by Moses Foster Administrator Inspected by the Court & ordered to record.

Ordered that William Foster of Tyger River Oversee the Road from Buck Branch up to its Junction with the Road Leading from Mr. Timmons's to the widow Bishops in place of Isham Foster & the Hands within the usual limits assertained in the former Order work thereon under his direction. Issued.

Ordered that Thomas Price have Licence upon giving Absalom Lancaster & James Saunders his Surities for his Lawful performance.

11 Ordered that Absalom Lancaster be Allowed the sum of twenty-four and three pence for Summoning Inquest & Executing a Negro

of James Lusk's, who was tried & Burnt, to be paid out of the County fund.

Ordered that Thomas Williamson be paid the sum of Two shillings & Ten pence, for Mantaining & Ironing said Negro in Jail. Issued.

The minutes were read & Signed by Baylis Earle, Esquire. Court then adjourned untill Court in Course.

At an Intermediate Court began and Held at the Court-House of Spartanburgh County on the Second Monday in September 1792. Present Their Honors Baylis Earle & James Jordan, Esquires.

The Last Will & Testament of William Tate Decd. Proven in open Court by the Evidences of Charles Hester & William Hester who say they saw John Hester witness the same, Ordered that the same be recorded.

An Inventory & appraisment of the Estate of Richard Harrison Esquire decd. return'd to Court by the Administrators ordered that they be filed.

Ordered that Obadiah Trimmier Esquire, Daniel McClaren, Joseph Dill & Jesse Tate appraise the estate of William Tate decd & Make return thereof by the Second Monday in April next. Issued.

A Deed of Conveyance from William Jameson & John Gowen Esq. proven in open Court by the Evidence of James Jordan Esquire according to Law, ordered to be recorded.

The Executors of the Estate of William Tate decd came into Court & took the Necessary oathes prescribed by Law.

12   A Deed of Gift from William Bratcher to Sarah Barnett proven in open Court by the Evidence of James Lanford & Joseph Burnett according to Law, Ordered to record.

Ordered that John James & Travice Reece Overseers the Road from this Court-House to where it Intersects the Road from the Iron-Works to Fords Mill in place of John Hammett & that all hands within three miles of said Road work thereon under their Jurisdiction. Issued.

Ordered that Fredrick Guttery oversee that part of the road which William Wier formerly did that leads from Camps Ferry on Broad River to this Court-House and all hands within five miles of said Road work thereon under his Jurisdiction. Issued.

Ordered that George Lamkin oversee that part of the Road which Frederick Guttery does not that leads from Camps Ferry on Broad River to this place, in place of Malachi Jones all hands within five miles to work theron accordingly. Issued.

Ordered that John Ford Junr. & Robert Miller Lieut.oversee the Road from the Narrow Passage on Tyger River to Patton's Ford on So. Tyger in place of Richard Barns & that all hands within three miles work thereon accordingly.

Ordered that Joel Trayler oversee the Road from Mr. Timmons's to the Narrow passage in place of Samuel Timmons & that Daniel Timmons warn the Hands within three miles of the same to work thereon accordingly.

William Shea came into Court being appointed Constable & took the Necessary Oaths prescribed by Law.

A Statement of the accounts due to & from the estate of James White decd return'd to Court by the Executors.

Present his Honor William Smith Esquire.

13 Ordered that the Child Durrel McBee which was pretended to be bound to Vardry McBee be delivered to the Care of its mother Rhoda McBee, alias Gibson & Jordan Gibson Her Husband.

Abraham Byce came into Court and acknowledged a Deed of Conveyance from Himself to Goen(?) Byce. Ordered to be recorded.

Ordered that Malachi Jones oversee the Road from Hammets Ford on Packolate to Lawsons Fork From Lawsons Fork to Fairforest Isham Harrison Esquire overseer. From Fair-Forest to the Cross Road Towards Fords mill Henry Cannon overseer. from the Cross Road to the Charleston Road in the fork of Tyger River Jesse Spencer overseer. from Charleston Road at Matthew Pattons to John Woodruffs, Obadiah Gresatt overseer. From John Woodruffs on Enoree leading by Susannah Hambys field and between two of Joseph Woodruffs fields striking the old Road below the Meeting House at the Corner of a Land Mark supposed to be Hugers, Joseph Woodruff & Robert Case(?) to lay off the same, William Moore overseer and that all hands within three miles of the said Road work thereon under their Jurisdiction.

Ordered that a Road be Laid out and opened from this Court House to that of Greenville respective to the report of James Jordan and William Benson Esquire.

The Inventory & appraisement of the Estate of George Louther decd. return'd to Court by Thomas Farrow Esquire Executor of said Estate Ordered that the same be filed.

Ordered that Thomas Farrow Esquire Executor of George Lowther decd Advertise twenty days & proceed to the sale of the Estate of said deceased at Twleve Months credit except sums under Ten Shillings which is to be paid at the Time of Selling.

Ordered that the County Treasurer pay James Faires three pounds for wintering Estrays

14 Agreeable to an Order of Court to us directed we have Viewed the Road & Unanimously agree that the Road is to Come from Charles McKnights Ford on North Packolate to a Certain place known by the name of the fish Pond on South Packolate, thence Crossing McDowell's Race paths & so on the same Course down to the Boiling Springs. John Young Senr., Wm. McMillan, David McDowell.

Ordered that John Anderson Oversee the Road from Charles McKnights Ford on North Packolate to a Certain Fish Pond on South Packolate And that John Young Senior Oversee from South Packolate to the Boiling Springs Meeting-House, all hands within five miles of said Road work their Jurisdiction accordingly. Issued.

Ordered that Credit be given on a Note against John Golightly in behalf of the County, for Twenty Shillings being part of the same & Heretofore paid.

Ordered that the Clerk & County Treasurer Examine the accounts between William Young Esquire & the County & the Treasurer pay him whatever may appear to be due him thereby, for his Extri Services while acting as Sheriff for this County. Done.

Ordered that the County Treasurer pay Bezel Lee & Samuel Ward two Shillings each per day for Guarding the Jail from the twenty first of July untill this day. Issued.

William Lancaster Presenting to Court Christopher Golightly as his deputy in the Clerks office, who was accepted by the same, thereupon quallifyed accordingly.

15   Ordered that the County Treasurer pay James Oates the sum of four Shillings for Summoning Witness's as a Constable in behalf of the State.

Ordered that Joseph Barnett Oversee the Road from Mr. McCrays at the old Iron-Works to the Rich Hill and that James Barnett warn the male Inhabitants within three miles of the same to work thereon under his Jurisdiction. Issued.

Ordered that Capt. William Benson take the Negro that George Bruton has as a County Charge named Anthony, and that he be allowed the sum of four pounds per year for Keeping the same to be paid by the County Treasurer.

Ordered that the minutes be read, which was accordingly done & Signed by Baylis Earle, Wm Smith, James Jordan, Judges.

Court then adjourned untill To-morrow 8 O'Clock.

Tuesday the 11th of September 1792. The Honorable Court Mett according to adjournment. Present Their Honors William Smith and Baylis Earle Esquires.

Ordered that the remaining part of the personal Estate of James White deceased be Exposed to sale by the Executors at Twelve Months Credit after their advertising the same Twenty days.

Ordered that a Road be laid out and opened from where a Road from Pinckney Court House Crosses this County line between this & Union & to direct a Course through this County the Straitest & Best way to Washington Court House in Washington District & to be directed thro' this County by Joseph Woodruff John Ford Junior

16   Tobias Bright & Joel Hembree and that from Union Line to where said Road strikes the waters of Cane Creek Benjamin Peak overseer, from Cane Creek to Gyer River William Meadows, overseer, from Tyger River to opposite William Lindsays, Nathaniel Woodruff, Junior, overseer. from Opposite William Lindseys to Enoree, William Hendrix, overseer. And that all persons within three miles of said Road work thereon under their Jurisdiction.

Ordered that Major John Gowen be paid by the County Treasurer the Sum of Six pounds Seventenn Shillings for his Public services.

Ordered that Joel Hembree & David Cook be bound as Surities on the Administration of the Estate of Edward Smith decd by Mary Smith in place of Richard Young.

Ordered that the minutes be read which was accordingly done & Signed by Wm Smith, Baylis Earle, Judges.

Court then adjourned untill Court in Course.

At an Intermediate Court began and Held at the Court House of Spartanburg County on the Second Monday in April 1793 Present his Honor William Smith Esquire.

A Lease & release from Adam Potter to David Smith acknowledged in open Court by the said Potter, Ordered to be recorded.

A Deed of Conveyance from Zachariah Bullock to David Smith, proven in open Court by the evidence of Adam Potter, Ordered to be recorded.

A Deed of Conveyance from David Smith to Nehemiah Norton proven in open Court by the Evidence of Adam Potter, ordered to be recorded.

17   The last will & Testament of William Wood Senior proven in open Court by the evidence of Sally Young, Ordered to be recorded.

Ordered that John Low oversee the Road from the Island ford upon Broad River to where Frederick Guttry begins to work.

Elizabeth Timmons daughter of Thomas Timmons came into Court and petitioned for Moses Timmons to be her Guardian, which was granted by the Court. Ordered that the said Moses Timmons enter into bond with two freehold Securities, of two hundred pounds for his faithful performance with the said Orphan According to Law.

Ordered that Bazel Lee & Samuel Ward be paid by the County Treasurer the sum of Ten pounds four shillings, for guarding the Jail of the County fifty one days.

Ordered that William Ford and John Ford appraise the Estate of James Fairis deceased.

Ordered that Thomas Price have Licence upon giving Enoch Floyd & Bazel Lee his Surities for his Lawful performance who signed a Bond in open Court for the performance.

Ordered that Alexander Alexander have licence to keep a public house of entertainment & retail Spirituous liquors upon giving Bazel Lee & Henry Wells his Surities for his Lawful performance which he did.

William Milikin a poor boy being presented to the Court by Robert Goodlett was thereupon bound to the said Robert Goodlett untill he arives to the age of Twenty one years, in which time the said Goodlett is to direct, with proportionable Education; & when he arives to the age aforesaid the said

Goodlett is to give him a new Suit of Clothes & A Horse Bridle & Saddle to the Value of Ten pounds by agreement the said Goodlett is alos to sign a bond of one Hundred pounds with two freehold Surities for his lawful preformance.

The Inventory & appraisment of Thomas Timmons deceased, returned to Court by the Administrator, Ordered to be filed.

18 An Inventory & Sale of the Estate of George Lowther deceased returned to the Court by Thomas Farrow Esquire, the Executor to the Estate of the said deceased. Ordered to be filed.

Ordered that Peter Smith oversee the Road from Captain James Smiths to the Shoals of Fairforest & the Inhabitants which are required by (sic) work thereon under his direction. Issued.

Ordered that the Jurisdiction of Jeremiah Tilman who is an Overseer from Nichols's old mill to where it Intersects the Road from Fords Mill to the Iron works Extend from the Charleston Road beyond said Mill to the same.

The Inventory & appraisment of the Estate of Richard Nalley deceased returned to Court by Abraham Nalley the administrator Ordered to be filed.

Ordered that Henry McCray, John Ford and Jason Moore view the two Roads in dispute between Henry Cannon & John Golightly near said Golightlys plantation & report to next June Court which of said Roads is most Useful for the Public Utility. Issued.

Ordered that the administrator of the Estate of Richard Nalley deceased proceed to the Sale of said deceaseds Estate on the Seventeenth day of May next at Nine months Credit for all sums above five shillings upon his giving twenty days Public notice of the time & place of the Sale.

Ordered that the Sheriff proceed to Sell the Estrays produced to him this Court To-morrow at two o Clock at Six months credit.

Ordered that Nathaniel Stokes, Turner Thomason & William Shea Constables be Summoned to attend next Court.

The minutes were read & signed by Wm Smith, Judge.

Court then adjourned untill To-morrow Nine O'Clock.

19 Tuesday the 9th of April 1793. The Honorable Court met according to adjournment. Present his Honor William Smith, Esquire.

Ordered that a Road be opened & Kept in good repair to go out of the Road that leads from Ralph Smiths deceased to Blackstocks to Cross Tyger River a little below Tods Mill thence to Peter Penals & there to fork & fork to go into the Charleston Road at Arnetts old place, the other Fork to pass Thomas Miles's from thence to Musgroves on Enoree, and that Thomas Miles & Peter Pinion oversee the said Roads.

Ordered that the old Road formerly leading by Daniel Grants be discontinued.

Ordered that Samuel Woodruff oversee the Road from John Woodruffs to Enoree, in place of William Moore and that all hands that are liable by law within three miles of the same, work thereon under his direction. Issued.

Ordered that the County Treasurer let John Burk have the Sum of three pounds of the County Money yearly, per assistance to Support William Axton & his Helpless family, agreeable to a petition of the neighbours of the said Burk. Issued.

Ordered that the widow Tacket a poor widow of this County be allow (sic) the sum of three pounds yearly out of the County Money by the Treasurer, for assistance twoards her support agreeable to a petition presented to the Court for that purpose.

Ordered that Capt. Henry Wells have licence to retail Spirituous liquors upon giving Isham Harrison Esquire & Jesse Connell his Surities who sign'd a Bond for that purpose in open Court.

Ordered that Agness Faires, William Fairis & Thomas Fairis have the full administration of the Estate of James Fairis deceased, upon their quallifying and giving Bond of Six Hundred pounds with good Security for their Performance.

20   On the application of Robert Smith by & with the Consent of Sarah Manton, mother of John Roach, the the said John Roach should be bound to the said Robert Smith untill he arives to the age of Twenty one years, the said Robert Smith in said Term to Teach the said John Roach the Handy Craft Trade of a Black Smith with the Knowledge in Arithmetic to the Single Rule of three Inverse, with other proportionable english education, and a good new Suit of Clothes at his freedom, which was granted by the Court.

Ordered that Major John Gowen be paid by the County Treasurer the sum of five pounds for his Extra Services as Sheriff for this County Also that he be allowed the Sum of five pounds Six shillings & Six pence for the Contingent Expences of Ann Carters Imprisonment.

Ordered that the minutes be read, which accordingly done & Signed by   Wm Smith, Judge.
Court then adjourned untill Court in Course.

At an Intermediate Court began and held at the Court-House of Spartanburgh on the 9th day of September 1793. Present their Honors William Smith and James Jordan, esquires.

A Power of Attorney from Peter Bennett to Major John Gowen proven in open Court by the evidence of William Easly Esquire Ordered to record.

Ordered that the Estrays produced to the Sheriff to be sold this Court, be sold tomorrow at three oClock.

Ordered that three pounds be allowed out of the County fund for the maintenance of Abraham Pettit who has become one of the poor of this County, agreeable to the Petition of Sundry Inhabitants of the same.

Ordered that the minutes be read, which was done & Signed by William Smith, James Jordan, Judges.
Court then adjourned untill To morrow 10 of the Clock.

Thursday the 10th day of September 1793. court met according to adjournment. Present his Honor William Smith Esquire.

A letter of freedom from Samuel Morrow to his Negro Poll proven in open Court by the evidence of Brittain Williford, according to Law, Ordered to be recorded.

Ordered that Isham Burks oversee the Road from North Carolina line near Jamesons Mill, to where it Joins Gowens Road in place of William Byrd. And that Isaac Spiva warn all hands within three miles which are liable by law to work thereon under his Jurisdiction.

Ordered that Benjamine McMekin be paid the sum of three pounds & ten shillings out of the County fund twelve months Hence for keeping a Negro named Anthony who has become a County Charge, said negro to be found Victualing & Cloathing as is common for Slaves.

Christopher Golightly being appointed Deputy Clerk of this County now resigns his office of the same and the Clerk recommending John Lancaster to succeed him thereon who was approved of by the Court and was thereupon quallifyed accordingly.

Ordered that James Southerland oversee the Road from Pattons ford in Tyger River to Alexander Alexander's Plantation in place of Alexander Evans, Matthew Patten to warn all hands within three miles to work thereon.

Ordered that the Road which Alexander Alexander is to oversee be turned from the lower end of his lane to Cross a Shoal on Jameys Creek below McCarleys old place, then to Intersect the same old Road at Henry Carleys old field, the nearst and best way for Convenience agreeable to a petition of a number of Inhabitants adjacent thereto.

Ordered that the minutes be read which was accordingly done & signed by William Smith, Judge.
Court then adjourned untill Court in Course.

At an Intermediate Court began and Holden at the Court-House of Spartanburgh County on the Second Monday in April AD 1794. Present His Honor William Smith Esquire.

Ordered that Thomas Price have Licence to Keep a Tavern upon giving Andrew Thomson & Jno Fed. Harmony, who were proposed as his Sureties.

Ordered that Jno. Frederick Harmony have licence to keep a Tavern, upon giving Andrew Thomson & Thomas Price who were proposed as his Sureties.

Ordered that Mr. Daniel White oversee the Road from the Boiling Spring Meeting Houseto the Bridge near Darbys Store on Packolate River, in place of John Young, And that James White & John Clerk warn the hands within three miles of the same to work under his direction. Issued.

Ordered that Robert Kimbell oversee the Road from the Boiling Spring Meeting-House to the Court House of this County, in place of John Burnett, and that Edmund Fowler warn the Hands in three miles of the same to work under his direction. Issued.

Ordered that Joel Smith oversee the Road from Wilies Fork to where it intersects the Road to Blackstocks Ford on Tyger River, in place of Thomas Williams. Issued.

23 Ordered that John Humphries oversee the Road from Gentleman Thomsons on Thickety Creek to Hammetts Ford on Packolate River, in place of Ignacius Griffin, and that William Wood warn the hands within three miles of the same to work thereon under his directions. Issued.

Ordered that John Harris oversee the Road from Hammetts Ford on Packolate River to the Ford on Lawsons Fork at the Old Iron-Works in place of Malachi Jones, Elijah Hammett to warn the Hands in three miles thereof to work under his directions. Issued.

A Power of Attorney from Abraham Markley to William Pool, H. S. proven in open Court by the evidence of James Pool. Ordered to Record.

James Pool came into Court and acknowledged a Deed of Conveyance fromhimself to William Pool, H. S. Ordered to be recorded.

On Application of William Crocker, Ordered that he have the full administration of the Estate of Arthur Crocker deceased, upon quallifying, signing a Bond and Complying with the requisites of the Law.

Ordered that Anthony Crocker, John Lukerery & Benjamin Howard appraise the Estate of Arthur Crocker deceased. Issued.

Ordered that Andrew Thomson, Robert Rodgers and Thomas Price appraise the Estate of Martha McCrory deceased and make due return thereof. Issued.

24 Ordered that Littleton Bagwell, Bazel Lee & Thomas Wells view the most Convenient way from this Court House to Hammetts ford on Packolate River, For a Public Road And make their return to next June Court. Issued.

Ordered that Samuel Ward Senior oversee the Road from this Court House to Joseph Harts meeting-House, in place of John James. Issued.

Ordered that three pounds PR Annum be allowed out of the County fund for the Support of Mary Brothers who has become one of the poor of this County, after some suitable person shall make application for the same to convert it to that use.

Ordered that Matthew Guttery oversee the Road from Gentl. Thomson's to said Gutrys Mill, in place of Joseph Price all his (sic) within three miles of the same to work thereon under his direction. Issued.

Ordered that Goldman Estrick a poor boy be bound unto James Hadder untill he arives to the age of twenty one years upon their Entering into an Indenture of apprenticeship, which they did in open court.

Ordered that Isaac Crow, George Bruton, and Thomas Moore Esquire, view the ground from Isaac Crows to Pattons Ford on Tyger River and make return to next Court whether there is no better way for a Road than where it is. Issued.

Edmund Clemons Junior and Ann Clemons children of Sarah Clemons alias Fowler by & with the Consent of their mother & the said Edmund Clemons, came into Court and Choosed the said Edmund Clemons their Guardian. Ordered that he act in that place.

25 upon giving Alexander Walker & John James who was offered as his Surities in a Bond of One thousand pounds for his lawful performance which was accordingly done.

Ordered that three pounds be paid out of the County fund Pr Annum towards the Support of James Crowder, who has become one of the poor of this County.

On application of Zacheus Wheeler, that Joseph Wade should be his Guardian. Ordered that the said Joseph Wade act in that place, upon giving a bond of Forty pounds with Micajah Barnett and Joroyal Barnett, his Surities for his lawful performance.

Ordered that the minutes be read which was accordingly done and Signed by William Smith, Judge.

Court adjourned untill To-morrow Nine O'Clock.

  Tuesday the 15th of April 1794.
Court met according to adjournment. Present his Honor William Smith, Esquire.

Ordered that three Constables be Summoned to attend next Court, to do their duty as Constables in time of Court. Issued.

Ordered that the Estrays which are produced to the Sheriff which are liable for sale, be sold at the adjournment of this Court.

Ordered that Mr. William Darby have Licence to keep public Entertainment & retail Spirituous Liquors upon giving Majr. John Gowen and James Saunders his Surities for his lawful performance.

26 Ordered that William Wells be paid out of the County fund the Sum of two pounds One Shillings and ten pence for his Contingent Expences heretofore with Estrays.

Ordered that William Simpson oversee the Road from the Rich Hill to the County Line towards McClellans Ford on Fairforest And that all hands within three miles thereof work thereon under his Direction. Issued.

Ordered that the Sheriff be paid out of the County fund the Sum of Six pounds and nine pence for returning Nonest Scieri Facias's against those that took up Estrays And those that were acquitted at the Counties Cost.

Ordered that the Clerk be paid the Sum of three pounds out of the County fund for his Services done for the Sciere Facias return'd nonest against those that took up estrays. Issued.

Ordered that the Sheriff be paid the sum of five pounds for his Extra Services for the year past.

Ordered that Wells Grifith oversee the Road from Lawsons fork at the old Iron-Works to the Cross Roads at James Saunders's. Issued.

Ordered that the minutes be read which was accordingly done & signed by   William Smith, Judge.

Court then adjourned untill Court in Course.

27 At an Intermediate Court began and Held at the Court House of the County of Spartanburgh on the Second Monday of September 1794. Present their Honors William Smith, James Jordan, Baylis Earle, Judges.

A Deed of Conveyance from Jarvais Cornwal to Baylis Earle Esquire acknowledged in open Court: Ordered to be recorded.

A deed of Conveyance from John Gowen Esquire to Bartholomew Groging acknowledged in open Court: Ordered to be recorded.

Ordered that Benjamin Clerke oversee the Road from McDowells Mill to the Boiling Spring Meeting-House, and that all hands within three miles thereof work thereon under his direction. Issued.

Ordered that Henry OVail oversee the Road leading by his House from the Shoals of fairforest to Wilies fork, in place of Josiah Culbertson and that the Male Inhabitants which are liable by law, work thereon under his directions, for the distance of three miles of the same. Issued.

Ordered that Elisha Hadden oversee the Road from the narrow passage Between the two Tygers in place of Robert Miller, and that within three miles of the same work thereon under his direction. Issued.

A Deed of Conveyance from Willey S Brown to Alexander Thomson acknowledged in open Court, Ordered to be recorded.

Ordered that Obadiah Wingo oversee that part of the Road laid out by Captain William Benson & James Jordan Esquire leading from the Court-House of this County to where it intersects Millers Road in place of James Ward, And that the working hands within three miles of the same work thereon under his direction, in order to keep the same in good repair. Issued.

28 Ordered that whereas John McElheny deceased by his last will and Testament left James Jordan Esquire his Executor, and he refusing to Serve That Francis Nevil Wayland & Anne McElheny widow of the said deceased have the full administration of the Estate of the said Deceased, upon Complying with the requisites of the law. Issued.

Ordered that Alexander Roddy oversee the Road from Old John Timmons's crossing Lawson fork to the Widow McDowells, and keep in good repair the Bridge across the Fork: And that the working hands within three miles of the same work thereon under his directions. Issued.

Ordered that the Road be opened from Isaac Crows along the dividing ridge between Enoree and Tyger Rivers to the old Indian Boundery line-- and that Joseph Woodruff oversee the same from Isaac Crows to Woodruffs Meeting-House; and that Francis Fowler oversee that part of the said Road from the Meeting House to the Green ponds at or near Joseph Fowlers old place, and that John Redman oversee from thence to the Boundery line, and that all hands within three miles thereof do work thereon under their directions.

Ordered that the minutes be read, which was accordingly done and signed by Baylis Earle, William Smith, James Jordan, Judges.
Court then adjourned untill To-morrow Nine O'Clock.

29   Tuesday the 9th of September 1794
Court met according to adjournment. Present their Honors. William Smith, Baylis Earle & James Jordan Esqrs.

Ordered that Jesse Connell, George Connell and David Golightly view the most convenient and best way for a Public Road, to be Struck out of a Road near Samuel Morrows and to come along the Ridge between Duchmans Creek and Wilies Fork to Arthur Hutchins, thence the ridge to David Golightlys, thence crossing fairforest between David Golightly's old place and Mitchells plantation, thro' said Golightlys plantation, thence thro' Jesse Connels land where it will be most convenient and the least Injurious to said Connell, thence the nearest & best way into the Road near James Saunders's to Intersect the Road to this Court-House. The said viewers to mark where the same shall go. And that the said David Golightly open oversee and keep in good repair the said Road all hands within three miles to work thereon under his direction.

A Deed of Conveyance from John Gray to Henry Petit, acknowledged in open Court. Ordered to be recorded.

Hugh Moore son of Patrick deceased came into court and prayed that Major John Henderson of Union County should be his Guardian which accordingly granted upon his signing a Bond of One hundred pounds for his lawful performance.

James Jordan Esquire reported to the Court that Isham Foster was duly quallityed before him to act as a Justice of the peace for this County, Ordered that the same be entered on the minutes.

Ordered that Joshua Downs have licence to retail Spirituous liquors upon signing a Bond agreeable to Law.

30 Ordered that William Foster serve as a Constable for this County upon taking the necessary Oaths prescribed by Law, which he did in open Court.

Ordered that Bazel Lee act as a Constable for this County, upon quallifying which he did accordingly.

Ordered that the Sheriff pay back to Malachi Jones the sum of two pounds fifteen shillings that appears due him collected by virtue of an Execution on a Judgment against him at last January Court for the sum of Ten pounds, upon forfeiture of Recognizance.

Ordered that Thomas Fod, George Bruton, John White, Tobias Bright & John Bragg view the most convenient and best way for a Road, to Strike off Blackstocks Road about a mile North of Ephraim Hills to Cross Tyger River the most convenient place below the fork, to Intersect the Laurens Road near Isaac Crows and make report of the same to next Court. Issued.

Ordered that Colo Thomas Moore, Joseph Woodruff and James Wofford view the most convenient and best way for a Road from John James's Mill on North Tyger River across South Tyger near the White oak Bottom from thence into Hites Road near Woodruffs Meeting-House, and make their report to next Court. Issued.

Ordered that what Estrays are produced to the sheriff this Court, liable for sale, be sold at the adjournment of the same according to Law. Issued.

Ordered that three Constables be Summoned to attend next Court, to execise their oficial duties. Issued.

Ordered that the minutes be read, which was accordingly done & Signed by William Smith, Baylis Earle, James Jordan, Judges.

Court then adjourned untill Court in Course.

31 At an Intermediate Court began and Held at Spartanburgh Court-House, on the Second Monday of April 1795. Present their Honours William Smith, James Jordan, Judges.

Samuel Miller Esquire being Elected Sheriff for this County produced his Commission from the Governor, Signed his bond and Quallify'd for the duties of his office.

The last Will and Testament of Arthur Simpson Deceased proved in open Court by Stephen Cruce, Richard Cruce and Robert Harriss according to Law. Ordered to be Recorded.

The last Will and Testament of Enoch Floyd Deceased proven in open Court by the Evidence of Andrew Thompson who made Oath that he saw Charles Bragg and Moore Bragg witness the same Together with himself. Ordered to Record.

Ordered that Edmond Snow act as Constable for this County, upon taking the necessary Oaths prescribed by Law, which he did in open Court.

The appraisment of the Estate of Dennis Lindsey Deceased, returned by the administratrix and ordered that she proceed to the sale of the same the 12th of May next, with a credit to purchasers of nine months Except Sums under one Dollar to be paid at the time of Sale.

Ordered that Robert Sterling oversee the Road from the Rich Hill to the County line towards McClebbens Ford on fairforest in place of William Simpson hands within three miles to work thereon. Issued.

32 Ordered that John Caldwell oversee the Road from Mr. Timmons's to the narrow passage in place of Joel Traylor; hands within three miles to work thereon. Issued.

On assignment upon a grant from Thomas Hays to Robert Armour proven before a Justice Ordered that it should be Recorded.

William Allen Executor in the will of Joseph Allen deceased came into open Court and took the oath prescribed by Law.

Ordered that Jonathan Harriss oversee the Road from the North side of Thickety which leads to the Cherokee Ford on Broad River to the County line in place of Thomas Cole. Hands within three Miles to work thereon. Issued.

Ordered that John Ross oversee the Road from Tates Ferry to the Meadows on the Cherokee Road. All hands within three miles to work thereon.

Ordered that the County Treasurer pay to the Widow Tackett (in proportion to the sum allowed her for a year) for six months past.

David Floyd Executor named in the will of Enoch Floyd deceased came into Court and took the oath prescribed by Law.

Ordered that Daniel Bragg act as Constable in this County upon taking the necessary oaths prescribed by Law, which he did in open Court.

33 Ordered that Thomas Price have Licence upon giving a Bond with Andrew Thomson and John F. Harmoning who were propsed as his Sureties.

Ordered that John F. Harmoning have Licence to keep Tavern on giving a bond with Andrew Thompson and Thomas Price, who were propsed as his Sureties.

Brittain Williford being recommended by Mr. Samuel Miller Sheriff of this County to serve as his deputy, who was approved of by the Court. And ordered that he be quallifyed which was accordingly done agreeable to Law.

Ordered that a resolution entered into by the Justices of the peace respecting the Estrays being kept at the appraisment Extend no farther than that of Estray Hogs.

Ordered that Alexander Alexander have Licence to Retail Spirituous Liquors upon giving Brittain Williford and John Tollison who were proposed, as his Sureties.

Ordered that the minutes be read, which was done and sign'd by William Smith, James Jordan, Judges.
Court then adjourn'd untill To morrow nine O Clock.

Tuesday the 14th 1795. Court met according to adjournment present his Honour James Jordan, Judge.

James Turner, Samuel Lancaster & George Bruton were quallifyed as Justices of the peace before William Smith Esquire, agreeable to his report.

34 Larkin Bethel being recommended to the Court by James Turner Esquire to act as a Constable was admitted and quallified according to Law.

According to a former order that Joseph Woodruff, James Wofford and Thomas Moore Esquire to View and lay off a Road from Capt. John James's Mill, to Mr. Shacklefords Meeting House on Hights Road. Report by Joseph Woodruff and James Wofford that they have marked and Laid off the same, But there is a bridge required across the South fork of Tyger River which report is defered for further consideration by the Court.

Nevil Wayland admr. of the Estate of John McElhany deceased return'd the Inventory and sale of the same.

Ordered that John Pace act as Constable in this County, upon taking the necessary oaths prescribed by Law, which he did in open Court.

Ordered that Thomas Green oversee the Road from the orebank Ford on Pacolate River to Frederick Gutry's Hog-pen at a Cross Road (in place of George Lamkin Esquire) all hands within three miles of the same to work thereon under his Directions. Issued.

Ordered that Justice Reynolds oversee the Road from this place to the ourbank ford on pacolate (in place of Wells Griffith) all hands within three (sic) of the same which are liable by Law to work thereon under his Directions. Issued.

35 Mary Young, wife of William Young, came into open court, and freely renounced to the Court all her right of Dower to twelve tracts of land wherein John and William Young hath impowered the Honourable Richard Winn Esquire to make Sale of.

Agreeable to a petition for a road from Captn. Daniel McClarens to intersect a road leading to Union Court House near the big meadows setting fourth that Daniel McClaren, Lewis Stanley and John Cooper lay off the same, and for said Stanley to open, oversee and keep the same in order, is granted by the Court, for the said to be effected agreeable to said Petition, all hands within three miles of the same which are liable by Law to work thereon under his Directions.

Ordered that the minutes be read which was Done and signed by James Jordan, Judge. Court then adjourn'd untill Court in Course.

36 At an Intermediate Court began and Held at the Court House of Spartanburgh County on the Second Monday of September 1795. Present their Honours William Smith, James Jordan, Judges.

Ordered that Captn. John Wright oversee and keep in good Repair, the Road from Pattons Ford on Tygar River to where Elisha Heddy oversees thereon--all hands within three miles of the same which are Liable by Law to work thereon under his Directions.   Issued.

Ordered that Joshua Downs have Licence to Keep Tavern, upon giving Isham Foster and John Foster his Sureties which he did by signing a bond in open Court.

Ordered that Henry Pettit oversee the Road from Gentleman Thomsons on Thickety to Hammetts Ford on Pacolate (in place of John Humphries) all withint three miles of the same which are liable by Law to work thereon under his Directions. Issued.

Agreeable to a presentment of the Grand Jury for a Road to be opened from Hammetts Ford on Pacolate, to Reynolds's Mill on Lawsons Fork from thence to the Court-House and requesting the Court to appoint Wm. T. Thomason, Zachariah Robertson and Vincent Wyatt to lay out the same, is accordingly granted by the Court & Ordered that they make their return to next Court. Issued.

37 Ordered that William Wells be allowed the sum of Two pounds Eighteen shillings & Six pence for Maintaining prisoners furnishing Guards & Estrays & Ct. and other contingent services for the County previous to this Court.

The last will and testament of James Miller deceased being proven in open court by the evidence of Francis Dodds, and David Drummons, Ordered to Record.

Ordered that George Bishop oversee the Road from the Boiling Springs to this Court-House (in place of Robert Kimbol) all hands within three miles of the same which are liable by Law to work thereon under his Directions. Issued.

Whereas Thomas Williamson was in June Session 1792, allowed the sum of five pounds & six pence for receiving and victualing William Morriss in Jail, and for keeping five Estrays. It is now Ordered that he be paid only the sum of Twelve shillings and Six pence for keeping the Estrays in lue (sic) thereof.

The Executors of the Estate of James Miller Deceased, took the oaths prescribed by Law as such.

Ordered that James Hooper Esquire be allowed the sum of Twenty five Shillings for Keeping and Wintering an Estray Horse. Copyed

Ordered that Coll. Thomas Moore, George Bruton & William Smith Esquires be appointed to left to the lowest bidder the building a bridge across Tyger River below the confluence of the North and South Tygers with an addition of Ten pounds from the County to a Subscription by the Neighbours thereunto if that is not Sufficient the sum of Fifteen pounds and no further.

38 Ordered that David Anderson and James Wofford View the most convenient and best way for a Road from Nichols's old Mill to David Andersons on Tyger River and from thence to Enoree River to where the Road is cleared the other side of the River the best and most convenient way to come the Road the other side near the Governor Shoo--(?).
And that Aaron Pinson oversee from Nichols Mill to South Tyger and Thomas Paden from South Tyger to Edward Arnolds Mill on Enoree. And open and Keep in good repair the same, all hands within three miles of the same which are liable by Law to work thereon under their directions.

Ordered that Benjamin McMaken be allowed in proportion for four Month. what he formerly was allowed for a year, for the

Keeping of a Negroe named Anthony which has become a County Charge.

Ordered that the Minutes be Read which was accordingly done and Signed by James Jordan, Wm. Smith, Judges.
Court then adjournd untill Court in Course.

39 At an Intermediate Court began and (sic) at the Court-House of Spartanburgh County on the Second Monday in April 1796. Present their Honours. James Jordan, William Smith, Judges.

John Lipscomb being appointed by the assembly as a Justice of the peace for this County, came into Court and took the oaths of office prescribed by Law.

Ordered that Samuel Neely oversee the Road from Nichols's old Mill to where it intersects the Road from Fords Mill to the Iron-Works (in place of Jeremiah Silman) all hands within three miles of the same to work thereon under his Directions. Issued.

The last Will and testament of Samuel Brice proven in open Court by the evidence of Thomas Paden, Francis Dodds, and John Caldwell. Ordered to Record.

Thomas Paden and Francis Dodds Executors of Samuel Brice decd. took the oaths required by Law.

Ordered that John James, Samuel Snoddy and Thomas Moore Esquire appraise the Estate of Samuel Brice deceased, and make due return thereof.

Nathan Lipscomb being appointed to act as constable in this county came into court and took the oaths of office prescribed by Law.

40 Ordered that Thomas Gillingwaters oversee the Road from the County line below Mr. Shippies to Mr. Thomsons (in place of Wm. Wilkins) all hands within three miles of the same which are liable by Law to work thereon under his directions. Issued.

the last will and testament of John King proven in open Court by the evidence of Wm. Ford--laid over for further proof.

Ordered that Alexander Alexander have Licence to keep tavern upon giving John Frederick Harmony and Thomas Price his Surities.

Ordered that John Fred. Harmony have Licence to Keep Tavern upon giving Alexander Alexander & Thomas Price who were proposed his Surities.

Ordered that Thomas Price have Licence to keep Tavern upon giving John Fred. Harmony and Alexander Alexander his Surities.

Ordered that the Estrays produced to the Sheriff be sold this evening.

Ordered that Jonathan Neasbett be allowed the sum of Ten shillings for Wintering an Estray Cow.

Ordered that Millie Gravatte have full administration on the Estate of Obadiah Gravatte deceased upon giving George Bruton

Joseph Woodruff and Alexander Evans as her Surities for her Lawful performance, and qualifying according to Law.

41 Ordered Wells Griffith be allowed the sum of three pounds Eight Shillings and Eight pence out of the County fund for Ironing putting in and Keeping in Jail Sundry persons.

The last will and testament of David Cooper deceased, proven in open court by the evidence of Obadiah Trimmier & Obadiah Watson, ordered to Record.

A bill of Sale from Thomas Williamson to Henry Onail acknowledged in open court. Ordered to Record.

Ordered that Moses Timmons oversee that part of the Road from the Court House of this County to that of Greenville, from where said Road Intersects Millers Road to Jamies Creek (in place of Samuel Jamison) all hands within three Miles of the same, which are liable by Law to work thereon under his directions. Issued.

David Burton quallified as an Executor on the Estate of John King deceased.

Ordered that Andrew Cowen oversee the Road from the Narrow passage to a certain crooked tree below James Hughes's (in place of Elisha Hedden) John Hughs warner. All hands within three miles of the same which are liable by Law to work thereon under his Directions. Issued.

42 Ordered that Edward Hooker, Richard Young and Jesse Spann review the Road from Isaac Crows to Musgroves on Enoree and make return thereof to next Court. Issued.

Ordered that fifteen Shillings be allowed Benjamin McMakin for Keeping two Stears & 3 Sheep as Estrays.

Ordered that Bazel Lee be allowed the sum of Twenty-five shillings for Keeping Estray Mare.

Ordered that the Minutes be Read which was done and Sign'd by Wm Smith, James Jordan, Judges.
Court then adjourn'd untill to-morrow nine o Clock.

Tuesday the 12th day of April 1796. Court met according to adjournment. Present their Honours Wm Smith, James Jordan, Judges.

Ordered David Bruton James Southerland and John Bragg appraise the estate of Obadiah Gravatte deceased and make their return thereon. George Bruton Esquire to qualify the appraisers. Issued.

The last Will and Testament of John King proven in open Court by the evidence of Charles Whitten, Ordered to be Recorded.

43 James King Executor of the Estate of John King deceased came into Court and qualified accordingly.

Ordered that George Bruton Esquire, Joseph Woodruff and Alexander Alexander appraise the Estate of John King deceased and make their Return thereon.

Ordered that Charles Hester have Licence to Keep Tavern on Giving George Lamkin and William Benson his Surities, which he did accordingly.

Thomas Clerk, Moses Casey Junior, Arias Brown, Isaac Pace and Hugh McMullen being qualified by the Judges of this Court Ordered that they act as constables in this county.

Ordered that three constables be summoned to next Court to practice their official duties.

Ordered that David Anderson oversee the Road from Captn. John James's House to South Tygar at David Andersons, John Durham from thence to Captn. Zadock Fords Muster Ground at the cross Road; Denny Anderson from thence to Enoree at sd. Denny Andersons. All hands within Three Miles of the same which are Liable by Law to work thereon under their Directions. Issued.

Ordered that Reubin Daniel oversee the Road from James Saunders's at the Cross Roads to this Court-House (in place of Job Soesby) all hands within three miles of the same which are liable by Law to work thereon under his Directions. Issued.

44 Ordered that Majr. John Gowen be paid out of the County fund the sum of five pounds nineteen Shillings and three pence for his Contingent Services done for the County while he was acting as a Sheriff for the same. Copyed.

Arnold Thomas being appointed to act as Constable in this County, came into Court and took the necessary oaths accordingly.

Ordered that the Estrays produced to the Sheriff be sold at the adjournment of Court.
Ordered that the Sheriff be paid out of the County funds the Extra fees allowed them by Law. Copyed.

Ordered that the Minutes be read which was done and sign'd by Wm Smith, James Jordan, Judges.
Court then adjourn'd untill Court in Course.

At an Intermediate Court began and Held at the Court-House of Spartanburgh on the second Monday in September 1796. present his Honour. James Jordan, Judge.

Ordered that William Turner oversee the Road from the boiling Springs to this Court House (in place of George Bishop) And hands within 3 Miles of the same to work thereon under his directions. Issued.

45 Ordered that Colo. Thomas Moore, Berryman D Shubate(?) Esquire & Isham Foster Esquire appraise the Estate of William Benson deceased and make due Return thereof.

The appraisment of the Estate of Obadiah Gravat deceased Return'd into open Court by the administratrix.

Present his Honour William Smith Esquire.

Ordered that Jacob Utly oversee the Road from this Court-House to where it Intersects Millers Road (in place of Obadiah Wingo) all hands within three Miles of the same which are liable by Law to Work thereon under his direction. Issued.

The appraisment of the Estate of John King deceased returned by the Executor.

The appraisment of the Estate of Samuel Brice deceased returned in open Court by the Executor.

Sarah King an Executrix of the Estate of John King deceased came into open court & took the oath of an Executrix prescribed by Law.

The appraisement and Vendue Bill of the Estate of Samuel Morrow deceased, Returnd by the Executor.

46 Ordered that Samuel Culbertson oversee the Road from Wilies fork to the Shoals on fairforest (in place of Henry ONail) all hands within three miles of the same which are liable by Law to work thereon under his directions. Issued.

Ordered that Nelley Benson & Gabriel Benson have the full administration on the Estate of William Benson deceased upon Signing a Bond & takeing the Necessary Oaths prescribed by Law, which they did in open Court.

Ordered that the administrators of the Estate of William Benson deceased, proceed to the sale of the said Deceaseds Estate on the second Thursday in december upon giving Twenty days Legal Notice, at Twelve Months Credit, all sums under Ten Shillings to be paid at the day of Sale.

William Simpson as Guardian of the person and Estate of Agnes Byrd came into open Court and Relinquished all his right & title of a Lease and Release made to him as a Guardian of the said Agness Byrd, to the said Agness Byrd, for which he was chosen Guardian.

The last will and Testament of Thomas Sexton deceased proven in open Court by the evidence of David Bruton & James Taylor Ordered to Record.

Ordered that Christopher Golightly oversee the Road from the Rich Hill to the old Iron works (in place of Joseph Barnett) all hands within three miles of the same which are liable by Law to work thereon under his directions. Issued.

47 Ordered that Joseph Dill oversee half the Road from the Cowpens to Tates Ferry on Broad River & John Turner the other half. All hands within three miles of the same which are liable by Law to work thereon under their Directions. Issued.

Ordered that Wells Griffith be allowed Twenty three shillings & four pence out of the County fund for Blacksmiths work done by Ironing prisoners in Jail. Copyed.

Alexander Walker appointed & accepted to act as County Treasurer for this County in place of William Benson who is deceased, and ordered that he make application to the administrators of the said William Benson for the papers pertaining to the County Treasury.

Ordered that William Smith Esquire proceed to the sale of two Estray cattle Told before him by Epraim Hill.

Ordered that the Estrays produced to this Court be sold by the Sheriff according to Law.

Ordered that Josiah Hatchet oversee the Road leading from Hurts Meeting-House to the Cross Roads (in place of Travice Reese) all hands within three miles of the same which are liable by Law to work thereon under his directions. Issued.

Ordered that William Wells have Licence to Keep public House & Retail Spiritous Liquors upon giving Moses Timmons and Wells Griffith his Surities.

Ordered that the Minutes be Read which was done & signed by William Smith, James Jordan, Judges.
Court then adjournd until Court in Course.

48 At an Intermediate Court began & Held for the County of Spartanburgh on the second Monday in April 1797. Present their Honours William Smith, Isham Harrison, Judges.

The last Will and Testament of Andrew Hendrix deceased, proven in open Court by the evidence of Andrew Thomson & John Erwin Ordered to Record.

Ordered that James Lankford Joseph Woodruff and John Erwin appraise the Estate of Andrew Hendrix deceased and make due Return thereof.

Ordered that Job Soseby oversee the Road from this Court-House to Peters Creek, leading to the Island ford on Broad River, and that William Shed oversee from Peter Creek to Pacolate River in place of William Garrett. All hands within three Miles of the same which are liable by Law to work thereon under their directions. Issued.

Ordered that Richard Beardan have the full administration on the Estate of John Beardan deceased, upon giving Brittain Williford & Thomas Biddenton, surities in a bond of Thirty-five pounds for his Lawful performance & qualifying as the Law directs, which he did in open Court.

Ordered that Brittain Williford, Thomas Williams & Bazel Trail appraise the Estate of John Beardan deceased, and make due return thereof.

49 The last will & Testament of Alexander Ray deceased proven in open Court by the evidence of Francis McDowell & William Ford who made oath that they saw John Hurt witness the same together with themselves.

Ordered that the Estate of John Beardan deceased be sold to the Highest bidder(in giving Twenty day public Notice) at twleve Months Credit for all sums above one dollar, and all under to be paid at the time of Sale.

Ordered that (on Information of William Simpson Esquire) David Brown & Robert Sterling be cited to next Court, to shew cause if any they have why the do not keep the Road on which they were appointed overseers in good Repair.

Ordered that Paul Castleberry oversee & Keep in good Repair that part of the canebrake From from Isaac Crows to Woodruffs Meeting house (in place of Joseph Woodruff) all hands within three Miles which are liable by Law to work thereon under his directions. Issued.

Ordered that Alexander Alexander have Licence to keep publick House & Retail Spiritous Liquors upon giving Henry Wells & Joseph Woodruff his Surities for his Lawful permance (sic).

Ordered that John Wright, David Tanner & John Bragg view & mark out the most conveniant and best way for a Road from said Tanners field in the fork of Tygar River to corss the bridge opposite George Fleys plantation to Intersect the Charleston Road thereat. Issued.

50 Ordered that the commissioners of the poor be allowed Twenty-five pounds out of the County fund when Collected for the use of the Poor.

Ordered that William Wells be allowed out of the County fund eleven & Eight pence for Keeping Two Estrays in January Court last. Copyed.

Ordered that the Minutes be Read which was done & Signed by William Smith, Isham Harrison, Judges.

Tuesday the 11th of April 1797. Court met according to adjournment. Present their Honors William Smith, Isham Harrison, Judges.

Ordered that the Sheriff of this County be paid five pounds out of the County fund for his Extra services for the year 1796. Copyed.

Ordered that the Clerk be allowed out of the fines and forfeitures of this County one pounds Six Shillings being a ballance of his Services done for the State from June Court 1793 to July Court 1796.

Ordered that William Underwood oversee the Road in place of Joel Hurt all hands within three Miles of the same to work thereon. Issued.

Ordered that Richard James oversee & keep in good Repair the Road from the old Iron Works to the Cross Road at Saunder's former dwellings, in place of Wells Griffith, all hands within three Miles of the same, which are liable by Law to work thereon under his directions. Issued.

51 Ordered that Alexander McKie have Licence to Keep public House & Retail Spiritous Liquors upon signing a bond for that purpose.

Ordered that the Minutes be read which was done and signed by William Smith, Isham Harrison, Judges.
Court then adjourn'd untill Court in Course.

At an Intermediate (sic) began and held at the Court-House of Spartanburgh County on the Second Monday in September 1797. Present their Honours, William Smith, Isham Harrison, Judges.

Ordered that William Crow have Licence to Keep Public House & Retail Liquors, upon Giving John Rainwaters & George Robuck his Surities for his Lawful performance.

Ordered that Thomas Price Have Licence to Keep public House & retail Liquors upon giving John Rainwater & Alexander Alexander his Surities for his Lawful performance.

Ordered that a Road be opened & kept in good Repair from blackstocks Road near Thomas Meadows's to Rodgers's Bridge on Tygar River, from thence to the Charlestown Road leading by Isaac Crows, to intersect the Charleston Road at Alexander Alexanders lane agreeable to the laying off, of Tobias Bright & Charles Burton And that Tobias Bright of the same from the bridge to Blackstocks Road, Thomas Shurly warner; and Alexander Alexander from his plantation to the bridge, Seal Beason warner. All hands within three Miles of the same which are liable by Law to work thereon under their Directions. Issued.

52 Ordered that a Road be opened & kept in good repair from David Tanners field in the fork of Tygar River to Cross the bridge opposite George Floyds plantation to intersect the Charleston Road thereat agreeable to the laying off, of John Wright & John Bragg; and that John Wright oversee the same; and the George Ison warn all hands within three Miles thereof which are liable by Law to work thereon. Issued.

The last will & Testament of Samuel Elder deceased proven in open Court by the evidence of William Otts & Hammon Elder Ordered to Record.

Thomas Moore and Samuel Otts came into Court & took the Necessary Oaths prescribed by Law, as Executors on the Estate of Samuel Elder deceased.

Ordered that Jesse Spiveer(?), Roland Jennings & Martins Otts appraise the Estate of Samuel Elder deceased. Issued.

Ordered that Reubin Matthews oversee & Keep in good repair the Road from the old Iron works, to Hammetts Ford on Pacolate River, all hands within three miles thereof to work thereon under his direction. Issued.

Ordered that Joseph Lively be allowed out of the County fund seven shillings for wintering an Estray Cow. Copyed.

Ordered that Lucy Wm & John Lemaster have full administration on the Estate of Ralph Lemaster deceased, on Signing Bond & qualifying agreeable to Law, which they did in open Court.

53 Ordered that Captain Daniel McClaren John Turner and John Lamkin Esquire, View and lay out a road the nearest and best way from Cherokee by Colonel Trimmiers to Camps old Meeting House then into the road that Leads from Spartan Court-House to Camps Ferry on Broad River and make report of the same at next Court.

Ordered that John Lukeroy, James Gosset and Richison Whitley appraise the Estate of Ralph Lemaster deceased.

Ordered that after Twenty days Notice the Estate of Ralph Lemaster be sold to the highest bidder at Twelve Months Credit.

Ordered that Malichi Jones, Zachariah Robertson and Nathan Ward, View and lay out a Road from Hammetts Ford on Pacolate, the nearest and best way to said Robertsons Ford on Lawsons fork, from thence to Spartanburgh Court-House and that Bazel Lee oversee the same. All hands within three Miles of the same to work thereon under his direction. Issued.

Smith Lipscomb being appointed to act as Constable (in place of Nathan Lipscomb) came into Court and took the necessary oaths of office prescribed by Law.

Ordered that James Ward, Obadiah Wingo & John Foster (Chinquepin) lay out a Road the best & nearest way from this Court House to Nichols's old Mill, and that William Wingo open and oversee the same. All hands within three Miles of the same to work thereon. Issued.

54 Ordered that William Wells have Licence to Retail Liquors, upon Giving John Foster & Obadiah Watson his Sureties for his Lawful performance.

Ordered that the Minutes be read which was done & Signed by William Smith, Isham Harrison, Judges. Court then adjourn'd 'till Tomorrow 10 O Clock.

Tuesday the 12th day of September 1797. Court met according to adjournment. Present thier Honours. William Smith, Isham Harrison, Judges.

Ordered that William Foster, Majr. William Foster F. F. and Isham Foster Esquire, View and report to next Court whether it is needful to open a Road from William McWilliams bridge to William Brannums from thence to Blackstocks road, or not.

Ordered that Robert McDowell oversee the Road from the Bridge upon Pacolate, to the boiling Springs Meeting-House in place of Daniel White, all hands within three Miles to work thereon.

Ordered that theClerk be paid out of the fines and forfeitures of this County, Nine pounds fifteen shillings, for his services done for the State from January Court 1797 to July Court 1797.

Ordered that Jonathan Harris have the liberty of opening and keeping in repair at his own Expence a road from the road near his House across the head of a branch, Intersecting the road leading to the Cherokee Ford on Broad River about a mile from his House. Issued.

55 Ordered that Drury McDaniel be allowed out of the County fund the sum of fourteen Shillings, for Keepin an Estray taken up by Abraham Whittemore, and Told before Thomas Moore Esquire.

Ordered that the Minutes be Read which was done & Signed by William Smith, Isham Harrison, Judges. Court then adjourn'd untill Court in Course.

At an Intermediate Court began and Held at the Court House of Spartanburgh County on the second Monday in April 1798. Present their Honours James Jordan, Isham Harrison, Judges.

Ordered that William Traylor, Oversee the Road from Moses Timmons's to the Narrow passage (in place of John Caldwell) and that Richard Pace warn all hands within three Miles to work thereon. Issued.

Ordered that Drury McDaniel oversee the Road from the Narrow passage to a certain Crooked tree below James Hughes's (in place of Andrew Coan) and that John Harris warn all hands within three Miles of the same to work thereon. Issued.

Ordered that John Tollison have Licence to Retail Liquors upon given John Golightly and Joseph Barnett his Surities for his Lawful performance.

Ordered that Justice Reynolds, George Lamkin Esquire, Wm Turner Thomason and

56 Vincent Wyatt View the best way for a Road from the fork of the Road from Lewis Cannons to Hewetts Cabbin into the Camp ferry Road, leading to Spartan Court House and Report to next Court thereon. Issued.

Ordered that Rolley Horton oversee the Road from the Island ford on Pacolate to the old boundary in place of George Lamkin Esq. and that James Lackey warn all hands within three miles of the same which are liable by Law to work thereon. Issued.

Ordered that Margaret Blackwood and James Blackwood have the full adminstration on the estate of Joseph Blackwood deceased upon Signing a Bond for that purpose and qualifying according to Law.

Ordered that William Thomson, William Lipscomb, and Obadiah Trimmier Esquire, View the Two Roads from Harrises to William Hesters and report to next Court which shall be a Public Road. Issued.

Ordered that George Bruton, Benjamin Wofford & Nathaniel Woodruff View the nearest and best Road from Pattons Ford on Tygar River to Benjamin Woffords on Enoree and make report of the same at next Court. Issued.

Ordered that David Lipscomb be allowed Ten shillings for wintering an Estray cow.

Ordered that Edward Hooker oversee & keep in good repair the road from Isaac Crows, down by Frederick Harmonings Store from thence to Musgroves Mill. All hands within three Miles of the same which are liable by Law to work thereon under his directions. Issued.

57 Ordered that John Frederick Harmoning have Licence to keep Tavern & retail Liquors upon giving John Williams & Bennett Langston his Surities for his Lawful performance.

Ordered that William Foster oversee and keep in good repair the Road from Nichols's old Mill to where it intersects the Road from Fords Mill to the Iron works (in place of Samuel Neely) all hands within three Miles of the same which are liable by Law to work thereon.

Ordered that a Road be opened and Kept in good repair from Cherokee to Colo. Trimmiers from thence to the old Meeting-House, and that a road be cut in the most direct manner from said Road, into the Cowpen Road, and that Obadiah Trimmier Esquire overse and Keep in good repair the same. All hands within three Miles thereof to work thereon.

Ordered that upon Examination by the Judges of the books and accompts of the former Co. Treasurer, to wit, William Benson, Esquire deceased, there appears a ballance due of seven pounds two Shillings & five pence, to the Estate of the said deceased And that the same be paid to the Administrator of the Estate the said deceased, out of the County fund.

Ordered that Alexander McKie have Licence to keep tavern and retail Spiritous Liquors upon giving Alexander Walker and George Connell his Surities for his Lawful performance.

Ordered that a Road from the lower bridge on South Pacolate to Brannons Shoal on Lawsons fork, from thence across the Creek along the ridge the left of Roland Johnsons, be opened and kept in good repair. and that William Brannon oversee

58 the same from Pacolate to Lawsons fork and Roland Johnson from thence to where it intersects Blackstocks Road, and that all hands within three Miles of the same to work thereon under their Directions. Issued.

Ordered that Alexander McKie be allowed out of the County fund Two pounds Eleven Shillings for his Contingent services as Jailor maintaining prisoners in Jail & Ct.

Ordered that Martha Thornton have the full administration on the Estate of her Husband Thomas Thornton deceased upon signing a Bond for that purpose & Qualifying according to Law.

Ordered that Thomas Williams, Thomas Compton & John Beardan appraise the Estate of Thomas Thornton deceased and make due Return thereof.

Ordered that George Keesee, Thomas McKnight & William McKnight appraise the estate of Joseph Blackwood deceased and make due return thereof. Issued.

Ordered that Zachariah Sparks oversee and keep in good repair the Road from the old Iron Works to the Cross Road near Peters Creek and all hands within three miles of the same which are liable by Law to work thereon under his directions.

59 Ordered that the Administratrix of the Estate of Thomas Thornton deceased proceed to the sale of the same at Twelve Months Credit, after giving Twenty days public Notice

Ordered that the administrators of the Estate of Joseph Blackwood Deceased, proceed to the sale of the same at Twelve months Credit, after giving Twenty days public Notice.

Ordered that Mary Chamblin and James Chamblin have the full administration of the Estate of Jesse Chamblin deceased, upon signing a bond for that purpose and qualifying according to Law.

Ordered that William Wilder, Thomas Miles & John Rainwater appraise the Estate of Jesse Chamblin deceased, and make due return thereof.

Order that the administrators of the Estate of Jesse Chamblin deceased, proceed to the sale of said Estate after giving Twenty days legal Notice thereof.

Ordered that the Sheriff be paid three pounds four Shillings & Six pence for services done in behalf of the State (Out of the County fund) by Virtue of his office.

Ordered that the Estrays which are liable for sale be sold this evening at the adjournment of Court.

Ordered that the Minutes be read which was done & sign'd by James Jordan, Isham Harrison, Judges.
Court then adjournd 'till Tomorrow Ten O Clock.

60 Tuesday the 10th of April 1798. Court met according to adjournment. Present their Honors. James Jordan, Isham Harrison, Judges.

The last will & Testament of Robert Lee Proven in open court by the evidence of Igantious Griffin & John Pearce also an addition or Codicil to said will was proven to be made by the said Testator by the evidence of James Wofford.

John Lee Executor of the Estate of Robert Lee deceased, came into Court and took the Oath of an Executor of said Estate.

Ordered that Edward Smith oversee the Green River Road from William Thomson to Gutry's Mill on Thickety and that Zachariah Blackwell oversee from thence to the State line of North Carolina. All hands within three Miles to work thereon.

Ordered that Alexander Alexander have Licence to Keep public House and retail Liquors upon Giving Anthony Foster and Brittain Williford his surities for his Lawful performance.

Ordered that William Hester have Licence to keep public House & Retail Liquors upon Giving William Thomson & William Lipscomb his Surities for his Lawful performance.

Ordered that a Road be opened from Jesse Matthews's to the fork of the main Court-House road that leads from the old Works and that Littleton Bagwell oversee & keep in good repair the same. All hands within three miles of

61 the same which are liable by Law to work thereon under his directions.

Ordered that the Sheriff be paid five pounds out of the County fund, for his Extra services for the year 1797.

Ordered that the Minutes be read which was done & sign'd by James Jordan, Isham Harrison, Judges.
Court then adjourn'd 'till Court in Course.

 An an Intermediate Court began to be holden at the Court house of Spartanburgh County on the Second Monday in September Seventeen hundred and Ninety Eight. Present their Honors William Smith, James Jordan & Isham Harrison, Esquires.

Ordered that John McCluer oversee (in place of John Anderson) the Road from Charles McKnights ford on North Pacolet to a certain fish pound (sic) on South Pacolet and That Thomas McCarrel & John Rogers warn the hands within three miles of the Same to work thereon under his Direction.

Ordered that Henry Young over see the Road from the Bridg on

South Pacolet to the North Carolina line (in place of Thomas Jackson) and that William Young and Jesse Dalton warn the hands within three miles thereof to work thereon under his Direction.

62 Ordered that Charles Morgan, View, lay out, open & keep in good repair, A Road from William Hester, to the County line of Union, intersecting a road leading to the Grindal Shoals, and that John Cooper warn the hands within three miles of the same to work thereon under his Direction.

Ordered that William T. Thomason oversee in place of Justice Reynolds the road from Spartanburgh Court House the Oar bank ford on Pacolet River. All hands within three miles to work thereon under his Directions.

Ordered that Moses Timmons have Licence to keep Tavern to retail Spiritous liquors upon giving William Wells & Henry Wells his Surities for his lawful performance.

The last will and Testament of Edward Linch being proven in open Court by the evidences of Aaron Casey & Benjamin Stone ordered to Record.

James Linch and John Casey Executors of the Estate of Edward Linch deceased came into open court and took the necessary oaths as Executors.

Moses Timmons came into court and give Satisfaction thereunto concerning a presentment of the grand Jury last Court respecting a Road. Therefore ordered the (sic) he be Dismissed from the presentment.

Ordered that Abraham Pool, William Stewart & Matthew Couch appraise the Estate of Edward Linch deceased & make due return

63 Ordered that James Turner, Alexander Walker, Michael Miller and John Redmond View the nearest and best way for a road from Kelleys Mill on Enoree to or near the forks of the Pacolet Extending to Bridges Ferry on Broad River and report thereon to next court.

Ordered that James Fowler Over See the road from Major John Gowens to the Cross Road called Passons road (in place of Samuel Fowler) All hands within three miles is to work thereon under his Direction.

Ordered that the minutes be red which was done and Signed by William Smith, James Jordan, I Harrison, Judges.
Court then adjourned untill Tomorrow ten O Clock.

Tuesday the 11th day of September 1798.
The Honourable Court met according to adjournment Present their Honors William Smith and Isham Harrison Esquires.

Mrs. Story Wood widow of John Wood deceased came into Court and Relinquished her right of aministration on said Estate whereupon Ordered that Robert Wood & John Wood have the full administration on said Estate upon Signing a bond for that purpose & Qualifying accordingly which they Did in Open Court.

64 Ordered that the Clerk be paid out of the fines and Forfeitures of this County the Sum of two pounds Eleven Shillings

and Six pence for Servises done for the State from July Court 1797 till July Court 1798.

Ordered that Isham Foster Esqr John Wood and William Foster of Tyger appraise the Estate of John Wood deceased and make due return thereof.

Ordered that the administrators of the Estate of John Wood Senr. Deceased proceeded to the Sale thereof after giving twenty days Publick Notice at twelve months Credit Except Sums under two Dollars which is to be paid upon the time of Sale.

Ordered that the Commissioners of the poor be paid Twenty pounds out of the County fund as soon as it can be collected by the County Treasurer.

Ordered that an Estray Cow Taken up by Jethro OSheal and Told before William Smith Esq. be sold by Esqr. Smith.

Ordered that a road be opened from Polley Woods Road up the Old Road by Majr. Fosters intersecting Blackstocks Road about a half Mile above Majr. Fosters and that Gideon See Over See & Keep in good repair the Same. All hands within three Miles to work thereon under his Direction.

Ordered that the Minutes be red which was done & signed by Court then adjourned untill Court in Course. William Smith, I Harrison, Judges.

65 At an Entermediate (sic) Court began and held at the Court House of Spartanburgh County on the Second Monday in April 1799.

Ordered that William Bishop Over See and keep in good repair the road from the Bridg on lawsons fork near the Widow Bishops to the Bridg on South Pacolet (in place of James Alexander) all hands within three miles to work thereon. Issued.

Ordered that Anthony Foster have Licence to Keep Publick Entertainment and retail Spirituous Liquors upon Giving Henry Wells and John Rainwaters his Sureties for his lawfull performance.

Ordered that John Wood Oversee the road from Buck Branch to the fork of the road near the Widow Bishops (in place of William Foster) and that Robert Foster warn the hands within three Miles to work thereon. Issued.

The last Will & Testament of John Shippy proven in Open Court by the Evidences of John Lipscomb Esqr. and Henry Littlejohn Ordered to record.

A Deed of Conveyance from Michael Miller to James Vernon acknowledged in Open Court and Ordered to record.

A Deed of Conveyance from Benjamin Jones to Michael Miller proven by the Evidence of James Jordon Esqr. according to Law. Ordered to Record.

66 The last will and Testament of James Wood Deceased proven in open Court by the Evidences James Dunnaway and Catharine Dunneway. Ordered to record.

Ordered that Thomas Price have Licence to retail Spiritous Liquors upon giving John F. Harmoning and Andrew Thomson his Sureties for his lawful performance.

Ordered that Alexander McKie have Licence to Retail Spiritous Liquors upon his giving Briton Williford & Alexander Walker his Sureties for his lawful performance.

Ordered that Daniel McKie have Licence to retail Spiritous Liquors & Keep bublock entertainment upon giving Alexander McKie and Drury McDaniel Esqr. his Sureties for his lawful performance.

Joseph Massey being Sworn Constable before Isham Harrison Ordered that he Act accordingly Isham Foster Esquire Qualifyd as a Justice of the peace Before James Jordan Esqr.

Livingston Bobo Being sworn as a constable before James Jordan Esqr ordered that he Act accordingly.

Lemuel Lancaster being sworn as a Constable before Isham Harrison Esqr Ordered that he Act in this County accordingly.

Ordered that the Estate of Zebulon Bragg Deceased be sold by the administrators at twelve months credit for all Sums above ten shillings after twenty days publick notice being given.

67 Ordered that Robert Stacy oversee the road from William Thompsons to the County Line of Union in place of John Lipscomb Esqr. and that the hands within three miles thereof to work thereon under his Direction.   Issued.

The last will and Testament of Stephen Wilson deceased proven in Open Court by the Evidences of Thomas Todd and Joseph Pelfrey. Ordered to record.

Reubin Wilson Executors of the Estate of Stephen Wilson deceased came into Open Court and took the Necessary Oathes of that Office prescribed by Law.

Smith Lipscomb came into Open Court and qualified as an Executor of James Wood deceased.

Ordered that William Thompson, Obadiah Watson & Henry McCray Esqr. appraise the Estate of James Wood deceased & Make due return thereof.

Ordered that Thomas Todd, Thomas Miles & Daniel Grant appraise the Estate of Stephen Wilson deceased and make due return thereof.

Samuel Shippy came into Court and qualified as an Executor of John Shippy deceased.

Ordered that William Lipscomb, William Wilkey & John Lipscomb appraise the estate of John Shippy deceased and make due return thereof.

Armistead Shumate qualified as an Executor of the Estate of Alexander Ray deceased to act (in place of Elizabeth Ray widow and Executrix of the said deceased) he being the present husband of the said Executrix.

68 Ordered that Sarah Ross have the full administration of the Estate of John Ross Deceased upon qualifying giving bond with Charles Hester, James Smith & Henry McCray Esqr. as Sureties for her lawful performance.

Ordered that James Smith, Charles Hester & Henry McCray Esqr. appraise the Estate of John Ross deceased and make due return thereon.

Ordered that Jethro Osheal be allowed Seven Shillings for wintering a cow and Earling told before Wm. Smith Esqr. Taken up by said OSheal to be paid out of the County fund.

Ordered that Alexander McKie be allowd. the sum of One pound fifteen shillings & Six pence out of the County fund for Keeping Estrays Jail locks & C.

Ordered that Jesse Reames Over See the road from the fork near the widow Bishops to the Creek at James Fowlers (in place of William Fields) and that Isaac Bishop warn the hands within three Miles to work thereon.   Issued.

Ordered that James Wofford, Colo. Thomas Moore & Joseph Woodruff View the ground and mark out a road from John Hughes to Woodruffs Meating House Commonly called Bethell   and make a Return thereof to July Court next. Issued.

Ordered that Isham Bobbit Over See the road from Peters Creek to this Court House (in place of Job Sosbee) and that Geo. Thomason warn the hands within three Miles to work thereon. Issued.

69 Ordered that John Arnold Oversee the road from Tates Ferry on Broad River to Lafeverses (in place of John Ross Deceased) Issued.

Ordered that John Nelson Oversee the Road from Warrens ford on Pacolet to the North Carolina line and the William Morriss warn the hands within three Miles to work thereon. Issued.

Ordered that Michael Miller, Benjamin McMekin and John Gowen Esqr. View the ground and lay out a road from Hills or Stoans Ironworks to the County line crossing South Pacolet and make their report to September Court next.

Briton Williford producing his Commission from the Governor as Sheriff of this County Signed his bond and qualified accordingly.

Willis Williford being recommended by the high Sheriff of this County to act as his Deputy was approved of by the Court and was qualified accordingly.

Ordered that John Hewit Over See the road from the County line near Blacks ford on Tyger River to Ephraim Hills old place John Red, warner and that Thomas Moore Oversee from thence to Where it Entersex (sic) Millers old road Samuel Elder, warner & that Jeremiah Silmon Senr Oversee from thence to the Buck Branch William Hammitt, warner, all hands within three miles to work thereon under their directions. Issued.

70 Absolam Lancaster being appointed a Justice of the peace for this County Was duly qualified Before Isham Harrison Esquire.

Ordered that William Fields be allowed the sum of Fourteen shillings out of the County funds for an Estray that was Sold which was Since proven to be the property of the said Fields.

Ordered that the Minutes be read which was accordingly done and signed by William Smith, James Jordan, Isham Harrison, Judges. Court then adjourned untill Court in Course.

END OF VOLUME

Index Prepared by Mary E. Phillips, Ft. Worth, Texas

_____ Bazel 78

Abanatha, James 65
Abbot(t), Matthew 264
  William 57
Acry, James 270
Adair, James 31
  Joseph 106, 122
Adams, ___ 26, 29, 43, 124
  Godfrey 131
  Robert 26
Adcock, Leonard 45, 73, 76, 83, 93, 103, 215, 223, 225
Aires (see Airs, Eyres), Henry 73, 78, 82, 135, 143
Airs (see Eyres), Henry 30, 57, 59, 69
Alderage, William 45
Alexander, Alexander 4, 21, 28, 33, 36(2), 45, 47, 62, 64, 72, 73, 79, 132(3), 163, 178, 199, 214, 130, 216, 237, 239(2), 243, 244, 246, 259, 267, 280, 283(2), 292(3), 293, 297, 298(2), 302
  Ann 46
  George 22, 62
  James 7, 27, 46, 56, 57, 59, 61, 69, 73, 77, 80, 83, 176, 186, 205, 227, 275, 304
  John 7, 17, 27, 29(2), 157, 167
  Joseph 164
  Joseph Jr. 178
  Mary 220, 227
  Matthew 27, 91, 106, 117, 112
  Robert 243
  Thomas 220, 221, 227, 275
  William 122
Alldredge, William 114, 128, 134(4), 138, 154
Allen, Allen 105
  Daniel 210, 216(2), 218, 221
  David 65, 147, 153(2), 177, 239, 265, 266
  David Jr. 258
  John 167
  Joseph 205(2), 289
  Rhoda 173
  William 173, 215, 242, 249, 266, 289
Allison, James 103
Amos, Daniel 147, 153(2), 215, 263
  Francis 55, 68, 110
  James 46, 62, 68, 203
Anderson, Abram 6
  Baley 3
  David 26, 28, 35, 45, 46, 215, 220, 222, 233, 239, 246, 248, 291, 294
  Denny 37, 46, 59, 138, 155, 168(3), 198, 204, 225(2), 239, 294
  James 203
  Jno. 6, 222, 231, 239, 246, 260, 278, 302
  Mariah 32
  Mary Ann 233
  Miriam 154
  Rebekah 220, 228, 233(2)
  Thomas 265
  Vincent 149
  William 44, 158, 231, 242, 263
Andrews, Abraham 230, 239, 240, 241
  Abram 119
Andrewson, David 69
  Isaac 121-122
Armour, Robert 114(2), 203, 210, 211(2), 289

Armstrong, John 92, 209, 220, 233, 235
  Martin 13, 17, 18, 69, 73, 81, 91, 94, 104(2), 106, 110, 112, 118, 119, 139, 157, 167, 174
  William 92
Arnett, ___ 281
  Ann 74, 84, 85, 95
  Edward 74, 84, 85, 95
Arnold, Ann 146(2)
  Benjamine 70, 155, 230, 239
  Bridges 250
  Edward 106, 145, 146, 153, 155, 162, 168, 197, 210
  John 19, 198, 204, 206, 306
  Rachel 183, 194
  Reader 250
Arnolds Mill 220
Arthur, Hargrove 229
Arwood, Zachariah 270
Atkison, John 40, 83
Austell, Amillira 37
  Milly 37
  William 260
Austin, Jesse 230
  William 145, 162, 168
Autry, Alexander 246, 253(2)
Avet, William 187
Axton, William 282

Babbitt, Isham 178, 205
Bagwell, Hayes 268
  John 5, 43, 152
  John Jr. 58
  Littleton 48, 58, 115, 128, 169, 172, 187, 222, 231
Baits, Henry 5
Baker, Robert 176, 212
Balender, ___ 52
Balenger, Edward 93, 129, 137, 193
Balsingame (see Blasingame), Thomas 48
Balue (see Belew), Elizabeth 93
Bankstone, Laurence 246
  Laurens 252
Banny, John 3
Barclay, James 42
  John 20, 31
Barkley, John 61, 78, 80
  William 80
Barnett, ___ 41
  Ambrose 40(2)
  Daniel 133, 152, 172, 203, 211, 225, 234, 237, 238
  James 279
  Jarayal 230
  Jeroyal 239
  John 203, 210, 258, 265, 266
  Joroyal 236, 239, 246, 250(2), 185
  Joseph 15, 16, 28, 35, 37, 39(2), 41, 81, 91, 97, 104, 112, 117, 147, 151, 170, 182, 210, 216, 258, 265, 279, 295, 300
  Micajah 133, 136, 197, 219, 224, 238, 285
  Richard 223
  Sarah 277
Barns, James 234
  Richard 277
  Samuel 265
Barrett, Ninian 136
  Reubin 84
  William 264
Barron, James 60, 87, 108(2), 131, 144
Barry (see Berry), Andrew 3, 27,

35, 39, 45, 46, 61, 75, 83, 92, 94, 96, 99, 101, 117, 120, 125, 132, 133, 159, 249, 254, 264, 271
  James 254
  John 3, 4, 5, 158, 239, 246, 254
  Richard 27, 29(2), 91, 105, 111, 133, 215(2), 222, 230, 239, 257(3)
Barton, Bavester 91
  Benjamine 86
  Elizabeth 91
  William 99, 204
Baswell, Gustavus 248
Bawcomb, Aaron 230, 239, 240, 241
Beach, John 56
Beard, Adam 181
  James 83, 93, 229(2), 231, 234, 241, 253, 255(2)
  John 83, 92, 147, 151, 170, 231, 252, 258, 259(2)
Beardan, Isaac 244
  John 258, 265, 266, 296(3), 301
  Richard 223, 296
  Thomas 239, 246
Bearden, Benjamine 244
  John 4, 28, 36, 45, 47(2), 48, 53, 54, 72, 162, 225
  John Jr. 102
  Thomas 82, 217
Beason (see Beeson, Beson), Benjamin 42, 106
  Seal 298
Beckham (see Beckum), John 258
Beckhum, William 91
Beddenton (see Biddenton), Thomas 219, 221
Beddington, Thomas 192
Beeson (see Beason, Beson), Benjamine 89
Beest, John 262
Belew (see Balue), Elizabeth 46
Bell, James 213(2)
  Samuel 112, 123, 137, 184
Bennett, ___ 43
  Daniel 27
  Elizabeth 183
  George 46, 56, 61
  James 46, 57, 59
  John 258, 266
  Peter 282
  Thomas 8, 30, 73, 77, 102, 106, 135, 188, 210, 216
  William 20, 32, 52, 71, 79, 84, 245(2), 251, 263
Benson, Abner 266
  Elias 266
  Elizabeth 266
  Gabriel 263(2), 264, 265(2), 266, 270, 295
  Joseph 266
  Nancy 266
  Nelley 295
  Nimrod 265
  Patience 266
  Polley 266
  Robert 265
  Thirsa 265
  Thomas 8, 63, 111
  William 5, 15, 28, 32, 35, 45, 46, 51, 59, 61(2), 85, 92, 99(2), 100, 102, 109, 110, 114, 128, 146, 167, 168, 179(2), 182(2), 191, 196, 199, 200, 202, 212(2), 221, 223(2), 263(2), 264, 266(2), 274, 278, 279, 286, 294(2),

295(3), 301
Willis 266
Bensong, William 3
Berge, George 57
Berk (see Burk), John 158
Berkly, Mary 29
Berry (see Barry), Andrew 54, 55
  Elizabeth 61
  George 60
Beshear, Hannah 244
Benson (see Beason, Beeson), Benjamine 73(2), 83(2)
Bethel, ___ 166
  Larkin 290
  Samson 148, 166, 187, 188(2), 209
Betterton, James 5, 119, 234, 264
  Thomas 210
Biddenton (see Beddenton), Thomas 296
Billis, John 246
Bingham, John 138, 194, 232, 238, 242, 247, 253, 258, 260
Bird (see Byrd), John 243
  Sarah 8, 20
  William 17, 19, 22, 23, 36, 45, 47, 276
Birdsong, John 20, 127, 134
  William 122, 137, 152
Bishop (see Byshop), Ann 28
  Edmund 28, 203, 264
  Edward 135
  George 178, 291, 294
  George Sr. 210
  Henry 160, 162, 186
  Isaac 128, 306
  John 28, 203, 210, 211(2), 212
  Robert 19
  Widow 4, 10, 26, 29, 85, 128, 149, 275, 304(2), 306
  William 28, 160(2), 230, 239, 240, 241, 304
Biswell, John 51
Biter, Moses 129, 140, 157
  William 188
Black, Robert 262, 268
Blackstock, ___ 32, 281
  James 77
  William 60, 77, 95, 100
Blackstock's ford 4, 72(2), 139, 284
Blackstock's Road 140, 237, 276, 288, 298, 299, 301, 304
Blackwell, James 7, 215
  Zachariah 171, 302
Blackwood, James 300
  Joseph 72, 83, 204, 300, 301 (2)
  Margaret 300
Blailock (see Blalock), John 6, 54
Blakely, Samuel 113(3)
Blalock (see Blailock), John 63, 87
  John Jr. 43
  John Sr. 43
Blanton, George 31
Blasingame, John 2, 82, 95, 100, 191, 192
  Thomas 51, 108, 127, 128, 136, 141, 162, 191, 195, 208, 212
  Thomas Jr. 65, 70, 125, 148, 176
Bloomer, William Pool 114
Bobbit, Isham 306
Bobo, Absalom 58
  Burrell 61, 69, 140, 239, 242, 264, 250, 253, 267, 268
  Burwell 39

Livingston 305
Sampson 4, 9, 39
Samson 17, 19, 53, 61, 69, 73, 76, 77, 83, 88, 89, 92, 127 (2), 128, 132, 139, 140(4), 170, 203, 212, 252, 267
Samson Jr. 265, 266
Spencer 19, 115, 129, 146, 151, 160, 167, 176, 206, 261
Spencer Jr. 135, 210
Spensor 54
Tilman 9, 272
Bogan, Isaac 3
Boican, Tobias 236(2)
Boid, Hugh 55
  John 104
  Sarah 104, 105
Bolston, Robert 88
Bonner, Benjamin 198, 204
  Briant 240
  Demps 186
  Dempsey 264
  Thomas 48(2), 107
Bookes (see Brooks), Peter 73
Boring, Joseph 160, 178
Borland, William 85
Bostick, William 238
Boswell, Gustavus 243, 244, 253
Bowen, Jacob 109
  John 118
  Jonathan 156, 164, 172, 173, 181, 182, 185, 274
Bowlens, ___ 176
Bowman, Cornelius 15
Braay, Andrew 5
Bracher (see Brashers, Bractcher), William 75, 78, 105, 135
Bragg, Charles 46, 47, 102, 288
  Daniel 257, 262, 289
  John 36, 61, 63, 64, 126, 127(2), 134, 142(2), 162(3), 164, 171, 175, 215, 222, 288, 293, 297, 298
  Moore 288
  Peter 36, 181, 215, 223, 225, 226
  Zebulon 164, 210, 256, 260, 261(2), 305
Bramblett, Newton 135
Bramlet(t), William 210, 216, 217, 219, 221, 258
Brammit, Thomas 6
Branch, Buck 306
Brandon, ___ 82
  Thomas 5, 73, 125, 129, 130, 142, 153
  William 73, 85, 215
Branham, William 4
Brannon, William 27, 29(2), 40, 226, 264, 266, 268, 301
Brannon's shoal 301
Brannums, William 299
Brashers (see Bracher, Bratcher), Brazal 9
  Jeremiah 80
  William 73
Bratcher, William 62, 72, 84, 129, 140(2), 141, 159(2), 277
Bratton, William 235
Brazel, William 21
Brewton (see Bruton), David 135
  George 172
Brice, Charles 213
  Samuel 292(3)
  Thomas 203, 210, 211(2)
Bridges, James 2
  John 137, 138(2)
Bridges Ferry 303
Bridgman, William 233, 235
Briggs, Frederick 27, 73
Bright, Albertis 4
  Alburtus 69, 91

James 36, 179, 267
Tobias 27, 28, 29(2), 46, 56, 57, 59, 61(2), 63, 64, 69, 83, 147, 151(2), 159, 161, 169, 180, 191, 238, 241, 279, 287, 298
Tobias Jr. 158
Briton, James 41
Brittain, William 214, 225, 227, 234(2), 236
Britton, William 235
Brock, David 243
Brookes, Peter 82
Brooks, ___ 137, 152, 229
  Isaac 122
  John 83, 203
  Mary 139
  Peter 16, 43, 54(2), 56(3), 61, 64, 72, 77, 78, 84, 87, 131, 133, 139, 152
  Sarah 54(2)
  Thomas 97, 112, 118, 122, 126, 133, 137, 139(3), 149
Brothers, Mary 284
Brown, Andrew 11, 53, 63
  Arias 106, 118, 120, 130, 140, 141, 152, 235, 240(2), 241 (2), 256, 260(2), 290, 294
  Benjamin 20, 28, 112, 118, 126
  Daniel 5(3), 9, 11, 13, 14(2), 15, 16, 19, 22, 23(2), 25, 26(3), 27(2), 28, 29(2), 30(2), 31, 32, 33(2), 41, 43, 44, 49, 52, 54, 57, 58, 60, 63, 65, 67(3), 68 (2), 74, 79, 82, 113, 130, 141
  David 6, 86, 119, 230, 240(2), 241(2), 244, 296
  Isaac 27, 32, 36
  Jacob 4, 11(2), 12(2), 13(2), 14, 15(2), 16, 20, 22, 24, 29, 30(2), 31, 33, 37, 38, 48, 49(2)
  James 44, 246, 253(2)
  John 19, 24, 28, 43, 52, 68, 91, 102, 114, 116, 118, 121, 135, 150, 159, 164, 165, 166, 171, 230, 239, 272
  Mark 270
  Randolph 237
  Roger 10
  Thomas 28, 52, 67, 73, 131, 222, 230, 232
  Vinson 129
  William 43, 62, 133
  Willey S. 203, 286
Browning, Luke 77
Brows, Arias 230
Bruce, Charles 54, 69, 73, 93, 96, 97, 99, 101, 103(2), 107(2), 109, 114(2), 118, 124, 125, 139, 145, 151(2), 152, 155, 159, 170, 175, 191, 201, 207, 213, 214, 248, 255
  Elijah 206
  William 147
Bruister, John 244, 254
Brummet, Thomas 53
Bruton, David 14, 186, 203, 211, 214, 216, 268, 293, 295
  George 3, 4, 5, 14, 17, 42, 69, 70, 83, 104, 143, 148, 149, 151, 162, 164, 171, 180, 191, 195, 204, 214, 216, 285, 287, 289, 291, 292, 293(2), 300
  George Jr. 104
  James 28, 37, 41, 69, 203
  John 215
  Jonas 239
  Samuel 223, 244
Brya, Edward Sr. 122

Bryan, William 138, 178
Bryant, William 83
Buckeby, Thomas 185
Buckston, Isaac 43
Buffington, Caroline
  Matilda 99
  Joseph 1, 4, 5, 6, 9, 10, 11,
    13, 15, 19, 28, 37, 44, 53
    (3), 55, 57, 63, 65, 67, 68,
    70, 75(2), 83, 90, 93, 99,
    100, 112, 130(2), 131, 143
    (2), 144, 145, 155, 156,
    163, 165, 175
  Mary 104
Buice, James 135
  William 222
Buise's Mill 87
Bull, Travill 60
Bullian, Thomas 64
Bullion, John 150
Bullock, Richard 200, 217
  Zachariah 67, 71, 280
Bumpass, Augustine 172, 219(2), 237
  Gabriel 172
  Robert 172
Burchfield, Joseph 50
Burgess, Richard 89
Buring, Joseph 151
Burk (see Berk), ___ 14, 27
  Aedamus (Judge) 1
  Isham 283
  John 113, 116, 215, 223, 225,
    226, 282
  Mary 116
  Polley 76, 105
Burnet(t), ___ 41
  Benjamin Jr. 41
  Benjamin Sr. 41
  James 191, 219, 232, 240,
    243(2), 244, 245
  John 158, 168, 275, 284
  Joseph 277
Burns, James 229, 235, 243
  Samuel 162, 267
Burrel(l), Peter 205
  Walter 72, 75, 83(2), 85,
    87, 89(2), 156, 161
Burt, John 112, 122
Burton, ___ 86
  Charles 107, 138(9), 143,
    148, 150, 152, 180, 191,
    213, 215, 221, 226, 238,
    251, 254(2), 264, 276, 298
  Culbert 215
  Cutbert 223
  David 191, 293
  George 18, 92, 147, 229
  George Jr. 104
  James 8, 83
  Jonas 246
  Joseph 67
  Nathaniel 107, 230, 240(2),
    241, 246, 252
  William 64, 78, 95, 129, 138
    (2)
Busey (see Bussey), Benjamin
    102, 115, 116, 118, 177,
    225, 237, 238, 274
  Samuel 230, 239, 241, 264
Bush, Thomas 107
Bussey (see Busey), Benjamine
    234
Butler, John 3, 27, 29(2), 30,
    39, 40, 56, 62, 64, 82,
    171
Byars, James 44
  John 44, 147, 153
Byas, James 264
Byce, Abraham 278
  Abram 132
  Goen (?) 278
Byrd (see Bird), Agnes 295
  James 139

William 129, 130, 139, 142,
    165, 274, 283
Byshop (see Bishop), Edmund 24

Calcock, Charles Jones 173
Caldwell, John 289, 292, 299
  William 7
Calhoun (see Colhoun), John Wm.
    256
  Thomas 58, 80, 92, 103
Callihan, Joel 69, 74, 86(2)
  John 68, 91
Calvert, Rolley 264
  Spencer 264
Camp, John 41, 50, 68(2), 72,
    75, 85, 86, 88, 104, 108
    (3), 122, 130, 136(2), 146
  Sarah 68, 85
  Susannah 85
  Thomas 85
  William 76, 86, 172
Camps ferry road 300
Camps meeting house 298
Campbell, John 19, 20, 145, 146,
    171
  Margaret 175, 195(2)
Candles, Alexander 53
Cane, Margaret 228
Cannon, Ellis 147, 153(2), 186
  Henry 115, 230, 239, 178, 281
  John 73, 115, 122
  Lewis 300
  Mason 91, 115, 252, 259
Cantrell, Benjamine 258
  Charles 246
  James 203
  John 152, 166, 170, 193, 194
    (3), 232, 233, 253, 275
Cantwell, John 162, 167, 172,
    182, 183(3), 197, 200, 209,
    212, 216, 222, 228, 230,
    240, 262
  Moses 226
Capshaw, Essix 163, 168, 206,
    207, 209, 220, 221, 225,
    242
Carden, Leonard 222, 232
Carley, Benjamin 73, 83(2)
  Henry 132, 283
  John 70
  William 132
Carmichael, Daniel 225, 236, 250
    (2), 251(2), 270
Carnes, John D. 129, 137
  Peter 54, 58, 74, 78, 79, 80,
    81(2), 82, 83, 87, 88(2),
    90, 95(3), 97, 98(2), 116,
    118, 120, 121, 122, 124,
    126(2)
  T. P. 57, 68
  Thomas P. 66, 74(2), 75, 79,
    88, 91, 92, 93, 94, 95(2),
    97(4), 98, 105, 106, 107,
    108, 109, 110, 114(2), 122
    (3), 123, 124(2), 126(3),
    127(2), 128(2), 130(3)
  Thomas Peter 72, 87, 89, 90
Carns, ___ 30
  Peter 24, 37, 38, 39, 48, 76,
    85
  T. P. 48
  Thomas Peter 18, 19, 24, 30,
    33
Carpenter, George 55
Carr, Hans 247, 257, 262, 263
Carrel(l), John 51, 215
  Nathl. 51
  Thomas 51
Carrells, John 10, 108
  Jno. Thomas 60
  Nathl. 44, 60, 108
  Thomas 108
Carrick, John 3

Carter, Ann 111, 172, 173, 282
  Charles 61, 105, 111
  Jesse 262
  Nancy 161
Carver, Andrew 222
  James 216, 217
  Richard 203, 210, 211(2)
Carwile, Zachariah 158
Cary, Thomas 158
Case, Moses 143
  Robert 278
Casey, Aaron 63, 133, 210, 216,
    217, 260, 267, 303
  Christopher 8, 12, 28, 39, 56,
    63, 143, 148
  Elizabeth 16
  Jacob 186, 217, 248(2), 256
  James 54, 61, 63, 72
  Jesse 36, 56(3), 160
  John 140, 303
  Levi 7, 143, 151
  Moses 17, 18, 56(3), 63, 79,
    83, 89, 132, 144, 242, 250,
    253, 255, 261, 267(3), 268
  Moses Jr. 294
  Randolf 7, 16
  Randolph 132, 144, 267
  Samuel 215
  Spencer 115, 205, 212, 219
  William 129, 151, 160, 210,
    216(2), 218, 221, 252
Castleberry, John 132
  Paul 28, 127, 158, 168, 215,
    296
  William 171, 181
Caully, Andrew 27
Cavin, John 14, 69, 70, 73, 78,
    82
  Joseph 135, 264
Center, Abner 164
  John 158
Chambery, Jacob 151
Chamblin, James 301
  Jesse 252, 301(3)
  Mary 301
Champion, Joseph 210, 216(2)
Chapman, Anne 229
  Isaac 241, 247
Chastain, James 111
  Joseph 158
Cheek, Ellis 120
Chesney, John 56, 63, 96, 129,
    222, 230, 232
  Richard 28, 55, 56, 63, 165,
    171, 175, 184, 215, 223,
    225, 226
Childers, Daniel 218
  David 210, 216(2), 221, 251
  Rachel 74(2)
  Richard 162
Childress, John 7, 14, 29
  Thomas 26
Childs, Hezekiah 56, 69, 148(2),
    272(3)
  Jeston 148, 272
  John 56, 73, 100, 148, 272
  Nathan 154, 273
  Nimrod 208
Chisham, John 50
Chism, John 41, 68(2), 75, 76,
    85, 88, 108(3), 122, 130,
    136, 146
Chumler, John 104, 105, 116,
    187, 189
  Mary 217
  Thomas 217
Chumley, Betsy 42
  Mary 42
  William 243
Chumlie, John 187
Clark (see Clerk(e)), Benjamine
    230
  James 51(2), 52, 60

Clarke (see Clark, Clerke), Benjamine 135, 239
　James 234, 236
Clayton, Augustine 158
　Austin 168
　Edward 151, 160
　Francis 151, 160
　John 159, 164, 196, 209
　Thomas 132
　William 9, 46, 47, 56, 61(2), 63, 64, 74, 78, 84(2), 85, 174, 194
　James 272
　Isham 264
　Moses 196, 209
Clements, Edmund W. 46
Clemins, John 18
Clemons, Ann 285
　Edmund 114, 245(2)
　Edmund Jr. 285
　Edmund W. 56, 61(3), 73, 85
　Sarah 285
Clerk(e) (see Clark, Clarke), Benjamine 150
　Benjamine Sr. 222, 286
　Christopher 102
　Edward 132
　Elijah 97, 126, 184
　Francis 185, 203, 205, 210, 211(2), 213
　James 71, 78, 85, 95(2), 108, 164, 166, 171, 175, 184, 225, 226, 227, 242
　John 283
　Lee 215, 222, 224
　Mary 184
　Samuel 166
　Thomas 167, 210, 294
Clowney, Samuel 140, 141
Coal (see Cole), Henry 222
Coan, Andrew 300
Coats, Bartan 124
　Bartin 64
　Barton 74(3)
Cobb, John 102, 230
　Ralph 90, 97, 103, 105(2), 121, 130
Cockrell, Lewis 247, 263
Cole (see Coal), Thomas 83, 215, 222, 274, 289
Colhoun (see Calhoun), Thomas 102
Colley, Andrew 102, 215, 223, 205, 225, 226(2), 232, 238, 242, 247, 253, 260, 267
　Samuel 215
　Susannah 266, 267, 269
Collins, Alexander 230
　John 24, 27, 29(2), 30, 73, 97, 98, 101, 122, 135, 140, 154(2), 224, 230, 236, 265(2)
　Joseph 230, 252
　Richard 24, 41, 64, 72, 73, 164, 165, 168, 203
Collins (see Cullins), Thomas 17, 98, 230(2), 235
　William 17, 224, 236(2)
Colo, John 129
Colter (see Coulter) Anthony 91
Colwall, John 102, 116
　William 102, 113, 116, 118, 149
Colwell, John 118
Compton, James 119
　Thomas 222, 232, 301
Compty, ___ 263
Connell, Ann 8, 60
　Avery 70, 95, 118, 121, 125
　Benjamine 223
　Frances 45
　Francis 8
　George 3, 6, 8, 17, 19, 20, 22, 23, 45, 114, 120, 121, 147, 151, 158, 165, 211,
218, 222, 232, 252, 287, 301
Giles 28, 32, 83, 92, 132, 136, 158, 165, 206, 212, 233
Giles Jr. 241
Jesse 8(3), 9, 10, 11(2), 13, 15(2), 27, 46, 57, 59, 60, 91, 104, 112, 147, 155, 158, 162, 165, 170, 182, 201, 202, 211, 218(2), 282, 287
Robert 12, 28, 35, 37, 41, 158, 162, 165, 170, 182, 201, 202, 211, 218(2), 282, 287
W. Giles 167
Conner, Boley 237
　Henry 97, 101
　James 101
　John 8, 10, 27, 32, 46, 57, 59, 74, 85, 124, 126, 142(2), 151, 154(2), 157(2), 224
　John Jr. 123
　John Sr. 164
　Maximilian 28, 35, 37, 41(2), 67, 75, 93, 112, 122, 130, 143, 247-248, 253, 262
　Robert 46, 210
　Uriah 10, 18, 129, 137
Conwell, Jno. 28
Cooglet, Robert 83
Cook, David 6, 171, 181, 230, 239, 280
　Eli 115
　John 234
　Thomas 72, 252, 259(2), 260
Coone, Henry 43
Cooper, David 165, 293
　Isaac 258
　James 165
　John 13, 14, 16, 21, 27, 28, 29(2), 31, 35, 37, 41, 44, 201, 213, 214, 216(2), 217, 218, 221, 222, 232, 239, 246, 249, 264, 290, 302
　Robert 75, 89
　Sios 259, 263, 266
Copeland, Alexander 244, 175, 182(3), 183, 192, 194, 244, 247, 271
Copelander, Alexander 133
Cornelius, Roland 8, 9, 10, 11, 13
　Rowland 14(2), 15, 29, 37, 41, 50, 72, 86, 92, 108(2), 131, 147
　Rowland Jr. 73, 108
　William 12
Cornwall, Daniel 171, 203, 224
　Edward 172
　Jarvis 200, 201, 286
Cornwell, Javis 191
Cosby, Sidner 97
　Sydney 112
Couch, Benjamine 36, 91, 168, 222, 230, 232
Drewry 208, 253(2)
Drury 246
Isaac 230
James 66
John 5, 31, 59, 62, 68(2), 79
Joseph 36, 56, 160, 164, 210, 219
Josiah 221
Long John 139
Matthew 3, 69, 143, 203, 210, 303
William 21, 51, 59, 79, 81
Coulter, Anthony 17, 18, 23, 105, 111
Counch, Millinton 16
Counnell (see Connell), Jesse 14

Coursey, William 122
Cowen, Andrew 230, 232, 293
　James 210, 216
　John 60, 128
Cox, Beverly 68(2), 77, 79, 8(
　Richard 203, 204
Craddock, Edmond 13
Cradock, Edmund 38
Crane, Dempson 248
　William 248
Credenton, Israel 210, 216(2), 221(3), 242, 249, 250, 253, 260
Cretohfield (see Critchfield, Crutchfield), Amos 184, 195
Crazie, George 175
Critchfield (see Cretchfield, Crutchfield), Amos 184, 195
Crocker, Anthony 119, 284
　Arthur 10, 19, 62, 203, 284(2)
　Arthur Sr. 62
　Solomon 75, 91, 105, 111, 258,
　William 3, 6, 17, 62, 76, 82, 114, 137, 171, 181, 230, 239, 240, 241, 284
Crofford, John 264
Crook, ___ 172
　James 186, 205, 222, 269
Cross, Edward 159, 172, 173(3)
　John 230, 239, 240, 241
Crow, ___ 20, 26
　Isaac 3, 16, 26, 28, 33, 42, 56, 62, 73, 83(2), 85, 87, 89, 126, 132(2), 213, 214(2), 219, 222, 230(2), 231, 238, 241, 242, 253, 285, 287, 288, 293, 296, 298, 300
　James 28, 36, 45, 47, 48, 52, 56(3), 132, 136, 203, 205, 211
　John 42, 62
　Mary 3, 6
　Thomas 11, 53
　William 33, 56, 60, 62, 64, 151, 153, 232, 260, 268, 273, 297
Crowder, Greenham 139
　James 116, 153, 192, 285
　Stephen 51
　Thomas 123
Crowther, James 49, 78, 84, 147, 231, 241
　Thomas 106, 146
Cruce, Isaac 75
　Richard 288
　Stephen 102, 288
Cruse, Isaac 6
Crutchfield (see Critchfield, Cretchfield), Amos 193
Culberson, Joseiah 28, 41
Culbertson, Harrison 55
　Josiah 17, 18, 31, 81, 127, 134, 151, 160, 159, 165, 206, 274, 286
　Samuel 3, 6, 81, 127, 134, 151, 160, 207, 210, 216, 295
Cullin(s) (see Collins), James 119, 126, 145, 152
Cunningham, John 237(2), 238, 270
　William 221
Curham, John 150

Dalton, Daniel 7
　Jeremiah 7, 18
　Jesse 303
Daniel, John 57, 263
　Reubin 294
Derby, Sarah 217(2), 220, 225(3), 231(?)
　William 138, 157, 196, 200,

207, 217(2), 225,(3), 231(2), 285
Darby's store 140, 283
Daugherty (see Dougherty, Dohertie), James 122, 124
  Thomas 106, 118, 120, 130, 140, 141, 142
David, Daniel 269
  Thomas 72, 83
Davidson, Alexander 86
  William 203
Davis, Benjamin 106, 119
  David 165, 171, 175, 228, 230, 232, 239
  David Jr. 222
  Evans 171, 210
  Iven 203
  Jesse 17, 92, 96, 99, 114, 235
  John 3, 6, 73, 168, 172(2), 180, 182, 183, 203, 210, 211(3), 215, 247, 265
  Joseph 264
  Larkin 120
  Nathaniel 4, 40, 143, 147, 153
  Neomi 200
  Peter 165, 166, 167, 170
  Thomas 3, 12, 19, 20(2), 46, 84, 86, 87, 128, 149, 223, 247
  Tullie 179
  Tully 174
  William 51, 71, 78, 85, 95, 166, 210, 216, 217
Davison, Robert 274
  William 115
Dean, Joel 164
Deavours (see Devors), George 162
Debnard (see Dennard), Thomas 13
Degraffenreed, Christopher 211
Delling, James 115
Dempsey, Barnet 251
  James 227, 233
Dennard (see Debnard), Jacob 54
  John 30
  Thomas 13, 16
Devine (see Divine), George 252
  James 43
  Thomas 274
Devors (see Deavours), George 19, 28
Dewberry (see Dubarry), Ann 58, 73, 111, 126
  Giles 73
  Irby 89
  James 252, 259, 260
  John 71
  Yearby 87
Dickson, Edward 18, 37
  Jeremiah 102
  John 19
  Joseph 130, 143, 155
  Reuben 28, 30, 35, 41, 44, 79, 96, 142
  Thomas 122
Dilingham, Vachel 3
Dill, Jane 94
  Joseph 230, 240(2), 241, 277, 295
Dinkins, John 50
Ditty, James 217
Divine, (see Devine), George 203, 257
  Thomas 165
Dixon, Reuben 14
  William 13
Dod, Frances 151, 158
  Francis 147
Dodd(s), Francis 28, 36, 45, 47, 83, 92, 165, 183, 215, 219, 222, 227, 291, 292(2)
  Jesse 179

Margaret 219(2), 240
Doeg, Thomas 36, 45, 56
Dohertie (see Daugherty, Dougherty), James 113, 118, 124, 126, 131(3), 136, 137(2), 142, 143(2), 144, 145(3), 147, 152, 153, 155(2), 156(4), 157
Doherty, James 138, 139
Dollar, Ambrose 43, 115, 199, 252
  Reubin 73, 83(2), 85, 87, 89
  Rubin 242
Domini, Henry 112, 113, 122
Dorgan, William 75
Dotey, John 84(2)
  Joseph 84
Dougherty (see Daugherty, Dohertie), James 83
  Thomas 78, 80
Doughty, John 94
Doutey, John 95, 96
Downs, Jonathan 80, 179
  Joshua 215, 233, 257, 287, 290
Drummons, David 291
Duberry (see Dewberry), Yearby 49
Duncan, William 73
Duff, Dennis 12
Duncan, John 141, 166
  William 83, 85, 78, 89, 129, 140, 141, 157, 203
Duncanson,   167, 176
Dundan, William 83
Dunlap, ___ 212, 213(2), 214, 232
Dunnaway, Catharine 304
  James 304
Durham, John 173, 220, 242, 249, 294

Ealy, John 269 (see Eley)
Earl, Justice Baylis 1, 2, 3, 4, 6, 7, 9, 10, 11, 14, 15, 16, 17, 18, 20, 21, 22, 24, 26, 27, 32, 34, 35, 38, 39, 41, 42, 44, 48, 49, 50, 51, 52, 54, 55, 58, 59, 61, 69, 71, 72, 74, 76, 77, 80, 81, 83, 84, 86, 99, 100, 101, 103, 106, 107, 108, 109, 118, 119, 132, 134, 135, 139, 141, 144, 153, 155, 158, 167, 168, 170, 171, 173, 175, 177, 179, 181, 183, 194, 200, 203, 204, 206, 207, 208, 210, 271, 273, 275, 276, 277, 279, 280, 286, 287, 288
  Baylis 13, 16, 45, 74, 77, 126, 127, 128, 129, 140(2), 141, 154(2), 165, 201, 267, 274
  John 45, 57, 70, 71(2), 77, 107, 110, 128, 158
  John B. 200, 201
  John Jr. 4
  Rebekah 110
  Samuel 45
Earnest, Henry 74, 89(2), 91, 127(2), 128, 139, 214, 215, 216
  Jacob 45, 133(2), 158
  William 28, 91, 105, 111, 199, 249(2)
Easlinger, George 217, 219
Easly, Millington 275
  William 160, 282
Edmundson, John 268
Edson, Graff 191, 195, 196, 207, 231, 232, 253, 254
Edwards, Joshua 210, 268
  Peter 33, 41, 44, 49, 50, 59,

80, 84, 118, 131, 158
  Potter 71
  Thomas 128
Eisen (see Eison, Ison), Frederick 78, 85, 95
  Jacob 125, 127, 178, 193, 195
Eison (see Eisen, Ison), Frederick 78, 85, 95
  Jacob 125, 127, 178, 193, 195
Elder, Alexander 30, 157, 163, 20 207(2), 211, 215, 217, 226, 227(2), 232
  Ephriam 102, 116, 118, 209
  Hammon 298
  Harmon 127
  James 81, 179, 198
  John 6(2), 10, 13, 21, 23, 30, 115, 140, 147, 156, 157, 161, 163, 203, 210, 211, 233, 240, 241, 250, 265
  John Jr. 212, 217, 226, 227(2)
  John Sr. 30
  Peter 17, 30, 58, 83, 93
  Robert 205, 212, 215, 223, 227, 241
  Samuel 127, 132, 136, 145, 147, 163, 272, 298(3), 306
  William 19, 21, 27, 114, 121, 150, 157, 158, 159, 163, 165
Eley, Jean 266
  John 266
English, James 119
Ervin, Robert 77
Erwin, John 163, 217, 228, 296(2),
  Joseph 104(2), 113, 123(2), 137(2)
Esterwood, Laurence 41
Estrick, Goldman 285
Evans (see Evins), Alexander 230, 264, 283, 293
  Daniel 217, 225
  Emmy 76
  Jabez 36
Evatt, James 230
  Thomas 215, 223, 225, 226
  William 230, 239, 240, 241
Evins (see Evans), Alexander 70, 83, 239
  David 77
  Robert 36, 39, 45
Eyres (see Ayres), Henry 257

Fair, Col. ___ 65, 70
Faires, Agness 282
  James 278
Fairis, James 280, 282(see Faris)
  Thomas 282
  William 282
Fallace (see Wallace), Elizabeth 229
Faning (see Fanning), James 72
Fannen, James 50, 64(2), 65, 73, 83(2), 85, 87, 148
Fanning, James 8
Faris, James 46, 56, 61(2), 69
Farmar, John 171
Farmer, Benjamin 265
  Ezekiel 194
  John 164, 175, 215
Farra, Thomas 13, 85, 94
Farrar, Jamor ___ 9, 10
  Thomas 18(3), 28, 35, 36, 45, 70, 72, 73, 74, 90, 95, 101(2), 118, 121(2)
Farrer, Thomas 50, 53
Farrow, Justice Thomas 44, 45, 46, 55, 58, 59, 60, 61, 63, 64, 65, 66, 67, 69, 70, 73, 74, 76, 77, 86, 88, 90, 91, 92, 95, 96, 98, 99, 101, 103, 104, 107, 109, 110, 112, 113, 114, 116, 117,

Farrow, Justice Thomas (con't)
119, 120, 123, 125, 132,
133, 136, 139, 141, 148,
167, 187, 188, 202, 207,
243, 246, 271, 278, 281
209, 249, 250
John 21, 22, 29, 30, 58, 65,
66, 70, 96, 112(2), 116,
123, 162, 210, 267
John Sr. 5, 11, 40
Landon 15, 16, 20, 32, 43, 46,
52, 68(2), 69, 71(2), 74,
77, 79(2), 80, 84, 86, 91,
96, 112, 118, 119, 123, 159,
160, 187, 206, 222, 258
Samuel 4, 5, 6, 12, 46(3), 48,
52, 54, 58, 65, 71, 73, 75,
79, 99(2), 109, 110, 113(2),
128, 134, 135, 139, 152, 156,
157, 160, 163, 166, 167, 169,
199, 201, 205(2), 206(2),
207(2), 208, 213, 214, 217,
218, 219, 221, 225, 226(2),
227(4), 228, 234, 235, 236,
237, 244, 248, 250, 253, 255,
256(2), 257, 258, 261, 264
Thomas 5(2), 17, 18, 25, 36,
42, 44, 46, 57, 71, 79, 80,
127, 142, 164, 186(2), 214,
228
William 5, 116, 134, 153, 162,
176, 209, 212(2), 213, 215,
217, 219, 221, 228, 232,
237, 243, 245, 263, 264,
269
Faugerson, John Hammett 119
Feals, William 232, 240
Ferguson's Creek 14
Few, Benjamin 99, 113, 114
Fewel(1), Glanley 231
Stanley 235
Fields, ___ 53
Jeremiah 71
William 16, 51, 107, 110, 135,
141, 149, 213, 218, 220,
223, 229, 306, 307
Finch, Daniel 184, 199(2), 201
Finley, James 252
Flanagan, Hugh 88, 89, 95
Flannagan, Hugh 91
William 77, 82
Fley, George 297
Flinn (see Flynn), James 244
Thomas 15, 28, 35, 37, 55
Floyd, Aaron 62(2), 147
Alexander 73, 83(2)
David 289
Enoch 14, 27, 62, 69, 280,
288, 289
George 298
Margaret 181
William 16, 27, 101, 135
Flynn (see Flinn), Thomas 74,
75, 112, 128, 137
Fod, Thomas 288
Foley, Mason 260, 264
Fonderin, John 4
Fondrin, Richard 124
William 124(2), 147, 171, 181
Ford, Ann 58
Elisha 49(2)
James 21
John 8, 21, 28, 35, 37, 44,
45, 69, 71, 133, 155, 162,
178, 180, 191, 192, 195,
209, 216, 262, 280, 281
Justice John 1, 2, 4, 6, 7, 8,
10, 11, 12, 14, 15, 23, 26,
47, 51, 58, 79, 80, 126,
134
John Jr. 46, 57, 59, 102,
159, 277, 279
John Sr. 215
Joseph 15

Major ___ 4
Manly 223
Philip 101
Samuel 46(2), 57, 59, 158
Spencer 46
William 8(2), 17, 18, 27, 29
(2), 30, 49(2), 59, 65, 68,
69, 73, 79, 80, 91, 105,
107, 108, 110, 111(2), 142,
145, 157, 159, 160, 177,
181, 182(2), 183(3), 184,
189, 193(3), 194(2), 196,
205, 210, 214, 216(3), 221,
223(2), 229, 232, 240, 247,
280, 292, 296
Zadock 3, 5, 185, 213, 219,
251, 260, 294
Justice Zadock 17, 18, 19, 21,
23, 24, 26, 29, 31, 32, 41,
44, 67, 69, 86, 88, 90, 99,
103, 117, 119, 123, 139,
148, 189, 207
Ford's mill 33, 50, 141, 176,
277, 281, 292, 300
Forrest, Owen 47
Forrister, Owen 47
Fortner, Thomas 33
Foster, Andrew 276
Anthony 248, 302, 304
Fielding 220, 231
Henry 119, 132, 230
Isham 3, 4, 8, 27, 36(2), 45,
60, 69, 73, 76, 77, 78, 81,
85, 86, 87, 92, 100, 101,
108, 148, 182, 196, 205,
211, 212, 222, 232, 233,
245, 247(2), 251, 253,
255, 257, 270, 276, 287,
290, 294, 299, 304, 305
James 37, 93, 206, 207
John 6, 36, 37, 45, 56(2), 62,
64, 67, 81, 102, 135, 151,
290, 299(2)
Major ___ 303
Moses 83, 147, 164, 171, 198,
204, 276
Rispey 206, 207
Rispy 93
Robert 8, 27, 62, 132, 136,
140, 141, 210, 216, 217(2),
218, 242, 249, 304
William 8, 17, 18, 36, 69, 73,
78, 82, 132, 136, 147, 151,
164, 171, 210, 216(2), 218,
221, 276, 287, 299, 300,
304
William, Major 299
Fourley, Hugh 158
Fowler, Abraham 83, 103, 208
Edmund 114, 122, 230, 239,
245(2), 275, 284
Francis 287
Jacob 208, 214(2), 236
James 128, 236, 303, 306
Jeremiah 99, 109, 110
John 149
Joseph 287
Samuel 26, 69, 149, 221, 303
Sarah 285
William 214
Francis, Mary 32
Freeman, Hugh 10, 27, 33, 44,
46, 60, 80, 85, 93, 100,
126, 127, 131, 139, 143,
144, 155, 195
French, Lepord 85
Liffert 252
Michael 264
Freneau, Peter 121
Frier, Richard 222
Fryar-Fryer, Richard 31, 231
Fuller, Stephen 130

Gaff, Martha 221
Galbraith, George 235
Galt, James 263
Garner, Adam 124, 127, 139, 140
John 107, 131
Garrett, Robert 231
William 132, 136, 164, 171,
204, 214(2), 228, 274, 296
William Sr. 133
Garrison, Paul 15, 81
Garvin, Thomas 18
Gaston, William 6, 23, 91
Gentry (see Jentry), Allen 256
Matthew 221
Nathaniel 91
Samuel
Giber, William 111
Gibbs, James 151, 152, 167, 199,
201, 202(2), 274
John 80, 100, 139, 147, 148
Jonathan 151
Phebe 30
Philip 30
Gibb's mountain 181
Gibson, George 114, 251, 255,
256
Gideon 179
Henry 99
John 151
Jordan 72, 76(2), 77(2), 88,
89, 99(2), 114(2), 252, 278
Nathan 179
Rhoda 278
William 246, 253(2)
Gilbert, Daniel 83
George 203, 237, 238
Jarvis 215
Samuel 164
William 17, 24, 58, 86, 126(2)
Gilbraith, George 212, 217, 229
Gillespie, John 221
Gilley, Charles 133
Francis 194
Gillingwaters, Thomas 210, 233,
292
Gilmore, James 17, 20, 22, 23,
148, 215, 223, 224, 225,
226(2)
James Jr. 175
Jason 19
Joseph 27
William 175
Gist, ___ 236(2), 237, 249, 256
(2)
Joseph 235, 243, 244
Joseph C. 256(2)
Sarah 243
William 218, 219
Godfrey, ___ 41
Golding, Ann 93
John 93
Good(e), Edward 162, 186(3), 189,
200(2), 201, 205
Golightly, Christopher 179, 279,
283, 295
David 3, 5, 8, 28, 35, 45, 46,
81(2), 89, 92, 105, 110,
115, 122, 146, 162, 169,
206, 246, 252, 262, 287
John 3, 6(2), 17(2), 28, 35,
36, 38, 45, 46, 75, 80, 101,
114, 120, 121(2), 132(2),
134, 136, 144, 146(4), 158,
165, 176, 178, 197, 222,
230(2), 231, 279, 281, 300
Shands 8, 9, 10, 11, 13, 14,
15, 36, 46, 56, 61, 63, 64,
114, 150, 164, 171, 215,
223, 258, 255, 266
Thomas 61
William 89, 110
Goodgion, Robert 8, 9, 10, 11,
12, 13, 14, 15, 28, 35(2),
45, 46, 49, 61, 64, 85, 92,

Goodgion, Robert (con't) 110, 125, 144, 145, 191, 200, 201, 205
Goodlett, David 3, 15, 28, 33, 35, 45, 46, 55, 56, 60, 101, 198, 202, 203, 228, 250, 257, 262, 275(2)
  Justice David 61, 62, 65, 69, 70, 71, 72, 74, 77, 80, 83, 84, 86, 90, 91, 92, 94, 95, 96, 98, 99, 100, 101-102, 103, 104, 109, 110, 112, 114, 116, 117, 119, 120, 125, 132, 134, 135, 136, 139, 141, 144, 147, 148, 151, 152, 172, 180, 187, 271, 272, 276
  Robert 280, 281
  Robert Sr. 3, 5, 254, 272
Goodwin, ___ 13, 22, 44
  C. 33
  Charles 8, 11, 15, 16(2), 23(2), 24, 31, 32, 39, 40(2), 53, 54, 56, 59, 103, 110(2), 112, 124
  Robert 131
Gordon, ___ 217
  George 2, 20, 26, 38, 223, 237, 242, 257, 265
  John 131, 144(2)
  Thomas 2, 17, 21, 24(2), 30, 37, 41, 50, 86, 90, 104, 105(2), 107, 108, 111, 114, 118, 126, 128, 131, 136, 138, 144, 154, 158, 162(2)
Gore, Thomas 177, 184, 204, 241, 247
Gore's mill 135
Gorman, Mary 36
  Thomas 31, 33, 36, 51
Gosset, James 298
  John 52
Gourley, Hugh 203, 210, 211(2)
Gowen, John 53, 64(2), 75(2), 76, 91, 94, 95, 99, 113, 121, 128, 129, 132, 134, 136, 148, 149(3), 154, 155, 167, 168(2), 182, 200, 201(2), 212, 214(2), 220, 221, 224, 236, 242, 261, 275, 277, 280, 282(2), 284, 286, 294, 303, 306
  William 181, 275
Gowen's mill 132, 283
Gowin, ___ 53
  John 8, 14, 17, 18, 26(2), 38, 42, 51
Gowney, Timothy 115
Grace, Catharine 133
Graham, Davis 40
  Elizabeth 76, 111(2), 116
  William 9(2), 44, 52, 57(2), 65, 67, 68, 71, 76, 77(2), 88, 126, 142
Grant, ___ 58
  Daniel 69, 192, 281, 305
  Deskin 14, 18, 37, 58, 115
  Diskin 172
  Thomas 74
  William 86, 97, 98
Gravatte (see Gresatt) Millie 292
  Obadiah 215, 222, 292, 293, 294
Gray, Abram 78, 84
  John 176, 228, 287
  Peter 264
  William 258, 265
Green, James 209
  Peter 162
  Thomas 70, 214(2), 290
Greenwood, Hugh 170, 176
Gressat (see Gravatte), Obadiah 278
Grice, Ignacious 158, 168, 189, 273, 284, 302
Young 184
Griffith, Wells 18, 28, 29(2), 35, 45, 46, 53, 56, 62, 65, 78, 81, 86, 157, 161, 202, 226, 230, 235(2), 237, 239, 286, 290, 293, 295, 296, 297
Grier, Thomas 65
Grimes, David 55, 171
Grines, David 171
Grist, John 187, 188
Grizzle, George 115, 124
  John 147, 222
Groce, Zachariah 264
Groging, Bartholomew 286
Guess, Sarah 28
Guiton (see Guyton), Moses 259
  Nathaniel 119
Gurrery, Frederick 86
Gutry, Frederick 290
Gutry's mill 284, 302
Guttery, Frederick 132, 136, 161(2), 277(2)
  Matthew 77, 84, 90, 110, 123, 149, 161(2), 166(2), 172, 284
Guttery's mill 273
Guttry, Frederick 280
Guyton (see Guiton), Nathaniel 35

Hacker, Catharine 221
  John 221
Hackney, Daniel 184
Hadden, Elisha 286
  James 258
  John 230
  Thomas 239
  William 222
Hadder, James 285
Haden, George 141
  George Jr. 72, 83(2), 85, 89, John 83, 93, 222, 232(2)
  William 141, 145, 149, 156, 164, 175, 191, 192(2)
Hadon, George Jr. 87
Hagan, James 230
  William 214, 221(2), 234, 247, 251
Hail(e), Daniel 30, 39
  John 123, 136, 139
Hall, James 130
  Joseph 26, 52(3), 66, 81, 137
Ham, James 36, 119, 123
Hamby, Isaac 91, 105, 111, 184, 193, 195, 230, 239, 264
  Isaac Jr. 178
  John 119, 268
  John Jr. 264
  Nathaniel 215, 258
  William 91, 104, 112
Hames, Jacob 180
Hamilton, Henry 20, 27, 31, 52, 66
  Peggy 155
  Peter 171
  Temperance 81, 106, 129, 141, 154, 155(2)
  Thomas 70, 81, 106, 109, 129, 130, 141, 146(3), 149, 154, 155(5), 162(2)
  see Hammilton
Hammet(t) (see Hammitt, Hemmett), Benjamin 174, 203, 210, 211(2)
  Daniel 270
  Elijah 174, 210, 284
  Elizabeth 207
  Jesse 94
  John 50, 56, 62, 69, 73, 81, 196, 199, 200, 211, 215, 218, 220, 221, 223, 225, 239, 277
  John Jr. 246(2), 247
  Nathaniel 173, 174
  William 102, 174, 212, 215, 225, 262, 267
Hammetts ford 7, 87, 89, 273, 278, 284(3), 291(2), 298(2)
Hammilton (see Hamilton), Henry 5, 12, 22, 28,
  Peter 28
Hammit (see Hammet(t), Hemmett), William 306
Hammits ford 4
Hammon, Noel 251, 256(2)
  Robert 132, 133(2)
Hampton, ___ 129, 250
  Edward 140(2), 141
  Richard 14, 20, 158, 163
  Samuel 237, 238, 249
  Wade 14, 20, 63(2), 121
Hamwell, William 64
Hand, Samuel 53
Hane, ___ 127
Haney (see Heaney), Thomas 27, 28, 35(2), 37, 46, 69, 81
Haning, ___ 172
  George 93, 110
Hannah, John 51
  Mary 28
  Robert 59, 80, 89
  Thomas 82, 129
Harden, Henry 230, 239, 240(2), 246, 247(2), 267
  John 209
Hardin, James 28, 44
Hardy, Charles 159
Hargrove, Henry 102, 248
  Hugh 183
  William 183
Harkney, Daniel 177
Harmoning, Frederick 300
  John F. 265, 289(2), 305
  John Frederick 300
Harmony, John F. 217
  John Frederick 283(2), 292(3)
Harper, ___ 53
Hance 51, 153(2), 215, 239
Hance Jr. 147
Hanee 225, 226
Hanie 223
Matthew 71, 130, 167, 203
Robert 2(2), 5, 54, 85, 91, 106, 118(2), 126(2), 129, 130, 133, 134, 142, 155, 163, 174, 221, 236, 264, 275
Samuel 171
Harris(s), Archer 231
  Elizabeth 207
  John 104, 174, 196, 222, 225, 238, 248, 262, 284, 300
  Jonathan 47, 56, 91, 97, 98, 147, 151, 158, 165, 220, 234, 250(2), 264, 269, 289, 299
  Richard 189, 210, 250, 251, 257, 258
  Robert 288
  Thomas 222, 230, 232
  Turner 64
  William 102
Harrison, Anna 167
  Isham 148, 155, 162, 167, 188, 189, 191, 196, 205, 207, 211, 222, 226, 230, 236, 238, 270, 272, 278
  Justice Isham 230, 231, 232, 233, 234, 235, 237, 238, 239, 240, 242, 244, 245, 247, 248, 249, 250, 252, 253, 254, 256, 258, 259, 260, 261, 263, 264, 276, 282, 296, 297, 299, 302, 303, 304, 305, 306, 307

J. 218
James 14, 20, 23, 33, 34, 37, 73, 75
Jonathan 36, 45, 112
Richard 91, 92, 95, 96(3), 97(2), 98(2), 125, 145(2), 151, 167, 169(2), 175, 188, 189(2)
Justice Richard 3, 8, 9, 10, 11(2), 14, 15(3), 17, 18, 19, 26, 27, 29, 31, 32, 35, 36, 37, 38, 39, 41, 44, 46, 46, 49, 54, 55, 56, 58, 59, 60, 61, 71, 72, 74, 75, 80, 81, 82, 83, 84, 86, 88, 90, 91, 93, 97, 99, 100, 101, 104, 107, 109, 112, 158, 163, 186(2), 187, 188, 277
Hart, Joseph 284
Philip 179, 191(2), 198
Hatch, Josiah 296
Hattaway, Susanah 39
Hawkins, Frederick 12, 23
Joshua 27, 29(2), 99, 129, 142, 145, 146
Samuel 152, 160, 166, 174
Hayes, Solomon 247
Thomas 98
Thomas Jr. 93
Hays, Henry 45, 58, 60, 81
Thomas 45, 46, 289
Haze, Thomas 67
Thomas Jr. 83
Head, James 46, 47, 56(2), 57, 102, 114, 116, 187
John 3, 4, 16, 41, 42, 63, 214, 222
Luerisa 56
Robert 30, 41, 143, 147, 272
Head's ford 16, 67, 112, 132, 229
Head's plantation 67, 229
Headen (see Hedden), John 37, 40
William 39, 40
Heaney (see Haney), Thomas 41, 45
Heard, Stephen 240
Hedden (see Headen), Elisha 293
Heddy, Elisha 290
Heirs, Henry 46
Hembree (see Hembry), Isaac 171
Joel 152, 157, 163, 164(2), 201, 221(3), 224, 231, 242, 249, 250, 253(2), 260, 263 (2), 264, 265(2), 270, 279, 280
John 114
William 158
Hembrick, Jeremiah 50
Hembry (see Hembree), Joel 127, 134
John 103
William 147, 170
Hemmett (see Hammett), William 223
Henderson, Allen 164
James 74, 75, 91, 166, 176(2), 177, 195, 208, 234, 243(2), 245, 254, 256, 260
John 107, 131, 287
Joseph 131, 144
Nathaniel 90, 195, 215, 223, 225, 226, 243, 244, 255, 261, 269
Robert 10
William 72, 116, 142, 167, 175, 181(3), 192, 201, 202 (3), 206, 207, 208
Hendrix, ___ 56, 129, 130, 142
Andrew 56, 185, 270, 296(2)
Anne 224
Elijah 210
Elizabeth 243
Isaac 15, 16, 79, 247, 251,
253, 256(3), 259, 260, 261, 270(2)
James 69
William 55, 73, 122, 241, 279
Henley, Len 200
Henly, Len 217
Henry, Abner 236
David 44, 67, 91
James 116
James Jr. 230
John 183
Herndon, Benjamin 24
Joseph 24
Herring, Elijah 268, 270
Herrington, Merrick 243
Hester, Abraham 220
Charles 35, 45, 46, 91, 104, 112, 119(3), 147, 151, 164, 171, 203, 211, 258, 266, 277, 294, 306(2)
John 277
Sarah 220
William 277, 300, 302, 303
Hewatt, John 171
Hewett, James 210, 217
Hewetts cabbin 300
Hewit(t) (see Huatt, Huitt), John 100(2), 106, 131, 306
William 100, 104, 109
Hickey, James 200, 239, 246, 251
Hickman, William 4
Hicks, David 176, 178(3), 235
James 225, 226
Hide, Moses 242, 249, 251, 256(2)
Hightower, John 32, 132, 136, 164, 204, 274
Thomas 37
William 119
Hightower's ford 274
Hill, Ephraim 211, 306
Epraim 295
Reubin 85
Solomon 229, 234, 235, 243
Thomas 122
William 33, 80, 131, 133, 136
Hill's ironworks 306
Hillen(e), Jesse 66
John 56, 58, 91
Mary 56, 58, 91
Hilsmore, History 15
Hindman, John 231
Hines, Absalom 86
Hobbs, Robert 22, 152, 156
Hodges, Richard 62
Hogan, Griffin 150
Michael 33, 41, 49(3), 50, 56, 59, 71, 78, 79, 80, 84, 96, 130, 141
Hogin, Michael 18
Holcom(b), James 54
John 32, 54
Sherard 132
Thomas 69, 73, 78, 82
Holeman, Comfort 76
John 131, 143
Holland, James 20
Reason 203, 211
Hollaway, Ann 28
Holley, Nicholas 63, 75, 87, 88, 89, 93, 94, 104, 109(2), 126, 126(2), 132, 134, 142 (2), 144, 152, 157, 162(3), 163(2), 164, 171, 181, 183, 193, 239, 246
Nichols 90
Holly, Nicholas 46, 200
Holmes, Frances 78
Jacob 147, 153(2)
John Bee 40
Holt, Charles 258
Hoof, Henry 96
Hooker, Benjamine 185
Edward 4, 9, 46, 58, 129, 224, 293, 300
Hooper, Enoch 199, 213
Edward 49
James 4, 28, 35, 40, 42, 45, 46, 56, 61(2), 63, 64, 83, 92, 151, 155, 158, 160, 162, 165(3), 166, 179, 186, 191, 199, 201, 209(2), 224, 232, 236, 260, 274, 291
Obediah 13, 14
Thomas 13
William 28
Hooper's ford 4
Horton, Rolley 265, 300
House, Laurence 49
Thomas 73, 222, 234
Hovers, Frederick 262(2), 266
Howard, Archer 234
Benjamine 222, 239, 246, 284
Nehemiah 65, 70, 95
Peter 19
Howel(l), James 9
Joseph 82, 94, 97, 183, 194, 228
Huatt (see Hewatt, Hewett, Hewit(t), Huitt), John 20
Hubburt, Lydia 76
Huckeby, John 249
Thomas 187
Hudgens, James 115
John 138, 185(3)
Huff, Henry Jr. 214
Henry Sr. 214
Philip 226, 233
Huger, ___ 278
Huggins, James 28, 35, 43, 54, 87, 202
Hughes, James 73, 81, 181, 293, 300
Joseph 239
Thomas 239, 246
Hughey, George 83, 135
Hughs, James 3, 6, 69
John 293
Huitt (see Hewatt, Hewett, Hewit, Huatt), John 90
Hull, John 33, 114, 115
Reubin 68
Humphries, David 151, 160, 210
John 185, 203, 284
Hunt, Charles 10, 57, 62
George 57, 60
McMakin 115
McMeekin 86, 91, 96
Hunter, Thomas 215
Hurt, Joel 176, 296, 297
Hurts Meeting House 296
Hutchens, Arthur 123, 175
Hutcheson, Arthur 164
Hutchins, Arthur 46, 133, 171, 287
Hutchison, Drewry 91
Drury 215
Elkenah 24, 33

Isaacks, Elijah 170, 176
Isam (see Isham, Isom, Eison), Frederick 60
Isham (see Eison, Ison), Frederick 39, 59
Jacob 39, 59
Ison (see Eison, Isam, Isham), Frederick 49(2), 51, 71

Jackson, Daniel 2, 87, 129
James 7, 40, 224, 256, 271(2)
John 175, 195, 198, 248, 256
Ralph 47
Samuel 17, 42, 46, 57, 85, 119, 134, 144, 224(3), 232, 248, 256, 271(3)
Samuel Jr. 46, 69, 114, 224
Thomas 3, 56, 69, 85, 106, 125,

Jackson, Thomas (con't) 168, 169,
    224, 256, 264, 271, 274,
    275, 303
  William 175, 177, 202(2), 207,
    208(3)
Jamerson, Robert 46
  Samuel 179
James, Charles 3, 5, 27, 86, 132,
    136, 164, 171, 222, 231,
    264
  John 8, 33(2), 83, 92, 158,
    164, 177, 184, 191(2), 196
    (2), 202, 237(2), 253, 256,
    258, 262, 267, 270, 277,
    284, 285, 288, 290, 292,
    294
  Philip 122
  Richard 15, 16, 164, 167(2),
    171, 172, 173, 175, 176,
    182(2), 193, 195(2), 196,
    209, 297
  Thomas 17, 195, 209
James' Creek 179, 193
Jameson, Henry 246, 252
  Robert 56, 61
  Samuel 210, 216, 258, 265
  William 69, 128, 277
Jameson's mill 139, 249, 283
Jamison (see Jemison), Samuel
  293
Janians (see Jenians), Rowland
  211
Jasper, Nicholas 19
Jemison (see Jamison), Robert
  4, 10, 27, 29
  William 26
Jemison's mill 26
Jenians (see Janians), Rowland
  92, 203, 210, 211, 214
Jenkens, Thomas 158
Jenkins, Thomas 130, 143
Jennings, John
Jentry (see Gentry), Samuel 96,
  188
Joel, Rispey 207
Johnson, ___ 27
  Claybrun, 246, 252
  Eady 139
  Ellis 102, 222
  Ezekiel 204, 219(2), 228
  James 252, 259
  John 11, 13, 27, 117(3), 122,
    133, 135, 195(2), 196, 237,
    238
  Margaret 156, 165, 220
  Michael 27
  Noel 121, 141, 160, 184
  Nowel 103
  Philip Jr. 206
  Randolph 102, 252, 259(2)
  Roland 301(2)
  Rowland 15, 16, 17, 28, 86,
    87(2), 91, 99, 105, 111(2),
    114, 198, 203, 210, 216,
    217, 219, 221(2)
  Samuel 217
Johnston, Ezekiel 232
  John 30, 69, 73, 77, 232
  Rowland 35, 46, 76, 81
Joice, Talley 81
Jones, ___ 26, 29, 112, 123,
    126, 234
  Benjamine 83, 93, 111, 177,
    218, 304
  Candace 110, 216
  David 237, 265
  David, Th. 198, 210
  Elizabeth 39, 137
  Henry 132, 136
  Hiram 86
  James 39, 56
  John 121, 133, 147, 176, 205,
    211, 218
  Joseph 43, 84, 110

Malichi 4, 73, 83, 85, 86, 87
    (2), 89, 164, 185, 197,
    210, 277, 278, 284, 285,
    298
  Thomas 83, 137, 230
Jordan, Alexander 222, 231
  Elias 192, 222
  James 19(3), 20, 26, 35, 48
    (2), 53, 72, 125, 128,
    179, 200, 206, 230, 277,
    286(2)
  Justice James 1, 6, 7, 8, 9,
    10, 11, 14, 15, 17, 18, 19,
    21, 23, 24, 26, 27, 32, 34,
    36, 38, 39, 41, 44, 46, 47,
    48, 49, 50, 51, 52, 54, 59,
    60, 61, 62, 63, 64, 65, 66,
    67, 69, 70, 71, 72, 73, 92,
    99, 100, 101, 104, 107, 114,
    116, 118, 119, 120, 122,
    125, 132, 134, 135, 136,
    139, 141, 144, 147, 148,
    149, 150, 153, 155, 158,
    159, 160, 163, 164, 165,
    168, 171, 173, 175, 177,
    179, 181, 183, 184, 187,
    189, 190, 192, 194, 197,
    198, 200, 203, 206, 207,
    208, 210, 211, 213, 215,
    216, 217, 218, 220, 222,
    223, 226, 227, 229, 231,
    232, 233, 234, 235, 236,
    237, 239, 240, 242, 244,
    245, 247, 248, 249, 250,
    252, 253, 254, 255, 256,
    258, 259, 260, 261, 263,
    264, 266, 267, 269, 270,
    271, 272, 273, 275, 277,
    278, 279, 282, 283, 286,
    287, 288, 289, 290, 292,
    293, 294, 296, 299, 302,
    303, 304, 305, 307
  John 153, 273
  Thomas 32, 133, 149, 151, 160,
    215
  Thomas T. 163
  William 136, 152, 198, 204,
    219, 273
Joslin, Daniel 106, 120, 130
Josling, Daniel 118
Jury, Curtis 13

Kain, John 198
Kean (see Keen), James 151, 241
Keating, Nicholas 150
Kearn, James 230
Keeler, Alexander 258
Keen (see Kean), James 8, 36,
    47, 48, 49, 53, 54, 59,
    240, 258, 265
Keenum, John 266
Deesee, George 301
Kelby, Adam 265
Kelley-Kelly, Daniel 6, 14, 56
    (2), 69
  Elijah 222, 230, 232
  John 45
Kelly's mill 303
Kelso, Joseph 230
  William 217(2)
Kemp, James 172, 179, 196
  Joseph 231
  Thomas 185
Kenedy, William 127, 134
Kenely, Joseph 160
Kerley, Henry 75
  William 15
Kerly, Henry 33
Kern, John D. 174
Kery, Thomas 31
Kezie (see Kizie), George 184,
    204, 255
Kilby, Adam 258

Kilgore, Benjamine 52(3), 66
Kilpatrick, ___ 4
  Alexander 150
  Robert 55
Kimbel(1), John 30(3), 57, 76,
    87, 92, 94, 106, 117(3),
    123, 239
  Robert 43, 48, 242, 259(2),
    275, 284
  Thomas 28, 91, 115, 122, 203,
    259(2)
Kimbol, Robert 215, 291
  Thomas 252
King, Ann 76
  James 293
  John 13, 42, 46, 97, 218, 222,
    227, 252, 258, 265, 266,
    292, 293(4), 295(2)
  Joseph 28
  Sarah 295
  Thomas 55
  William 162
Kirby, Henry 42
Kirconnell, John 18
Kirk, George 210, 216(2), 217,
    218, 219
Kirkendale, ___ 131
Kirkindale, ___ 144
Kirkland, John 215, 223, 225,
    226
  Joseph 28
  Zachariah 118
Kithcart, Samuel 151, 246, 252,
    253
Kivel, Benjamin 168
Kizer, ___ 247
Kizie (see Kezie), George 177,
    252
Knight, Jacob 254
Knox, Samuel 47, 195
Koon, Henry 115, 145
  James 45, 60
Kusee, George 242

Lackey (see Larkey), James 300
  John 171
  Salley 174
Lafevers, (see Lefever), ___ 306
Lambert, John 130
Lamkin, George 73, 130, 131,
    143, 144, 163, 175, 226,
    230, 239, 240, 250, 258(2),
    277, 290, 294, 300(2)
  John 298
Lancaster, Aaron 219(2)
  Absalom 27, 26, 45, 47, 86,
    148, 170, 191, 196,
    211, 229, 239, 248, 256,
    257, 270, 276(2), 306
  John 256, 257, 261, 268, 270,
    283
  Larkin 64, 135, 136, 148, 162,
    226
  Lemuel 305
  Samuel 3, 6, 17, 77, 177, 232,
    248, 249, 251, 254, 261,
    289
  Justice Samuel 27, 28, 29, 31,
    34, 35, 36, 44, 54, 55, 58,
    59, 60, 61, 62, 63, 64, 66,
    67, 69, 70, 72, 74, 77, 79,
    83, 84, 92, 94, 95, 100,
    101, 103, 104, 106, 118,
    125, 132, 148, 189, 224,
    271
  W. 148, 170, 226
  W. S. 127
  William 64, 89, 98, 113, 117,
    149, 178, 232, 262, 272,
    275, 279
Landers, Matthew 106, 109
Landford, James 264
Lands, John 56

Lanford (see Lansford), Janes 277
Langford, Nathan 135
Langley, Thomas 119, 214, 227, 233
Langston, ___ 43, 52, 71
  Bennett 71, 300
  Caleb 184
  Hezekiah 39
  Jaconias 43
  Jechonias 63, 73
  John 32, 42, 43, 53, 54, 55(5), 71, 79, 84
  Joseph 23
  Samuel 9
  Sarah 9
Lankford, James 296
Lansford, Swanson 220, 233, 242, 247, 270
  Lanford
Larkey (see Lackey), John 181
  Salley 166, 174
Laurence, James 193
  Randolph 220
Law, Jonathan 103, 171
  John 258
Lawson, John 32, 36
  Reubin 36, 70(2)
Lawson's Fork 4, 7, 10, 32, 39, 53, 73, 85, 128, 133, 139, 149, 277, 278, 284, 286, 287, 291, 298-99, 301(2)
Laxon, James 188
Laxton, Betty 76
  James 87
Lay (see Ley), Francis 200
Layton, Stephen 65, 70
Lea (see Lee), Sarah 270
Leach (see Leech), John 34
Leath, John 232
Ledbetter, Daniel 203
Lee (see Lea), Barzel 120
  Bazel 18, 58, 69, 73, 82, 86, 91, 95, 96(2), 97, 98, 99, 113, 114, 137, 145, 155, 179, 183, 184, 199, 201(2), 202, 209, 212, 220, 233, 245, 257, 258, 262, 279, 280(3), 284, 287, 293, 299
  James 7, 58, 123, 236, 137(2), 242, 259
  John 246, 302
  Richard 95, 223, 225, 226, 242, 249(2), 254, 262, 263 (2), 268
  Robert 302(2)
  William 213, 246, 253(2)
Leech (see Leach), David 94
  John 3, 27, 61(2), 62, 63, 64, 73, 83(2), 85, 87, 222, 265(3)
  Sarah 265(2)
Leek, ___ 213, 217
  Joseph 205
Lefever (see Lafever), John 89, 131, 212, 262(2), 266
Legate, Elias 102(2)
Lemaster, John 189, 298
  Lucy 298
  Ralph 298(3)
  William 258, 298
Lewis, Abel 74
  Beverly 210, 216
  David 3, 17(2), 18, 62(2), 103 (2), 191
  David Jr. 17, 19, 20, 22, 23, 46, 62
  Elizabeth 142
  Ephraim 106, 115
  George 74, 194
  Isaiah 147, 209
  Joel 62, 139
  Margaret 223, 226
  Peggy 18

Peter 27, 53, 74, 126
Polly 18
Richard 28, 35, 45, 46, 120, 136, 271
Seth 52
Widow ___ 139
William 51, 199, 209, 264
William Terrell 24
Ley (see Lay), Francis 208, 215, 221
Lidson, ___ 67
Liles, Thomas 255
Linch (see Lynch), Edward 303(3)
  James 303
Lindsay, Mary 229
  William 279
Lindsey, Carlton 109(2), 118, 127(2), 138, 174
  John 20, 80, 82, 89, 103, 126, 127, 134, 143
  Joshua 109
  Mary 204, 236
  William 29, 46, 69, 155, 198
Lipscomb, ___ 206
  David 300
  John 233, 241, 260, 292, 304, 305(2)
  Nathan 292, 299
  Smith 299, 305
  William 3, 5, 8, 17, 67(2), 69, 73(2), 75, 77, 84, 91, 100, 104(2), 112, 147, 148, 151(2), 152, 170, 183, 199, 214, 216, 300, 302, 305
Lissenby, Reubin 261
Littleton, Charles 119, 199
  Henry 304
Lively, Joseph 199(2), 201, 298
Livingston, John 63
  Joseph 184
Lockart, Thomas 200
  William 102
Loftis, Job 246
Logan, James 118, 134, 191, 201, 242, 253
Long, Christopher 10, 46, 83
Louther (see Lowther), George 278
Low (see Lowe), John 280
  Jonathan 184
Lowden, George 56, 62, 64
Lowder, George 153, 273
Lowe (see Low), Jonathan 45
Lowrie, Samuel 249, 256(2)
Lowry, Jane 106
  Thomas 16
Lowther (see Louther), George 164, 167, 184, 278, 281
  Thomas 228
Luallen, William 161(2)
Lucas, Jeremiah 28, 35, 56(2), 69, 73(2), 77
  John 56, 136
Lucus, John 271(3), 272, 273
  Rachel 271(2)
Lukerery, John 284
Lukeroy, John 298
Lusk, ___ 59
  James 42, 44, 48, 54, 57(2), 69(2), 73, 75, 77, 117, 118, 124, 134, 138(2), 150, 154(2), 213, 218, 222, 229, 231, 274(2), 277
  Robert 51
Lynch (see Linch), Edward 16, 67, 132, 198, 204, 206
  Isaach 229
  John 258
  William 3, 9, 11

McAbee, Charles 221
  Elisha 116
  Lacey 239, 246, 247(2)
  Mary 58, 116
  William 183
McBee-MacBee, ___ 138
  Betsy 241, 245(2)
  Burrell 137
  Durrel 278
  John 48
  Lucy 76
  Polley 76, 105
  Rhoda 36, 37, 40, 93, 111, 278
  Silas 65, 72, 76, 120
  Vardry 6, 10, 14, 21, 24, 28(2), 39(2), 36, 37, 40, 41, 42(2), 50(3), 51(2), 54, 65, 66, 67(2), 71, 78, 83, 91, 103, 110(3), 111 (3), 113, 125, 127, 128, 129, 130, 137(3), 142, 145, 156, 164, 170(2), 193, 241, 244, 247, 250, 251, 274, 278
McBeth, Alexander 199, 209, 222, 225, 228, 231, 250, 265(2), 266
McCall, Samuel 212
McCarley, ___ 283
  David 45, 158, 168, 176, 178, 209, 212, 239, 246(2), 247
  James 36
  Mose 46
McCarrell, John 147, 153(2)
  Thomas 302
McCarroll, John 240
McCarter, Alexander 46, 151, 160, 177, 184, 240, 259
  Charles 176, 178(2)
  George 239, 246, 247
  John 62, 115, 122, 183, 199, 246
  Margaret 259(2)
  Mary 182, 259
  Matilda 259
McClain-MacClain, Charles 46, 56, 61(2), 63, 64, 184
  Daniel 17
McClaren, Daniel 151, 158, 159, 165, 177, 243, 244, 245, 250(3), 252, 256, 261, 277, 290, 298
McClarin, Daniel 3, 33
McClary, Daniel 4, 5, 114, 121
McCle, Jane 141
McClebben's Ford 288
McClellan's Ford 285
McClure, Caty 160
  James 154(3), 160, 161, 169
  John 54, 69, 73, 78, 82, 153, 160, 240, 302
  Samuel 128, 138, 153, 154, 198, 204, 246
  William 153, 158, 160, 184, 192(2), 201
McCollock, John 49
McCowin, William 18
McCrary, Henry 120, 161(2)
McCravies, John 71
McCray, ___ 279
  H. 243
  Henry 97, 98, 113, 117, 149, 152(2), 156(4), 157, 169, 172, 178, 207, 209, 212(2), 216, 228, 229, 230, 233, 236(3), 239, 240, 251, 254(2), 261, 262, 263, 281, 305, 306(2)
  Martha 149
McCree, David 47
  John 53
McCrory, Jane 243
  John 272

317

McCrory, Margaret 184
  Martha 284
  Thomas 151, 243(2)
McCroy, Martha 184
McCullock, John 19, 54(2), 55, 58, 61
McDaniel, ___ 172
  Drewry 176, 177, 184, 260
  Drury 299, 300, 305
  Thornton 152
  William 188, 205, 230, 259, 267
  Zachariah 267
McDowall, Charles 26
  David 9, 10, 27, 33, 112
  James 4, 17, 31, 40
  Robert 3, 17, 19, 20, 22, 23, 32, 65
  William 8, 13, 28, 32
McDowall's mill 8
McDowell, David 44, 46, 60, 69, 73, 77(2), 80, 85, 87, 91, 93, 104, 106, 121, 122, 131, 139, 141, 143, 148, 151, 158, 159, 165, 177, 184, 245, 246, 252, 278
  Francis 296
  George 172
  James 135, 239, 246
  John 180
  Joseph 46
  Robert 14, 60, 65, 69, 73, 78, 82, 141, 247, 249, 255(2), 266, 269, 299
  Sarah 172
  Widow ___ 287
  William 44, 55, 61, 62, 64, 74(2), 85, 172(2), 186, 173, 204, 210, 216, 220, 261, 264
  Justice William 61, 62, 69, 70, 72, 83, 84, 97, 99, 100, 101, 102, 104, 105, 120, 132, 271
McDowell's mill 44, 121, 122(2), 286
McElhany, James 6, 7, 8
  John 8, 183, 290
McElheney, Alexr. 40
  John 56, 76
McElhenny, John 51
McElheny, Alexander 22, 27
  Anne 286
  James 33(2), 93, 96(2)
  John 60, 72, 83, 84, 92(2), 94, 95(3), 99, 104, 126, 132, 140, 141, 168, 169, 170, 175, 182(2), 183(2), 193(3), 194(2), 200(2), 247, 286
  William 101
McElrath (see McElwrath), John 248
  Michael 248
  Nathaniel 239, 246
McElray, John 138
McElroy, John 128, 130, 153
McElwane, James 10(2)
McElwayne, James 41, 52, 212
McElwrath, John 151, 160, 198, 204
McGaughey, John 104, 105
  Michael 104, 105
McGore, John 248
McGowen, James 104, 123, 137
  John 113
  William 164, 172, 175, 195, 197, 202, 210, 212, 246, 252, 256
McGrew, John 209
McGuire, John 64, 78, 119(3), 239, 238(2)
McHughes, James 189
McInvail, John 150

McKein, Hugh 102
McKie, Alexander 254, 258(2), 261, 297, 301(2), 305(2), 306
  Daniel 305
  Michael 196, 216
  Patrick 194
McKinney, John 72
McKneely, David 54(2)
McKnight-MacKnight, Charles 41, 43, 50, 56, 60, 61(2), 71, 83, 89, 91, 100, 118(2), 126, 133, 139, 148, 150, 159, 170, 209, 220, 233, 235, 278(2), 302
  David 220, 233, 235
  James 122, 204
  John 10, 56, 61, 63, 64, 132, 136, 144, 203, 264
  Thomas 17, 18, 56, 61(2), 63, 64, 115, 122, 133, 135, 167, 175, 181(3), 192, 194, 199, 201, 202(3), 203, 206, 207, 208, 301
  William 122, 301
McMahan, John 115, 122
McMaken, Benjamin 291
McMakin, Benjamine 146, 293
McMekin, Benjamine 150, 169, 172, 175, 177, 180, 182(2), 183, 191, 221, 252, 254, 265, 283, 306
McMikin, Benjamine 114, 121, 168(2)
McMillan, Robert 85
  William 63, 64, 100, 135, 148, 278
McMillen, Hugh 139
McMillian, Robert 10
McMillin, Robert 28, 36, 45, 47, 48, 53, 54, 159
  William 22, 56, 62, 133, 159
McMullan, William 138, 271
McMullen-MacMullen, Andrew 259, 264
  Hugh 205, 294
  John 176
  William 61(2), 139
McNeely, David 59
McNees, ___ 10
  Robert 217
McNelly, David 54
McVarnan, John 115
McVey, Eli 198(2), 209, 213, 231
McWilliams, William 73, 83, 183, 195, 245(2), 299

Mabery (see Mayberry), Charles 194
  Thomas 194
Mabrey, Thomas 149
Machan, Henry 3, 6
Mackaboy, Matthew 45
Maddox, Michael 120
Mahany (see Mehaney), ___ 87
Mangham, ___ 152
Manton, Sarah 282
Mapp, John 3, 19, 36, 45, 47, 45, 69, 73, 77
  Littleton 64, 119, 173
  Littleton Jr. 91, 105, 111
Markley, Abraham 284
Martin, Charity 155
  Goerge 183, 193, 214(2)
  James 231, 243, 244
  John 11, 12, 40
  Peter 40, 44, 50
  Philemon 73, 84, 149, 175
  Phillip 8
Martindale, John 100
Mason (see Mayson), Broadrick 198

Mason, Frances 184
  Francis 199(2), 201
  John 182, 183
Massey (see Massy), Joseph 305
Massingale, Blake 267
  Thomas 209
Massy, William 184
Matthews, ___ 250
  James 237, 238, 249
  Jesse 212, 302
  Reubin 90, 298
Mattis, Reubin 124, 193
Maxwell, John 176, 195, 208, 211
Maybery (see Mabery), Charles 207
  Thomas 199
Mayes, Andrew 114, 128, 134(4)
  James 134, 198, 239, 244
  John 134
Mayfield, Dianna 197
  Millie 197
Mayson (see Mason), Broadrick 239, 246(2), 247
  Francis 264
Meadows, John 238
  Thomas 298
  William 279
Means, Hugh 138
  Joseph 130, 143, 144
Mechie (see Michie), Patrick 173, 182
Mehaney (see Mahany), Margaret 173
Merchant, William 185, 219, 242
Mercy, William 69
Meredith, Henry 69, 112(2), 119, 123(2), 127, 140, 143(3), 267
Meridith, Henry 62, 67
Merridith, Henry 141
Merrik, Tilley 121
Michie (see Mechie), Patric 176
  Patrick 165
Michison (see Mitchison), Edward 81, 88
  William 81, 168
Miles, Charles 66, 78, 111(2)
  Michael 181, 183
  Thomas 46, 57, 59, 102, 116, 118, 184, 199, 260, 261, 281, 301, 305
Milican, Andrew 56, 61(2), 63, 64
  James 51, 60
  Thomas 91
  William 81
Milikan, Robert Jr. 102
Milikin (see Millican, Millikin), Andrew 131, 144
  James 181, 202
  John 108
  Mary 186
  Robert 116, 118, 135
  Thomas 104, 112, 118, 150, 159, 164, 186
  William 118, 181,184, 254, 280
Mill, Nicholas 4
Miller, ___ 247
  Byares 4
  David 9-10
  George 117
  James 50, 81, 82, 105, 222, 242, 244, 291(2)
  John 14, 27, 138, 146, 164, 171, 175, 222, 258, 264, 266
  Michael 2, 76, 94(2), 132, 144, 145, 146(5), 179, 184, 202, 230, 239, 242, 268, 303, 304(2), 306
  Nathaniel 14(2), 39, 48
  Robert 14, 50, 83, 93, 133,

184, 199(2), 201, 229, 239, 242, 277, 286
Samuel 104, 114, 121, 138, 171, 183, 199, 209, 224, 235, 242, 258(2), 266, 288, 289
Sheriff ___ 238
Stephen 28, 96, 113, 117, 125
William 50, 176, 178, 203, 210, 265
Miller's Road 179, 276, 286, 293, 294, 306
Millican (see Milican, Milikin, Milikin, Millikin), James 44
Milligar (see Millinghan), Andrew 19, 22, 23
James 27, 36
Thomas 19, 20, 22, 23
Millikin (see Milican, Milikin, Milikin, Millican), William 177, 202
Millinghan, Andrew 17
Thomas 17
William 17
Milson, William S. 262, 268
Mitchel(1), Joseph 70(2)
Lemuel 57
Martha 57
Robert 57
Samuel 57
Mitchell's plantation 287
Mitcheson, William 49
Mitchison, Edward 3, 5, 22, 38, 52, 60
Moffatt (see Muffatt), Henry 14, 17, 19, 20(2), 22, 23, 27, 29, 130
Monger, Henrh 97
Monjoy, Jordan 42
Monk, William 119
Monroe, Daniel 65(2), 145, 157
Montgomery, James 61, 168
John 65, 70, 253
Robert Jr. 218
William 59
Moody, Rebekah 181
Thomas 23
William 183, 196, 199
Moore, Aaron 114, 121, 150, 158
Abraham 36, 150, 199(3), 201, 258, 264, 266
Charles 3, 5, 6, 20, 31, 42, 43, 49(2), 60, 64, 67, 68 (5), 79, 81, 83, 92
George 77
George B. 208, 213(2), 233, 243
Hugh 198, 204(2), 246, 251, 254(2), 287
James 119, 198, 238, 239, 246(2)
Jason 17, 19, 20, 22, 23, 102, 116(2), 118, 178, 238, 246, 250, 252, 276
Jeremiah 36, 132
John 13, 17, 60, 87, 106, 108(2), 131, 144, 158, 163, 165, 179, 198, 274
Joseph 160, 165, 248, 274
Patrick 287
Samuel 267
Thomas 6, 83, 85, 148, 159, 172, 180, 181, 187, 188, 195, 204, 207, 217, 224, 251, 252, 257, 276, 285, 288, 290, 291, 292, 294, 298, 299, 306(2)
William 20, 31, 42, 60, 78, 80, 94, 109, 115, 122, 135, 187, 188, 193, 204(3), 224, 278, 282
Morgan, Charles 250, 252, 259(2),

266, 268, 302
Henry 59, 112, 147, 153
Henry Jr. 135
Isaac 8, 179
J. 128
Joshua 88
William 250
Morris(s) (see Morros), ___ 33
Betsey 76
Israel 3, 5, 14, 19, 23, 29, 30(3), 45, 50, 72, 76, 85, 86, 87, 92(3), 94, 100, 108(2), 113(4), 125, 129, 130, 131, 142, 143, 144, 145, 146
James 67, 78
John 18, 171, 198
Joseph 18(2), 91, 130, 133, 204, 219, 239
Richard 147, 153(2), 183
Thomas 58
William 18, 121, 155, 157, 161, 165, 170, 171, 291, 306
William Sr. 171
Morrison, ___ 80
Alexander 269
Morros (see Morris(s)), Samuel 132
Morrow, John 252
Robert 73
Samuel 114, 121, 136, 147, 151, 158, 223, 224(3), 227, 250, 252, 283, 287, 295
Samuel Sr. 215
Thomas 26, 43, 60, 89
Morse (see Moss), ___ 74
Agness 174
Ebenezar 13, 20, 26, 42, 55, 58, 59, 62, 63, 68, 69, 71, 75, 78, 79, 81, 88, 89, 91, 97, 115, 117(2), 123, 124, 128, 132, 136, 139, 163, 167, 177, 184, 185, 200, 208, 215, 219, 247, 251, 253, 255, 256(2), 259, 260 (2), 261, 270(2), 274
James 252
Mason 188, 208
Obadiah 132, 239, 264
Travice 89, 113, 141, 160
Travis 124(2)
William 70
Morton, David 40
Moss (see Morse), Ebenezar 7, 20, 41, 42, 44, 46
Travis 124(2)
Motlow, John 2, 87, 179, 198, 206, 247
Mucklehany, ___ 234
Muffatt (see Moffatt), Henry 115
Mulnex, Matthew 123
Murrell, Drewry 127, 134
Murry, ___ 167, 176
Nicholas 243
Thomas 239
Musgrove, ___ 53, 293
Beaks 11
Berks 22, 31
Edward 22
Edward B. 92
Edward Beeks 63, 77, 81(3), 82, 84
Musgrove's mill 300

Naile, Henry 180
John 104(2), 113, 123(2), 137(2), 180
Nails, John 86
Nalley, Abraham 89, 171, 281
Abram 75, 132
Richard 55, 171(2), 281(2)

Nally, Abraham 40
Richard 2
Neal (see Neel), David 57, 143, 184
William 87, 176
Nealy, Mary 244
Neasbitt (see Nesbitt), Agness 142
James 142, 199(2), 201, 249
Jeremiah 59
John 114, 121, 132, 158, 165, 211, 212
Jonathan 91, 106, 118, 120, 130, 132, 136, 140, 141, 142(2), 164, 198, 204, 292
Joseph 73, 83(2), 85, 87, 89, 115, 203, 211
Nathan 106
Robert 73, 144, 121, 164
Samuel 54, 71, 91, 104, 107, 112, 122, 129, 132, 136, 142, 158, 175, 230, 239(2), 247, 248
Nebuhr, John David 224
Neel (see Neal), David 62, 64
Jeremiah 12, 27, 31
William 2
Neely, Samuel 292, 300
Nelly, Samuel 39
Nelson, John 103, 246, 253, 306
Robert 8
Nesbit(t) (see Neasbitt), James 184
John 3, 6, 28, 35, 36, 203
Jonathan 171
Robert 7, 28, 247, 271
Samuel 7, 50, 54, 70, 223
Nevins, Alexander 132
Newman, George 119
Reuben 102, 116, 118, 174, 203, 211
Simpson 264
Simson 147, 153(2), 214
William 243
Nibbs, ___ 226(2), 227, 228
William 165, 222
Nichol(s), ___ 147
Jno. 7(2), 8, 59, 146
Nichol's old mill 220, 281, 291, 292, 299, 300
Nickoll, John 36
Nickol's mill 21
Nobbs, Mr. ___ 166, 171
Nobles, Erasmus 265, 267(3)
Noel, David 132
Norris(s), Israel 85
James 28, 36, 45, 47, 48, 52, 54, 69, 73, 82, 122, 132, 135, 136, 207
Northward, Benjamin 91
Norton, Nehemiah 280
Thomas 246
Nott, ___ 169, 173, 176, 177, 185, 193, 199, 206, 209(2), 212, 215, 221, 215, 221, 224, 227, 228, 236(2), 237, 250(2), 251, 256, 260, 262, 266, 268
Abraham 237, 240, 242, 244, 249(2)
Abram 159, 205, 207, 208, 211, 214, 225
Nunn, William 86, 118

Oates, James 164, 279
Martin 184, 199(2), 201
Maryan 274
Oats, James 252
Martin 28, 35
O'Barr, Michael 263, 268
Robert 263
O'Kean, Henry 168

319

Oliphant, James 3, 22, 24, 173
  Obadiah 73, 84
Olliver, Jelson 264
O'Nail, Henry 207, 293, 295
  John 227, 231
Osheals, Elizabeth 37
  Jethro 270, 304, 306
  John 42, 184, 199(2)
Osling, John 56
  Samuel 127, 134
Otterson, Samuel 127, 134
Ottis, James 259(2)
Otts, Martin 298
  Samuel 298
  William 298
Ovail, Henry 286
Owen(s), Hardy 195
  William 176

Pace, Isaac 256, 260, 294
  John 120, 183, 199, 214, 226, 265, 290
  Richard 166, 176, 177, 299
Pack, John 83, 158
  Sarah 233
  Simon 233, 234
Paden (see Pedan), Thomas 46, 55, 83, 92, 150, 159, 170, 198, 204, 220, 291, 292(2)
Page, Robert 171, 184, 199(2)
Parker, John 30, 42
  Robert 109(2), 118, 127(2), 138
  Thomas 91
Parkinson, George 7, 14, 15(2), 169
Parkison, George 33, 194
Parks, Thomas 197, 213, 219
  William 261
Parsons, Major ___ 14, 29, 42, 51, 60, 65(2), 80
Passon, ___ 128(2)
  Lucy 154
  Major ___ 129, 139, 142
Passon's road 149(2), 303
Patrick, ___ 49
Patten (see Patton), Matthew 283
Patterson, James 102
  William 93, 95, 98, 102, 109
Patton (see Patten), John 4, 5, 14, 42, 70
  Matthew 132, 215, 223, 278
Paul, Andrew 47, 67, 75, 82(2), 97, 107, 117, 152
  John 75
Peace, Hugh 13
Peaks, Benjamin 279
  James 239
Pearce (see Pierce), John 302
Pearson, Anthony 198, 204, 206
  Joel 255
  William 255, 261
Pebes, John 243
Pedan (see Paden), David 24, 40
  John 24
  Samuel 24
  Thomas 35, 40, 45
Peeler, Alexander 207
Pelfrey, Joseph 305
Penals (see Penials, Pinion), Peter 281
Pendleton, Judge Henry 1
Penial (see Penals, Pinion), Peter 261
Pennington, ___ 17
  Jacob 81, 102
  John 22(2), 38(2), 42, 52(2), 66, 135, 138, 183, 185, 199, 225(2), 239, 246
Penny, John 132
  Thomas 94, 147, 153(2)
Perce (see Pierce), Hugh 14, 15(2), 16, 27, 30, 33, 42, 43
Pervines, Moses 132
Peters, Sarah 229
Peters' Creek 296, 301, 306
Peterson, Peter 264(2)
Pettitt (see Pettit), Benjamin 164
  Henry 287
Pettice, George 35
Pettis (see Pettus), George 28
Pettit (see Petitt), Abraham 282
  Henrh 73, 83, 291
  Joshua 82
Pettus, George 36, 47(2), 51, 52, 54(3), 59, 95, 108
Petty, Joshua 88, 89, 94
Pharis, James 28, 35
Philips, Benjamine 131, 144(2)
  James 12, 40
  Stephen 102, 116, 118, 177
  Thomas 165
Pierce (see Pearce, Perce), Hugh 93, 107, 111, 114, 123, 131, 136, 137(2), 144
Pierceon, Anthony 119
Piles, ___ 10
  John 102
Pinckney, Charles 120, 121
Pinion (see Penals), Peter 198, 281
Pinson, Aaron 147, 153(2), 291
Piper, B. 218
  Benjamine 119, 211
  John 232, 268
  Robert 276
Pipes, John 126, 247, 248, 249, 253, 261, 263, 268
Poesy (see Posey), John 265, 276
Pollard, William 239, 246
Polson, Joseph 2
Pool, Abraham 192, 201, 303
  George 180(2)
  James 197, 284(2)
  William 92, 107, 136, 158, 182, 183, 196, 205
  William (H.S.) 111, 114, 117, 284(2)
  William (J.M.) 105, 121, 126, 128, 137, 142, 145, 152, 155, 164
  William (Taylor) 92, 147, 151
Pool's iron works 133
Poole, George 4
  James 13, 14, 29, 76, 219(2), 220
  William 5, 8, 19, 35, 37, 38(2), 39, 41, 45, 50(2), 51, 53, 55, 66, 69(2), 70(2), 72(2), 73, 75(2), 77(2), 82(2), 90, 97, 193, 209, 229
  William (J.M.) 4, 145, 171, 230
  William (Taylor) 3, 17, 28, 121, 203, 211, 239, 246
Poor's ford 122
Pore, Holley 131
Porter, James 21
  Samuel 10, 32, 28(2), 45, 51, 67, 127, 129, 146
Posey (see Poesy), John 49, 83, 92, 147, 151, 158, 165, 177, 184, 258
Potter, ___ 138
  Adam 12, 67, 137, 143, 148, 280(2)
Powell, James 31
  Mark 46, 63, 143, 148, 200, 208, 215, 221, 241, 244
  Richard 153
Power(s), Francis 115, 120, 145(2), 166, 171, 181, 203, 210, 211(2)
Hollaway 176, 194
  James 111
  Joseph 49(2), 91, 105(2)
  Mary 185, 187(2)
  Nathaniel 267, 269, 270
Prestrage, Joshua 73, 83(2), 85, 87, 89
Prewet (see Prewit, Pruitt), David 151
  Thomas 178
Prewit(t) (see Prewet, Pruitt), David 62, 69, 73, 78, 82
  Drewry 83
  Moses 140
  Samuel 246, 252, 253
  Snoden 115
  Thomas 135
Price, Hugh 7
  Joseph 273, 284
  Thomas 88, 94(3), 119, 149, 172, 180, 184, 191, 196, 199(3), 201, 223(2), 225, 246, 252, 262, 276, 280, 283(2), 284, 289(2), 292(3), 298, 305
Price's store 143
Prince, Henry 26, 50, 111(3)
  Mary 63
  Mrs. ___ 4
  Richard 57, 66
  Robert 17, 63
  Widow ___ 37
  William 2, 3(2), 8, 28, 35, 58, 69, 71, 101
Prior, Richard 135
Pritchett, ___ 131
  John 131, 144(2)
Procter-Proctor, Moses 12, 40, 149
  Susannah 166
Pruitt (see Prewet, Prewitt), David 4
Pugh, Edmund 129, 140
Pulliam, Isham 165

Quarles, David 248, 258
  Thomas 258
Quin(n), ___ 131
  Hugh 131, 133, 144(2)
  Joseph 138

Raburn, John 45
  Richard 45
Rainey, Benjamin 81
Rainwater, John 69, 198, 232, 297, 298, 301, 304
Rakestraw, James 21
  Jesse 20, 21, 26, 29, 34, 204, 218, 233, 234, 241
  Robert 218, 233, 234, 241
Rampley-Ramply, Mary 231
  William 158, 168, 222, 231(2)
Ramsey, Ephraim 102, 103, 105(2), 111, 224
Ray, Alexander 17, 19, 144, 191(2), 223, 226, 240(3), 258, 296, 305
  Andrew 151, 160, 215, 223, 225
  Elizabeth 305
Reams, Jesse 28, 30, 36, 45, 94, 135, 306
Reaves, Jordan 151
  William 158, 168, 203, 210
Red, Dudley 16, 23, 51, 108, 126, 133, 140, 173, 181, 183, 196(4), 197, 199
  John 306
  Joseph 2
Reddy, Laurens 41

Redman, John 3, 6, 17, 18, 26, 69, 177, 184, 193, 195, 287
  Samuel 84, 85, 116, 141, 151, 153, 166
  William 84, 85, 116, 141, 151, 153, 165, 166, 274
Redmond, John 303
Reece, Ephraim 46, 87, 88, 90, 147, 153(2)
  Thomas 58, 143
  Travice 147, 153(2), 277
Reed (see Reid), Isaac 219
Reese, Travice 296
Reid (see Reed), William 178
Reiner, John George 166, 172
Rennolds, ___ 52
Reynolds, Elias 225
  Furney 191(2), 192, 214
  Henry 191(2), 192, 214
  John 187, 191(2), 192, 214
  Justice 201, 202(2), 215, 225(2), 235(2), 237(2), 238, 244, 247, 249, 250, 259, 261, 263, 268, 290, 300, 303
  William 66, 94, 96, 191(2), 192, 214
Reynold's mill 291
Rholds (see Roads, Rodes), Benjamine 181
  Benjamine Jr. 171
  Christopher 198, 204(2)
Rice, James 87
  Joseph 158
  Margaret 220
Richards, Thomas 229(2), 234, 241, 253
Richardson, Charles 248
Richey (see Ritchey), James 6, 8, 11, 13, 14, 15
Rickman, William 40, 91, 125, 130, 137, 156, 231, 243, 244(2), 250(3), 252, 256
Right, William 6
Rightsford, William 235
Riner, George 156
Ritchey (see Richie), James 10
Rizner-Riznor, Valentine 131, 144
Roach, John 282
Roads (see Rhodes, Rodes), Benjamin 42, 62(2)
Robbin, William 130
Roberds, Michael B. 173
  William 229
Roberts, Jane 161, 166, 169(2)
  Jean 169
  Martha 107
  Michael B. 108, 111, 126, 151, 152
  Obadiah 113
  Richard 152, 161, 166, 169
  Robert 102(2), 105
  Thomas 102, 104, 105, 107, 135
  William 102, 104, 105, 107(2), 109, 133, 136, 154, 160, 189
Robertson, Elizabeth 157, 206
  Israel 264, 272(2)
  James 157
  John 209, 212, 234, 242
  Joseph 157, 198, 204
  Nathaniel 31, 91, 115, 132, 164, 171, 198, 204
  Thomas 83
  William 171, 257, 266
  Zachariah 69, 73, 157, 186, 196(2), 197, 198, 204, 291, 298
Robertson's ford 298
Robinson, John 12
  William 165

Robison, Henry Sr. 19
  Nathaniel 16, 23
  Zachariah 37
Robuck (see Roebuck), ___ 82
  Benjamin 60
  George 52, 297
  John 60
Rodden (see Roden), ___ 80, 85, 87, 93, 131, 143
  Thomas 195
Roddy, Alexander 172, 191, 194, 216, 222, 240, 253, 287
Rodes (see Rhodes, Roads), Christopher Jr. 119
Rodgers (see Rogers), ___ 41
  Daniel 258, 265, 266
  Robert 119, 203, 210, 211(2), 241, 284
  Thomas 151, 198, 204, 206-207
  William 226, 243, 258, 265, 266
Rodger's bridge 238, 298
Rodin, ___ 44
  Thomas 46
Roesee Roden
Roebuck (see Robuck), ___ 72, 74, 82(2), 84, 95
  Benja. 82(2), 85
  George 3, 79, 82, 83, 131, 139, 150, 152, 159, 164, 171, 198, 212, 214, 217, 228, 232, 243, 263, 269
  John 43, 56, 61, 64, 78(2), 82, 83, 87, 104, 105, 113, 116, 117, 118, 120(2), 121, 128, 131, 139, 152, 171, 231, 243, 247, 264
Rogers (see Rodgers), John 302
  Wilson 41
Rolston, Robert 94
Roson, John 72
Ross, Ellis 52
  James 52
  John 11, 56, 61, 215, 239, 289, 306(3)
  Sarah 306
Rountree (see Trountree), James 196
  William 138, 155, 168(3), 196, 197
Rowland, George 264
Ruse, Ephraim 35
Rush, Matthias 247, 253
  William 149
Russ, Ephraim 28
Russell, Jeremiah 12
  John 8, 26, 50, 111(3)
  Thomas C. 53(2), 70
  Thomas Commander 37
Rutherford, James 229
Ryan, John 129
Ryner, George 66

Saffold, ___ 54
  Isham 50, 86, 130, 143
Safford, Isham 50
Safold, ___ 22, 24, 29, 44, 49
  Isham 12, 38, 41
Salley, John 132, 169
  Susannah 169
Salmon, George 6, 8, 82, 93, 94, 104, 188, 190
Sanders, John 99, 114(2)
  Lewis 114
  Richard 50, 77
Saratt (see Seratt, Serratt), John 122
  Samuel 44
Saterfield, James 167, 199, 201
Satterfield, James 184, 199
Saunders, ___ 297
  Ann 184
  Elizabeth 161, 174

Saunders, James 153, 169, 174, 205, 276, 285, 286, 287, 294
  John 99
  Mary 154
  Richard 165, 169, 181, 274
Saxon, ___ 215, 218
  Benjamine H. 200, 215(2)
  Charles 9
  Joshua 80
Scott, Bazel 226
Scruggs, Charles 119
  Drewry 64(2), 250
  John 56
Scurry, Nichols 49
  Thomas 12, 23, 68(2)
Seaborne, ___ 52
See, Gideon 304
Selman, Jeremiah 146, 147, 178, 184, 193, 200, 211, 218, 220, 221, 248
  Thomas 115, 122
Seratt, John 49(2)
Serratt (see Saratt, Sarratt), John 107, 119
  Samuel 165
Sexton, Thomas 295
Shackleford, ___ 290
Shands, Anthony 246
  John 3, 69, 138, 151
Shannon, John 23, 24, 30, 41(2), 50, 52, 54, 70, 71, 129
Shaver, Henry 172, 180, 181
Shaw, ___ 13, 43
  Daniel 64(2), 129
  W. 20
  William 4, 7, 9(2), 22, 23(2), 24(2), 25, 26, 28(2), 30 (2), 31, 32, 35, 37, 38, 41, 42, 44, 47, 48, 52, 53(2), 54, 59(2), 63, 64 (2), 65(2), 66, 67, 68(2), 71, 72, 75, 78(2), 79(2), 81, 85(2), 88(2), 89(2), 93(2), 94(2), 95(2), 97, 109(2), 110(2), 111(2), 112, 113(2), 114, 119, 120, 124, 125, 131, 133, 136, 137(4), 139, 140, 141(2), 142(2), 143(2), 144(3), 145(3), 146(3), 151, 152, 153, 154(3), 156, 157, 159 (2), 160(2), 162, 163(4), 164, 167, 168, 169(2), 175, 176, 179, 181(3), 182, 191, 193(2), 194(2), 199, 202
Shea, William 278, 281
Sheals (see Shields), Jeremiah 146
Shed, William 115, 122, 198, 296
Shelton, ___ 29
Sherdon, Dennis 115, 120, 145(2)
Sherley (see Shurley), Thomas 91
Shields (see Sheals), Jeremiah 143
Shippies, ___ 292
Shippy(s), 233
  Daniel 135, 136
  John 27, 132, 148, 149, 170, 258, 273, 304, 305(2)
  Samuel 305
Shoemate, Berryman 189
Shumat, Berryman D. 267
Shumate, Armistead 305
  Benjamine D. 265
  Berryman D. 230, 239, 255, 257, 260, 267, 294
Shurbet, Samuel 187
Shurley (see Sherley), Thomas 111, 150
  William 105, 164
Shurly, Thomas 298
Shute, Casper C. 241

Silman, Benjamine 20, 31, 37, 38(2), 40, 42, 43, 60, 68 (5), 79, 81
  Jeremiah 32, 39, 292
  Thomas 68, 81
Silmon, Jeremiah Sr. 306
Silvey, Francis 197
  Stephen 197S
Simmons, Abner 15
  James 198
  William 77, 82, 146
Simpson, Arthur 288
  Crofford 231
  William 8, 9, 10, 11, 13, 14, 27, 69, 86, 115, 183, 199, 269, 285, 288, 295, 296
Simson, Arthur 151, 212
  Crofford 227
  Jean 212
Sinckley, Elizabeth 180
Sinkley, Elizabeth 180
Sinyard, Jonathan 136
Skelton, ___ 22, 44, 49
  Mark 216
Sloan, Adam 246, 252
  George Tho. 262
  John 247, 256, 257, 262, 263
Sloan's ironwork 121, 179
Slone, John 167
Slone's iron works 133, 135
Smith, ___ 11, 30, 40, 65, 70
  Agnes 66
  Ann 60
  Buckner 76, 88, 90, 125, 169, 171, 181, 210, 216, 217, 218, 221, 252, 259
  Catharine 66(2)
  Charles 17, 19, 22, 23, 83, 93, 110
  David 132, 136, 206, 280(3)
  Edward 15, 49, 77, 84, 116, 271, 280, 302
  Elisha 45, 145, 163, 187
  Fleming-Flemming 3, 4, 6, 36, 45, 47, 49(2), 52, 54, 69, 73, 78, 82, 258, 266
  Getis 73
  Giles 32, 60
  Handcock 2, 42, 48, 66, 102, 123, 124, 137, 153, 191
  Isham 37
  James 4, 17, 19, 20, 22, 23, 30, 42, 47, 49(2), 57, 59, 61, 62, 66(3), 82, 84, 86, 114, 115, 117, 121, 123, 128, 134(4), 136, 147, 162 (2), 176, 177, 182(2), 193, 195(2), 200, 209, 212, 215, 218(2), 222, 223, 225, 228, 229, 233(2), 234(2), 238, 241(2), 246, 251, 253, 257, 281, 306(2)
  Jane 66
  Joel 57, 140, 164, 171, 175, 284
  John 8(2), 9, 10, 11(2), 13, 14, 15, 28, 43, 47(2), 83, 85, 93, 95, 97, 113, 121, 124, 151, 158, 159, 170, 182, 184
  Josel 54
  Joshua 47(2), 90, 125
  Leonard 60, 72, 74, 82(5)
  Mary 116, 280
  Millington 216
  Paul 43, 60
  Peter 66, 135, 178, 218, 229, 281
  Ralph 22, 53, 60, 281
  Reubin 4, 36, 45, 47, 83, 93 (2), 94
  Robert 132(2), 137, 197, 282
  Samuel 91, 105, 111
  Spencer 66, 229

Tod 62
Widow ___ 4(2), 72
William 2, 3(2), 4, 8, 11, 15, 16, 19, 27, 28, 33, 36(3), 45, 46, 49(2), 52, 58, 60, 61, 66(2), 72, 77, 95, 100, 123(2), 127, 129, 131, 144, 147, 166, 168, 178, 184, 187, 191, 194(3), 195, 200, 205, 208, 214, 216, 218(2), 224, 238, 241, 250, 251, 257, 258, 278, 291, 295
Wm. Jr. 191, 194, 227
Wm. Sr. 214, 227, 228, 235
Justice William 69, 72, 74, 77, 80, 82, 83, 86, 88, 90, 91, 92, 94, 95, 96, 97, 98, 99, 100, 101, 103, 104, 107, 109, 112, 113, 114, 115, 117, 118, 119, 120, 125, 132, 134, 135, 136, 139, 141, 144, 147, 148, 149, 150, 153, 155, 158, 159, 160, 163, 164, 165, 168, 170, 171, 173, 175, 177, 179, 181, 183, 184, 190, 192, 194, 196, 198, 200, 203, 204, 206, 207, 208, 210, 211, 213, 215, 216, 217, 218, 220, 222, 224, 226, 227, 229, 231, 232, 233, 235, 236, 237, 238, 239, 263, 266, 267, 269, 270, 271, 272, 273, 275, 276, 279, 280, 281, 282, 283, 285, 286, 287, 288, 289, 290, 292, 293, 294, 296, 297, 299, 302, 303, 304, 306, 307
Zophar 17, 140, 141
Smithson, Marsoncock 94
  Mason Cox 60
Snody, John 171, 210, 216, 252
  Samuel 246
  Samuel N. 266
Snoddy, John 21, 27, 29(2), 33, 56, 83, 92, 147, 151, 164
  Samuel 102, 239, 265, 292
  William 27
Snow, Edmund 288
  John 267
  Levi 268, 269
  Moses
Snowden, John 243
Solmon, George 206
Sosbee, Job 170, 306
Sosby, Job 274
Sosebee, Job 177
Soseby, Job 294, 296
Sossbery, Job 151
Southerland, James 178, 230, 239, 261, 264, 283, 293
  John 246
Space, ___ 27
  Amos 11, 13, 27
Span(n), ___ 175
  Jeremiah 185, 208, 213(2), 228, 235
  Jesse 47, 198, 242, 267, 293
  Moses 47, 178
  Thomas 47, 172, 178, 184, 199 (2)
Sparks, Matthew 246, 252, 253
  Zachariah 70, 301
Spears, John 243, 244, 250
Spelce, John 191, 201, 223, 224, 228
  Joseph 201
Spelcer, John 199
Spelee, John 128, 129
Spencer, Benjamin 102, 124, 125(3)
  Jesse 83, 150, 230, 239, 278
  John 172

Susannah 150
Spiler, William 127
Spiller, Warrington 154, 252, 259(2), 273
  William 154, 173
Spiva, Isaac 283
Spiveer, Jesse 298
Sprinkle, Michael 6, 58, 107, 143, 147, 272
Spurgeon-Spurgion, Elizabeth 58, 167
  John 14
Spurgin, Elizabeth 20
  John 20
Stacy, Robert 305
Staggs, Samuel 166, 167, 170(2)
  Thomas 176
  William 170
Standley, Ezekiel 178, 188
Stanley, Lewis 203, 290
Steen, John 57, 110, 128, 131, 137
Stephens (see Stevens), Anne 184
  Daniel 106, 204
Stephenson (see Stevenson), Alexander 141
  Daniel 85
  Hugh 141, 153, 175, 183, 195, 199, 204, 231, 255, 256
  Hugh Jr. 225
  James 151
  William 147, 222, 225, 231
Sterling, Robert 35, 45, 46, 72, 81, 179, 198, 239, 246, 288, 296
  Sarah 81
  William 28, 31, 36, 45, 47, 54, 178, 184, 193, 195
Stevens (see Stephens), Elijah 184
Stevenson (see Stephenson), Hugh 256
Steward, Edward 209
Stewart, ___ 145
  Alexander 241, 242, 244
  Edward 198, 207, 213, 223, 247
  Elizabeth 156, 164, 175, 191, 192(2)
  Samuel 70, 92, 118, 121, 125
  William 200, 212, 246, 303
Still, Thomas 70, 71, 129, 142
Stoaks (see Stokes), Nathaniel 36, 45
Stoans (see Stone) ironworks 306
Stokes (see Stoaks), Absalom 180
  Edward 48
  Ignacius 266
  John 195
  Nathaniel 47, 48, 53, 54, 119, 148, 166, 169, 178, 184, 198, 275, 281
Stone (see Stoan), Benjamin 12, 73, 83(2), 85, 87, 89, 184, 199(2)
  Caleb 63, 226, 233
  Christopher 226, 233, 246, 252, 267
  Edward 136, 246
  Edward Sr. 69, 132
  John 3, 158, 168, 198, 204, 206, 243, 246, 253
  Jonathan 28, 36, 43, 45, 47, 48, 53, 54
  Thomas 258, 265, 266, 269
  William 184, 223, 252
Story, George 204, 206
  George Jr. 198
  George Sr. 44
  John 198, 204, 206
Stouval, John 178
  Mary 13
Strawder, Jemp 75

Streemathead, John 171
Stron, John 235
Stroud, Thomas 246
Strow, John 229, 234
Stubblefield, Edward 119, 178
Suddeth, William 83, 92
Suddoth, William 123, 132, 133, 286, 138, 170
Sullivan, Dennis 228, 252
  Elizabeth 226
  Ezekiel 103
  Rebekah (2), 103
Sulser, Matthias 19
Sumner, Ann 76
  Holland 37, 39, 48, 51(2), 65, 70, 76, 80, 88, 108, 125, 126, 127, 128, 129, 133, 136, 142, 145, 148
  Mills 127
Sutin, William 153
Sutton, James 246
Swan(n), James 43, 93
Swanson, William 37
Sweny, Bernard Wm. 174(2), 248, 253(2)
Syms, Charles 127, 134
Symmes, Daniel 36
  Robert 36
Symms, Daniel 13, 15, 18(3)
  Robert 119, 198
Synard, James 255, 169

Tacket, Widow 282, 289
  William 119
Taliaferro (see Toliaferro, Tolliaferro), Zachariah 93
Tanner, David 246, 252, 297, 298
  James 221
  John 274, 276
  Josiah 8, 24, 28, 56, 69, 71, 114, 121, 150, 152, 159, 189, 206, 216
Tap, John 188
Tarket, John 178
Tarrance, Andrew 234
Tarry, James 12
  Joseph 12
  William 21, 29
Tate, ___ 131
  Jesse 19, 91, 131, 144(2), 264, 277
  William 8, 17, 18, 23, 28, 35, 45, 46, 48(2), 49, 61, 91, 102, 103, 127, 170, 171, 277(3)
  William Jr. 18
  Tate's ferry 4, 16, 289, 295, 306
Taylor, Agnes 76
  Bayley 15, 21, 22, 72, 83(2), 85, 89
  George 33, 40, 67, 80, 92, 110(2), 111, 124, 128(2), 151, 160, 187, 192, 197, 202, 212, 217, 231, 243, 245, 259, 263, 270
  James 175, 179, 184, 295
  Joel 60
  John 261
  Micajah 83
  William 135, 187, 188, 192, 211
  William Poole 90, 170
Temple, Jesse 215, 258
Templeman, Aaron 268
Templeton, Aaron 252
Tenant, ___ 172
  William Peter 173
Terly, Isham 23
Terrell, James 272
Terrill, James 76, 91, 99, 100, 115, 122, 130, 131, 133, 136, 137(2), 152, 156, 272
  Micajah 122
  Simon 137
Terry, John 219
  Joseph 120
Thomas, Col. ___ 92
  J. Jr. 22(2), 76
  John 9, 29, 42, 44, 65, 122
  John Jr. 39, 53, 57, 65(2), 70, 75, 88, 89, 99, 101, 120, 121, 132, 144, 149, 163, 182
  Justice John Jr.1,3, 100
  Thomas 294
  William 182
  William D. 110, 111, 182, 184, 216, 221
Thomason, Arnold 209, 239, 245, 246(2), 247, 262
  George 87, 257, 266, 306
  Turner 135, 150, 182, 212, 275, 281
  William 51, 204
  William T. 188, 198, 199, 209, 243, 259, 291, 303
  William Turner 3(2), 4, 18, 92, 120, 262, 300
Thompson, Andrew 288
  Waddy 234, 235, 240
  William 233, 305(2)
Thomson, ___ 9, 12, 65, 112, 206, 228, 233, 250, 256, 262, 266, 268, 284(2), 291, 292
  Absalom 17
  Alexander 246, 252, 258, 286
  Andrew 47, 59, 119, 149, 150, 171, 172, 178, 283(2), 284, 289(2), 296, 305
  Betty 50
  Burrell 112, 123(2), 141, 143 (3), 147, 159, 176, 189, 195, 208, 212, 228
  Burwell 24, 39
  Elijah 252
  Elisha 164, 182
  Elizabeth 68, 71, 126, 128, 142, 217
  Hugh 247(2), 263, 268(2)
  Jeremiah 27, 47, 64, 159
  John 48, 228
  Joseph 24, 28, 35-36, 45, 46, 50, 56, 61(2), 62(2), 63, 64, 69, 73, 77, 222
  Joseph Jr. 167
  Lucy 175, 182, 189, 192, 201
  Richard 63, 246, 252, 254
  Robert 80
  Samuel 88, 102, 116, 118, 166, 167, 208, 222, 228
  Swann 54
  Waddy 198, 225, 228, 247, 254, 257(2), 260, 269
  William 4, 8(2), 36, 41, 44, 45, 46, 50, 53, 56, 57, 63, 69(2), 73, 75, 77, 83, 84, 89, 102, 118, 124(2), 131, 132, 137, 152, 158, 165, 197, 198, 200, 201, 204, 205, 214, 215, 220, 234, 242, 251, 254(2), 261, 273(3), 300, 302(2)
  William Turner 69, 86
Thornton, Josiah 165, 171, 175, 210, 214, 219, 221
  Luke 150
  Martha 301
  Thomas 4, 210, 217, 219, 221, 224, 301(3)
Tichey, James 9
Tickle, Leather 225, 226, 227, 236
Tillett, Francis 211
Tilman, Benjamine 110
  Jeremiah 15, 195, 281
Timmons, ___ 21, 179, 276, 277, 289
  Abner 10, 16
  Daniel 277
  Elizabeth 280
  James 258
  John 10, 28, 29, 62, 95, 102, 109, 218, 228(2), 264, 287
  Moses 15, 16, 28, 35, 37, 41, 62, 92, 115, 122, 218, 228 (2), 236, 250(2), 251, 252, 257(3), 280, 293, 296, 299, 302(2)
  Samuel 135, 147, 153(2), 183, 199, 277
  Thomas 218, 228(2), 280, 281
Tinsley, ___ 176
  James 202
  Ransom 183, 199, 218
  Thomas 147
  William 4, 208
Tipping, John 80
  Philip 75, 89, 93, 94, 104, 109(2)
  William 231
Tippins, John 24
Tod, ___ 158
  Thomas 9(4), 27, 28, 35, 37, 52(3), 63, 68, 69, 71, 73, 75(2), 77, 78(2), 79, 88, 89, 97, 132, 143, 163, 170, 183, 187, 195
  Winthrop 163
Tod's mill 281
Todd, Thomas 49(3), 136, 246, 305(2)
Toliaferro (see Taliaferro, Tolliaferro), ___ 172, 225
  Z. 233
  Zachariah 97, 118, 126, 142 (2), 145, 146, 153, 154(2), 155, 156, 157, 160, 163(2), 168, 176(2), 180, 181, 191, 207, 208, 209(2), 225(2), 243
Tollason, John 52, 130, 137, 138, 159
Tolleson, John 184
Tolliaferro, ___ 269(2)
  Richard 259, 270
  Zachariah 143, 162, 168, 211, 221, 249, 253, 255
Tollison, John 114, 121, 149, 150, 172, 177, 180, 181, 289, 300
Toney, Timothy 69
  William 268
Toney's ford 53
Towers, William 239, 247
Trail, Basil 203, 211
  Bazel 252, 296
  David 224
Trailor (see Traylor), William 198
Trammall, David 101
  Samson 135
  William 108
  Zilpha 108
Tramel, ___ 60
Trammel(2), ___ 41, 43, 89
  Elizabeth 96, 97(2)
  Peter 13
  Thomas 48, 55
  William 97(2)
Trammill, David 38
  Thomas Jr. 42
Traylor (see Trailor), Jesse 178, 184, 193, 195
  Joel 114, 121, 132, 136, 164, 171, 264, 277, 289
  Josiah 37
  Mary 230
  Richard 239, 246

Traylor, William 195, 204, 206, 230(2), 239, 299
Tremia, John 3
  Obediah 3
Trimia, Obediah 11
Trimmier, Col. ___ 298, 300
  John 187, 207, 230, 239, 261
  Obediah 39, 204, 206, 221, 241, 252, 254, 262, 277, 293, 300(2)
  Justice Obediah 34, 35, 36, 37, 38, 41, 42, 45, 46, 49, 50, 51, 54, 63, 65, 66, 67, 69, 70, 75, 76, 86, 90, 99, 100, 109, 116, 123, 134, 135, 137, 169, 187, 189
Trountree (see Rountree), William 196
Tucker, John 192, 201, 229, 259
  Samuel 192
  Starling 120
Turner, Ann 37
  Benjamine 250, 251, 257
  Darby 239, 246, 247(2)
  George 37(2), 39, 151
  Henry 39, 40, 50, 69, 73, 78, 82, 148, 214(2), 222(2), 230, 232, 243, 248, 249, 253, 261, 272
  Henry Jr. 226
  Henry Sr. 16, 41
  Holland 102
  James 7, 119, 133, 222, 230, 232, 246, 252, 289, 290, 303
  John 45, 221, 258, 263, 265, 295, 298
  Lewis 41
  Pleasant 270
  Richard 214(2), 226, 239, 246
  Samuel 133, 171, 181, 192, 214(2)
  William 148, 203, 238(2), 245, 272, 294
Turpin, ___ 12, 23(3), 29, 40, 44, 45, 48(2)
  Wadsworth 43
  William 18(3)
Tyger, William Smith 158

Underwood, John 252
  Thomas 50, 56, 61(2), 63, 64, 132, 136, 170, 230, 239, 258
  William 4, 36, 45, 297
Ursary, Robert 7
  William 7
Ussery, William 209
Utley, Jacob 258, 265, 294
  John 270

Vanderhorss, John 1
Vanderver, John 222
Vanderhorst, Arnoldus 237
Varner, Peter 175
Vaughan, John 194, 215, 222
Vaughn, George 129
  John 168, 182, 242
  Joseph 12
  Stephen 36
Veal, Morris 218, 228, 229, 234, 238, 241
Venable-Veneble-Venible, Joseph 8, 9, 10, 11(2), 30, 36, 45, 47, 48, 53, 54, 65, 70, 102, 115, 132, 136, 155, 163, 174, 175, 182(2), 186, 192, 194, 218(2), 220, 230, 239, 240, 241, 272
  Joseph Jr. 218
  Larkin 224, 225, 237
  Richard 220, 252

William 36, 123, 124, 125(3), 126, 130, 142(2), 142, 224, 225, 247, 249, 255(2), 269
Vernon, Alexander 8, 9, 10, 11, 13, 14, 15, 17, 28
  James 36, 45, 51, 210, 216, 232, 235, 240, 304
  John 122, 222, 230, 232
Vice, John 3, 69, 118, 198, 204
Vincent, Jesse 269
  William 241, 251, 255(3), 257, 269
Vinson, Capt. ___ 11
  David 47, 56

Wade, Edmund 274
  John 64(2), 81, 96, 130
  Joseph 178, 285
Wadsworth, ___ 12(2), 13(2), 16(2), 17(2), 23(2), 29, 40, 44, 45, 48(2), 87(2), 90, 100
  Thomas 2, 8, 15, 16, 17, 18(3), 19, 21, 23, 24, 26(3), 27, 29, 32, 47, 49
Wakefield, Charles 26
  Mary 32
  William 32
Walden, Henry 57, 66
  Nathan 178, 184, 193, 195
Waldrop, John 81
  Shadrack 64
Waldrope, ___ 21
  Benjamine 252, 259
  Elizabeth 66, 125
  Iley 198
  Isaiah 178
  James 29
  John 220, 252, 259(2)
  Michael 128
  Shadrack 57, 62, 132, 136, 167, 198, 204, 206, 258, 265, 266
  Thomas 66
  William 102, 117, 124, 198, 204, 206
Walker, Alexander 36, 57, 83, 92, 147, 150, 151, 158(2), 161, 165, 198, 204, 263, 285, 295, 301, 303, 305
  Daniel 45, 174, 212
  Eleanor 48
  Felix 39, 45, 127, 156
  George 69, 75, 81, 88, 92, 108, 109, 112, 122, 124(2), 126, 131, 221, 241, 245
  Henry 57, 62, 64
  Jane 27
  Jeremiah 124, 196, 205
  John 8, 99, 168, 178(2)
  John Fh. 178
  Nelly 127
  Rice 122
  Thomas 151, 153, 156, 163, 168
  William 37, 48, 130, 166, 174(2)
  Zachariah 48
  Zedikiah 164
Walton, William 206(2)
Ward, James 93, 99, 179, 253(2), 286, 299
  John 8, 9, 10, 11, 13, 14, 15, 109, 130, 146, 149, 152, 155(3), 162(2), 205
  Moses 4, 119
  Nathan 115, 122, 198, 204(2), 259, 298
  Nathan Jr. 252, 259
  Samuel 62, 81, 87, 279, 280, 284
  Samuel Jr. 87
Warner, Wettinhal 29
Warren, Joseph 103, 131, 135,

144, 147
Reubin 204, 239, 246
Thomas 7, 11, 56, 62, 64, 67, 91
Warren's ford 133, 306
Waters, Charles 5, 6, 10(2), 11, 31, 33, 51, 68, 79, 80, 95
  Elizabeth 36
  Nicholas 226
  Philemon B. 245
  Westwood 11(2), 20(2), 21(2), 22, 31, 36, 51, 59, 79, 80, 81(2)
Watkins, William 164
  Willis 130, 141
Watson, John 27, 29(2), 33, 56, 57, 132, 236
  Obadiah 99, 236(3), 256, 257(4), 270, 293, 299, 305
Watts, William 165
Wayland, Francis 16
  Francis N. 59, 74, 83, 183
  Francis Nevil 13, 15, 19, 86, 89, 286
  Nevil 24, 48, 51, 72, 73, 83, 86, 88, 115, 140, 141, 165, 168, 182, 183, 184, 194, 198, 211, 218, 220, 249, 290
Webb, Jeremiah 3
  William 83
Webster, William 254
Weir (see Wier), William 28
Wells, David 262
  Ezekiel 22, 151
  Henry 4, 8, 28, 35, 46, 47, 48, 50, 113, 146, 135, 162, 167(2), 169, 179, 196, 205, 214, 263, 276(3), 280, 282, 297, 303, 304
  John 178, 184, 193, 195, 239, 246, 247(2)
  Philip 197
  Thomas 196, 198, 204, 206, 207, 284
  William 47(2), 179, 201, 235, 242, 245, 248, 257, 285, 291, 296, 297, 299, 303
West, George 74
  John 183
  Joseph 127, 134
  Osborn 265
  Osburn 258
  Robert 257
  Walter 134
  William 12, 40, 160(3), 162
Westmoreland, John 123, 148, 185, 258
  Thomas 239, 246(2), 247
Weston, John 89
Whitby, Richard 264
Wheeler, William 274
  Zacheus 285
White, ___ 138
  Ann 57(3), 66, 117, 125
  Aquilla 87
  Daniel 188, 229, 232, 240, 244, 252, 259(2), 283, 299
  David 252, 264
  Henry 15, 16, 57(3), 66
  Justice Henry 1, 2, 4, 9, 17, 18, 21, 23, 30, 31, 32, 35, 44, 46, 47, 49, 50, 51, 55
  James 3, 8, 21, 28, 33, 35, 44, 58, 84, 138, 278, 279, 283
  James T. 272
  James Taylor 43, 136, 140, 141, 179, 271

324

White, John 15, 66, 93, 96, 98, 102, 107, 171, 181, 210, 216, 287
  Moses 218
  Reubin 209
  Robert 48, 178, 184, 188, 193, 195, 218(2), 227
  Samuel 225
  Thomas 135, 169
Whitley, Richison 298
Whittemore, ___ 108
  Abraham 224, 299
  John 96, 98, 104, 105, 106, 108, 118, 122, 223
  Saphira 185(2), 186
Whitten, Charles 222, 293
Whitworth, Fendol 206
  Thomas 44, 206(2)
Wier (see Weir), William 44, 45, 47, 48, 51(2), 53, 54, 86, 90, 114, 115, 277
Wier's creek road 69
Wilder, William 57, 60, 62, 64, 68, 79(2), 119, 257, 261, 264, 269, 301
Willie's fork 72(2), 284, 286, 287, 295
Wilkey, William 305
Wilkins, William 37(3), 135, 203, 211, 216, 273, 292
Wilkison, William 197, 212
Williams, Abram 156, 157
  Edward 273
  George 264
  Henry 187
  James 63, 72(2)
  John 10, 28, 32, 36, 45, 69, 83, 106, 108, 129(2), 140(2), 141, 157, 159, 172, 173(2), 248, 38, 300
  Martin 22
  Mary 63, 75(2)
  Polley 76
  Thomas 6, 47(2), 69, 72, 76, 88, 115, 122, 183, 199, 209, 224, 284, 296, 301
  William M. 83
Williamson, John 147
  Thomas 1, 3, 4, 5(2), 8, 15, 17, 18, 27, 35(2), 38, 41, 67, 80, 91(2), 101, 104, 105, 110, 111, 112, 118, 120, 125, 137, 146, 148, 150, 151, 159, 164, 167, 170(3), 171, 218, 272, 274, 276(2), 277, 291, 293
  William 8, 80(2)
Williford, Briton 305, 306
  Brittain 56, 62, 64, 69, 73, 75, 77, 78, 84, 118, 138, 151, 152, 171, 181, 209(2), 214, 219(2), 224, 248, 251, 253, 254(2), 260, 264, 283, 289(2), 296(2), 302
  Stephen 14, 37, 42, 43, 59, 60, 68, 108, 115, 129
  Wilie 244
  Willis 306
Willis(s), Richard 27, 210, 216
  Stephen 58
Wilson, ___ 218
  Mrs. ___ 109
  Fennell 264
  James 164, 171, 175, 198, 204, 206
  Jason 91
  John 16, 246
  L. 256
  Reubin 305
  Stephen 53, 69, 73, 76, 88, 91, 104, 112, 150, 159, 170, 198, 204, 258, 266, 305(3)
  Thomas 33, 44, 77, 84

W. 256
William S. 255
Wingo, Oba. 135
  Obadiah 189, 210, 216, 286, 294, 299
  William 299
Winn, Richard 290
Winthrop, ___ 158
Wise, William 36, 44
Wofford, Absolom 17
  Benjamine 12(2), 21, 23, 43 (2), 63, 70, 74, 80, 81, 88, 89, 92, 95(2), 96, 98, 102, 103, 105, 106, 112 (3), 118, 119, 123(3), 127 (4), 128, 129, 130, 136, 137, 139, 140(4), 141(2), 143(5), 144, 146(2), 151, 152, 154, 155(2), 166, 167 (2), 168, 169, 172, 175(2), 176, 177, 179, 182(2), 183 (4), 185(2), 189, 192, 193, 194(3), 196(2), 197, 200, 201, 202(2), 207, 208(4), 209, 214(2), 215, 216, 218 (2), 219, 220(2), 221, 228, 233(3), 242(2), 247(2), 249(2), 251, 256, 263, 268(3), 269(2), 270(2), 300
  Benjamine Jr. 268, 269
  C. Gasdain Benjamin 28
  Isaac 115, 146, 153(2), 254
  James 8, 9, 10, 11, 13, 14, 15, 28, 37, 87, 97, 98, 104, 154(2), 199, 203, 220, 243, 247, 254, 255 (2), 288, 290, 291, 302, 306
  Jeremiah 244, 248, 253
  John 28, 36, 37, 45, 83, 93, 122, 140, 183, 199, 232, 249, 251, 252, 254
  John Jr. 181
  Joseph 8, 10, 11, 27, 28, 36, 37, 39, 42, 43, 45, 48(2), 48, 53, 73, 75, 78, 95, 121, 152, 159, 164, 171, 176, 191, 192, 195, 208, 213, 233, 252
  Nathaniel 199, 241, 251, 255 (3), 257
  Sarah 268, 269
  William 138, 144, 153, 163, 176, 196(2), 197, 209, 228, 238, 246, 250, 253(2), 268, 269
  William Jr. 13, 36, 39, 45, 47, 48, 55, 57, 62, 64, 69, 83, 114
  William Sr. 10(2), 11, 12, 15, 18, 30, 75, 83, 89, 105, 110, 114, 119, 124, 131
Wolf, Henry 2, 13, 87
Wood, ___ 53, 110, 115
  Henry 178
  Henry Machen 24, 117, 145, 274
  Justice Henry Machen 1, 4, 6, 7, 8, 9, 10, 11-12, 14, 15, 69, 72
  James 113, 115(2), 117, 183, 269, 304, 305(2)
  John 7(2), 11, 15, 18, 21, 27, 53, 70, 71, 76, 82, 129, 140(4), 141, 151, 246, 252, 302, 304(2)
  Mary 45, 104, 113, 115
  Michael 183, 246
  Moses 45, 87(2), 97, 104, 112, 113, 118(2), 126, 137, 139 (4), 144
  Penuel 252
  Polley 304
  Robert 178, 184, 193, 195, 199, 252, 259(2), 260, 302
Mrs. Story 303
  Thomas 6, 14, 16, 20, 27, 42, 53
  William 5, 36, 42, 45, 47, 48, 50, 51, 53, 54, 57, 59, 66, 68, 87, 108, 126, 157, 161, 167, 170, 188(3), 189, 190, 197, 249, 261, 274, 280, 284
  Justice William 1, 2, 67
  William Jr. 100, 168
Woodruff, ___ 198
  Fielding 49
  Jacob 248
  John 178, 184, 193, 195, 246, 257, 278, 282
  Joseph 26, 69, 180, 184, 195, 204, 230(2), 253, 259, 263, 278, 279, 287, 288, 290, 293(2), 296(2), 297, 306
  Nathaniel 178, 204, 277, 300
  Samuel 282
  Thomas 203, 210, 239, 246, 247(2)
Woodruff's meeting house 296, 306
Woody, Henry 154
Wooten, Nathaniel 62
  William 4
Wooton, John 71, 129, 142, 145, 184
  John Sr. 129(2)
  Nathaniel 159
Woottin, John 44
Wright, John 238, 244, 258, 265, 290, 297, 298
Wyatt, Abram 147, 153(2), 214 (2)
  Henry 48(2), 229
  Isaac 204
  James 133, 203, 210, 211(2)
  James Jr. 83, 93
  Thomas 2, 76, 91, 104, 112, 115, 120, 135(2), 136, 140, 141, 145, 151, 170, 204, 271
  Vincent 198, 204, 291, 300
  William 57

Yancey, James 2(2), 4(2), 6, 9 (3), 10(2), 11(2), 12(3), 13(2), 14, 15, 16(3), 17 (2), 19(2), 20(2), 21, 22, 23(4), 24(3), 25, 26(2), 27, 29(3), 30, 32, 33(2), 38(2), 43, 44, 49, 52(2), 53(4), 54(2), 63(2), 65, 2, 68(2), 113
Yearby, Isham 17
Yearly, Isham 22
Yerly, Isham 19
Young, ___ 53, 54, 55(5), 74
  Ezekial 83
  Henry 106, 115, 178, 221, 268, 275(2), 302
  Isaac 69, 73, 77, 133, 174, 177, 184, 188, 199, 246, 253
  John 51, 62, 91, 100, 102, 104, 112, 114, 132, 136, 15 158, 165, 168, 170, 188, 190, 243, 283, 290
  John Jr. 117, 150, 178
  John Sr. 1(2), 28, 35, 139, 148, 183, 199, 247
  John D. 127, 216, 255, 256, 262(3), 267, 268, 274
  Joseph 176
  Joshua 77
  Nathl. 42, 54, 252
  Patty 42, 43, 55
  Richard 116, 127, 171, 177, 184(2), 267, 280, 293

Young, Robert 161, 165
  Sally 280
  Samuel 232
  Thomas 69, 73, 78, 82, 198
  William 1(4), 6, 36, 40, 41,
    45, 52(2), 80, 117, 129,
    137, 158, 162, 188, 189,
    274, 275, 279, 290, 302

www.ingramcontent.com/pod-product-compliance
Lightning Source LLC
Chambersburg PA
CBHW020055020526
44112CB00031B/181